READINGS IN
CULTURAL
CONTEXTS

READINGS IN CULTURAL CONTEXTS

JUDITH N. MARTIN

THOMAS K. NAKAYAMA

LISA A. FLORES

ARIZONA STATE UNIVERSITY

MAYFIELD PUBLISHING COMPANY

Mountain View, California

London • Toronto

Library of Congress Cataloging-in-Publication Data
Readings in cultural contexts / [edited by] Judith N. Martin, Thomas K. Nakayama, Lisa A. Flores.
    p. cm.
  Includes index.
  ISBN 0-7674-0061-5
  1. Intercultural communication. 2. Communication and culture.
3. Multiculturalism. 4. Ethnicity. I. Martin, Judith N. II. Nakayama, Thomas K. III. Flores, Lisa A.
GN345.6.R43 1997
303.48′2—dc21
                                                97-22675
                                                   CIP

Manufactured in the United States of America
10 9 8 7 6 5 4 3 2 1

Mayfield Publishing Company
1280 Villa Street
Mountain View, California 94041

Sponsoring editor, Holly J. Allen; *production editor,* Lynn Rabin Bauer; *manuscript editor,* Darlene Bledsoe; *design and art manager,* Susan Breitbard; *text and cover designer,* Joan Greenfield; *cover artist,* J. W. Stewart; *manufacturing manager,* Randy Hurst. The text was set in 9/11 New Aster by G&S Typesetters and printed on 45# Quebecor Matte by Quebecor Printing Book Group.

Acknowledgments and copyrights continue at the back of the book on page 497, which constitutes an extension of the copyright page.

CONTENTS

◈ PREFACE

The field of intercultural communication is currently undergoing great changes. There is now no dominant paradigm, but rather several distinct, complementary, and contradictory paradigms. Students and instructors are faced with multiple, sometimes contradictory choices: Do we accept only social science–based research? Is it important to incorporate narratives or ethnographic findings? Should instructors introduce political issues into intercultural communication courses? These challenges prompted two of the editors of this collection, Martin and Nakayama, to write *Intercultural Communication in Contexts*, which examines multiple perspectives in intercultural communication and explores ways that professors and students can begin to answer these difficult questions.

It is also useful, however, to expose students to more in-depth exemplars of the best intercultural communication scholarship across the various paradigms. Hence, we present this edited collection to reflect the current paradigm shift and to help students and professors better understand the unique and complementary contributions of diverse research perspectives. The essays in the 10 parts of *Readings in Cultural Contexts* range from classic writings to more recent scholarship.

We begin the book by presenting a dialectical approach, or framework, that admits the complexities of intercultural communication and allows for multiple ways of understanding. We then identify three different perspectives: social science, interpretive, and critical. The subsequent essays reflect these multiple ways of understanding and writing about intercultural communication. The essays include narratives, ethnographic studies, and textual and media analyses, as well as the more traditional social-science reports. In addition to conceptual issues, many of the essays address practical guidelines for meeting intercultural challenges faced in daily life.

FEATURES

- ◆ The book presents a broad (macro) conceptual framework for contextualizing intercultural communication knowledge from dialectical approaches.

- ◆ Clearly written essays offer insight into particular examples and foci of intercultural communication in both domestic and international contexts.

- ◆ Author voices reflect a diversity of ethnicity, gender, and research orientations.

- ◆ Material is presented in a tone and style that is accessible to students.

- ◆ Practical as well as conceptual concerns are addressed.

- ◆ Questions to consider, found at the beginning of each part, guide students as they read the essays.

- ◆ Discussion questions at the end of each essay begin a dialogue on the essays and help students get into a dialectical framework.

- ◆ An entire section is devoted to each of the following topics not typically covered in existing intercultural communication readers: history, cultural spaces, popular culture, and ethics.

Not only are the topics covered of emerging interest in intercultural communication, but the conceptual dialectical framework for connecting and understanding these disparate forms of knowledge is unique. Students are presented with a variety of conceptual "hooks" for understanding the interconnections and intersections of experiential knowledge, social scientific knowledge, historical knowledge, and other forms of knowledge.

OVERVIEW

We begin with essays that explore the foundations of intercultural communication. The first essay presents our integrative dialectical framework, which reflects and connects the diversity of perspective and contributions in the field of intercultural communication. Other essays in Part One describe the history of the field and the strengths and limitations of current work. These essays also highlight contemporary issues in intercultural communication scholarship, such as the role of objectivity, experience, and context.

After establishing an overview and foundation for further reading, the book focuses on issues of identity in Part Two. These essays explore the multifaceted and dynamic connections among identity, culture, and communication. The contributing authors discuss ethnic, gender, race, class, and religious identities from a variety of perspectives and methods, including textual analysis, ethnography, and narrative.

Part Three examines the centrality of history in intercultural communication. The readings show how history influences various international and domestic communication settings in the United States, Europe, the Middle East, and South Africa.

The next part discusses language and its role in intercultural communication. Essays in Part Four describe the rules for speaking in specific communities, both international and domestic (for example, Native American public speaking and leave-taking in Colombia). Other essays describe how language can facilitate (by language accommodation, for example) or inhibit intercultural communication (for example, by reinforcing stereotypes).

In Part Five, the essays explore cultural spaces and practices in specific contexts. Readings analyze verbal and nonverbal cultural practices in a variety of specific locations: European and American business contexts, print media in Korea and the United States, a U.S. working-class neighborhood, and an American Indian gaming casino.

Part Six examines popular culture and intercultural communication, including the ways people consume and resist messages from television, movies, and sports. The essays also explore how popular culture influences our perceptions of other cultures and subsequent intercultural communication.

The essays in Part Seven discuss a variety of intercultural transitions—sojourns overseas, reentry shock upon return, and "passing" from one race or class to another. The essays discuss transition issues including the role of language, friendships, and culture learning, and they provide practical guidelines for easing transitions.

Part Eight focuses on intercultural relationships. These essays examine the role of culture in various kinds of relationships: family, work, friendship, and romantic. The contributing authors offer ways to think about relationships as well as practical suggestions for developing intercultural relationships and meeting both the joys and challenges of these relationships.

The essays in Part Nine explore conflict, communication, and culture, offering cross-cultural comparisons of conflict management in both international and domestic settings. The essays range from descriptive empirical studies to very practical suggestions for dealing with intercultural conflict, and they explore interpersonal, global, and mediated conflict.

Finally, Part Ten addresses ethical issues in intercultural communication. These essays provide conceptual frameworks for understanding ethical issues and offer specific guidelines for ethical communication in both research and practice.

ACKNOWLEDGMENTS

First, we thank our Mayfield editor, Holly J. Allen, for initiating and supporting this project from the conceptualization to the publishing of this collection. Without her patience, advice, and commitment, this work would never have been realized. We also thank all the authors for their essays. They contributed high-quality, often cutting-edge scholarship, responded thoughtfully and promptly to reviewers' suggestions, and met the sometimes difficult deadlines.

We also thank Regina E. Spellers, our editorial assistant at ASU. She was the liaison and contact person for the three editors (one of whom was out of town on sabbatical), the Mayfield staff, and the 50-plus authors. Regina somehow managed to keep us all connected; she responded graciously and efficiently to the many requests, completed the required tasks while meeting the heavy demands of graduate study, and still maintained her sense of humor.

To the reviewers—Donal Carbaugh, University of Massachusetts; Hui-Ching Chang, University of Illinois at Chicago; Robbin D. Crabtree, New Mexico State University; Victoria DeFrancisco, University of Northern Iowa; Randy K. Dillon, Southwest Missouri State University; Natalie Dollar, Oregon State University; Bradford "J" Hall, University of New Mexico; Mark Lawrence McPhail, University of Utah; Nagesh Rao, University of New Mexico; Gust A. Yep, San Francisco State University—we owe a great deal of thanks for challenging our thinking about the conceptualization and framework of the book and for helping us clarify our material. Because of their insightful and timely work, the book represents the very best of current scholarship.

Thanks also go to the Mayfield staff for making it all work—to Lynn Rabin Bauer, production editor; Darlene Bledsoe, copyeditor; and JoAnne Naples, permissions editor. They were consistently available and helpful.

Finally, to our partners (Ronald S. Chaldu, David L. Karbonski, and Marouf A. Hasian, Jr.), friends, colleagues, and students, we owe our thanks for contributing in ways many times not realized—for allowing us to work on this project when we might have (and sometimes should have) been doing other things.

CONTRIBUTORS

Mike Allen is an associate professor at the University of Wisconsin, Milwaukee. His research focus is on the methodology of quantitative synthesis of existing data or meta-analysis. He has co-edited two books and authored over two dozen meta-analyses on various aspects of communication, including self-disclosure, persuasion, sexual preference, pornography, culture, and racial self-image.

James Baldwin (1924–1987) was an important U.S. writer who had a significant voice in racial issues, particularly in the late 1950s and 1960s. He grew up in Harlem and then moved to Paris; he later lived in both France and the United States. He was active in the U.S. Civil Rights movement. Many of Baldwin's works dealt with sexuality as well as racial issues. Author of many books, he is well known for *Go Tell It on the Mountain* (1953), *Notes of a Native Son* (1955), *Giovanni's Room* (1956), *Nobody Knows My Name* (1961), *Another Country* (1962), and *The Fire Next Time* (1963).

John R. Baldwin is an assistant professor at Illinois State University. His research and publications focus on interethnic communication, intercultural relationships, and intolerance. He is particularly interested in the role of race, ethnicity, and culture in relationships.

Mary Catherine Bateson is Clarence Robinson Professor of Anthropology and English at George Mason University. She has written on a variety of linguistic and anthropological topics and is the author of a memoir of her parents, Gregory Bateson and Margaret Mead, entitled *With a Daughter's Eye*. Other recent books include *Composing a Life* and *Thinking AIDS*.

Detine L. Bowers is the founder and president of several organizations dedicated to communicating inner peace and instituting global transformation through peace communication. She holds a Ph.D. in Communication from Purdue University. Her research interests include both spiritual and intercultural communication. She has published in the areas of African American rhetoric and intercultural communication.

Dwight E. Brooks is an assistant professor of Telecommunications at Indiana University, Bloomington. His teaching and research focus on cultural studies, with particular emphasis on advertising and consumer culture, African Americans and media, and broadcast and cable programming.

Benjamin J. Broome is a professor of Communication at George Mason University, where he teaches intercultural communication, group design and problem solving, and conflict resolution. His recent experience as a senior Fulbright scholar contributed to his book, *Journey Through the Greek Mosaic,* which is a guide for Americans living, studying, working, and traveling in Greece. His earlier work with Native American tribes in the United States and Mexico has been published in numerous international journals.

Deborah A. Cai is an assistant professor of Speech Communication at the University of Maryland at College Park. She teaches, researches, and publishes in the areas of intercultural communication and conflict management and effective communication in intercultural business negotiation.

Donal Carbaugh is a professor of Communication at the University of Massachusetts, Amherst. One of the leading scholars in cultural communication, his writings focus on the development of a communication theory of sociocultural interaction integrating identity issues, forms of action, and emotional expression. His edited volume, *Cultural Communication and Intercultural Contact* (1990), received the Distinguished Scholarship Award by the Speech Communication Association's International and Intercultural Communication Division.

Ling Chen is an assistant professor of Communication at the University of Oklahoma, Norman. Her major areas of interest are intercultural interpersonal communication, Chinese communication, language, and social interaction. Her work has been published in various journals including *Communication Monographs, International Journal of Intercultural Relations,* and *Research on Language and Social Interaction.*

Mary Jane Collier is an associate professor in the University of Denver's School of Communication. She is editor of Volumes 23–25 of the *International and Intercultural Communication Annual.* Her primary research areas include cultural identities, cultural and intercultural relationships, and intercultural communication competence. Her work has appeared in international and national journals.

Leda M. Cooks is an assistant professor of Communication at the University of Massachusetts, Amherst, where she teaches courses in intercultural communication, conflict, mediation, critical pedagogy, and interpersonal communication. Her research has focused on the dynamics of power in mediated and face-to-face communication and has been published in *Western Communication Journal, Women's Studies in Communication, Communication Quarterly,* and *Negotiation Journal.*

Frederick C. Corey is an associate professor of Communication at Arizona State University. He writes in the areas of performance studies, gay culture, and personal narrative.

Karen Lynnette Dace is an assistant professor of Communication at the University of Utah and holds a joint appointment with the Ethnic Studies Program. Her research interests include small group communication, interracial communication, and African American women's discourse. Her work has appeared in the *Western Journal of Black Studies* and the *International and Intercultural Communication Annual* and is regularly presented at the annual meetings of the Speech Communication and Popular Culture Associations.

Fernando Delgado is an assistant professor of Communication Studies at Arizona State University West and is affiliated with the Hispanic Research Center at Arizona State University. His teaching and extensive publications focus on the politics of identity and representation in popular culture (sports, music, television, and film).

Michel Dion is a sociologist at the National Center of Scientific Research in France (C.N.R.S.). He has conducted research in the area of religion and politics in France, Romania, and Brazil. He has authored or co-authored seven books and published over 100 journal articles, chapters, and reviews.

Carley H. Dodd is dean of the Graduate School and professor of Communication at Abilene Christian University. His eight books and numerous papers address many communication issues, including an emphasis on studying relationships from a variety of family systems and cultures.

Kristine L. Fitch is an associate professor of Communication at the University of Colorado, Boulder. She was a Fulbright Doctoral Fellow in Colombia in 1987 and has published in many journals. Her research interests include cultural approaches to interpersonal communication, methodological approaches to cultural comparison, and culturally contextualized conversational analysis.

Lisa A. Flores is an assistant professor of Communication at Arizona State University. She received her Ph.D. in Speech Communication from the University of Georgia in 1991. Her research is in the areas of culture, communication, and feminism, with an emphasis on U.S. cultural discourses of race, ethnicity, and gender.

Anita K. Foeman is a professor of Communication at West Chester University in Pennsylvania. She teaches and researches in the areas of interpersonal, organizational, and intercultural communication.

Howard Giles is a professor and chair of the Communication department at the University of California, Santa Barbara, with affiliate positions in Psychology and Linguistics. His research interests include many areas of intergroup communication—intercultural, intergenerational, and police-community relations. He has edited numerous books on language attitude and communication accommodation, including *Contexts of Accommodation* (1991) with Justine and Nicholas Coupland.

Douglas R. Golden earned his B.A. in Rhetoric from the University of Illinois at Urbana-Champaign. He is currently completing his M.A. in Communication at Arizona State University. His research interests include intercultural communication and Jewish identity.

María Cristina González is director of Campus Communities and an adjunct professor of Communication at Arizona State University. Her work explores how various forms of social organization, including culture, constrain and enable self-expression and human communication. She regularly takes graduate students on field courses to learn the "four seasons approach" to ethnography and is an active member of the poetry community in Phoenix, Arizona.

Bradford "J" Hall is an associate professor of Communication at the University of New Mexico. His research and publications focus on intercultural conflict and how people use everyday talk to establish, maintain, and transform their social identities. He is currently investigating narratives of prejudice.

Edward T. Hall is an internationally known anthropologist and author. He was a partner in Edward T. Hall Associates with his wife **Mildred Reed Hall.** This pioneering firm, founded in 1961, specialized in intercultural communication, providing lectures and consultations to international businesses, foundations, and government agencies. His most recent book is *West of the Thirties: Discoveries Among the Navajo and Hopi.* He co-authored with Mildred Reed Hall *Understanding Cultural Differences: Germans, French and Americans* and *Hidden Differences: Doing Business with the Japanese.* His earlier books—*The Silent Language, The Hidden Dimension, Beyond Culture,* and *The Dance of Life*—have been translated into 20 languages

Rona Tamiko Halualani is a doctoral student in Communication at Arizona State University. She earned her M.A. in Communication Studies at California State University, Sacramento. Her research interests include intercultural communication, cultural and critical studies, Asian Pacific American communication, and media/film studies.

Marouf A. Hasian, Jr., is an assistant professor of Communication at Arizona State University. He is the author of *The Rhetoric of Eugenics in Anglo-American Thought.* His research areas include law and rhetoric, intercultural communication and postcolonial discourse, the rhetoric of science, and freedom of expression.

Michael L. Hecht is a professor of Communication at Pennsylvania State University and the author of numerous articles and book chapters in interpersonal, interethnic, and nonverbal communication. His research includes investigations of ethnicity and identity, and he is currently working to create culturally sensitive drug prevention material for adolescents.

Radha S. Hegde is an assistant professor of Communication at Rutgers University, where she teaches interpersonal and intercultural communication. Her research and publications focus on issues of race and gender with particular interest in South Asian immigrants in the United States.

Geert Hofstede is an emeritus professor of Organizational Anthropology and International Management at the University of Limburg at Maastricht, the Netherlands. He has conducted extensive research in the area of national and organizational cultures. His best-known books are *Culture's Consequences: International Differences in Work-Related Values* (1980) and *Cultures and Organizations: Software of the Mind* (1991).

Fred E. Jandt is a professor of Communication Studies at California State University, San Bernardino. His research interests are culture and conflict studies. His publications include *Intercultural Communication: An Introduction* (1995) and *Win-Win Negotiating: Turning Conflict into Agreement* (1985), which is available in seven languages.

Min-Sun Kim is an associate professor of Communication at the University of Hawaii at Manoa. Her research interests include the role of cognition in conversational styles among people of different cultural groups. Her articles have appeared in many journals, including *Human Communication Research, Communication Monographs,* and the *Howard Journal of Communications.*

Young Yun Kim is a professor of Communication at the University of Oklahoma in Norman. Her research activities address the cross-cultural adaptation of immigrants, sojourners, and native-born ethnic minorities. Among her most recent books are *Communicating with Strangers,* with W. Gudykunst (1997) and *Becoming Intercultural: An Integrative Theory of Communication and Cross-Cultural Adaptation* (1998).

Janis L. King is an associate professor of Communication and Mass Media at Southwest Missouri State University, where she teaches rhetorical criticism, persuasion, and argumentation. She investigates how people, particularly Native Americans and women, use persuasion to present their positions during public conflict situations.

Wendy Leeds-Hurwitz is a professor and chair of the Department of Communication at the University of Wisconsin, Parkside. She is the author of *Communication in Everyday Life: A Social Interpretation* (1989) and *Semiotics and Communication: Signs, Codes, Culture* (1993), as well as numerous journal articles and book chapters.

Dorothy Leland is currently director of the Women's Studies Center and an associate professor of Philosophy at Florida Atlantic University. Previously, she worked at Purdue University, where she and Jacqueline Martinez were colleagues.

Judith N. Martin is an associate professor of Communication at Arizona State University. Her research and publications focus on intercultural communication and transitions, ethnic and racial identity, and communication competence.

Jacqueline M. Martinez in an assistant professor of Communication and Women's Studies at Purdue University, where she teaches courses in semiotics, phenomenology, and feminist theory. She has published essays on Chicana/lesbian and gay studies and sexual harassment.

Mark Lawrence McPhail is an associate professor of Communication at the University of Utah. His research interests include rhetorical theory and epistemology, contemporary race relations, discourse and power, and Eastern philosophy. His work has appeared in many journals and he is the author of two books, *The Rhetoric of Racism* and *Zen in the Art of Rhetoric: An Inquiry into Coherence.*

Dreama G. Moon is a doctoral candidate in Communication at Arizona State University. Her research focuses on issues of culture, communication, and identity. She is currently investigating the ways in which white women are enculturated into social relations of racial domination and white supremacy.

Thomas K. Nakayama received his Ph.D. from the University of Iowa. He is currently associate professor in the Department of Communication and affiliate faculty in the Interdisciplinary Humanities Program and the Women's Studies Program at Arizona State University. He writes in the areas of cultural studies and rhetoric, focusing particularly on issues of race, gender, and sexuality.

Teresa A. Nance is an associate professor of Communication Arts at Villanova University and is a member of the Africana Studies Program. Her areas of teaching and research include classroom communication and African American learning styles.

T. A. Niles is a doctoral candidate in Communication in Arizona State University's Interdisciplinary Ph.D. Program. He is currently investigating relationships among communication, culture, and ethnic and racial identity.

Kimberly A. Noels received her Ph.D. from the University of Ottawa. She is currently a visiting postdoctoral fellow of Communication at the University of California, Santa Barbara. Her research interests include intercultural communication processes—particularly as they relate to ethnic identity—stress and adjustment, other acculturation phenomena, and social psychological aspects of second language learning.

Peter Ogom Nwosu is an associate professor of Communication Studies at California State University, Sacramento, and a nationally recognized contributor and consultant on intercultural training and development. His scholarly writings and presentations include a recent book, *Communication and the Transformation of Society: A Developing Region's Perspective*. He currently serves as associate editor of the *Journal of African Communications* and is an editorial board member of the *Howard Journal of Communications*.

Melanie Payne is currently completing her M.A. in Communication at Arizona State University. Her research focuses on a critical understanding of domestic race relations, which includes issues like affirmative action and interracial relationships.

Gerry Philipsen is professor of Speech Communication at the University of Washington. He pioneered an area of scholarship known as cultural communication—ethnography of communication studies describing communication patterns of various speech communities. He has recently published *Speaking Culturally: Explorations in Social Communication*.

Donald L. Rubin holds a joint appointment as professor and head of the Department of Speech Communication and professor in the Department of Language Education's Program in Linguistics at the University of Georgia. He teaches courses in intercultural communication and applied linguistics, and his research focuses on various aspects of oral and written language variation. He is editor of *Composing Social Identity in Written Language* (1995).

Ellen Seiter is professor of Communication at the University of California at San Diego. She investigates questions of gender, audiences, and media technology. She is also interested in the social construction of race and gender and whiteness. Her latest book is *Researching Television Audiences* (Oxford University Press). She is also the author of *Sold Separately: Children and Parents in Consumer Culture* and the co-editor of *Remote Control: Television, Audiences and Social Power*.

Robert M. Shuter is a professor and chair of the Department of Communication Studies at Marquette University. His research has been published in a variety of journals including *Communication Monographs, Journal of Communication,* and *Journal of Social Psychology,* as well as the *Wall Street Journal* and *New York Times*.

Shelley L. Smith is an instructor of Communication at Concordia College in St. Paul, Minnesota, and an education specialist at the University of Minnesota's Office of Preparing Future Faculty. She has been involved in international, intercultural, and diversity education as a teacher and trainer for 15 years in the United States and abroad.

Regina E. Spellers earned her M.B.A. from the University of Bridgeport in Connecticut. She is presently a doctoral candidate in Arizona State University's Interdisciplinary Ph.D. Program in Communication, where her research interests include ethnic identity and organizational socialization.

Melissa Steyn is a faculty member in the Professional Communication Unit at the University of Cape Town, South Africa. As a Fulbright scholar, she received her M.A. from Arizona State University. She is co-editor of *Cultural Synergy in South Africa: Weaving Strands of Africa and Europe* (1996) and currently writes about "whiteness" in a changing South Africa.

Dolores V. Tanno is an associate professor of Communication Studies at California State University, San Bernardino. Her research interest integrates rhetoric, intercultural communication, and communications. Her publications include a book, *Politics, Communication, and Culture,* and various articles published in journals such as the *International Journal of Intercultural Relations* and the *Howard Journal of Communications.*

Jacqueline Taylor is a professor of Communication and associate dean of Graduate Studies in the College of Liberal Arts and Sciences at DePaul University. She is the author of *Grace Paley: Illuminating the Dark Lives* (1990) and of various articles in the area of performance studies. Her recent work focuses on autobiographical performance.

Stella Ting-Toomey is a professor of Speech Communication at California State University, Fullerton. One of the top international experts in intercultural communication, she has written or edited several books and numerous journal articles and book chapters. Her writings have focused on facework negotiation, ethnic identity, and cross-cultural conflict.

Angharad N. Valdivia is a Research Assistant Professor at the Institute of Communications Research at the University of Illinois. Her research interests include transnational approaches to the study of gender and culture, focusing on both Latin American and U.S. Latina women. Her work has been published in *Chasqui, Women and Language,* the review of *Education/Pedagogy/Cultural Studies,* and the *Journal of International Communications.* She is the editor of *Feminism, Multiculturalism, and the Media* (1995, Sage).

Kathleen Wong(Lau) has been an instructor of Public Policy Analysis and Intercultural Communication at the Woodrow Wilson Summer Institute at the Graduate School of Public Policy at the University of California at Berkeley. Her research interests include ethnic, racial, class, and gender identity and intercultural communication as well as multiculturalist policies and practices in higher education.

Gust A. Yep is an associate professor of Speech and Communication Studies at San Francisco State University. His work on communication, identity, and health issues has appeared in numerous books and journals including *AIDS Education and Prevention, Hispanic Journal of Behavioral Sciences, International Quarterly of Community Health Education, Journal of American Health,* and *Journal of Social Behavior.*

TO THE STUDENT

In putting together this collection of readings, we tried to include a range of perspectives, although we cannot represent every kind of dialectic or every variation of intercultural communication scholarship. Each author contributes something to our understanding—perhaps an insight about cross-cultural differences; or an in-depth look at how culture and communication are intertwined; or probing looks at the importance of social, political, and historical contexts; or explorations of how power plays into intercultural communication.

Each section of this book represents a common topic addressed by intercultural communication scholars. Parts Two and Three address what is brought to an intercultural encounter: our identity and historical influences. We then turn to language processes (Part Four) as well as cultural spaces and nonverbal aspects (Part Five) of intercultural communication. Part Six explores popular culture, and Part Seven addresses issues in making cultural transitions. The next two sections address relationship issues, building intercultural relationships (Part Eight) and dealing with conflict (Part Nine). Part Ten addresses ethical issues in the practice and study of intercultural communication.

In each part we tried to include examples of three types of scholarship—social science, interpretive, and critical. We have also tried to provide a balance of international and domestic studies. However, it is important to realize that

1. Research cannot always be neatly categorized into one of these three types, but you should be able to recognize the author's stance on some of the issues and dialectics identified in the first reading in Part One.

2. Some topics will be more heavily represented by one particular perspective. For example, the readings in Parts Three (history) and Six (popular culture) are heavily represented by critical scholars—because social scientists and interpretive researchers have been less concerned with these topics.

Here are some general questions you may want to keep in mind as you read the various essays:

How does the reading portray culture and communication? As static, like a snapshot? or as dynamic? As cultural? or as idiosyncratic?

Are authors after objective knowledge? Do they approach their scholarship objectively? Subjectively?

What is the relationship between cultural notions and communication? Is it causal? Is it contested?

Does the reading address the importance of context? Is communication assumed to be consistent across many contexts or to vary contextually?

Does the reading address issues of power?

Perhaps most important, what does the essay contribute that helps you better understand your communication with others? Or how might the ideas in the reading help you improve your skills in communicating across ethnic, racial, gender, national, and sexual orientation boundaries?

READINGS IN
CULTURAL
CONTEXTS

PART ONE

THINKING ABOUT INTERCULTURAL COMMUNICATION

In recent years, research in intercultural communication has engaged in debates over questions of purpose, perspective, and method. Within these debates have been arguments about why we study intercultural communication. Some scholars propose that we need to address real practical issues, such as international business or domestic discussions of affirmative action, and that scholars are in a unique position to develop strategies for more effective communication in these contexts. Others propose that intercultural communication research should aim to share knowledge about culture in ways that can address power inequities.

Questions about the goals of intercultural communication inevitably raise other issues around the perspective of the researcher and the most appropriate methods for studying intercultural communication. Objectivity is a primary concern for scholars who are worried about imposing cultural biases on research; however, researchers increasingly question objectivity and quantitative analyses. Can any researcher be truly objective? Aren't all researchers (and their research) influenced by personal and cultural biases? Interested in the role of power and identity, these scholars propose turning to multiple forms of knowledge and various methods or analyses.

In Part One we enter into these debates and listen to the different arguments.

Consider these questions as you read the articles in this part:

How can intercultural communication be conceptualized?

What are the best ways to study intercultural communication?

What are issues of concern to intercultural specialists and practitioners?

The first reading, "A Dialectical Approach to Intercultural Communication," outlines a unique approach that provides a broad framework for understanding the various perspectives of intercultural communication. We (Martin, Nakayama, and Flores) identify various dialectics that emphasize the relational and processual aspects of intercultural communication behavior and research. In addition, a dialectical approach means holding contradictory notions simultaneously. We identify three types of intercultural communication research—social science, interpretive, and critical—and note how each, when seen through a dialectic lens, yields unique and complementary insights.

In the second reading, "Notes in the History of Intercultural Communication," Wendy Leeds-Hurwitz describes the beginning of the field, when post–World War II global activities led Congress to establish the Foreign Service Institute to train diplomats. Here, E. T. Hall and other anthropologists and linguists developed innovative ways to study culture and communication. Leeds-Hurwitz shows how interest in identifying broad cultural differences evolved. She also identifies the pragmatic, interdisciplinary, and international foci that influence the field to this day.

After establishing an overview of the field and its historical foundations, we turn to different ways of understanding and researching. We look at several issues in communication research: What should be the focus? Which cultures should we study? By what means?

Deborah A. Cai, in "Issues in Conducting Cross-Cultural Survey Research," identifies several challenges in social science research. She is interested in studying cross-cultural differences and emphasizes that assumptions and interpretations of communication behavior may not easily transfer from a researcher's home culture to a different culture. She also describes specific problems that arise in objective intercultural research—problems in sampling, survey instruments, survey administration, and comparing survey results.

Robert M. Shuter, in "Revisiting the Centrality of Culture," emphasizes the importance of studying communication in context. He promotes culture-specific studies that identify shared communication rules in specific communities/cultures. He also points out the limitations of our knowledge at this point, that vast areas of the world have been ignored in communication research: Africa, South and Central America, and the Middle East. He outlines the importance of culture in the next century for global business, understanding ethnic and racial tensions within societies, and coping with worldwide technological advances.

1

A DIALECTICAL APPROACH TO INTERCULTURAL COMMUNICATION

JUDITH N. MARTIN / THOMAS K. NAKAYAMA / LISA A. FLORES

We live in a world of increasing intercultural and international contacts. Sometimes these interactions are on an interpersonal level; sometimes they occur in organizational settings or political arenas. They are often facilitated by technological inventions such as jet travel, the Internet, and satellite transmissions of news events. The possibilities for intercultural communication are far greater than ever before. Yet, we know that these intercultural interactions include moments of conflict, friendship, hatred, romance, war, and an array of other experiences. The kinds of intercultural experiences that we face and the ways they occur often make intercultural communication a difficult field of study. It is not just interpersonal interaction, nor is it simply social interaction—it is quite complex indeed. Consequently, you need to think in more complex ways about intercultural interactions. There are no simple answers or easy items to memorize about any culture. Cultures are dynamic—as you are—and this ever-changing nature makes any attempt at static pieces of knowledge problematic.

A Dialectical Approach

Because of the dynamic nature of intercultural communication, we emphasize a *dialectical approach* to thinking about intercultural interaction. Many different kinds of dialectics have developed over thousands of years. Think about the judicial model, for example, in which the prosecution and the defense present the best cases they can from which the truth is to emerge. This dialectical relationship is rather oppositional. In many psychoanalytic models, however, the analyst and the analysand (patient) are not in an oppositional relationship, but rather in a helping, enabling dialectic. This text does not offer a comprehensive

overview of these differing forms of dialectic; however, it does introduce you to dialectical ways of considering intercultural communication.

A dialectical approach emphasizes the *processual, relational, and contradictory* nature of intercultural communication. In other words, you will encounter many different kinds of intercultural knowledge. For example, some culture-specific information will tell you how closely people in that culture tend to stand to each other. Other studies will give you historical background that might help explain certain antagonisms felt toward and by members of that culture. These various kinds of knowledge need to be understood in relation to one another to help you better understand the culture you are studying.

A dialectical approach to intercultural interaction emphasizes the *processual* character of understanding. Cultures change and so do individuals. In this dynamic mixture, we cannot assume that someone has particular characteristics simply because he or she belongs to a certain culture. We change over our lifetime, and this dynamic nature of personhood needs to be considered in intercultural communication. The culture of the United States today is not the same as the culture of the United States in the 1950s or even in the 1970s. Many assumptions about gender, sexuality, race or ethnicity, age, and so forth have been drastically reconfigured. Thus, intergroup relationships need to be viewed dynamically. For example, terrorist activities, such as the bombing of the Federal Building in Oklahoma City, have forced us to reconsider how we think about terrorism, about the threat of White supremacy groups, and about the safety some of us feel in the U.S. culture. These changes have influenced U.S. culture, much as future changes will influence any culture as well.

A dialectical approach also emphasizes the *relational* rather than individual aspects and persons. In studying intercultural communication, the dialectical perspective emphasizes the relationship between *aspects* of intercultural communication, and the importance of viewing these holistically and not in isolation. Can we understand culture without understanding communication and vice versa? Can we understand the conflict in the former Yugoslavia by only looking at the Serbian experience? Can we understand race relations in America without looking at the many different relationships among Blacks, Hispanics, Whites, and other groups?

The dialectical approach stresses the importance of relationship in intercultural communication encounters. Further, we cannot understand a relationship by only looking at two individuals' motivations, actions, and behaviors. A relationship has something unique that goes beyond the sum of two individuals. Intercultural communication scholar Muneo Yoshikawa (1987) describes this as the "dynamic in-betweeness" of a relationship—what exists beyond the two persons.

A more challenging aspect of the dialectical approach is that it requires holding two *contradictory* ideas simultaneously. This is contrary to most formal education in the United States. Most of our assumptions about learning and knowledge assume dichotomy and mutual exclusivity (e.g., multiple-choice and true/false tests). Dichotomies—good-evil, planets-earth, arteries-veins, air-water, man-animal—form the core of our philosophical, scientific, and religious traditions.

In contrast, a dialectical approach recognizes a need to transcend these dichotomies. This perspective is well known in Eastern countries and is based on the logic of *soku* (not-one, not-two). It emphasizes that the world is neither monistic nor dualistic (Nakayama, 1973, pp. 24–29). It is a way of seeing things as they are, recognizing the interdependent and complementary aspects of the seeming opposites (Yoshikawa, 1988, p. 187). For example, can we be wise and stupid at the same time? Of course. Can the strong also be weak? Of course; a strong tree branch, by bending and giving, doesn't break. Is it sometimes difficult to take a dialectical approach? Yes, but it seems very appropriate to studying intercultural communication because intercultural communication is about stepping outside normal frames of reference and trying to understand other worldviews.

Use a dialectical approach in understanding both the practice and the study of everyday intercultural communication. First, look at how to apply this approach to the practice of everyday intercultural communication.

The Dialectics of Intercultural Communication Practice

Communication scholar Leslie A. Baxter (1988) has identified three contradictory dialectic tensions that most of us recognize in relationships. For example, we sometimes feel the need to be both connected and autonomous in relationships with our parents and with others. We may also feel the need for novelty and predictability simultaneously, and the need to be open and yet private in our relationships. Six different dialectics come into play, taking into consideration the four building blocks of intercultural communication: culture, communication, context, and power. (See Figure 1.)

Cultural-Individual Dialectic

Intercultural communication is both cultural and individual, or idiosyncratic—that is, you may have some behaviors not shared by anyone else, perhaps a unique way of wrinkling your nose or a unique way of using language. However, you may also share communication patterns with those who have shaped you (family) and with whom you share other cultural practices. For example, Judith, one of the authors, shares some language patterns with other Americans of Pennsylvania Dutch heritage, such as saying "Is the ice cream all?" when she means "Is the ice cream all gone?" She may also share some patterns with other women—a preference for hi-context (indirect) communication. She shares other communication patterns with other White people; for example, assuming that communication competence mainly involves being polite and nice and not thinking very often about issues of power in her interactions with others. And yet, her communication cannot be reduced to the sum parts of all her group memberships: gender, ethnicity, race, and so forth.

So in studying intercultural communication,

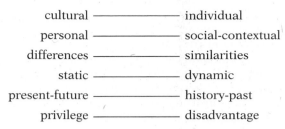

cultural ——————— individual

personal ——————— social-contextual

differences ——————— similarities

static ——————— dynamic

present-future ——————— history-past

privilege ——————— disadvantage

FIGURE 1 *Intercultural Communication Dialectics*

we will sometimes talk about communication patterns that are shared by particular groups (gender, ethnicity, etc.) and yet we always have to remember not to assume that group membership completely determines communication. This kind of rigid categorization leads to stereotyping.

Personal-Social (Contextual) Dialectic

This dialectic involves the role of context in intercultural communication. A dialectical perspective emphasizes the relationship between someone's personal characteristics and social, contextual behavior; that is, in some contexts we enact particular social roles that give meaning to our messages. For example, when lawyers, financial planners, or physicians communicate on specific topics, their messages may be interpreted in particular ways. In other contexts, messages may be interpreted differently.

As students and professors, we communicate in particular ways in classroom contexts, and our messages are interpreted in particular ways. Outside the classroom, in study group sessions, at football games, or at faculty meetings, we may communicate differently, expressing different aspects of ourselves. In understanding intercultural communication, we have to understand that we sometimes communicate as members of social groups, yet we also always communicate from our personal identities.

Differences-Similarities Dialectic

A dialectical approach recognizes the importance of similarities and differences in understanding intercultural communication. Real, important differences exist between various cultural groups. Women and men do communicate differently in

some contexts; so do Japanese and Americans. In real life, however, there are a great many similarities in human experience and ways of communicating.

There is a tendency sometimes to overemphasize group differences in intercultural communication—in a way that can set up false dichotomies and rigid expectations. Difference and similarity can coexist in intercultural communication interactions. For example, two men, one British and one Japanese, learn that they are going to be fathers. As men, they may share an initial joy and pride in parenthood, but differences in national culture, age, or religion might lead one to rejoice in the perpetuation of the family name while the other anticipates the father-child relationship. The cultural differences here may serve to complement the similarities and bring both men to a fuller appreciation of parenthood. Yet, consider another scenario: Israelis and Palestinians share a love for their holy city, Jerusalem. This similarity may be outweighed by the historical differences in meanings of Jerusalem so that the differences work in opposition. So, it is important to see how differences and similarities work in cooperation or in opposition.

Static-Dynamic Dialectic

The static-dynamic dialectic highlights the ever-changing nature of culture and cultural practices but also underscores the tendency to think about these things as constant. Some general cultural patterns remain relatively consistent over time, such as the emphasis in the United States on innovation, on liking things "new and improved." However, specific cultural practices, such as language, often vary substantially. For example, sociolinguists' descriptions of Black English or White counterculture language in the 1970s appear outdated when compared with contemporary language patterns. So thinking about culture and cultural practices as both static and dynamic helps us navigate through a diverse world.

Present-Future/History-Past Dialectic

A dialectic exists between the history-past and the present-future—that is, we need to balance an understanding of both the past and the present. Also, the past is always seen through the lens of the present. Consider the responses to Oliver Stone's film *Nixon*. The film was criticized because of the interpretation Mr. Stone made of (now) historical events and persons. Yet, as Mr. Stone pointed out, we are always telling our versions of history. How do we know what "really" happened in the first 100 years of U.S. history?

Understanding African American and White interaction in the United States is incomplete without understanding the history of slavery and the African diaspora. At the same time, contexts today are different from contexts 100 years ago. Many influential factors precede and succeed any intercultural interaction and give meaning to that interaction.

Privilege-Disadvantage Dialectic

This dialectic concerns the role of power in intercultural communication. As individuals, we carry and communicate various types of privilege and disadvantage. These may be in the form of political preference, social position, or status. For example, if members of wealthy nations travel to less wealthy countries, the intercultural interactions between these two groups will certainly be influenced by their differential in economic power. A colleague recounted a recent experience of being a U.S. tourist in Banff, Canada, and seeing many signs in upscale shops in Japanese rather than in English. She described how the Canadian shopkeepers seemed much more interested in interacting with Japanese tourists than with U.S. tourists.

Hierarchies and power differentials may not always be this clear. And people may be simultaneously privileged and disadvantaged, or privileged in some contexts and disadvantaged in others.

The question for us as we study intercultural communication is, How does understanding these dialectics change our approach to intercultural communication? We might also ask, How do we, as scholars and practitioners of intercultural communication, use these dialectics in our daily intercultural interactions?

The dialectics themselves suggest that these questions are complicated, for as mentioned ear-

lier, there are no easy answers. However, as an intercultural communicator, each of us can use our knowledge of these dialectics to guide our intercultural communication. One important thing to remember is that when we communicate across cultures, we can never just communicate with the individual. Instead, because we are always situated, to some degree, within our cultural identities, we bring those cultural identities to our interaction. Similarities, differences, power, context—they are always with us.

The Dialectics of Studying Intercultural Communication

This dialectical approach can also be extended to intercultural communication research, where there are many different ways to think about and study culture and communication. Some of the same dialectics discussed above also apply to intercultural research: Some intercultural communication researchers concentrate on identifying cultural differences; some seek similarities in communication patterns. Some think of culture and communication as fairly static entities; others see them as more fluid and dynamic. In addition, some scholars do qualitative analysis of poetry, folk tales, or media, while others gather quantitative data such as from survey questionnaires. Obviously, scholars disagree on the best way to study and understand intercultural communication.

This question of what counts as research knowledge is not just an academic debate because we all "do research" in informal ways. For example, we, the authors, might ask ourselves how we understand each other—across age, gender, sexual orientation, ethnicity. What kinds of knowledge about intercultural communication might help us understand each other? Television shows about Japanese or Pennsylvania Dutch culture? Results of surveys about male-female communication? Our experiences with other Japanese Americans, White, and Latino/a individuals? Studying the history of gender, race, and ethnicity in U.S. contexts? How we approach and answer these questions may influence what we know about each other, how we treat each other, and how or whether our relationship develops.

Additional dialectics having to do with research assumptions and methods are given in the three descriptions of intercultural communication research that follow. They illustrate three different ways to study and report on the issue of interethnic conflict. As you read these examples, think about which study is more appealing to you. What does each tell us about intercultural conflict? How does each study approach the dialectics discussed earlier?

The study in the first example attempted to discover if differences exist between the ways in which African American and White males and females deal with interpersonal conflict. A questionnaire about preferred styles of handling conflicts was completed by 123 Black and 180 White college students. It used a 30-item scale that measures three conflict communication styles: control, nonconfrontational, and solution oriented. Based on previous research, 12 hypotheses were posed. Results of the statistical analyses (MANOVA, and *t* tests) revealed that 4 hypotheses were supported, and 8 were not. The results showed that

1. Males, both Black and White, tended to use more indirect, nonconfrontational strategies than did females.
2. Black females, overall, tended to use slightly more direct, controlling conflict strategies.
3. White females, overall, tended to use more active solution-oriented conflict strategies (Ting-Toomey, 1986).

The study in the second example used ethnographic research methods (participant-observation, observation, interviews). The researchers spent a great deal of time observing and interacting with both Athabaskan and English speakers in northern Canada. Athabaskan language is related to many languages spoken by Native peoples in Canada and the United States. The researchers identified four differences in language use by Athabaskan and English speakers and concluded that these four differences often lead to intercultural misunderstandings and conflict:

1. *Presentation of self:* When first meeting someone, Athabaskans speak little, whereas English speakers talk a lot. When they know someone well and feel very comfortable, Athabaskans speak a lot; English speakers are more comfortable with silence.

2. *Distribution of talk:* In beginning conversations, the English speaker talks first; the Athabaskan rule is to wait. So when the two interact, the English speaker usually has control of the topic. Athabaskan speech has more and longer pauses. These differences in rules mean that an English speaker almost always has the floor, and an Athabaskan gets very little time.

3. *Information structure:* In English, information structure, or knowing how to interpret a statement, is shown by prosody (intonation, stress, tone of voice). For example, if you say "He told me so," it means something different from "*He* told me so." In Athabaskan, information structure is expressed by morphemes (suffixes or words at beginning or end of a phrase). When English speakers learn Athabaskan, they use stress and intonation; in speaking English, Athabaskans try to insert word endings to show emphasis. Both groups of speakers sound halting and confusing to the other group.

4. *Content organization:* Athabaskan organizes conversations and narratives in sections of twos and fours; English speakers, in threes. The result is that speakers sometimes feel they are out of synchrony with each other. English speakers feel Athabaskan stories are a little too long or points are irrelevant; Athabaskans feel that English speakers leave something out—the fourth part.

These differences in discourse rules often lead to stereotyping and conflict. Athabaskan speakers see English speakers as too talkative—always talking first, bragging, asking too many questions, interrupting. English speakers stereotype Athabaskans as being too silent, avoiding situations of talking, being too indirect, only wanting to talk to close acquaintances, and playing down their own abilities (Scollon & Wong-Scollon, 1990).

The study in the third example, which is grounded in critical theory, analyzes the centrality of land in dominant and Native American representations of Indians. The researcher's goal is to examine the ways land figures into political struggles of Native Americans. Beginning with a historical frame on discussions around land, the study traces two bodies of literature on Native Americans. The first, which comes predominantly from Western sources, exoticizes the relationship between Native Americans and land. Native American discourse, the second body of literature, offers a more complex picture of the importance of land to Native Americans. The researcher describes these contradictory discourses regarding Native peoples and their land:

> The political combat over land is wrapped in a complex of oppositional discourses, contradictory representations, and diverse cultural constructions. . . . The land is constructed in . . . narratives of dominance and survivance, historical and current simulations of the Indian by Native and North Americans.
>
> In contrast to the people who inhabited the expanse, the land itself was represented in early texts by romanticized images of Indians engraved on the landscape. While the Spanish were debating the ambiguous humanity of the Indians, the rough, earthy beauty of the new territory was symbolized by pairs of Indian men and women . . . framed in the exoticism of flora and fauna. . . . Images of the Princess and the squaw accommodate the colonial experience, the western expansion of settlement, and the development of the land over which we continue to struggle.
>
> Across Native America today, writing about the land reflects the differing experiences and practices of individuals and communities, even nations. But these differences are absorbed in an appeal to communality related to two distinct but intertwined cultural conceptions of the earth. . . . [S]urvival stories speak of land as a specific cultural construct articulated to the physical environment, an expanse of territory which locates the ideology, identity, and practice of a particular nation or community.
>
> With their small population and meager financial means, it is this ideological stance, this "difference," that distinguishes Native Americans in the minds of both Indians and others. . . . Indian resistance is cultural persis-

tence; and it is voiced in strategies of direct and indirect opposition. . . . From this position, Indian "spiritness" asserts the promise of political autonomy, economic possibility, and cultural survival.

> The vague consciousness expressed in narratives of survival and dominance is not a paradigm for Native American cultural construction of the land. Indian discourses of the land affirm that space is cognitively and politically marked in metaphorical and real expressions of politics and ideology. (Valaskakis, 1996)

All three examples explore the notion of intercultural (interethnic) conflict, but in different ways. Which do you like the best? Why? Which seems to reveal the most about intercultural conflict? These examples represent three different kinds of scholarship. Each reflects different assumptions about culture, communication, and research goals and methods. Each takes a position with respect to the six dialectics discussed previously. So we can now extend our dialectical framework to include research dialectics (see Figure 2.)

Let's examine each dialectic, answering the following questions:

1. What is the goal of the researcher?
2. What is the relationship between culture and communication? (causal-reciprocal-contested dialectic)
3. What counts as knowledge? (reductionist-holistic dialectic)
4. What are the best methods for studying and reporting intercultural communication? (objective-subjective dialectic)
5. What is the researcher's view of intercultural communication practice—with respect to the six research dialectics?

Social Science Research

The first example is a good demonstration of social science study. The goal of this type of research is to describe and ultimately to predict, through hypotheses, conflict behavior. The

Social Science   Interpretive   Critical

Practice Dialectics

cultural ——————— individual

personal ——————— social-contextual

differences ——————— similarities

static ——————— dynamic

present-future ——————— history-past

privilege ——————— disadvantage

Research Dialectics

causal —— reciprocal —— contested

reductionist ——————— holistic

objective ——————— subjective

FIGURE 2 *Three Intercultural Communication Research Perspectives*

hypotheses are usually drawn from previous research, and knowledge is accumulated in very systematic, incremental ways. Since only four hypotheses were confirmed in this study, a follow-up study may revise hypotheses, and either refine the theory or add another variable, or both. For example, perhaps conflict style depends on the type of conflict encountered.

In this type of research, culture and communication are often seen as two causal variables; that is, they are linked together in very explicit, causal ways. In this study, culture (ethnicity-gender) determines communication (conflict style). The hypotheses suggest that one's ethnicity or race and gender will determine one's preferred strategies for managing conflict. Black and White males and females use different strategies, as predicted by the theory and hypotheses.

What counts as knowledge? Knowledge is approached in a reductionist way—that is, the researcher breaks down communication and culture into specific, measurable variables (e.g., gender, conflict styles). These variables are then measured and a causal relationship is established, often through statistical calculations.

What methods are used by social science researchers? The social science researcher empha-

sizes objectivity and tries to remain separate from participants in the research. In this example, the researcher mailed or distributed questionnaires to college students without knowing the people who participated in the study. These objective methods are similar to those used in psychology and sociology, such as survey questionnaires, observation, and standardized tests. After data are gathered, the analysis is often quantitative—that is, large numbers of individuals participate in the study and supply information that is then analyzed by statistical methods to establish quantitative relationships.

What is the best way to report knowledge? Usually in an objective, neutral manner. As seen in this example, the researcher tries to be as unbiased and objective as possible and often follows a set format for reporting research studies: theoretical background, research questions or hypotheses, methods, results, and discussion.

How do you think a social science researcher sees intercultural communication practice? Perhaps you can tell from this example that communication is studied as rather static, cultural, and personal; that is, we can learn something from a "snapshot" of communication behaviors that are assumed to be connected to the cultural background of individuals and are consistent in a variety of contexts.

To summarize, social science researchers generally emphasize cultural, static, personal, and present-oriented aspects of communication. They are often interested in identifying differences and not as interested in issues of power or privilege. Culture and communication are causally related, and research and research reporting emphasize objectivity.

Interpretive

The second example discussed earlier is interpretive research. The goal of interpretive researchers is generally to describe, rather than predict. Interpretive researchers usually see the relationship between culture and communication as a reciprocal one. Culture and communication are intertwined and dynamic. Culture is shaped through communication; communication is shaped and influenced by culture. They often look for patterns or regularities of communication, rather than universal or predictable relationships.

In the second example, the researchers describe different patterns of talk of Athabaskan and English speakers. They observed that different patterns of talk sometimes lead to conflict, but they did not begin their study with a prediction that ethnicity would produce certain kinds of talk or conflict.

What counts as knowledge? Information gathered in a more holistic and subjective way. Interpretive researchers emphasize the importance of seeing cultural communication in a holistic way; for example, beginning with general communication patterns of Athabaskan and English speakers. They did not approach their study with previously defined categories or variables. In terms of approaching and reporting research, interpretive researchers tend to be more subjective and qualitative—that is, they emphasize that getting close to people may provide unique insights not gained by more objective methods. Thus, many use ethnographic methods (borrowed from anthropology or sociolinguistics): participant-observation, observation, and interviews. As seen in the second example, conclusions about the Athabaskan and English communication patterns were arrived at after a long time of carefully observing and interacting with both Athabaskans and English speakers.

Another type of interpretive research is rhetorical analysis in which researchers might turn to films, television programs, newspaper articles, or even speeches from particular cultures to assess public images and representations of culture and intercultural communication. For example, a researcher might turn to *Star Trek* to find models of effective intercultural communication. Another possible study might involve analyzing newspaper accounts of a social issue, such as affirmative action, that would have implications for cultural interaction. Researchers are not involved in the subject of these studies, but they do approach the studies in a subjective, holistic mind-set.

Rhetorical scholars, then, might seek to uncover the rhetorical strategies used to mask or highlight culture. While they might rely on particular tools in their analysis (e.g., identifying metaphors), they do not explicitly predict what they will find. Instead, they are likely to let the findings emerge from the data.

Unlike this study, interpretive researchers often study communication patterns in one cultural group—rather than looking for cultural differences. They often prefer to do more in-depth analysis of communication rules in several contexts in one speech community. Contexts are important to the interpretive researcher.

To summarize, interpretive researchers are generally interested in individual similarities among or within a group of people; culture and communication are seen as dynamic and emerging. Understanding communication in context is very important. Like the social science researcher, interpretive researchers are not as interested in privilege-disadvantage dialectic. They approach research and report research in a more holistic and subjective way than do social science researchers.

Critical

A third kind of scholarship shares many of the same assumptions as the interpretive, but the goal of the research is to produce societal change. In critical research, culture is seen as a site of struggle for various meanings. There is no easy or direct relationship between culture and communication—that is, there is no assumption that everyone in a cultural group will communicate in the same way. Rather, competing groups have competing meanings, and in those competitions the boundaries of cultures are negotiated.

In the third example, the researcher examined the various discourses and competing meanings for the relationship of Indians to their land. This complicated relationship can only be understood by examining the historical, political, and economic forces that affect understandings of culture, conflict, and communication. The example also illustrates the importance of locating power and resistance in intercultural interactions.

What counts as knowledge within this approach? Here, the material existence (or nonexistence) of a nation with specific land boundaries is only as significant as the meanings that are given to that nation. Knowledge is situated within cultural boundaries so that questions of proof or validity are recognized as specific cultural constructions of the definition of knowledge. As shown in our third example, a critical approach focuses on the communication texts where these meanings are located. In what ways are American Indians not simply Canadians or U.S. Americans? How do cultural texts portray them?

Critical researchers are also sensitive to which groups are more and less empowered to create these texts, whether on television or in movies, magazines, and newspapers. The notion of power here is crucial to understanding how these indigenous cultural groups are both manipulated and dominated by the dominant cultural groups. Power is also important in understanding how cultural groups resist meanings and maintain their own ways of understanding the world.

Critical methods are varied and frequently include analysis of media and other popular culture texts. The cultural discourses about "Indianness" are communicated through messages, and critical researchers often turn to these cultural texts. It is important, however, to note that critical researchers are also attentive to how these texts circulate in society, as well as the political, economic, and social differences between and among these cultural groups that form the foundation of much of this communication. A critical researcher does not assume that everyone can and does communicate from equivalent positions in society, nor that everyone is listened to in the same ways.

What are the best formats for reporting research? Narratives, stories, and dialogues that incorporate social statistics, such as data on hate crimes against certain cultural groups as well as income and educational differences, help us to better understand how these cultural texts are relevant in a given society. Critical researchers utilize a wide range of data and discourses to understand how intercultural communication is influenced by the social context in which it occurs. Thus, the forms for presenting critical research are quite varied and responsive to different ways of understanding different cultural texts and experiences.

To summarize, critical researchers are generally interested in individual experiences and similarities among or within a group of people, within the context of unequal relations of power. In this perspective, culture and communication

are seen as dynamic and emerging, but also as contested. These contestations lead to empowering and disempowering different cultural groups in different ways. Critical researchers attempt to interpret and understand how this happens so that differing ways of intercultural communication can be undertaken to change contemporary ways of living and the attendant material conditions.

Understanding communication in context, particularly the macrocontexts (social, political, historical) is very important. Unlike social science and interpretive researchers, critical scholars are very interested in privilege-disadvantage dialectic. Like interpretive researchers, critical scholars approach research and report research holistically and subjectively.

Conclusion

Whereas most intercultural communication texts include one or two types of scholarship, we, the authors, believe that each of the three perspectives we discussed contributes something to the understanding of communication. Each represents one angle or one view of a very complicated topic—the intersections of culture and communication. Actually, it's more a matter of what each considers important. Most scholars would agree on the components of intercultural communication: culture, communication, context, power. But they would disagree on the relative importance of each, how they are interrelated, and the *best* methods for understanding intercultural communication.

Let's look more closely at what each kind of research contributes. *Social science research,* by taking "objective snapshots" of communication behavior, has helped us identify broad cultural *differences* in language and nonverbal behavior among various groups, as illustrated in the example of conflict styles of Blacks and Whites. This research has also helped us identify important variables, such as gender, ethnicity, and national culture, that influence and help us predict the intercultural communication process, both successes and failures. For example, scholars have identified factors that influence success in overseas sojourns as well as factors that determine how people accommodate their language in intercultural interactions.

Interpretive research, with an emphasis on *context*, has given us in-depth understanding of communication rules in very specific communities (e.g., Athabaskan and English). It shows us how communication often varies with context—within the same cultural community; for example, researchers have identified rules for speaking in places and contexts in working-class communities, for leave-taking in Colombian social contexts, and for Native American and White students in classroom contexts. Interpretive researchers concentrate on the shared communication rules, and their research helps us understand how communication, culture, and identity are dynamically and holistically intertwined.

Critical researchers have provided us with insights on the role of *power* in intercultural interactions, as well as the influence of historical, political, economic, and social forces on intercultural interaction. For example, critical researchers have examined the role of history in interracial interactions in the United States and in Arab-Israeli relations. They have also looked at how media images present contradictory messages about various cultural groups, how historical forces impact individuals' personal identity and development of interpersonal relationships across gender, ethnic, and sexual orientation. Their research efforts are focused on understanding how power works, so that these power relations can be challenged for disempowered groups.

We can get a more complete picture of the complexities of intercultural communication by gleaning knowledge yielded from all three perspectives. While research is based on different and sometimes contradictory assumptions, taking a dialectical approach means living with some apparent contradictions and looking at intercultural communication from a variety of different angles.

REFERENCES

Baxter, L. A. (1988). A dialectical perspective on communication strategies in relationship development. In S. W. Duck (Ed.), *A handbook of personal relationships* (pp. 257–273). New York: John Wiley & Sons Ltd.

Carbaugh, D. (1988). Comments on "culture" in communication inquiry. *Communication Reports, 1,* 38–41.

Hall, S. (1992). Cultural studies and its theoretical legacies. In L. Grossberg, C. Nelson, & P. Treichler (Eds.), *Cultural studies* (pp. 277–294). New York: Routledge.

Hofstede, G. (1984). *Culture's consequences.* Beverly Hills, CA: Sage.

Martin, J. N., & Nakayama, T. K. (1997). *Intercultural communication in contexts.* Mountain View, CA: Mayfield.

Nakayama, N. (1973). *Mujunteki, sosoku no ronri.* Kyoto: Hyakkaen.

Philipsen, G. (1992). *Speaking culturally: Explorations in social communication.* Albany: State University of New York Press.

Scollon, R., & Wong-Scollon, S. (1990). Athabaskan-English interethnic communication. In D. Carbaugh (Ed.), *Cultural communication and intercultural contact* (pp. 259–287). Hillsdale, NJ: Lawrence Erlbaum.

Ting-Toomey, S. (1986). Conflict communication styles in Black and White subjective cultures. In Y. Y. Kim (Ed.), *Interethnic communication: Current research* (pp. 75–88). International and Intercultural Communication Annual 10. Newbury Park, CA: Sage.

Valaskakis, G. G. (1996). Indian country: Negotiating the meaning of land in Native America. In C. Nelson & D. P. Gaonkar (Eds.), *Disciplinarity and dissent in cultural studies* (pp. 149–169). New York: Routledge.

Yoshikawa, M. J. (1987). The double-swing model of intercultural communication between the East and the West. In D. L. Kincaid (Ed.), *Communication theory: Eastern and Western perspectives* (pp. 319–329). New York: Academic Press.

Yoshikawa, M. J. (1988). Cross-cultural adaptation and perceptual development. In Y. Y. Kim & W. B. Gudykunst (Eds.), *Cross cultural adaptation: Current approaches* (pp. 140–148). International and Intercultural Communication Annual 11. Newbury Park, CA: Sage.

KEY TERMS

dialectic	interpretive
methodology	critical
culture	research
social science	

DISCUSSION QUESTIONS

1. The authors identified six dialectics of intercultural communication practice. Can you think of other dialectics that might apply to intercultural interactions?

2. How might a dialectical perspective help us understand contemporary intercultural incidents, for example, the different perceptions of Whites and Blacks toward the O. J. Simpson trial?

3. How does using these three approaches (social science, interpretive, and critical) provide a more comprehensive picture of intercultural interaction than any one approach?

4. If you were conducting intercultural communication research, which of the three approaches would you prefer? Why?

5. How might a critical researcher conduct an investigation of different conflict resolution styles used by Anglo-Americans and Chicano(a)s? Would a critical researcher be interested in investigating this topic? If so, what kinds of methods might be used?

2

NOTES IN THE HISTORY OF INTERCULTURAL COMMUNICATION: THE FOREIGN SERVICE INSTITUTE AND THE MANDATE FOR INTERCULTURAL TRAINING[1]

WENDY LEEDS-HURWITZ

Many articles discussing some aspect of intercultural communication begin with a paragraph in which the author reviews the history of the field and the major early publications. Typically, Edward Hall's book *The Silent Language*, published in 1959, is listed as the first work in the field, and often specifically mentioned as the crucial starting point.[2] The lack of attention to his motives and sources for the work is not surprising, since the young field still has little history written about it. But no book develops without a context, and no author invents a field without a reason. This study will look at the context in which Hall's work was produced and will describe some of the events that led to the creation of the field of intercultural communication. Using this historical record, I argue that the parameters of the field were established in response to a particular set of problems. If we are to understand why we include some topics as appropriate and do not consider other types of work, we must understand the exigencies that generated the first study of intercultural communication.

Briefly, I will argue that intercultural communication emerged from occurrences at the Foreign Service Institute (FSI) of the U.S. Department of State (DOS) between 1946 and 1956. Because intercultural communication grew out of the need to apply abstract anthropological concepts to the practical world of foreign service diplomats, this early focus on training American diplomats led to the later, now standard use of intercultural communication training. Only recently (beginning with Gudykunst, 1983) has intercultural communication begun to discuss theoretical approaches; initially the concepts were accompanied only by examples, not by an elaboration of theory. In their first writings on the subject Hall (1959) and Hall and Whyte (1960) made no explicit attempt to create a new academic field with a novel research tradition (Winkin, 1984, p. 17). Establishing a new academic field was, rather, a secondary phase, based on Hall's early attempt to translate anthropological insights into cultural differences to an audience that wanted immediate and practical applications, not research studies.

My discussion offers four major arguments: first, that Hall's work was important to the development of the field of intercultural communication; second, that Hall's work originated in and was shaped by the specific context of the FSI; third, that this context resulted in a number of crucial decisions, which were continued by later researchers; and fourth, that these decisions illuminate some features of the contemporary literature. Assuming that the readers of this article will be most familiar with the contemporary literature, my effort will focus upon illuminating the historical context which set the stage for the current practices in the field.

The following specific connections between the work of Hall (and others) at the FSI and current intercultural communication research will be demonstrated:

1. Instead of the traditional anthropological focus on a *single* culture at a time, or at best, a comparison of two, Hall responded to the critique of his foreign service students by stressing interaction between members of different cultures. Hall is most explicit about this in a publication written jointly with William Foote Whyte:

   > In the past, anthropologists have been primarily concerned with the internal pattern of a given culture. In giving attention to intercultural problems, they have examined the impact of one culture upon another. Very little attention has been given to the actual communication process between representatives of different cultures (Hall & Whyte, 1960, p. 12).

   This shift from viewing cultures one at a time to studying interactions between members of different cultures has been enormously influential on the study of intercultural com-

munication and is what most completely defines the field today.

2. Hall narrowed the focus of study from culture as a general concept (macroanalysis) to smaller units within culture (microanalysis). This occurred in response to a particular problem: the students in the FSI classes had no interest in generalizations or specific examples that applied to countries other than the ones to which they were assigned; they wanted concrete, immediately useful details provided to them before they left the US, and they thought it appropriate that the anthropologists involved in their training should focus their energy on this level of culture.[3] Hall, eventually agreeing that the complaints of his students were justified, began the move from a focus on the entire culture to specific small moments of interaction.

3. Hall enlarged the concept of culture to include the study of communication; he viewed much of his work as an extension of anthropological insight to a new topic, interaction between members of two or more different cultures. Those who study intercultural communication continue to use the concepts taken from anthropology in the 1940s and 1950s (culture, ethnocentrism, etc.), but this cross-fertilization moved primarily in one direction: now only a few anthropologists study proxemics, time, kinesics or paralanguage, or focus on interactions between members of different cultures. Although anthropology and intercultural communication were once closely allied, the two fields have grown apart as reflected in the shift from the qualitative methods of anthropology to the quantitative methods of communication generally used in intercultural communication today and in the recent surge of interest in applying traditional American communication theories to intercultural contexts. While intercultural communication sprang from anthropological insights, it has been on its own for some thirty years, and some shift in focus was predictable.

4. Implicit in Hall's work is the view that communication is patterned, learned, and analyz-

able, just as culture had been previously described. (Others later stated these insights more explicitly, but he implies them and should be given some credit for the ideas.) Researchers today make the same assumptions about communication. Without these assumptions, we could not have the abstract theorizing about intercultural communication that now marks the field.

5. Hall decided that the majority of information potentially available about a culture was not really essential in situations of face-to-face interaction with members of that culture: only a small percentage of the total need be known. Thus he delineated several types of microcultural behavior as the focus of study: tone of voice, gestures, time, and spatial relationships. That intercultural research still pays extensive attention to these types of interaction over many other possibilities is a tribute to the influence of his work.

6. Several aspects of the training established by Hall are accepted as part of the repertoire of training procedures used today: (a) Hall created teaching materials out of experiences abroad which students in the training sessions were willing to provide; (b) Hall encouraged his students to meet with foreign nationals as part of the preparation for a trip abroad, as one way to increase their knowledge of other cultures; and (c) Hall presented his insights as a beginning for his students, but assumed they would continue the learning process once they arrived at their destination.

7. Hall and his colleagues at FSI are responsible for the use of descriptive linguistics as the basic model for intercultural communication, a model which still implicitly serves as the basis for much current research. Explicit discussion of linguistic terminology is currently enjoying a renaissance through attention to what are now termed the "etic" and "emic" approaches to intercultural communication.

8. Hall expanded his audience beyond foreign diplomats to include all those involved in international business, today one of the largest markets for intercultural training.

Intercultural communication continues to serve the function of training Americans to go abroad, although it has grown substantially beyond this initial mission to include such areas as the training of foreign students, recent immigrants, and teachers who work with students of different cultural backgrounds; it has established a university base now, and many practitioners engage in research, as well as teaching large numbers of undergraduate students the basics of an intercultural communication approach.

The innovations listed here were picked up by the fledgling field of communication, and they were crucial in the establishment of the area known as intercultural communication. They are today hallmarks of intercultural communication.

Background: The Foreign Service Institute

The story of intercultural communication begins at the Foreign Service Institute. In the 1940s many persons recognized that American diplomats were not fully effective abroad, since they often did not speak the language and usually knew little of the host culture. After World War II Americans began to reevaluate their knowledge and understanding of other countries, both in terms of their languages and in terms of their cultural assumptions. Along with general concern about the ability of Americans to interact with foreign nationals, the training and knowledge of American diplomats were issues, since deficiencies in those areas have substantial repercussions. In 1946 Congress passed the Foreign Service Act, which reorganized the Foreign Service, and established a Foreign Service Institute to provide both initial training and in-service training on a regular basis throughout the careers of Foreign Service Officers and other staff members.[4]

As one part of the preparation of the bill, in 1945 the *American Foreign Service Journal* sponsored a contest for ideas to improve the training program of the Foreign Service; Foreign Service personnel from around the world contributed essays. Those judged to be the best were published as a series of articles in the journal, and the comments are fascinating. Many themes recur, among them the recommendation for better language training. Because American representatives abroad were often not well trained in foreign languages, many contributors argued that they would be more successful if they had fluency in at least one language other than English.[5] Many authors also urged fuller education about the history, political structure, economics, and international relations with the United States, not only of the country to which the diplomat would be sent, but of the entire geographic region.

About the same time, a series of articles not submitted for the contest, but generally addressing the issue of change in the Foreign Service, was published. One of these specifically criticized the generally limited language fluency in the foreign service and highlighted the need for individuals who knew more than basic grammar and who could converse in a language other than English (Pappano, 1946). In an unpublished history of the beginnings of FSI, Boswell points out that "Prior to 1946 the American Foreign Service placed less emphasis on language qualifications for entry than any other nation's foreign service" (1948, p. 38). He attributed the deficiency to the poor language training available in American schools.

One factor which changed attitudes towards language training in the Foreign Service was the extensive language training program begun by the Army during World War II, which demonstrated the feasibility of language training on a large scale. Little excuse remained for Foreign Service diplomats to have inadequate language skills (Boswell, 1948, p. 38).

In 1939 Mortimer Graves, then the Executive Secretary of the American Council of Learned Societies (ACLS), reasoned that linguists who were capable of analyzing Native American Indian languages (often funded through ACLS grants) should be able to analyze other, perhaps more politically useful, languages. Convinced that worldwide conflict was inevitable, he obtained funding from the Rockefeller Foundation to put a small group of linguists to work. Mary Haas, the first hired, was asked to analyze Thai from native speakers, to prepare basic teaching materials, and then to teach a group of students the language, combining the spoken words of native speakers with the written materials she had prepared (Cowan, 1975, 1987; see also Smith, 1946, and Murray, 1983, pp. 113–120).

When the United States formally entered World War II, Graves brought J Milton Cowan to Washington; together they organized the linguists to serve the war effort through what became known as the Intensive Language Program (ILP). Those who had been inducted served on the military side of the project, and those who had not participated as civilians through the ACLS. Henry Lee Smith, Jr., who was trained as a linguist, was in the Army Reserves at the time; he was recalled to active duty and put in charge of the military side (Cowan, 1975; Maddox, 1949).

The method, developed as the "linguistic method" of language training, became the "Army method." Instead of the traditional focus on learning to read and write a language and on grammar as the key to a language, the method emphasized appropriate use of the spoken language, an innovative approach. Because the classroom teacher was a native speaker, students heard the idiomatic usage and pronunciation. These native speakers were under the close supervision of professional linguists, who worked with them on consistent organization of the materials. Ideally the material was organized as a series of natural speech situations: asking directions, going shopping, finding housing, etc. Through this division of labor, a small number of linguists supervised a large number of native speakers, and dozens of languages could be taught simultaneously with a minimum of full-time staff members (Smith, 1946).

Initially the Army program, formally one part of the larger Army Specialized Training Program (ASTP), was to serve 1,500 of the brightest and most qualified Army recruits. However, believing that having a larger number of soldiers qualified to speak a variety of languages was desirable, officials increased the number of participants to 15,000. Not all of the techniques that had been established for 1,500 transferred easily to the larger group, but, on the whole, the program was remarkably effective (see Cowan, 1975). The primary problem with ASTP was not in the training, but in the follow-through. For various reasons, soldiers trained to speak particular languages were assigned randomly and only rarely were able to use their linguistic training.

All of these efforts came together when the Foreign Service Institute was officially established. Because of the experience within an Army setting and due in part to the widespread agreement of a need for language training within the Foreign Service, FSI was immediately able to establish a language training program that had already been developed, tested, and proven effective. Frank Hopkins, the first Director of FSI, had studied linguistics and anthropology while at Harvard and had been impressed there with the work of Clyde Kluckhohn. "Hopkins was the linchpin in recruiting Haxie [Henry Lee] Smith and in the bringing of Social Science into FSI" (Hall, personal correspondence). Smith moved from the Army, where he had been serving as Director of the Language School, to a position as Director of Language Studies in the Division of Training Services for the Foreign Service in 1946; when the new Foreign Service Institute was formally established in 1947, he was made director of the School of Languages, one of the four schools established within FSI. Smith was later responsible for recruiting well-known linguist George L. Trager into the School of Languages, as well as Edward Kennard, an anthropologist who ran the School of Area Studies (Hall, personal correspondence). Bringing to FSI the knowledge of how to run a linguistically based language training program, Smith adapted his experience to a new audience.

Smith maintained the model of native speakers in the classroom, combined with trained linguists available to prepare additional written materials where these were needed, although much of this work had already been prepared under ILP and ASTP auspices. The linguists could also work occasionally with the students. For the classes in descriptive linguistics, linguists such as Trager prepared the materials.

Trager summarized the basic approach quite well in this statement, described as the efforts of the entire group working together:

> Language has been indicated as being only one of the systematic arrangements of cultural items

that societies possess. A culture consists of many such systems—language, social organization, religion, technology, law, etc. Each of these cultural systems other than language is dependent on language for its organization and existence, but otherwise constitutes an independent system whose patterning may be described. In theory, when one has arrived at the separate statements of each such cultural system, one can then proceed to a comparison with the linguistic system. The full statement of the point-by-point and pattern-by-pattern relations between the language and any of the other cultural systems will contain all the "meanings" of the linguistic forms, and will constitute the metalinguistics of that culture (Trager, 1950, p. 7).

Two important assumptions are apparent here: first, that the analysis of culture was dependent upon a prior linguistic model; and second, that linguistic meaning comes not from words alone but from a combination of the linguistic and what was then termed the "metalinguistic" levels. Both ideas are basic to Hall's 1959 book; both have influenced the contemporary field of intercultural communication.

The other members of the group to which Trager refers were: John M. Echols, Charles A. Ferguson, Carleton T. Hodge, Charles F. Hockett, Edward A. Kennard, Henry Hoenigswald, and John Kepke. Trager, Ferguson, and Hodge all had the advantage of having worked previously with Smith within the Army program. Edward Hall came into the group later than the others, in 1951, and frequently served a different administrative structure, although he was part of the FSI staff, and did participate in most of the orientation programs for Foreign Service personnel. In addition to learning how to speak a particular language, the students attended a seminar on general linguistics and another on discussing general principles for analyzing human societies (Maddox, 1949). There Hall found his role, working to ensure that the students obtained general anthropological training to complement their specific language training. Shortly before Hall's arrival, Edward Kennard published an article describing the role of anthropology at the FSI, in which he mentions developing the course, "Understanding

Foreign Peoples," to combine anthropological insights with actual Foreign Service experiences (Kennard, 1948).

Although a full member of the FSI staff with the rank of professor, Hall was under a different administrative branch of the Department of State, the Technical Cooperation Authority (TCA) also widely referred to as Point IV (Hall, personal correspondence). He worked closely with the linguists and anthropologists at FSI from 1951 to 1955 to provide the training TCA required, since no separate staff was available (Hall, 1956, p. 4). A contemporary described TCA as "a stepchild in the organization [FSI]" for various reasons, a fact that did not facilitate its work (Gordon, 1955). Hall points out that FSI acquired a reputation for having a large number of anthropologists. Later problems were attributed to the inappropriate numbers of anthropologists on staff, and two new directors were sent into the organization with orders to "get rid of the anthropologists" (Hall, 1956, p. 5). Hall writes in detail about the administrative problems that academics in government faced: many of them could not use the proper procedures effectively, seeing them as unnecessary interference. Thus, they spent an inordinate amount of time trying to get their work done, and struggling to offer the training they were hired to provide (Hall, 1955). The basic four-week training course that Hall and the others offered to Point IV technicians was a modified version of the training given to foreign service personnel, including beginning instruction in the language of the country of assignment, orientation to the mission and its philosophy, limited study of the country and area, and a small amount of time devoted to anthropological and linguistic generalizations, including culture as a concept, change as a process, and common American assumptions (Hall, 1955, p. 6).

Microcultural Analysis

The idea of culture, one of the central concepts taught in the anthropology seminars, was, and still is, one of the cornerstones of intercultural communication. Today, of course, the notion that each group of people has what can be described as a unique culture, consisting of traditional ways

of doing things, traditional objects, oral traditions and belief systems, is taken for granted. In the 1940s and 1950s this was a newer concept, requiring extensive discussion. Much to the astonishment of the anthropologists, many participants in the seminars viewed the concept itself as vague and viewed discussing it as a waste of time; instead, they wanted concrete information about how to interact with persons in the specific culture to which they were being sent. As Hall later wrote, "There seemed to be no 'practical' value attached to either what the anthropologist did or what he made of his discoveries" (1959, p. 32). Faced with this reaction, Hall resolved to focus on what he termed microcultural analysis: on tone of voice, gestures, time, and spatial relationships as aspects of communication (1956, p. 10). These smaller units of a culture, having obvious and immediate impact on interaction between members of different cultures, were very attractive to the Foreign Service personnel. Hall writes: "Microcultural analysis, when used, seems to be much more acceptable and more readily handled by the layman" (1956, p. 10). Thus, the focus of his training efforts gradually became all those parts of culture which are learned and used without conscious notice. By the time he published *The Silent Language*, this emphasis on aspects of interaction generally ignored by others was even more obvious: "If this book has a message it is that we must learn to understand the 'out-of-awareness' aspects of communication. We must never assume that we are fully aware of what we communicate to someone else" (1959, p. 38).

Sometimes Hall termed these discussions "informal culture," which he contrasts with "formal culture," defined as traditional parts of knowledge, and "technical culture," the most explicit elements of knowledge, and those generally associated with particular sciences or technologies (1959, pp. 63–91, especially the chart on p. 92; see also 1960a, p. 158). In presenting this scheme, Hall emphasized that although lay persons assumed that informal culture has no rules or patterns governing it, the job of the anthropologist was to prove otherwise. At one time he explained informal culture through an extended description of the difference between what we assume schools are supposed to teach students, the formal and technical, and what they really teach, the informal. In the latter category he included: all things are subservient to time; bureaucracies are real; what happens in the classroom is a game, and the teachers set the rule; and the teacher's primary mission is to keep order (Hall, 1971, pp. 230–231).

While discussing the complexity of the cultural systems governing interaction, Hall provides a clear statement of culture as a system of patterns which must be learned:

> [T]he anthropologist knows that in spite of their *apparent* complexity, cultural systems are so organized that their content can be learned and controlled by all *normal* members of the group. Anything that can be learned has structure and can ultimately be analyzed and described. The anthropologist also knows that what he is looking for are patterned distinctions that transcend individual differences and are closely integrated into the social matrix in which they occur (1963b, p. 1006).

The extension from this view of culture to assuming that communication, as culture's counterpart, is equally patterned, learned, and analyzable is implicit in Hall's work, although others, writing later, made the point explicit. These assumptions about culture and communication and the ways in which they are similar lie at the heart of much current research in intercultural communication. Hall's influence here is crucial. Hall views culture as communication, and others after him have had to come to terms with the ways in which the two overlap.

For Hall, the practical implication of this theoretical extension of culture into communication was the feasibility of training those going overseas to attend *deliberately* to the more subtle aspects of interaction and to understand more fully the implications of their own behavior for others. Hall notes that the beginnings of his awareness of cultural impact on behavior occurred through observing his own interactions with others. While preparing the orientation materials for Americans going overseas, he was surrounded by people who represented many of the major languages and cultures of the world, some of whom would stop by his office to visit. "I would find myself impelled (as though pulled by hidden strings) to hold myself, sit, respond, and listen in quite different ways. I noted that when I was with Germans I would (without thinking) hold myself stiffly, while with Latin Americans I would be caught up and involved" (1969, p. 379). It was exactly this sort of awareness of behavior that he then tried to foster in others. His instruction stressed understanding that others do not necessarily interpret our behavior as we do nor as we expect them to. Unlike typical anthropology students, the students in these classes were unwilling to arrive in a culture and simply observe interaction for several months before trying to draw conclusions as to what was occurring. In response, Hall gradually concluded that the majority of information potentially available about a culture was not really essential in situations of face-to-face interaction with members of that culture: only a small percentage of the total need be known, although that portion was critical.

One problem in implementing this insight was the dearth of information at the level of microcultural analysis. Hall had to create his own materials, primarily using details about experiences abroad which students in the training sessions were willing to provide. In addition, Hall was able to travel abroad to check the effectiveness of his program; he specifically listened to the problems Americans were having once they arrived at their destinations (E. Hall, 1976, p. 68). These stories served as an additional resource for improving training.

In his earliest articles Hall already demonstrated what was to become a mark of his approach: providing a few generalizations, along with a large number of specific examples documenting interaction differences between members of different cultures. His students at FSI encouraged this approach, because they would tolerate only a few theoretical statements, although they paid attention to concrete details of real occurrences and were able to learn from them by drawing their own generalizations. This style also served him well with a broader audience, although scholars within intercultural communication, who hope for more extensive, less anecdotal, perhaps more traditionally academic, studies, sometimes criticize it. As late as 1979 Nwanko suggested that most intercultural communication instructors "focus on the identification of communication barriers and on description and application rather than theory-building" (1979, p. 329). This can be attributed largely to the origins of the field as a practical tool for training diplomats rather than as discipline based within a university setting, where the focus would have been on abstract theorizing. By 1983 this had changed with the publication of a volume specifically devoted to theories within intercultural communication (Gudykunst, 1983).

Hall notes that the four weeks total training time for the general sessions as well as specific language training only permitted an orienting of students; he saw four months as ideal. A series of shortcuts designed to maximize the amount of learning possible despite a lack of available teaching time were used to make the endeavor feasible. For example, he mentions the need to put Americans in touch with someone from the local culture with the task of discovering how many times they had to meet with someone in the country before they could begin official business. Through such assignments, Americans destined for the Middle East learned not to pursue business too quickly (Friedman, 1979, p. 50). Intercultural communication training still takes this approach of providing basic orientation to some problems that occur in intercultural interaction, leaving the balance of the learning to the student.

Proxemics, Time, Paralanguage, Kinesics

Major early statements on proxemics and nonverbal communication developed out of the training program at the Foreign Service Institute. In trying to adapt anthropological concepts for presentation to a new audience, Hall and the others established a whole new series of concepts: Hall's *proxemics* and related discussions of the use of *time*, occasionally called chronemics, Trager's *paralanguage*, and Birdwhistell's *kinesics*, were all initially begun by the group of linguists and anthropologists who were involved in the training courses presented through FSI. These areas are today standard parts of courses on intercultural communication and of most shorter training sessions, as well as standard parts of much research in other areas of communication.

Not until 1963 did Hall separate his work on cultural differences in use of space from the other aspects of microcultural analysis, and give it the name now popular, "proxemics." He reported having considered a series of other possible labels, including: "topology," "chaology," the study of empty space, "oriology," the study of boundaries, "choriology," the study of organized space. But he decided that proxemics was most descriptive (1963a, p. 422). Since the widespread adoption of a new field of study is often delayed until a name has been chosen, this choice of a name was critical. Later, in 1972, he reunited the various aspects of nonverbal communication, saying "Proxemics represents one of several such out-of-awareness systems which fall within the general rubric paracommunication" (1972, p. 274; 1964a). "Paracommunication," not a term generally used in the field then or now, served as one of a series of ways of referring to the entire complex of what are today more generally termed nonverbal "channels" of communication. Other early terms included Trager's "metalinguistics," again not the term of choice today.

The materials Trager wrote while at FSI between 1948 and 1953 allude to metalinguistics and the importance of extending the study of linguistics to more than words (Trager, 1950). Originally, all nonverbal communication was categorized under the rubric "metalinguistics," and all was viewed as being potentially of equal interest to linguists. Trager saw no reason for linguists to limit themselves to the study of language, arguing that nonverbal behaviors had an influence both on language choice and on how such choices were interpreted by participants in an interaction. Since virtually no one else was studying nonverbal communication at the time, there was little competition, and no one to complain if Trager and the others crossed the boundary between language and other aspects of culture and/or communication to "trespass" on territory covered in other disciplines. Although Trager's seminal article on paralanguage was not published until 1958, after research experience with *The Natural History of an Interview* team, among other influences (Leeds-Hurwitz, 1987), his position on the significance of that research was established while he was at FSI, as a direct result of the effort to put linguistic generalizations into a form which diplomats would be able to appreciate and put to immediate use.

Trager not only published general statements on the importance of metalinguistics as an extension of language study and the specific programmatic statement for research in paralanguage, but he was also the group member most directly involved in Hall's writings. In all of his early publications, Hall credits Trager as a collaborator. The draft for *The Silent Language* was actually published jointly, as *The Analysis of Culture*. This jointly authored text was issued only as a prepublication draft, by FSI in 1953, although at various times Hall commented that it was to be published shortly. Trager later decided it was not the best possible analysis, commenting in 1971: "No other edition ever published; no published criticism or discussion. GLT has completely replaced this scheme by another" (F. Trager, 1971, p. 18). His assessment reflects his effort to refine his work rather than substantive disagreements with the content of the work. In a parallel fashion, Hall also revised his understandings of intercultural communication as the years went by. He noted "My own description (Hall 1959) does not deviate in any significant degree from the joint version. However, I have come to feel that it was somewhat oversimplified and this I shall attempt to correct" (1964b, p. 155). In *The Silent Language* Hall sometimes uses the plural first person form and refers often to an idea or a problem as being a joint effort between himself and Trager (see pp. 13, 36, 66, 97, 120, 171, 176). In later publications Trager's role has become significantly reduced, though still noticeable.

Since one of Hall's major statements about his work was published in *Current Anthropology* and accorded the CA treatment (being subjected to critique by peers, their comments published with the article), Trager had the opportunity to comment in print on the development of the work. After objecting to a rather minor linguistic point (Hockett's comment that language has the characteristic of duality, which he feels Hall has misunderstood and consequently misused), he adds that he is able to "commend this article unreservedly" (1968, p. 105). As this statement shows, and as Hall confirms, any disagreements were minor (Hall, personal correspondence).

Although Ray L. Birdwhistell was at FSI only during the summer of 1952, his publication of *Introduction to Kinesics* through FSI established his reputation as the expert in that area of communication. In spite of his brief tenure, discussion at FSI during the time, particularly the need to focus attention on a microanalytic level, influenced his work. Like Trager he was later a part of *The Natural History of an Interview* team and developed his early insights in that context, adapting them to a new audience of psychiatrists. As with the study of proxemics, time, and paralanguage, kinesics obviously can be and now is fruitfully applied to almost any context of interaction. But all four originated with a particular context in mind, a context which shaped the way they developed.

My concern here is not to distinguish between the specific contributions of each member of the group at FSI, but rather to stress the importance of understanding that the influential work produced at FSI was partly due to the particular combination of talents drawn together at one time and place for a single purpose. As the person most immediately involved with Hall's work, Trager merited the title of co-author on the original major publication, but the presence of other scholars was equally significant since their ideas contributed to the whole. Although it is customary to attribute specific ideas to individual writers, sometimes an unusually fortuitous combination of individuals, brought together for the purposes of a specific research agenda, can encourage the development of new insights by all. Because he is the author of most of the early work on intercultural communication, giving Hall sole credit for the ideas is easy. However, the catalyst of the particular context, and informal discussions with particular individuals available, may well have been crucial to his thinking.

The Linguistic Model

Modelling paralanguage, kinesics, and proxemics after the analysis of language provided by descriptive linguistics was a deliberate attempt to make at least some aspects of culture as readily available to verbalization, and as readily taught, as language. Linguistics in the 1940s had acquired the reputation of being the most "scientific" of the social and behavioral sciences, and the FSI group wanted anthropology to be equally scientific. That two of the most influential descriptive linguists of the 1950s, Smith and Trager, were part of the group of peers Hall found at FSI was obviously a contributing factor. Not only did linguistics as a whole have the reputation of being scientific, but representatives were available daily and influenced Hall's ideas as they developed. Hall emphasized that the material he included in microcultural analysis was intended to be learned "in much the same way that language is learned" (1956, p. 10), eventually making explicit the connection between linguistic analysis and cultural analysis: "Language is the most technical of the message systems. It is used as a model for the analysis of the others" (1959, p. 38). In later writings he related this parallel more specifically to microcultural analysis:

> A microcultural investigation and analysis properly conducted can provide material which can be compared in the same way that phonetic and phonemic material from different languages can be compared. The results of such studies are quite specific and can therefore be taught in much the same way that language can be taught. (Hall, 1960b, p. 122; see also 1960c)

Occasionally Hall has been explicit about why he saw the linguistic model as a particularly useful one, as when he specifically listed the strengths of linguistics: "it has distinguished between *etic* and *emic* events . . . and has been able to handle greater and greater complexity" (Hall 1964b, p. 155). He wished to utilize these strengths in intercultural communication. If anything, the linguistic model is even more important today to intercultural communication research, as the concepts of "etic" and "emic," in a slightly adapted form, are undergoing a strong resurgence as key terms in the field.

For many of the same reasons that prompted Hall to utilize the model of descriptive linguistics in developing proxemics, Trager and Birdwhistell used descriptive linguistics as their model in developing paralanguage and kinesics. Trager's interest in paralanguage was an extension of his interest in language; he considered it obvious that paralanguage as a field of study would closely parallel formal linguistic analysis of language (Trager, 1958). Although the majority of his early work focused on a rather abstract level of analysis, developing the categories to be used in studying paralinguistic behavior, he subsequently published a description of paralinguistic behavior for a Native American language, Taos (Trager, 1960). Later authors described in detail the problems that divergent paralinguistic norms can cause when members of different cultures attempt to interact (such as Gumperz, 1982), the application of the topic most directly relevant to the study of intercultural communication. Birdwhistell has been equally explicit about the deliberate use of descriptive linguistics as the model for kinesic analysis in his outlines of the historical development of kinesics, and about the influence of linguists such as Trager and Smith on his ideas (Birdwhistell, 1952, 1968, 1970). Hall was responsible for recommending to Kennard that Birdwhistell be brought into the FSI group; his intention was to permit him to work with the linguists there in refining his early model of kinesics (Hall, personal correspondence).

In addition to the ready and appropriate model linguistics provided for analysis of human symbolic behavior, Hall points out that the linguists at FSI were more successful in their efforts to teach language than the anthropologists were in their efforts to teach culture and adds that this disparity led to direct comparisons of the methodologies of the two fields (1960b, p. 118). "Trager and Smith thought that if language is a part of culture, and can be taught so that people speak with little or no accent, why would it not be possible to analyze the rest of culture in such a way so that people could learn by doing and thereby remove the accent from their behavior?" (Hall 1960a, pp. 157–158). This provided yet another reason to use a linguistic model.

Culture and Communication

One goal of Hall's work was to extend the anthropological view of culture to include communication.[6] At the time anthropologists paid attention to large cultural systems (e.g., economics or kinship) only and did not document directly interaction patterns in any detail. Statements relating culture and communication abound in his work; both *The Silent Language* and *The Hidden Dimension* have entire chapters devoted to the subject. In the early work, culture is seen as primary, communication as secondary, since it is only one aspect of culture. In the later work, Hall suggests "culture is basically a communicative process" (1968, p. 89), thus reversing the order: communication is now viewed as primary. In light of this, it is important to note that *The Silent Language* was proposed as the first presentation of "the complete theory of culture as communication" (1959, p. 41), not as the establishment of a new field to be called intercultural communication, not even as an outline of proxemics and/or the study of time as new foci for research.

Much of Hall's work is explicit about citing anthropological precedents, from the grandfather of American anthropology, Franz Boas (who "laid the foundation of the view which I hold that communication constitutes the core of culture and indeed of life itself," 1966, p. 1) to the most significant of the early American linguists: Edward Sapir, Leonard Bloomfield, and Benjamin Lee Whorf (see 1966, pp. 1–2). Indeed, Whorf's essays were first gathered together and published by FSI during Hall's tenure there (Whorf, 1952). Whorf's influence on Hall's work is obvious in *The Silent Language*, where he is called "one of the first to speak technically about the implications of differences which influence the way in which man experiences the universe" (p. 113). In *The Hidden Dimension*, Hall specifically says: "The thesis of this book and of *The Silent Language*, which preceded it, is that the principles laid down by Whorf and his fellow linguists in relation to language apply to the rest of human behavior as well—in fact to all culture" (1966, p. 2; see also Hall, 1984, p. 36).

The changing connections between intercultural communication and anthropology merit explicit comment. Culture as a concept had been and still is traditionally the domain of anthropology. Yet, for a variety of reasons, many of them political and bureaucratic in nature, anthropologists were no longer a part of FSI after the late 1950s. For other reasons relevant to disciplinary boundaries in American universities, anthropologists are not generally involved in intercultural communication as currently taught, whether as a full course or as a workshop.

Hall's first publication on intercultural communication, in 1955, was titled "The Anthropology of Manners," not "proxemics" or "the silent language," and not "intercultural communication." He suggests that:

> The role of the anthropologist in preparing people for service overseas is to open their eyes and sensitize them to the subtle qualities of behavior—tone of voice, gestures, space and time relationships—that so often build up feelings of frustration and hostility in other people with a different culture. Whether we are going to live in a particular foreign country or travel in many, we need a frame of reference that will enable us to observe and learn the significance of differences in manners. Progress is being made in this anthropological study, but it is also showing us how little is known about human behavior (1955, p. 89).

Hall's focus on establishing a "frame of reference" that would enable one to *observe* better and that would help us to discover the *significant differences* in manners (or, as more commonly described today, interaction styles), has remained important in the field. His emphasis on how much is still to be discovered, rather than what had already been learned, was an appropriate emphasis for a new field. His statement also illustrates how Hall clearly positioned his new field in relation to the discipline of anthropology, not communication. Only in looking back on the past 30 years of work do we know communication would provide an intellectual home to the new field rather than anthropology; in the 1950s there was no way to predict its future course. My suggestion is not that anthropology in some way abandoned intercultural communication, but that the expanding field of communication turned out to be an appropriate "foster home" for the new research into intercultural interaction, readily accepting the "infant" as a member of the extended "family."

Anthropology originally addressed an academic audience, along with a smaller group in various government agencies. The original audience of intercultural communication was the reverse: primarily a sector of government (Foreign Service officers) with a small audience among academics. But this division changed over time. Intercultural communication today addresses a varied audience: Americans who travel for pleasure or business or school as well as foreign nationals coming to this country for any of the same reasons. Hall himself made this shift away from the original audience of diplomats. In at least one article, Hall (1960d) drew explicit connections between his work with diplomats and what has become one of the largest groups interested in the results of intercultural communication research and training: international business. The rationale for this new, broader audience assumed that the same wide variety of factors that played a role in diplomatic interactions must play an equal role in business. Even in this early application, Hall saw the value of the case study approach; a major section of his article describes how a business deal "soured" due to cultural differences in timing, use of space, etc. Comparable case studies still abound in intercultural communication training today as one of the best ways to provide participants concrete examples of problems caused by cultural differences in communication patterns.

Conclusion

FSI hired some of the best linguists and anthropologists of the day to train members of the Foreign Service. These academics had to adapt their knowledge for the new audience in a variety of ways; this adaptation led to new ideas about their work and to a burst of creativity in the late 1940s and early 1950s. The need to teach immediately practical aspects of their subject led to the study of small elements of culture, rather than the traditional topics anthropologists taught their college students. This shift, in turn, led to the creation of new fields of research, all centered on the role of nonverbal communication in social interaction: proxemics, time, kinesics, paralanguage. Since the academics who had been assembled were not adept at nor interested in the political maneuvering necessary to survive in the federal

bureaucracy, the group was disbanded in the mid-1950s. But by that time their role in establishing what is now known as the field of intercultural communication had been completed and their influence assured.

Hall's writings have been instrumental in the development of intercultural communication as it is currently practiced; further, since Hall's approach was created in response to the context provided by the FSI, the field today owes much to the explicit requests of a small group of diplomats in the 1940s and 1950s for a way to apply general anthropological insights to specific problems of international discourse. Intercultural communication as a field obviously has changed in many ways over the past 40 years, and no doubt will continue to change; understanding the roots of our own discipline and the reasons for some of the decisions that have come to be accepted as doctrine can only increase our ability to deliberately shape it to meet future needs.

NOTES

Wendy Leeds-Hurwitz wishes to thank Ray Birdwhistell, J Milton Cowan, Edward T. Hall, Charles F. Hockett, Steve Murray, and Yves Winkin for their comments and suggestions, as well as William Bennett, of the FSI Library, and William Turley, of the Office of Personnel, DOS, for archival assistance.

1. The majority of the footnotes and many of the references in the original article have been omitted here. See the original publication for complete documentation of the historical analyses provided (*Quarterly Journal of Speech, 76*, 1990, 262–281).

2. For example, Condon calls it "the work with which many scholars credit the current interest in intercultural communication studies" (1981, p. 255); see also Dodd, 1982, p. 7; Gudykunst, 1985; Singer, 1987, p. 85; and Klopf, 1987, p. 17. Although it is generally acknowledged that Hall (1959) includes the first use of the phrase "intercultural communication," in his earlier writings Hall used several variants of the phrase ("intercultural tensions" and "inter-cultural problems" in Hall (1950) clearly refer to the same topic, for example). Hall was not, however, the first to use the term "intercultural" (for an earlier usage, see Benedict, 1941).

3. As Hall reports, "Foreign Service officers in

particular used to take great delight in saying that what the anthropologists told them about working with the Navajo didn't do them much good, for we didn't have an embassy on the Navajo reservation" (1959, p. 36).

4. See Harrington (1946) and Lampson (1946) for descriptions of the legislation and the Institute it established; an unidentified author also provided the basic outline of the legislation as soon as it was passed, in "The Principal Features of the Foreign Service Act of 1946" (Anonymous, 1946), available at the FSI library.

5. Some authors argued as late as 1960 that language ability was only a minor criteria for success as a diplomat. One author even went so far as to suggest: "Selecting, training and promoting Foreign Service officers on the basis of foreign language skill [something that was often mentioned, but never done] is a little like picking chorus girls for moles and dimples. From the balcony it doesn't matter" (Bradford, 1960, p. 25).

6. Hall was not the first anthropologist to make this suggestion; Mead made a strikingly similar statement a little earlier when she said: "The whole mesh of human social life might logically, and perhaps, in other contexts, fruitfully, be treated as a system of human communications" (1948b, p. 9). However, she did not carry the statement through to its logical conclusion, as Hall did.

REFERENCES

Anonymous. (1946). US Foreign Service. *Fortune Magazine, 34,* 81–86, 198–207.

Benedict, R. (1941). Race problems in America. *Annals of the American Academy of Political and Social Sciences, 216.*

Birdwhistell, R. L. (1952). *Introduction to kinesics.* Washington, DC: Foreign Service Institute.

Birdwhistell, R. L. (1968). Kinesics. *International Encyclopedia of the Social Sciences, 8,* 379–385.

Birdwhistell, R. L. (1970). *Kinesics and context: Essays on body motion communication.* Philadelphia: University of Pennsylvania Press.

Boswell, W. P. (1948). The Foreign Service Institute: A case study. (Unpublished manuscript available at the Foreign Service Institute library.)

Bradford, S. (1960). Over the river and into the language course. *American Foreign Service Journal, 37,* 24–25.

Condon, J. (1981). Values and ethics in communication across cultures: Some notes on the North American case. *Communication, 6,* 255–265.

Cowan, J M. (1975). Peace and war. *LSA [Linguistic Society of America] Bulletin, 64,* 28–34.

Cowan, J M. (1987). The whimsical Bloomfield. *Historigraphia Linguistica, 14,* 23–37.

Dodd, C. H. (1982). *Dynamics of intercultural communication.* Dubuque, IA: William C. Brown Company.

Friedman, K. (1979). Learning the Arabs' silent language. *Psychology Today,* August, 45–54.

Gordon, L. (1955). Organization for the conduct of foreign policy. *American Foreign Service Journal, 32,* 18–20, 46–48.

Gudykunst, W. B. (1983). *Intercultural communication theory: Current perspectives.* Beverly Hills, CA: Sage.

Gudykunst, W. B. (1985). Intercultural communication: Current status and proposed directions. In B. Dervin & M. J. Voigt (Eds.), *Progress in communication sciences,* vol. 6 (pp. 1–46). Norwood, NJ: Ablex Publishing Corporation.

Gumperz, J. J. (1982). *Discourse strategies.* Cambridge, England: Cambridge University Press.

Hall, E. (1976). How cultures collide: Interview with Edward T. Hall. *Psychology Today,* July, 66–97.

Hall, E. T. (1950). Military government on Truk. *Human Organization, 9,* 25–30.

Hall, E. T. (1955). The anthropology of manners. *Scientific American, 192,* 85–89.

Hall, E. T. (1956). Orientation and training in government for work overseas. *Human Organization, 15,* 4–10.

Hall, E. T. (1959). *The silent language.* Garden City, NY: Doubleday and Company.

Hall, E. T. (1960a). Linguistic models in the analysis of culture. In W. M. Austin (Ed.), *Report of the ninth annual round table meeting on linguistics and language study* (pp. 157–158). Washington, DC: Georgetown University Press.

Hall, E. T. (1960b). A microcultural analysis of time. In A. F. C. Wallace (Ed.), *Selected papers of the Fifth International Congress of Anthropological and Ethnological Sciences, 1956* (pp. 118–122). Philadelphia: University of Pennsylvania Press.

Hall, E. T. (1960c). The language of space. *Landscape, 10,* 41–45.

Hall, E. T. (1960d). The silent language in overseas business. *Harvard Business Review, 38,* 87–96.

Hall, E. T. (1963a). Proxemics: The study of man's spatial relations. In Arden House Conference on Medicine and Anthropology, *Man's image in medicine and anthropology* (pp. 422–445). New York: International Universities Press.

Hall, E. T. (1963b). A system for the notation of proxemic behavior. *American Anthropologist, 65,* 1003–1026.

Hall, E. T. (1964a). Silent assumptions in social communication. In D. McK. Rioch & E. A. Weinstein (Eds.), *Disorders of communication: Proceedings of the Association for Research in Nervous and Mental Disease, 1962* (pp. 41–53). Baltimore, MD: Williams and Wilkins Company.

Hall, E. T. (1964b). Adumbration in intercultural communication. *American Anthropologist, 66,* 154–163.

Hall, E. T. (1966). *The hidden dimension.* Garden City, NY: Doubleday and Company.

Hall, E. T. (1968). Proxemics. *Current Anthropology, 9,* 83–108.

Hall, E. T. (1969). Listening behavior: Some cultural differences. *Phi Delta Kappan, 50,* 379–380.

Hall, E. T. (1971). The paradox of culture. In B. Landis & E. S. Tauber (Eds.), *In the name of life: Essays in honor of Erich Fromm* (pp. 218–235). New York: Holt, Rinehart and Winston.

Hall, E. T. (1972). Silent assumptions in social communication. In J. Laver & S. Hutcheson (Eds.), *Communication in face-to-face interaction* (pp. 274–288). Middlesex, England: Penguin.

Hall, E. T. (1984). *The dance of life: The other dimension of time.* Garden City, NY: Doubleday and Company.

Hall, E. T., & Trager, G. L. (1953). *The analysis of culture.* Washington, DC: Foreign Service Institute.

Hall, E. T., & Whyte, W. F. (1960). Intercultural communication: A guide to men of action. *Human Organization, 19,* 5–12.

Harrington, J. F. (1946). How the legislation developed. *American Foreign Service Journal, 23,* 7–9, 52.

Kennard, E. A. (1948). Cultural anthropology and the Foreign Service. *American Foreign Service Journal, 25,* 18–19, 42, 44.

Klopf, D. W. (1987). *Intercultural encounters: The fundamentals of intercultural communications.* Englewood, NJ: Morton Publishing Company.

Lampson, E. T. (1946). A Foreign Service Institute. *American Foreign Service Journal, 23,* 12–13, 43–44.

Leeds-Hurwitz, W. (1987). The social history of the *Natural History of an Interview:* A multidisciplinary investigation of social communication. *Research on Language and Social Interaction, 20,* 1–51.

Maddox, W. (1949). The Institute's program of language instruction. *American Foreign Service Journal, 26,* 12–14, 36, 38, 40, 42.

Mead, M. (1948). Some cultural approaches to communication problems. In L. Bryson (Ed.), *The communication of ideas* (pp. 9–26). New York: Institute for Religious and Social Studies.

Murray, S. O. (1983). *Group formation in social science.* Edmonton, Canada: Linguistic Research, Inc.

Nwanko, R. L. (1979). Intercultural communication: A critical review. *Quarterly Journal of Speech, 65,* 324–346.

Pappano, A. E. (1946). Language study in the Foreign Service. *American Foreign Service Journal, 23,* 30–31, 40.

Singer, M. R. (1987). *Intercultural communication: A perceptual approach.* Englewood Cliffs, NJ: Prentice-Hall.

Smith, H. L., Jr. (1946). Language training for the Foreign Service and the Department of State. *American Foreign Service Journal, 23,* 11–13, 43–44, 47.

Trager, F. H. (Ed.). (1971). An annotated bibliography of the publications and writings of George L. Trager through 1970. *Studies in Linguistics,* Occasional Paper #12.

Trager, G. L. (1950). The field of linguistics. *Studies in Linguistics,* Occasional Paper #1.

Trager, G. L. (1958). Paralanguage: A first approximation. *Studies in Linguistics, 13,* 1–12.

Trager, G. L. (1960). Taos III: Paralanguage. *Anthropological Linguistics, 2,* 24–30.

Trager, G. L. (1968). Comment. *Current Anthropology, 9,* 105.

Whorf, B. L. (1952). *Collected papers in metalinguistics.* Washington, DC: Foreign Service Institute.

Winkin, Y. (1984). Le développement de la "communication interculturelle" aux Etats-Unis: Un aperçu critique. *Les Cahiers de Psychologie Sociale, 24,* 16–27.

KEY TERMS

history
intercultural commu-
   nication training

Foreign Service Institute
application

DISCUSSION QUESTIONS

1. What is the Foreign Service Institute? Why is it important in the study of inter-

cultural communication? What happened to it?

2. Why is it important to take an interdisciplinary approach to understanding intercultural communication? What did Hall believe?

3. What aspects of intercultural communication were emphasized by the FSI focus on intercultural training? What aspects were overlooked or obscured by the focus on training?

3
ISSUES IN CONDUCTING CROSS-CULTURAL SURVEY RESEARCH

DEBORAH A. CAI

Conducting communication research in a foreign culture can be time-consuming and expensive but also important and rewarding. Attention to special methodological issues can yield quality research that provides insight into cross-cultural similarities and differences in attitudes and behaviors affecting communication. In most research methods books, however, little attention is given to the unique issues that arise in cross-cultural research, particularly when using social science methodologies such as experiments, ability, personality and attitude tests, and surveys and interviews (Bhawuk & Triandis, 1996). Researchers Johnson and Tuttle (1989) warn, "As social scientists doing research in cultures other than the ones into which we have been socialized, we run the risk of wrongly interpreting the process of communication and the variables that determine the outcomes of these activities" (p. 463).

This essay addresses some of the key challenges of using one social science research method—survey research. Some of the questions addressed are, How do we choose a population when extending our research to new cultural contexts? What survey instrument(s) should we use? How do we use the survey instrument? How are

we able to compare results across cultures? And finally, what are some solutions to intercultural research problems?

As an example to illustrate and answer some of these questions, I draw on my own experience in conducting research in China, although cross-cultural research within the United States presents some of the same challenges (Stanfield II & Dennis, 1993). During a recent project, I was especially interested in investigating communication patterns among the elderly in China. Similar survey research had already been conducted in the United States, so a collection of pretested survey scales and measurements were available. My plan was to extend this research to a new cultural population. Having received grants to pay for my research and travel, I headed to China for a summer of collecting survey data among elderly Chinese. A national organization in China had promised to assist me with my research. I had substantial experience living and working in China and was aware of one of the unwritten rules for conducting cross-cultural research: Most everything will go differently from what is planned.

This, in fact, was the truth. Although the

national organization had promised to assist me, the city representatives said they knew nothing about the project and therefore could not help. Fortunately, I had a workable backup plan prepared for just such an occasion, and with the help of Chinese friends, the survey was translated, printed, and administered, and the data collected. While I monitored the data collection, I had to yield to those more expert on Chinese language and culture: Chinese people willing to assist and oversee the project to its completion. As with most cross-cultural research, extensive preparation and contingency plans, knowledge of the culture, plenty of time, ample resources, and trustworthy people from the host culture helped ensure the success of my research project. But let's back up a bit and examine the issues I had to resolve in preparation for my work in China.

Who Should Be Studied?

The first methodological issue in cross-cultural research is the selection of a population: who you are going to study. Assuming you have a research question that merits cross-cultural comparisons, you must determine what cultures will be surveyed and the populations to be surveyed within these cultural groups. Researchers usually choose a particular cultural group for two reasons: (1) They have knowledge of or access to (or both) particular cultural groups, and (2) the research question leads to or away from certain cultures. First, researchers tend to study cultural groups with whom they are familiar. This is important because the more they understand the particular culture, the better they can anticipate cultural issues that may affect the research. Furthermore, they may know people from the culture who can serve as coinvestigators and provide assistance with the research project. As you will see throughout this essay, the more knowledge the researcher has about the culture, the greater the likelihood of obtaining quality results.

In addition to knowledge about and access to a particular culture, the research questions also influence the selection of a particular culture to study. Consider, for example, wanting to understand voting behavior in different cultures.

Surveying people in the United States and other nations with democratic governments would be appropriate for this study. Surveying people in nondemocratic countries where voting is less common is not likely to produce very useful results. Similarly, looking at the way people handle organizational conflict between managers and employees may be appropriate in Japan and Korea, but conducting this study among Indians in the highlands of Mexico does not seem reasonable. Thus, the research questions guide which culture groups are appropriate to study and which are not.

Once you have determined the culture groups, consider what specific population will be surveyed within the culture. Normally, random sampling is the ideal for social scientific research. Random sampling is the "method of drawing a portion (or sample) of a population . . . so that each member of the population . . . has an equal chance of being selected" (Kerlinger, 1986, p. 110). But this is often not possible when doing cross-cultural research. Western techniques used to achieve randomness are more likely to produce a very distorted picture of the society. Intercultural research, particularly in developing countries, often does not afford the luxury of randomly selecting names from a phone book, and university students are generally not a representative population of most cultures. These methods, because of economic circumstances, may reach only the elite of the culture being studied (Johnson & Tuttle, 1989). Consequently, choosing a sample may involve more ingenious means.

In cross-cultural settings, demographic differences play an important role. Class and other societal differences are frequently more pronounced, particularly in non-Western nations, because of political systems, the effects and influence of religion, economic stratification, and so on. Researchers need to know whether the research should focus on a national population as a whole or on some particular ethnic or regional group.

Frequently, cross-cultural researchers want to study "national" cultures—that is, they want to know about the people from one or more countries. For example, my goal for the research in China was to find out about certain attitudes and behaviors of elderly Chinese when they communicate. This information would then be compared to data from several other cultures, resulting in a comparison of national cultures. In contrast, I could compare ethnic cultures; that is, I could compare Chinese who speak Mandarin in Mainland China with those who speak Cantonese in southern China and Hong Kong or with those who speak Taiwanese and Hakke in Taiwan. These are all various ethnic groups within different "Chinese" countries.

Targeting any culture population must be done with care. To draw accurate comparisons between two or more cultures and attribute behavioral and attitudinal differences to "culture," populations of all the cultures studied must be in as similar a way as possible. Yet, because of time and money constraints, researchers often resort to "convenience samples": using the group of people most easily accessible to the researchers. This type of sample is problematic for two reasons. First, often the group most available to American researchers is more Westernized than the general population researchers think they are studying because those accessible are also those who generally have more frequent contact with foreigners. In the mid-1970s, the U.S. Information Agency conducted research in Iran on elite groups, assuming they were the primary decision makers in the country. But this neglected the more traditional groups in the country and focused on the group most exposed to Western ideas. The result was a distorted image of the society. This eventually resulted in serious problems for U.S.-Iran relations (Johnson & Tuttle, 1989).

A second reason convenience samples are problematic is that often the most easily accessible group from another culture is college and university students, either studying in the United States or within their own countries. More so than any groups of people available to researchers within other countries, international students in the United States are more likely to be Westernized through acculturation—adjustment to a second culture as a result of living within the culture. Even college and university students within their own cultures often represent a third culture because they are the most Westernized of their culture, often educated in Western traditions (John-

son & Tuttle, 1989). Another problem is that college students from the United States and other countries are likely to be very different from each other in ways not related to culture. To be a university student in some countries means that your family has a certain level of political connectedness or has attained a certain economic status. Also, in many countries university status is only attained by the top 2 to 3% academically of all students and may require very competitive and difficult testing to qualify (Messick, 1988). These differences from the qualifications of U.S. students entering college or university mean that the two populations, U.S. students and international students, may be quite different from each other socioeconomically. Thus, any differences in responses to the research between the two groups could possibly be caused more by social and economic factors than by culture. Despite these drawbacks, studies still compare college students within the United States with college students from one or more other countries, but this is usually because of convenience rather than design.

As one solution to the problem of finding representative populations, quota sampling may be carefully used to obtain an appropriate sample of the population. Researchers using this type of sampling first determine the composition of the entire population in terms of socioeconomic factors, education levels, gender, and age differences; second, they set certain quotas that represent the given population; and third, they seek out participants from the culture until those quotas are met. For example, Johnson and Tims (1985) conducted a quota sample to examine the opinions of eight specific elite groups in Mexico. This would involve determining the ratios of the groups to each other and then seeking participants until representative ratios are met. As another solution, Johnson and Tuttle (1989) suggest "cluster sampling"—the use of intact villages or families or classes of students in cultures where social and family groupings are the norm—as a viable alternative to random sampling. They suggest that this is also helpful when researchers lack mobility because of underdeveloped transportation, have difficulty in accessing subjects, or lack resources to conduct a full-scale random sample in a country. Sekaran (1983) points out that although true random sampling is always the preferred method of selecting research participants, nonrandom samples can still be valuable because they guide future research and the selection of future samples more purposefully.

What Survey Instrument Should Be Used?

After determining who will participate in the research, careful consideration is given to the survey "instrument." Unfortunately, the simple replication of previous studies or the use of standard scales and questionnaires previously used in the United States is often not a good idea when doing cross-cultural research. For the questionnaire to be cross-culturally appropriate, four types of "equivalence" need to be achieved (Brislin, 1993).

1. Vocabulary equivalence is the process of simply translating the questionnaire from one language and vocabulary into another, such as from English into Japanese. While this may seem like an obvious step, it is often not used when the participants have knowledge of the original survey language. Although not translating the survey may save time, using the native language of participants helps them to think in their own cultural terms. Thinking in a second language such as English may encourage participants to think also in U.S. American or Western concepts rather than in their own culture. Thus, whenever possible it is best to provide a language translation of the questionnaire.

2. Idiomatic equivalence goes beyond vocabulary translation and considers the appropriate cultural idiomatic expressions. For example, in English we express emotions by referencing our heart, as in "downhearted" or "lighthearted"; through references of constraint, as in "freed up," "pressured," or "depressed"; or through expression of certain colors, as in "feeling blue" or "seeing red." In Hmong, however, reference is made to the liver to express emotion, so that fretting over an uncompleted task is to have an "unsettled liver," or involvement in a highly emotional or bitter conflict such as divorce is to suffer

from a "rotten liver," but to feel happy is to have a "pleasant liver" (Dunnigan, McNall, & Mortimer, 1993). Capturing these differences in idiomatic expression is important to achieving accurate understanding and responses in survey research.

3. Experiential equivalence is considering whether the targeted cultures have had experience with the concept in question. For example, in preparing a project to study private business management practices in China, I wanted to adapt scales that had been successfully used among U.S. business managers. When considering experiential equivalence, however, it became evident that many of the terms that we accept as common managerial jargon in the United States were likely to have no cultural applicability to business managers in China. "Strategic planning," "organizational vision," "work teams," and "job rotation" are just some examples of terms that managers in the United States would readily recognize and understand. But interviews with Chinese managers confirmed what we expected—these concepts were completely foreign to them. Using a standardized questionnaire that included these Western concepts would have been a waste of time and money, as well as producing results that would likely be an inaccurate reflection of Chinese management.

4. Conceptual equivalence is necessary. Although words may be directly translatable, connotations may be significantly different. For example, "propaganda" has a negative political connotation in the United States, but in China it carries a positive connotation of promoting what is good about the country. Similarly, people in the West think of profit as something desirable to obtain through business practices, but profit is historically viewed as resulting from the exploitation of others and thus undesirable in former Soviet-bloc countries. So, questions that a researcher believes to be tapping a particular construct may in fact tap a completely different one. In English, dolphins are thought of as "Flipper"—cute, helpful, friendly ocean mammals; in Japanese, dolphins are called "sea pigs"—not

a very endearing term—because they are viewed as thieves of good fish from the fishermen. This conceptual difference illustrates the importance of having a cultural understanding of terminology used in the survey.

To manage difficulties of translating surveys for cross-cultural use, two general prescriptions are offered. First, translation-backtranslation is an important procedure that should be used to prepare surveys for use in different languages. Translation-backtranslation involves two different native speakers of the target language. One native speaker carefully translates the questionnaire into the desired language, giving consideration to the four equivalences mentioned above. On completing the translation, the other native speaker "backtranslates," or translates the questionnaire back into English without looking at the original English version. Through this process, researchers can check on the accuracy of the translated version based on how accurately it translates back into English. On one occasion, I had a questionnaire translated into Chinese. The translation looked great on first glance, but the backtranslation revealed that terms such as "conservative" and "liberal" had been translated into Chinese with the meanings of "open" and "closed." Obviously, the connotation of these terms had not been captured, and the translation had to be altered.

If the translated and backtranslated versions are similar, the researcher can stop there; if not, he or she should continue with a process of decentering. Decentering means going back and forth between two texts with two different sets of translators until there are two versions of the text that are almost identical (Brislin, 1986; Bhawuk & Triandis, 1996).

Even after backtranslating and decentering, there may be errors in the appropriateness or accuracy of the survey. Thus, the second prescription is to pretest any instrument within the culture before using it. Besides connotations, questions may be affected by cultural values such as our understandings about age, family, gender, and so on. For example, the initial survey research I was planning to use among the Chinese elderly defined "elderly" as ages 65 to 85 and "middle aged" as 45 to 55. These age ranges were based on Western concepts of the terms. But in China, someone who is 55 is viewed as "elderly." Someone who is 65 is considered very old, and someone who lives to be 85 is highly revered beyond being simply viewed as "elderly." These differences reflect differences in the values toward age in the United States and China. In the United States, we prefer youth and try to avoid becoming old; but in China, becoming old is good because age is associated with wisdom and knowledge and thus is granted more social respect.

Differences in decision-making processes, different views of time, the importance of what a person does versus who a person is, and the value of an idea versus the value of relationships are just some of the many differences that must be understood from various cultural perspectives when preparing questionnaires for cross-cultural use (Triandis & Albert, 1987). For example, an international organization evaluating member performance may have difficulty making comparisons if members in past-oriented societies report past performance, members in future-oriented societies report projected performances, and members in present-oriented societies report current performance. Once again, this requires ability on the part of the researcher, often with the assistance of persons from the cultures themselves, to understand how concepts may be understood differently across cultures.

How Should the Survey Be Administered?

There are several important considerations related to how surveys are administered in cross-cultural situations. Johnson and Tuttle (1989) argue, "Nothing, from the handling of pencils to the administer's eye or head movements, should be taken for granted" when administering tests for people unfamiliar with them (p. 475). Experience with surveys, literacy, confidentiality, and response biases are four main issues of administering surveys.

Prior Experience

In most societies around the world, people are not as accustomed to being surveyed as we are in the

United States. Participation in an "experiment" can be such a novel experience in cross-cultural settings that news travels fast throughout the region. Furthermore, participants may find that they gain social status by announcing their participation and then disclosing information about the experiment to other possible participants despite researchers' requests not to reveal the content of the survey. These are potential confounds that researchers have to be aware of and deal with effectively to protect the quality of the data collected (Johnson & Tuttle, 1989).

Because U.S. Americans are frequently asked to complete questionnaires or evaluation forms for products, courses, or research projects, they have become accustomed to the format of questionnaires and the use of scaled items asking them to rate issues, attitudes, or behaviors on a scale of 1 to 7, where 1 represents some quality such as "very good" and 7 represents the opposite, "very bad." Yet this is a mathematically conceptual notion catering to Western culture that may not be appropriate for many non-Western cultures. The idea of attaching a number to a felt attitude or belief is one that is not familiar and is not consistent with the more concrete or intuitional thinking processes that are prevalent in much of the non-Western world (Hines, 1993). In many cultures, surveys are not commonplace. I found among the elderly in China that most had never completed such a task before. Consequently, a handful of surveys were returned with zigzag patterns of circled numbers down the page or straight lines of 7s or 1s circled—a result of lack of experience with survey questions on the part of the participants and lack of careful explanation of how to use them on my part. That people in many cultures are not accustomed to being observed or questioned or to completing questionnaires can be a problem for researchers.

Literacy

Another problem with written surveys is the lack of literacy that exists within many cultures. To get around this problem, surveys can be administered orally, yet conducting verbal interviews still carries a number of possible confounds. In some places, just the presence of a tape player may bring about undesired, theatrical responses, or induce fear that the foreign researcher represents some feared government agency or organization such as the CIA (Sarbaugh, 1984). In order to obtain the most valid responses, researchers may in some cases be required to memorize questions and responses as they simply converse with subjects.

Confidentiality

An important part of doing research is promising participants that their responses will remain confidential and that the participants will not be identified as having responded in any particular way. But the Western promise of confidentiality is not believed by individuals in many countries. In some cultures, confidentiality is a nonexistent concept as we know it. Particularly in totalitarian societies, people may not be willing to participate if they suspect any possible risk of their responses becoming known to government officials. Furthermore, researchers should expect that national agencies or governments supporting the research or allowing it to take place, or both, may demand information about the groups and topics studied (Tafoya, 1984).

The fear of having responses identified or traced may prevent participants from answering honestly or from answering at all. This problem must be taken into consideration by researchers. For example, Adler, Campbell, and Laurent (1989) report that they requested less demographic information from participants in Chinese organizations to ensure that people could not be identified. Although the additional demographic information, such as the person's position and department, would help interpretation of the data, protection of anonymity and the importance of encouraging participants to provide accurate information prevented the researchers from asking such detailed questions. Consideration must be given to the type of questions asked and the feasibility of reaching the desired population to answer the research question.

A similar problem arose for me when administering the questionnaire among the elderly in China. Surveys administered in the United States often include a written statement at the top promising anonymity to the participants. Although anonymity was orally promised to the Chinese participants and was preserved, Chinese assistants with the project recommended that a written statement promising anonymity not be included. They argued that the written statement would be more likely to arouse people's suspicions that anonymity would indeed *not* be preserved.

Biases

In addition to biases that can normally occur in survey research, four types of potential bias are unique to cross-cultural research (Hines, 1993; Sekaran, 1983). The first is a "courtesy bias." As observed in some Asian cultures, participants respond to surveys administered by foreigners by providing answers that they think the foreign researcher wants to hear. This type of bias interferes with quality responses and prevents obtaining accurate results. The second bias is a "sucker bias," which occurs when participants believe that outsiders, or foreigners, are fair game for deception, so responses are fabricated and not accurate.

A third type is a "culture-based bias," which emerges from aspects of the culture, such as values, norms, and information that is available. For example, because of the Japanese value of humility, Japanese participants are likely to underestimate their achievements. In contrast, within some Middle Eastern cultures it is acceptable to exaggerate achievements (Mitchell, 1969; Sekaran, 1983). Thus, results may be skewed in one direction or another based on what is appropriate communication within the culture itself. A similar problem emerges based on the ability of people within the culture to answer questions accurately. Questions such as date of birth may be much more problematic in cultures where dating is counted differently than in the West, or when the date of birth is not as important and therefore not remembered, or when records are not accurately maintained or are not accessible.

Another example of a culture-based bias is when there are taboos regarding with whom an outsider may speak. In group societies, for example, it is appropriate only for the leader or head of the community or tribe to speak, and the leader speaks on behalf of the group as a whole.

Furthermore, in this type of society, individual opinions will generally not differ, or not be spoken, from what the leader has expressed. In other cultures, certain individuals are "expected" to know certain things and will not admit lack of knowledge or they risk losing status (Sarbaugh, 1984). In these situations, surveys may result in responses, but the responses are not necessarily reliable.

The fourth bias is an "appropriateness bias," which deals with the appropriateness or acceptability of the questions being asked on the survey. For example, in some cultures it is not appropriate or acceptable to discuss sexual practices; in others, people may be unwilling to discuss political opinions or issues related to religious practices. In these cases, participants may be fearful, hesitant, or unwilling to respond to questions honestly (Hines, 1993).

Solutions

A primary way of dealing with problems of administering surveys is to work with researchers or assistants from the host cultures being studied (Kuechler, 1987). Usually, having the foreign researcher assisted by people from the host culture is most effective. Extra-careful measures must be taken, however, in the selection and training of national assistants. For example, care must be given not to violate cultural norms of status and role. Choosing assistants from a substantially lower or higher class than those being surveyed may result in participants giving equally false information to the assistant as they would to the foreign researcher, not wanting the assistant to have access to their truthful responses. Furthermore, research assistants from the host culture may not be trained or experienced in conducting research with the same rigorous requirements as those expected in Western scientific research. Role play of an interview situation as well as detailed training and instruction on the collection and recording of information need to be managed carefully.

On the other hand, national interviewers may be able to "hear" what national subjects are saying and provide insight into the questions and responses beyond the actual wording in ways that foreign researchers may miss. Particularly in high-context cultures where more of the message is implied than explicitly expressed in verbal form, this insight by national assistants is valuable for Western researchers who may not be accustomed to interpreting implicit communication.

How Should the Results Be Compared?

To interpret results and make comparative claims across cultures, there are three recommendations for data collection. First, uniform procedures should be used across all the cultures being surveyed (Sekaran, 1983). In other words, the same instrument, appropriately translated, should be administered to similar populations through similar methods. If students are surveyed in a classroom in the United States, then a similar population of students should be surveyed, also within the classroom, in the comparative culture, rather than surveying a group of workers in their homes to be compared to the U.S. student population.

Second, data should be collected in the various cultures within a short time period. Only several weeks or a few months should pass between the time data is collected in the different cultures. Long periods of time can affect the data quality due to "history effects": changes in the culture caused by the passing of time and the occurrence of political and societal events. Collecting data within a close time frame prevents history effects from changing the responses.

Third, longitudinal rather than cross-sectional data is preferable (Kuechler, 1987; Sekaran, 1983). Cross-sectional data is obtained when the survey is administered at one point in time. This gives a sort of "snapshot" image of the culture. But this "snapshot" may not be accurate. As an example, let's say we want to understand the general political attitudes of the Norwegian communities in Minnesota. After determining how to contact members of this population, we conduct our survey. But as it happens, we ran our survey in late October, just prior to the U.S. presidential elections when attention to media coverage and concern over political issues tends to be heightened. While our results may be interesting, they may not reflect this particular population's typical views on political issues. To combat this "cross-sectional" perspective of culture, we instead conduct the survey at several points in time. This "longitudinal" information provides us with a more accurate picture of the population by allowing us to see general trends in responses over time.

Conclusion

It has been said that the true test of a theory is how well it holds up across cultural contexts (Sarbaugh, 1984; Johnson & Tuttle, 1989). The issues discussed here are only some of the many careful considerations of doing intercultural survey research. There are no specific intercultural research methods; there are just many more aspects of the research that must be carefully thought through and prepared for. Researchers must expect and prepare for the fact that there are many more possible confounds in data collection when doing research across cultures.

Several recommendations can be made for achieving the best possible results from cross-cultural research situations. Spending time in the culture before conducting the research to become familiar with the general population and cultural ways is an important beginning. Bias and overgeneralization about the culture threaten the accuracy of the research if the researcher doesn't have enough cultural understanding. It is important that the researcher be thoroughly knowledgeable about the culture, including its language and its social, political, economic, ideological, and psychological makeup. Tafoya (1984) points out that spending six months or less within a culture is not enough time to understand the local conditions that are likely to affect the data. Consequently, this necessary level of cultural knowledge is not always possible for foreign researchers.

The value of having at least one national researcher, therefore, to assist the foreign researcher cannot be underestimated. The indigenous researcher can clarify how to appropriately study constructs, whether the right questions are being addressed, what potential history effects might exist, and so on (Carter, 1966; Sarbaugh, 1984; Johnson & Tuttle, 1989). The foreign researcher should be aware, however, that indigenous assistants may tend to overgeneralize about their own culture, just as we tend to overgeneralize about our own.

Finally, multiple methods for collecting data are useful for gaining a fuller understanding of the research question (Hines, 1993). A variety of methods, both quantitative and qualitative, should be incorporated into the research plan whenever possible. Looking at any research question using more than one method provides better and fuller understanding of the question (Babbie, 1995). Preliminary qualitative research including unstructured interviews and ethnography can provide valuable information, such as what questions to ask and how variables may relate differently than expected, when preparing for larger research projects (Hines, 1993; Johnson & Tuttle, 1989).

The bottom line of intercultural research is that researchers need to know the cultures they are studying and take precautions for their own fallibility in understanding cultures that are not their own. But although this type of research may involve many complex hurdles, it is rich with possibilities for new and fascinating discoveries.

REFERENCES

Adler, N. J., Campbell, N., & Laurent, A. (1989, Spring). In search of appropriate methodology: From outside the People's Republic of China looking in. *Journal of International Business Studies*, 61–74.

Babbie, E. (1995). *The practice of social research*. 7th ed. New York: Wadsworth.

Bhawuk, D. P. S., & Triandis, H. C. (1996). The role of culture theory in the study of culture and intercultural training. In D. Landis & R. S. Bhagat (Eds.), *Handbook of intercultural training* 2nd ed. (pp. 17–34). Thousand Oaks, CA: Sage.

Brislin, R. (1986). The wording and translation of research instruments. In W. J. Lonner & J. W. Berry (Eds.), *Field methods in cross-cultural research* (pp. 137–164). Newbury Park, CA: Sage.

Brislin, R. (1993). *Understanding culture's influence on behavior*. Fort Worth, TX: Harcourt Brace Jovanovich.

Carter, R. E., Jr. (1966). Some problems and distinctions in cross-cultured research. *The American Behavioral Scientist, IX*, 23–24.

Dunnigan, T., McNall, M., & Mortimer, J. T. (1993). The problem of metaphorical nonequivalence in cross-cultural survey research: Comparing the mental health statuses of Hmong refugee and general population adolescents. *Journal of Cross-Cultural Psychology, 24*(3), 344–365.

Hines, A. M. (1993). Linking qualitative and quantitative methods in cross-cultural survey research: Techniques from cognitive science. *American Journal of Community Psychology, 21*(6), 729–746.

Johnson, J. D., & Tims, A. R. (1985). Communication factors related to closer international ties. *Human Communication Research, 12*, 259–273.

Johnson, J. D., & Tuttle, F. (1989). Problems in intercultural research. In M. K. Asante & W. B. Gudykunst (Eds.), *Handbook of international and intercultural communication* (pp. 461–483). Newbury Park, CA: Sage.

Kerlinger, F. N. (1986). *Foundations of behavioral research*. Chicago: Holt, Rinehart & Winston.

Kuechler, M. (1987). The utility of surveys for cross-national research. *Social Science Research, 16*, 229–244.

Messick, D. M. (1988). On the limitations of cross-cultural research in social psychology. In M. H. Bond (Ed.), *The cross-cultural challenge to social psychology* (pp. 41–47). Newbury Park, CA: Sage.

Mitchell, R. E. (1969). Survey materials collected in developing countries: Sampling, measurement, and interviewing obstacles to intra- and inter-national comparisons. In J. Boddewyn (Ed.), *Comparative management and marketing* (pp. 232–252). Glenview, IL: Scott, Foresman & Co.

Sarbaugh, L. E. (1984). An overview of selected approaches. In Y. Y. Kim & W. B. Gudykunst (Eds.), *Methods for intercultural communication research* (pp. 67–81). Beverly Hills, CA: Sage.

Sekaran, U. (1983, Fall). Methodological and theoretical issues and advancements in cross-cultural research. *Journal of International Business Studies*, 61–73.

Stanfield, J. H., II, & Dennis, R. M. (Eds.). (1993). *Race and ethnicity in research methods*. Newbury Park, CA: Sage.

Tafoya, D. W. (1984). Research and cultural phenomena. In Y. Y. Kim & W. B. Gudykunst (Eds.), *Methods for intercultural communication research* (pp. 47–65). Beverly Hills, CA: Sage.

Triandis, H. C., & Albert, R. D. (1987). Cross-cultural perspectives. In F. M. Jablin, L. L. Putnam, K. H. Roberts, & L. W. Porter (Eds.), *Handbook of organizational communication* (pp. 264–295). Newbury Park, CA: Sage.

KEY TERMS

methodology   translation
social science   surveys
research

DISCUSSION QUESTIONS

1. What are the primary issues related to doing survey research across cultures? Select a culture and consider what particular methodological issues might have to be considered for conducting research within that culture.

2. How can researchers ensure that the concepts being studied in one culture are the same when studying them in another culture?

3. Cai mentions several biases that may arise in cross-cultural research. Can you think of other types of bias, including culture-based biases, that may arise?

4. Select a research question related to communication. Walk through the process of preparing to study that question in both the United States and one other culture.

5. Besides those offered in the reading, what are some other problems intercultural researchers may encounter? What could researchers do to either prevent those problems or deal with them effectively?

4
REVISITING THE CENTRALITY OF CULTURE

ROBERT M. SHUTER

Intercultural communication has been examined for many years by communication scholars, with the term first appearing in Edward Hall's *Silent Language* published in 1959. Edward Hall is an anthropologist with a keen interest in human interaction. His early writings on culture and communication influenced many disciplines, including speech communication where they spawned a new field of inquiry: intercultural communication.

Edward Hall's (1959, 1966, 1976) research reflects the regimen and passion of an anthropologist: a deep regard for culture explored principally by descriptive, qualitative methods. A theoretician as well, Hall (1976) developed communication theories like high context/low context cultures, which he used to categorize societies and explain communication in which particular cultural groups engage. His theories are intracultural in nature; that is they are generated from

an understanding of shared values and interaction patterns *within* similar societies. However, he applies these theories interculturally to explain communication issues between dissimilar national cultures.

Unlike Hall, researchers in communication who conduct intercultural research do not generally exhibit in their published studies a passion for culture, an interest in descriptive research, or a desire to generate intracultural theories of communication. Instead, much of the published research in intercultural communication, particularly in the national and regional speech-communication journals, is conducted to refine existing communication theories: culture serves principally as a research laboratory for testing the validity of communication paradigms.[1]

While this research agenda has produced significant insights on selected communication theories, it has virtually ignored the heart and soul of intercultural research: culture. As a result, intercultural researchers, as documented in the following section, have produced few published investigations of global regions, scattered examinations of communication in particular societies, and scant intracultural communication theories that can be applied interculturally. The challenge for intercultural communication in the 1990s and the 21st century, as argued in this essay, is to develop a research direction and teaching agenda that returns culture to preeminence and reflects the roots of the field as represented in Edward Hall's early research.

Research on Intercultural Communication: A 10-Year Overview

Between 1980 and 1990, 51 intercultural communication studies were published in the national and regional speech-communication journals, and the overwhelming majority of these articles are theory validation studies, not cultural research. Theory validation research conducted interculturally is aimed at testing the validity and generalizability of extant communication theories like uncertainty reduction (Gudykunst, 1988), initial interaction (Shuter, 1982), intercultural communication competence (Hwang, Chase, & Kelly, 1980), communication apprehension (McCroskey, Fayer, & Richmond, 1985), intercultural adaptation (Kim, 1987, 1988), and relationship development (Cronen & Shuter, 1983)—the theories most frequently examined in intercultural research over the last decade. For example, Gudykunst's multiple investigations on uncertainty reduction are important contributions to the literature in terms of furthering our understanding of how this communication theory operates interculturally. The investigations are not designed to explore the rich cultural landscape of a particular country or world region. Although theory validation is often classified as etic research, it is not, at least according to John Pike's (1966) original discussion of etic and emic, "as standpoints of the description of behavior" (p. 37).

For Pike, a linguist and anthropologist, etic researchers use predetermined analytical categories for investigating language behavior within particular societies with the principal aim of describing cultural patterns. Although these cultural descriptions may help generate unified theories of human behavior, the etic researcher is first and foremost interested in cultural description, much like the emic investigator who also describes cultural patterns without being guided by external predetermined analytical categories and schemes.

Etic and emic similarities and differences are best stated, writes Pike (1966),

> . . . in the words of Sapir who anticipated this position years ago: "It is impossible to say what an individual is doing unless we have tacitly accepted the arbitrary modes of interpretation that social tradition is constantly suggesting to us from the very moment of our birth. Let anyone who doubts this try the experiment of making a painstaking report (an etic one) of the action of a group of natives engaged in some activity, say religious, to which he has not the cultural key (i.e., a knowledge of the emic system). If he is a skillful writer, he may succeed in giving a picturesque account of what he sees and hears or thinks he sees and hears, but the chances of his being able to give an accurate picture of what happens in terms of what would be intelligible and acceptable to the natives are practically nil. He will be guilty of all manner of distortion." (p. 39)

Intercultural studies in national and regional speech-communication journals are of neither an etic nor emic nature: they are products of a nomothetic model developed in psychology that drives communication research and aims at identifying laws of human interaction rather than describing cultural patterns (Shuter, 1985a). Since the nomothetic model regulates culture to a laboratory for refining theory and generating laws, it is not surprising that a 10-year review of national and regional journals did not uncover a series of studies dedicated to a global region or a line of research on a particular culture except Japan.

For example, between 1980 and 1990 not a single study has been published in the national or regional speech-communication journals on Africa, South and Central America, or Southeast

Asia. European investigations include just four studies scattered among Sweden, USSR (Corcoran, 1983), Britain (Bass, 1989), and France (Ting-Toomey, 1988). In East Asia, one study examines the region, and the remaining investigations focus on Japan and Korea (Gudykunst, Sodetani, & Sonada, 1987). Taiwan and People's Republic of China are not examined in separate studies. There are a few studies on the Middle East, principally investigating Israel (Frank, 1981; Katriel, 1987) and Iran (Heisey & Trebing, 1983), and one additional investigation on South Asia (Carlson, 1986).

It is possible that the nomothetic bias of the discipline serves as an obstacle for accepting etic or emic intercultural investigations in national or regional journals. This may be the case; however, in examining the published studies between 1980 and 1990 in the *International and Intercultural Communication Annual*—the only speech-communication journal dedicated to intercultural studies—one finds publishing patterns similar to those found in the national and regional speech-communication journals. First, there is not a line of research on any global region, and only East Asia (Cushman & King, 1985), Europe (Hopper & Doany, 1989), and the Middle East (Griefat & Katriel, 1989; Hopper & Doany, 1989) are examined in more than one investigation. Africa, South and Central America, and Southeast Asia are not explored in studies published in the *Annual* since 1980.

Moreover, the emphasis of communication studies in the *Annual* has been on communication theory validation and the development of intercultural communication theory. While the *Annual* has made significant contributions to the discipline, its dedication to theory development has resulted in a paucity of research on world regions and single cultures.

Not surprisingly, the last 10 years has also resulted in few studies of an intracultural nature in national and regional speech-communication journals except for scattered investigations on selected U.S. and European co-cultures (Booth-Butterfield & Jordan, 1989; Campbell, 1986). A co-culture is a cultural group within a particular country and normally includes ethnicity, race, and religion and can be extended to age and gender as well. Co-culture is synonymous with subculture; however, the prefix "sub" expresses a subordinate social position, whereas "co-culture" communicates equality: multiple cultures living co-equally within a nation.

Because intracultural investigations tend to focus on a particular society, they are not perceived as being easily translated into intercultural communication theory. For this reason, researchers tend to avoid conducting intracultural studies and instead execute comparative intercultural investigations.

Intercultural Communication Research Between 1991 and 1995: How Central Is Culture?

In comparing the intercultural communication studies published in the 1980s with cross-national investigations of the 1990s, it is clear that similarities and differences in the role culture plays exist in the research of both decades. Between 1991 and 1995, approximately 30 studies were published in the national and regional journals in speech communication, which somewhat exceeds the publishing rate for intercultural studies in the 1980s over a five-year period. Like the 1980s, the intercultural communication research of the past five years ignores most of the regions of the world and, unlike the last decade, concentrates principally on a single world region. The overwhelming majority of these studies examine East Asia, with China receiving the most attention (Xiao, 1996a, 1996b; Ma, 1992), followed by Korea (Singelis & Brown, 1995), Taiwan (Singelis & Brown, 1995), and Japan (Cupach & Imahori, 1993). Only two investigations focus on Europe (Carbaugh, 1993; Stohl, 1993); one study examines the Middle East (Katriel, 1994); and no published research in these journals is reported on Africa, South and Southeast Asia, and Central and South America. The significant increase in published studies on China is noteworthy and may be related to the increase in Chinese and Taiwanese scholars in the discipline, as evidenced by the authors of these investigations.

Most of the intercultural investigations published in the 1990s in major national and regional journals are still theory validation studies in which culture functions primarily as a laboratory for testing the generalizability of communication theories like compliance gaining (Fitch, 1994), verbal aggression (Suzuki & Rancer, 1994), and conversational constraints (Kim, 1994). However, the last five years have also produced some excellent examples of intracultural communication research on co-cultures, world regions, and specific countries (Carbaugh, 1993; Flores, 1996; Martin, Hammer, & Bradford, 1994; Orbe, 1995). For example, Orbe's research delves into African American communication with the goal of increasing our understanding of this co-culture, which he achieves by critiquing past studies on African Americans. The Chinese scholarship is also worth noting because it consists of several in-depth investigations on Chinese rhetoric and communication (Xiao, 1996a, 1996b; Ma, 1992). And unlike the 1980s, a few cross-national studies have been published on communication within East Asia comparing, for example, China and Korea or Taiwan and Korea (Singelis & Brown, 1995; Kim, 1994). This is an important research trend because it provides close examination of cultural variability in East Asia, which in the 1980s was often treated in the literature as a homogenous world region. Still, too few intercultural investigations are found in the national and regional journals, and most of the world is virtually uninvestigated in these journals in terms of theory validation studies or intracultural research.

Turning to the *Annual on International and Intercultural Communication*, one finds similar research trends that are identified in the national and regional journals. Published research concentrates on East Asia, with China, Korea, Taiwan, and Japan receiving most attention (Gao, 1991; Won-Doornink, 1991; Greenburg, Ku, & Li, 1992). Africa, Central and South America, and Europe as well as South and Southeast Asia are examined in only a few investigations (Sanders, Wiseman, & Matz, 1991; Archer & Fitch, 1994; Cushman & King, 1994). Unlike the national and regional journals, most research in the *Annual* is conducted interculturally, with comparisons always made to the United States. Only one investigation is intracultural in nature, focusing exclusively on a single co-culture, country, or specific world region. It appears, then, that the national and regional journals in the field have devoted more attention than the *Annual* in the past five years to examining specific co-cultures, countries, and world regions rather than primarily publishing intercultural studies that almost always contain a U.S. sample.

In summary, intercultural communication research between 1980 and 1995 has provided important validation studies of communication paradigms and significant breakthroughs in development of intercultural communication theory. However, the published research has neglected people, context, and national culture. As a result, interculturalists have provided precious few data-based insights into how *specific* societies, world regions, and ethnic groups communicate. It is time for a change in direction.

Intercultural Communication in the 1990s and the 21st Century: A Cultural Imperative

Culture is the most important global communication issue in the 1990s and the 21st century. New cultural coalitions and alliances are redefining global relationships. Western Europe, for example, struggles with the continued development of the European Economic Community, which strives to unify European trading regulations within the Common Market without dismantling national cultural traditions that provide the historical and contemporary identity of each member country (Bruce, 1988; Montet, 1989). While Western Europe evolves into a unified marketplace, North America wonders about the development of "fortress" Europe—a monolithic cultural bloc that may prevent North American products and communication from successfully penetrating the European Community (Reimer, 1989; Rosenbaum, 1989).

As Western Europe attempts to harmonize cultural differences to achieve trade unification, Eastern European countries proclaim their cultural independence by changing their political systems and celebrating age-old cultural values, traditions, and communication patterns (Berend, 1988). With the diminution of Soviet control of Eastern Europe, there is a resurgence of national cultures in countries that have traditionally surrendered a significant degree of cultural and political independence to the Soviets.

Culture dominates the Pacific Basin as well, with Japan reordering its relationships with East and Southeast Asian countries to develop what some have described as the Pacific equivalent to the European Community (Yahuda, 1988; Yang, 1989). As Japan, Korea, Taiwan, Hong Kong, and Singapore develop sustained and cooperative trading relationships, these countries, at the same time, retain distinct cultural identities that are carefully preserved but sometimes cause cultural rifts between them (Pearce, 1988; Tank, 1987).

Culture is also the central theme in Africa, the Middle East, South Asia, and Central and South America. These diverse cultural regions struggle with maintaining traditional cultural systems while developing technological and communications infrastructures that may threaten cultural and religious values and national identities (Kelly, 1988; Kwarteng, 1988; Shamsuddin, 1988).

Culture is also the dominant issue within global societies (Rosen & Weissbrodt, 1988). In the United States, for example, cultural tensions are the result of long-standing conflicts between co-cultures as well as more recent communication issues posed by immigration into North America (Roberts, 1988). Countries in Africa, Latin America, the Middle East, and South Asia struggle with co-culture tensions and confrontations fueled by racial divisions, religious and cultural differences, and tribal identifications (Kelly, 1988; Rupesinghe, 1988; Weissbrodt, 1988). Societies within Eastern and Western Europe are also coping with serious intracultural communication issues that have evolved from age-old ethnic divisions and more recent changes in immigration patterns.

Compelling global conditions require intercultural researchers to alter their research agenda and return culture to preeminence in their studies. This can be accomplished by examining intra-cultural patterns of interaction within societies and world regions.

An Intracultural Communication Research Agenda for the 1990s and the 21st Century

Intracultural research identifies and examines communication patterns endemic to a particular country or co-culture within a society. Patterns are "those common, unstated experiences which members of a given culture share, communicate without knowing, and which form the backdrop against which all other events are judged" (Hall, 1966, p. 4). They are, according to Ruth Benedict (1934), the cultural forms and processes that are an integral part of every society. When cultural patterns are linked to communication, the terms refer to the shared, recurring, and culturally derived ways of interacting that are manifested in the ebb and flow of human transactions within a society.

Pattern research tends to be descriptive in nature: it details the form and function of communicative behavior within a society. Methodologically, it can be conducted either quantitatively or qualitatively in a research laboratory, field study, or rhetorical analysis of primary and secondary sources. This type of research, as indicated earlier, is not often published in communication journals, but scattered examples of pattern studies on culture and communication are found in the literature (Condon, 1984; Katriel, 1986; Philipsen, 1975; Shuter, 1979, 1982, 1985b, 1990; Wiseman & Shuter, 1994). This type of research generates cultural data that not only increases understanding of a society, but also serves as a springboard for developing intracultural communication theory.

Unlike intercultural theory, an intracultural perspective marries culture and communication theory and hence produces communication paradigms about a co-culture, country, or world region. The approach to theory development is best exemplified in Kincaid's (1987) *Communication Theory: Eastern and Western Perspectives*, which identifies differences and similarities between Korean, Chinese, Japanese, and Indian communication theories. While Kincaid's book stops short of identifying different Western communication theories—French versus British communication theory, for example—it is a most significant contribution in intracultural communication theory development.

Intracultural communication theory is critically important for several reasons. First, it provides a conceptual framework for analyzing interaction within a society and world region. Second, intracultural theories demonstrate the inextricable linkage between communication patterns and sociocultural forces. And, last, it provides a conceptual basis for making intercultural communication comparisons between dissimilar societies.

With an intracultural perspective, researchers can concentrate on developing a line of research on a society or world region. This approach should produce comprehensive communication data on countries and world regions as well as establish the foundation for developing culture specialists—researchers and teachers who are experts on a particular country and world region. Culture specialists in communication are vital if global and co-cultural conflicts are to be understood and ameliorated.

An intracultural perspective also has implications for teaching intercultural communication. With comprehensive intracultural data, teachers should be able to design multiple courses in intercultural communication that focus on interaction within a society and world region—a marked improvement over many intercultural curricula that currently consist of a single course offering called intercultural communication. For example, with sufficient intracultural data, a series of communication classes could be offered on Africa, East Asia, or South Asia, with seminars also available on specific countries within these regions. Currently, this type of curriculum is not easily developed because intercultural researchers have devoted limited attention to intracultural communication. Without an expanded intercultural curriculum, it will be difficult to develop students and teachers who are culture specialists in communication.

The 21st century requires interculturalists who understand both culture and communication—professionals with a deep understanding of specific countries and world regions. By continuing the intracultural research trend of the past five years and also expanding future analysis to co-cultures, countries, and world regions that have been neglected, we may, at some point, be able to modify undergraduate and graduate programs in intercultural communication to reflect the central role of culture in communication.

NOTES

For this essay, the speech-communication journals reviewed for intercultural communication research included Communication Studies, Communication Monographs, Communication Quarterly, Human Communication Research, Quarterly Journal of Speech, Southern Communication Journal, *and* Western Journal of Speech-Communication.

1. An exception should be noted. The *Howard Journal of Communications*, although not included within the boundaries of research reviewed in this essay, has published descriptive, culture-centered studies.

SUGGESTED READINGS

The following references provide a comprehensive listing of intercultural communication research published between 1985 and 1995 not cited in the essay.

Uncertainty Reduction and Culture

Gudykunst, W. B., Chua, E., & Gray, A. (1987). Cultural dissimilarities and uncertainty reduction processes. In M. McLaughlin (Ed.), *Communication yearbook* (Vol. 10). New Brunswick, NJ: Transaction.

Gudykunst, W. B., & Nishida, T. (1984). Individual and cultural influences on uncertainty reduction. *Communication Monographs, 51,* 23–26.

Gudykunst, W. B., Yang, S. M., & Nishida, T. (1985). A cross-cultural test of uncertainty reduction theory. *Human Communication Research, 11,* 407–454.

Initial Interaction and Culture

Gudykunst, W. B., & Hammer, M. (1987). The effects of ethnicity, gender, and dyadic composition on uncertainty reduction in initial interaction. *Journal of Black Studies, 18,* 191–214.

Nakanishi, M. (1986). Perceptions of self-disclosure in initial interaction: A Japanese sample. *Human Communication Research, 13,* 176–190.

Intercultural Communication Competence

Hammer, M. (1984). The effects of an intercultural communication workshop on participants' intercultural communication competence. *Communication Quarterly, 32,* 352–362.

Nishida, H. (1985). Japanese intercultural communication competence and cross-cultural adjustment. *International Journal of Intercultural Relations, 9,* 247–269.

Communication Apprehension

Watson, A. K., Monroe, E., & Atterson, H. (1989). Comparison of communication apprehension across cultures: American and Swedish children. *Communication Quarterly, 37,* 67–76.

Relationship Development and Culture

Gudykunst, W. B. (1983). Similarities and differences in perceptions of initial intracultural and intercultural encounters: An exploratory investigation. *Southern Communication Journal, 27,* 49–65.

Gudykunst, W. B. (1985). An exploratory comparison of close intracultural and intercultural friendships. *Communication Quarterly, 33,* 270–283.

Intracultural Communication Research

Martin, J., Hecht, M., & Larkey, L. (1994). Conversational improvement strategies for interethnic communication: African American and European American. *Communication Monographs, 61,* 236–255.

Nakayama, T., & Krizek, R. (1995). Whiteness: A strategic rhetoric. *Quarterly Journal of Speech, 81,* 291–309.

Park, M.-S., & Kim, M.-S. (1992). Communication practices in Korea. *Communication Quarterly,* 40, 398–404.

Rigsby, E. (1993). African American rhetoric and the "profession." *Western Journal of Communication, 57,* 191–199.

Co-cultural Communication Research

Gudykunst, W. B., & Kim, Y. Y. (1986). *Interethnic communication.* Newbury Park, CA: Sage.

Hammerback, J., & Jensen, R. (1980). The rhetorical words of Cesar Chavez and Reises Tijerina. *Western Journal of Speech-Communication, 44,* 166–176.

Jensen, R., & Hammerback, J. (1980). Radical nationalism among Chicanos: The rhetoric of Jose Angel Gutierrez. *Western Journal of Speech Communication, 44,* 191–222.

Lake, R. (1983). Enacting red power: The consummatory function in Native American protest rhetoric. *Quarterly Journal of Speech, 72,* 434–445.

Stanback, M., & Pearce, W. B. (1981). Talking to "the man": Some communication strategies used by members of subordinate social groups. *Quarterly Journal of Speech, 67,* 21–30.

Korea, Japan, China, and Taiwan

Chang, H.-C., & Holt, G. R. (1991a). The concept of yuan and Chinese interpersonal relationships. In S. Ting-Toomey (Ed.), *Cross-cultural interpersonal communication.* Newbury Park, CA: Sage.

Chang, H.-C., & Holt, G. R. (1991b). More than relationship: Chinese interaction and the principle of Kuan-Hsi. *Communication Quarterly, 39,* 251–271.

Chang, H.-C., & Holt, G. R. (1996). The changing Chinese interpersonal world: Popular themes in interpersonal communication books in modern Taiwan. *Communication Quarterly, 44,* 85–106.

Chen, G.-M., & Chung, J. (1994). The impact of Confucianism on organizational communication. *Communication Quarterly, 42,* 93–105.

Gao, G., & Gudykunst, W. B. (1995). Attributional confidence, perceived similarity, and network involvement in Chinese and American romantic relationships. *Communication Quarterly, 43,* 431–445.

Gudykunst, W. B., Yang, S. M., & Nishida, T. (1985). A cross-cultural test of uncertainty reduction theory. *Human Communication Research, 11,* 407–454.

Klopf, D. (1991). Japanese communication practices: Recent comparative research. *Communication Quarterly, 39,* 130–143.

Park, M.-S., & Kim, M.-S. (1992). Communication practices in Korea. *Communication Quarterly, 40,* 398–404.

Yum, J. O. (1982). Communication diversity and information acquisition among Korean immigrants in Hawaii. *Human Communication Research, 8,* 154–159.

East Asia

Kume, T. (1985). Managerial attitudes toward decision making: North America and Japan. *International and Intercultural Communication Annual, 9,* 231–252.

Okabe, R. (1983). Cultural assumptions of East and West: Japan and the United States. *International and Intercultural Communication Annual, 7,* 21–41.

Yum, J. O. (1988a). Locus of control and communication patterns of immigrants. *International and Intercultural Communication Annual, 9,* 191–211.

Yum, J. O. (1988b). The impact of Confucianism on interpersonal relationships and communication patterns in East Asia. *Communication Monographs, 55,* 374–388.

Europe

Magiste, E. (1988). Changes in lateralization pattern of two immigrant groups in Sweden. *International and Intercultural Communication Annual, 9,* 233–251.

Punetha, D., Giles, H., & Young, L. (1988). Interethnic perceptions and relative deprivation: British data. *International and Intercultural Communication Annual, 9,* 252–266.

REFERENCES

Archer, L., & Fitch, K. (1994). Communication in multinational organizations in the United States and Western Europe. In R. Wiseman & R. Shuter (Eds.), *Communicating in multina-tional organizations* (pp. 75–93). Newbury Park, CA: Sage.

Bass, J. (1989). An efficient humanitarianism: The British slave trade debates, 1791–1792. *Quarterly Journal of Speech, 75,* 152–165.

Benedict, R. (1934). *Patterns of culture.* New York: Morrow.

Berend, I. (1988). Crisis and reform in East-Central Europe. *Studia Diplomatica, 41,* 257–267.

Booth-Butterfield, M., & Jordan, F. (1989). Communication adaptation among racially homogeneous and heterogeneous groups. *Southern Communication Journal, 54,* 253–272.

Bruce, L. (1988). Where adversaries converge. *International Management, 43,* 70–73.

Campbell, K. (1986). Style and content in rhetoric of early Afro-American feminists. *Quarterly Journal of Speech, 72,* 434–445.

Carbaugh, D. (1993). "Soul" and "self": Soviet and American cultures in conversation. *Quarterly Journal of Speech, 79,* 182–190.

Carlson, C. (1986). Gandhi and the comic frame: Ad bellum purificandum. *Quarterly Journal of Speech, 72,* 446–455.

Condon, J. C. (1984). *With respect to the Japanese.* Yarmouth, ME: Intercultural Press.

Corcoran, F. (1983). The bear in the backyard: Myth, ideology, and victimage ritual in Soviet funerals. *Communication Monographs, 50,* 305–320.

Cronen, V., & Shuter, R. (1983). Forming intercultural bonds. In W. B. Gudykunst (Ed.), *Intercultural communication theory.* Beverly Hills, CA: Sage.

Cupach, W., & Imahori, T. (1993). Managing social predicaments created by others: A comparison of Japanese and American facework. *Western Journal of Communication, 57,* 431–444.

Cushman, D., & King, S. (1985). National and organizational cultures in conflict resolution: Japan, the United States, and Yugoslavia. *International and Intercultural Communication Annual, 9,* 114–135.

Cushman, D., & King, S. (1994). Communication in multinational organizations in the United States and Western Europe. In R. Wiseman & R. Shuter (Eds.), *Communicating in multinational organizations* (pp. 94–116). Newbury Park, CA: Sage.

Fitch, K. (1994). A cross-cultural study of directive

sequences and some implications for compliance-gaining research. *Communication Monographs, 61,* 185–209.

Flores, L. (1996). Creating discursive space through a rhetoric of difference: Chicana feminists craft a homeland. *Quarterly Journal of Speech, 82,* 142–156.

Frank, D. (1981). Shalom achshave: Rituals of the Israeli peace movement. *Communication Monographs, 48,* 165–182.

Gao, G. (1991). Stability of romantic relationships in China and the United States. In S. Ting-Toomey (Ed.), *Cross-cultural interpersonal communication.* Newbury Park, CA: Sage.

Greenburg, B., Ku, L., & Li, H. (1992). Parental mediation of children's mass media behaviors in China, Japan, Korea, Taiwan, and the United States. *International and Intercultural Communication,* 150–171.

Griefat, Y., & Katriel, T. (1989). Life demands musayara: Communication and culture among Arabs in Israel. *International and Intercultural Communication Annual, 13,* 121–138.

Gudykunst, W. B. (1988). Uncertainty and anxiety. In Y. Y. Kim & W. B. Gudykunst (Eds.), *Theories in intercultural communication.* Newbury Park, CA: Sage.

Gudykunst, W. B., Sodetani, L., & Sonada, K. (1987). Uncertainty reduction in Japanese-American and Caucasian relationships in Hawaii. *Western Journal of Speech-Communication, 51,* 256–278.

Hall, E. (1959). *The silent language.* Garden City, NY: Doubleday.

Hall, E. (1966). *The hidden dimension.* Garden City, NY: Doubleday.

Hall, E. (1976). *Beyond culture.* Garden City, NY: Doubleday.

Heisey, R., & Trebing, D. (1983). A comparison of the rhetorical visions and strategies of the Shah's white revolution and the Ayatollah's Islamic revolution. *Communication Monographs, 50,* 158–174.

Hopper, R., & Doany, N. (1989). Telephone openings and conversational universals: A study in three languages. *International and Intercultural Communication Annual, 13,* 157–179.

Hwang, J., Chase, L., & Kelly, C. (1980). An intercultural examination of communication competence. *Communication, 9,* 70–79.

Katriel, T. (1986). *Talking straight: Dugri speech in Israeli Sabra culture.* Cambridge, England: Cambridge University Press.

Katriel, T. (1987). Rhetoric in flames: Fire inscriptions in Israeli youth movement ceremonials. *Quarterly Journal of Speech, 73,* 444–459.

Katriel, T. (1994). Sites of memory: Discourses of the past in Israeli pioneering settlement museums. *Quarterly Journal of Speech, 80,* 1–20.

Kelly, J. (1988). Class conflict or ethnic oppression: The cost of being Indian in rural Bolivia. *Rural Sociology, 53,* 399–420.

Kim, M. S. (1994). Cross-cultural comparisons of perceived conversational constraints. *Human Communication Research, 21,* 128–151.

Kim, Y. Y. (1987). Facilitation immigrant adaptation: The role of communication. In T. C. Albrecht, M. B. Adelman, et al. (Eds.), *Communicating social support* (pp. 192–211). Newbury Park, CA: Sage.

Kim, Y. Y. (1988). *Communication and cross-cultural adaptation: An integrative theory.* Avon, England: Multilingual Matters.

Kincaid, L. (1987). *Communication theory: Eastern and Western perspectives.* London: Academic Press.

Kwarteng, C. (1988). Difficulties in economic integration: The case of ECOWAS. *Transafrica Forum, 5*(88), 17–25.

Ma, R. (1992). The role of unofficial intermediaries in interpersonal conflicts in the Chinese culture. *Communication Quarterly, 40,* 269–278.

Martin, J., Hammer, M., & Bradford, L. (1994). The influence of cultural and situational contexts on Hispanic and non-Hispanic communication competence behaviors. *Communication Quarterly, 42,* 160–179.

McCroskey, J. C., Fayer, J. M., & Richmond, V. (1985). Don't speak to me in English: Communication apprehension in Puerto Rico. *Communication Quarterly, 33,* 185–192.

Montet, M. (1989). Europe's spiritual organs. *International Management, 44,* 38–39.

Orbe, M. (1995). African American communication research: Toward a deeper understanding of interethnic communication. *Western Journal of Communication, 59,* 61–78.

Pearce, J. (1988). Free port, no trade restrictions,

Mark Singapore Development. *Business Japan, 33*, 31–32.

Philipsen, G. (1975). Speaking "like a man" in teamsterville. *Quarterly Journal of Speech, 61*, 13–22.

Pike, J. (1966). *Language in relation to a unified theory of the structure of human behavior.* The Hague, The Netherlands: Mouton.

Reimer, B. (1989, March 27). Europe may slap a quota on General Hospital. *Business Week*, 46–47.

Roberts, A. (1988). Racism sent and received: Americans and Vietnamese view one another. *Research in Race and Ethnic Relations, 5*, 75–97.

Rosen, S., & Weissbrodt, D. (1988). The 39th session of the UN sub-commission on prevention of discrimination and protection of minorities. *Human Rights Quarterly, 10*, 487–508.

Rosenbaum, A. (1989). Fortress or facade: A unified EC is far from finished. *Industry Week, 238*, 54–55.

Rupesinghe, K. (1988). Ethnic conflicts in South Asia. *Journal of Peace Research, 25*, 337–350.

Sanders, J., Wiseman, R., & Matz, I. (1991). Uncertainty reduction in acquaintance relationships in Ghana and the United States. In S. Ting-Toomey (Ed.), *Cross-cultural interpersonal communication.* Newbury Park, CA: Sage.

Shamsuddin, M. (1988). UNESCO and the flow of information: A case study. *Pakistan Horizon, 41*, 31–49.

Shuter, R. (1979). The Dap in the military: Hand-to-hand communication. *Journal of Communication, 29*, 136–142.

Shuter, R. (1982). Initial interaction of American blacks and whites in interracial and intraracial dyads. *Journal of Social Psychology, 117*, 45–52.

Shuter, R. (1985a). The Hmong of Laos: Orality, communication, and acculturation. In L. Samovar & R. Porter (Eds.), *Intercultural communication: A reader* (4th ed., pp. 102–108). Belmont, CA: Wadsworth.

Shuter, R. (1985b). Nomothetic and ideographic approaches to developing an intercultural communication curriculum. Paper presented at the annual convention of Speech Communication Association, Chicago.

Shuter, R. (1990). [Entire special issue devoted to intracultural communication.] *Southern Communication Journal, 55* (Spring).

Singelis, T., & Brown, W. (1995). Culture, self, and collectivist communication: Linking culture to individual behavior. *Human Communication Research, 21*, 354–389.

Stohl, C. (1993). European managers' interpretations of participation: a semantic network analysis. *Human Communication Research, 20*, 97–117.

Suzuki, S., & Rancer, A. (1994). Argumentativeness and verbal aggressiveness: Testing for conceptual and measurement equivalence across cultures. *Communication Monographs, 61*, 256–263.

Tank, A. (1987, April). Korea's Japanese jinx. *Management Today*, 88–90.

Ting-Toomey, S. (1988). Rhetorical sensitivity style in three cultures: France, Japan, and the United States. *Central States Speech Journal, 39*, 28–36.

Weissbrodt, D. (1988). Country related and thematic developments at the 1988 session of the UN commission on human rights. *Human Rights Quarterly, 10*, 544–558.

Wiseman, R. L., & Shuter, R. (Eds.). (1994). *Communication in multi-national organizations.* Newbury Park, CA: Sage.

Won-Doornink, M. (1991). Self-disclosure and reciprocity in South Korean and U.S. male dyads. *Cross-cultural interpersonal communication.* Newbury Park, CA: Sage.

Xiao, X. (1996a). From the hierarchical ren to egalitarianism: A case of cross-cultural rhetoric mediation. *Quarterly Journal of Speech, 82*, 38–54.

Xiao, X. (1996b). China encounters Darwinism: A case of intercultural bias. *Quarterly Journal of Speech, 82*, 83–99.

Yahuda, M. (1988). The Pacific community: Not yet. *Pacific Review, 1*, 119–127.

Yang, D. J. (1990, April 10). Japan builds a new power base: Its emerging clout in East Asia could come at America's expense. *Business Week*, 42–45.

KEY TERMS

centrality	intracultural communication
culture	
intercultural studies	

DISCUSSION QUESTIONS

1. Why is culture so important to intercultural communication?
2. Why is it desirable to understand communication in specific co-cultures, countries, and world regions?
3. How can your current intercultural communication class be modified to make "culture" more central to it?
4. Can you think of a country or world region that you would like to know more about with respect to its communication? Why?
5. What occupations need to know about communication in co-cultures and countries of the world? Why?

PART TWO

IDENTITY AND INTERCULTURAL COMMUNICATION

This part focuses on a fundamental construct—identity—and inter-cultural communication. As individuals, as members of social groups and national cultures, we come to intercultural encounters with a wealth of experiences, beliefs, needs, and interests, all of which affect our inter-cultural communication. The complexities of our identities often mean that at particular times or in certain situations, aspects of our identities become more or less important. Sometimes, we communicate from our gendered positions, speaking as women or men. At other times, our ethnic or racial identity may be important. In intercultural situations, our iden-tity positions shape our understanding of the world around us. Through research that investigates identity, we can begin to understand the impact of our complex and multiple identities on intercultural interactions.

Consider these questions as you read the articles in this part:

How do these readings view identity (static or dynamic)?

How do they approach the study of identity and communication (objectively or subjectively)?

What is the relationship between identity and communication? Does identity shape our communication, or does communication shape our identity?

Is it possible to have many different identities?

Does the sense of who we are change from context to context?

What role does power play in our sense of self-identity?

Does it matter if people see our identities differently from how we see our own identities?

The essays in this section describe identity in various ways—from a fairly consistent set of categories to seeing it as complex, dynamic, socially constructed, and having contradictory and competing facets. Identity may be either generational, gender, ethnic, racial, or religious, or any combination of those terms. Methods range from the more objective media analysis and literature reviews to the more subjective interviews and introspection of personal journeys.

Teresa A. Nance and Anita K. Foeman explore biracial identity in "On Being Biracial in the United States." They take a fairly objective view of identity, review the social psychological development of identity, and critique early "deficit" models of biracial identity. These models were based on an ethnocentric notion that biracial individuals have to choose between their racial backgrounds, and that the dominant racial background would prevail. The authors propose, instead, a model based on the notion that racial identity is socially constructed. To illustrate, they outline a three-stage communication model that shows how parents can help their children develop "healthy" biracial identities.

In "Jewish American Identity," authors Douglas R. Golden, T. A. Niles, and Michael L. Hecht outline a more interpretive framework for understanding identity. They emphasize the dynamic nature of identity and suggest that identities are created, maintained, and negotiated through communication. They note the ambiguity of U.S. Jewish identity—that it can be hidden, can be viewed as religious or ethnic, and can incorporate some views about the Holocaust. They describe "layered" aspects of Jewish identity (personal, enactment, relational, and communal). Their insights are gleaned from both media analysis and ethnographic interviewing.

Regina E. Spellers, in "Happy to Be Nappy: Embracing an Afrocentric Aesthetic for Beauty," traces the development of one fundamental aspect of identity: self-image. She takes a more contextual, power-based approach. Using an Afrocentric framework, she recounts her self-conscious struggle with and ultimate rejection of dominant U.S. knowledge claims about beauty. She points out the macrocontexts (social, political, historical) that play an important role in how minority individuals develop a sense of self-image.

We then turn to discussions of how individuals develop and juggle multiple, dynamic identities within social and political contextual constraints. In "My Three Cultures: Navigating the Multicultural Identity Landscape," Gust A. Yep, an Asianlatinoamerican, describes in a personal story how he navigates and integrates his three ethnic cultural heritages. He describes the internal conflicts (in his family relationships) and external conflicts (stereotyping, rigid expectations) that arise as identities are created and co-created in communication within social and political inequities. He emphasizes the fluidity of identity and shows how negotiating identity from the margins can be empowering and liberating.

The final reading explores the intersections of race, class, and gender within societal structures. In "Chicana y Chicana: Dialogue on Race, Class, and Chicana Identity," Dorothy Leland and Jacqueline M. Martinez use a dialogue format to relate their personal stories of how they each came to assume a Chicana identity. Their narratives illustrate the intersections of class, gender, and sexual orientation. They note that as Chicanas, they assume a political consciousness, which may be absent from other identities. They explore the problems of dichotomizing identity—making people choose between identities—and describe the resulting violence when people (like Leland's and Martinez's parents) erase part of their heritage. Finally, they describe contradictions and ambivalence they feel when others assume they are White, or don't care that they are Chicanas.

5
ON BEING BIRACIAL IN THE UNITED STATES

TERESA A. NANCE / ANITA K. FOEMAN

These children have always been boxed and labeled, like they are goods, and damaged goods at that. Before it was words like half breed, half caste, mongrel, children with an identity conflict. Then the instructions came that they were black whether they feel it or not. It makes me so mad, they are both, not just black; we need new words to describe that identity, instead of just holding up placards and getting them to queue behind them. ("Choosing Sides," 1992, p. 14)

In the above quote, a Black social worker laments the bureaucratic convention that forces an "official" identity on biracial children. This lament highlights some of the communication issues and dilemmas experienced by biracial individuals. Who should decide ethnic and racial labels? What are the messages sent by society and the government to biracial individuals concerning their identity? What are the consequences when an individual's avowed identity is different from the label imposed by others? The answers to these questions are not easy and often reflect the interplay of race and power within our society.

Issues concerning biracial identity are becoming increasingly important as the biracial population in the United States grows. According to the article "Interracial Baby Boom" in *The Futurist* (1993), between 1968 and 1989, children born to parents of different races increased from 1% of total births to 3.4% (p. 54). Miller and Rotheram-Borus (1994) estimate that approximately 2 million multiracial people reside in the United States (p. 147).

For Black and White parents, births increased from 8,700 in 1968 to 45,000 in 1989. Births to Japanese and White parents have also increased. In fact, in the United States today, Japanese–White parents account for 39% more births than Japanese–Japanese parents. Similarly, between 1968 and 1989, births to Chinese–White parents more than tripled, from 1,000 to over 3,800.

As Susan Kalish (1992) of the Population Reference Bureau observes somewhat optimistically:

the upward trend toward more mixed births is a sign that the social meaning of race in the United States may be undergoing subtle shifts. It suggests that forces similar to those that softened the historical isolation of European ethnic immigrants over time may now be at work making somewhat more permeable the stubborn barriers of race. (p. 55)

This essay explores issues surrounding biracial identity formation and communication strategies that facilitate the development of a healthy biracial identity in children. There has been very little scholarship on biracial identity development and even less concerning the communication issues of biracial identity. This exploratory essay is part of a larger investigation of interracial families and is based on previous writing and our own experiences in multiracial families.

First, we discuss the social psychological mechanisms of identity formation and explore the meaning of race as an identity category in the United States today. We then describe the development of biracial identity. Finally, we relate what we understand to be the formative functions of communication in the process of positive self-development to the biracial child.

Identity Formation

Identity formation, especially among adolescents, has generated much interest and work since the renowned psychologist Erik Erikson (1968) proposed his eight stages of psychosocial development. Central to Erikson's development stages is the understanding that each phase involves a particular crisis that must be resolved before the person moves on to the next phase. Symbolic interactionists and communication theorists built on the foundation of Erikson's work. They stress that identities are not created by the self alone but are co-created through communication with others. Consequently, it is through interactions with significant others in our lives that we learn how to judge ourselves and others. We also learn from others how our social world is divided into categories and where we fit with respect to those categories, that is, to gender, race, and ethnicity (Hecht, Collier, & Ribeau, 1993).

While some of these lessons are taught intentionally, many lessons are simply deduced from everyday verbal, written, mediated, and nonverbal communication messages that are a part of our daily lives. And sometimes these messages conflict with how we see ourselves. The identity that we avow may not be the one that is ascribed to us by others. For example, biracial people are sometimes forced to place themselves in a category where they do not fit (Nakayama, 1997). As described in other readings in this book (see Yep; Leland & Martinez), ethnic, gender, and sexual orientation identity formation is a complex, communicative process.

Before describing how biracial identity is developed, let's examine how thinking about racial categories and identity has evolved in the United States.

The Social Construction of Race

Recent thought on race has shifted from an emphasis on physical characteristics to the social meanings of race. Contemporary theories suggest much of what we "know" is based on social myth rather than on scientific fact. Root (1992) calls the system we have for specifying race "simple and irrational" (p. 6). To better understand this charge, it is necessary to put the process of race-defining into a historical context.

During the early part of the 19th century, as the newly formed United States struggled to establish economic solvency, it was imperative that cheap forms of labor be readily available. Africans had been enslaved since the early part of the

17th century but did not accumulate in number until the 19th century. The Africans were "ideal" as slaves because in addition to their physical prowess and ability to withstand the heat, their skin color provided the necessary ingredient in the determination of race.

Long after the physical enslavement of African Americans ended, the cultural and economic enslavement continued. The popular myth that "one drop of Black blood made one an African American" can certainly be seen as derived from these old laws. The simple truth is that it's not really about blood at all. It's really about cultural dominance and power.

> People with no discernible African genotype or phenotype were regarded as Black on the basis of the fact that they had grandfathers or other remote relatives who were socially regarded as Black and they had no choice in the matter. . . . The boundaries were drawn in this manner to maintain an absolute wall surrounding White dominance. (Spickard, 1992, p. 16)

In many ways the one-drop myth can be seen as a means to concretize the boundaries between Black and White Americans. It makes sure that current labels, whether descriptively useful or not, are maintained so that a system that tends to oppress members without the correct label is also carefully maintained. Consequently, anyone accepting the one-drop rule means internalizing the oppression of the dominant group, buying into the system of racial domination (Spickard, 1992, p. 19).

The great irony here is that most scientists (biologists and physical anthropologists) acknowledge the essential commonality of all humans and see races as geographically and biologically diverging populations. Spickard (1992) states, "The so-called races are not biological categories at all; rather, they are primarily social divisions that rely only partly on physical markers such as skin color to identify group membership" (p. 17).

In other words, for scientists, there is more racially that unites us as human beings than separates us. The real issue is one of political control. The process of racial labeling starts with geography, culture, and family ties, and it runs through

Minority Identity[1]	Majority Identity[2]	Biracial Identity[3]
1. Conformity	1. Contact	1. Awareness of differentness and dissonance
2. Dissonance	2. Disintegration	2. Struggle for acceptance
3. Resistance/denial	3. Reintegration	3. Self-acceptance and assertion
4. Introspection	4. Pseudo-independent	
5. Synergetic articulation	5. Autonomy	

[1]Ponterotto & Pedersen, 1993
[2]Helms, 1990
[3]Kich, 1992

FIGURE 1   *Stages of Racial Identity Formation*

economics and politics to biology, and not the other way around. It has also led to the rather rigid dichotomization of racial categories—one is either White or not White, and people often feel uneasy when they are unable to categorize individuals (Omi & Winant, 1994).

Racial Identity Formation

Given this historical context of racial categorization in the United States, it is not surprising that racial identity seems to develop differently for majority and minority members. While all young people pass through predictable phases of racial identity formation, minorities (e.g., African Americans, Hispanic Americans) develop racial awareness and identities earlier than Whites. This is the result of the imbalance of power and segregation in contemporary society. White children do not need to attend to the norms and values of minority groups unless they have direct exposure in their neighborhoods and schools. Minority children, however, are exposed to and compare themselves to White cultural norms through television, books, and other media (Miller & Rotheram-Borus, 1994, pp. 152–153).

How do we develop a sense of racial identity? And is biracial identity different from monoracial identity? As shown in Figure 1, minority identity formation usually involves an initial stage of conformity, of internalizing negative messages from society. This is followed by dissonance, then by a stage of positive, even superior feelings about

race, and finally by a secure sense of racial identity where all races can be accepted and even appreciated (Cross, 1978; Parham & Williams, 1993; Ponterotto & Pedersen, 1993).

In contrast, majority identity begins with unawareness of racial categories, then evolves to a passive acceptance of privilege in a racialized society, and may evolve to a stage of pseudo-independence and resistance to racist assumptions. Finally, it reaches an autonomy stage. The point is that the developmental process for monoracial adolescents (both majority and minority) follows a linear course, and the final identity is absolutely unambiguous (Miller & Rotheram-Borus, 1994).

For the biracial adolescent, however, the development of a biracial identity is not so easily understood. What roles are played by the child's self-identification, the family's attitudes, or society's label? Which racial group's label will have a more powerful influence on family and self-labeling? Society may rely on physical characteristics to assign identity, whereas the family may see bloodlines as most important. What happens when the child's self-label contradicts society's label (Miller & Rotheram-Borus, 1994, p. 151)?

Biracial Identity Formation

Glamour magazine replied to an anxious reader in 1955:

> Many colored men are fine people . . . but scientists do not yet know if it is wise for two such

very different races as white and black to marry, for sometimes the children of mixed marriages seem to inherit the worst characteristics of each race. ("Choosing Sides," 1992, p. 14)

The Deficit Perspective

Most of the early social psychological literature about biracial people in this country focused on the products of unions between Black and White parents. Biracial people were described as "marginal" people who lived tormented lives of self-doubt and social ostracism. As social outcasts, they existed between two different cultures and were not allowed into the social center of either racial group to become "whole" selves. Consequently, such peripheral social placement left them scarred and incomplete. They developed marginal personalities (Poston, 1990, p. 152). The belief was that the marginal person was destined to drift back and forth between two conflicting sets of values and lifestyles.

A closer look at this deficit model reveals it to be based on a truly ethnocentric framework. Implicit in each of the limitations is the assumption that the dominant culture is naturally better than the minority culture and that the essential struggle for all biracial individuals is to find a way to gain acceptance into the dominant culture. The deficit model does not recognize that the negative effects observed in biracial individuals may have been caused by the dominant culture's prejudicial attitudes and behavior and *not* by a defect caused by the race of one's parents.

Contemporary Models

As shown in Figure 1, more recent models of biracial identity development are less ethnocentric and differ somewhat from the monoracial models (Jacobs, 1992; Kich, 1992). A first stage is *awareness of differentness and dissonance*, where the child realizes that he or she is different from others and doesn't fit into a neat racial category. The child also becomes aware that others don't share the same self-perceptions. A second stage is the *struggle for acceptance*, in which the child deals with the ambiguity of identity and place. At this stage children openly experiment with and explore both cultures, and they may intensify their

struggles by actively and consciously choosing between cultures (Alexander, 1994; Herring, 1994). The third stage is *self-acceptance and assertion*, when the child is more self-expressive and less defensive, and has a more secure sense of self and a biracial self-concept.

It is important to note that biracial development is different from monoracial development in at least two ways. First, it is more ambiguous. That is, biracial adolescents may resolve their identity status in several ways, whereas models developed for monoracial people have a single end state—one has or has not resolved one's racial identity (Root, 1992; Miller & Rotheram-Borus, 1994). Biracial adolescents may identify with one group, both groups, or a new group (for example, biracial people), or they may accept community labels (Root, 1992).

Second, identity development is more cyclical than linear; there may be a cyclic reenactment of the three stages described above. As individuals mature, they may sometimes experience the same three phases with greater intensity and awareness (Herring, 1994, p. 179).

In direct contradiction to the earlier deficit model, some evidence suggests that biracial children may have advantages over monoracial children in that exposure to different cultural patterns increases both behavioral and cognitive flexibility. This flexibility facilitates the development of a multicultural identity. Biracial children who have been exposed to norms, values, and beliefs of both their heritage races may have bicultural identities as well as biracial status (Bennett, 1993; Ramirez & Castenada, 1974).

The Communication Game Plan

What are communication strategies that facilitate the development of a healthy biracial identity in children? First, what we know about biracial identity challenges us to think in new ways about racial identity development; static and dichotomous thinking about race are not useful. Second, we need to recognize that identity development occurs in the context of a racialized society. Because of U.S. history and our notions about race, society will often force a child to choose between the two heritage races, and depending on their physical characteristics, biracial children may face discrimination.

Kerwin et al. (1993) found that many of the parents of biracial children anticipated the fact that their children would confront racial discrimination. Not surprisingly, there was some difference between the White and Black parents' attitudes. The Black parent was the one who typically felt the need to prepare specifically for dealing with racial prejudice and bigotry (p. 225). Miller and Miller (1990) have argued that parents of biracial children best prepare themselves and their children for the challenge of coping with many of society's insensitivities by adopting a "minority orientation": "Without some orientation toward a minority agenda, a child cannot reconcile or cope with the conflict between African-American culture and majority culture or place this conflict in a relevant context" (p. 177).

Parents must teach their children how to recognize racialized language and situations and respond accordingly. Racial disharmony and polarization exists just as traffic exists. Responsible parents must inform their children about the dangers of living with racism just as they inform them about the dangers of living with cars.

Given that we know that children learn important lessons about who they are and how to behave from their interactions with others, and given the fact that ideas about race are socially constructed and not biologically preordained, we felt we needed to articulate a positive and proactive role that communication could play in this process. The following steps are languaged to relate to the experience of a developing child and are somewhat analogous to the three stages of biracial identity development shown in Figure 1.

Step One: Awareness

In this initial stage, parents of biracial children need to recognize the messages about identity and race that exist within their environment. These messages can be categorized as personal messages (the messages about identity coming from the immediate family and extended family members), social messages (those generated by significant others such as neighbors, schoolteach-

ers, and religious and social groups), and mass media messages (those in readily available forms of mass communication such as television, radio, movies, newspapers, magazines, etc.).

Personal Messages

Parents of biracial children begin the process of heightening their children's perception of racial identity messages by locating the source of their own assumptions about race. We know that in dealing with other people, we often try to figure out the reason why people behave as they do. We first need to figure out our own attitudes and behaviors.

For example, it is important to discover if family members mirror the inequities of the broader social structure within the family. For example, are light-skinned children favored more than dark-skinned ones? Is the child with dark skin treated differently by immediate or extended family members? For example, the grandmother of one adopted biracial child treated her like a souvenir from Africa. In all families, issues of hierarchy and bonding patterns are established early on—and will be magnified if family members are also treated differentially by the larger society (Miller & Rotheram-Borus, 1994, p. 155).

Once people know their own positions and know that they are responsible for their own behaviors, they will impose that same standard of accountability on others as well. Consequently, when we try to make sense of the behaviors of others, we will seek to attribute a cause to an observed behavior.

According to this process, known in the communication literature as attribution, individuals can choose to assign cause to others' behaviors based on either external or internal causes. If we assume that circumstances or environment dictate behavior, then external causes are seen as the cause of the behavior. If, however, we understand that the person's behavior is uniquely his or her own, then we would conclude that internal reasons produced the behavior.

Race becomes problematic when added to the process of attribution, because race, in and of itself, is used as the cause and explanation of behavior. Statements such as "African Americans are natural athletes," "Asians work hard," and "White folks are smart and rich" reveal this problem. Other such race-based assumptions can include statements about perseverance, honesty, and beauty.

Within the context of family conversation, seemingly innocent statements and observations can be the source of identity difficulties for biracial children. For example, the uncle of one biracial little boy was heard to comment, "He'll be a great ballplayer someday because he'll be smart and strong!" Because the child's father is White and his mother is Black, the uncle's statement presumes that the child would be heir to the intelligence of his father's race and the athleticism of his mother's.

Parents need to hear these kinds of generalizations as disturbing and help their child (as appropriate to the child's age and maturity) hear both the complimentary explicit message and the dangerous implicit message of racial stereotyping. Given the comment made above, a parent could say to the child, "If you want to be a great athlete, you will have to work hard on your body and your mind to succeed."

Social Messages

As children grow older and begin to move in social circles where parents are not always present, it becomes important that they learn to detect racialized "self-messages" on their own. For example, one parent reported that her 5-year-old daughter came home one day and recounted a playground conversation in which a little boy (who happened to be White) told her she couldn't be the queen. As the other children began to play, the little girl challenged the boy and asked why she couldn't be the queen. The boy explained simply that "queens are never Black."

The critical point in this story is that the little girl asked, "Why can't I be queen?" If she had simply accepted the roles as unequally distributed, she could attribute her being passed over for the part to any number of reasons. Because she asked the question, she brought the issue to the fore and allowed her mother, the teacher, and the boy's parents to deal with the issue.

We are not suggesting here that parents burden their children with heavy conversations about race, nor are we suggesting that parents make

children suspect everyone with whom they interact of being a closet racist. We are saying, however, that it is important to deal with conversations about race directly and honestly with an emphasis on recognizing the potential of the good and positive in every situation. An important aspect of the first stage of identity development is for the child to work through his or her awareness of racial issues and the dissonance of not belonging to one racial category (Jacobs, 1992).

When parents make race a natural part of their family dialogue, children are able to recognize and respond to comments and observations that are inappropriate. They will also know how to bring such statements to the attention of responsible adults who can provide assistance if needed.

Media Messages

Media messages need to be addressed as well. Helping children appreciate the ways in which other people provide them with messages about themselves that they may or may not accept is an especially important lesson for any biracial person to learn. When the son of one of the authors was watching the old television show *The Jeffersons*, he was perplexed by the term "zebra" used to refer to a biracial character on the show. Even after receiving an explanation that the term referred to the fact that the character had a parent who was Black and a parent who was White, the child concluded that the reference was "silly." It made no sense to him because zebras "are not people and they don't have a race." Clearly, he dismissed what he heard on television and recognized the comment as senseless.

Whether listening to irrational statements about race on situation comedies, or to well-meaning but condescending statements from a relative, the biracial child who has been made aware that such statements reflect the attitude of the language user and not some sort of "truth" is empowered to meet the challenge of living in our current racialized society.

Step Two: Coping

Learning to respond effectively to the racialized messages from the environment is the next step in the process as the child struggles for acceptance. It is important here for parents to understand the relationship between two important concepts: self-concept and self-esteem. Self-concept is the socially constructed image one has of oneself, and self-esteem is the value one has for oneself as well as one's perception of worth. As one's self-esteem rises and falls, the image one has of one's self is correspondingly influenced. It is certainly important for parents of all children to praise them and reinforce their overall self-concept. It is particularly important for parents of biracial children to monitor those aspects of their child's life that might influence the value the child holds for the "self" that may be grounded in race (Herring, 1994, p. 181).

Let's take the example of a biracial child (whose parents are White and Black) from a stable home environment, who has a relatively strong self-concept and is doing reasonably well in school. She sees herself as smart, athletic, and pretty well liked at the school. In a routine meeting with her guidance counselor, however, she is told that few Black students do well in an upper-level math course she has selected and that she might do better in a lower-level class.

In order for this child to cope with this challenge to her sense of self, her parents should provide her with the ability to understand that the guidance counselor's statement is an assumption about who she is and what she is capable of doing. The first step in helping children cope with damaging racialized messages is to instill in them a strong belief in their intrinsic worth. The children must believe that while they are not always perfect and will make mistakes, they are inherently good and worthwhile people.

Psychologist Jacobs (1992) describes four ways in which parents can help the biracial child develop a healthy self-esteem. First, they can *foster ego strength* by providing strong familial attachments. Ego strength is important for all children but especially important for the biracial child. Second, parents need to provide biracial children with a *biracial label* or a similar label (e.g., that their child belongs to the human race and color is not important).

Third, parents need to understand that their children's *racial ambivalence* is part of a normal developmental stage. More important, they should encourage children to verbalize racial thoughts and feelings. It is very important in this stage that parents allow and encourage open discussions. In a society where race is not easily discussed openly and productively, the family may be the only place where the child feels safe to vent ambivalence or anger or both. Through verbalization, the child can find ways to channel anger and work through the developmental process (Gibbs, 1989).

Finally, to the extent that it is possible, parents should *provide a multiracial and multiethnic environment*. Recent evidence shows that positive intergroup relationships in the community contribute to high self-esteem of biracial children, while cross-racial tensions can lead to negative adjustment (Miller & Rotheram-Borus, 1994, p. 156). This type of environment not only contributes a great deal to the identity development of the child but can also provide communicative and emotional support for parents as well as children (Jacobs, 1992).

Given a starting point of "I know I'm an ok and worthwhile person," parents can work with their children to develop sets of appropriate responses. For example, in response to the situation outlined above, a younger child can be prepared to say, "Thank you for your suggestion. I'm not comfortable with what you are telling me now. I think my parents should probably continue this conversation with you." An older child may deal with the comment more directly by saying, "I am not comfortable with your comments and here's why. . . ."

In designing coping responses, biracial children and their parents should recognize the communication principle that meaning is not inherent in words or situations. Meaning is simultaneously created by people interacting with one another. When people communicate, they seek to create a common ground of understanding. Consequently, coping responses should acknowledge the response of the other and at the same time point out that some incongruency exists.

Many biracial students have developed their own repertoire of coping responses. For example, one young woman responded to the inevitable question "Are you Black or White?" with the response, "I'm 100% both." A well-meaning relative asked the parents of a biracial baby whether or not they thought the baby would have "good hair." The child's balding father quipped, "In this family, any hair is good hair!"

Children must learn to accept some messages, reject others, and ignore still others. Figuring out ahead of time the kind of responses to give in potentially negative situations gives children the confidence to face new and different situations with confidence.

Step Three: Emergence

Out of a strong sense of self, and a confidence that comes from understanding how labels are created and used, biracial children should reach a point of selecting and creating their own labels. As noted above, parents can offer the "biracial" label as a place to start. By doing this, parents are teaching their children that they should and can control the labels that categorize them. Children also learn that categories are created by people and are inherent in social life. This valuable lesson is a powerful one for all biracial people to understand.

One interesting feature of the emergence stage of this model is that the control of the stage shifts from the parent to the child. As Erikson (1968) described it, the primary developmental task of adolescents in Western culture is to establish their personal identity, of which racial identity is an important part.

Of course, the way in which this stage unfolds is directly related to the quality of the work done in the previous stages. From a communication perspective, in this stage biracial children become more self-expressive and less defensive or reactive. Both cultures are understood and valued. Biracial children can discern racialized messages from the environment, develop sets of appropriate responses, and create a place where they establish the ways in which they can define themselves (Herring, 1994; Jacobs, 1992). What makes this process so interesting is that the place the children define for themselves may not be the one initially envisioned by the parents.

One of the authors has a son named Jesse. He has attended university functions sponsored by African American faculty and students since he was a baby. When he was 8 years old, Jesse was talking to an engineering student who suggested that when he was old enough to attend the university, he should join an organization for Black engineers. Jesse thought about the suggestion and then shook his head, informing the engineering student that he couldn't join the group because he wasn't Black.

His mother was taken aback by his comment because she thought she had been diligent in helping Jesse and his brother craft their dual racial identity. As she was about to challenge Jesse's remark, she had another thought. She explained to Jesse that some people use the term Black to refer to African Americans.

When Jesse heard this, he started to shake his head again. With his hazel eyes, tightly curled light brown hair and tawny skin color, he concluded, "That's ridiculous, because I'm a White African American." Jesse's comment clearly indicated that he had figured out his place in our racialized society.

Jesse's mother also realized the simple truth that most parents of biracial children will never live the life of a biracial person. They can only prepare their children to live happy and productive lives and then watch from the sidelines to see how it all turns out. As children grow in age and experience, their ability to discern racialized messages, craft coping responses, and create communication space for themselves will also develop and change. The ultimate measure of any parent's success is the healthy and productive functioning of their children.

Summary

The issue of biracial identity development grows more important as the number of biracial children grows. Understanding the social construction of racial categories and the process of biracial identity formation is only the beginning. Parents of biracial children have the very real task of preparing their children to handle themselves in a racially troubled society. Working through the three stages of the communication—awareness, coping, and emergence—provides parents and children with a method for beginning to address this serious but manageable situation.

REFERENCES

Alexander, S. (1994). Vietnamese Amerasians: Dilemmas of individual identity and family cohesion. In E. P. Salett & D. R. Koslow (Eds.), *Race, ethnicity and self: Identity in multicultural perspective* (pp. 198–216). Washington, DC: Multi-Cultural Institute.

Bennett, J. M. (1993). Cultural marginality: Identity issues in intercultural training. In R. M. Paige (Ed.), *Education for the intercultural experience* (pp. 109–136). Yarmouth, ME: Intercultural Press.

Choosing sides. (1992, February 7). *New Statesman & Society, 5,* 14–15.

Cross, W. E. (1978). The Thomas and Cross models of psychological nigrescence: A review. *Journal of Black Psychology, 5*(1), 13–31.

Erikson, E. H. (1968). *Identity: Youth and crisis.* New York: W. W. Norton & Company.

Gibbs, J. T. (1989). Biracial adolescents. In J. T. Gibbs & L. N. Huang (Eds.), *Children of color: Psychological interventions with minority youth* (pp. 322–350). San Francisco: Jossey-Bass.

Hecht, M. L., Collier, M. J., & Ribeau, S. A. (1993). *African American communication: Ethnic identity and cultural interpretation.* Newbury Park, CA: Sage.

Helms, J. E. (1990). Toward a model of white racial identity development. In J. E. Helms (Ed.), *Black and White racial identity: Theory, research, and practice* (pp. 49–66). New York: Greenwood Press.

Herring, R. D. (1994). Native American Indian identity: A people of many peoples. In E. P. Salett & D. R. Koslow (Eds.), *Race, ethnicity and self: Identity in multicultural perspective* (pp. 170–197). Washington, DC: MultiCultural Institute.

Interracial baby boom: Ethnic lines blurring in the U.S. (1993, May–June). *The Futurist, 27,* 54–55.

Jacobs, J. H. (1992). Identity development in biracial children. In M. P. P. Root (Ed.), *Racially mixed people in America* (pp. 190–206). Newbury Park, CA: Sage.

Kalish, S. (1992). Interracial baby boomlet in progress? *Population Today,* 1875 Connecticut Avenue, N.W., Suite 520, Washington, DC 20009–5728.

Kerwin, C., Ponterotto, J. G., Jackson, B. L., & Harris, A. (1993). Racial identity in biracial children: A qualitative investigation. *Journal of Counseling Psychology, 40*(2), 221–231.

Kich, G. K. (1992). The developmental process of asserting a biracial, bicultural identity. In M. P. P. Root (Ed.), *Racially mixed people in America* (pp. 304–317). Newbury Park, CA: Sage.

Miller, R. L., & Miller, B. (1990). Mothering the biracial child: Bridging the gaps between African American and white parenting styles. *Women and Therapy, 10*(1–2), 169–179.

Miller, R. L., & Rotheram-Borus, M. J. (1994). Growing up biracial in the United States. In E. P. Salett & D. R. Koslow (Eds.), *Race, ethnicity and self: Identity in multicultural perspective* (pp. 143–169). Washington, DC: MultiCultural Institute.

Nakayama, T. K. (1997). Dis/orienting identities. In A. González, M. Houston, & V. Chen (Eds.), *Our voices* (2nd ed., pp. 14–21). Los Angeles: Roxbury.

Omi, M., & Winant, H. (1994). *Racial formation in the United States from the 1960s–1980s* (2nd ed.). New York: Routledge.

Parham, T. A., & Williams, P. T. (1993). The relationship of demographic and background factors to racial identity attitudes. *The Journal of Black Psychology, 19,* 17–24.

Ponterotto, J. G., & Pedersen, P. B. (1993). *Preventing prejudice: A guide for counselors and educators.* Newbury Park, CA: Sage.

Poston, W. S. C. (1990). The biracial identity development model: A needed addition. *Journal of Counseling and Development, 69,* 152–155.

Ramirez, M., III, & Castenada, A. (1974). *Cultural democracy, bicognitive development and education.* New York: Academic Press.

Root, M. P. P. (1990). Resolving "other" status: Identity development of biracial individuals. *Women and Therapy, 9*(1–2), 185–205.

Root, M. P. P. (1992). Within, between and beyond race. In M. P. P. Root (Ed.), *Racially mixed people in America* (pp. 3–11). Newbury Park, CA: Sage.

Spickard, P. R. (1992). The illogic of American racial categories. In M. P. P. Root (Ed.), *Racially mixed people in America* (pp. 12–23). Newbury Park, CA: Sage.

Stonequist, E. (1937). *The marginal man: A study in personality and culture conflict.* New York: Russell and Russell.

Wardle, F. (1987). Are you sensitive to interracial children's special identity needs? *Young Children, 42,* 53–59.

KEY TERMS

biracial   identity
coping strategies   race

DISCUSSION QUESTIONS

1. What does it mean to say that race is a "social construction"? How do you define yourself racially? How comfortable are you with your definition?

2. Why were people of mixed racial heritage previously called "marginal"? How did that influence the way they were treated?

3. What advice do the authors give parents of biracial children to help them construct their own coping strategies? Take any one of the examples given in the section entitled "Step Two: Coping" and create your own response.

4. What makes "emergence" so difficult for parents of biracial children?

6

JEWISH AMERICAN IDENTITY

DOUGLAS R. GOLDEN / T. A. NILES / MICHAEL L. HECHT

I find it hard to identify myself as a Jew around other people. I don't wear a star or letter or anything. I'm not able to wear a kepah (yarmulke) because I'm a girl. Maybe I should wear a star, but once in school one of the girls asked the rabbi how to show people she was Jewish. He said she should take out her chain with the letter on it and wave it in people's faces. But I don't know, I just can't do that. Maybe I should. But when I'm in a bus I always get up and give an older person my seat. (Roiphe, 1981, p. 111)

This excerpt from an interview with an American Jewish teenager illustrates the saliency and problematic elements of her Jewish identity. From this small passage, her Jewish American identity is seen as a function of several different levels: how she feels about herself, how she wants others to regard her, how her actions represent her, and how she is connected to a certain community. Thus, "identity is both an individual and social construct emerging in a dialectic between the two" (Hecht, Collier, & Ribeau, 1993, p. 50). As a result of this dialectic tension, identity, often seen as an enduring trait, also possesses a dynamic quality. In the above situation, the teenager's self-concept and self-image, her relationships, the community with which she aligns herself, and her enactments in everyday life are continuously interacting to define a Jewish American identity.

The passage above also illustrates one of several characteristics that make Jewish American identity a problematic concept. The fact that she must find a way to symbolize her identity also shows her ability to "closet," or hide, her identity if she so desires and to answer for herself if, when, and how to express her Jewish American identity. Because she has no visible physical traits that define her as "Jewish," she can choose to show others that she is Jewish or she can also simply be an American or a teenage girl. Many Jews in America neither have visible "Jewish" characteristics such as a Jewish-sounding name nor choose to wear a traditional Jewish head covering; thus, revealing and concealing their Jewishness is a function of their Jewish identity. Weiss (1996), for example, admits: "I am a Chinese menu Jew; I pick and choose the values of my background that I wish to keep" (p. 27). In effect, being Jewish, like many other ethnicities in America, "has become a subjective identity, invoked at will by the individual" (Waters, 1990, p. 7).

The complex nature of Jewish American identity is compounded by the various ways of answering the basic question, Who is a Jew? In Jewish rabbinic law, the matrilineal principle answers that to be Jewish, one's mother must be Jewish. Also, through conversion, one can become Jewish. In recent years, however, the Reform Movement has adopted a nonlineal principle in which a child with one Jewish parent who is raised Jewish is considered Jewish.

This set of religious principles that define one as Jewish by *descent*, however, is only one means of determining who is a Jew. Being Jewish also may include the process of *assent* in which certain *chosen* strategies define one's Jewishness (Krausz, 1993). An embrace of modernism and individualism has transformed religious life to meet the needs of the individual (Meyer, 1990). Thus, instead of complying with the norms of a closed community of Jews, many Jewish Americans move toward considerations of what is meaningful for them as individuals. So, Jewish Americans now *choose* their way of being Jewish, whether it be through "believing in a Jewish God, embracing certain moral or social precepts, pursuing certain Jewish practices, pursuing Zionist [Jewish nationalist movement] activities, adopting a certain kind of persona or lexicon . . . , and so on" (Krausz, 1993, p. 273).

Jewishness-by-assent can be broken into religious and other cultural components. The former involves the degree of acceptance of one God and other beliefs connected with Jewish religious practices and observances; the latter focuses on an "identification with Jewish history" (Krausz, 1993), ancestry, and/or values, attitudes, and beliefs. In the premodern times some would argue that these elements were inseparable (Meyer, 1990). In contemporary America, however, we have seen a weakening of the religious component (e.g., understanding and participating in religious services) creating an increasing base of secular Jewry that has separated considerations of religion from considerations of group identification.

The publisher's letter in a recent issue of *Davka: Jewish Cultural Revolution* poignantly illustrates this philosophy: "It does not matter if you have green hair, body piercings, or tattoos and feel more at home in a mosh pit than a *shul* [synagogue], wear a black caftan and dance your soul to ecstasy, or belong to all the possible lifestyles that lie between: you're a Jew and you belong" (Kaufman, 1993, p. 3). Thus, the unique intersection of religious and other cultural possibilities in Jewish America creates a problematic and ambiguous identity.

Another factor that adds to the ambiguous character of Jewish identity is the history of anti-Jewish discrimination and prejudice (anti-Semitism) throughout the world and in the United States. Jewish people have a long history of victimization that is stored as a collective memory and often used to construct Jewish identity. Fein (1994) describes a Jewish identity that is constructed all too often as a reaction to the Holocaust:

> Why not intermarry? Because of Auschwitz. Why not assimilate? Because too much Jewish blood has been spilled. We may march behind the star of David, but it is the swastika that urges us on. . . . Our slogan is not a blessing, but a curse: "Never again!" (p. 10)

The Holocaust remains a "constant background factor . . . affecting the way Jews see themselves and the way they perceive their relationship to the non-Jewish world" (Simon, 1989). Also, Jewish American history is marred by the presence of anti-Semitic barriers that confined Jews to certain occupations and excluded them from mainstream corporate management (Sacks, 1994). The Jewish-American response to anti-Semitism has been as diverse as the types of Jewish identities in America. Some Jews have internalized stereotypes and become "what the group labeling them as Other has determined them to be" (Gilman, 1986, p. 12). Others see anti-Semitism as something that obligates them to strengthen ties with the Jewish community or religion, or both (Fein, 1994).

To reiterate, as a result of the ability to closet one's Jewish identity, the complexities of defining one's Jewishness, and a history of anti-Semitism,

Jewish identity has been shown to be an ambiguous and dynamic process that is difficult to pinpoint. The aim here is to view Jewish American identity and its idiosyncrasies through the lens of a communication perspective.

Communication Theory of Identity

The Communication Theory of Identity states that "identity is 'stored' within individuals, relationships, and groups and is communicated between relational partners and group members" (Hecht et al., 1993, p. 166). Four "locations," or layers, have emerged as perspectives for understanding identity. These four (sometimes competing, sometimes complementary) layers illustrate identity as being problematic as they push and pull each other toward adopting a number of different identities. The *personal layer* focuses on one's self-cognition, spiritual self, self-concept, and sense of well-being. The *enactment layer* deals with how messages express identity. The *relational layer* deals with how one's identity emerges through one's relationships with others and how relationships themselves possess their own identities. Finally, the *communal layer* involves an identity that is shared among a certain group of people or a particular community. A community possesses its own identity and represents the shared identities of its members. These frames of identity can work together or create dialectical oppositions (Hecht et al., 1993).

The premise of the communication theory of identity is that interaction is central to the identity process. Several propositions show how communication and identity shape each other.

- Identity is formed, maintained, and modified through social interaction.
- Identity influences interaction through shaping expectations and motivating behavior.
- Identity is enacted in social interaction, and the conditions of interaction influence identity enactments.
- Identity is an individual and social event. (Hecht et al., 1993)

In essence, communication shapes identity while identity shapes communication. When the four layers of identity are considered simultaneously, the formation of identity can be seen as a negotiation or conversation between and among the individual, the enactments, the relationship, and the community or any combination of the four.

Through our own research interpreting a Jewish media image and an ethnographic study of a Jewish fraternity along with examples drawn from published ethnographies and interviews, we will illustrate the emergent and dialectical processes of Jewish American identity. First, we will explore Jewish identity from each of the four layers of identity; then, we will illustrate how these four layers intersect in the identity process.

Personal Jewish Identity

"As a characteristic of the individual, identity has been known as self-concept or self-image and provides an understanding of how individuals define themselves in general as well as in particular situations" (Hecht, 1993, p. 79). Although personal identity resides within the individual, the personal layer does not exist independently of the other three layers. Personal Jewish identity, therefore, emerges from and with other influences such as one's community, relationships, actions, and other identities (e.g., gender and occupation). The Jewish American identity of any given individual is a process that is also situationally emergent (Collier & Thomas, 1988; Hecht et al., 1993) and is a source of expectations and motivations (Hecht, 1993; Hecht et al., 1993).

Various studies indicate that personal identity also influences how individuals interpret mass communication, and how meaning is created differently by individual viewers of television shows, movies, or news programs (Wolfe, 1992). In our own study of Jewish American viewers' reactions to certain themes on the *Northern Exposure* television show, we found that different interpretations were attached to the themes, images, and narratives of the show. For example, some perceived Joel's Jewishness and his identity as a New Yorker as inseparable, while others saw the two characteristics as distinct aspects of Joel's identity. One Jewish New Yorker we interviewed said that "one almost assumes that the East Coast tradition is a Jewish tradition . . . and *Northern Exposure* illustrates that." A small-town Wisconsin Jew, however, resented the portrayal and felt that Joel's enactments did not accurately portray Jewish characteristics. The variety of interpretations illustrates that Jewish identity and images and interpretations of Jewish identity are neither universally shared nor monolithic. Each American Jewish person creates his or her own Jewish identity through the interaction of various layers and unique experiences, and uses this identity to interpret the social world.

An interesting process that relates to the interpenetration of the personal layer and other layers is the internalization of stereotypes. When stereotypic communal images are internalized as personal identity, it is often called "Jewish self-hatred" or "Jewish anti-Semitism" (Gilman, 1986). Gilman has characterized Jewish self-hatred as a result of American Jews' acceptance of the Jewish stereotypes generated by non-Jewish Americans. This occurs as a product of assimilation: "The more one attempts to identify with those who have labeled one as different, the more one accepts the values, social structures, and attitudes of this determining group, the farther away from true acceptability one seems to be" (pp. 2–3).

This process helps to shape one's personal identity, but is a product of an interaction with other layers. Bershtel and Graubard (1992) interviewed several self-hating Jews. One woman in this collection expressed that "[my family was] always talking about problems and moaning and whining. That is Jewish to me: whining. And I whine to this day, and I hate it" (Bershtel & Graubard, 1992, p. 9). Thus, this woman dislikes that she is a whiner (personal layer), but that she connects whining with being Jewish is a product of a stereotype that was formulated by the group to which she is trying to assimilate (communal layer).

Jewish American Enacted Identity

Not only is identity a property of the individual, but it is also found in communication. "Identities are enacted in social interaction through communication and may be defined as those messages" (Hecht, 1993, p. 79). When enacting Jewish customs, practices, and observances, one is expressing values, affirming beliefs, and reinforcing fundamental commitments and rejections that connect one directly with elements of group identity. The enactment layer of identity thus allows us to view the emergent quality of Jewish identity through Jewish actions (or nonactions).

Studies of Jewish identity have closely examined the enactment layer as an indicator of one's individual Jewish identity. These studies have consistently focused on such formal enactments as ritual behavior, formal organizational participation, Jewish social ties, and charity giving (Medding, Tobin, Fishman, & Rimor, 1992). Furthermore, Medding et al. point out that certain situations and events in one's life bring Jewish identity to a conscious level. Choosing a marriage partner, the birth and raising of a child, decisions about raising children, and reactions to prejudice are all occasions in which Jewish identity can emerge through the choices made and their subsequent enactments. These enactments usually occur in coordination with the other three identity layers. On a relationship layer, for example, a couple can choose to send their child to a Jewish day school. On a personal layer, one can wear a Star of David. Through these enactments, Jewish identity is both experienced and expressed.

One particular episode of *Northern Exposure* illustrates how identity emerges through one's enactments: Joel Fleishman's uncle dies, and Joel promises his aunt that he will find a *minyan* (a quorum of 10 Jewish men needed to say certain prayers) so he can say the *Kaddish* (memorial prayer) for his uncle. The townspeople of Cicely then work together to find 9 more Jews for Joel. During the search, Joel doubts that Buck, one of the "recruits," was Jewish, so he asks him to say the *Shema* (a prayer that most Jews know). Buck recites the prayer, thereby enacting a Jewish identity. The members of Cicely discuss other enactments, such as displaying a sense of humor, using a particular last name, or being smart, as possible indications that a person is Jewish. Other episodes present Joel's argumentative style and his dour demeanor. In these cases, Jewish identity is attributed through certain enactments characterized (perhaps stereotypically) as Jewish.

The *Northern Exposure* episodes show how identity emerges through the enactments of an individual; however, communal groups can be the source of enactments as well. For example, in a study of an all-Jewish fraternity at a large Southwest university conducted by Golden (1996), communal identity was explored through the fraternity's enactments. One of the members mentioned that:

> We do get involved in Hillel [the Jewish student union] because we want some of their guys to become our members. . . . So, like we volunteer our services as ushers at the High Holy Day services, we put together a Passover Seder, and we do some philanthropies with them. (p. 34)

Through the fraternity's communal enactments of volunteering at High Holy Day services and doing other activities and rituals with the Jewish student union, a Jewish identity emerges.

The fraternity's enactments illustrate that how an individual or organization chooses to act or not to act is a function of Jewish identity. This includes engaging in behaviors that disclose or mask one's Jewish identity. One of the authors, for example, has remarked to another, "You don't have to let others know you are Jewish!" As illustrated by the young woman on the bus who expressed concern about identifying herself as a Jew around other people, the fact that Jewish Americans often cannot be identified by their physical appearance alone allows those who may not want their "Jewishness" to be known to closet, or hide, their identity. Closeting one's membership in a particular group is not uncommon within groups that have been stigmatized, discriminated against, or otherwise oppressed. Within some African American communities, this phenomenon has been called "passing," and many individuals with names that indicate membership in other stigmatized ethnic groups have changed their names to sound more "American."

Hiding one's group membership when one internally acknowledges being a member of the group may represent an *equivocation,* or compromise, of one's identity and, in effect, one's self. Such a compromise ultimately is the result of apprehension about the consequences of having one's group identity known or the result of holding negative attitudes, beliefs, and feelings about one's own group. Feelings of apprehension are often present because of a historical stigma attached to one's identity and the negative consequences (e.g., verbal and physical abuse) suffered by individuals who share that identity. In some cases, however, although there may be little fear of negative consequences, individuals may choose to hide their identity because they have accepted negative evaluations of their group. In either case, one is likely to experience discomfort and self-doubt, because the possibility always exists that one might be "found out" and criticized by both in-group and out-group members.

Jewish American Relational Identity

The relational layer focuses on identity as mutually constructed in social interaction (Hecht, 1993): "People define themselves in terms of their relationships" and "the relationships, themselves, take on identities" (p. 80). A person, therefore, can retain personal identity while also participating in the negotiation of a shared relational identity (e.g., marriage, groups of friends, and families). The relational level is about who associates with whom and how this association contributes to the construction and enactment of identity. From certain relationships a Jewish identity can emerge.

A couple is an excellent context to explore the relational layer of identity. From the beginning of a relationship between two Jewish people, a Jewish relational identity may be created through the negotiation of the personal identities of the individuals and the enactments of the couple. Did they meet through a Jewish organization? Do they go to Synagogue together (if at all)? Did they have a traditional Jewish wedding? Do they send their children to Jewish day school? Do they belong to Jewish groups? In part, the way these questions are answered both reflects *and* constitutes the couple's Jewish identity.

When one parent is not Jewish, these questions become more problematic. In a study of Jewish identity and intermarriage, Medding et al. (1992) found that in a mixed marriage, "the likelihood of creating an unambiguous Jewish identity [in the household] . . . is virtually nil" (p. 37). Although some intermarried couples make a conscious decision to have a Jewish family (i.e., send their children to Jewish day school and celebrate exclusively Jewish holidays), a vast majority of these intermarried households incorporate aspects of both traditions. Examples of the latter include having a "Hanukah bush" or sequentially celebrating Hanukah and Christmas to combine a family's Christian and Jewish heritages. Mixed-marriage households often create permeable boundaries between what is Jewish and what is not.

Relationships between Jewish and non-Jewish partners are the norm on television. More often than not, Jewish male characters have romantic relationships with non-Jewish women on prime-time television (Pearl & Pearl, 1993). Programs such as *L.A. Law, thirtysomething, Mad About You,* and *Northern Exposure* all portray relationships in which Jews and non-Jews are paired together. In the television drama *thirtysomething,* Michael Steadman, a Jewish baby boomer, and his non-Jewish wife, Hope, are unable to decide whether to have a Jewish ritual circumcision for their newborn son. Ultimately, their decision to have the ceremony is a "public declaration" of the family's Jewish relational identity (Pearl & Pearl, 1993).

Jewish American Communal Identity

The communal layer enables us to explore identity as "something held by a group of people which, in turn, bonds the group together" (Hecht, 1993, p. 80). On this layer, identity emerges from groups and networks. Jewish organizations, religious movements, and the media are all sites in which Jewish identity can be viewed on the communal layer.

The above-mentioned fraternity, for example, possesses a communal Jewish identity. This identity, in turn, creates communally held expectations. Thus, a commonly understood expectation of the fraternity is that all the members are Jewish. The idea of Jewish membership is salient in the myths of the fraternity, which has implications for how the members as a collective and as individuals present themselves to Jewish and non-Jewish underclassmen. Golden (1996) gives the following description of how a member of the fraternity recruits (or rushes) students on campus:

So he (a fraternity member) comes up with certain questions like, "What are you doing for the holidays?" and if they (recruits) don't say Rosh Hashanah or Passover or the High Holy Days, or something like that, then he'll actually say "what are you doing for such and such [Jewish] holiday?" and if they act whimmed, (i.e., confused) that means that they are not Jewish and then he pretty much gives the cold shoulder. (p. 19)

Although the recruit does not need to observe Jewish laws or holidays or even know much about Judaism, a fundamental knowledge of Jewish American life and a Jewish self-identification are necessary to become a member. Thus, the fraternity's communally held Jewish identity is enacted (giving "the cold shoulder") in recruiting and is reflected in the expectations of its members.

Television is also an excellent setting in which to explore the communal layer of Jewish identity. "Since the beginnings of television, Jewish themes and characters have been a steady element in popular television shows, from dramas and situation comedies to miniseries and made-for-TV movies" (Pearl & Pearl, 1993, p. 25). As the Jewish community, for many, no longer plays the same role it used to in the formation of Jewish identity, those who do not belong to a strong traditional Jewish community learn and gain insight about Jewish traditions, the Jewish community, and Jewish life from nontraditional sources such as television shows and other forms of mass media. Thus, television has some interesting implications for the formation and enactment of a Jewish communal identity.

Pearl and Pearl (1993) discuss a number of studies that have demonstrated that TV depictions are often absorbed and emulated by viewers and have the potential to affect viewers' behaviors, attitudes, knowledge, and understanding of the world. Although Hawkins and Pingree (1981) have pointed out that television probably does not shape culture, their research has shown that television does make a contribution to the creation of social reality. Pearl and Pearl (1993) illustrated the significant impact that television has on Jewish identity by claiming that an expertly done episode of *The Wonder Years* that dealt with a Bar Mitzvah had a positive effect on Jewish youngsters and their views of Jewish rituals. *Northern Exposure* also shows rituals, discusses Jewish theology, and portrays characteristic Jewish personality traits. These presentations, therefore, can impact the identities of Jewish American viewers.

Television programming not only contributes to the shaping of social reality but is also an enactment of communal identities and beliefs. The writers, producers, directors, and actors on a television program enact and perpetuate communal perceptions of Jewish identity when they create a television show. Many of the characters found on television shows are projections of those who create them. Sy Dukane, a coproducer of *The Home Court,* noted that the Jewish main character was a natural character for him and his partner to write about and stated that "we were also writing from our own experiences. . . . We're both Jewish, and so it was easier to do that" ("In the Spotlight," 1995, p. 4). Thus, the salient issues within the Jewish community are made visible through Jewish portrayals on television. Intermarriage, assimilation, and ritual portrayals are therefore salient off the screen and on. Prell (1992) has said that "the power of these cultural representations does not lie in their accurate descriptions, but in their ability to synthesize the feelings and the anxieties about living in American society" (p. 22).

The state of Israel, itself, is a problematic aspect of communal identity for some. Do Jews, particularly American Jews, accept Israel's policies and celebrate its break with historical victimization? Many American Jews have no identification with Israel as a part of their Jewish identity, whereas other American Jews use Israel as a basis for their Jewish identity.

Interpenetration of Frames

As illustrated by this discussion of Jewish American identity, identity is a process that incorporates the personal, the relationship, the enactment, and the communal levels. These four layers should be understood as interpenetrating and inseparable. Each layer only serves as a method to focus on identity in a variety of contexts. For example, one's personal identity feeds off one's relations while at the same time the individual contributes to a relational identity. The boundaries between these two layers are fluid and undefined. Where

does one's personal identity end and a relational identity begin?

An illustration of the interpenetration of the four levels concerns intermarriage. One's personal Jewish identity creates motivations and expectations that help to decide whether one will pursue intimate relations only with Jews. Over 50% of American Jews have non-Jewish spouses. On a personal level, this reflects the feelings one has toward Jewish law, the beliefs one has concerning a multicultural America, and the saliency of one's Jewishness. In part, a relational identity reflects the individual identities of each person in the relationship. Also, the identity of the relationship (i.e., as a mixed marriage) is created through the enactments of the couple. Finally, the identity of the relationship is a function of the pressures of the Jewish community. Some Jewish communities choose to marginalize intermarried couples, while others seek to reach out to them. Thus the couple's relational identity is drawn from a negotiation of personal identities, the enactments of the couple, and the input of the community(ies) to which they belong(ed).

The frequency with which Jewish Americans are intermarrying also recreates Jewish communal identity. "The 1.3 million gentile spouses and the children of these intermarried couples are radically changing the anatomy of the Jewish community and blurring the lines of who exactly is a Jew" (Beiser, 1996, p. 26). Mixed marriages are a reality in America and are portrayed as normal on the media. These images, viewed and understood as the norm by many Jewish Americans, help to create personal expectations and motivations for Jewish Americans. Thus, the phenomenon of intermarriage can be seen as an identity issue that is a function of all four levels of identity.

Conclusion

This essay discusses Jewish American identity. In it we apply the Communication Theory of Identity (Hecht, 1993) to examine personal, enacted, relational, and communal identities and the interpenetration of these four layers. We have attempted to unpack some of the problematic elements of this identity group without imposing stereotypical constructions. The diversity among

Jewish Americans is great, and it is impossible to understand the process of Jewish identity as one type of person, action, relationship, or community.

One of the problematic elements of Jewish American identity is Jewish Americans' phenotypically White appearance. They can "pass" as White—they are often "racially" grouped this way—and many would self-identify this way. Jews can, and often do, claim the benefits of "Whiteness," although Jews are typically among the top-five hate-crime victim groups, and one can find active and virulent anti-Semitism on the Internet. Faced with potential censure and discrimination, afforded the opportunity to assimilate or pass, challenged by the demands of religious and cultural practice, do Jewish Americans maintain their Jewish identities, closet these identities, or change them? What effects do these identity processes have? Does closeting equivocate or compromise one's identity? If a Jewish American chooses not to enact that identity when he or she perceives it to be salient and appropriate, does this influence that person's sense of self? How?

It was our goal in this essay to provide an introduction to Jewish American identity and raise questions about this community and identity groups in general. How well does our knowledge of Jewish Americans apply to Jews worldwide; to other American identity groups? Is the closeting of Jewish American identity similar to that of gay men and lesbians? What do Jewish Americans perceived to be "passing" have in common with members of other groups perceived to be passing? One thing is clear. Jewish Americans share a unique history that weaves together factors such as religion, persecution, minority status, ghettoization, and liberation. Jewish American culture has evolved through immigration, the Holocaust, the creation of Israel, and the emerging American middle class. So we end with a question. Who are Jewish Americans, and what can we learn about and from them?

REFERENCES

Beiser, V. (1996, September 6). Intermarried with children. *The Jerusalem Report, 7,* 26–30.

Bershtel, S., & Graubard, A. (1992). *Saving remnants: Feeling Jewish in America.* New York: The Free Press.

Collier, M. J., & Thomas, M. (1988). Cultural identity: An interpretive perspective. In Y. Y. Kim & W. B. Gudykunst (Eds.), *Theories in intercultural communication* (pp. 99–120). Newbury Park, CA: Sage.

Fein, L. (1994). *Smashing idols: And other prescriptions for Jewish continuity.* New York: Nathan Cummings Foundation.

Gilman, S. L. (1986). *Jewish self hatred: Anti-Semitism and the hidden language of the Jews.* Baltimore: Johns Hopkins University Press.

Golden, D. R. (1996). *What's so Jewish about a Jewish fraternity? Interpreting Jewish communal identity.* Unpublished manuscript, Arizona State University.

Hawkins, R. P., & Pingree, S. (1981). Using television to construct social reality. *Journal of Broadcasting, 25,* 347–364.

Hecht, M. L. (1993). 2002—A research odyssey: Toward the development of a communication theory of identity. *Communication Monographs, 60,* 76–81.

Hecht, M. L., Collier, M. J., & Ribeau, S. (1993). *African American communication: Ethnic identity and cultural interpretations.* Newbury Park, CA: Sage.

In the spotlight. (1995, September). *Jewish Televimage Report, 5,* 3–4.

Kaufman, A. (1993, Spring–Summer). Publisher's letter. *Davka: Jewish Cultural Revolution, 1,* 3.

Krausz, M. (1993). On being Jewish. In D. Goldberg & M. Krausz (Eds.), *Jewish identity* (pp. 264–278). Philadelphia: Temple University Press.

Medding, P. Y., Tobin, G. A., Fishman, S. B., & Rimor, M. (1992). *Jewish identity in conversionary and mixed marriages.* New York: American Jewish Committee.

Meyer, M. (1990). *Jewish identity in the modern world.* Seattle: University of Washington Press.

Pearl, J., & Pearl, J. (1993). All in the Jewish family: Understanding, utilizing and enhancing images of intermarriage and other Jewish family relationships on popular television. *Journal of Jewish Communal Service, 69,* 24–39.

Prell, R. E. (1992). The begetting of America's Jews: Seeds of American Jewish identity in the representations of American Jewish women. *Journal of Jewish Communal Service, 69,* 4–23.

Roiphe, A. (1981). *Generation without memory: Jewish journey in Christian America.* New York: The Linden Press.

Sacks, K. (1994). How did Jews become white folks? In S. Gregory & R. Sunjek (Eds.), *Race* (pp. 78–102). New Brunswick, NJ: Rutgers University Press.

Simon, H. (1989). *Jewish identity: A social psychological perspective* (2nd ed.). New Brunswick, NJ: Transaction Publishers.

Waters, M. C. (1990). *Ethnic options: Choosing identities in America.* Berkeley: University of California Press.

Weiss, P. (1996, January 29). Letting go. *New Yorker,* 24–33.

Wolfe, A. S. (1992). Who's gotta have it? The ownership of meaning and mass media texts. *Critical Studies in Mass Communication, 9,* 261–276.

KEY TERMS

Jewish identity	layers
communal identity	equivocation
relational identity	closeting
enacted identity	intermarriage
personal identity	

DISCUSSION QUESTIONS

1. Golden, Niles, and Hecht discuss intermarriage as a situation in which all the layers of identity interact. What other examples can you think of in which several layers interact?

2. What does the essay tell us about the role of communication in the process of identity?

3. The essay suggests that there are a variety of ways to enact Jewish identity. If one has a Jewish mother, belongs to several Jewish organizations, and knows Hebrew, but also is a practicing Buddhist, what can we say about this person's Jewish identity?

4. The essay discusses the process of internalizing stereotypes. How does this process play out within other ethnic/racial/gender groups?

5. Golden, Niles, and Hecht explain that Jewish Americans can choose to engage in behaviors that disclose or mask their Jewish identity. Is this different for other identity groups? What are the implications of having this choice?

7

HAPPY TO BE NAPPY! EMBRACING AN AFROCENTRIC AESTHETIC FOR BEAUTY

REGINA E. SPELLERS

Her beauty cannot be measured with standards
of a colonized mind darker than blue
her blackness unblemished her features are
broad and striking . . . .
— Me'Shell N'Degeocello

Beauty is in the eye of the beholder. Beauty is only skin deep. But who is the beholder? And whose

skin can be beautiful? For women of color in the United States, this is a very critical question. It is a question that has the potential to transform one's self-concept and reconfigure one's identity. In this essay, I utilize my own personal narrative to illustrate how a critical investigation of the creation, acceptance, and maintenance of dominant knowledge claims about beauty can lead to a paradigm shift—a different way of viewing the world than previously encountered. Specifically, I interrogate how one takes an Afrocentric worldview and moves from valuing mainstream standards of beauty to embracing a conception of beauty that evolves from one's personal ideology. Race, class, gender, sexuality, and, I argue, beauty are social constructs that are salient in American culture. This paper interrogates the degree to which beauty has been sociopolitically constructed in the United States and how as a text, the corporeal can be used to resist the dominant interpretation of female beauty. As performance studies scholars Carol Simpson Stern and Bruce Henderson (1993) suggest,

> In many ways, the body has become a kind of text, or even a set of texts, that we remake not only as we grow up physically and go through puberty and other physical stages but also as we reflect on and engage in psychological and sociopolitical dimensions of experience. (p. 317)

Central to understanding how we co-create social constructs is the idea that through self-awareness and self-conscious struggle we can control the degree to which social constructs influence how we act and think. In this paper I share my experiences of experimenting with different ways of styling my hair. My personal story is interwoven with a discussion of three theoretical frameworks that guide my analysis of dominant knowledge claims about beauty: the idea that one's personal story impacts his or her perception of reality, that individuals co-create their reality, and that telling one's personal story can be empowering. Finally, I offer an Afrocentric framework that provides a way to deconstruct existing standards of beauty.

Roots

On my vanity table in my bedroom sits a picture of me when I was 5 years old. This photograph was taken on picture day, one of the highlights of a kindergartner's life. I am wearing a new dress, and my hair is neatly styled in two ponytails with Shirley Temple curls dangling about my shoulders. No doubt, my mother's beautician had "pressed" my hair for the occasion. "Pressing" is a technique that can be hazardous to your health. If the person styling your hair has a slip of hand, you can be burned. If the hot comb is left too long in your hair, your hair can be burned. If you flinch during the process of getting your hair pressed, you can be labeled tenderheaded.

My heart goes out to the tenderheaded child. Being tenderheaded in the Black community means that you cannot withstand the pull of your hair through the hot comb; that your scalp cries out in agony when the relaxer meets your naps; that tight braids strain your scalp so much that your eyes want to pop out of your head. Your mama, or whoever does your hair, scolds you, rolling her eyes in disbelief, "You have the nerve to be tenderheaded with this thick head of hair full of naps? Shame on you!"

And you feel ashamed. You learn how to detest the natural kink of your hair. You never marvel at the rich coarseness of its texture. You do not say, "I am happy to be nappy." Instead, you come down with a bad case of blonde ambition. You desire hair that is longer, bouncier, straighter, and shinier than your own. You invest in potions and lotions, gels and pomades that hold the unspoken promise of good hair; pretty hair; Indian-looking hair, baby hair, kinda curly/kinda straight hair, hair like a White person's hair; hair that is anything but nappy. You convince yourself that it is absolutely necessary to get your hair chemically treated on a regular basis in order to have beautiful, healthy hair. Good hair. You get your hair dyed, fired, and laid to the side in an effort to suppress the natural kinky, nappy curl of your hair. You are not convinced that Black is beautiful. You do not say, "I am happy to be nappy." Shame on you. Shame on me.

The first theoretical framework in this essay suggests that personal stories can give insight into how people construct their lives (Madison, 1993). Social constructs evolve out of culture. My experience of race, class, gender, sex, ethnicity, and identity may be different from your experience. I am a woman of color. Like the theme suggested in Lorraine Hansberry's (1969) play, I am young, gifted, and Black. My experiences of reality as a Black woman are shaped by the time and place of my birth, my social networks, my gender, and among other things, my race and ethnicity. Taken together, all of these factors make up my story. We all have a story. However, in traditional social science research, some histories and herstories are given prime-time status, whereas other stories—my story—the stories of the everyday lived experience of Black women in the United States, are often marginalized (James, 1997). This means that I do not often hear my story. Communication scholar Sidney Ribeau (1997) writes that "these omissions separate the academic world from the realities students encounter in daily life and see on television and film" (p. 23).

In her book entitled *Black Feminist Thought: Knowledge, Consciousness and the Politics of Empowerment*, Patricia Hill Collins (1991) investigates why the Black female experience in the United States tends to be a neglected area of inquiry in the social sciences. She suggests that "maintaining the invisibility of Black women and our ideas is critical in structuring patterned relations of race, gender, and class inequality that pervade the entire social structure" (p. 5). Silencing the stories of marginalized groups aids in the creation of a dominant discourse. By studying personal stories, the tendency to naturalize one's experiences of reality as a universal experience of reality becomes minimized and we come to understand that there are different ways of knowing. The personal story presented in this paper interrogates dominant knowledge claims about beauty that may give insights into what it means to be Black and female in America.

The practice of silencing certain voices in traditional social science research is only one way dominant discourse is created. Often when the experiences of marginalized groups are discussed, they are framed in opposition to the experience of dominant groups, which functions both to marginalize racioethnic groups and center Whiteness as the dominant paradigm. The result is what Collins (1991) calls either/or dichotomous thinking: us/them, right/wrong, Black/White. By conceptualizing phenomena in an oppositional framework, the articulation of difference becomes polarized and equated with claims of superiority/inferiority. She also argues that images of the Black woman as "the Other" provide ideological justification for race, gender, and class oppression:

> Finally, because oppositional dichotomies rarely represent different but equal relationships, they are inherently unstable. Tension is resolved by subordinating one half of the dichotomy to the other. Thus whites rule Blacks, men dominate women, reason is thought superior to emotion in ascertaining truth, facts supersede opinion in evaluating knowledge, and subjects rule objects. The foundations of a complex social hierarchy become grounded in the interwoven concepts of either/or dichotomous thinking, oppositional difference, and objectification. (p. 70)

One way to subvert the practice of framing marginalized discourse in opposition to dominant discourse in traditional social science research is to tell our stories in our voices (e.g., González, Houston, & Chen, 1997). Centering marginalized discourse in an autonomous framework rather than a framework of opposition emancipates us from dichotomous thinking and suggests that difference has utility and meaning.

Black Barbie

Although I was not tenderheaded, I did have long, thick, nappy hair. Reflecting on the different techniques I employed to style my hair, I can now see that there were periods in my life where I unconsciously defined my appearance in relationship to Eurocentric standards that value a particular kind of external beauty. By the time I reached high school, I had graduated from my press-and-curl days and now had a permanent relaxer or a perm. I had traded the inconvenience of having to endure the hot comb every 2 weeks to instead having to "touch up" my perm every 6 to 8 weeks at the salon. Like pressing, a perm also straightens the natural kink of my hair. In between salon visits, I would style my own hair. Learning to do my own hair took some practice. I struggled with techniques to get my hair as straight and shiny as possible without damaging it. Eventually, though, after religiously reading Black hairstyle magazines and getting advice from other Black women, I developed a beauty ritual that, albeit time consuming, resulted in the bouncy shiny curls I so desired. I could flip and bounce my hair with the best of them. I was Black Barbie.

The second framework that guides this essay assumes that individuals actively construct their reality. Berger and Luckman (1967) argue that we create social constructs, and in turn, we are created by them (James, 1997, p. 46). Viewing race as a social construct, sociologists Omi and Winant (1994) argue that the manner in which racial categories are defined and utilized in the United States is linked to economic and political changes within a society and that one can trace how race is socially constructed in the United States by conducting a sociopolitical analysis of history. They cite the experience of Blacks in the United States to illustrate their claim that the sociopolitical history of this country is characterized by a legacy of oppression. During the period in U.S. history when Black Africans were enslaved here, having dark skin was associated with being inferior, and in turn, this definition became a way to justify slavery. As described by John Hope Franklin (1995):

> The presence of persons of African descent, almost from the beginning had helped whites to define ethnicity and to establish and maintain the conditions by which it could be controlled. If their color and race, their condition of servitude, and their generally degraded position did not set them apart, the laws and customs surrounding them more than accomplished that feat. . . . It was not enough for Americans, already somewhat guilt-ridden for maintaining slavery in a free society, to exclude blacks from American society on the basis of race and condition of servitude. They proceeded from that point to argue that Negroes were inferior morally, intellectually, and physically. (p. 28)

Particular meanings, stereotypes, and myths that compromise racial ideology can be linked to specific historical moments and continuities. The system of racial meanings established in the United States is based on the practice of one group asserting power over other groups in order to justify control of economic resources (Omi & Winant, 1994).

Ruth Frankenberg (1993) describes how, in her study of the social construction of Whiteness in the United States, social constructs serve to marginalize certain groups: "given male domination within white culture, the 'protection' or 'salvation' of white women and their supposedly civilized sexuality has been the alibi for a range of atrocities from genocide and lynching to segregation and immigration control" (p. 76). The association of inferiority with certain phenotypical features also played an important role in the U.S. government's extermination policy of American Indians, the anti-Chinese movement in California prior to World War II, and the establishment of detention camps for Japanese Americans on the West Coast of the United States during World War II. These historical examples illustrate that race is socially constructed and how, as a social construct, defining certain racial groups as inferior serves to position the dominant group as being superior.

Stern and Henderson (1993) argue that social constructs also have material consequences:

> . . . As long as we live in a racist society, the concept of race will continue to be important; we may envision a world in which this concept has disappeared, but until then, we need to confront its meaning in the lives of those people whose bodies are constructed along racial lines.
>
> In America, the issue of race has centered most consistently and devastatingly on the lives of African-Americans, in large part, of course, to their enslavement for economic purposes from the colonial period to the end of the Civil War and their continued economic disadvantage today. In recent years, more attention has been paid to the racism practiced historically . . . against . . . Native Americans, Hispanic-Americans, and Asian-Americans. In fact, so potent a concern is racism that the term *people of color* has been coined to provide an umbrella description for all those groups who have experienced oppression because they are not members

of the dominant European-American or "white" culture. (pp. 324–325)

Investigating epistemological standpoints that are rooted in dominant knowledge claims (for example, about aesthetics) encourages discussion about how this particular way of seeing impacts members of nondominant groups.

Nap Attack

For members of marginalized groups, constructing identity in a racist environment can be a complex and difficult task. The challenge is to positively reconstruct one's self-image within the context of a system of racial domination. Although I do not position myself, as the title of Marlon Riggs's film suggests, the judge of what "Black is and Black ain't," I do struggle daily against the subtle seduction of images that suggest my brown skin, my nappy hair, my full lips are not beautiful. Cultural studies scholar bell hooks (1992) describes how being subjects of and subjected to a European gaze creates the potential for Blacks to internalize racism:

> Opening a magazine or book, turning on the television set, watching a film, or looking at photographs in public spaces, we are most likely to see images of black people that reinforce and reinscribe white supremacy. Those images may be constructed by white people who have not divested of racism, or by people of color/black people who may see the world through the lens of white supremacy-internalized racism. (p. 1)

Learning to value self involves investigating ways in which one has embraced practices and ideologies that promote self-hatred.

Starting my first real job in a large corporation, I wanted a new executive look that encompassed a new hairstyle. Ponytails were fine for bad hair days (which for me usually meant that I was having a nap attack—the natural kink and curl of my hair rebelled and resisted all of the mechanisms designed to suppress it), but I needed a style that was polished and sophisticated. Still perming my hair, I decided to cut my hair in a short bob. Although the style gave me peace of mind (I no longer debated over how to wear my hair), I grew tired of the beauty ritual my permed hair required. I wanted simplicity. I wanted low maintenance. Braids were an option because the upkeep was minimal. A braided style required a beauty ritual but not an extensive one. But, I wondered, is this style for me? Will I be viewed as unprofessional/too ethnic/too Black? I agonized over these questions and sought advice from other Black women and men working in white-collar corporate America. They spoke from experience. The consensus was that wearing braids would probably be frowned upon in a work environment where the values of the corporate culture are synonymous with the values of the dominant culture, but that you also have to be happy. Happy? Happy. Happy to be nappy.

Closely related to the second framework, the third framework that guides this essay stems from a personal sense of purpose, of empowerment, legacy, and resilience. In the legacy of Marsha Houston (1992) and so many other scholars who often write with a keen sense of purpose, I am writing for my life. I am telling my story because if I do not, who will? Alice Walker (1983) expresses how having a sense of purpose guides her work:

> In my own work I write not only what I want to read—understanding fully and indelibly that if I don't do it no one else is so vitally interested, or capable of doing it to my satisfaction—I write all the things that I should have been able to read. (p. 13)

While my own personal story is unique, it can also have relevance for others. This is echoed by Navita Cummings James (1997):

> [N]o one story is so unique or idiosyncratic that it cannot provide us insight into the overall human experience. One of the most powerful ways to gain an understanding of "the other" (e.g., a person from a culture other than one's own) is to hear or read the story of "the other" in his or her own words. (p. 47)

Like these scholars, I am also motivated to tell my story, hoping that as a member of a marginalized group that has historically been oppressed in America, I may give critical insights into the experience of oppression.

I cannot, however, separate thought from action. The very act of telling my story is one of resistance. In my experience, publicly speaking about internalized racism in the Black community, particularly of the struggle of believing Black to be beautiful for ourselves, is taboo. It is painful to speak of how one's race is represented in the mass media knowing that some of the negative stereotypical images were created by members of our community. bell hooks (1992) suggests that it is also painful to articulate this issue of representation because to do so one must not only critique how Whiteness has been centered as the dominant paradigm, but also interrogate how one has played a role in sustaining this position:

> To face these wounds, to heal them, progressive black people and our allies in struggle must be willing to grant the effort to critically intervene and transform the world of image making authority of place in our political movements of liberation and self determination (be they anti-imperialist, feminist, gay rights, black liberation, or all of the above and more). If this were the case, we would be ever mindful of the need to make radical intervention. We would consider crucial both the kind of images we produce and the way we critically write and talk about images. And most important, we would rise to the challenge to speak that which has not been spoken. (p. 4)

By centering our stories, in our voices, even when our stories are about how we see ourselves aesthetically, we become empowered. We open up a space for healing. We create an opportunity for our stories to be heard and to be meaningful in a context that has traditionally negated their significance.

Free Your Mind, the Rest Will Follow

I am presently a long way from my press-and-curl days. My once-shoulder-length hair is now cut into a short Afro. Today, I am happy to be nappy.

For me, being happy to be nappy is a state of mind that allows me to feel liberated, to understand that I have the right to define who I am and that this definition is ever changing. My past experiences experimenting with different hairstyles is part of a journey that I do not regret. They have brought me to a place where I understand that there is value in the self-conscious struggle that often results from the discrepancy between how we define ourselves and how we are defined by others. Given that there is a dynamic contrast between how we see ourselves and how others see us, how is it possible to resist conceptions of self that promote self-hatred while at the same time engage in the process of reconstructing our identity?

One solution is through the process of decolonization, which challenges us to rethink our acceptance of images that support and maintain our oppression and promotes the conscious effort to reject nonaffirming images of self. bell hooks (1992) suggests that the complex process of decolonization is a critical, difficult, and painful process for all colonized people, in particular for Black folks in America. It is critical for colonized individuals because the practice of exalting Whiteness as the ideal negatively impacts their self-identity (p. 3). It is difficult to achieve because America is a White supremacist society in which marginalized and nonmarginalized people are still shackled to the promise of mainstream success (p. 17). It is a painful process because it forces you to see the wounds of your self-hate; "often it leaves us ravaged by repressed rage, feeling weary, dispirited, and sometimes just plain old brokenhearted" (p. 4).

Images, deeply woven with ideology, determine not only how we think about others but how we think about ourselves. Learning to resist dominant knowledge claims about beauty is an ongoing process. Equating beauty with being White, blonde, young, thin, and having blue eyes has material consequences for all women. White American females who judge their appearance from a Eurocentric standard of beauty also fall victim to dominant knowledge claims about beauty (Collins, 1991, p. 79). I propose, however, that while the dominant perspective on who can be beautiful in American society is destructive for all women, it has additional dire implications for women of color. Any attempts to meet these dominant beauty standards require women of color not only to remake themselves but to denounce and negate their personal value. Writing on this subject, Collins suggests that "African-American women experience the pain of never being able to live up to externally defined standards of beauty—standards applied to us by white men, Black men, and, most painfully, one another" (p. 80). Negative images of Black women serve to reinforce dominant ideology about beauty:

> From the mammies, Jezebels, and breeder women of slavery to the smiling Aunt Jemimas on pancake mix boxes, ubiquitous Black prostitutes, and ever-present welfare mothers of contemporary popular culture, the nexus of negative stereotypical images applied to African-American women has been fundamental to Black women's oppression. (p. 7)

Resisting the temptation to internalize these and other negative images of self requires self-conscious struggle.

The pain of being subjugated to a gaze that seeks to dominate and colonize can often lead to denial:

> Many black folks refuse to look at our present condition because they do not want to see images that might compel them to militancy. But militancy is an alternative to madness. And many of us are entering the realm of the insane. Like Pecola, in Toni Morrison's *The Bluest Eye*, black folks turn away from reality because the pain of awareness is so great. Yet it is only by becoming more fully aware that we begin to see clearly. (hooks, 1992, p. 6)

It is through decolonization and self-conscious struggle that one begins the journey to heal the wounds of self-hate and emancipate oneself from the prison of a colonized mind. Through the act of self-definition, one begins the journey of a changed consciousness, which becomes a way of transcending images that limit the view we have of ourselves. This change can be empowering.

Behold the Quiltmaker

Redefining beauty is a crucial step in deconstructing social constructs that value and uphold one group while simultaneously devaluing and degrading another group(s). Constructing a definition of beauty that simply suggests what was good is now bad and what was bad is now good, however, does not adequately challenge the existing dichotomous framework characteristic of dominant ideology. As Collins (1991) suggests,

> But proclaiming Black women "beautiful" and white women "ugly" merely replaces one set of controlling images with another and fails to challenge how Eurocentric masculinist aesthetics foster an ideology of domination. Current standards require either/or dichotomous thinking: in order for one individual to be judged beautiful, another individual—the Other—must be deemed ugly. Accepting this underlying assumption avoids a more basic question concerning the connection among controlling images, either/or dichotomous thinking, and unequal power relationships. (p. 88)

What is required, then, is a perspective that not only deconstructs existing standards of beauty but also emancipates beholders of beauty from judging who can and cannot be beautiful based on external or ornamental qualities or both.

Afrocentric theory is such a perspective. It provides a means to deconstruct and redefine existing standards of beauty. A central assumption in Afrocentric thought is that of centeredness. The Afrocentric idea "is a strategy to seek one's centrality or one's human agency from the fringes or the periphery. . . . [I]t rejects the notions and practices of hegemonic or alleged universal tendencies and practices of a given paradigm" (Bekerie, 1994, pp. 136–137). For this reason, this perspective has important implications for deconstructing and redefining existing standards of beauty. As the leading proponent of Afrocentricity Molefi Kete Asante (1995) writes, "Our aim is to open fields of inquiry and to expand human dialogue around questions of social, economic, historical, and cultural concern. . . . Our methods are meant to establish a clear line of discourse that may be followed by others" (p. 3). Afrocentricity provides a framework that can be utilized by all to center their discourse in a particular cultural context. Bekerie (1994) argues that

> Afrocentricity is an intellectual pursuit that endorses humanistic mission. This mission is pursued by first affirming our own humanity. It is pursued by defining and naming phenomena that emanate from our own experience. . . . Afrocentric theory is a theory of being a subject. It is about exercising one's agency. It is a theory that seeks to empower, free the mind, and ring the bell of harmony. (p. 148)

Theorizing about beauty from an Afrocentric orientation provides an alternative to the dichotomous way in which this social construct has been traditionally conceptualized.

Patricia Hill Collins (1991) and others offer quiltmaking as an example of an Afrocentric feminist aesthetic for beauty.

> . . . African-American women quiltmakers do not seem interested in a uniform color scheme but use several methods of playing with colors to create unpredictability and movement (Wahlman & Scully, 1983, in Brown, 1989, p. 922). For example, a strong color may be juxtaposed with another strong color, or with a weak one. Contrast is used to structure or organize. Overall, the symmetry in African-American quilts does not come from uniformity as it does in Euro-American quilts. Rather, symmetry comes through diversity. (Collins, p. 89)

The emphasis on diversity, rather than either/or conceptualizations of beauty, creates a space for all women to be beautiful. As Collins suggests,

> The Afrocentric notions of diversity in community and functional beauty potentially heal many of the oppositional dichotomies inherent in Western social thought. From an Afrocentric perspective, women's beauty is not based solely on physical criteria because mind, spirit, and body are not conceptualized as separate, oppositional spheres. Instead, all are central in aesthetic assessments of individuals and their creations. . . . Moreover, participation is not based on conformity but instead is seen as individual uniqueness that enhances the overall "beauty" of the group. Using such criteria, no individual is inherently beautiful because beauty is not a state of being. Instead beauty is always defined in a context as a state of becoming. (p. 89)

The pieces of cloth once deemed scrap become useful when taken together as a whole. The quiltmaker is the beholder of beauty and utilizes her creativity to self-define that which is beautiful.

Conclusion

I have tried to show how one's personal story gives insight into how we construct our identity and how our identity is socio-politically constructed. As socially constructed in the United States, gender (Frankenberg, 1993), race (Martinez, 1995), age, class, and beauty have significant material consequences. The process of decolonization suggests that individuals must take an active role in reconstructing themselves within particular cultural contexts. hooks (1992) argues that "all whites (as well as everyone else within white supremacist culture) have learned to overvalue 'whiteness' even as they simultaneously learn to devalue blackness" (p. 12). A critical examination of how we, as co-creators of this interpretation of dominant ideology, can decolonize our minds, has critical implications for subverting dichotomous thinking. Investigating dominant knowledge claims about beauty requires a critical examination of the beholder of beauty—those who possess the power to define who is beautiful. Rejecting controlling and oppressive images of Black womanhood often requires self-evaluation. Through self-conscious struggle, we critically examine who we were, who we are, and who we are becoming.

REFERENCES

Asante, M. (1995). *Malcolm X as a cultural hero.* Trenton, NJ: Africa World Press, Inc.

Bekerie, A. (1994). The four corners of a circle: Afrocentricity as a model of synthesis. *Journal of Black Studies, 25,* 131–149.

Berger, P. L., & Luckman, C. (1967). *The socialization of reality.* Garden City, NY: Anchor Books.

Brown, E. B. (1989). African-American women's quilting: A framework for conceptualizing and teaching African-American women's history. *Signs, 14,* 921–929.

Collins, P. H. (1991). *Black feminist thought: Knowledge, consciousness and the politics of empowerment.* New York: Routledge & Chapman and Hall.

Frankenberg, R. (1993). *White women, race matters: The social construction of whiteness.* Minneapolis, MN: University of Minnesota Press.

Franklin, J. H. (1995). Ethnicity in American life: The historical perspective. In A. Aguirre & D. Baker (Eds.), *Sources: Notable selections in race and ethnicity* (pp. 24–32). Guilford, CT: Dushkin Publishing Group.

González, A., Houston, M., & Chen, V. (1997). *Our voices: Essays in culture, ethnicity, and communication* (2nd ed.). Los Angeles: Roxbury Publishing Company.

Hansberry, L. (1969). *To be young, gifted and black.* New York: Signet.

hooks, b. (1992). *Black looks: Race and representation.* Boston: South End Press.

Houston, M. (1992). The politics of difference: Race, class, and women's communication. In L. F. Rakow (Ed.), *Women making meaning* (pp. 45–59). New York: Routledge.

James, N. C. (1997). When Miss America was always white. In A. González, M. Houston, & V. Chen (Eds.), *Our voices: Essays in culture, ethnicity, and communication* (pp. 46–51). (2nd ed.). Los Angeles: Roxbury Publishing Company.

Madison, D. S. (1993). "That was my occupation": Oral narrative, performance, and Black feminist thought. *Text and Performance Quarterly, 13,* 213–232.

Martinez, E. (1995). Beyond black/white: The racism of our time. In A. Aguirre & D. Baker (Eds.), *Sources: Notable selections in race and ethnicity* (pp. 79–90). Guilford, CT: Dushkin Publishing Group.

N'Degeocello, M. (1993). Untitled. On *Plantation lullabies* [CD]. New York: Maverick.

Omi, M., & Winant, H. (1994). *Racial formations in the United States from the 1960s to the 1990s.* New York: Routledge.

Ribeau, S. (1997). How I came to know "In self-realization there is truth." In A. González, M. Houston, & V. Chen (Eds.), *Our voices: Essays in culture, ethnicity, and communication* (pp. 21–27). (2nd ed.). Los Angeles: Roxbury Publishing Company.

Riggs, M. T. (Producer/Director), & Atkinson, N. (Co-Producer). (1994). Black is, black ain't. [Video]. Available from California Newsreel, 149 9th Street, San Francisco, CA 94103.

Stern, C. S., & Henderson, B. (1993). *Performance: Texts and contexts.* White Plains, NY: Longman Publishing Group.

Walker, A. (1983). *In search of our mother's gardens.* New York: Harcourt Brace Jovanovich.

Wahlman, M., & Scully, J. (1983). Aesthetic principles of Afro-American quilts. In W. Ferris (Ed.), *Afro-American folk arts and crafts* (pp. 79–97). Boston: G. K. Hall.

KEY TERMS

Afrocentric	marginalize
decolonize	social construct
ideology	

DISCUSSION QUESTIONS

1. Spellers discusses dominant discourse and marginalized discourse in terms of how beauty is conceptualized in the United States. Can you think of other dominant knowledge claims that may conflict with the experience of members of marginalized groups?

2. The author views the body as text. How does this inform our understanding of communication?

3. Can one's personal story be viewed as scholarship?

4. Spellers's essay suggests that we are co-creators of our identities. Who or what co-creates our identity with us?

5. What does this essay tell us about diversity? How is diversity defined in this essay?

8

MY THREE CULTURES: NAVIGATING THE MULTICULTURAL IDENTITY LANDSCAPE[1]

GUST A. YEP

[We] cannot enter the struggle as objects in order later *[emphasis in the original] to become human beings.* —Paulo Freire

I am Asianlatinoamerican.[2] Although I have never been to China, I am racially what my parents describe as "100% pure Chinese." During my formative years, we lived in Peru, South America, and later moved to the United States. I learned to speak Chinese first, mainly to communicate with my grandmother, a traditional Chinese woman who rarely ventured beyond the boundaries of the Chinese community in Lima. I then learned to speak Spanish in school in Peru, where we lived until I finished high school at the age of 15. I started learning English when I came to the United States to attend college. After completing my doctorate, I started my university teaching career in Los Angeles, California, and I am currently teaching in San Francisco and residing in the city with my two Pomeranians, Tyler and Dino. I am trilingual (English, Spanish, Chinese) and I speak all three languages with a slight accent. I used to be concerned about the accent in my speech, but in recent years I have adopted a different attitude: My accent might simply be an indication that I probably speak more languages than my conversational partner. I "look Asian American," yet at times my Latino culture is most prominent in some communication settings. I strongly identify with all three cultures, and they are more or less integrated into this complex entity that I label as my "multicultural self." Such integration,[3] however, is an ongoing process. In this essay, I explore how I negotiate this multicultural identity in my daily communication experiences. More specifically, I discuss (1) the nature of identity, (2) the co-creation and re-creation of my identity in

everyday encounters, and (3) the negotiation of identity as a liberation process.

The Nature of Identity

Broadly defined, identity is a person's conception of self within a particular social, geographical, cultural, and political context. Identity gives the individual a sense of self and personhood and an intepretive frame of experience (Hecht, Collier, & Ribeau, 1993). Identity is abstract, complex, multidimensional, fluid, and amorphous (Cupach & Imahori, 1993). People have multiple identities—ethnic, racial, occupational, socioeconomic, sexual, gender, and relational—which Cupach and Imahori describe as "interconnected cultural identities" (p. 114).

Collier and Thomas (1988), consistent with Geertz's (1973) conceptualization of culture as historically transmitted systems, define cultural identity as "identification with and perceived acceptance into a group that has shared systems of symbols and meanings as well as norms/rules for conduct" (p. 113). Sarup (1996) further notes, "identity is a construction, a consequence of a process of interaction between people, institutions and practices" (p. 11). In short, cultural identity is a social construction that gives the individual an ontological status (a sense of "being") and expectations for social behavior (ways of "acting").

Cultural identity can be characterized as political, fluid, and nonsummative. First, cultural identity is political (Appiah, 1996; Harvey, 1993; Moraga, 1983; Sarup, 1996; Thornton, 1992). Cultural identity separates individuals on the basis of ingroup-outgroup differences. Appiah (1996) elaborates, "if other people organize their solidarity around cultures different from ours, this makes them, to that extent, different from us in ways that matter to us deeply" (p. 39). Such contrasting loyalties are necessarily associated with political power. Citing Ernesto Laclau's work, Sarup (1996) maintains that

> the relations between groups are constituted as relations of power; each group insists on its difference on the basis of the exclusion and subordination of other groups. . . . If the oppressed is defined by its difference from the oppressor, such a difference is an essential component of the identity of the oppressed. But in that case, the latter cannot assert its identity without asserting that of the oppressor as well. (pp. 59–60)

A dominant group, to maintain its status in the hierarchy, will seek to keep others in lower positions. One powerful way to accomplish this is through discursive practices.

"Why won't you just be like everybody else?" is a remark that I have often heard directed to people of color or to other people who do not conform to the "norm." Underlying this seemingly innocuous remark are cultural conceptions of power and privilege. Who is this entity called "everybody else"? It is the dominant group who determines who and what is normal or deviant, desirable or undesirable, right or wrong, successful or unsuccessful, beautiful or ugly, human or subhuman, native or alien, us or them. Being like "everybody else," the identification to the dominant group, takes on a natural appearance, remains unnamed and unquestioned, and therefore disguises and hides power relations between the oppressor and the oppressed. For people of color (or other marginalized groups), "being like everybody else" is a double bind: Regardless of how we attempt to be like the dominant group, our very presence would almost automatically label us as the "other." This assimilationist view directs the marginalized person to try harder and harder to adhere, obey, and follow the rules of the dominant group—rules that he or she can never fully and completely participate in creating.

For an individual with a multicultural identity, this can be a site of multiple tensions. People who are multicultural and multiracial are often expected to choose and privilege one aspect of their background over others, and such tension can be manifested externally or internally or both. Thornton (1992) notes that while some multiracial individuals are demanding political representation through the creation of a unique census category, others are concerned about losing political power associated with their primary racial identity. He cites the example of an African American/Native American man who believes that a distinct multiracial category will dilute African American political representation. For Moraga (1983), this tension is both external and internal. As a fair-skinned Latina lesbian, she describes her struggle with her own internalized racism ("light skin is better"), classism ("feeling superior to poor and uneducated Mexicans"), and heterosexism ("heterosexuality is better"), which eventually propelled her to political activism.

Being monoracial and multicultural, my own experience with my multicultural identity has brought about internal and external conflicts. As a child in a Chinese family, I was expected to always listen to my parents, never question their authority, and never demand an explanation for their actions toward me. My primary duty was to excel in school and consequently, I was expected to do school-related work every day, year-round. I never had a weekend to relax or a summer to play. Being about a full school year ahead in my math, I questioned my father one summer day about the purpose of doing school work every day when all my friends were having fun. He was surprised that I questioned him. After giving me an explanation, he told me in Chinese, "You are becoming like a white ghost" (which can be translated into English as "You are becoming 'too Westernized'"). Although I felt like saying that I have never lived anywhere but the West, I could not think of further upsetting my father.

I have also experienced external conflicts with my multicultural identity. Although I always introduce myself as multicultural during my first class meeting with students, some inevitably express that they are very glad to have an "Asian professor teaching communication courses." These students seem to be genuinely delighted to have an Asian role model. Given that both Asians and Latinos are underrepresented in the communication discipline, I sometimes feel that I am not properly representing the Latino part of me. Although I have become more comfortable with the persistent internal and external tensions associated with my multicultural identity in recent years, I am always mindful of them in my everyday interaction.

Second, cultural identity is fluid (Martin & Nakayama, 1997; Sarup, 1996). In other words, one's cultural identity is ever evolving, growing, and changing. It is never static; as Sarup (1996) notes, "identity [has] to do not with being but with becoming" (p. 6). I have experienced—and will continue to experience—many subtle and profound changes in my multicultural identity. I still recall my attempts to repress my Chinese identity during my adolescent years. Whether this was a product of adolescent rebellion against parental insistence that I should be Chinese above all else or a sense of identification with my Latino peers or a fascination with my new American culture seems immaterial. During my college years, I slowly started reembracing the Chinese in me. I started having a deep appreciation for Chinese philosophy, wisdom, and the hardships that many Chinese have endured in foreign lands. I became interested in my family story—why and how they left China during the Communist Revolution. I also became fascinated by how Asian Americans give voice and legitimacy to their own experiences through oral histories and literature.

Third, cultural identity is nonsummative (Cupach & Imahori, 1993). In other words, one's cultural identity is not a simple addition of the component parts of one's cultural background. To put it another way, one cannot get a complete sense of my multicultural identity by simply adding my Chinese, Latino, and American parts. I am more than the sum of those individual parts. The combination of my experiences, values, beliefs, and perceptions in all three cultures constitutes a new gestalt, a fluid entity that I describe as my "multicultural self." This can be observed when I speak to my family over the telephone. We usually start our conversation in one language (usually Chinese), then I would start speaking English and Spanish, and in a few minutes we have a phone conversation using all three languages.

Typically, when I speak Chinese with my parents, I feel more like a child and would often behave differently than an independent and free-thinking adult. I switch to English when I have something serious to discuss and to Spanish when I have strong emotions to express. However, I cannot say that those cultural parts of me only "come out" when I speak in that language, for I have directly and openly disagreed with my parents in Chinese, expressed my love for them in English, and discussed my plans to redesign my home in Spanish. My identity transcends the boundaries of those individual cultural components.

The Co-creation and Re-creation of Identity

Cultural identities are co-created and re-created in everyday interaction. In other words, we create our identities with those individuals with whom we interact (co-creation) and in the context of specific communication episodes and encounters (re-creation). The process of co-creation and re-creation of identity can only occur through *dialogue*. Freire (1970) writes:

> Dialogue is the encounter between [people], mediated by the world, in order to name the world. Hence, dialogue cannot occur between those who want to name the world and those who do not wish this naming—between those who deny others the right to speak their word and those whose right to speak has been denied them. (p. 69)

Put in another way, co-creation of identity cannot occur when there is an attempt on the part of one of the communicators to, consciously or unconsciously, dominate the other physically or symbolically. This process of domination between oppressor and oppressed is, in Freire's terms, "by prescription." He further maintains that "every prescription represents the imposition of one individual's choice upon another, transforming the consciousness of the person prescribed to into one that conforms with the prescriber's consciousness" (p. 29). Genuine co-creation of identity becomes difficult when asymmetrical power relations exist.

In my daily encounters, I have experienced numerous instances in which the other interactant attempted to prescribe a label, an identity for me. A long time ago, when I was involved in a play for a church fundraiser, the director demanded, "Show your Oriental anger!" I first thought that I did not hear him correctly. I was completely dumbfounded when he repeated the same command. I objected to the label "Oriental" and I was not sure what "Oriental anger" was. Finally, I uttered, "I do not understand you. . . . How does anger come to have a derogatory ethnic label? Is it supposed to be different from your (an older man's) anger, a woman's anger, or some other form of anger?" I then proceeded to tell him that if we were going to work together, we needed to come up with labels that were comfortable and agreeable to both of us. He did not understand.

Although this process of prescription is not always necessarily a conscious or a malicious one, we need to be mindful of it and its potential harm. When we allow this process to occur, we are tacitly choosing to participate in a transaction as *objects*—not subjects (in the above example, I would not have been an active agent in the communication but rather a passive fulfillment of whatever characteristics, attributes, and expectations the director had of an "Oriental" and his particular brand of anger, "Oriental anger"). In other words, we are not affirming our humanity as free agents with a capacity and potential to create, to construct, to wonder, and to venture when we are reduced to the status of objects or things (Freire, 1970). To put it differently, *both* interactants are responsible for this process of identity creation. If one prescribes, the other needs to be aware that unless the prescription is resisted and the transaction redefined (in the same example above, I reclaimed my subject position, in the end, by negotiating the terms of interaction that were acceptable to both of us), a true co-creation of identity cannot occur.

Freire's (1970) notion of prescription resonates with Cupach and Imahori's (1993) concept of "identity freezing." They maintain that identity freezing occurs when one interactant imposes an objective and public identity (like a stereotype, whether positive or negative) on the other (Cupach & Imahori). For example, if I tell an Asian student that she must be good with numbers (presumably a positive stereotype), I am freezing her identity and prescribing our relationship. With this example, I also want to point out that prescription and identity freezing are not necessarily restricted to intercultural encounters but are applicable to intracultural relations as well.

As I indicated earlier, to co-create and re-create identities, we need to participate in the process, in Freire's (1970) terms, "as subjects of the transformation" (p. 108). When someone tells me, "You are not a typical university professor," I often ask what they mean by the statement. In the process, we usually uncover some stereotypical attributes of university professors that I do not possess (I do not smoke a pipe; I do not have gray hair (yet); I am not absent-minded) and some stereotypical qualities that I do possess (I am nearsighted; I am constantly reading; I am nerdy). I usually follow up this discussion with another question, "What does it mean to you that I am not a 'typical university professor'?" This usually prompts a discussion that allows both of us to co-create and re-create ourselves as we develop a greater sense of connectedness and understanding of each other's perception of self and interpretive frame of reference.

Fundamental in dialogue or dialogical action is cooperation. Freire (1970) further notes that cooperation "can only be achieved through communication" (p. 149). In other words, communication is intrinsic to the process of co-creation and re-creation of one's cultural identity. Another example appears to be in order. I have been a member of the La Raza Caucus of the National Communication Association (NCA) since I was a graduate student. As the name might indicate, the primary focus of the La Raza Caucus is on Chicano(a) and Latino(a) culture and communication, and most members are of Latin descent. Although some members of the caucus attempted to prescribe, or "freeze," my Asian identity, most welcomed my presence. We entered the dialogue as subjects mutually defining our unique cultural identities. Through communication, we have achieved, over the years, a great sense of understanding, fondness, and familiarity with each other, and I became the first Asianlatinoamerican to serve as chair of the caucus.

The Negotiation of Identity as a Liberation Process

Negotiating identities is a process involving both parties. Freire (1970) describes this as a "process of liberation" (p. 28) in which both oppressor and oppressed find freedom.

Because of my multicultural identity, I have felt, at times, that "I am neither here nor there." Although San Francisco is a city characterized by a rich cultural, ethnic, social, gender, and sexual diversity, I sometimes feel like a foreigner in the crowded streets of Chinatown or Clement (another predominantly Chinese populated area), the congested streets in the Mission (a predominantly Latino district), or the busy streets in the Marina (a predominantly affluent Euro American area). For many Chinese Americans, I am "not quite Chinese." For many Latinos, I am "not quite Latin." For many Euro Americans, I am "a person of color." This view of marginality, of "otherness," is one of isolation, invisibility, alienation, and deprivation.

Otherness represents the undesirable, degraded, exiled, suppressed, deviant, disenfranchised, and incongruous elements of the "ideal order." As I stated earlier, otherness and the ideal order must exist together for they are the opposing extremes of a dichotomy. Dichotomies, according to Sarup (1996),

> are exercises in power and at the same time their disguise. They split the human world into a group for whom the ideal order is to be erected, and another which is for the unfitting, the uncontrollable, the incongruous and the ambivalent. (p. 9)

If I were to subscribe to this view of otherness, I would have automatically accepted a less privileged subject position.

I endorse another view of marginality. Marginality may also be conceptualized as resembling Turner's (1990) notion of liminality, a threshold or space "in between" states. He further elaborates, "The attributes of liminality or of liminal personae ('threshold people') are necessarily ambiguous, since this condition and these persons elude or slip through the network of classifications that normally locate states and positions in cultural space" (p. 147). Reminiscent of Turner's notion of liminality, hooks (1990) maintains that marginality is a "space of radical openness" (p. 149). Although such space is never a safe place, hooks argues that it is necessary to locate oneself there to find alternatives, envision possibilities, and create a future. In other words, marginality can be a position and place of resistance to the dominant power. Citing her earlier book *Feminist Theory: From Margin to Center*, hooks further explains her view of marginality as a site of radical possibility:

> To be in the margin is to be part of the whole but outside the main body. . . . Living as we did—on the edge—we developed a particular way of seeing reality. We looked both from the outside in and from the inside out. We focused our attention on the center as well as on the margin. We understood both. . . . This sense of wholeness . . . provided us with an oppositional worldview—a mode of seeing unknown to most of our oppressors, . . . [and] strengthened our sense of self and solidarity. (p. 149)

This view of marginality is empowering and liberating. Negotiating one's identity from the cultural margins can allow us to see things from both the center and the margins—a perspective that those who attempt to prescribe labels for us simply do not have.

Although the margins are our sites of resistance and survival, Trinh Minh-ha (1995) cautions that if we reclaim the margins "as our exclusive territory, [the oppressors] happily approve, for the divisions between margin and center should be preserved, and as clearly demarcated as possible, if the two positions are to remain intact in their power relations" (p. 216). To challenge these power relations, she calls for the work of displacement. Minh-ha further elaborates, "by displacing, it never allows this classifying world to exert its classificatory power without returning it to its own ethnocentric classifications" (p. 216). The active creation and re-creation of our own identities are acts of displacement.

Summary and Conclusions

In this essay, I have explored the political, fluid, and nonsummative nature of cultural identity. I maintain that cultural identities are co-created and re-created in interaction only when dialogue, cooperation, and communication—not prescription or identity freezing—exist between interactants. I also argue that negotiation of identity from the margins—and engaging in acts of displacement—can empower us to enter the dialogue as subjects rather than powerless objects or prescribed labels.

NOTES

1. The title invokes James Clifford's (1992) notion of travel and traveling identities. Smith and Katz (1993) argue that "travelling provides a means for conceptualizing the interplay among people that are no longer so separate or inaccessible one to the other. Travel . . . suggests social, political and cultural identity as an amalgam, the intricacy of which defies the comparative simplicity of 'identity'" (p. 78). However, I do not intend to imply a "spatial essentialism"—that is, the view that multicultural identities are fixed in absolute spaces. I am suggesting quite the contrary: a landscape metaphor to indicate that "multicultural identity spaces" are fluid and constantly evolving terrains with ever changing colors, fragrances, shapes, and sizes. I dedicate this essay to my parents.

2. I am using this label to imply an integration of my three cultures. This term places all three cultures together without separation, division, or hyphenation that might imply disconnection between them. Further, I do not intend to suggest that my multicultural identity is linear and hierarchical—Asian, then Latino, and finally American—as the label might appear to indicate. Such a label is a limitation of language.

3. The term "integration" is used here to indicate union, connection, and unification. However, I do not claim that such integration is necessarily harmonious and free of tension. In fact, I argue that tension is vital in the process of self-definition, identity negotiation, and personal liberation.

REFERENCES

Appiah, K. A. (1996). Identity: Political not cultural. In M. Garber, R. L. Walkowitz, & P. B. Franklin (Eds.), *Fieldwork: Sites in literary and cultural studies* (pp. 34–40). New York: Routledge.

Clifford, J. (1992). Traveling cultures. In L. Grossberg, C. Nelson, & P. Treichler (Eds.), *Cultural studies* (pp. 96–116). New York: Routledge.

Collier, M. J., & Thomas, M. (1988). Cultural identity: An interpretive perspective. *International and Intercultural Communication Annual, 12,* 99–120.

Cupach, W. R., & Imahori, T. T. (1993). Identity management theory: Communication competence in intercultural episodes and relationships. *International and Intercultural Communication Annual, 17,* 112–131.

Freire, P. (1970). *Pedagogy of the oppressed.* New York: Continuum.

Geertz, C. (1973). *The interpretation of cultures.* New York: Basic Books.

Harvey, D. (1993). Class relations, social justice and the politics of difference. In M. Keith & S. Pile (Eds.), *Place and the politics of identity* (pp. 41–66). London: Routledge.

Hecht, M. L., Collier, M. J., & Ribeau, S. A. (1993). *African American communication: Ethnic identity and cultural interpretation.* Newbury Park, CA: Sage.

hooks, b. (1990). *Yearning: Race, gender, and cultural politics.* Boston: South End Press.

Martin, J. N., & Nakayama, T. K. (1997). *Intercultural communication in contexts.* Mountain View, CA: Mayfield.

Minh-ha, T. T. (1995). No master territories. In B. Ashcroft, G. Griffiths, & H. Tiffin (Eds.), *The post-colonial studies reader* (pp. 215–218). London: Routledge.

Moraga, C. (1983). La güera. In C. Moraga & G. Anzaldúa (Eds.), *This bridge called my back: Writings by radical women of color* (pp. 27–34). New York: Kitchen Table Press.

Sarup, M. (1996). *Identity, culture and the postmodern world.* Athens, GA: University of Georgia Press.

Smith, N., & Katz, C. (1993). Grounding metaphor: Towards a spatialized politics. In M. Keith & S. Pile (Eds.), *Place and the politics of identity* (pp. 67–83). London: Routledge.

Thornton, M. C. (1992). Is multiracial status unique? The personal and social experience. In M. P. P. Root (Ed.), *Racially mixed people in America* (pp. 321–325). Newbury Park, CA: Sage.

Turner, V. (1990). Liminality and community. In J. C. Alexander & S. Seidman (Eds.), *Culture and society: Contemporary debates* (pp. 147–154). New York: Cambridge University Press.

KEY TERMS

cultural identity
identity freezing
liminality
marginality

negotiation of identity
otherness
power

DISCUSSION QUESTIONS

1. Yep's essay starts with Paulo Freire's quote "[We] cannot enter the struggle as objects in order *later* to become human beings." How does the essay explain and illustrate this quote?

2. Yep suggests that we have multiple identities. What does he mean? What types of identities do you have when you are communicating with someone from the same culture? Someone from a different culture?

3. Yep observes that power is inherent in relations between groups. How is power manifested in those relationships? How is power related to "otherness"? How is power related to identity?

4. How are cultural identities co-created and re-created? Describe a communication situation in which you co-created and re-created your own identities. Describe a situation in which your identity was prescribed by the other communicator.

5. Yep presents two views of marginality. How are they similar? Different?

9

CHICANA Y CHICANA: DIALOGUE ON RACE, CLASS, AND CHICANA IDENTITY [1]

DOROTHY LELAND / JACQUELINE M. MARTINEZ

Situating Ourselves in Theory and Practice

One way of understanding how people make sense of their everyday world is to look at how culture functions as context. The meanings ascribed to any experience or perception are mediated by various cultural contexts (Hall, 1981). Identifying these contexts and how they function to correlate specific perceptions or behaviors with

their interpretations help people to understand how they come to construct the very meanings they take from their everyday experiences.

This paper is the product of the effort of two academic feminists to explore with each other our processes of coming to consciousness as Chicana.

---

[1] This paper was originally presented in 1995 at a Women's Studies colloquium at Purdue University, West Lafayette, Indiana.

Working through the academic context in which we share a common commitment to feminist and phenomenological work (Young, 1990; Bartky, 1990) we have come to grapple with very personal issues of our own life experiences and ethnic identities. The paper has been written in dialogue form to reflect the actual path we took in reaching our more abstract, theoretical conclusions. Through our dialogue we explore the very processes by which we come to both political and personal consciousness regarding the racism and classism that have contextualized the development of our ethnic identities.

Sharing this very personal dialogue with a larger audience seems risky. We offer up fragments of our lives as the stuff out of which theory gets made. As academics, we expect our theory and even our method to be criticized. But we must trust our audience to receive with openness the lived experiences we share; it is, after all, this recovery of lived experience that so typifies the work of radical women of color within U.S. feminist theorizing (Moraga & Anzaldúa, 1981; Anzaldúa, 1990).

Since the mid-1980s, the signifier "woman of color" has become a familiar inhabitant of feminist discourse. Today, there are books and essays written by self-identified "women of color." There are women of color caucuses, panels, and special events associated with our professional organizations. But it is our belief that academic feminism has not yet sufficiently explored what this signifier means—what it has been and can be constructed to represent.

In this paper we problematize the category "woman of color" by exploring how it has been and remains both problematical and hopeful for us. We look at how race, ethnicity, and class issues have affected our willingness to identify as "women of color" and at how these same issues affect the willingness of others to place us in that category. In the process, we explore how our assimilation into the dominant "Anglo" culture of the American Southwest reveals the racism and classism inherent in it, how our assimilation has created for us powerful barriers to assuming non-conflictual racial and ethnic identities, and how we struggle against even as we are restrained by the racism of this culture.

Dialogue on Race, Class, and Chicana Identity

DL: Like many people who live in the United States, my ethnicity is multiple and complex. I come from many peoples and countries. But the origins that are alive for me, that define and perplex me, are only two. I am the daughter of a Texan father and Mexican mother—a borderland creature, Tex-Mex.

Somewhere along the way, in the schoolyard and town in which I grew up, I learned to be white and not Mexican. I learned that Mexicans are brown—browner than me. I learned that Mexicans were those browner "others" who worked in the fields that white people owned.

Yet, even as I learned this, I traveled each summer to Mexico to visit my grandparents. My grandfather, Don Tomas, was a proud charro and businessman. But I remember him best as a storyteller. From my grandfather I inhaled rich images of his boyhood in the state of Sinaloa, growing up in a socialist colony, fleeing Mexico in a boxcar during the revolution. My grandfather wrote books about his adventures, transcribed dying native languages, and translated the diaries of Spanish explorers.

My grandmother would prepare feasts of tamales and boiled beans in honor of our visits. When she didn't want us to understand, she spoke Spanish. Daily we walked a dirt path to the local bakery, where she would buy hard crusted rolls and pastries sprinkled with sugar. On the days we went to the meat market, I worried about the buzzing flies.

Once we visited the town of Los Mochis, where my mother was born. My grandparents chatted happily with old friends and relatives. But my mother, who was educated in the United States and spoke perfect Anglo English, seemed to have nothing to say. As we grew up, she never—not even once—talked about her childhood in Mexico. Somewhere along the way, she learned to be ashamed.

There is one more thing I need to say.

My twin brother has blond, nappy hair and blue eyes. When he was in high school, he cut his hair short to silence the white teens who teased him about his "Afro." But I am the darkest of my siblings. My brothers and sisters some-times used my darkness as a threat, hinting that I might not be a "real" member of the family. "You were adopted," they taunted, "a poor child abandoned on the streets of Mexico." I learned early the ostracizing, stigmatizing reality of white racism.

So, for a long time I became white and not Mexican.

JM: Like many people who live in the United States, my ethnicity is multiple and complex. I come from many peoples and countries. But I have always considered myself, first and fore-most, a Californian. As a very young girl, I was always very proud of my name "Martinez." I knew it made me different—something to do with Mexico. In my childhood imagina-tion it meant "great people," "proud warriors," "fighting spirit." I don't know where I got this, except from my father's very quiet and deter-mined way.

But in the "real" world of people, outside of my child's imagination, my name has always, for as long as I can remember, prompted the ques-tion, "Do you speak Spanish?" I learned that being named Martinez meant being Mexican, meant speaking Spanish. Because I didn't speak Spanish, I wasn't a real Mexican. I learned that Mexicans were the "low-riders" who lived in San Fernando, in the barrios, who spoke differently than I did.

My father has always been mostly silent about his life while growing up. One of my most prominent memories of my father during my own childhood was his rare but impactful story-telling about the poverty within which he grew up. Short and to the point, left with no word to follow, his stories always confused me.

My grandmother was visiting us once when I was a little girl. She was making beans and tor-tillas for us. As she spread the beans out on the table, carefully sorting out the chunks of dirt and small rocks from the beans, my father told me how he remembered her doing that when he was a little boy, except that as the family sat around that table sorting the dirt from the beans, they looked at all the food they had for the week. As they sat around the table, my father

and his brother and sister knew that that was all the food they had.

I was a little girl. We went to visit some rela-tives in Santa Ana, the occasion of a wedding or birthday, I think. Everyone spoke Spanish, there were all kinds of foods I didn't recognize but saw my father eat knowingly. Mexican music, dress, and decorations were all around. Years later, on some unknown occasion, my father tells me how those people, my relatives in Santa Ana, used to laugh and make fun of him because his family was so poor. But after my father had moved to California, worked his way through UCLA and earned a very good living as a corporate man-ager, then they invited him to their parties and celebrations. These stories told me that being poor, more than being Mexican, was the condi-tion by which one suffered discrimination.

There was something I sensed about my father's suffering that told me that it was dan-gerous to ask for explanations. Both he and my grandmother: stiff-lipped, straight-backed—we didn't talk about the past. Being poor and Mexi-can was something we couldn't talk about. It was something hidden, dangerous, evil. I learned never to ask questions.

DL: Our stories are different, yet at important junctures so much the same. When Jackie and I talk, Chicana to Chicana, we erase silences that painfully define who we are. We discover com-mon experiences that unite us as Mexicana, ex-periences that no Anglo shares. Talking Chicana to Chicana, we become more whole, more in touch with our race and ancestry.

Chicana is a consciously assumed identity. To be Chicana or Chicano, one must be Mexican American. But not all Mexican Americans are Chicana or Chicano. Identifying as Chicana or Chicano requires assuming a certain political consciousness, a resistance to being totally as-similated into Anglo culture, a commitment to bonding the surviving fragments from shared pasts into a proud and creative future. A Chi-cana can be light or dark skinned. But she is not white. Whiteness is a racist category that severs the Chicana from her ethnic and racial identity.

Because Anglos identify me as white, I will always have white privilege. But I grew up with the inherent contradictions of a racist-defined color spectrum inside my home and family. My blood is mixed, and my heritage defies white/non-white classification.

JM: Anglos identify me as white, my name an "oddity," or the sign of a Mexican family that "made it"—a Mexican that can do America proud. My father went from a childhood of extreme poverty to a life filled with the signs of middle-class white America. The more middle-class he became, the less his ethnic heritage mattered, the more he could be seen as white. I've come to see how those signs of "middle-class and thus white" do violence to everyone for the erasures they enact. They've done violence to my father by putting him in an either/or position. He chose *not* to have his family live the poverty he did—a decision that funneled him into whiteness and erased his own private retention of his ethnic heritage and family history of struggle and survival. My father talks about his life in terms of survival. I see how it is class, more so and differently from race, that defines my father's self-understanding.

Signs of middle-class achievement have done violence to me, robbing me of a space to live with my father's history. They do violence to us all by erasing my, Dorothy's, and others' ethnicity, making it easy to see us simply as white, and thus working against the possibility of speaking Chicana to Chicana.

The designator "woman of color" has been, at times, a perplexing one for me. I have been in conversations with white colleagues about the need to have more women of color in the academy. It seems like such discussions have the best of motivations behind them. But I wonder, why such passion and insistence on needing women of color here when these folks are so able to erase whatever non-white presence I bring to these very conversations? Such moments freeze me in silence. What do I say? Do I insist that they identify me as a woman of color and make myself the subject of the conversation? This is a very uncomfortable thing to do—suddenly my body and my presence become the object of our discussion. Or do I simply go along and agree with this abstract commitment to women of color and let the erasure of my own ethnicity

stand? What kind of racism gets expressed here? How do we see the need for more women of color in the academy when we are unable to see the color and difference in those who are non-white? I bear the signifier of the name—Hispanic, not white. Yet still, simple assumptions erase my ethnicity. I need the sign WOMEN OF COLOR as a designator to help create alliances in an oppositional consciousness to the power, privilege, and authority of middle-class whiteness that so dominates U.S. America. But when this designation is taken (especially by white people) as simple and self-apparent, it reinforces the logic of racism: one is white or isn't. It is, fittingly, among my Chicana, Asian, Black, and Native American colleagues that my color gains the greatest space to live.

For those of us who are not white, contradictions abound. Personal lives filled with contradictions bear struggle lived deep in the body. For those of us in the academy, we often embrace theorizing, writing, creative art—something to find expression that is not available within the received practices of a racist culture. This process is, for me, the ongoing assertion of Chicana identity.

DL: I do not (yet) know how to make art or theory from my way of being Chicana. Perhaps the identity is for me too thin—ethereal like a spirit I have not yet met.

My grandparents and mother are buried in Mexico. My cousin, Miquel, lives near the graveyard and visits with their spirits. The graves are covered with large rocks following the local Pai Pai Indian custom. When I visited the graves a few years ago, I knew that I too would be buried there. I feel a connection with the earth and rocks—some strange peace and sense of belonging.

Loss and longing to touch cultural roots define my way of being Chicana. Like Jackie, I do not speak Spanish. But I know phrases and songs—especially songs—from fragments of childhood memories. I am Chicana when I sing the songs. I am Chicana when my soul opens to bright Indian colors—vibrant yellows, oranges, reds, pinks, browns, and blues. I am Chicana when I crave a lunch of beans and corn tortillas.

Perhaps the loss and longing is for my

mother, who slowly went mad as I grew up. Anglo medicine said she was paranoid-schizophrenic; she said she was possessed. Sometimes she assumed separate identities as a saint and as a devil. Her saint name was Maria; her devil name, Mr. Underwood.

I remember a psychiatrist commenting on the Mr. Underwood name—the Underwood deviled ham product with the pitchforked devil logo its obvious source. Only recently have I wondered about the devil's gender and the saint name, the equally obvious Maria.

Jackie, Chicana to Chicana, I'll tell you one more story. Before my mother died, she underwent a ritual exorcism, arranged by family in Southern California. I was here, in Indiana, but promised to observe the hours of the ritual sitting in silence. I lit a candle and listened to a recording of Mozart's Requiem.

Later my brother told me that during the exorcism there was a good spirit in the room; he believes the spirit was me. I don't believe in spirits, good or bad. I am far too Anglo and modern European for that. But I am comforted by the cheap plastic statues that ward off snakes and other ominous things by the grave where my mother is buried.

In this comfort—in affirming it—I am also Chicana.

JM: Dorothy, *mi amiga,* Chicana to Chicana, we speak from places of such pain, loss and longing, perplexity, danger and possibility. As I live with your words and hear my own—for the first time, in a way, because of their nearness to yours—I feel a familiar kindling deep inside that I have learned to walk away from.

It's a kindling that was first nourished by my grandmother on my mother's mostly Anglo side. But I have American Indian heritage on my mother's side as well. I grew up hearing stories about how my grandfather's great-grandmother was a pure-blood Tennessee Cherokee. My grandfather knew this, as the story goes, because oil was found on a reservation there and my grandfather's family had a genealogy done to find out if they were entitled to any of it.

My grandmother was a deeply spiritual woman, and though she often evoked the name of Jesus Christ, she was spiritual in a no-man

kind of way. I never associated her spirituality with church or buildings or the image of Christ crucified. I associated her spirituality with the desert—incomprehensibly beautiful, the earth, the magic of a desert sunset. After dinner, walking with my grandmother, holding her hand as she swung her arms vigorously in front and behind her shouting for all the earth and sky to hear "Oh Joy, Oh Joy, Oh Joy," in a continuous refrain.

My grandmother has always known that I'm an Indian. I grew up, it seems, telling her stories about my past life as an Indian. She knew my stories to be true, and she always nurtured my belief in a spirit world that lives in the earth and sky, far beyond this ordinary world we live in. Though I have no recollection of telling my grandmother these stories, the spirit world that she helped me to live in has always been so very real for me; the desert a deeply spiritual place.

But I haven't been able to spend much time living in that world. I learned that my Indian wasn't a real Indian. I learned that there could be no connection between my ethnicity and those old stories I used to tell my grandmother. I learned that there was no connection between the fact of my name, which I got from my father, and the fact of the Indian-spirituality I got from my maternal grandmother.

Throughout my life, I've felt only tiny prods, here and there, kindlings that spark deep within my feeling-spirit. I felt it when I first joined the Chicano Student Organization at Cal. State, Northridge. I felt it when I attended the National Association of Chicano Studies meeting and felt overwhelmed with warmth and senses of possibility as I spent those days roaming among rooms full of brown women and men talking about this brownness, whiteness, struggle, and racism. I felt it as I sat in the audience and listened to Joy Harjo read her poetry about the Native people, their struggles. And then, as I spoke with her afterward and she asked me about my life, where I'm from, the Indian in me. A connection so deep that I could only barely stumble out a few words, taken as I was by her seeing Indian in me.

These tiny prods here and there, as this speaking with you, Chicana to Chicana, are joy for me. They contain an incredible sense of possibility. But they are also much more than joy and possibility. They are also laced with danger, serious danger, paralyzing danger.

I came to the academy so that I could live those parts of me that have been erased. All of my studies, my reading, writing, and speaking are part of that effort to live and become that which has been silenced in my life. This is not an abstract effort—it is a concrete effort of struggle that I engage every day.

I've always been a theoretician, beginning in those very early days when my father's stories gave me great pause; theorizing has always been about figuring things out, about understanding, discovery and possibility. As I grew up, my discovery of my lesbianism became the most pressing site of conscious struggle. I understood the profundity of cultural erasure most obviously here. Realizing that I was a lesbian led me to understand how that knowledge about myself was hidden by cultural biases that gave me no way to understand feelings that I had always had. Through this struggle I came also to understand the erasures and hidden presences of my ethnic heritage, and thus came to see the common ways in which cultural norms can rob us of who we are.

Now that I'm in the academy, I can read and write "as a Chicana," but that is fraught with just as many dangers. I haven't felt smart enough about racism and my own life and heritage to be able to outsmart the racisms at work. I've been tokenized for my name, served the interests of white racism.

DL: I came to the academy to escape from the small town where I grew up. I still hate that place, so full of mean-spirited prejudice and sick bigotry. This town was one of the first in the United States to declare English as its "official" language—a blatant effort to rob the large Mexican immigrant population of even the semblance of democratic right.

When I entered the academy, I never declared myself as "Hispanic" on those forms in which institutions attempt to quantify the ethnic and racial mix of their student population. At first, this was because I recognized myself only as white. But as I learned to see through race and class stereotypes and the deeply hidden

fears I had of being discovered as Mexican, my motivation changed. As I filled out those forms, I would say to myself, "You do not get to count me. That would be too easy. I do not embody the differences you fear."

I viewed this as a small attempt to thwart the interests of white racism. I'm not the sort of Hispanic who makes Anglos uncomfortable: I have neither the stereotypical name nor look. Lately I've adopted a somewhat different strategy: now I check both the "white" and "Hispanic" boxes, even though you are supposed to declare yourself as only one. It is a little protest against the logic of racism that says you must be either one or the other—which recognizes only blood that is pure.

I have similar problems with the signifier "woman of color." Jackie, you claim it as an oppositional space from which to speak. But I feel fraudulent assuming this identity. I'll try to explain why.

I have white-skin privilege by virtue of the fact that the dominant culture does not identify me as "being colored." "Color" is a signifier of visibility—of a presumed otherness and inferiority based on how one looks. No matter what my actual skin shade, if my skin or facial features or speech patterns fail to mark me as being "of color," I do not suffer in the eyes of the dominant culture the stigma of that mark.

When the signifier "women of color" first emerged in feminist circles, it was used to designate a vast and undifferentiated arena of otherness. African Americans, Asian Americans, Hispanic Americans, Native Americans, and so forth—were lumped together as women of color. But this categorization simply replicates the extant racist white/colored dichotomy. Today, "people of color" still signifies "people who are black" to most North Americans. Since I have not borne the stigma of "being colored" in white eyes, it feels fraudulent to attempt to claim the oppositional space, women of color, as my own.

But neither am I white if being white means not being Chicana.

I'm talking about what Cherríe Moraga (1983) calls the "white wash of cultural identity." Cherríe, who grew up in a town fifteen miles northwest of the community where I was Anglicized, explains:

> No one ever quite told me this (that light is right), but I knew that being light was something valued in my family (who were all Chicano, with the exception of my father). In fact, everything about my upbringing . . . attempted to bleach me of what color I did have. (p. 28)

So, Jackie, this is what I've been trying to say. Like Cherríe, I am a woman best described as "one who has been bleached." And like most bleached women, when I am lucky, blotches of brown bleed through.

JM: Feeling fraudulent. I've felt that all my life, beginning with the question, "Do you speak Spanish?" Interesting how that question came mostly from white people. Interesting how the places I've felt most fraudulent are among white people. Interesting how in the Chicano Studies Department at UCSB I was welcomed, my difference from others not used to mark me as fraudulent. Interesting how my students there, just like the ones at the East Coast Chicano Students Association's annual Pachanga, looked to me for advice about being a Chicana in the academy, advice about how they might pursue their own lives. Interesting how in conversations with my Chicana friends my identity as Chicana is simply taken as a basis upon which we come to understand our similarities and differences so as to engage a common struggle.

DL: Amongst Chicanas, there is greater recognition of our differences. Some of us are gay; some of us are not. Some of us come from the *haciendados* and merchant classes; some of us have only worked the land of others. Some of us are more European; some of us more Mayan or *mestizo*. We have dark and light skins; blond and black hair, short and tall statures.

Anglo culture tends to construct all Mexicans as being "the same." Where I grew up, being Mexican meant being poor, brown, and ignorant. The migrants who journeyed north to pick fruit and work the fields had different ways: they lived in shacks, their children went without shoes, they spoke a language that signified their lack of education and stupidity.

Escaping poverty required becoming Anglicized, whited. Only good English would allow you to become something other than a "stupid Mexican." Wearing Anglo suits, adopting Anglo customs, living in Anglo homes: these were and are signs of one's escape from being a dark blot on a white cultural landscape.

Many Anglos do not realize that Mexico is a class-and-race-stratified society. The less Indian, the more European, the more wealth: the better. This racist and classist heritage travels across borders, creating powerful internal pressures to adopt the garb, customs, and speech of white middle-class America. This pressure has affected all Mexican Americans despite our race and class differences. It forms a common locus of Chicana experience and resistance.

JM: My father felt his identity most poignantly as poor, dirt poor. He came to achieve all of the signs of middle class. I've worked hard to understand my father's life. In brief conversations here and there, almost always stilted, full of hesitancy of both sides—I've come to understand that his achievement of Anglo markers have been in an absolutely dedicated effort to be faithful to *la familia*. Not an assimilator or a cop-out on his race, but a testament to the power and dignity of people who are ostracized for being poor. He proved himself better. But in a society where racism and classism are twins, his very success economically has meant the erasure of this ethnicity. My father's very life can be seen as an example of how racism and classism are intertwined. Because he aspired to provide for his family what he did not have in his birth family, Anglo culture could recognize him in its own racist terms. To succumb to a single trajectory in understanding of how people are positioned by race, class, gender, or sexuality, is to reinscribe those very oppressions we are trying to subvert. This is the lesson I am learning.

Conclusion

At the beginning of this piece, we promised to problematize the category "woman of color" by exploring how it has been and remains problematical for us. We hope we have succeeded in this.

Both of us were born "la güera": fair skinned. This physiognomic trait has shaped our experience both inside and outside Anglo and Chicana communities. But the trait itself would not have assumed for us or others the significance it has outside of a racist culture. Being fair skinned has enabled us to reap the benefits of white privilege. But passing or being labeled by others as white has also meant ethnic invisibility. This is because Anglo culture has constructed "Mexican" as a homogenous group—as those brown-skinned "beaners," "wetbacks," and "spicks."

For both of us, identifying as Chicana has meant resisting total assimilation into Anglo culture and whiteness. This identification is a political act, an interruption of the bleaching process that attempts to launder out *mestizo* blood and spirit, as if it were an ominous stain on an otherwise superior cloth of white Anglo identity. Thus, when our Anglo feminist friends identify us as white, we simultaneously understand and resist. We understand that we share the privileges accorded to fair-skinned persons in a racist culture. But we resist because the sense in which they are white is profoundly different from the sense in which we are white. Anglos do not become white through a process of bleaching: their being seen and treated as white does not entail an erasure of cultural roots and ethnic identities.

REFERENCES

Anzaldúa, G. (Ed.). (1990). *Making face, making soul/haciendo caras: Creative and critical perspectives by women of color.* San Francisco: Aunt Lute Foundation.

Bartky, S. L. (1990). *Femininity and domination. Studies in the phenomenology of oppression.* New York: Routledge.

Hall, E. T. (1981). *Beyond culture.* New York: Doubleday.

Moraga, C. (1983). La güera. In C. Moraga & G. Anzaldúa (Eds.), *This bridge called my back: Writings by radical women of color* (pp. 27–34). New York: Kitchen Table, Women of Color Press.

Moraga, C., and Anzaldúa, G. (Eds.). (1983). *This bridge called my back: Writings by radical women of color.* New York: Kitchen Table, Women of Color Press.

Young, I. M. (1990). *Throwing like a girl and other essays in feminist philosophy and social theory.* Bloomington: Indiana University Press.

KEY TERMS

Chicana	classism
racism	ethnic identity

DISCUSSION QUESTIONS

1. Both Leland and Martinez describe their relationships to the Spanish language. How are their relationships to Spanish similar and different? What connections do they make between Spanish and their Chicana identities? How might their perspectives help us understand some of the issues at work in questions of bi- or multilingual education?

2. Having a consciousness of class differences is important to each author's development of ethnic identity. Yet, this class consciousness was, in some ways, more difficult to develop than ethnic issues. Why? How do you think, within mainstream culture, we are or are not able to talk about class issues?

3. The authors have different perspectives on identifying themselves as women of color. What are these differences? What are the political issues at work for each author? How does Martinez use woman of color in her own political struggles? What does Leland's point about not embodying the difference that Anglos fear say about the nature of racism?

4. What is the significance of Leland's story about the Maria/Mr. Underwood identities that her mother developed later in life?

5. What is the significance of Martinez's identification of herself as a lesbian? What role does her lesbian consciousness play in relation to her ethnic and class consciousness?

PART THREE

HISTORY AND INTERCULTURAL COMMUNICATION

Many different kinds of histories influence intercultural communication. Asking parents and grandparents about family history and where they come from is one way that people come to understand who they are. Another basis for our cultural identities comes from the ways in which different cultural groups understand the past. Think about what significance the Holocaust, Hiroshima and Nagasaki, the Rodney King incident, or the Stonewall incident has for different cultural groups. In what ways are these historical events important in the construction and maintenance of various cultural identities? The histories that we learned in school as well as the most common and well-known histories are not necessarily the most important to us. Often, different cultural groups have different understandings about the past.

Research in intercultural communication has examined conflict and cooperation, attitudes and beliefs, dimensions of cultural variability, and interpersonal relations between members of different cultures, but it has only recently focused on how history influences intercultural interaction. Much about the relationship between history and intercultural communication remains unexplored. Yet, we know that any historical event can have many different interpretations and meanings for many different cultural groups. These interpretations have important implications for understanding cultural group identity and intercultural communication.

Collective memories and cultural interpretations of history have emerged as central in our understanding of cultural differences in attitudes, beliefs, values, and behaviors. Scholars have argued that events such as the Vietnam War have no single meaning across cultures but, instead, have different cultural and historic accounts within cultures, co-cultures, and even social groups. These culturally located histories help us explain contemporary relations and guide us in our understanding of intercultural conflict and communication.

At the same time that scholars assess the multiple meanings in history, they also recognize the need for broader knowledge of global histories. No longer can we afford to ignore the histories of any place or people. As we see more signs of the global village, we realize the limitations of our historic knowledge. In order to better situate ourselves to understand intercultural communication, we must understand more about the various ways in which different cultural groups in the present understand the past.

This part is not intended to give a comprehensive understanding of the past; instead, it is designed to help us see how we might think about the past. The essays expand our knowledge of history and its implications for intercultural communication. Addressing both the idea of competing histories and the gaps in knowledge of history, the authors in this section extend our awareness of the relationship between history and intercultural communication.

Consider these questions as you read the articles in this part:

How do the histories of some of your own cultural groups (ethnic, national, and family) influence your cultural identities?

What historical events have shaped how you think about your own cultural identity? How do historical events influence how you think about other cultural groups?

How is your understanding of a historical event influenced by your cultural group membership? For example, what interpretations are possible for Pearl Harbor? the Alamo? the Civil War?

If you are going to interact with members of another culture (whether for tourism, business, or other purposes), how much history of that culture should you learn?

In "Intercultural Histories and Mass-Mediated Identities," Marouf A. Hasian, Jr., builds on the work of cultural critics who have examined the ways in which mass media influences the creation of intercultural relations. By reviewing how mass media in various cultures construct the Arab-Israeli conflict, we gain an appreciation of the complexities of particular communication practices that facilitate or hinder the coproduction of social identities. In most of the media constructions, the creation of the "other" becomes a precondition for one's belonging to one or the other camp. This binarism and polarization precludes the parties from contemplating constructive imaginary histories that could alter present realities.

In "Who Are You and What Have You Done with the Real Hottentots?" Melissa Steyn uncovers the various histories told about the settlement of South Africa. Her analysis shows that the different histories are in conflict and lead to different conclusions about who has more legitimate claims to the land. The significance of history as a major influence in intercultural communication is clear because these competing histories are incompatible.

The last three essays focus on the intersections of domestic and international histories. In "Stranger in the Village," writer James Baldwin recounts his experience of living in a tiny Swiss village whose inhabitants had never seen an African American before. He uses this experience to explore the unique historical contexts of race relations in the United States. He points out that the United States, unlike Europe, was founded *on* the oppression of Africans, and that the histories and destinies of African Americans and Whites in the United States are inextricably intertwined. Baldwin explores how these histories present challenges and opportunities for all peoples of the United States.

"Crossing an Irish Border" is about Irish Americans, cultural identity, illegal immigration, and sexual difference. In this essay, Frederick C. Corey uses the metaphor of the border as a way of interrogating social and personal territory. He questions his own family's telling of their history and his own relationship to Ireland and the United States.

In the last reading, Kathleen Wong(Lau) examines identities and "Migration Across Generations." She looks at how Asian American immigrants sometimes retain an identity from their host country over generations that bears little relationship to contemporary life in the "old country." She explores how this "imagined community" and the heterogeneity in the Asian American community affects communication across generations. She points out that immigrant identity can only be understood in relation to historical, economic, and political forces and contexts in which migration or immigration or both occurs.

10

INTERCULTURAL HISTORIES AND MASS-MEDIATED IDENTITIES: THE RE-IMAGINING OF THE ARAB-ISRAELI CONFLICT

MAROUF A. HASIAN, JR.

As Carbaugh (1990) recently observed, cultural communication and intercultural contact is often created from "different social fabrics" (p. 15), and nowhere is this more evident than the volatile relationship that exists between Israeli and Arab cultures. The recent media coverage of archeological tunnels and national disputes reminds us of the need to find symbolic means of communication that will allow for peaceful resolution of conflicts. Issues of cultural and communication studies need to deal with discursive elements of social relations and ideological oppositions.

Although there are a plethora of constructive ways to try to understand some of these divergent social fabrics, I feel that one of the best ways of analyzing these situations is by explicating some of the symbolic constructions that are implicated in the creation of such conflicts. Geertz once argued that the notion of "culture" itself was a "historically transmitted pattern of meaning that" is embodied in an inherited structure of symbolic forms (quoted in Carbaugh, 1990, p. 20). If this is indeed the case, then we need to sensitize ourselves to the ways in which intercultural relations are not only represented but constituted (Charland, 1987). This means not only understanding the personal skills at the microlevel of analysis, but also the larger histories, cultural memories, and social facts that circulate as the taken-for-granteds of communities that need to coexist. For example, the clash of belief systems can create situations where there is "cognitive discrepancy" (Bar-Tal, 1990) that helps to perpetuate polarization.

This obviously has important ramifications for many different cultural conflicts, including the Arab-Israeli situation. As Bar-Tal (1990) recently noted, the "Middle Eastern conflict is one of the longest conflicts of our century" (p. 7). Culturally and politically, isn't this a situation where we have *several* oppressed people who stand on the margins of Western civilization? Do we not have at least two "Oriental" (Said, 1978/1979) cultures that are mirror images of each other? In place of reasoned deliberation we have

> those bloated signifiers "Arab" and "Jew" [that] have accrued a set of vile and ugly characteristics—terrorists, child-killers, primitives on one side; bloodsuckers, occupiers, fascists on the other. Even more depressing is the fact that these images and stereotypes have become institutionalized through children's literature. This is true both in Israel and throughout the Arab world, as each side shapes and colors its own respective demons with facile, terrifying, and extremely effective propaganda. This demonization only diverts attention from common problems that get more urgent and pressing every day. (Alcalay, 1993, p. 280)

As long as these constructs are uncritically circulating in the public sphere, we will continually be asked to simply choose sides and perpetuate the existence of these deadly binaries.

I argue that improved intercultural relations in the Middle East depend on a re-imagining of the histories and identities of the region. Extending the work of Anderson (1983/1986), I believe that cultural sensitivities can be improved when we understand how communities have imagined themselves as distinct races or nations. For example, how have Arabs, Israelis, and Palestinians constructed themselves or been represented within complex symbolic systems? These discursively constructed individuals, places, and histories have created belief systems that are frozen (Bar-Tal, 1990) in time, and this is what prevents some cultures from seeing or hearing the "Other."

In order to unfreeze some of these stereotypes, we need approaches that look at the interrelationship among intercultural communication, history, and collective memory. How we remember the past alters the ways in which we think about our present and our future. For example, the recent controversy over the opening of an Israeli tunnel in Jerusalem sparked a new Intifada (uprising), which has exacerbated tensions in the region.

In this essay, I follow Foucault (1980) in claiming that scholars and students can perform critical genealogies that can augment traditional unilinear studies of the histories of cultures. Rather than assume the existence of one true or correct history, this stance asks readers to assume that there are always multiple histories that have been written by social agents who have clear agendas. For example, in the recent *Enola Gay* controversy, the curators at the Smithsonian Institution were interested in presenting a story of the dropping of the atomic bomb that was radically different from the story of air force veterans. From an intercultural perspective, we might want to look at the ways that motivated agents embedded in cultural contexts create histories about the bombing and circulate this information through elite and vernacular texts. Vernacular texts are documents that contain the commonsense ideas that ordinary citizens use in their daily lives, whereas elite texts involve professional modes of discourse that circulate within intellectual circles (Ono & Sloop, 1995).

In order to illustrate the heuristic value of engaging in such criticism, I have divided this essay into five sections. The first segment highlights the ways in which genealogical criticism differs from more traditional historical approaches to intercultural conundrums. The second part begins to apply some of these theoretical arguments by looking at the prefigurations, characterizations, and other social constructions that have been historically crafted at one particularly important

time in Arab-Israeli relations—the public display in 1917 of the Balfour Declaration, which pledged British support for a Jewish national home in Palestine. The third section briefly outlines some of the conflicting narratives and myths that were circulated in the Anglo American press between 1917 and time of the 1987 Intifada. The fourth section illustrates how the Anglo American press is reporting the Arab-Israeli conflict today. Finally, I provide a brief assessment of the findings of the essay.

Intercultural Histories, Collective Memories, and Genealogical Criticism

In order for an individual, group, or nation to form any type of intercultural relationship, ways of creating bridges and new identities that reformulate existing stereotypes must be found. In most existing theories of historiography, this often translates into a battle over representations, where each side attempts to archive the past in order to disprove the "false" claims that are being promulgated by the other side. For example, imagine the feelings of the Israeli archeologist who is digging in some of the ancient sites of Israel, trying to show that Jews have been living in Sumeria and Judea for thousands of years. For such a researcher, finding pottery and other relics of the past serves as an operative way of legitimizing Israeli claims that the present state of Israel simply stands on ruins of a much older Israel. Theoretically, no amount of debate can alter the "fact" that an artifact can be carbon dated and linked to a particular period.

Yet at the same time, imagine the interpersonal conflict that must be involved in linking such archeological digs to the politics of the present. Palestinians could argue that they have never denied the presence of Jews or Israelis in the areas, or that those individuals who have lived in this region in the past have had little relation to the Russian immigrants or other Europeans who helped "colonize" the region. What might initially appear to be a simple archeological dig can be interpreted as an attempt at an erasure of culture or revision of history. In such situations, vilification and invective are some of the likely results when findings that valorize certain characterizations from the past are exhibited in museums. What one community might regard as the recovery of the past is simultaneously interpreted by the neighbors as fabricated history.

How one relates to a member of a different or similar culture clearly influences the intercultural communication that takes place between these communities. When groups do not have the opportunity to co-create history, or when one elite tale or vernacular narrative takes primacy over other interpretations, we may have a coherent and consistent history, but this clarity has come at the cost of altering the possibilities of improving communications. As Bar-Tal (1990) explains, debates within the Israeli-Palestinian conflict are tied to the "salience and centrality of beliefs as well as the effects of the underlying needs" of the parties involved (p. 13). Within these tales, one's *own* culture's historical markers or memory is presented as discovered truth, and intercultural conflicts are treated as examples of dogmatic intransigence on the part of outsiders who simply do not understand. Disagreement is treated as a temporary problem that will disappear as soon as one's enemies are educated to the truth of one's own culture.

By extending Foucault's work, researchers can improve our intercultural dialogues by helping us become sensitive to the ways in which our own values and beliefs are inextricably related to our images of the "Other" (Ono & Sloop, 1992). I invite scholars to engage in genealogical investigations that problematize the taken-for-granteds of orthodox interpretations of the Arab-Israeli conflict. My purpose in this essay therefore goes beyond simply claiming that the United States or other Western nations "misrepresent" a particular side in the conflict. Rather, I believe that intercultural relations are facilitated by negotiated readings (Liebes & Ribak, 1994) that look at the ways in which local knowledges become selectively incorporated into the evening news in both the Near East and the West. In the process of telling one culture's truths, we forget the rhetoricity of these claims.

The orthodox approaches to history teach us much because they are created by motivated

scholars who want to see behind the discourse in order to get to the reality underneath. Yet in the process of validating their findings, they oftentimes bracket out the influence of politics and cultural persuasion. In order to counter the raising of monolithic voices, critical theories have recently invited us to perform critical genealogical investigations in which researchers pay attention to the ways that power "flows, circulates, and defines" relationships of domination and freedom (Ono & Sloop, 1992, p. 50). From an intercultural perspective, such a stance invites individuals to go beyond simply expressing personal standards and beliefs in order to coproduce new values and standards of communication. This means renegotiating histories by understanding the uncertainties, complexities, and ambiguities that exist in prior histories that often marginalize the contributions of the "Other" in the effacements of the past.

For such critics, a culture's "history" is not something either discovered or recovered by privileged social actors who are interested in explaining present situations. Nor is it retrieval of dispassionate archival information that has escaped the ravages of the everyday world. Rather, genealogies are histories that are also created by ordinary individuals who have themselves created micro- and macrolanguages that influence our intercultural communicative practices. This type of approach asks that a scholar follow Foucault in appreciating the relationship that exists between "discourse and social functions" (Nakayama, 1988, p. 66).

In order to apply this framework to debates over Israeli and Palestinian cultures, I begin my re-imaginative tale by reviewing some of the essentialist assumptions that have been built into influential histories since 1917. In retelling this tale, I highlight the different stereotypes and assumptions that will become parts of recurring narratives that have helped alter the intercultural habits of diverse cultures and communities.

The Signification of the Balfour Declaration in the Anglo American Press, 1917

If you ask most Arabs or Israelis about the significance of the Balfour Declaration (November 2,

1917), their answers will provide you with a wealth of information on the origins of an ancient intercultural conflict. At the same time, most Anglo American accounts of the conflict punctuate time by chronicling the ways that the Balfour treaty managed to promise the same piece of land to different communities. Prior to 1917, most of the information about Levantine culture (i.e., culture of the region of Palestine) that circulated in the English and American popular presses came from travelogues and books published by missionaries who had been sent to the area. Most came back with stories of deserts and barren lands occupied by roving Bedouins who did not seem to have any interest in agriculture. For many of these sojourners, Palestine was an area that was occupied by Jews, Gentiles, and Moslems, and the holy city of Jerusalem was considered to be the center of civilization in the Near East.

Living during a time in which people worshiped the power of science, technology, and efficiency, many elites around the world hoped that after World War I progress would come to a region that had been marked by intercultural fighting since the time of the Crusades. In 1917 England found itself in the midst of war. British leaders publicized the signing of an ambiguous document known as the Balfour Declaration that promised support for a Jewish state in Palestine and at the same time recommended that the rights of the Arabs in the region be respected. For many modern-day critics trying to understand the history of the Arab-Israeli conflict, this is considered to be a crucial stage in the formation of "nations" in the region. Davidson (1994), for example, has argued that the Balfour Declaration was a document that reflected the Western image of English and American leaders who constructed a vision of the Holy Land that was based on Christian fundamentalist ideology and Western imperialism (p. 125).

Yet an analysis of the press reports during that period reveals a complex picture of intercultural relations. The Balfour Declaration created a great deal of tension for the Arabs and Jews living in Palestine at the time, but in the West, the passage of this document seemed to signal to many contemporaries a hopeful end of many forms of anti-Semitism. Many Jews who had ambivalent feelings about assimilation hoped that the rediscovery of a "Jewish homeland" meant that at long last the European powers were providing shelters from the pogroms on the Continent.

For months before the Balfour Declaration, the Allied forces had been discussing the benefits that would come from the creation of a Jewish nation. The *New York Times* reported on April 15, 1917, that a British report claimed:

> Our invasion of Palestine is dictated by imperious strategical necessity . . . the Syrian plateau has been rightly regarded as the strategic portal into Egypt. . . . What should we do with Palestine thus liberated from the century old Turkish grip? . . . We should revive the Jewish Palestine of old, and allow the Jews to realize their dreams of Zion in their homeland.
> ("Objects," p. 14)

On the surface, the Balfour Declaration seemed to be a simple military decision, but it became a contested site for both Palestinians and Israelis, who argued for the correct interpretation of its edicts.

Anti-Semitism in Europe and other places has a long history, and during World War I, the debates over the Balfour treaty transformed Jews from being members of a clannish, separate race into potential allies. At the same time, politicians like England's prime minister, Lloyd George, and his foreign secretary, Arthur Balfour, saw the importance of building on the image of Palestine as a land that had been an important part of the Christian religion. By encouraging the emigration of Jews to Palestine, British leaders hoped to allow the *recovery* of both lands and identities that had biblical origins.

Yet in the process of creating this new Jewish homeland, many Arabs who lived on the land disappeared as social agents. Although some voices raised in Europe worried about the "Musselman inhabitants" (Curzon, 1917, quoted in Davidson, 1994, p. 126), the majority of decision makers hoped that Arabs and Jews would live in peace under the benevolent guidance of the British Mandate system, which grew out of the Treaty of Versailles following the end of World War I. At other times, the Arabs of the region were simply configured as temporary denizens who could have made the desert bloom. Other characterizations of the time included the belief that this was a complacent race ruled by Arab landlords who were willing to sell the land to the highest bidders. Within such Orientalist accounts of Palestine (Said, 1978/1979), the Arab "Other" was someone who resembled the Philistines that Anglo Americans recognized from their Sunday sermons (Grabill, 1971).

Unfortunately, anti-Semitic feelings against many Jews did not disappear following the passage of the Balfour treaty. Conspiracy tales that circulated on several continents claimed that banking interests had influenced British leaders in their decision to support the creation of a Jewish homeland. At the same time, if there was any improvement in relations between Jews and Christians in the West, it came at the price of redefining Palestine as a geographic area that might become a part of civilization. The *Washington Post* reported on November 20, 1917, that

> millions of ardent Christians are fervently hoping that the near future will witness the Holy Land reclaimed from the control of the Moslem who for centuries has held uninterrupted sway over the birthplace of the Christian religion. . . . (Quoted in Davidson, 1994)

Needless to say, such characterizations made the establishment of intercultural relations in the region difficult because of the conflicting histories that were involved in describing the inhabitants of Palestine before and after the Balfour Declaration.

Arab-Israeli Narratives and Myths and the Configuration of the "Other": 1917–1987

For the next 60 years following the signing of the Balfour treaty, Moslems, Jews, and Christians constantly carried on discursive and material battles over the right to represent a land that some have called Palestine. Battles were fought in 1948, 1967, and 1973 that enlarged the scope of Israel after every confrontation. This was a period of time when a large Arab population in the region

witnessed the arrival of millions of Zionist Jews who were intent on returning to the land that had been promised them by right and might. Tragically, both Arab nationalists and Israeli Zionists encouraged the separation and segregation of their peoples because of supposed racial, religious, and cultural differences. In the process, they created myriads of new histories that would later become sound bytes on television news. As a result, several different reconfigurations of time and place are used to explain how one land rightfully belongs to "us" and not to "them."

In the Arab and Palestinian histories that recounted events between 1917 and 1987, this region had supposedly been more than 90% Arab prior to the signing of the Balfour treaty. Following this event, Jews immigrated to the region because they were under the protection of the British Mandate forces. Arab nationalists in 1936 tried to reclaim the land for their own people in the 1930s (one of the first Intifadas), but British and Jewish settlement forces crushed the rebellion. In many of these tales, 1948 was a key year in this chronicle of Arab woes because it was the year of the uprooting and dispossession of an entire nation that had to make room for what Israelis called an ingathering of Jews in Palestine from all parts of the world (Bar-Tal, 1990, p. 8). In such renditions, Israelis are not portrayed as pioneers, but rather as strangers who flee a Nazi Europe at the expense of an indigenous people. In the Palestinian versions of these events, the rising population of the Jews in the region looks like a large conspiracy, where an endless flotilla of boats keeps bringing in a Jewish population to Palestine in order to fulfill the Zionist dream of returning Jewish communities to their Middle Eastern homeland—a major movement that would later be called Zionism. The wars that followed can be explained by the ways in which American military might has been allied with Israeli power in a systematic attempt to extend Western imperialism.

In Israeli tales of the same events, the Balfour Declaration is believed to be simply the *ratification* of preexisting rights that date back to biblical times. In such narratives, Palestine is renamed Judea and Sumeria because these are the ancient names for lands that have always belonged to Israel. The Zionist characters that appear in the histories between 1917 and 1987 describe a community of pioneer settlers who remember the tales of Masada and the importance of being steadfast in a hostile land (Zerubavel, 1995). In 1973, for example, one Israeli information center document entitled *History from 1880* included this material from the *Encyclopedia Judaica:*

> The merging of two trends—the rationally intellectual and the emotionally traditional—gave birth not only to Zionism as an organized political effort, but also to the beginnings of the pioneering movement of the late 19th century, which laid the foundations, on the soil of Erez Israel, for the economic, social and cultural rebirth of the Jewish nation. The land itself seemed eminently suitable for the purpose; a marginal province of the weak Ottoman Empire, sparsely inhabited by a population consisting of various religious groups and seemingly lacking any national consciousness of ambitions of its own; a motherland waiting to be redeemed from centuries of neglect and decay by its legitimate sons. (Quoted in Bar-Tal, 1990, p. 9)

Many Israelis thus saw immigration to the region as an activity that could be defended on political, religious, social, and economic grounds.

These conflicting narratives are not only recorded in history books and in political tracts—they are fragments that circulate within the broader rhetorical culture. They provide the structural elements that are used to create stereotypes that influence the ways in which we memorialize the past and configure the future. In Palestinian tales, the narrativized histories that signify the Israeli as colonizer allow for a form of self-identification where wearers of the *kufiyya* (the checkered headdress worn by Palestinian Arabs) are freedom fighters rather than terrorists. At the same time, Israeli settlers on the West Bank are viewed as interlopers or pawns of international Zionism, simply the latest wave of infidels who have tried to rule Jerusalem since the time of Saladin.

In Israeli folk tales and media stories, greater Israel is depicted as a lonely nation surrounded by hundreds of millions of Arabs. Angered that the Western media focuses attention on the victimization tales of Palestinians, many Israelis try to remind viewers that at different times in their nation's history, Israelis have been at war with Egypt, Syria, Lebanon, Jordan, and Iraq. Israel's major problems often are presented as security issues in which many Palestinians are portrayed as common criminals and terrorists who are bent on driving Israel back into the ocean.

The Past Is the Prologue: Deciphering the Anglo American Press Representations of the Arab-Israeli Conflict

Arab and Israeli histories are complex structures in and of themselves, but when we add on the layers of Anglo American press representations, we multiply the number of distortions and stereotypes that circulate within the public sphere. Although some critics contend that American-Israeli relations have often created an apologetic rhetoric for Israeli policies (Chomsky, 1983), this tells only a part of the story. In both the attacks and defenses of Israeli policy, we can see the ways that historical claims influence the trajectory of intercultural relations.

Recent press reactions to the bombing of the Murrah Federal Building in Oklahoma City illustrate the ways that many Americans have stereotyped Arabs in the wake of the Iraqi conflict. Yet these are simply the latest manifestations of a much older intercultural phenomenon. As Shaheen (1985) once explained:

> Today's most obvious stereotype is that of the Arab. It is magnified and given credence around the clock through television programs, motion pictures, novels, news reports, and even comic books. The image of the Arab is so pervasive that it threatens to engulf public opinion and ultimately influence American foreign policy in the Middle East. The greater the distance we are from any group, including the Arabs, the greater the reliance upon preconceived images about that group. . . . Arabs are portrayed as extremely wealthy, as sex maniacs and white slavers. They are described as terrorists, their society as

violent, and their religion, Islam as radical. (pp. 161–162)

The advent of the Intifada (1987–1993) simply reinforced the view that Israelis were dealing with tribal nations of emotional human beings that had difficulty listening to reason and argument. Palestinian supporters of Saddam Hussein became guilty by association. For many Americans who have observed the Arab-Israeli conflicts through the mediated texts of television, the battle for Palestine seemed to be an eternal battle that has been prophesied since biblical times. The Palestinian revolt thus became a mass-mediated spectacle, and viewers shook their heads as they saw the "violent demonstrations, blocking roads, burning tires, and attacking Israeli soldiers and civilians with stones and Molotov cocktails" (Liebes & Ribak, 1994, p. 110). In such renditions of the tale, complex social, economic, and political issues were often reduced to stories of the need to contain violence and terrorism in order to maintain order. In a traumatic transvaluation of time and space, Americans anxiously worried that terrorism could spread to this country if international problems were not quickly settled on a White House lawn.

Assessment

This exploratory essay has argued that intercultural scholars need to appreciate the ways that historical prefigurations influence the ways that particular communities create their own self-identities and images of the "Other." Using a case study of the Arab-Israeli conflict, I have argued that unilinear histories are always distortions because they achieve their clarity by bracketing out the politics of the past. Events dating from the Balfour treaty to the coverage of the Intifada have been influenced both by prior prefigurations and by our present needs. Intercultural communication occurs at both micro and macro levels, and it is imperative that we understand some of the histories that are involved in our key international conflicts. I believe that it is imperative that we try to understand the ways that our notions of nationalism are tied to issues of power, knowledge, and

discourse. We need new imaginations that take into account our differences while at the same time remembering the humanities of the "Other."

REFERENCES

Alcalay, A. (1993). *After Jews and Arabs: Remaking Levantine culture.* Minneapolis: University of Minnesota Press.

Anderson, B. (1986). *Imagined communities: Reflections on the origin and spread of nationalism.* London: Verso Editions. (Original work published in 1983)

Bar-Tal, D. (1990). Israeli-Palestinian conflict: A cognitive analysis. *International Journal of Intercultural Relations, 14,* 7–29.

Carbaugh, D. (1990). Toward a perspective on cultural communication and intercultural contact. *Semiotica, 80,* 15–35.

Charland, M. (1987). Constitutive rhetoric: The case of the Peuple Québécois. *Quarterly Journal of Speech, 73,* 133–150.

Chomsky, N. (1983). *The fateful triangle: The United States, Israel, and the Palestinians.* Boston: South End Press.

Davidson, L. (1994). Historical ignorance and popular perception: The case of U.S. perceptions of Palestine, 1917. *Middle East Policy, 3,* 125–147.

Foucault, M. (1980). *Power/knowledge: Selected interviews and other writings by Michel Foucault* (C. Gordon, Trans.). New York: Pantheon Books.

Grabill, J. (1971). *Protestant diplomacy and the Near East: Missionary influence on American policy, 1810–1927.* Minneapolis: University of Minnesota Press.

Liebes, T., & Ribak, R. (1994). In defense of negotiated readings: How moderates on each side of the conflict interpret Intifada news. *Journal of Communication, 44,* 108–124.

Nakayama, T. K. (1988). "Model Minority" and the media: Discourse on Asian Americans. *Journal of Communication Inquiry, 12,* 65–73.

Objects of advance into holy land. (1917, April 15). *The New York Times,* p. 14.

Ono, K. A., & Sloop, J. M. (1992). Commitment to Telos—A sustained critical rhetoric. *Communication Monographs, 59,* 48–60.

Ono, K. A., & Sloop, J. M. (1995). The critique of

vernacular discourse. *Communication Monographs, 62,* 19–46.

Said, E. (1979). *Orientalism.* New York: Vintage Books. (Original work published in 1978)

Shaheen, J. G. (1985). Media coverage of the Middle East: Perception and foreign policy. *The Annals of the American Academy of Political and Social Science, 482,* 160–175.

Zerubavel, Y. (1995). *Recovered roots: Collective memory and the making of Israeli national tradition.* Chicago: University of Chicago Press.

KEY TERMS

Balfour

British Mandate
 system

Levantine

Zionism

Intifada

Israel

Orientalism

Palestine

vernacular

DISCUSSION QUESTIONS

1. What is vernacular discourse and how can this be traced in cultural studies?
2. If different cultures create various histories, then how do we know when media representations have accurately represented those cultures?
3. Can you think of key documents other than the Balfour Declaration that have been a part of intercultural conflicts?
4. What are the political meanings of the terms *Israel* and *Palestine*?
5. What does it mean for discourse to be "constitutive"?

11

WHO ARE YOU AND WHAT HAVE YOU DONE WITH THE REAL HOTTENTOTS? THE LEGACY OF CONTESTED COLONIAL NARRATIVES OF SETTLEMENT IN THE NEW SOUTH AFRICA

MELISSA STEYN

Southernmost Africa has played a notable role in the meeting of Europe and its "others" since Europe first caught the whiff of potential wealth and power that could come from trade and expansion beyond its own continent. The strategically placed Cape of Good Hope, midway between Europe and the East, became a focus for rivalry between the Dutch and English. The first White settlement was Dutch, and was intended as a halfway post for the Dutch East India Company to provide fresh food and water for sailors en route to the East. During the Napoleonic wars, the English challenged Dutch ownership of the territory, and the Cape changed hands a few times before the English finally established their supremacy.

The Afrikaner people (descendants of Dutch settlers, intermarried with settlers from other parts of Europe) strove throughout their history to be independent of Europe and, in particular, the English. They made a strong claim to their right to occupy the land they had chosen as their home, naming themselves and their language (Afrikaans) after the continent, Africa. The English-speaking White group, on the other hand, retained much stronger political, economic, cultural, and intellectual ties with the Metropolitan areas of Euro-America. South Africa was a consequential piece in the British imperial scheme of things—the South African Embassy in London has pride of place on Trafalgar Square, a measure of the significance attached to this colony until South Africa became a republic in 1961.

This White history, long told as *the* story of the country in South African schools, was superimposed upon, and irrevocably changed the course of, the much older history of the indigenous peoples. Along the Cape coastal region, Stone Age peoples—the Khoikhoi and the San (known in colonial discourse as Hottentots and Bushmen)—had lived as hunters, stockbreeders, and food-gatherers for a vast number of centuries (Davidson, 1995). Iron Age people, later to be called the Bantu, had been living further inland since A.D. 300 (Davidson). They were cattle-farmers and agriculturists, and had a high degree of social organization. At the time of early European settlement, they were in the process of nation-building (Unterhalter, 1995) and possessed iron-tipped spears with which they could defend themselves.

The arrival and subsequent migration inland of Europeans set up conflicting interests, and contested realities, that are actually still unresolved today. The New South Africa, heralded by the first democratic elections in April 1994 and the inauguration of Nelson Mandela as president, still deals with the legacy of conflict established in the initial scenario sketched above. The New Constitution is the latest attempt to find a workable dispensation that will provide for the coexistence of all the groups who regard South Africa as home. The Bill of Rights to which the constitution and laws of the country are accountable enshrines the human dignity, equality, and freedom of all South Africans. In this, the New South Africa represents a dramatic revision of the dynamics established in early colonization, dynamics that were entrenched through 300 years of White supremacist rule, and found their apotheosis when institutionalized as the infamous policy of apartheid.

Although the historical events that led to the specific nature of intercultural relations within South Africa are unique to the circumstances within the country, they bear a family resemblance to events and relationships established in other places into which Europeans expanded their empires. This broader history has to be seen against the background of European attitudes toward the countries they colonized, and how they viewed Europe and its role in global relations and history. This article explores some aspects of how Europe framed its African enterprise in terms of a social identity that the European imagination linked to skin color. The article gives some account of the counternarratives that the indigenous people constructed in opposition to the European view, then it briefly looks at some of the consequences of these constructions for present intercultural communication in the New South Africa. A short article such as this cannot map the complexities of intercultural perceptions throughout the history of South Africa. Inevitably, it contains oversimplifications. Nevertheless, as Nederveen Pieterse (1995) notes, "The economic, political and legal aspects of apartheid have repeatedly been discussed, but studies of the 'culture of apartheid' and of the South African popular culture in which the discourse of apartheid was shaped, imagined and transmitted are rare" (p. 102). This article is an offering toward that end.

Europe's Story About Europe

Long before colonialism, Europe had an image of itself as the center of the world. During the medieval period, this centrality was related to faith in the role Christendom was to play in the redemption of the world. By the 16th century this ethnocentric self-image had come to include the notion of Europe as the global nexus of commerce. From there it was a short step to viewing itself as deserving of owning the world, literally and figuratively. A view of history was constructed in which Europe was conceived of as the "inside," or center, and the rest of the world as the "outside," or periphery. As a result of the unique intellectual or spiritual qualities inherent in Europeans, "progress" would diffuse to the rest of the globe from this center (Blaut, 1993). This scheme takes as its fundamental premise the inequality of human beings; the "inner processes" of Europe are believed to be superior to the less rational, less innovative, and less creative inner processes of the periphery. It follows, therefore, that the normal and logical way for the rest of the world to change for the better is through the flow of people, ideas, and products from Europe outward. In (always inadequate) compensation for the gift of civilization that Europe brings, it would receive material wealth from the lands it influences culturally (Blaut, 1993, p. 16).

All non-Europe was conceived of as stagnant, noninnovative, backward. Some of the territories in non-Europe (such as China) were constructed as having had some rationality and culture at certain stages of their history, which they had lost as a consequence of lacking the European "essence" that alone could sustain progress. Although some earlier classical and medieval conceptions of Africa had been favorable, by the time of colonization Africa was seen as always having been irredeemably lacking in anything remotely akin to the European essence. It was the limit case of the "other"—irrational, prehistoric, the "dark" continent.

Europe's Stories About Africa

In constructing their view of Africa, Europeans drew on discourses that had been around in Europe for centuries. They gave these discourses a new "spin" to provide justification for imperialism. Three examples of these discourses are discussed below.

The Savage

The notion of the "savage" had previously been associated with the regions of Europe that were the last to be cultivated. In the European imagination, these areas were inhabited by "beings who were on the border-line between human and animal, myth and reality, like the *Homo ferus* who was raised by wolves, and the *Homo sylvestris*, or man of the woods" (Nederveen Pieterse, 1995, p. 30). The savage was the "human minus culture." Once Europe started widening its mental landscape, the notion of the savage was applied to those who

lived outside of Europe. The African savage was regarded as the most "cultureless," and demonstrated the least potential for upliftment. Africans were part of nature, wild inhabitants of dense African jungles, incapable of cultural creativity or historical agency. Whatever social sophistication Europeans found in Africa had to be explained away. As Mudimbe (1988) puts it:

> Since Africans could produce nothing of value, the technique of Yoruba statuary must have come from the Egyptians; Benin art must be a Portuguese creation; the architecture of Zimbabwe was due to Arab technicians; and Hausa and Bugunda statecraft were inventions of white invaders. (p. 13)

Brantlinger (1985) points out that viewing Africans as "unimprovable" necessitated that they would permanently need "civilized" masters. The construction also furnished the "central fantasy of imperialism" (p. 181), namely that there existed a "natural" laboring class, which would remain in a servile relationship to its entrepreneurial European masters indefinitely.

The southern African territory that the settlers occupied was thus perceived to be devoid of any people who had any significance in themselves with whom a European could relate equally. The Dutch were outraged at the unwillingness of the Khoisan people to enter into a servile relationship and imported slaves to compensate for the "inadequacy" of the indigenous people. One of the major reasons for the migration of Afrikaners into the interior, known as the Great Trek, was the decision of the then British authorities to free the slaves owned by the farmers.

Although the indigenous African people were never chattel slaves as in the American South, they were subjected to systems of unfree labor practice throughout South Africa's history. The notion that a good government would protect the interests of White capital through restrictive labor legislation remained one of the central assumptions of Afrikaner society through generations, and was entrenched in apartheid laws (Fredrickson, 1981). So, too, the belief that Black people were naturally suited to menial labor found expression in a separate education system introduced by the chief engineer of the apartheid system, Dr. Hendrik Verwoerd. The curricula were quite specifically designed to comply with the "nature and requirements of the black people" (Coetzer, 1992) and did not include, for example, mathematics.

Science

A second source of justification for the relative position of Europe to the rest of the world was found in the discourses of science, elevated by Enlightenment faith in rationality and reason. Science provided "proof" of the naturalness, the necessity of the European diffusional model outlined above. The classificatory scheme known as the chain of being, which categorized the universe and then placed the categories in hierarchical order from the lowest to the highest, had been present in European thought since Aristotle. It laid out the "natural order of things." The science of race enabled Western scientists to give this notion new clothes, especially in the guise of the Late Victorian notion of social evolution. Using the methodologies of science—measurement, "objective" description, theory construction—a human hierarchy could be fixed as biologically determined. All the branches of science involved in researching race managed to reach the same conclusion: the superiority of the Caucasian race (especially the male of the species).

Yet again, the place that Africa occupied in the European imagination is demonstrated by the niche allocated to Africans in this scientific hierarchy. The positioning of Africans, particularly the Pygmies and the Hottentots, in the undefined space between human and animal, the "missing link," clearly provided a useful moral ambiguity. Africans could be classified out of the genus *Homo* and established as a separate species, fundamentally different, and thus naturalized into an irrevocably inferior position. Brantlinger (1985) sums it up:

> Evolutionary thought seems almost calculated to legitimize imperialism. The theory that man

evolved through distinct stages—from barbarism to civilization—led to a self-congratulatory anthropology that actively promoted the belief in the inferiority—indeed the bestiality—of the African. (p. 184)

The Cape was the first outpost of anthropology in Africa. Descriptions of the Khoi and San "form the basis of the early European ethnography" (Nederveen Pieterse, 1995, p. 102). The influence of this science is evident in the following description by an anthropologist of 1851:

> A row of seven dirty, squalid, natives came to meet us. . . . They had Hottentot features, but were of a darker colour, and a most ill-looking appearance; some had trousers, some coats of skin, and they clicked, and howled, and chattered, and behaved like baboons. (Quoted in Nederveen Pieterse, 1995, p. 103)

Lord Milner, the British High Commissioner in South Africa at the turn of the century, evidenced the same belief in Social Darwinism:

> The white man must rule, because he is elevated by many, many steps above the black man; steps which it will take the latter centuries to climb, and which it is quite possible that the vast bulk of the population may never be able to climb at all. (Quoted in Fredrickson, 1981, p. 195)

The role such discourses played in shaping and justifying the culture of apartheid, where blacks were not regarded as "developed" enough to have equal rights, is only too evident.

Christian Narratives

A third discourse that was recycled in the service of colonialism was provided by Christian narratives. It was seen as appropriate that a different set of moral imperatives should pertain to saved souls as opposed to heathens. Nederveen Pieterse (1995) puts it succinctly: "The view of Africa as a continent condemned to eternal servitude was eminently suited to a theological assessment of slavery. Its attractiveness was that the unity of creation remained intact while an exceptional position was yet justified for Africans" (p. 44). Not only was the colonial servitude of Africans thus sanctioned, but the colonizers could retain their sense of moral rectitude. In fact, they accumulated what JanMohamed (1985) has referred to as "surplus morality." All evil and undesirable qualities could be projected onto those who were oppressed, leaving the colonizer "pure."

Religion played a major role in creating the popular culture in which apartheid thinking could come to be supported by the majority of the White populace. The Afrikaner people were staunch Calvinists, believing that as a chosen people in a promised land, they were entitled to subjugate the heathen tribes they encountered. This was not a proselytizing version of Protestantism; the early settlers preferred to leave the heathens in their heathendom and thus maintain the "proper" relationship between the groups (Fredrickson, 1981). The often quoted words of an Afrikaner woman explaining why they chose to migrate inland after the British decision to emancipate the slaves reveals these attitudes:

> It is not so much their freedom which drove us to such lengths as their being placed on an equal footing with Christians, contrary to the laws of God, and the natural distinction of race and colour, so that it was intolerable for any decent Christian to bow down beneath such a yoke, wherefore we rather withdrew in order thus to preserve our doctrines in purity.
> (Quoted in De Villiers, 1987, p. 101)

The Colonial Imagination

Relations between the Europeans who came to settle in South Africa and the indigenous Africans were shaped from the start not only by Europe's technological advantage but also by its psychological needs. What Europeans saw and experienced as they moved inland and interacted with Africans had as much to do with the manner in which their imaginations had been shaped by discourses, such as those previously discussed, as with what they actually encountered in the country. The meeting between the cultures was given a particular intensity in that Africa had been con-

structed as the most extreme opposite of Europe. A mental pattern of opposites was set up in which Europeans occupied one side of a set of binaries, and Africans the other. Undoubtedly the single most important marker on which the binary oppositions were pinned was appearance, particularly skin color. "Whiteness" guaranteed the other exemplary qualities listed beneath it, just as "Blackness" entailed the whole list beneath it. Here are some of the typical binaries:

Europeans	Africans
White	Black
Christian	heathen
honest	untrustworthy
civilized	savage
intelligent, rational	emotional, instinctual
inventive	imitative
cultured	natural
adult	childlike
scientific	superstitious
progressing, modern	stagnating, primeval
ordered, restrained	anarchical, spontaneous
knowledgeable, conscious	ignorant, unconscious
predictable, certain	mysterious, undependable
loyal to duty	self-gratifying

This psychological map emphasizes the role that the unconscious played in the narrative that European settlers constructed of their mission in Africa. The drive to power, personal inflation, fear, desires, sexual fantasy—all played their part in developing the story. Such unconscious material probably always features in relationships between cultures, particularly where they have become established as enemies or compete for resources. The unequal power between the South African Whites and the indigenous people, however, provided the circumstances where the European settlers did not have these stereotypes challenged in equal, intersubjective relationships. They did not have to humanize the images they had of Africans, or take African perceptions, feelings, and beliefs seriously and thus be changed by them. The consequence has been that many of these powerful collective preconceptions were able to continue through generations, particularly once apartheid enforced separation.

In its extreme racism South Africa was typical of all the colonial countries in southern Africa—Rhodesia, Mozambique, Angola, and Kenya. Perhaps in part because White people in South Africa never attained the numerical majority Europeans achieved in other settler societies such as the United States, Canada, New Zealand, and Australia, South African Whites held on to the ideology of Whiteness more fanatically than settler colonies on other continents.[1] The demographic fact of a numerical White minority greatly influenced intercultural relations within the country. In order to retain the position of supremacy they felt entitled to, Whites resorted to harsh measures, yet they could never achieve the security experienced where White immigration had been more vigorous and where the indigenous populations were greatly reduced. The fear of Black revenge, the fear of majority takeover, and the fear of annihilation have always worked beneath the surface of White material comfort.

Talking Back: Counterstories

The Native African cultures were oral cultures. The absence of written records from an African perspective, coupled with the fact that the settlers controlled the symbolic resources of the country, meant that Whites could largely determine what accounts would be preserved for posterity in highly biased historical records. Nevertheless, there can be little doubt about the broad contours of how the involuntary intercultural experience was constructed by the local inhabitants. Their "remembered history,"[2] a construction of life before colonization, has been important to African resistance discourse, as this quotation from Nelson Mandela's speech at the Rivonia trial of 1962 illustrates:

> The structure and organization of early African societies in this country fascinated me very

much and greatly influenced the evolution of my political outlook. . . . There were no classes, no rich or poor and no exploitation of man by man . . . in such a society are contained the seeds of revolutionary democracy in which none will be held in slavery or servitude, and in which poverty, want and insecurity shall be no more. (Mandela, 1994, p. 391)

The contrast between this construction of a harmonious, prosperous past prior to European settlement contrasts starkly with both the European construction of savage precolonial Africa discussed above, and also, sadly, with the poverty that Africa now deals with as a legacy of its colonial past and a reality of its neocolonial present.

As early as 1655, the local people informed the Dutch East India Company's commander at the Cape that they regarded the occupied territory as their own land, but their claim was summarily dismissed. The hatred the local people felt for the invaders who deprived them of their livelihood and drove them to poverty was evidenced in numerous acts of resistance—"Bushmen wars," the murder of "collaborators," nocturnal raiding attacks and destruction of settler livestock, absconding from service with horses and guns—the list goes on. In time many of the Hottentots were "tamed" into colonial employ, but as Newton-King (1992) points out, the master-servant relationship became the site of daily struggle, albeit in subtle ways:

> Every trivial conflict over the performance of daily chores raised echoes of the more fundamental conflict over mastery of the land and its people. The master-servant relationship became a battleground upon which the terms of white dominance were at stake. (p. 111)

The typical South African dynamic in which indigenous people were servants, and thus caretakers of settler property and lifestyle, yet also perpetually under suspicion of being enemies, was established early in the country's history. This is also true of the tendency of indigenous people to live up to the self-fulfilling prophecies mobilized by the projections of Whites: The colonized worked without energy or commitment, thus supporting the notion that they were lazy and untrustworthy; many came to rely on plunder for their subsistence, "proving" the preconception that they were thieves.

Given the inversions of reality with which colonial discourse operated, a fair indication of the indigenous people's descriptions of European settlement can probably be inferred from what the settlers said about the local people. The colonial stereotype of the Bantu people as warlike aggressors engaged in mutual intertribal bloodlust (thus necessitating "civilized" government) is a case in point. As Davidson (1995) observes:

> There is little or no reason to believe the later white-racist stereotype of "tribal massacre" among pre-colonial African clans. What we know of their ideas of justice, usually preferring punishment by compensation to any other sanction, and of the emphasis they placed on the conservation of manpower, always in short supply, suggests customs of warfare among these peoples that could have had no tolerance of mass killing. . . . Yet the wars of dispossession and their consequences changed all that. Blood-stained years followed as the constant pressure of advancing white settlement thrust one community against another in a kind of "shunting process" which, by copious evidence, became ever more destructive. . . . (p. 270)

In other words, the logic of blaming the victim provided alibis for Whites to "exculpate the principal culprit, namely, violent white dispossession of African land and labour" (p. 273).

Davidson's analysis indicates the point made by postcolonial writers, namely, the interconnectedness of the psyches of the colonizers and colonized. According to Unterhalter (1995), the process of African nation-building that was underway before White migration did not include the notion of "race." She maintains that the "incursion of settler and colonial forces against African kingdoms forced them to formulate a racially inscribed notion of their attackers as 'the European'" (p. 211), and thus they came to think of themselves as Black. A major aspect of this racialization was the process of internalizing the valuation that came with being Black, believing themselves to be "less than" the Whites (Sonn, 1996), who could main-

tain this impression through superior education and unequal access to resources.

A tactic of colonial rule was to exaggerate "ethnic" differences of the dominated population, "while simultaneously officially downplaying similar diversities among the settler population" (Unterhalter, 1995, p. 214). This was the familiar "divide and rule" policy. Africans were governed in terms of these divisions, eventually institutionalized in the "homelands" policy of apartheid. Although identifying with this divided ethnic identity did not further African resistance, the ascription of a Black race proved capable of appropriation for the purposes of resistance. Again Unterhalter sums it up:

> Partly as a defence against this forced subordination, the population classified as non-white mobilized politically and ideologically in organizations that simultaneously both opposed segregation under imposed racial categories and entrenched a racial identity. . . . The notion of "black" delineated a common experience of oppression and became widely used in a broad range of opposition movements. With this meaning it gained a particular ideological force for opposition organizations. . . . (pp. 225, 232)

The Legacy Today

The intertwining of imagined, imposed, and self-ascribed identities described in this article attests to the difficulty of sorting out the legacy of colonialism now that the African majority rules the country. Although African nation-building once again has come to the fore, there can be no retrieval of a pure and innocent African past, nor can White South Africans be de-Europeanized. Moreover, not all sections of these societies have been equally affected by the 300 years of coexistence. Many Africans do not even speak a European language. As Nederveen Pieterse and Parekh (1995) argue, colonialism introduced "one new idiom, one new strand, in the complex mosaic of the societies subjected to it" (p. 2). They continue:

> Decolonization cannot consist in discarding what is deemed to be alien. Colonialism evolved

a new consciousness out of a subtle mixture of the old and new; decolonization has to follow the same route. It requires not the restoration of a historically continuous and allegedly pure precolonial heritage, but an imaginative creation of a new form of consciousness and way of life. (p. 3)

It is this creative process that the New South Africa is undertaking. Given the long and complex history of domination, the new consciousness is not likely to evolve immediately or simply. South Africa is not anomalous in attempting this task of realigning the relationship between the people of European descent and the descendants of those whose lives and livelihoods were irrevocably changed by their encounter with European expansion. It is part of the broader postcolonial process of reassessment of the role Europe and European systems of knowledge have played in world history since the period of the Enlightenment, a reassessment that accompanies a shift in global power dynamics.

When the elections of April 1994, which ended apartheid and the era of official racism, passed peacefully despite all expectations to the contrary, South Africa was in a state of euphoria. Since then, dealing with the inheritance of systemic inequalities has been at the forefront of the national agenda. But deep-seated differences in interpretation of these inequalities—narratives that have been told, recycled, resisted, or silenced for three centuries and that both created, maintained, and subverted the inequalities also need to be addressed. The minds of both Black and White South Africans need to be decolonized. Renegotiating social identities in the New South Africa is one of the most profound collective psychological experiences occurring in the contemporary world, and the adjustment of intercultural relationships within the country is a dramatic test of the human capacity to change social reality. The delicate balance of dealing with past injustices honestly and yet maintaining faith in each other is challenging indeed.

There is currently a tendency in the country to blame the system of apartheid per se for what went wrong in the society. This enables a great deal of face-saving, as private citizens can main-

tain a measure of innocence. The Truth and Reconciliation Commission provides a mechanism that allows those who were in key positions in the military or police, for example, to be identified as the culprits, exceptions to the ordinary citizens who bore no part in the system. Moreover, apartheid can be ascribed to a temporary aberration from "normal" Western values.[3] Instead, this article has argued, along with others (see Derrida, 1985), that apartheid was a logical, if extreme and anachronistic, manifestation of belief systems that were part of the popular mental landscape inherited from Europe.

Although psychological mechanisms such as blaming apartheid may be useful in the short term for facilitating a *modus vivendi* through the early transition process, a far more deep-moving transformation is needed. Many White South Africans still harbor the lack of faith in Africa and Africans bequeathed by the colonial frame of reference. Just as the failure of the old "homelands" policy was ascribed by apartheid proponents to the inherent inability of Blacks to govern a country, so many Whites attribute the inevitable difficulties of transition to the New South Africa—a coded reference to Black mismanagement—rather than to the real causes that lie in psychological and socioeconomic circumstances established over centuries. This type of thinking largely motivates the emigration of Whites to countries that are more supportive of White identity. It also places Whites who remain in the country in an ambivalent relationship to a successful new dispensation. For the sake of their future, Whites need safety and prosperity, yet many are not predisposed to expect it, or to recognize and acknowledge successes that do occur. This does not contribute to a constructive environment. White status is still high through association with the greater internationalism of Western culture, seen to be the key to economic competitiveness. (Though obviously such internalized colonialism is contested by more Africanist thinkers.)

The transfer of power, however, means that Whites can no longer unilaterally define issues or maintain unchallenged constructions. Politically, they no longer own the country, its people, and its resources—the logical order of colonialism has been reversed.[4] Although some manage to redeploy old psychological strategies to render themselves impervious to new insights, the blinkers caused by colonial racist thinking are challenged in the new order. Issues become visible to Whites for the first time as resources are allocated to address needs previously given the lowest priority, and a more realistic sense of what has to be accomplished develops.

The initial postelection honeymoon is over. Old fears have not disappeared in the face of disturbing trends such as rocketing crime rates. I suspect that this crime bears some family resemblance to the raiding of the early White settlements—looting taken in compensation for a deep-seated sense of injustice done. Despite the many difficulties, though, a great deal of energy in the country is directed at societal reconstruction. One of the factors that gives intercultural relations within South Africa their particular intensity is that South Africans are aware that the stakes are very high. The survival of the country depends on the successful interdependence of the different cultures and their ability to overcome the negative aspects of their heritage while drawing on their many strengths. The stage is set for much greater syncretism in the future, and shifts toward a more synergistic, inclusive South Africanism are encouraging. Whether this possibility will win out over the tendency for the cultures to polarize will depend largely on how South Africans reframe the narratives that have shaped their society.

For some of us the excitement of witnessing an extraordinary era of cultural and historical redefinition has not dissipated. In my own family, the grandchild of a White ex-cabinet minister in the apartheid government is dating the son of a previously exiled "colored" member of the African National Congress, now a member of Parliament. The young couple feels accepted in both homes. Even two years ago that could have qualified as the definition of the impossible. In these times of change and uncertainty in South Africa, we are encouraged by such micromiracles.

NOTES

1. Although Fredrickson (1981) maintains that the United States and South Africa share the unflat-

tering distinction that they "have manifested over long periods of time a tendency to push the principle of differentiation by race to its logical outcome—a kind of *Herrenvolk* society in which people of color, however numerous or acculturated they may be, are treated as permanent aliens or outsiders" (pp. xi–xii).

2. Davidson (1995) writes about this remembered history: "These [Iron Age] communities evolved their own ideologies of self-acceptance and worked out their own patterns and customs of mutual tolerance. In this southern land of beaming climate, good and often virgin soil for crops and cattle, and abundant extra protein in the form of game both big and small, they evidently prospered; and this prosperity is what their remembered history, in so far as very distant years are ever remembered, certainly combines to suggest" (p. 265).

3. Of course, the mechanism also allows for face-saving on the part of the greater Western community, which has been able to construct White South Africans as "others," and thereby not acknowledge commonalities.

4. At a literal level, by far the greatest part of the country is owned by Whites, particularly farmers. This unresolved issue is likely to be the site where contesting narratives will be played out for a long time to come.

REFERENCES

Blaut, J. M. (1993). *The colonizer's model of the world: Geographical diffusionism and Eurocentric history.* New York: The Guilford Press.

Brantlinger, P. (1985). Victorians and Africans: The genealogy of the myth of the dark continent. *Critical Inquiry, 12,* 166–203.

Coetzer, P. W. (1992). The era of apartheid, 1948–1961. In T. Cameron & S. B. Spies (Eds.), *A new illustrated history of South Africa.* Johannesburg: Southern Book Publishers and Human and Rousseau.

Davidson, B. (1995). *Africa in history: Themes and outlines.* Revised and expanded edition. New York: Touchstone.

Derrida, J. (1985). Racism's last word. *Critical Inquiry, 12,* 290–299.

De Villiers, M. (1987). *White tribe dreaming: Apartheid's bitter roots as witnessed by eight genera-

tions of an Afrikaner family. New York: Penguin.

Fredrickson, G. M. (1981). *White supremacy: A comparative study of American and South African history.* New York: Oxford University Press.

JanMohamed, A. R. (1985). The economy of Manichean allegory: The function of racial difference in colonialist literature. *Critical Inquiry, 12,* 59–97.

Mandela, N. (1994). *Long walk to freedom.* London: Abacus.

Mudimbe, Y. Y. (1988). *The invention of Africa: Gnosis, philosophy, and the order of knowledge.* Bloomington: Indiana University Press.

Nederveen Pieterse, J. (1995). *White on black: Images of Africa and blacks in Western popular culture.* New Haven: Yale University Press.

Nederveen Pieterse, J., & Parekh, B. (1995). *The decolonization of the imagination: Culture, knowledge and power.* London: Zed Books.

Newton-King, S. (1992). Khoisan resistance to colonial expansion, 1700–1828. In T. Cameron & S. B. Spies (Eds.), *A new illustrated history of South Africa.* Johannesburg: Southern Book Publishers and Human and Rousseau.

Sonn, J. (1996). Rewriting the "White-is-right" model: Towards an inclusive society. In M. E. Steyn & K. B. Motshabi (Eds.), *Cultural synergy in South Africa: Weaving strands of Africa and Europe.* Randburg: Knowledge Resources.

Unterhalter, E. (1995). Constructing race, class and gender: State and opposition strategies in South Africa. In D. Stasiulis & N. Yuval-Davis (Eds.), *Unsettling settler societies: Articulations of gender, race, ethnicity and class.* London: Sage.

KEY WORDS

apartheid	discourse
binaries	narratives
blaming the victim	"others"
chain of being	postcolonialism
colonialism	social evolution
decolonization	Whiteness
demographics	

DISCUSSION QUESTIONS

1. This article stresses the role the unconscious plays in intercultural relations (desires, fears, the drive to power, feelings of inferiority and superiority). Can you think of ways in which such unconscious factors influence intercultural communication between Americans and groups with which they have dealings, such as the Japanese, for example? What would you say is the value of becoming conscious of the extent to which our imaginations play a part in intercultural interactions? Can you suggest ways in which we can counter this tendency?

2. Steyn maintains that there are "family resemblances" between the dynamics established in the relations between Europeans and Africans at the time of European expansion, and relations between European settlers and indigenous people elsewhere. What similarities or differences or both can you see between what she describes and the relations between White Americans and their "others"? Think particularly of how the discourses of the savage, of science, and of Christianity have been played out on the North American continent.

3. According to Steyn, intercultural relations in South Africa have been greatly influenced by the demographic fact of Whites being numerically in the minority. Would you like to speculate on how intercultural relations in the United States might have been different if Whites had remained a small settler society? Do you think the current shift in demographics in the United States is affecting intercultural relations? How? Why?

4. Many of the stereotypes with which Europeans arrived at the Cape at the time of early colonization have been "recycled" in the face of changing circumstances in South Africa, rather than disappearing completely. Can you suggest why stereotypes can be so hardy? Can you think of stereotypes that have been or are being recycled within the United States?

5. An implication of the discussion in this article is that binary thinking in intercultural communication is very dangerous. Think of a group with whom you have intercultural contact, and try to identify binaries that tend to operate in relations with this group. Can you see a relationship between the way the binaries are set up and the relative power of the groups?

12
STRANGER IN THE VILLAGE

JAMES BALDWIN

From all available evidence no black man had ever set foot in this tiny Swiss village before I came. I was told before arriving that I would probably be a "sight" for the village; I took this to mean that people of my complexion were rarely seen in Switzerland, and also that city people are always something of a "sight" outside of the city. It did not occur to me—possibly because I am an American—that there could be people anywhere who had never seen a Negro.

It is a fact that cannot be explained on the basis of the inaccessibility of the village. The village is very high, but it is only four hours from Milan and three hours from Lausanne. It is true that it is virtually unknown. Few people making plans for a holiday would elect to come here. On the other hand, the villagers are able, presumably, to come and go as they please—which they do: to another town at the foot of the mountain, with a population of approximately five thousand, the nearest place to see a movie or go to the bank. In the village there is no movie house, no bank, no library, no theater; very few radios, one jeep, one station wagon; and, at the moment, one typewriter, mine, an invention which the woman next door to me here had never seen. There are about six hundred people living here, all Catholic—I conclude this from the fact that the Catholic church is open all year round, whereas the Protestant chapel, set off on a hill a little removed from the village, is open only in the summertime when the tourists arrive. There are four or five hotels, all closed now, and four or five *bistros*, of which, however, only two do any business during the winter. These two do not do a great deal, for life in the village seems to end around nine or ten o'clock. There are a few stores, butcher, taker, *épicerie*, a hardware store, and a money-changer—who cannot change travelers' checks, but must send them down to the bank, an operation which takes two or three days. There is

something called the *Ballet Haus*, closed in the winter and used for God knows what, certainly not ballet, during the summer. There seems to be only one schoolhouse in the village, and this for the quite young children; I suppose this to mean that their older brothers and sisters at some point descend from these mountains in order to complete their education—possibly, again, to the town just below. The landscape is absolutely forbidding, mountains towering on all four sides, ice and snow as far as the eye can reach. In this white wilderness, men and women and children move all day, carrying washing, wood, buckets of milk or water, sometimes skiing on Sunday afternoons. All week long boys and young men are to be seen shoveling snow off the rooftops, or dragging wood down from the forest in sleds.

The village's only real attraction, which explains the tourist season, is the hot spring water. A disquietingly high proportion of these tourists are cripples, or semicripples, who come year after year—from other parts of Switzerland, usually—to take the waters. This lends the village, at the height of the season, a rather terrifying air of sanctity, as though it were a lesser Lourdes. There is often something beautiful, there is always something awful, in the spectacle of a person who has lost one of his faculties, a faculty he never questioned until it was gone, and who struggles to recover it. Yet people remain people, on crutches or indeed on deathbeds; and wherever I passed, the first summer I was here, among the native villagers or among the lame, a wind passed with me—of astonishment, curiosity, amusement, and outrage. That first summer I stayed two weeks and never intended to return. But I did return in the winter, to work; the village offers, obviously, no distractions whatever and has the further advantage of being extremely cheap. Now it is winter again, a year later, and I am here again.

Everyone in the village knows my name, though they scarcely ever use it, knows that I come from America—though, this, apparently, they will never really believe: black men come from Africa—and everyone knows that I am the friend of the son of a woman who was born here, and that I am staying in their chalet. But I remain as much a stranger today as I was the first day I arrived, and the children shout *Neger! Neger!* as I walk along the streets.

It must be admitted that in the beginning I was far too shocked to have any real reaction. In so far as I reacted at all, I reacted by trying to be pleasant—it being a great part of the American Negro's education (long before he goes to school) that he must make people "like" him. This smile-and-the-world-smiles-with-you routine worked about as well in this situation as it had in the situation for which it was designed, which is to say that it did not work at all. No one, after all, can be liked whose human weight and complexity cannot be, or has not been, admitted. My smile was simply another unheard-of phenomenon which allowed them to see my teeth—they did not, really, see my smile and I began to think that, should I take to snarling, no one would notice any difference. All of the physical characteristics of the Negro which had caused me, in America, a very different and almost forgotten pain were nothing less than miraculous—or infernal—in the eyes of the village people. Some thought my hair was the color of tar, that it had the texture of wire, or the texture of cotton. It was jocularly suggested that I might let it all grow long and make myself a winter coat. If I sat in the sun for more than five minutes some daring creature was certain to come along and gingerly put his fingers on my hair, as though he were afraid of an electric shock, or put his hand on my hand, astonished that the color did not rub off. In all of this, in which it must be conceded there was the charm of genuine wonder and in which there was certainly no element of intentional unkindness, there was yet no suggestion that I was human: I was simply a living wonder.

I knew that they did not mean to be unkind, and I know it now; it is necessary, nevertheless, for me to repeat this to myself each time that I walk out of the chalet. The children who shout *Neger!* have no way of knowing the echoes this sound raises in me. They are brimming with good humor and the more daring swell with pride when I stop to speak with them. Just the same, there are days when I cannot pause and smile, when I have no heart to play with them; when, indeed, I mutter sourly to myself, exactly as I muttered on the streets of a city these children have never seen, when I was no bigger than these children are now: *Your* mother *was a nigger.* Joyce is right about history being a nightmare—but it may be the nightmare from which no one *can* awaken. People are trapped in history and history is trapped in them.

There is a custom in the village—I am told it is repeated in many villages—of "buying" African natives for the purpose of converting them to Christianity. There stands in the church all year round a small box with a slot for money, decorated with a black figurine, and into this box the villagers drop their francs. During the *carnaval* which precedes Lent, two village children have their faces blackened—out of which bloodless darkness their blue eyes shine like ice—and fantastic horsehair wigs are placed on their blond heads; thus disguised, they solicit among the villagers for money for the missionaries in Africa. Between the box in the church and the blackened children, the village "bought" last year six or eight African natives. This was reported to me with pride by the wife of one of the *bistro* owners and I was careful to express astonishment and pleasure at the solicitude shown by the village for the souls of black folk. The *bistro* owner's wife beamed with a pleasure far more genuine than my own and seemed to feel that I might now breathe more easily concerning the souls of at least six of my kinsmen.

I tried not to think of these so lately baptized kinsmen, of the price paid for them, or the peculiar price they themselves would pay, and said nothing about my father, who having taken his own conversion too literally never, at bottom, forgave the white world (which he described as heathen) for having saddled him with a Christ in whom, to judge at least from their treatment of him, they themselves no longer believed. I thought of white men arriving for the first time in an African village, strangers there, as I am a stranger here, and tried to imagine the astounded populace touching their hair and marveling at the color of their skin. But there is a great difference between being the first white man to be seen by Africans and being the first black man to be seen by whites. The white man takes the astonishment as tribute, for he arrives to conquer and to convert the natives, whose inferiority in relation to himself is not even to be questioned; whereas I, without a thought of conquest, find myself among a people whose culture controls me, has even, in a sense, created me, people who have cost me more in anguish and rage than they will ever know, who yet do not even know of my existence. The astonishment with which I might have greeted them, should they have stumbled into my African village a few hundred years ago, might have rejoiced their hearts. But the astonishment with which they greet me today can only poison mine.

And this is so despite everything I may do to feel differently, despite my friendly conversations with the *bistro* owner's wife, despite their three-year-old son who has at last become my friend, despite the *saluts* and *bonsoirs* which I exchange with people as I walk, despite the fact that I know that no individual can be taken to task for what history is doing, or has done. I say that the culture of these people controls me—but they can scarcely be held responsible for European culture. America comes out of Europe, but these people have never seen America, nor have most of them seen more of Europe than the hamlet at the foot of their mountain. Yet they move with an authority which I shall never have; and they regard me, quite rightly, not only as a stranger in their village but as a suspect late-comer, bearing no credentials, to everything they have—however unconsciously—inherited.

For this village, even were it incomparably more remote and incredibly more primitive, is the West, the West onto which I have been so strangely grafted. These people cannot be, from the point of view of power, strangers anywhere in the world; they have made the modern world, in effect, even if they do not know it. The most

illiterate among them is related, in a way that I am not, to Dante, Shakespeare, Michelangelo, Aeschylus, Da Vinci, Rembrandt, and Racine; the cathedral at Chartres says something to them which it cannot say to me, as indeed would New York's Empire State Building, should anyone here ever see it. Out of their hymns and dances come Beethoven and Bach. Go back a few centuries and they are in their full glory—but I am in Africa, watching the conquerors arrive.

The rage of the disesteemed is personally fruitless, but it is also absolutely inevitable; this rage, so generally discounted, so little understood even among the people whose daily bread it is, is one of the things that makes history. Rage can only with difficulty, and never entirely, be brought under the domination of the intelligence and is therefore not susceptible to any arguments whatever. This is a fact which ordinary representatives of the *Herrenvolk*, having never felt this rage and being unable to imagine it, quite fail to understand. Also, rage cannot be hidden, it can only be dissembled. This dissembling deludes the thoughtless, and strengthens rage and adds, to rage, contempt. There are, no doubt, as many ways of coping with the resulting complex of tensions as there are black men in the world, but no black man can hope ever to be entirely liberated from this internal warfare—rage, dissembling, and contempt having inevitably accompanied his first realization of the power of white men. What is crucial here is that, since white men represent in the black man's world so heavy a weight, white men have for black men a reality which is far from being reciprocal; and hence all black men have toward all white men an attitude which is designed, really, either to rob the white man of the jewel of his naïveté, or else to make it cost him dear.

The black man insists, by whatever means he finds at his disposal, that the white man cease to regard him as an exotic rarity and recognize him as a human being. This is a very charged and difficult moment, for there is a great deal of will power involved in the white man's naïveté. Most people are not naturally reflective any more than they are naturally malicious, and the white man prefers to keep the black man at a certain human remove because it is easier for him thus to preserve his simplicity and avoid being called to account for crimes committed by his forefathers, or his neighbors. He is inescapably aware, nevertheless, that he is in a better position in the world than black men are, nor can he quite put to death the suspicion that he is hated by black men therefore. He does not wish to be hated, neither does he wish to change places, and at this point in his uneasiness he can scarcely avoid having recourse to those legends which white men have created about black men, the most usual effect of which is that the white man finds himself enmeshed, so to speak, in his own language which describes hell, as well as the attributes which lead one to hell, as being as black as night.

Every legend, moreover, contains its residuum of truth, and the root function of language is to control the universe by describing it. It is of quite considerable significance that black men remain, in the imagination, and in overwhelming numbers in fact, beyond the disciplines of salvation; and this despite the fact that the West has been "buying" African natives for centuries. There is, I should hazard, an instantaneous necessity to be divorced from this so visibly unsaved stranger, in whose heart, moreover, one cannot guess what dreams of vengeance are being nourished; and, at the same time, there are few things on earth more attractive than the idea of the unspeakable liberty which is allowed the unredeemed. When, beneath the black mask, a human being begins to make himself felt one cannot escape a certain awful wonder as to what kind of human being it is. What one's imagination makes of other people is dictated, of course, by the laws of one's own personality and it is one of the ironies of black-white relations that, by means of what the white man imagines the black man to be, the black man is enabled to know who the white man is.

I have said, for example, that I am as much a stranger in this village today as I was the first summer I arrived, but this is not quite true. The villagers wonder less about the texture of my hair than they did then, and wonder rather more about me. And the fact that their wonder now exists on another level is reflected in their attitudes and in their eyes. There are the children who make those delightful, hilarious, sometimes astonishingly grave overtures of friendship in the unpredictable fashion of children; other children, having been taught that the devil is a black man, scream in genuine anguish as I approach. Some of the older women never pass without a friendly greeting, never pass, indeed, if it seems that they will be able to engage me in conversation; other women look down or look away or rather contemptuously smirk. Some of the men drink with me and suggest that I learn how to ski—partly, I gather, because they cannot imagine what I would look like on skis—and want to know if I am married, and ask questions about my *métier*. But some of the men have accused *le sale nègre*—behind my back—of stealing wood and there is already in the eyes of some of them that peculiar, intent, paranoiac malevolence which one sometimes surprises in the eyes of American white men when, out walking with their Sunday girl, they see a Negro male approach.

There is a dreadful abyss between the streets of this village and the streets of the city in which I was born, between the children who shout *Neger!* today and those who shouted *Nigger!* yesterday—the abyss is experience, the American experience. The syllable hurled behind me today expresses, above all, wonder: I am a stranger here. But I am not a stranger in America and the same syllable riding on the American air expresses the war my presence has occasioned in the American soul.

For this village brings home to me this fact: that there was a day, and not really a very distant day, when Americans were scarcely Americans at all but discontented Europeans, facing a great unconquered continent and strolling, say, into a marketplace and seeing black men for the first time. The shock this spectacle afforded is suggested, surely, by the promptness with which they decided that these black men were not really men but cattle. It is true that the necessity on the part of the settlers of the New World of reconciling their moral assumptions with the fact—and the necessity—of slavery enhanced immensely the charm of this idea, and it is also true that this idea expresses, with a truly American bluntness, the attitude which to varying extents all masters have had toward all slaves.

But between all former slaves and slave-owners and the drama which begins for Americans over three hundred years ago at Jamestown, there are at least two differences to be observed. The American Negro slave could not suppose, for one thing, as slaves in past epochs had supposed and often done, that he would ever be able to wrest the power from his master's hands. This was a supposition which the modern era, which was to bring about such vast changes in the aims and dimensions of power, put to death; it only begins, in unprecedented fashion, and with dreadful implications, to be resurrected today. But even had this supposition persisted with undiminished force, the American Negro slave could not have used it to lend his condition dignity, for the reason that this supposition rests on another: that the slave in exile yet remains related to his past, has some means—if only in memory—of revering and sustaining the forms of his former life, is able, in short, to maintain his identity.

This was not the case with the American Negro slave. He is unique among the black men of the world in that his past was taken from him, almost literally, at one blow. One wonders what on earth the first slave found to say to the first dark child he bore. I am told that there are Haitians able to trace their ancestry back to African kings, but any American Negro wishing to go back so far will find his journey through time abruptly arrested by the signature on the bill of sale which served as the entrance paper for his ancestor. At the time—to say nothing of the circumstances—of the enslavement of the captive black man who was to become the American Negro, there was not the remotest possibility that he would ever take power from his master's hands. There was no reason to suppose that his situation would ever change, nor was there, shortly, anything to indicate that his situation had ever been different. It was his necessity, in the words of E. Franklin Frazier, to find a "motive for living under American culture or die." The identity of the American Negro comes out of this extreme situation, and the evolution of this identity was a source of the most intolerable anxiety in the minds and the lives of his masters.

For the history of the American Negro is unique also in this: that the question of his humanity, and of his rights therefore as a human being, became a burning one for several generations of Americans, so burning a question that it ultimately became one of those used to divide the nation. It is out of this argument that the venom of the epithet *Nigger!* is derived. It is an argument which Europe has never had, and hence Europe quite sincerely fails to understand how or why the argument arose in the first place, why its effects are so frequently disastrous and always so unpredictable, why it refuses until today to be entirely settled. Europe's black possessions remained—and do remain—in Europe's colonies, at which remove they represented no threat whatever to European identity. If they posed any problem at all for the European conscience, it was a problem which remained comfortingly abstract: in effect, the black man, *as a man*, did not exist for Europe. But in America, even as a slave, he was an inescapable part of the general social fabric and no American could escape having an attitude toward him. Americans attempt until today to make an abstraction of the Negro, but the very nature of these abstractions reveals the tremendous effects the presence of the Negro has had on the American character.

When one considers the history of the Negro in America it is of the greatest importance to recognize that the moral beliefs of a person, or a people, are never really as tenuous as life—which is not moral—very often causes them to appear; these create for them a frame of reference and a necessary hope, the hope being that when life has done its worst they will be enabled to rise above themselves and to triumph over life. Life would scarcely be bearable if this hope did not exist. Again, even when the worst has been said, to betray a belief is not by any means to have put oneself beyond its power; the betrayal of a belief is not the same thing as ceasing to believe. If this were not so there would be no moral standards in the world at all. Yet one must also recognize that morality is based on ideas and that all ideas are dangerous—dangerous because ideas can only lead to action and where the action leads no man can say. And dangerous in this respect: that confronted with the impossibility of remaining faithful to one's beliefs, and the equal impossibility of becoming free of them, one can be driven to the most inhuman excesses. The ideas on which American beliefs are based are not, though Americans often seem to think so, ideas which originated in America. They came out of Europe. And the establishment of democracy on the American continent was scarcely as radical a break with the past as was the necessity, which Americans faced, of broadening this concept to include black men.

This was, literally, a hard necessity. It was impossible, for one thing, for Americans to abandon their beliefs, not only because these beliefs alone seemed able to justify the sacrifices they had endured and the blood that they had spilled, but also because these beliefs afforded them their only bulwark against a moral chaos as absolute as the physical chaos of the continent it was their destiny to conquer. But in the situation in which Americans found themselves, these beliefs threatened an idea which, whether or not one likes to think so, is the very warp and woof of the heritage of the West, the idea of white supremacy.

Americans have made themselves notorious by the shrillness and the brutality with which they have insisted on this idea, but they did not invent it; and it has escaped the world's notice that those very excesses of which Americans have been guilty imply a certain, unprecedented uneasiness over the idea's life and power, if not, indeed, the idea's validity. The idea of white supremacy rests simply on the fact that white men are the creators of civilization (the present civilization, which is the only one that matters; all previous civilizations are simply "contributions" to our own) and are therefore civilization's guardians and defenders. Thus it was impossible for Americans to accept the black man as one of themselves, for to do so was to jeopardize their status as white men. But not so to accept him was to deny his human reality, his human weight and complexity, and the strain of denying the overwhelmingly undeniable forced Americans into rationalizations so fantastic that they approached the pathological.

At the root of the American Negro problem is the necessity of the American white man to find a way of living with the Negro in order to be able to live with himself. And the history of this problem can be reduced to the means used by Americans—lynch law and law, segregation and legal acceptance, terrorization and concession—either to come to terms with this necessity, or to find a way around it, or (most usually) to find a way of doing both these things at once. The resulting spectacle, at once foolish and dreadful, led someone to make the quite accurate observation that "the Negro-in-America is a form of insanity which overtakes white men."

In this long battle, a battle by no means finished, the unforeseeable effects of which will be felt by many future generations, the white man's motive was the protection of his identity; the black man was motivated by the need to establish an identity. And despite the terrorization which the Negro in America endured and endures sporadically until today, despite the cruel and totally inescapable ambivalence of his status in his country, the battle for his identity has long ago been won. He is not a visitor to the West, but a citizen there, an American; as American as the Americans who despise him, the Americans who fear him, the Americans who love him—the Americans who became less than themselves, or rose to be greater than themselves by virtue of the fact that the challenge he represented was inescapable. He is perhaps the only black man in the world whose relationship to white men is more terrible, more subtle, and more meaningful than the relationship of bitter possessed to uncertain possessor. His survival depended, and his development depends, on his ability to turn his peculiar status in the Western world to his own advantage and, it may be, to the very great advantage of that world. It remains for him to fashion out of his experience that which will give him sustenance, and a voice.

The cathedral at Chartres, I have said, says something to the people of this village which it cannot say to me; but it is important to understand that this cathedral says something to me which it cannot say to them. Perhaps they are struck by the power of the spires, the glory of the windows; but they have known God, after all, longer than I have known him, and in a different way, and I am terrified by the slippery bottomless well to be found in the crypt, down which heretics were hurled to death, and by the obscene, inescapable gargoyles jutting out of the stone and seeming to say that God and the devil can never be divorced. I doubt that the villagers think of the devil when they face a cathedral because they have never been identified with the devil. But I must accept the status which myth, if nothing else, gives me in the West before I can hope to change the myth.

Yet, if the American Negro has arrived at his identity by virtue of the absoluteness of his estrangement from his past, American white men still nourish the illusion that there is some means of recovering the European innocence, of returning to a state in which black men do not exist. This is one of the greatest errors Americans can make. The identity they fought so hard to protect has, by virtue of that battle, undergone a change: Americans are as unlike any other white people in the world as it is possible to be. I do not think, for example, that it is too much to suggest that the American vision of the world—which allows so little reality, generally speaking, for any of the darker forces in human life, which tends until today to paint moral issues in glaring black and white—owes a great deal to the battle waged by Americans to maintain between themselves and black men a human separation which could not be bridged. It is only now beginning to be borne in on us—very faintly, it must be admitted, very slowly, and very much against our will—that this vision of the world is dangerously inaccurate, and perfectly useless. For it protects our moral high-mindedness at the terrible expense of weakening our grasp of reality. People who shut their eyes to reality simply invite their own destruction, and anyone who insists on remaining in a state of innocence long after that innocence is dead turns himself into a monster.

The time has come to realize that the interracial drama acted out on the American continent has not only created a new black man, it has created a new white man, too. No road whatever will lead Americans back to the simplicity of this European village where white men still have the luxury of looking on me as a stranger. I am not, really, a stranger any longer for any American alive. One of the things that distinguishes Americans from other people is that no other people has ever been so deeply involved in the lives of black men, and vice versa. This fact faced, with all its implications, it can be seen that the history of the American Negro problem is not merely shameful, it is also something of an achievement. For even

when the worst has been said, it must also be added that the perpetual challenge posed by this problem was always, somehow, perpetually met. It is precisely this black-white experience which may prove of indispensable value to us in the world we face today. This world is white no longer, and it will never be white again.

KEY TERMS

Africa	rage
America/American	slavery/slaves
Black/negro	stranger
Europe	West, the
history	White (man, people)
identity	

DISCUSSION QUESTIONS

1. What exactly does Baldwin mean by the phrase "Stranger in the Village"? Have you ever experienced that feeling of strangeness? When? Where?

2. In much intercultural literature, there is talk that as a world, we are moving toward a "global village." What does Baldwin's essay tell us about our progress toward that global village?

3. As Baldwin recounts his experiences of strangeness, he notes that the people in the village did not mean to be unkind. Even when the children shouted *Neger!*," and when people suggested he let his hair grow long and make it into a coat. And yet, as he tells the story, he is also clear about the fact that he did feel pain, in spite of the intentions of the villagers. This question of the role of intentionality persists in intercultural communication. How can we reconcile misunderstandings across cultures that are not intentional? Or, do we need to?

4. According to Baldwin, how has U.S. history shaped Blackness and Black identity? What does Baldwin's essay tell us about the influence of history on today's daily experiences?

5. How are Baldwin's experiences of his identity as an African American man in the United States different from his experiences as a Black man in the Swiss village? How do the different historical experiences in Switzerland and the United States affect his different sense of himself and his different experiences of being Black?

13
CROSSING AN IRISH BORDER

FREDERICK C. COREY

In 1967 I was confirmed under the name of Joseph. This name was not my choice. We were at a Holy Confirmation rehearsal, in a combined class of fourth- and fifth-grade boys, and my brother Bob and I were in line. Sister Mary Stevens announced that today we would practice with our names. I raised my hand, and when called upon, I said, "Sister, I have not yet selected my Holy Confirmation name." "Well, blow me down said Popeye," Sister bellowed. "How many of you have not yet selected a name?" A slew of us raised our hands, and Sister was aghast. She swung her arm and marched down the aisle, pointing to each of us in succession, "John. Joseph. John. Joseph," until she reached the end. My brother Bob became John. The names lacked distinction. My oldest brother's name is John Joseph. He was confirmed during the era of the Singing Nun, and he selected Dominique.

Joseph. I never intended to be Joseph, just as I never intended to work "in the field." I was trained as a literary critic. I can scan a poem with the best of them, excavate a metaphor, and trace a symbol to its rhizome. I took an interest in fieldwork when, on my first sabbatical, I decided to conduct an ethnographic study of gay men in Irish pubs (Corey, 1996). I am still intrigued by the metaphor of "fieldwork": the comparison between research and the earth, between a cultural space and a pasture suitable for tillage. The metaphor appears to have its roots in farming. The researcher enters the field to see how things grow, develop, endure a life cycle. The metaphor has its limits, though, for fieldwork does not always embody the simplicity, serenity, or charm so often associated with pastoral life. Joseph, quite by chance, was no farmer. He was a carpenter. He built things.

Many contemporary writers are fieldworkers and carpenters. Although they do visit the pastures and watch things grow, they also labor in the shop, building things. They till, cultivate, and fertilize. They carve, sand, level, curve, and design

little bureau drawers in which to hide ideas, such as old rings from ex-lovers. Contemporary writers herd sheep, build doors, turn the soil, and get splinters. Are the metaphors yet exhausted? Contemporary writers—the postmodern crew—are strong like the fieldworker, clever like the carpenter. They can make things fit like the carpenter and make things bloom like the fieldworker. But wait: The postmodernist is also the cartographer, the person who maps the terrain, excavates the topography of discourse, and traces the landscape of cultural identity. A fieldworker, a carpenter, and a cartographer. The postmodern writer is a busy person.

This is an essay about Irish America, cultural identity, illegal immigration, and sexual difference. This is where we are going. How we are going to get there is quite another matter. I have a story to tell, but I want to place this story in the context of communication theory. The problem is, no one theory seems to be a good fit; so I will borrow several theoretical concepts, put them together, and build a place for my story. Here, I am like a carpenter.

The idea of building a theoretical framework to analyze a communication event is not new. In his book *Democracy in an Age of Colonization*, Deetz (1992) advocates an integrative analytical approach in communication studies (p. 66). Integrating theoretical constructs gives the communication scholar an opportunity to "reveal a stream with many forces that provide many new channels to cut, cross, and bridge" (p. 6). In the same spirit, Allport (1979) argues that critical questions may not be answered with one theoretical approach, that there "is no master key. Rather, what we have is a ring of keys, each of which opens one gate of understanding" (p. 208). Some people, some very wise people, might well disagree with the principle of integrating theoretical concepts, and some might say that the concepts I am about to mix do not mix well.

For better or worse, I do not know, but in this essay I have blended principles of social constructionism, personal narrative, autoethnography, literary criticism, cartography, and fieldwork. From Eve Kosofsky Sedgwick (1985, 1990) I borrow ideas on how to engage in a subversive reading of desire as it is constructed in literary discourse. In his famous analyses of the history of sexuality, Michel Foucault (1976/1978, 1984/1985) argues well for the contextualization of desire, and a series of writers (e.g., Greenberg, 1988; Halperin, 1995; Stein, 1990) followed with cogent discussions of sexuality as a social construction. Although I acknowledge the debates over the social constructionism (see, for example, Mohr, 1992) and believe in a biological foundation of sexuality, I lean toward the belief that sexuality-as-cultural-practice is constructed through social discourse. My interests in the construction of sexuality, literary discourse, and questions of identity have led me toward autoethnography (Crawford, 1996), or the (re)placement of myself in the cultural texts I analyze. Autoethnography is a blending of the autobiography and the study of a people; in this case, I blend my own story with the literary and cultural texts of Irish in America. Crawford (1996) writes: "Autoethnography orchestrates fragments of awareness—apprehended/projected and recalled/reconstructed—into narratives and alternative text forms which (re)present events and other social actors as they are evoked from a changeable and contestable self" (p. 167). Such evocations may be more suited to an entire book, certainly, but in this essay I scan address some central themes of silence and speech, sexuality, and immigration. Finally, I turn to Deleuze and Guattari (1991/1994), Browning (1996), and Bell and Valentine (1995), from whom I borrow principles of territorialization, geography, and the mapping of discourse. In short, I pledge my allegiance not to a flag that symbolizes a traditional theoretical perspective, but to the winds that destabilize that flag.

"We are not Irish," my mother would say, "we are American. Now, go do your homework." St. Patrick's Day was never a celebration at our house. The day would come and go with barely a notice. No hats, no green beer, no sing-alongs. Not until I spent a sabbatical in Ireland did I see just how Irish I was in habit and attitude. There was the food, of course, the beef stews, roasted chickens, simple salads, and the habit of heating dinner plates in the oven before serving. But there were also the quirks of everyday life: spending an inordinate amount of energy decorating the most unattractive corner in the backyard, attending to the front door of the house no matter how wretched the rest of the house appeared, treating the local library or bookstore like a community center, and telling stories that weave from point to point without ever having any point at all.

On a lark, I spent a week in a tiny town called Dingle, in County Kerry, on the western shores of Ireland. I took to riding my bike out to Slea Head, a breathtaking jolt of earth set against the Atlantic Ocean. One day I watched the blue sky disappear within seconds, and suddenly the fog was so thick I could not find my bicycle. I was unnerved as I groped through the thickness of the beach. When at last I found my bike, I started to make my way across what I thought was the road. I stumbled upon a shepherd, an old man with a dog at his side, and I asked him which way was the town. "What you need is a pint," he said. "You won't make it to the town you won't." I tried anyway. Lost, not knowing which way was anywhere, I found myself in Dunquin. In the distance, I saw the silhouette of a large building and at my feet a small sign saying THE GREAT BLASKET CENTER. I made my way to the building.

The fog was beginning to roll away, but I decided to stay in the museum until I could see clearly the way back to Dingle. I would learn about the Blasket Islands, some remote chunks of land deserted by their final 21 residents in 1953 (Mac Conghail, 1987; Thomson, 1988). Some photographs on a gallery wall caught my eye. I walked directly to the photographs and studied the two men, looking dashing and sporty, and then a photograph of one of the men, alone, with a wispy look on his face, and a caption stating the photo was of Maurice O'Sullivan, taken by his "good friend, George Thomson." This photograph captivated me at numerous levels. The photograph looked for all the world like a photograph in my parents' scrapbooks, and although all photographs from the 1920s look similar, this one was particularly familiar. The guy looked like a relative, with the same cheeks, same jaw, same pose, same attitude. I would never know who he looked like. He may have looked like a Gratton, one of my mother's uncles, maybe Joseph, who was born around 1878, or Henry, who worked for an electric company and was electrocuted, or Howard, who simply "had no progeny." Howard. All I know of Howard is that he left no progeny. The men in the photographs looked like boyfriends is what they looked like. I know boyfriends when I see them.

The next day I went to the local library and read about "the boyfriends" for hours. Maurice O'Sullivan was a writer, and he is best known for his autobiography, *Twenty Years a-Growing*. My gay radar, or gaydar, as we say, went off when I saw the introduction by E. M. Forrester, and as I read the book, I discovered yet another Irish custom, an indirection of discourse that simultaneously spoke eloquently of the truth yet never named the unmentionable. The two men loved each other. When O'Sullivan met Thomson in 1923, O'Sullivan was tending sheep. The sun, he writes, "was yellowing in the west and a lark singing above. Indeed, little bird, you have me beguiled, said I to myself. Just then the earth shook beneath me" (O'Sullivan, 1933, p. 220). The two men became the closest of friends, spending all of their time together, but they were faced with a dilemma: O'Sullivan had plans for America, but Thomson was English, a scholar with a career in Britain. Eventually, Thomson persuaded O'Sullivan to move to Dublin to join the police force. When O'Sullivan was admitted to the Civic Guard, Thomson said, "you have made your white coat" (p. 283), an Irish phrase that is said to a woman when she finds a husband, meaning "you are settled for life."

I proceed with caution as I venture into the discursive territory of the relationship between O'Sullivan and Thomson. I make no claims that the two men were lovers in the way two men might be lovers today. In her discussions of love between men, the literary critic Eve Kosofsky Sedgwick (1990) writes about homosexuality in the English novel:

> "Modern sexuality" and hence modern homosexuality are so intimately entangled with the historically distinctive contexts and structures that now count as *knowledge* that such "knowledge" can scarcely be a transparent window

onto a separate realm of sexuality but, rather, itself constitutes that sexuality. (p. 44)

I do not take what I know today and assume that O'Sullivan knew what I know, or that he viewed sexuality in a way similar to the way I view sexuality. Rather, I engage in a dissident reading of the text (Sinfield, 1994) and forsake the assumption that the two men are heterosexual. I read the novel looking for signs of the (in)visible homosexual-heterosexual binary, of the unspeakable border dispute. Irish culture constitutes the backdrop for my interpretation.

The scenes in *Twenty Years a-Growing* are tender and affectionate, but never explicitly sexual. We never enter the bedroom. When O'Sullivan arrives in Dublin, Thomson meets him at the train station. They go to Thomson's flat. They close the bedroom door at 4:00 in the morning, and, one sentence later, open the door at 11:00 with "the two of us awake, talking and conversing" (p. 273). *You can take me to the bedroom door*, my mother would say of sex in movies and novels, *but you don't need to take me inside the bedroom. Just leave the door closed.* How to map the discourse of the unspoken? Irish law would have prevented any discussion of same-sex desire. Part One Section Two of the Censorship of Publications Act forbade literary discussions of "sexual immorality or unnatural vice," and as John Broderick, an Irish writer born in 1927, observes, "the Irish are pathological about homosexuality. . . . it was one of the things that was absolutely unspeakable and which they would never admit to" (quoted in Carlson, 1990, p. 46).

Once a year, in cities such as Boston and New York, gay men and lesbians do battle with the Ancient Order of Hibernians to be included in the St. Patrick's Day parade. Gay men and lesbians want to march under a banner that identifies their sexuality, and the Ancient Order of Hibernians refuses, usually with the argument that it is not possible to be Irish *and* gay or lesbian. The parade organizers, who are named well, express genuine bafflement. They do not understand how someone could be Irish *and* gay or lesbian, and the basis of their argument has far less to do with the pope than some might imagine. The pope merely serves as "expert testimony." The essence of the problem is that same-sex desire in ancient Hibernia—the literary word for Ireland—did not exist as discourse. Queer desires were unspeakable. Contemporary Ireland now boasts some of the most liberal laws in all of Europe (Rose, 1994), and Irish gays and lesbians are mapping new terrains of sexual discourse (Dublin Lesbian and Gay Men's Collectives, 1986; Finnegan, 1994; O'Carroll & Collins, 1995; Pettitt, 1996). But the Ancient Order of Hibernians are not contemporary. They are a preservation of historical discourse. Their journey from Ireland to America constitutes a transportation of epoch.

While in Cork, I took a day trip to the port city, Cobh, and tried to imagine what it must have been like when my ancestors left Ireland. I had never given the emigration much thought, and certainly the topic was never discussed when I was a child. The details are sketchy at best: They left during the famines, probably around 1850, and landed in what was then British North America and is now Canada. They probably landed in Gross Ile and one by one made their way through the provinces to northern Michigan and Wisconsin. The path is vague. Discourse has obscured the map. The names I know: Corey, Sullivan, Nichol, Gratton. My great-grandmother, Josephine Sophia Ramesbotham, was born in Chatham, New Brunswick, in 1854, and she met my great-grandfather, Patrick Scott Gratton, a farmer, through her occupation. She taught English. When they moved to the United States is a mystery. There are no records of the move because *all of the records were destroyed in a terrible church fire.* My mother does not know for certain if her mother, Flora Gratton, was born in the United States. "She was very proud of being American," my mother tells me, "and resented any questions at school about her children's nationality. We were instructed to answer always that we were American. When the Irish hoopla would start around St. Patrick's Day, she would say, 'I wonder if Ireland is so great why we are all here?'" When I raised my eyebrows over this rather incredulous story, my mother assured me that not once has the possibility of illegal immigration ever been raised, and I was being overly suspicious. Two weeks later, my mother told me that over lunch she asked Bishop Harrington what he thought, and he said that there were a lot of church fires,

Faith, a lot of church fires. Wink. The luck of the Irish.

My father's family, by contrast, is completely American, and to suggest otherwise is an affront to the family name. My great-grandfather fought in the Civil War, for goodness sake, and received from President Lincoln a plot of land in Chelsea, Michigan. Nana had relatives in Belfast, and my father's father had a drinking problem, so we never talked about him. That my father was born in Canada was a matter of chance, nothing more, and when we crossed the border between Detroit and Windsor for a day trip or a vacation, we were to sit in the back of the station wagon and not say a word. Not one word. "All American citizens," my father would say. Once, the border guard asked about the place of birth. "The United States," my father said. This was the only time I have known my father to lie outright.

A border is deceptive. How is it possible to lie through deception? My father was an American soldier in World War II. Why should he have to explain his birth to the border patrol? He is of the Irishmen who "defined themselves not only as Americans but as Americans of a superpatriotic kind" (Shannon, 1963, p. 132). Would not a discussion of birthplace excavate an unnecessary historical discourse of the Irish and their border instabilities? The onset of "Wisconsin Fever" and "Michigan Fever" brought the laborers from New Brunswick to the United States, often by way of Maine (Fitzgerald & King, 1990). The Irish, then, who were British subjects, crossed the Atlantic, landed in Canada, migrated to the United States, reentered Canada, and found their way back to the United States. Borders were for crossing, and perhaps my father, like the United States census takers of the 19th century, considered a person Irish only if that person were *born* in Ireland. Information about the descendants of the Irish, particularly those with ties to Canada, is unreliable at best, and more accurately lost (Fitzgerald & King, 1990; McDonald, 1954/1976).

"Borders are," writes Batten (1996) of the poetry of Paul Muldoon, "troublesome in Ireland" (p. 175). There is the border between Northern Ireland and The Republic, between English and Irish law, between the colonizer and the colonized. There are the borders between Catholic

and Celtic traditions, the patriarchy and matri-
archy, censorship and the Irish devotion to literature. The Irish poet has a way with words, yet has
been silenced. Batten writes,

> At the borders of the linguistically competent
> self, the self colonized by the Law, metaphors
> cross easily from self to world, and vice versa,
> precisely because no checkpoints are required
> along a border that appears to guarantee a pri-
> vate self and a public world. (pp. 174–175)

What of the border between heterosexuality
and homosexuality? In the time of Maurice O'Sullivan, no Irish word for homosexual existed. The
Irish words for same-sex desire—*homaighneasach* for men and *Leispiach* for women—were
not established until the 1970s, and the etymolo-
gies of these words are based not in the Irish language but in the Greek, suggesting that not only
the words but their ideas are imports. There were
English words, such as buggery or inversion, but
no Irish words. How could Maurice O'Sullivan
have been *homaighneasach*? The word did not exist. Thomson, like a character out of an English
novel, outgrew his affection for O'Sullivan. He returned to England, took a wife, established a career and a name as a scholar (Enright, 1988).
How very English. As for O'Sullivan, he too took a
wife, but his career as a police officer never took
off, never became his "white coat." He tried to
write a second book but failed.

O'Sullivan did not commit suicide. He
drowned in the placid waters off Salthill, a holiday
beach just north of Galway.

In their discussion of what they call "geophilosophy," Deleuze and Guattari (1991/1994) write
that "thinking takes place in the relationship of
territory and the earth" (p. 85). We may well never
know the geophilosophy of sexuality on the Blasket Islands, and we will never know what O'Sullivan was thinking as he drowned in the waters off
Salthill. I shall never know what my father was
thinking when he told the border police he was
born in the United States, but now, as an adult, I
have the tools to interpret relationships between
what people say and where people are, between
beings and borders. The line between the United
States and Canada is a river, the Detroit River, and

it is a friendly, albeit murky, crossing. The Detroit
River is a fluid moment in the history of national identity. The border is a "plane of imma-
nence" (Deleuze & Guattari, 1991/1994, pp. 35–
60), which is not entirely unlike the border between silence and speech. I have 5 siblings, 36 first
cousins, and the good Lord only knows how many
relations on the historical plateau of the earth. I
am the only homo. Or, more aptly put, I am the
only one to cross the hetero-homo border and
claim a queer identity. I am going to say something, but I do not want to be quoted out of context, and I do not want to be conveniently misunderstood: I was born heterosexual. On the map of
my Irish Catholic history, all roads were built of
the discourse of heterosexuality. I turned off that
road and followed a road I knew to be a truer,
more honest road. I crossed a border. I spoke the
words, "I am gay." Are there now or have there
ever been any gays or lesbians in my family? I
have my suspects, but such suspicions constitute dangerous territories. I shall say nothing of
Jessica, who was born in 1927. Jessica did not
want to be a girl, says my mother, because men
had more career options. Jessica had a Ph.D. in
biology and was a research scientist. Jessica never
married. I shall say nothing of the photographs of
men who send my gaydar into high alert, and I
shall say not a word, not one word, about the
priests. Let us say simply this: If there were any
gay men or lesbians, *all of the records were destroyed in a terrible church fire.*

When I deterritorialize my own map, I am
able to view the history of my terrain as "the set of
conditions, however recent they may be, from
which one turns away in order to become, that is
to say, in order to create something new" (Deleuze
& Guattari, 1991/1994, p. 96). Throughout this essay, I have explored "borders" as the conditions
from which I turn as I move through questions of
identity. These borders are deceiving and deceit-
ful. The border between gay and straight is a
discursive territory, disturbed by language and
culture, silence and speech, censorship and literature. The border between Irish and American is
also a discursive territory, disturbed by fact and
fiction, memory and history, truth and the essence of truth. The line between gay and straight,
like the line between Irish and American, is not

an absolute, but rather an ongoing construction. The line is shifted, altered, shaved, and nurtured. My ancestors created "something new," an American identity, by blurring the lines of immigration.

I, too, create "something new" when I interface the autobiography with ethnography. When I tell my own story and place that story against the portrait of a people, I bring history to the moment and ground my identity. I accomplish this construction of a "newness" through "various stories of vicarious truths" (Crawford, 1996, p. 168), and a modest attempt to map the discourse of the unspoken. Maurice O'Sullivan could not have written about a sexual desire for his "good friend." In Irish culture, such a desire would have been unspeakable. My ancestors could not have talked openly of illegal immigration, for this, too, would have been unspeakable. What, then, to make of my scandalous discourse? I offer the possibility of O'Sullivan as a queer. I offer a possibility of illegal immigration. I depolice the border of the silence surrounding sexual desire in Irish culture, and I interrogate the crossing of the Canadian-American border by my ancestors. I build a place for discourse, for talk of possibilities, disturbing as such discourse is to an Irish pattern of denial. My awareness is evoked from this changeable and contestable self, within a changeable and contestable culture.

We can learn not to deny our own sexual desires, and we can learn how to venture into the silences—the unspoken terrains—of the cultures from which we come. When we tell our stories against the cultural backdrops that nourish those stories, we transcend self-indulgence and contribute to a rewrite of the governing, cultural narrative (Corey, in press). That is, the personal narrative interrupts social discourse. My claims of desire disturb discursive assumptions of heterosexuality, and through the personal narrative, the body of the self, which has been colonized by cultural law, is policed not by a border patrol, but by the capacities of language. A story, then, is rooted in cultural norms, but through language, a storyteller is able to construct a form of identity, reshape memory, sand a rough moment, curve a straight line, or build a bureau of clandestine drawers in which to hide things, things such as a place of birth, a line of flight, an undeveloped thought, or the pleasure of a name.

REFERENCES

Allport, G. W. (1979). *The nature of prejudice* (Rev. ed.). Reading, MA: Addison-Wesley.

Batten, G. (1996). "He could barely tell one from the other": The borderline disorders of Paul Muldoon's poetry. *South Atlantic Quarterly, 95,* 171–204.

Bell, D. & Valentine, G. (Eds.). (1995). *Mapping desire: Geographies of sexualities.* New York: Routledge.

Browning, F. (1996). *A queer geography: Journeys toward a sexual self.* New York: Crown.

Carlson, J. (1990). *Banned in Ireland: Censorship and the Irish writer.* London: Routledge.

Corey, F. C. (1996). Performing sexualities in an Irish pub. *Text and Performance Quarterly, 16,* 146–160.

Corey, F. C. (In press). The personal: Against the master narrative. In S. J. Dailey (Ed.), *The future of performance studies: The next millennium.* Annandale, VA: Speech Communication Association.

Crawford, L. (1996). Personal ethnography. *Communication Monographs, 63,* 158–170.

Deetz, S. (1992). *Democracy in an age of colonization.* Albany: SUNY Press.

Deleuze, G., & Guattari, F. (1994). *What is philosophy?* (H. Tomlinson & G. Burchell, Trans.). New York: Columbia University Press. (Original work published 1991).

Dublin Lesbian and Gay Men's Collectives. (Eds.). (1986). *Out for ourselves: The lives of Irish lesbians and gay men.* Dublin: Womens Community Press.

Enright, T. (1988). George Thomson: A memoir. In G. Thomson, *Island home: The Blasket heritage* (pp. 117–150). Wolfeboro, NH: Brandon.

Finnegan, B. (Ed.). (1994). *Quare fellas: New Irish gay writing.* Dublin: Basement Press.

Fitzgerald, M. E., & King, J. A. (1990). *The uncounted Irish in Canada and the United States.* Toronto: Meany.

Foucault, M. (1978). *The history of sexuality. Volume I: An introduction* (R. Hurley, Trans.). New York: Random House. (Original work published 1976)

Foucault, M. (1985). *The history of sexuality. Volume II: The use of pleasure* (R. Hurley, Trans.). New York: Random House. (Original work published 1984)

Greenberg, D. F. (1988). *The construction of homosexuality.* Chicago: University of Chicago Press.

Halperin, D. M. (1995). *Saint Foucault: Towards a gay hagiography.* Oxford: Oxford University Press.

Mac Conghail, M. (1987). *The Blaskets: A Kerry island library.* Dublin: Country House.

McDonald, G. (1976). *History of the Irish in Wisconsin in the nineteenth century.* New York: Arno. (Reprint of doctoral dissertation, Catholic University of America, published by the Catholic University of America Press, Washington, DC, 1954)

Mohr, R. D. (1992). *Gay ideas: Outing and other controversies.* Boston: Beacon.

O'Carroll, I., & Collins, E. (Eds.). (1995). *Lesbian and gay visions of Ireland: Towards the twenty-first century.* London: Cassell.

O'Sullivan, M. (1933). *Twenty years a-growing* (M. L. Davies & G. Thomson, Trans.). New York: Viking.

Pettitt, L. (1996). G(ay)uinness is good for you. *South Atlantic Quarterly, 95,* 205–212.

Rose, K. (1994). *Diverse communities: The evolution of lesbian and gay politics in Ireland.* Cork, Ireland: Cork University Press.

Sedgwick, E. K. (1985). *Between men: English literature and male homosexual desire.* New York: Columbia University Press.

Sedgwick, E. K. (1990). *Epistemology of the closet.* Berkeley: University of California Press.

Shannon, W. V. (1963). *The American Irish.* New York: Macmillan.

Sinfield, A. (1994). *Cultural politics—queer reading.* Philadelphia: University of Pennsylvania Press.

Stein, E. (Ed.). (1990). *Forms of desire: Sexual orientation and the social constructionist controversy.* New York: Garland.

Thomson, G. (1988). *Island home: The Blasket heritage.* Wolfeboro, NH: Brandon.

KEY TERMS

gay	personal narrative
sexuality	mapping
Irish	immigration
fieldwork	social constructionism
autoethnography	

DISCUSSION QUESTIONS

1. In what way is "coming out of the closet" similar to "crossing a border"?
2. What are some of the relationships between language and identity? Is it possible for a person to be homosexual if no word exists to describe such a love?
3. The author claims that when we tell our stories against the cultural backdrops that nourish these stories, we transcend self-indulgence and contribute to a rewrite of the governing, cultural narrative. Do you agree or disagree?
4. If being homosexual is not part of Irish tradition, should lesbians and gay men be allowed to participate in the traditional St. Patrick's Day parade?
5. What are some of the borders you have crossed?

14

MIGRATION ACROSS GENERATIONS: WHOSE IDENTITY IS AUTHENTIC?

KATHLEEN WONG(LAU)

In many movies and popular novels by Asian Americans, particularly Chinese Americans Amy Tan and Maxine Hong Kingston, Chinese Americans are portrayed as struggling with issues of identity that stretch across generations and centuries of traditional Chinese thought and values

(Kingston, 1976; Tan, 1989). The younger generation is seen to struggle with the conflicting conservative immigrant traditional values of Chinese Confucianism and the individualistic values of U.S. Americanism. Though these fictional models may be informative about some American-born Chinese, they are indicative of a shrinking proportion of Chinese Americans. The 1990 U.S. census reports 37% of Asian Americans were native-born Americans, compared to 92% of the general population. For Chinese Americans the number of native-born Americans is only 30.7% (Min, 1995). The characters of these popular novels may give some insight about the experiences of American-born children of Chinese immigrants who immigrated from the 19th century through the 1960s. These immigrants came mostly from rural areas of southern China through the port of Hong Kong at a time when rural Chinese culture was imbued with Confucian values, especially in regard to family structures (Sodowsky, Kwan, & Pannu, 1995). The cultures of these countries have been preserved in the minds and subsequent practices of immigrants, seemingly frozen at the time of immigration (Anderson, 1983).

This phenomenon of preserving ethnic cultural practices has been common among all immigrants throughout the migrant history of the United States (Anderson, 1983; Ignatiev, 1995). One still finds Italian American neighborhoods in Boston and Polish American neighborhoods in Chicago (Takaki, 1993). Immigrants preserve their identities and cultural practices in an effort to survive in a hostile society where dominant cultural values often conflict with traditional values and economic opportunities are scarce. Immigrants often pool economic resources and experiential knowledge, help one another find employment, learn to negotiate bureaucracy, learn English, find familiar foods, and celebrate familiar holidays. Immigrants also learn to avoid becoming victims of unscrupulous employers, landlords, and others who may take advantage of new arrivals (Wei, 1993). Many Asian American communities have created these immigrant communities as primary landing places for new immigrants, who ultimately move to Asian American suburbs or predominantly White suburbs once social and economic security are attained (Fong,

1994). Often immigrant communities in the United States have preserved practices over generations that are rarely even practiced by their cohorts in the home country, as these countries have continued to modernize since the time of an individual's immigration and absence.

Thus we have the incongruous phenomenon of Greek American cultural experts going back to Greece to play traditional Greek songs, perform traditional Greek dances, and cook traditional Greek dishes during festivals designed for U.S. Americans. Many of these cultural practices may be unfamiliar to their Greek hosts except in stories passed down from grandparents. The following quote is from a recent Greek immigrant who teaches Greek folk dance and music in the United States to Greek Americans:

> Greeks in Greece are currently interested in disco and fashions from Milan. There is a new form of music called urban music, which is like traditional Greek music and disco. I think Greek Americans whose ancestors immigrated to America generations ago are usually quite shocked when they get there. (personal interview with anonymous participant; July 1994)

The experience of my parents returning to Hong Kong in 1980 for the first time in 20 years after their immigration to the United States illustrates a similar clash of conceptions of "Chinese" culture across the recent history of their own lives. The cosmopolitan capitalistic Hong Kong they encountered upon their arrival shocked and saddened them. Hong Kong resembled Manhattan more in its values than it did the Chinese city they remembered in their young adulthood. My mother had stated, "Now I feel as if I truly belong nowhere. When I am here [Hong Kong], I feel so American. When I am home in America, I feel so Chinese." The Chinese values she had so carefully preserved for her children and family now seemed to exist only among the group of Chinese American immigrants whom we saw several times a month and at special holidays back home in the United States—thousands of miles away from Hong Kong and Asia.

The following quotes illustrate how markedly different my mother's experiences are from those of recent Chinese American immigrants in the 1990s. The first quote is from a conversation that my husband and I had with my young immigrant cousin about his difficulty in adjusting to living with us in the United States. The second quote is from a conversation I had with my parents that same week. These examples caution us about the complexity of what it means to be of Chinese descent in America across migration waves:

> ABCs [American-born Chinese] are so old-fashioned. You are young, but it is like you live in old Chinese history books—you are SO old-fashioned and strict! You celebrate August Moon festival. You know how to make wonton and potstickers. Only poor people cook. You have money, but you order white rice in fancy restaurants. How embarrassing! *I can't believe you are Chinese.* Chinese are supposed to be "tight," you know, good dressers, good in business, "tight" cars, go out to eat all the time, cell phones. (cousin, personal conversation, 1995)

> Chinese people are honorable people. We respect our elders, value family, cherish children, and we are honest. Chinese people look at what is inside a person, not focus on smooth talk and nice dress like Americans [White Americans] do. I don't trust them [Hong Kongese]. They are upper crusty. . . . All they care about is money and buying things, nice cars, clothes, watches—spend money. They are supposed to take care of those less fortunate in society, be thrifty. *They aren't very Chinese.* (parents, personal conversation, 1995)

Race, Ethnicity, and Identity

Whose identity is more Chinese or Chinese American? Whose is more authentic? To choose one or the other is a grave mistake. Identity is fluid and shaped through experience. Identity formation arises in interaction and is a function not only of the individual and his or her relation to the ethnic or racial group but of that group's place in the wider social setting (Rosenthal, 1987). In intercultural communication, communicative interaction at the individual as well as group level is the focus

of study in identity formation. Intercultural communication is an overall encompassing term. In recent literature in intercultural communication, communication has come to include everyday discourse in conversations, mediated discourses in textbooks, news media, popular culture, advertising, and other types of communication. Thus the conversations we have, the movies we watch, and the books we read all serve to mediate our identity formation. We, in turn, impact the identity formation of others by our everyday discourses and our influence on the media and popular culture.

From this standpoint, the relationships within ethnic and racial groups are more complex than what appears on the surface. Questions of identity, ethnicity, and race often become confusing and complex. The popular media, the press, and even scholars often interchange race and ethnicity or combine these concepts with a slash using "race/ethnicity" rather than selecting one or the other. Students often ask, "What is the difference between race and ethnicity?" The reason for this confusion is that concepts of both race and ethnicity include notions of social construction and identity formation. Though for many centuries we believed that race was biologically based, we now know that the notion of race is really the result of the social process of grouping people we *believe* to be different based on what we *perceive* are inherent genetic immutable differences. The process has been described as *racializing* (Goldberg, 1993). In anthropology and many of the social sciences, the traditional concept of ethnicity is based on the notion of collective cultural practices that are part of the socialization of groups in specific isolated geographical communities.

In the present political and social context, concepts of race and ethnicity become further entangled when groups appropriate either or both of these notions for similar political resistance. Individuals may often base their identity and group formation to specifically resist being discriminated against based on others' beliefs of racial or ethnic inferiority. As a result, we often connect specific ethnic practices with specific racial groups. However, in the previous examples of Greek Americans and Hong Kong Americans, traditional concepts of race and ethnicity in and of themselves provide little explanatory power for the phenomena in these instances of intercultural and intracultural interaction. How would one describe Greek American or Chinese American ethnicity in these instances? It would be helpful to develop a framework for understanding a more dynamic way of looking at racial and ethnic identity formation. The following section examines a framework in the specific instances of Asian American identity formation with implications for more widespread application of these concepts.

Frameworks for Asian American Identity

In intercultural communication literature Asian Americans are often described as possessing characteristics of a specific ethnic (Chinese American, Japanese American, Indonesian American) or racial (Asian or Pacific Islander) group. There is a long list of characteristics such as collectivism, face-saving, filial respect, and preference for uncertainty reduction. These characteristics are believed to originate from traditional beliefs based in Confucianism rooted in the Asian continent. Although these characteristics may prove true for a portion of U.S. Americans of Asian descent, they are not representative for many Asian Americans.

Asian Americans are a heterogeneous group, speaking many different languages in addition to English, each incomprehensible to another. Asian Americans practice many different religions, ranging from the Christianity of Chinese American Baptists to Buddhism, Hinduism, and Islam (Sodowsky et al., 1995). Asian American immigrants also arrive from Asian countries that have had centuries or decades of national and ethnic conflict. These conflicts have resulted in wars and hostilities, many of which still exist in Asia. Asian Americans may trace their ancestors to differing regions, decades, and centuries—each with its own unique values, historical relations, and cultural practices.

It is easy to accept, given evidence, that all ethnic groups are heterogeneous. We must be cautious, however, that knowledge of heterogeneity doesn't encourage us to only make longer lists of ethnic characteristics. The common frame used to understand Asian Americans in social science is to provide a large overarching laundry list of characteristics or dimensions of ethnic identity. These identities describe class, gender, and cultural practices as characteristics of ethnic groups influenced by the culture of the country of origin, not as effects of *ethnic and racial formation across time, generations, regions, and countries.* It is more productive and informative to conceptualize Asian American identity as the ever changing effects of individual and group experiences of migration, of historical contact with other Asian groups, other people of color, and White U.S. Americans. These effects are complex, involving the formation of beliefs about social status, economic status, institutions, the home country, relationship of the United States to the outside world, and preservation of cultural values.

The Diaspora and Imagined Communities

Metaphors of the *diaspora* and of the *imagined community* are helpful for examining ethnic and racial identity. A diaspora is the dispersion of a minority group of people among a majority group beyond the borders of the minority's homeland. The notion of imagining a community describes the ways in which all people construct a collective community to which they identify and belong. Beliefs about nationalism, patriotism, and what it means to be a U.S. American are constructed this way. For example, a Nebraskan using communication through the stories she tells constructs an imagined community of Nebraskans from a specific location with specific beliefs. She constructs this community even though she may not know all Nebraskans or even a significant percentage of them. Yet she identifies herself as part of this community and shares common stories about what it means to be Nebraskan. She imagines that other Nebraskans are in the diaspora in the greater United States, having come from this community even though the neighborhood she left in childhood may be unrecognizable today.

Similarly, immigrants often preserve and incorporate dimensions of their cultural practices in the diaspora, often constructing their ethnic identity around beliefs and memories of cultural values and practices that existed in their home country at the time of immigration. As waves of immigrants arrive over many generations from countries that experience tremendous global, political, cultural, and technological change, we find that these imagined communities often clash even as different waves of immigrants arrive from the same locale in Asia. Notions of "authentic" ethnic identity in ethnic communities in the United States create much intracultural friction, especially among American-born and immigrant communities.

In this framework of ethnic formation, who represents the Chinese American perspective, much less the Asian American perspective? Chinese communities struggle with differences across class, relations to technology, cultural history, traditional legacies, and traditional family hierarchies. In July 1997 Hong Kong will revert back to Communist China from the United Kingdom; as a result, many Chinese immigrants from Hong Kong have already emigrated to the United States and other countries. Many are descendants of Chinese who immigrated to Hong Kong decades ago after fleeing the Communists. As China fires missiles over Taiwan to encourage its "One China Policy," we can see how complicated and fraught with conflict the development of an ethnic Chinese American identity can be. Although non-Chinese others may see you and communicate to you as being simply Asian, Asian American, Chinese American, or Chinese, you may see yourself as being ethnically Taiwanese American, or Hong Kongese American, distinct from Chinese Americans who trace their ancestral home to mainland China. The difficulties of identity formation are even more problematic when labeling assumes that every Asian-looking person is Chinese, or more derogatory terms such as Oriental or Chink.

These dynamics with the larger White communities can create great tensions for many ethnic minorities in the United States, where communities struggle with tremendous differences not only with the larger dominant White majority, but also within their own ethnic communities on how to handle this seeming effort to lump people of Asian descent together. The following is an example of the ambivalent situation a Korean American student faced when encountering a well-meaning White colleague:

> A White woman acquaintance at my university pulled me aside and in a serious voice announced that she understood what I had been talking about all these months about ethnicity and race. "I saw the movie *The Joy Luck Club* with my husband over the weekend. I feel so close to you now, like I understand you so much better! Chinese women are so lucky to have relationships with their mothers with such deep emotions!" I felt confused and speechless and didn't know where to begin. In addition to the fact that I am not Chinese American, I wondered what in the world this woman and her husband have fantasized about my life and family relations based on this Hollywood movie.
> (G. Kim, conversation in a graduate seminar class, 1994)

Under these circumstances, ethnic minorities often create a larger, more strategic *political identity* such as "Asian American identity." This imagined community is one in which individuals are unified in their beliefs about being similarly discriminated against and share similar histories of struggle in the diaspora of Asians in the United States. In many ways the community is one of strategic racial formation designed to recognize and resist racial oppression. It is this process of political identity formation that allows for Asian Americans and Pacific Islanders to encompass the same diasporic community regardless of the extreme complex and sometimes problematic histories of languages and conflict in home countries. It is this same process that allows for Asian American Pacific Islanders to form coalitions with other groups of color to fight common causes of discrimination and stereotyping often based on perceptions of race.

Consider the experience I had while attending a recent regional academic communication conference in a large hotel in the American Pacific Northwest: I am in the hotel restaurant and walking to my table to sit with my colleagues. Although I am dressed in typical professional conventioneer clothing and am wearing a conference name tag, I am grabbed twice by unfamiliar White communication professors who demand that I seat them. One White male professor grabs my upper arm tightly and barks, "I said, Clear my table!"

My experience is eerily similar to those experienced by Cornel West, bell hooks, Gloria Anzaldúa, Ronald Takaki, Maxine Hong Kingston, and other scholars of color in similar professional settings, where White people that you know generally exhibit a level of respect and genuine friendship and those that you don't know are likely to racialize you and stereotype you to be one of "the help."

What does it mean to be Chinese, Chinese American, and Asian American in the United States in the 1990s? There is not now, nor has there ever been, an easy or stable answer. Trying to pinpoint and understand what ethnic and racial identity means in the United States is like shooting at a moving target. I am an American-born woman of Chinese descent, born of working-class immigrant parents in the United States. The experiences of the Korean American graduate student and myself illustrate the different ways in which the identities of people of Asian descent can be very complex and at times very problematic even in academia. To some White colleagues I can be different things: a Chinese American woman with deep secrets about her past, or a laborer in food service, or one of the thousands of people of color who clean our offices, maintain our campuses, and serve our food. These colleagues shape their perceptions of my identity not by who I am as a Chinese American, but by assigning simplistic ethnic and class characteristics based on their own perceptions of my physical appearance, my race, my Chineseness and Asianness. This process is racialization, or racial stereotyping. My own perception of my identity is often in shockingly sharp conflict with how others perceive and assign my identity.

Being an Asian American means being faced with the difficult dilemma of constantly having to contradict preconceived ethnic and racial stereotypes of Asians and Asian Americans, or of letting these stereotypes pass, knowing that they will continue to be imposed on others. It means being wary that one's whole identity does not become merely a reaction to these stereotypes, while rec-ognizing that these struggles are a part of the formation of my identity as an American. These struggles are part of my imagined community of fellow strugglers. Though I do not know Cornel West, bell hooks, or Maxine Hong Kingston personally, we all share a sense of community through our writings and through our ethnic and strategic racial identity formation.

This formation of a collective identity is not without its problems. Asian Americans struggle with relationships with other people of color in the United States. For an Asian American, identifying as a person of color who is concerned about the core issues of social and economic empowerment for marginalized people can often mean having to take an uncomfortable look at racial, social, and economic privilege in relationship to the status of other ethnic American groups. For example, during a university class for gifted students of color that I taught in 1996, a session on Asian American/African American conflict became heated as a discussion about Asian immigrant entrepreneurship in African American communities unfolded. Students began taking sides, which left some Asian and Asian American students questioning their own loyalties to their own ethnic and racial group against their solidarity with African American students in a joint struggle to improve the lives of all marginalized people. "Why do I feel pressured to choose? Can't I be Asian American AND a person of color?!" an exasperated Chinese American woman asked me.

Many Asian Americans who immigrated to the United States after 1965, with the exception of refugees, immigrated largely from urban areas of Asia. Unlike their predecessors who arrived from poor rural farming areas with little money and resources, many recent immigrants arrive with advanced college degrees and investment capital. Most Americans—including Asian Americans—are unaware that through changing immigration criteria, the federal government has encouraged the immigration of this class of affluent merchants in order to bolster the American economy (Ikemoto, 1995; Min, 1995; Sodowsky et al., 1995). Many recent Asian American immigrants arrive with little understanding of American class dynamics, especially in regard to racial dynamics.

They may not understand their actions in the context of racial formation in the United States and may still be struggling with their own ethnic and racial identity here. The media, as we saw in the simplistic portrayals of Korean merchants and African American residents of Los Angeles after the Rodney King verdicts, does not assist immigrants or the public at large in understanding the complex, problematic, and tragic race relations in the United States that go well beyond whether Korean Americans and African Americans have conflicting communication styles and disparate economic opportunity (Ikemoto, 1995).

Intercultural communication should not and cannot study Asian American communication in isolation from the historical, social, political, economic, and racial dynamics of the peoples of the United States and of the larger world. Examining ethnicity and race within the framework of the diaspora and imagined communities can help us understand the complexities and challenges of intercultural and intracultural communication. We must use this framework to examine identity as a process, as an effect of discourses about racial and ethnic formation that stretches across continents, history, generations, governments, and peoples. Using the metaphors of diaspora and imagined communities, we can examine the discourses that we use or are exposed to that both help us and hinder us in shaping notions of community. These communities should be viewed as fluid and ever changing as new immigrants arrive, new generations are born, new alliances are formed, old alliances are broken, and events such as wars and conflicts and other common concerns arise around the world.

REFERENCES

Anderson, B. (1983). *Imagined communities.* London: Verso.

Fong, T. (1994). *The first suburban Chinatown: The remaking of Monterey Park.* Philadelphia: Temple University Press.

Goldberg, D. T. (1993). *Racist culture: Philosophy and the politics of meaning.* Oxford: Blackwell.

Ignatiev, N. (1995). *How the Irish became white.* New York: Routledge.

Ikemoto, L. (1995). Traces of the master narrative in the story of African American/Korean American conflict: How we constructed "Los Angeles." In R. Delgado (Ed.), *Critical race theory: The cutting edge* (pp. 305–315). Philadelphia: Temple University Press.

Kingston, M. H. (1976). *The woman warrior: Memoirs of a girlhood among ghosts.* New York: Alfred A. Knopf.

Min, P. G. (1995). *Asian Americans: Contemporary trends and issues.* Thousand Oaks, CA: Sage.

Rosenthal, D. A. (1987). Ethnic identity development in adolescents. In J. S. Phinney & M. J. Rotheram (Eds.), *Children's ethnic socialization: Pluralism and development* (pp. 156–179). Newbury Park, CA: Sage.

Sodowsky, R. G., Kwan, K. L. K., & Pannu, R. (1995). Ethnic identity of Asians in the United States. In J. Ponterotto, J. M. Casas, L. A. Suzuki, & C. M. Alexander (Eds.), *Handbook of multicultural counseling* (pp. 123–154). Thousand Oaks, CA: Sage.

Takaki, R. (1993). *A different mirror.* Boston: Little, Brown.

Tan, A. (1989). *The joy luck club.* New York: G. P. Putnam's Sons.

Wei, W. (1993). *The Asian American movement.* Philadelphia: Temple University Press.

Wong, K. S. (1993). Our lives, our histories. In D. Shoem, L. Frankel, X. Zuniga, & E. Lewis (Eds.), *Multicultural teaching in the university* (pp. 87–94). Wesport, CT: Praeger.

KEY TERMS

Asian American identity

diaspora

imagined communities

intercultural communication

migration

identity

DISCUSSION QUESTIONS

1. Wong(Lau) uses the metaphors of the diaspora and imagined communities. Using these concepts, discuss examples of diasporic formation and imagined communities on your campus. How would these considerations impact your communication in these groups?

2. In communication literature, especially in intercultural literature, the concept of context in the shaping of communication is often emphasized. This essay helps us understand the importance of looking at the experience of migration in identity formation. What other types of contextual considerations could be relevant? Discuss your own experiences.

3. What does Wong(Lau)'s essay suggest about the possible ways in which people may identify with the terms "Asian American," "Chinese American," or "people of color"? Discuss these terms using the concepts of race and ethnicity.

4. What types of communication discourses are out there about Asian Americans and specific ethnic Asian Americans? Identify the source and the message. How might these discourses impact the identity formation of Americans of Asian descent? How might they impact Americans of non-Asian descent?

5. Discuss the power of communication in identity formation and community formation. In what ways do groups persist in maintaining diasporic communities over time? Start with larger imagined national and regional communities such as the United States, the South, and New England and move to smaller, more specific ones. Where did you learn about these regional and ethnic characteristics, even if you haven't had contact with these communities? What does this tell us about intercultural communication?

PART FOUR

LANGUAGE, DISCOURSE, AND INTERCULTURAL COMMUNICATION

Language can serve to strengthen community and cultural identity; it can also be a source of misunderstanding and an obstacle in intercultural interaction. The essays in this part explore various aspects of language used in intercultural encounters—from a very specific sociolinguistic feature like accent, to broad language use across contexts, to pragmatics or discourse (language in use) in very specific contexts. These essays show how language can be predicted to influence or reflect attitudes or both, or how it can be studied as rituals that are intimately and reciprocally linked to cultural norms and identity.

Consider these questions as you read the articles in this part:

What kind of everyday language rituals do you know or use?

How much does your language vary from context to context?

What role does power play in language use? Does language use vary with the degree of power felt by an individual?

The first two readings seek to theoretically explain and predict language use in intercultural encounters—from a social science perspective.

The next three interpretive essays explore language use in specific contexts (Colombian, Chinese, and U.S. social contexts; Native American and Japanese students in U.S. classrooms). The last reading emphasizes the role of power in language use in public speaking contexts.

The first essay, "Communication Accommodation in Intercultural Encounters," explores how speakers adapt their language in intercultural interactions. Howard Giles and Kimberly A. Noels describe a social science theory, Communication Accommodation Theory, that predicts how and when individuals will seek to diverge or converge in their communication with others. They stress the importance language has in our cultural (e.g., ethnic) identity and outline the assumptions of the theory. They point out that under certain conditions, individuals will try to minimize differences and converge with the other speaker—that is, they will "mirror" the other's tone, rate, accent, and so forth. In some encounters, however, speakers will emphasize cultural differences and diverge in speech, particularly when power inequities exist. Note that the research reviewed here is objective, and this social science theory is unique in that it incorporates notions of power.

In "Help! My Professor (or Doctor or Boss) Doesn't Talk English," Donald L. Rubin describes how a sociolinguistic dynamic—accent—affects perceptions and stereotyping. He describes a typical U.S. college interaction—international instructors and college students—but also provides examples from health care and business interactions. He draws his conclusions from a series of objective social science studies that show, in each case, how accent or *perceptions* of accent result in "listening barriers." He then gives practical suggestions for overcoming the tendency to negatively stereotype on the basis of accent.

We extend the U.S. classroom focus to more subjective, interpretive research. Donal Carbaugh, in "'I can't do that!' but I 'can actually see around corners,'" explores the contrasts between Native American and White communication rules in U.S. classroom contexts. Based on personal experiences and ethnographic interviews, he describes the communication among the Blackfeet, which emphasizes listener-active silence more than public speaking skills. He shows how their communication patterns are in direct contradiction to typical demands of U.S. classrooms, where public speaking is a highly valued skill. Note that while he describes cultural differences, he does not start his study with an assumption of finding particular differences. Rather, these differences emerge from in-depth, qualitative study. He describes the reciprocal dynamic between types of discourse and deeply held cultural values and meanings. He suggests that, though difficult, teachers should carefully consider what they are asking Native American students to "undo" and what each group can learn from the other.

In "Ritual as Part of Everyday Life," Bradford "J" Hall (no relation to E. T. Hall) describes the importance of language in everyday rituals, "symbolic acts that pay homage to some ideal or object." He refutes the assumptions that rituals are outdated or meaningless or only occur in religious contexts. Note that he also assumes a reciprocal, dynamic relationship between culture and language. By examining everyday rituals in various contexts in several countries—Japan, Colombia, and the United States—he reveals the universal and important roles rituals play in community life, regardless of the community.

The next essay provides a good example of Brad Hall's "everyday ritual" based on interpretive ethnographic research. In "A Ritual for

Attempting Leave-Taking in Colombia," Kristine Fitch analyzed conversations that took place between Colombians at social occasions and argues that in these social gatherings, special relationships, or *vínculos,* are formed. These relationships lead to particular ways of saying good-bye. She shows how these language rituals, as cultural expressions, serve to strengthen interpersonal bonds in social contexts.

Moving to a critical perspective, Detine L. Bowers explores how power differentials can affect language use in public or mediated contexts. In "When Outsiders Encounter Insiders in Speaking," she first explores the rhetorical "rules of racial standing" that apply to oppressed collectives by dominant institutions (such as media). Bowers suggests that rhetorical rules vary for powerful and less powerful groups. Two such rules are that Blacks who disparage other Blacks or voice outrageous opinions are granted enhanced standing. She then shows how these rules play out in TV shows. She also offers strategies that oppressed minorities can use to reverse the rhetorical condition.

15
COMMUNICATION ACCOMMODATION IN INTERCULTURAL ENCOUNTERS

HOWARD GILES / KIMBERLY A. NOELS

When members of two cultural groups come together, they often have to make choices about whose communication system to use and how much to accommodate each other. Consider back-packers in a European youth hostel at the end of a day on the road. Travelers from the four corners of the world, including Germans, Israelis, Australians, South Africans, Iranians, Americans, and Japanese, come together in the common room to prepare their meals. They discuss the details of their latest adventure, share their impressions of the city in which they have arrived, and seek advice on the next place to visit. How will they communicate? What language will serve? For those who can speak each other's language, how will they decide which linguistic code to use? The process of negotiating these decisions and their behavioral implications is the concern of the theory covered in this chapter, Communication Accommodation Theory (CAT). We will begin with a discussion of the importance of language for interethnic relations. The fundamental tenets of CAT will then be outlined, including the notions of convergence and divergence, followed by a consideration of some recent research findings.

The Importance of Language in Intercultural Relations and Communication

Despite the complexities of negotiating a language for intergroup communication, few scholars have investigated language behaviors and processes in intercultural encounters. This is surprising given worldwide prominence of language issues in intercultural interactions, and particularly in conflict-ridden interactions (Clément, 1996). Consider the following examples.

The official language of the Ottoman Empire, which had been in use for over 400 years, was suppressed in 1922 in an effort to promote a modern version of the language. It was felt that this linguistic change to modern Turkish would discourage identification with the old empire and encourage linguistic identification with central Asia. Elsewhere, in an attempt to distinguish their language from Serbo-Croatian, Macedonian writers in Yugoslavia began to incorporate words and grammatical structures used in rural areas in an effort to develop a new standard of the language. This attempt to change the language occurred at the same time as Macedonians strove for a separate Macedonian republic in Yugoslavia.

During the 1976 Soweto riots in South Africa, many Blacks and Whites were killed. These riots occurred at a time when Blacks were protesting the White government's insistence that the Afrikaans language be used in the education of Black students. As expressed by Black leaders,

> the situation has unearthed the innermost frustrations of Black people which were hidden from the outside world. Although there is a prevalent belief in some quarters that Afrikaans as a medium of instruction was not a direct positive factor in these riots, this is not so. Afrikaans was forced down Black students just as much as the Trust Land Act, pass laws, and migratory labour. (reported in *The Times* [London, June 23, 1979], cited in Giles & Coupland, 1991, p. 95)

As a symbol of White domination and oppression, Blacks most certainly perceived the enforced use of Afrikaans in the school system as an abhorrent and inexcusable attack on their social identity.

More recently in Canada, concerns over cultural autonomy and language maintenance threaten to divide Canadians. In a 1995 provincial referendum, 49% of the Quebec population voted to remove themselves as a province from Canada, a percentage only slightly less than the 51% who decided to stay in Confederation. This concern over cultural maintenance centers to a large extent on linguistic issues: The Quebec government passed legislation requiring that commercial signs be printed primarily in French and that French be the primary language of instruction for most non-French-speaking immigrant children (Lemco, 1992).

Finally, concern over language issues remains an important facet of ethnic relations in the United States. In response to the diversity of languages spoken in some areas, many states have declared English as their official language. These movements are also evident at the federal level. Identity issues have often centered in these debates, for those who are both for and against official language policies. For instance, Republican House Representative Norman Shumway (1992) wrote

> [English] has been the "glue" which has held us together, forging strength and unity from our rich cultural diversity. From our earliest days, despite our melting pot inheritance, English has been the language in which we expressed the goals, objectives, ideals, principles and duties of our form of government. It is the language in which the Declaration of Independence and the Constitution are written. . . . And in my view, it is the primary language in which our government should continue to function. (pp. 121–122)

Elsewhere, in opposition to an officially monolingual society, columnist Montaner (1992) writes

> We quarrel, are jealous, love, and hate with certain words, with certain tones, with certain inflections of the voice learned in childhood and adapted to a given set of gestures that also cannot be transported into another language. . . . We cannot do without our own tongue without brutally mutilating our individual consciousness. . . . If this is so, is it reasonable to ask millions of human beings to do without this fundamental part of their lives solely so that others are not inconvenienced . . . ? (p. 164)

Why Is Language So Important for Interethnic Relations?

According to Giles and Coupland (1991), there are at least three reasons: Language is often a criterion for group membership, it is a cue for ethnic identity, and it is a means of facilitating ingroup[1] cohesion.

There are different criteria for membership in an ethnic group, including ancestry, physical features, religion, and so on. Most ethnic groups also have a distinct language or dialect, and the ability to use this language may be necessary for group membership. To illustrate, there was a common saying in Hispanic communities in the southwestern United States in the 1970s: "A Mexican American who can't speak Spanish should choke on his chili beans!" Even when there are clear and distinctive criteria for ethnic group membership, such as skin color, an ethnic language variety often remains a critical attribute. When he met his African "brothers" in Sierra Leone, one African American member of the Peace Corps was surprised and dismayed when they called him *oyimbo* (White man) because of his standard American English and behavior (Hancock, 1974).

Language has been shown to be an important aspect of ethnic identity, more important even than cultural background for many social groups, albeit not for all. For instance, Smolicz (1984) argued that Dutch people in Australia did not consider language to be central to their identity, although Polish and Greek people did. Taylor, Bassili, and Aboud (1973) found, however, that some French Canadians felt closer to an English Canadian who spoke French than to a French Canadian who did not. In a similar vein, Clément, Gauthier, and Noels (1993) examined Franco Ontarian adolescents who spoke French most often or English most often. Their results showed that although both groups learned French as their native language, Francophones who spoke primarily English identified less strongly with the Francophone group and more

---

[1] The term "ingroup" refers to the group to which the individual belongs. The term "outgroup" refers to any group to which the individual does *not* belong.

with the Anglophone group than did those who spoke primarily French. For many groups, then, the language used is closely connected to feelings of ethnic identity.

Language is also important for ensuring within-group cohesion. Kim (1988) suggests that the linguistic code, as one of the primary media through which the daily activities of human affairs are conducted, can well be described as a carrier of culture. By sharing a common language for communication, individuals also share a common manner of interacting in the social world. Moreover, this shared commodity carries symbolic value: Fishman (1977) suggests provocatively that language "can become the ultimate symbol of ethnicity, since in expressing, referring to, and evoking something else in addition to itself, it becomes valued in itself" (p. 25). Naturally enough, people are very emotionally attached to this ethnic symbol, so much so that ethnic group members using a language and speech style other than that of their group may be labeled cultural traitors by fellow group members. Indeed, recent Internet graffiti from the United States on the Punjab Usenet group (cited by Sachdev, 1995) illustrates how important language may be for within-group solidarity: "To any Punjabi out there, whether you are a Hindu, Muslim, or Sikh. If you speak Hindi or Urdu instead of Punjabi, you are a serious disgrace to your culture and you shouldn't call yourself a Punjabi!" (p. 175).

At the same time, it is important to note that members of an ethnic group need not speak the language so long as they have it available; indeed, "ethnicity is frequently related more to the symbol of a separate language than to its actual use by all members of a group" (De Vos, 1975, p. 15). Gaelic, Welsh, and Breton are all examples of languages that are not spoken by the majority of those who identify with their respective groups, but that are nevertheless highly valued as aspects of ethnic identity. Moreover, De Vos argues that, even without a distinct language, "group identity can . . . be maintained by minor differences in linguistic patterns and by style of gesture" (p. 16). For example, many immigrants may speak their host language, but with a distinctive accent and with words and phrases borrowed from their own ethnic tradition, culture, and religion. In a similar

way, many Australians are reexamining the influence of American and European traditions on Australian culture and are considering the nature of a distinctive Australian identity. In an article about the Australian Renaissance ("Ockerism") in the *London Observer Review* (June 27, 1976), language was considered to be a central aspect of this issue:

> Americanization of the language is much more significantly pervasive than the high incidence of skate-boards and roadside fast food parlors. . . . The American invasion of the Australian stomach was always on the cards. But the invasion of the language is less easy to laugh off. (cited in Giles & Coupland, 1991, p. 100)

Language is hence often important for intercultural relations because (1) it serves to classify people as members of a particular ethnic group, (2) it is important for their identity as an ethnic group member, and (3) it can be used to emphasize solidarity between ingroup members and to exclude outgroup members from ingroup transactions.

Communication Accommodation Theory

Having established that language behaviors have diverse and complex implications for interethnic relations, we move now to consider how it is that communicators fashion their self- (and also group) presentations via language. The framework used to describe and explain these communicative behaviors is Communication Accommodation Theory (CAT). According to CAT, we are motivated to use language in different ways to achieve a desired level of social distance between ourselves and our listener. Each of us often accommodates verbally and nonverbally to others—and is aware of others accommodating to us (or *not*, as can be the case) on many levels. Such experiences are common in settings such as the classroom, the courtroom, business and commerce, and so forth. To illustrate, referring to the travelers in the youth hostel described in the introduction, an American traveler from Georgia may use a standard U.S. American accent (such as the accent used by television anchorpersons on national television) while talking with a fellow-traveler from Vermont. Upon returning home to Georgia, he may switch back to the accent more typical of that part of the country. It may even be argued that there are no occasions in which we do not adjust our language style to take into account what we believe to be the perspective of the person with whom we are interacting.

There are many kinds of accommodative acts, many reasons for accommodating, and many consequences arising from accommodation. In the following sections, the fundamental strategies of convergence and divergence and their complexities are addressed first. We then examine the synchrony between speakers' intentions and actual behavior, and listeners' interpretations. Finally, we consider how social beliefs, such as stereotypes and norms, guide accommodation, although not always in ways that lead to successful interactions.

Convergence and Divergence

Convergence can be defined as a strategy whereby individuals adapt their communicative behavior on one or a number of linguistic, paralinguistic, and nonverbal features in such a way as to become more similar to their interlocutor's behavior. Among the many communicative behaviors that may be modified are languages and dialects, and characteristics found within language groups, such as speech rate, pauses, utterance length, phonological variants, smiling, and gaze. Although most studies have been conducted in the West and in English-language settings, convergence on temporal, phonological, or language-switching dimensions has been noted in many different languages, including Hungarian, Frisian and Dutch, Hebrew, Taiwanese Mandarin, Japanese, Cantonese, and Thai (see sources in Giles, Coupland, & Coupland, 1991).

As suggested earlier, motives for converging vary widely. Certainly, converging to a common linguistic style can improve the effectiveness of communication (Gallois, Giles, Jones, Cargile, & Ota, 1995)—the similarity in speech styles between interlocutors has been associated with pre-dictability (Berger & Bradac, 1982) and intelligibility (Triandis, 1960). Another motive that has received considerable attention since the inception of the theory (Giles, 1973) is the desire to gain approval from one's interlocutor. The premise is that the more similar we are to our interlocutor, the more he or she will like us and the better able we will be to gain social rewards from them. Indeed, convergence is generally associated with more positive evaluations (Bourhis, Giles, & Lambert, 1975). This tendency, however, may be constrained by several factors that are discussed later in this essay.

Divergence refers to the way in which speakers accentuate speech and nonverbal differences between themselves and others. Divergence is designed to emphasize distinctiveness from one's interlocutor, usually on the basis of group membership. Following the premises of Tajfel's (1978) Social Identity Theory, CAT maintains that individuals categorize the social world into groups, and derive a part of their identity and self-esteem (called "social identity") from groups to which they belong. Assuming that people are motivated to maintain self-esteem, they will tend to differentiate their own group from other groups, provided they are pleased to belong to that group.

Consistent with the idea that people will try to differentiate themselves linguistically from others when their social identity is strong, Bourhis and Giles (1976) designed an experiment to demonstrate the use of accent divergence among Welsh people in an interethnic context. The study was conducted in a language laboratory where people who placed a strong value on their national group membership and its language were learning the Welsh language (only about 26% of Welsh people at that time, as now, could speak their national tongue). During one of their weekly sessions, Welsh people were asked to help in a survey concerned with second language learning techniques. The questions in the survey were presented to them verbally, in English, in their individual booths by a very English-sounding speaker, who at one point arrogantly challenged their reasons for learning what he called a "dying language with a dismal future." As expected, the informants diverged by broadening their Welsh accents when replying to the perceived threat to their ethnic identity, compared to emotionally neutral questions asked earlier. Moreover, some informants began introducing Welsh words and phrases into their answers. One Welsh woman did not reply for a while, and then was heard to conjugate a pejorative verb gently into the microphone.

A phenomenon similar to divergence is *maintenance,* in which a person continues in his or her original speech style, in spite of the convergence or divergence of the interlocutor. Maintenance is often evaluated in the same way as divergence (Bourhis, 1979).

Further Distinctions in Convergence and Divergence: Direction, Degree, and Mutuality of Accommodation

The complementary nature of convergence and divergence is summarized in Figure 1. Individuals may speak the language of the outgroup with no trace of an accent, such that they can pass as a member of that group, or they may affect a slight to heavy accent to hint at their ingroup origins. Alternatively they may maintain their original language but speak more slowly to help the outgroup member understand. Finally, they may completely diverge (i.e., show no convergence) by using the ingroup language at the usual speed used by native speakers. One might accommodate on one feature, such as accent, but at other times on multiple features, for example, by adjusting word choice and speech rate in addition to accent. Moreover, convergence (or divergence) on some features of a language does not imply that there will be convergence (or divergence) on all features.

Accommodation is not a one-way process. As outlined in Figure 2 (p. 144), within a communicative episode, each interlocutor can converge, diverge, or maintain, although not necessarily to the same extent as the partner. When accommodation is approximately equal for both partners, it is said to be symmetrical. At other times one partner may converge or diverge to the greater or lesser extent, or fail to react (i.e., maintain), or behave in a contrasting manner. This is called asymmetrical accommodation. Thus, although convergence and divergence are complementary concepts, they can both occur in a communication episode and in different ways for each interactant. Moreover, as complex as accommodation is, its complexity is amplified further when one considers how speakers interpret their own and their listeners' intentions subjectively.

Objective, Subjective, and Psychological Accommodation

There are several levels on which accommodation phenomena can be investigated. The previous discussion focuses on objective accommodation, that is, on actual communicative behavior, as assessed through direct observation of linguistic exchanges in an interaction. The examination of accommodation, however, is not restricted to this behavioral level, but includes, perhaps more interestingly, an examination of the intentions of speakers and the perceptions of listeners. These latter two levels are termed psychological and subjective accommodation, respectively. A speaker's intention is often consistent with actual behavior, but this need not always be the case. For example, referring back to the example in the introduction, one of the American travelers may

FIGURE 1   *Some Increasing Variants of Convergence and Divergence*
(Source: Adapted from Giles, Bourhis, & Taylor, 1977.)

Linguistic Dimensions	Increasing Convergence	Increasing Divergence
1. Outgroup language with nativelike pronunciation	↑	
2. Outgroup language with features of ingroup pronunciation		
3. Ingroup language with slow speech rate		
4. Ingroup language with normal speech rate		↓

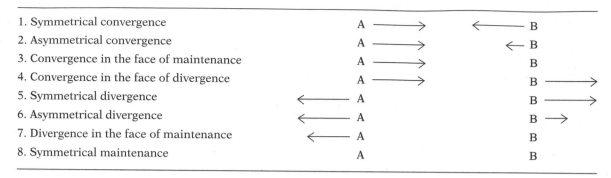

1. Symmetrical convergence	A ⟶	⟵ B
2. Asymmetrical convergence	A ⟶	← B
3. Convergence in the face of maintenance	A ⟶	B
4. Convergence in the face of divergence	A ⟶	B ⟶
5. Symmetrical divergence	⟵ A	B ⟶
6. Asymmetrical divergence	⟵ A	B →
7. Divergence in the face of maintenance	⟵ A	B
8. Symmetrical maintenance	A	B

FIGURE 2   *Degree, Direction, and Mutuality of Accommodation*
(Source: Adapted from Gallois and Giles [in press].)

decide to adopt a Spanish accent in order to accommodate a Spanish fellow-wanderer. This accent may not, however, truly represent the Spanish speaker's accent or in any way correspond with an actual Spanish accent. Similarly, speakers may converge to their listener objectively, but the intent behind this convergence may not be to indicate intimacy with the listener but to exclude the listener from the language group. For instance, Woolard (1989) reports of a language norm in Spain to the effect that Catalan should only be spoken between Catalans, such that Castillian speakers who attempted to speak Catalan would likely receive a reply in Castillian. In an empirical examination of correspondence between speakers' intentions and their actual behavior, Thakerar, Giles, and Cheshire (1982) examined student nurses in conversations with their supervisors. Contrary to objective measures that indicated that their behavior became less similar to the supervisors', the nurses maintained their behavior did not change.

Subjective accommodation refers to the listener's interpretation of the speaker's act. Like psychological accommodation, subjective accommodation does not necessarily correspond with objective behavior. Returning to the example of the interaction between the Spanish and English speakers, the Spanish speaker may not be familiar enough with English to notice that the English speaker has altered his or her language or may not recognize the change as a shift to a Spanish accent. Similarly, even if the change in behavior is perceived, the Spanish speaker's interpretation

may not be consistent with the English speaker's intention—the Spanish speaker may see it as a rude joke, as mimicry of his or her imperfect English. In a similar vein, Giles and Smith (1979) varied convergence on three linguistic characteristics—pronunciation, speech rate, and message content—and found that convergence on any one level was viewed positively but that convergence on all three levels was viewed negatively. Thus, in spite of the greater similarity that objective convergence implies, the listener may not interpret this behavior as actually indicating greater intimacy.

Optimal Level of Accommodation: Stereotypes and Norms

The mismatch between objective accommodation on one hand, and psychological and subjective accommodation on the other, implies that interactants have some notion of an optimal level of accommodation (Giles & Smith, 1979); that is, speakers and listeners have beliefs and expectations that act as guidelines for what is appropriate and acceptable accommodation behavior. Two such guidelines are stereotypes regarding outgroup members (and their level of communicative competence) and beliefs about the appropriate norms regarding language use.

Stereotypes   Stereotypes about characteristics of outgroup members are often associated with expectations about how they will respond in a social encounter. Returning to the interaction between the American and Spanish travelers, the American may expect Spanish people to be emotional and sociable, and alter his or her behavior to become similarly expressive and outgoing. Using the stereotype as a guideline for communication, the American may risk offending the travel-weary Spaniard, who in fact sees such behavior as boisterous and intrusive. In this scenario, the American could be said to overaccommodate the Spaniard. Other expectations regarding characteristics and behaviors of outgroups may similarly affect convergence. For instance, the person who thinks that his or her interlocutor could not reasonably be expected to be fluent in the speaker's language may not see divergence or maintenance in a negative light. In line with this notion, Simard, Taylor, and Giles (1976) found that nonconvergence on the part of the interlocutor that was the result of linguistic incompetence was viewed less negatively than nonconvergence that was perceived to be the result of a lack of effort.

Norms   In addition to stereotypes regarding outgroup members, norms regarding language use can also influence the extent of convergence and divergence, and the manner in which these accommodation phenomena are evaluated. According to DeRidder, Schruijer, and Tripathi (1992), when two groups coexist in a society for a long period of time, they establish norms for how members from the two groups should interact with each other. Extending this idea to the realm of language, these norms may constrain the extent to which one can converge or diverge. For instance, Bourhis (1991) found that despite the fact that the French-speaking population was a majority in provincial government offices in New Brunswick, Canada, both Anglophones and Francophones reported using English more often than French when interacting across language groups. Moreover, regardless of the level of English competence, Francophones were more likely to converge to English, even when the English speaker was a subordinate employee. The same was not true of English speakers, who usually maintained their use of English even when interacting with French-speaking superiors. Thus, intergroup norms for language use overrode the importance that demographic representation could have had

in affecting patterns of language use. Adherence to norms may also moderate our impressions of others. Simard, Taylor, and Giles (1976) found that when attempts to converge were perceived as a reaction to situational pressures forcing them to converge, convergence was viewed less positively than when it was seen as an attempt to reduce intercultural distance between the two speakers.

A pervasive norm is that individuals will converge to the language of the group with greater ethnolinguistic vitality, who often speak what is termed the standard or prestige variety of a language. Ethnolinguistic vitality refers to the power of a language group, in terms of its demographic representation, institutional support in areas such as government and education, and social prestige (Giles, Bourhis, & Taylor, 1977). Thus, all other factors being equal, it would be expected that Latinos converge to English speakers in the United States, Francophones converge to Anglophones in Canada, and Turkish speakers converge to German speakers in Germany. This straightforward hypothesis is complicated by the fact that different dialects may compete as a standard language. To illustrate, although French remains a prestigious language in Tunisia since France's attempt to colonize that country up until the 1940s, Tunisian Arabic is widely accepted as a marker of "real" Tunisians. Lawson-Sako and Sachdev (1996) investigated convergence, divergence, and code-switching in Tunisian pedestrians who were randomly approached by either Arab Tunisians or White Europeans who asked for directions to the local post office. Half of the pedestrians were asked for directions to the post office in Tunisian Arabic and half in French. The researchers expected that a Tunisian confederate asking for information in Tunisian Arabic would receive a reply in Tunisian Arabic, and a European would receive one in French. Although respondents generally converged to the language of the researcher, they were more likely to converge if the request was presented in Tunisian Arabic. They were more likely to use code-switching strategies or to diverge if addressed in French. Thus, despite the prestige of French, Tunisians were likely to signal their distinctiveness from their former colonizers.

Further complexities are evident when one

considers that different dialects may have varying appeal for different groups of people. For instance, Al-Khatib (1995) explains that although Modern Standard Arabic may be the standard dialect in Jordan, the urban variety of Jordanian Arabic is also highly regarded, albeit more so by women than by men. In an investigation of the impact of interlocutor sex on linguistic accommodation, Al-Khatib examined the use of phonological variants of the two dialects by speakers on a phone-in radio show. As expected, men were more standardized in their linguistic behavior, and women were less standardized and more urbanized.

The importance of gender in determining adherence to different linguistic styles is further illustrated in a study by Willemyns, Gallois, Callan, and Pittam (in press). Undergraduates applying for a job as a research assistant received two interviews, one from an interviewer who spoke in a broad Australian English accent and one from an interviewer who spoke in a cultivated accent. Male applicants diverged from cultivated-accented females, particularly if they identified with the broad accent. As pointed out by Willemyns and his colleagues, this is consistent with the premises of CAT that the stronger a person's loyalty to their language, the more he or she will emphasize distinctiveness between groups. Women, however, did not change their accent, suggesting that they are more accommodative than men.

In addition to considering intergroup norms, situational norms may further affect the extent and evaluation of language use. For instance, in the study by Willemyns et al. (in press), applicants used broader accents when talking with the broad-accented interviewer than when talking with the cultivated-accented interviewer. There was, however, no evidence of convergence to the cultivated-accented interviewer. The authors suggest that possibly the formal nature of the interview situation primed the applicants to speak with as cultivated an accent as possible. Depending on the formality of the situation, convergence and divergence may be more or less positively viewed. Coté and Clément (1994) presented students with hypothetical interactions between a Francophone and an Anglophone. In less intimate, task-oriented settings, Anglophone interlocutors who used English were evaluated less favorably than those who used French; but in intimate situations, the language used by the Anglophone interlocutor did not affect their evaluations. The authors suggested that in intimate situations, expectancies regarding appropriate language behavior may be more relaxed and flexible than in task-oriented situations. Thus, the positivity of convergence may be situationally bound.

Epilogue

This essay has focused on the importance that language has in intercultural relations. It suggested that language helps to categorize, symbolize, and give coherence to cultural groups. Because language is often an important aspect of ethnic identity, how we use it can emphasize how closely we identify with the people with whom we interact, so that by converging our linguistic style to others', we generally wish to indicate closeness, and by diverging in our linguistic style, we generally imply distance. Space precludes a discussion of many other issues addressed by CAT, such as accommodative strategies at the discourse level or greater elaboration of the issues of under- and overaccommodation, but more extensive treatments can be found elsewhere (e.g., Gallois et al., 1995; Gallois & Giles, in press; Giles & Coupland, 1991; Giles et al., 1991). The present discussion does suggest, however, that satisfying communicative exchanges may require a delicate balance of convergence to demonstrate willingness to communicate, as well as divergence to promote a healthy sense of group identity (see Cargile & Giles, 1996).

We have seen that interactants have expectations regarding the optimal level of convergence and divergence, expectations that may be based on stereotypes about outgroup members and norms for intergroup interactions and situationally acceptable behavior. Individuals' linguistic choices may correspond with their intentions and with listeners' interpretations, but there is oftentimes a mismatch between these aspects of accommodation. In intercultural interactions, it is not difficult to imagine the potential for miscommunication that can result if interactants do not share common assumptions about group characteristics and appropriate intergroup behavior across different situations.

It is also important to note that CAT's utility in explaining intercultural relations extends beyond the microinteractions discussed here, to more macrolevel ones, including issues of language learning, language maintenance and shift, and creolization. With its attention to intergroup communication strategies, CAT can readily be applied to other intergroup settings, such as encounters between genders, across generations, and between people who are physically challenged and those who are not. However CAT is applied, the perspective emphasizes that intercultural communication or communication in general is often not so much about the exchange of referential information as it is about social connectedness and the negotiation of social identities.

REFERENCES

Al-Khatib, M. (1995). The impact of interlocutor sex on linguistic accommodation: A case study of Jordan radio phone-in programs. *Multilingua, 14*, 133–150.

Berger, C. R., & Bradac, J. J. (1982). *Language and social knowledge.* London: Edward Arnold.

Bourhis, R. Y. (1979). Language in ethnic interaction. A social psychological approach. In H. Giles & B. Saint-Jacques (Eds.), *Language and ethnic relations* (pp. 117–141). Oxford: Pergamon.

Bourhis, R. Y. (1991). Organizational communication and accommodation: Toward some conceptual and empirical links. In H. Giles, J. Coupland, & N. Coupland (Eds.), *Contexts of accommodation* (pp. 270–303). Cambridge: Cambridge University Press.

Bourhis, R. Y., & Giles, H. (1976). The language of intergroup distinctiveness. In H. Giles (Ed.), *Language, ethnicity and intergroup relations* (pp. 119–135). London: Academic Press.

Bourhis, R. Y., Giles, H., & Lambert, W. E. (1975). Social consequences of accommodating one's style of speech: A cross-national investigation. *International Journal of the Sociology of Language, 6*, 55–72.

Cargile, A. C., & Giles, H. (1996). Intercultural communication training: Review, critique, and a new theoretical framework. In B. R. Burleson (Ed.), *Communication yearbook, vol. 19* (pp. 385–423). Thousand Oaks, CA: Sage.

Clément, R. (1996). Prologue: Social psychology and intergroup communication. *Journal of Language and Social Psychology, 15*, 222–229.

Clément, R., Gauthier, R. M., & Noels, K. A. (1993). Choix langagiers en milieu minoritaire: attitudes et identité concomitantes. *Canadian Journal of Behavioral Science, 25*, 149–164.

Coté, P., & Clément, R. (1994). Language attitudes: An interactive situated approach. *Language and Communication, 14*, 237–251.

DeRidder, R., Schruijer, S. G. L., & Tripathi, R. C. (1992). Norm violation as a precipitating factor of negative intergroup relations. In R. DeRidder & R. C. Tripathi (Eds.), *Norm violation and intergroup relations* (pp. 3–38). Oxford: Clarendon Press.

De Vos, G. (1975). Ethnic pluralism: Conflict and accommodation. In G. De Vos & K. Romanucci-Ross (Eds.), *Ethnic identity: Cultural continuity and change* (pp. 5–41). Palo Alto, CA: Mayfield.

Fishman, J. A. (1977). Language and ethnicity. In H. Giles (Ed.), *Language, ethnicity, and intergroup relations* (pp. 15–58). London: Academic Press.

Gallois, C., & Giles, H. (in press). Accommodating mutual influence in intergroup encounters. In M. Palmer (Ed.), *Mutual influence.* New York: Guilford.

Gallois, C., Giles, H., Jones, E., Cargile, A. C., & Ota, H. (1995). Accommodating intercultural encounters: Elaborations and extensions. In R. Wiseman (Ed.), *Intercultural Communication Theory* (pp. 115–147). Thousand Oaks, CA: Sage.

Giles, H. (1973). Accent mobility: A model and some data. *Anthropological Linguistics, 15*, 87–109.

Giles, H., Bourhis, R. Y., & Taylor, D. M. (1977). Towards a theory of language in ethnic group relations. In H. Giles (Ed.), *Language and intergroup relations* (pp. 307–348). London: Academic Press.

Giles, H., Coupland, J., & Coupland, N. (Eds.). (1991). *Contexts of accommodation: Develop-*

ments in applied sociolinguistics. Cambridge: Cambridge University Press.

Giles, H., & Coupland, N. (1991). *Language: Contexts and consequences.* Pacific Grove, CA: Brooks/Cole.

Giles, H., & Smith, P. M. (1979). Accommodation theory: Optimal levels of convergence. In H. Giles & R. St. Clair (Eds.), *Language and social psychology* (pp. 45–65). Oxford: Blackwell.

Hancock, I. F. (1974, Spring/Fall). Identity, equality, and standard language. *Florida FL Reporter,* 49–52, 101–102.

Kim, Y. Y. (1988). *Communication and cross-cultural adaptation.* Clevedon, Avon: Multilingual Matters.

Lawson-Sako, S., & Sachdev, I. (1996). Ethnolinguistic communication in Tunisian streets: Convergence and divergence. In Y. Suleiman (Ed.), *Language and identity in the Middle East and North Africa* (pp. 61–79). Richmond, Surrey: Curzon Press.

Lemco, J. (1992). Quebec's "distinctive character" and the question of minority rights. In J. Crawford (Ed.), *Language loyalties: A source book on the official English controversy* (pp. 423–433). Chicago: Chicago University Press.

Montaner, C. A. (1992). "Talk English—you are in the United States." In J. Crawford (Ed.), *Language loyalties: A source book on the official English controversy* (pp. 163–165). Chicago: University of Chicago Press.

Sachdev, I. (1995). Predicting Punjabi linguistic identity: From high to low in-group vitality contexts. *International Journal of Punjab Studies, 2,* 175–194.

Shumway, N. (1992). Preserve the primacy of English. In J. Crawford (Ed.), *Language loyalties: A source book on the official English controversy* (pp. 121–123). Chicago: University of Chicago Press.

Simard, L., Taylor, D. M., & Giles, H. (1976). Attribution processes and interpersonal accommodation in a bilingual setting. *Language and Speech, 19,* 374–387.

Smolicz, J. J. (1984). Minority languages and the core values of culture: Changing policies and ethnic response in Australia. *Journal of Multilingual and Multicultural Development, 5,* 23–41.

Tajfel, H. (Ed.). (1978). *Differentiation between social groups.* London: Academic Press.

Taylor, D. M., Bassili, J. N., and Aboud, F. (1973). Dimensions of ethnic identity: An example from Quebec. *Journal of Social Psychology, 89,* 185–192.

Thakerar, J. N., Giles, H., & Cheshire, J. (1982). Psychological and linguistic parameters of speech accommodation theory. In C. Fraser & K. R. Scherer (Eds.), *Advances in the social psychology of language* (pp. 205–255). Cambridge: Cambridge University Press.

Triandis, H. C. (1960). Cognitive similarity and communication in a dyad. *Human Relations, 13,* 175–183.

Wilemyns, M., Gallois, C., Callan, V. J., & Pittam, J. (in press). Accent accommodation in the job interview: Impact of interviewer accent and gender. *Journal of Language and Social Psychology.*

Woolard, K. A. (1989). *Double talk: Bilingualism and the politics of ethnicity in Catalonia.* Stanford, CA: Stanford University Press.

KEY TERMS

accommodation	underaccommodation
linguistic accommodation	Communication Accommodation Theory
objective accommodation	convergence
optimal level	divergence
overaccommodation	ethnolinguistic vitality
psychological accommodation	ingroup
	intergroup differentiation
	maintenance
subjective accommodation	outgroup
	Social Identity Theory

DISCUSSION QUESTIONS

1. Drawing from your own experience, what might be the implications of CAT for learning a second language? Using the constructs of convergence and divergence, discuss how well an individual might learn a second language and how often he or she might be inclined to use it.

2. As pointed out in this essay, CAT can be applied in a variety of intergroup contexts (e.g., intercultural, intergenerational, intergender, etc.). Consider how CAT might be useful in describing

interactions between grandparents and their teen-aged grandchildren. How does the application of the theory in this context differ from the intercultural context—or does it?

3. Reflect on your travels to other areas where people do not speak your native language. How did you decide on which language to use to speak with the people from that country? Was the reaction of the other person to your language choice positive, neutral, or negative? How would CAT explain why this reaction happened?

16

HELP! MY PROFESSOR (OR DOCTOR OR BOSS) DOESN'T TALK ENGLISH!

DONALD L. RUBIN

On his way to the first meeting of his Introduction to Business Accounting class, marketing major Greg Hanover[1] was feeling that familiar sickly sweet sensation in the pit of his stomach—half anticipation and half fear—that always accompanied him during the first week of class. As he approached the classroom, he saw his friend Barbara Coleman, another junior in marketing, hovering just outside the doorway. Greg and Barbara had taken two classes together last year, and they would occasionally get together to study before an exam.

"Hey," called Greg, "looks like the dynamic duo is back together again to fight the Battle of Accounting this fall. Let's go do it, partner."

"Hey, Greg! Awright!" Then, with her smile waning, Barbara continued, "But I don't know about this here accounting class. I just can't risk getting a bad grade in it. I need at least a B."

"Well, it's a required class; you've got to take it anyway, so we'll just bust our chops and do it. Right? I mean it may not be the most exciting stuff, but we'll do okay, and really I can see that you kinda need this stuff."

"It's not that. Have you looked to see who's teaching it?"

Barbara motioned with her head for Greg to glance into the room. The instructor was standing at the podium, looking over some notes, shuffling papers until the official start of class period. Barbara rolled her eyes and raised her eyebrows.

"Yeah, so, it's some TA. You always get graduate students teaching these intro classes. So what?"

"I'm sorry," Barbara said with finality in her voice, "I just can't go through another killer class with a teacher who doesn't speak English. I mean, math is not my best subject. So at least I need a guy who can speak the language when he's doing problems at the board. This summer I took stat from this Chinese guy. And I mean he was smart and everything I guess, but geez I couldn't understand a word he said. And everybody in the class was the same way. Some of them even went to the department chair to complain. Most people just stopped going because they could learn just as much on their own. I even went to the tutor and everything—but that lady was from some damn place too and it was just as hopeless with her. I mean, I was lucky I even got a D in that class. So

I said, from now on I'm not going to take any more classes from foreigners."

"So what are you gonna do?" asked Greg.

"I'm going to the section that's scheduled for 3:20 this afternoon and see who's teaching it. I might have to move my work schedule around, but it'll be worth it to me even if I have to take a closing shift one or two days a week. I just can't take another class from a guy who can't talk English. And if the teacher for that 3:20 class is another one of them, I dunno. . . . I gotta go. See ya! Good luck, sucker."

"Hey," Greg called after Barbara, "you've still got my number? Let me know what you find out about that afternoon class, okay? Give me a call!"

International Instructors on U.S. Campuses

Many readers will find that the preceding conversation between Greg and Barbara strikes a familiar chord. It is an instance of what communication researcher Nagesh Rao (1995) has called the Oh No! syndrome. In one survey (Rubin & Smith, 1988), more than two out of every five students reported that they had withdrawn from a class or switched classes when they found that their teacher was a non-native speaker of English.[2] Nearly three out of five agreed with Barbara in the vignette above and attributed a poor grade in at least one class to the poor communication skills of an international instructor.[3]

It's an ever more common scenario. The number of international instructors in U.S. colleges and universities is on the rise. Already by 1987

---

[2] Some institutional data (Norris, 1991; Oppenheim, 1996) suggest that students actually "vote with their feet" when they encounter international teaching assistants much less frequently than their survey responses indicated.

[3] The perception of students that international instructors damage their grades does not generally comport with actual institutional data. On average, students who enroll in class sections taught by international teaching assistants do just as well on examinations (Jacobs & Friedman, 1988) and on final course grades (Norris, 1991) as students who are taught by U.S. teaching assistants.

40% of the junior faculty teaching mathematics at U.S. institutions had received their own degrees overseas (Smith, Byrd, Nelson, Barrett, & Constantinides, 1992). Less than a decade later, nearly one-third of *all* graduate teaching assistants (i.e., faculty-in-training across all disciplines, not just the math-intensive fields) at some major universities were not native speakers of English (Oppenheim, 1996). In a number of math-intensive fields such as computer science and physics, well over half the doctoral candidates who are qualifying to teach at the college level are not U.S. citizens. In large universities, the student who graduates without ever encountering an international instructor is rare indeed; many have encountered four or more international instructors in four years of college (Fox & Gay, 1994; Plakans, in press; Rubin & Smith, 1988).

Ethnolinguistic Minority Speakers in Positions of Authority

The growing internationalization of the college professoriate is just one case of a broader social trend regarding ethnolinguistic minorities in the United States. In the past, ethnolinguistic minorities in this country almost always occupied subservient social strata—disproportionately undereducated, politically powerless, economically exploited. To be sure, ethnolinguistic minorities more often than not continue to occupy underclass positions in the United States. But as this nation moves toward greater infusion of cultural heterogeneity throughout its various sectors and strata, the phenomenon of ethnolinguistic minority speakers in positions of relative authority or power becomes increasingly frequent. Thus, as we have seen, it is now commonplace on most North American college campuses for Chinese or Arab or Latino instructors to occupy positions of relative authority over mainstream Anglo students (i.e., the teacher's institutional authority over the student).

A parallel situation occurs in the health care context. Increasing numbers of physicians are internationals, many of whom do not speak standard American varieties of English. As a rough correlate of national and ethnolinguistic diversity among the ranks of physicians, the American Medical Association estimated that 21.4% of all U.S. physicians licensed in 1990 were international medical graduates, perhaps a quarter of whom were U.S. citizens (Roback, Randolph, & Seidman, 1992). Between 1970 and 1992, the number of international medical graduates practicing in the United States increased 132% (U.S. Department of Commerce, 1994). Apparently these physicians are subject to the same sort of Oh No! syndrome as are international instructors. As evidence, consider the following introduction to a letter to advice columnist Abigail Van Buren:

> Dear Abby: So many physicians today seem to be of foreign extraction. I have no problem with that, if one can understand them. However, my gynecologist's new partner is Asian, and I often leave his office wondering what he has told me. . . . ("Patient Irked by Doctors with Accents," 1990, p. E2)

Another parallel situation emerges in employment contexts, in which upper-level managers of multinational corporations are often non-U.S. nationals, often not speakers of mainstream North American Englishes. For example, in 1989, within just the relatively isolated state of Georgia, Japanese trade officials estimated that about 200 manufacturing and commercial establishments maintained Japanese national management teams to supervise U.S. workers (Rubin, DeHart, & Heintzman, 1991). The not uncommon antipathy of mainstream North Americans toward Japanese managers was the premise of the popular 1980s comedy film *Gung Ho*. Here too, then, we see ethnolinguistic minorities in positions of power. In complex but increasingly common social dynamics such as these, how do listeners evaluate the speech patterns of such speakers?

Some Dimensions of Language Variation

Before we proceed much further discussing linguistic stereotypes, it is necessary to describe exactly who is subject to such stereotyping. I am going to label these speakers by means of an admittedly clumsy—but I think informative—

acronym. I will call them NNSMNAEs. The acronym stands for the mouthful, "Non-Native Speakers of Mainstream North American Englishes." We need to use this acronym as a consciousness-raising device. It reminds us that no one group or nationality owns the English language. It reminds us that we tend to judge a speaker's English language skills to be wanting mainly when that speaker's style fails to match our own. And it reminds us that the lines of demarcation between who counts as a standard English speaker and who is linguistically deviant can be fuzzy indeed.

Consider, for example, Chakravathi ("Chaki") Ghoshal. Chaki is a graduate teaching assistant in educational psychology. To look at him, he is clearly a person of color, and behind his back, at least one Anglo student has referred to him as a "sand nigger." Chaki's English is marked by language features that set him apart from North American speakers. For example, he pronounces the consonant "v" like the sound /w/ (e.g., "a wery big book"). Occasionally, his sentence structures sound odd, though not technically ungrammatical (e.g., "The question, it is not so very difficult were you to break it down"). Chaki grew up in a household in which English was spoken most often, with Hindi spoken mainly in the presence of his grandparents. He attended a school in which most academic subjects were taught in English from first grade. His own undergraduate college education in Bombay was conducted entirely in English. And yet when he first taught at a U.S. college, a delegation of students complained that Chaki was "a foreigner who can't speak English." To the contrary, Chaki *is* a native speaker of English, but the variety of English he speaks is an Indian English (Kachru, 1970). To accuse Chaki of not being a native English speaker is both an insult to him and an embarrassment for his accusers. The accusation also maligns the marvelous breadth and flexibility of the English language.

The United States receives large numbers of immigrants and sojourners from nations such as Jamaica in the Caribbean, Nigeria in central Africa, and Guam in the Pacific, as well as India and Pakistan in South Asia. Many residents of these nations speak English as their native languages, but they are not the same varieties of

English one typically hears in Nebraska or Connecticut. They speak what have become known as "world Englishes." It is important to appreciate that just because one does not speak a North American English, one may still be wholly proficient in a world English. U.S. students who would like to grab a share of the emerging global economy would be wise to become comfortable at least in world Englishes (if not in some second or third language), the *lingua franca* for communication of international trade and technical information.

Consider now the case of Hilda Estrada-Jackson. Hilda teaches an introduction to art history. Her mother is from a Puerto Rican background, though she grew up in New York City, as did Hilda. Hilda's father is African American, also a native New Yorker. Although Hilda can conduct rudimentary conversations in Spanish ("restaurant Spanish" her cousins in Puerto Rico call it), not much was really spoken in her home. Indeed, much of the Spanish Hilda did hear at home and on the streets of East Harlem was a kind of hybrid "Spanglish." When Hilda lectures or answers a student question, her sentence structure is quite standard, but her pronunciation marks her as culturally different from her students. She may say something that sounds a little like /Chew gunna halfta figyo that out yosef, my fren./

Hilda feels that students challenge her credibility and authority more vociferously than they challenge her Anglo colleagues. She suspects that her students prejudge her to be academically inept (at least until they take her first exam!) because they stereotype her based on her skin color and her language patterns. Clearly Hilda is a native speaker of North American English, but it is not a *mainstream* language variety like that of most of her students.

Finally, meet Li Wen Shu, a laboratory assistant in the nutritional science department. Wen Shu is a native speaker of Cantonese. He started learning English as a high school junior. (Prior to that time English was not a frequently taught language in the People's Republic of China, and even afterward, most language teaching materials and models came from the British Council.) He has been living in the United States for 6 years now, always choosing to room with a North American roommate, so as to improve his English skills. While he knows much current slang, he still misses the allusions of many common sayings and cliches such as "bone tired" or "easy as pie." Like many second language speakers, he has difficulty recognizing when people are joking around or being sarcastic in English, and he long ago abandoned any hope that English speakers would appreciate his own attempts at a light-hearted tone. Wen Shu has become quite proficient in English, but he may never quite master native English speaker patterns. Thus his speech will always mark him as "foreign."

We see, then, that deviations from mainstream North American English patterns can derive from various sources and can be manifest in a variety of ways. NNSMNAEs may mark their "otherness" by means of nonstandard pronunciation (what linguists call "phonology"), different ways of forming words ("morphology"), different choices and uses of words ("lexicon" and "semantics"), or variant sentence structures ("syntax").

One source of language interference that especially troubles mainstream listeners relates to the way language is used in social contexts ("pragmatics"). For example, a teaching assistant may say "Now it is the time for your question" rather than "Does anyone have any questions before we move on?" Students may perceive this teaching assistant as gruff or rigid, and perhaps they will not feel comfortable voicing the questions that are on their minds. In truth, this instructor may care a great deal about student learning but simply has not quite mastered North American norms for inviting inquiry (Myers, 1994).

Another type of language interference that seems to deeply affect listeners' impressions of NNSMNAEs pertains to the category of "prosody." Prosody refers to features that overlay words, such as stress and sentence intonation. Prosody gives our speech rhythm, melody, and emphasis. In typical Mainstream North American English (MNAE) declarative sentences, we drop our voices at the ends of sentences, and we usually do not stress each syllable equally. To mention but one example, in contrast, it is common for native Mandarin Chinese speakers to violate these MNAE patterns for prosody. As a result, it can seem to some North American listeners as if the Chinese speaker of English is shouting or scolding. Indeed, some studies conclude that prosody exerts more impact than even vowel and consonant pronunciation on listeners' judgments of speaker proficiency (see review in Munro & Derwing, 1995).

Linguistic Stereotyping

Some of the earliest and most influential research on how a speaker's language variety can trigger listeners' stereotyped evaluations was conducted in the 1960s in Quebec (for a comprehensive review of language and attitude research, see Bradac, 1990). Researchers wanted to determine how listeners in that ethnolinguistically fractious setting would react to speakers solely on the basis of language choice—French vs. English. But the researchers knew that listeners react not only to *group* identities deriving from language choice, but also to *idiosyncratic* personality factors signaled by such highly individual vocal cues as voice quality (nasal, resonant, etc.) and pitch (high or low). They therefore developed the "matched guise technique" (Lambert, Hodgson, Gardner, & Fillenbaum, 1960), which has served ever since as a methodological mainstay of language and attitude research. Matched guise research uses a speaker who is competent in more than one language variety to produce speech samples. When comparing reactions to, for example, a French speech sample and an English speech sample produced by the same speaker, researchers can be confident that any measurable differences in listener attitude are due solely to the contrasting language varieties.

Using the matched guise technique in the French Canadian context, researchers found that listeners formed very strong impressions of speakers based on very brief speech sample. The sociopolitical climate in Quebec has changed considerably since those studies were conducted (see for example Guimond & Palmer, 1993), but at that time, Francophone Québécois constituted a distinct underclass, whereas Anglophone Quebecers controlled most financial and governmental resources. Language attitudes paralleled this social stratification. When listeners heard a speaker talk-

ing in French, they judged the speaker to be less intelligent and less capable than when the very same speaker spoke in English. These linguistic stereotypes were similar for both Anglophone and Francophone listeners, leading to the conclusion that many French speakers in Quebec suffered from a kind of "linguistic self-hatred." Perhaps of greatest concern was the impact of language attitudes in educational settings. Teachers judged French-speaking children to have lower scholastic potential than their English-speaking peers. Teachers tended to give a low grade to a composition attributed to a French-speaking child, while the very same composition attributed to an English-speaking child received a higher grade (Seligman, Tucker, & Lambert, 1972).

Inspired by these studies of language and attitude in French Canada, U.S. researchers began to consider whether similar processes contributed in particular to stereotyped interracial perceptions. Not surprisingly—but still sad to say—it was found for example that Spanish-accented speakers suffered at job interviews. When listening to a Spanish-accented guise, personnel officers judged a job applicant eligible for a janitorial job, whereas the same person speaking in a MNAE might be judged management trainee material (de la Zerda & Hopper, 1979).

In school settings, educators were trying to understand why children who spoke Black English Vernacular (BEV) tended to achieve more poorly than children who spoke MNAEs. There are no barriers to learning inherent in BEV grammatical structure (Labov, 1972). Instead, teachers' linguistic stereotypes may contribute to student failure. When teachers hear students speaking BEV, they may expect those students to be less intelligent and less academically oriented. These teacher expectations can become self-fulfilling; that is, teachers may give less assistance and encouragement to the BEV speakers, and hence over time those children do indeed become academically less skilled than MNAE speakers (Williams, 1976). Thus the nonstandard language variety is not itself the cause of student failure, but teachers' reactions to that language variety may contribute to failure in school. Even when there is no linguistic basis for judging a student, if a teacher determines that a student belongs to an ethnolinguistic minority group, that teacher may *perceive* more nonstandard features in the student's language and devalue the student's school achievement accordingly (Pichè, Rubin, Turner, & Michlin, 1978).

The "Foreign Teacher Problem"[4]

The case of NNSMNAE college instructors is the obverse of these earlier studies of teacher expectancy and language attitudes. Here we have students judging their teachers rather than the other way around, teachers who are "others" vis-à-vis the dominant culture, and a curious power dynamic wherein teachers would surely possess high authority were it not for the compromising impact of their ethnolinguistic identities.

Negative reactions to "foreign" teachers are legion. College newspapers, as well as the wider circulation press, periodically investigate or editorialize about the "problem." Typical is this lead article from the *St. Louis Post Dispatch:* "For some college students, the classes taught in the ivory tower sound more like something out of the tower of Babel. They say they can't understand—much less learn from—some of the foreign graduate students teaching their classes" (Casmier, 1993, p. 1). State legislators and regents have in many instances joined the chorus decrying

"foreign" instructors' inadequate teaching skills (Monoson & Thomas, 1993).

The overwhelming complaint is that "foreign" teachers lack sufficient English proficiency. They are too hard to understand. Their lectures are incomprehensible, they fail to understand students' questions, and in any event their responses to student questions are just as undecipherable as are the lectures that caused the confusion in the first place. Students who are frustrated by their NNSMNAE instructors usually give up on their teachers and seek other information resources—other classmates or bearing down with the textbook—or else they just plain give up (Fox & Gay, 1994; Plakans, in press).

Universities across the United States have responded to student, legislative, and administrative complaints with programs to "remediate" instructors' English skills (see review in Smith et al., 1992). Usually these programs are targeted to graduate student teaching assistants (TAs), perhaps in part because it is politically more expedient to dictate requirements for graduate assistants than for full-fledged faculty members. While initially focusing on strictly linguistic skills such as pronunciation and classroom vocabulary, these TA testing and remediation programs have evolved so that they now address a wide range of instructional skills—for example, how to formulate good test questions, how to write a clear syllabus, how to conduct a lively discussion, even how to appreciate cultural diversity among U.S. undergraduates. In fact, these "foreign" TA workshops are the kinds of training experiences that would be of benefit to *all* college teachers, regardless of experience and regardless of ethnolinguistic background.

Stereotyping in the Perception of NNSMNAE Instructors

If these language "remediation" programs have the felicitous outcome of improving NNSMNAEs' teaching skills, perhaps that is fine. But just how justified are they? Are NNSMNAE instructors really so difficult to understand? No doubt some NNSMNAE instructors do lack adequate English skills and should never be thrust to the front of a

---

[4]I place the phrase "foreign teacher problem" in quotes because I want readers to think about the implications of each of its terms. The term "foreign" itself carries negative connotations (the term "international" is more neutral) because it conveys the sense that a person so labeled is like an invading body, not to be embraced by the society, but eventually to be isolated and expelled. Moreover, the salient issue may or may not be the instructor's overseas birth. Britishers or Canadians are not generally regarded as part of the "foreign teacher problem"; their particular international status might even be seen as an advantage in a teacher. On the other hand, U.S.-born teachers of Latino backgrounds cannot legitimately be called "foreign," yet they very likely are included in the "problem." And briefly, interrogate the nature of the term "problem" here. Why should a teacher with a broad background and multilingual ability be defined as a "problem"? If there were a "problem," to whom does it rightfully belong—to the international instructors or to the U.S. students? Who is in the best position to fix any such "problem"?

classroom. But all of our prior knowledge about linguistic stereotyping suggests that we had better look carefully at any accounts that attribute blame only to those who diverge from the ethnolinguistic mainstream.

First, let's ask by what criterion we should be judging the English language proficiency of NNSMNAEs. The bottom line in evaluating the speech performance of any teacher ought to be intelligibility and comprehensibility. Can the instructor be understood? Comprehensibility and intelligibility are not the same as subjective judgments of speech accentedness or foreignness. In one study (Munro & Derwing, 1995), college students rated a set of tape-recorded speech samples as highly accented—even some speech that (unknown to them) was produced by MNAE speakers. On the other hand, when those same students listened to those very same speech samples on another occasion, they comprehended the speech quite well. Just because you think an individual speaks with a strong accent does not mean you can't understand that person.

Next, let's consider the validity of our judgments of speech accentedness. A number of studies suggest that many U.S. students cannot distinguish between accents from different nationalities (e.g., between native speakers of British English and Malaysian; see Gill, 1994). Also, U.S. students aren't very acute in distinguishing different degrees of accentedness (e.g., between highly and moderately Chinese-accented English; see Rubin & Smith, 1988). I believe that each of us has a sort of "threshold of foreignness." When we feel (for reasons that are not fully understood) that a speaker's accent falls beyond some limit of tolerable divergence from MNAE, we perceptually lump that speaker together with other NNSMNAE speakers. In effect, we write off the speaker as just one more incomprehensible "foreigner."

Now we are ready to see how these perceptual processes operate in our judgments of NNSMNAE college teachers (summaries of relevant research can be found in Rubin, 1992, and in Smith et al., 1992). We know from end-of-term course evaluation data that international instructors are generally judged to be poorer teachers than their U.S.-born colleagues. Students regard NNSMNAE instructors as relatively less approachable, less enthusiastic, less interpersonally attentive, and less fair.

These perceptions of NNSMNAE instructors can be influenced by a variety of factors. Some of these factors are indeed instructionally relevant. For example, instructors with stronger English proficiency (as independently measured) or those who use personal anecdotes to help convey information fare relatively well. But judgments of language proficiency and teaching competence are also susceptible to factors that should be extraneous. For example, the nationality of a speaker (e.g., Sudanese vs. Italian vs. Iranian in one research study) or attributed institutional status (professor vs. TA) can affect students' reactions to the very same speech sample (Brown, 1992). A student's own background and experience also influence his or her impressions of NNSMNAE teachers. Students with liberal arts majors seem to be more tolerant than agriculture students (Fox & Gay, 1994; Plakans, in press). Students in more advanced classes register more positive evaluations than students in introductory ones (Oppenheim, 1996).

Students' stereotyped expectations of NNSMNAE teachers are foregrounded in a series of studies in which I have been involved. In these studies, for example, students who thought an instructor (whether international or U.S. born) was physically attractive generally had more positive perceptions of the instructor's accent and teaching competence. (This is adding insult to injury for those of us who resemble Gene Hackman more than Robert Redford!) More to the point of this story about ethnolinguistic identity, student judgments of instructors were not sensitive to *actual* differences in degree of accentedness. However, judgments of instructors were affected by listeners' *perceptions* of accentedness. Teachers whom students *heard* speak with a strong accent—regardless of the reality of those accents—received relatively poor ratings.

In addition, students' perceptions of the cultural "otherness" of the teacher exerted equally strong impact. Specifically, the degree to which students saw a teacher as more Asian-like and less Caucasian-like negatively influenced their evaluations of that teacher. These findings are consistent with others that examine how students on predominantly White campuses perceive Black teachers (Hendrix, 1995).

To explore how students respond to the very ethnicity of NNSMNAE instructors—apart from any language differences—I devised a very simple experiment.[5] 'Students heard a lecture tape-recorded by a MNAE speaker (a speech teacher from central Ohio). In one condition the students were shown a slide of an Asian face, and told that this was the face of the instructor to whom they were listening. In the other condition they were shown a Caucasian face. When students thought they were listening to an Asian, they perceived the instructor to speak with a marked accent—that is, students *heard* a "foreign" accent just because they were looking at an Asian face. Even more distressing, students recalled significantly less information when they thought they were listening to an Asian. They found the Asian's speech to be less comprehensible than the Caucasian's, even though in reality *it was the very same MNAE speech*. This is about the clearest possible evidence of stereotyped expectations in operation. One expects an Asian instructor to be incomprehensible, and so one in fact comprehends less.

Why are U.S. undergraduates so likely to harbor distorted perceptions of NNSMNAE teachers? Perhaps students have heard college folklore conveying horror stories about "foreign" teachers, and this creates high levels of anxiety. This anxiety throws up an "affective filter" that prevents students from listening accurately. We do know that direct experience with NNSMNAEs can dispel that tendency to distort. Students who have had relatively large numbers of classes from NNSMNAEs can comprehend accented speech with greater accuracy, and their attitudes toward NNSMNAEs are less negative.

This pattern of results, incidentally, is generally consistent with findings regarding NNSMNAEs in other professional or higher-status settings. In the case of Japanese managers in a sales organization, for example, U.S. listeners had rela-

tively positive attitudes when they judged the manager to be speaking with a MNAE accent. Even when the manager was in fact using a "Japanese-typical" persuasive strategy, listeners regarded him positively, as long as they mistakenly thought that his persuasive strategy was American-like (Rubin et al., 1991). In the case of South Asian physicians, U.S. listeners did a poor job of discriminating a moderate Indian accent from a stronger one. But when they *believed* they were listening to a South Asian, they found this doctor to be cold and unsympathetic. They did not like this person. Interestingly, though, in terms of medical competence, U.S. patients were not uncomfortable with the expertise of a "foreign" doctor. Their comprehension was not measurably impaired by listening to a NNSMNAE physician, but that is because their overall comprehension of the medical topic was so poor even when listening to an identified MNAE speaker, that it could hardly have been made any worse (Rubin et al., in press).

Strategies for Dealing with Linguistic Stereotypes

I do not believe that you or I or anyone else is a "bad person" for harboring linguistic stereotypes. Stereotyping is inevitable and in fact has some adaptive value for us. What I do believe is that we must all acknowledge and explore our stereotypes and then figure out how to deal with those stereotypes so that we can treat people in an equitable fashion, according to their merits rather than according to our expectations.

In the case of NNSMNAE instructors, their merits—if we allow ourselves to come to know them—are likely to be rather impressive. In many countries, the proportion of the population with access to higher education is less than a tenth of the U.S. norm (about 45% of the U.S. adult population has had at least some college course work). A college graduate from one of these nations, therefore, must possess extraordinary qualities. And then imagine the degree of competence and dedication it takes for one of these overseas graduates to function at a U.S. university level (even if not perfectly) in a second language! College stu-

---

[5] This study has now been replicated and extended, with similar results. This gives me a degree of confidence in its conclusions.

dents in the United States are indeed fortunate to be able to draw upon the intellectual elite from across the planet.

In order to capitalize on the invaluable resource that NNSMNAE teachers—or physicians or corporate managers—represent for us in the United States, we need first off to accept that successful intercultural communication occurs when *both* parties in an interaction make efforts to accommodate each other. To be sure, many NNSM-NAEs can use improvement of their English language and instructional communication skills, and we can be grateful that so many universities have initiated instructional development workshops for that purpose. At the same time, members of the mainstream host culture also need to accommodate. In fact, when we consider which parties are under the least stress in U.S. culture, which have the greatest degree of discretion and choice in their behaviors, and which have the most to gain from a successful classroom interaction—it makes sense to think that MNAE speakers might do a sizable share of the accommodating in these encounters.

A number of experts have laid out principles for effective intercultural communication behaviors in general (see, for example, review in Martin, 1993), and for effective student-teacher intercultural interactions in particular (e.g., Fox & Gay, 1994; Plakans, in press; vom Saal, 1987). From these, we can extract some concrete recommendations for MNAE-speaking students (or patients or workers) to take responsibility for effective communication with NNSMNAE instructors (or doctors or bosses):

♦ *It's okay to talk about language and cultural differences.* Most sojourners from another culture are delighted to have a chance to speak about the customs with which they grew up. The trick is to avoid putting the other on the defensive, as if you are attacking the person for being different. But if you approach the subject of cultural differences as a curious, open-minded ethnographer, you might be able to say such things as, "I see. In your college classes in Japan, the lecturer made a point of never making eye contact with students? And you all saw that as a sign of the

teacher's credibility? That's pretty strange to me because in the United States. . . ."

♦ *Respond empathically.* Put yourself in the shoes of an instructor who is trying to function in a second language and culture, whose interpersonal support system may reside thousands of miles away, and who feels "on the line" to prove competence every time that person stands in front of your class. What would you want and need to hear were you in such a position? Perhaps you'd like to hear someone acknowledging your efforts—and occasionally your successes. Perhaps you'd like to hear someone commiserating with you about shared problems. You might find yourself saying things like, "Your must find it incredibly frustrating having students wandering in and out of class the first week of the term. The registration situation at this stupid university is outrageous. I bet you've had problems yourself getting into some of your graduate courses. . . ."

♦ *Focus on what you can understand rather than on what you miss.* Exact recall of information in a typical academic lecture is actually fairly low, even when the teacher is a speaker of MNAE. And besides, most lectures contain a degree of redundancy. You should not be put off if not every word your instructor is saying is intelligible to you. Work on getting the gist. If the topic makes sense to you, congratulations. You're comprehending. If it doesn't make so much sense, see the following advice about listening actively.

♦ *Listen actively.* In the United States, we often expect a speaker to take the lion's share of responsibility for clarity. We tend to blame the speaker's inadequacies for communication failure. We expect our teachers to be explicit about the significance of some topic in class or about course assignments. In other cultures, however, it can actually be rude to speak too explicitly. Listeners are given credit for making sense and are expected to draw their own conclusions. That is just one reason why it is important for students to ask questions, to paraphrase, and to check perceptions with NNSMNAE instructors. But you'll need to do so in a way that does not come across as challenging your teacher's authority. Take ownership of your questions. You might find yourself saying something like, "This idea of a standard error of measurement is a little confusing to me, and I want to make sure I understand how it's different from a plain old standard deviation, which we talked about a couple of weeks ago. Here's what I understood you to be saying about that. . . ." In some cultures, students do not ask questions in the middle of class; they wait until afterward or for the privacy of the instructor's office hour. You might want to visit your instructor during office hours of the first week of class. Ask the instructor if it's okay for you to ask questions during the lectures. If negotiated in this manner, your instructor might be very pleased to have you as a classroom ally.

♦ *Take a stand against prejudice.* A class is a kind of culture unto itself. It has a set of characteristic norms and values and communication practices, just like a larger culture. In some classroom cultures, a norm of intolerance toward NNSMNAEs begins to take root when the first student says "Oh no!" and the second student rolls her eyes and the third student slams his book and the fourth student mutters under her breath. If you don't stand up and turn this behavior around, it will escalate, and only the most skilled teacher will be able to keep the classroom climate from utterly deteriorating. Talk to your fellow students in the hallway during class break. You might find yourself telling them, "Give this prof a break. What are you tearing her down for before she even gets started?" Get together with another like-minded student in the class and make conscious efforts to give the teacher positive, public feedback during class (you can do this without being too soupy). If despite your efforts the prejudice expressed in the class becomes too virulent, have the courage to find institutional channels for complaining against those who would sabotage your learning.

♦ *Don't panic. Be patient.* Many of the studies cited in this chapter point to the same conclusion. When we expose ourselves to NNSM-

NAE speech, and have positive expectations about doing so, we gradually accommodate to it. We become more effective listeners. This is a tremendous benefit for anyone who intends to function at top potential in a multicultural-multilingual nation and in an interdependent global community. It is a benefit that extends beyond what you learn or do not learn about the subject matter of a particular class. It is a benefit lost to those who throw up their hands and walk out of any situation in which they encounter a NNSMNAE.

Remember Barbara Coleman from the scenario that opened this chapter? Pity her.

REFERENCES

Bradac, J. J. (1990). Language attitudes and impression formation. In H. Giles & W. P. Robinson (Eds.), *Handbook of language and social psychology* (pp. 387–412). New York: Wiley.

Brown, K. (1992). American college student attitudes toward non-native instructors. *Multilingua, 11,* 249–265.

Casmier, S. (1993, April 25). English debate renews. *St. Louis Post Dispatch,* 1, 9.

de la Zerda, N., & Hopper, R. (1979). Employment interviewers' reactions to Mexican American speech. *Communication Monographs, 46,* 126–134.

Fox, W., & Gay, G. (1994). Functions and effects of international teaching assistants. *Review of Higher Education, 18,* 1–24.

Gill, M. M. (1994). Accent and stereotypes: Their effect on perceptions of teachers and lecture comprehension. *Journal of Applied Communication Research, 22,* 348–361.

Guimond, S., & Palmer, D. L. (1993). Developmental changes in ingroup favouritism among bilingual and unilingual Francophone and Anglophone students. *Journal of Language and Social Psychology, 12,* 318–351.

Hendrix, K. G. (in press). Student perceptions of the influence of race on professor credibility. *Howard Journal of Communications.*

Jacobs, L., & Friedman, C. (1988). Student achievement under foreign teaching associates compared with native teaching associates. *Journal of Higher Education, 59*, 551–563.

Kachru, B. (1970). Some style features of South Asian English. In K. Goodwin (Ed.), *National identity*. London: Heinemann Educational Books.

Labov, W. (1972). *Language in the inner city*. Philadelphia: University of Pennsylvania Press.

Lambert, W., Hodgson, R., Gardner, R., & Fillenbaum, S. (1960). Evaluational reactions to spoken languages. *Journal of Abnormal and Social Psychology, 60*, 44–51.

Martin, J. N. (1993). Intercultural communication competence: A review. In R. L. Wiseman & J. Koester (Eds.), *Intercultural communication competence* (pp. 16–32). Newbury Park, CA: Sage.

Monoson, P. K., & Thomas, C. F. (1993). Oral proficiency policies for faculty in U.S. higher education. *Review of Higher Education, 16*, 127–140.

Munro, M. J., & Derwing, T. M. (1995). Foreign accent, comprehensibility, and intelligibility in the speech of second language learners. *Language Learning, 45*, 73–97.

Myers, C. L. (1994). Question-based discourse in science labs: Issues for ITAs. In C. Madden and C. Myers (Eds.), *Discourse and performance of international teaching assistants* (pp. 83–102). Alexandria, VA: TESOL.

Norris, T. (1991). Nonnative English-speaking teaching assistants and student performance. *Research in Higher Education, 32*, 433–448.

Oppenheim, N. (1996, April). *Undergraduate learning from nonnative English-speaking teaching assistants*. Paper presented at the Annual Meeting of the American Educational Research Association, New York.

Patient irked by doctors with accents. (1990, May 11). *Atlanta Journal and Constitution*, E2.

Pichè, G. L., Rubin, D. L., Turner, L. J., & Michlin, M. L. (1978). Effects of nonstandard dialect features in written compositions on teachers' subjective evaluations of students and composition quality. *Research in the Teaching of English, 12*, 107–118.

Plakans, B. S. (in press). Undergraduate experiences with and attitudes toward international teaching assistants. *TESOL Quarterly*.

Rao, N. (1995, May). *The Oh No! syndrome: A language expectation model explains initial encounters between U.S. undergraduates and foreign teaching assistants*. Paper presented at the International Communication Association convention, Albuquerque, New Mexico.

Roback, G., Randolph, L., & Seidman, B. (1992). *Physician characteristics and distribution in the U.S.* Chicago: American Medical Association.

Rubin, D. L. (1992). Nonlanguage factors affecting undergraduates' judgments of nonnative English-speaking teaching assistants. *Research in Higher Education, 33*, 511–531.

Rubin, D. L., DeHart, J., & Heintzman, M. (1991). Effects of accented speech and culture-typical compliance-gaining style on subordinates' impressions of managers. *International Journal of Intercultural Relations, 15*, 267–283.

Rubin, D. L., Healy, P., Zath, R., Gardiner, T. C., & Moore, C. P. (in press). Non-native physicians as message sources: Effects of accent and ethnicity on patients' responses to AIDS prevention counseling. *Health Communication*.

Rubin, D. L., & Smith, K. A. (1988). Effects of accent, ethnicity, and lecture topic on undergraduates' perceptions of nonnative English-speaking teaching assistants. *International Journal of Intercultural Relations, 14*, 337–353.

Seligman, C. R., Tucker, C. R., & Lambert, W. E. (1972). The effects of speech style and other attributes on teachers' attitudes toward pupils. *Language in Society, 1*, 131–142.

Smith, R. M., Byrd, P., Nelson, G. L., Barrett, R. P., & Constantinides, J. C. (1992). *Crossing pedagogical oceans: International teaching assistants in U.S. undergraduate education*. ASHE-ERIC Higher Education Report No. 8. Washington, DC: George Washington University School of Education and Human Development.

United States Department of Commerce. (1994). *Statistical abstract of the United States 1994*. Washington, DC: United States Printing Office.

vom Saal, D. R. (1987). The undergraduate experience and international teaching assistants. In N. Chism (Ed.), *Institutional responsibilities and responses in the employment and education of teaching assistants: Readings from a national conference* (pp. 267–274). Columbus: Ohio State University Center for Teaching Excellence.

Williams, F. (1976). *Explorations in the linguistic attitudes of teachers*. Rowley, MA: Newbury House.

KEY TERMS

accented speech
ethnolinguistic
    minorities
instructional
    communication
intercultural
    competence
international
    instructors

language and attitude
    research
linguistic stereotypes
listening (active)
managers
matched guise technique
non-native speakers
physicians

DISCUSSION QUESTIONS

1. In the scenario with which this essay begins, the students make a whole string of inferences about the instructor on the basis of very limited information. How does this process of attribution work? Can you think of instances outside the classroom where these attribution processes also occur? Have you ever been the object of attributions that others have made about you on the basis of very limited information?

2. The author uses a very imposing label, "non-native speakers of mainstream North American Englishes" (NNSMNAE). Do you agree that this label is useful? What is included and what is excluded by each of the modifiers? For example,

why does the author say "North American Englishes"? Why not just "American English," or just plain "English"?

3. The essay proposes that effective communication is the responsibility of both speaker and listener. According to the essay, listeners sometimes are obliged to work extra hard to understand a speaker. Do you agree with this position? Is this what you learned in your basic public speaking class? Exactly what is the obligation of the listener to the speaker in intra- and intercultural contexts?

4. The essay describes some research in which potential patients regard NNSMNAE physicians to be as competent as U.S. mainstream physicians. Still, they did not like the "foreign" doctors. Can you think of some situations in which you have had these ambivalent feelings about groups of individuals? That is, you admire certain qualities in members of this group but dislike others.

5. At the end of the essay, you are challenged to stand up against expressions of prejudice among your peers. Have you ever heard a friend make a snide or disparaging remark about NNSMNAEs? What did you do in that situation? Do you really see any point in following the charge that this essay gives you?

17

"I CAN'T DO THAT!" BUT I "CAN ACTUALLY SEE AROUND CORNERS": AMERICAN INDIAN STUDENTS AND THE STUDY OF PUBLIC "COMMUNICATION"

DONAL CARBAUGH

"I can't do that!" The young woman was talking to me in my office about a required speech to be delivered in a public speaking course. The first as-

signment involved preparing and delivering a five to seven minute speech that demonstrated a basic process or principle. We had been going over—in class and now again in my office—some of the possible tactics one might use to design and produce such a speech when her hands trembled, her eyes watered, and with her head bowed she exclaimed forcefully through clenched teeth, "I can't do that!"

I remember vividly her highly intense emotional response. In fact, her reaction was so intense that I began immediately to search for possible reasons for her expressed difficulties, so I could help formulate possible and productive courses of action for her. While it took years for me to eventually understand even some of her concerns, some of the meanings in her exclamation that she "can't do that," we nonetheless worked hard together, for hours, to prepare for the delivery of her first speech—which turned out to be a very painful event for everyone involved, especially her.

The young woman in this opening story is Ms. Mina Running Eagle, a member of the Blackfeet Indian Nation which is centered upon a reservation in Montana, USA.[1] Over the next semesters and years of my teaching, I had occasion to contact several Blackfeet students in communication classrooms. Not all, nor even most were like Mina, but in her reaction we can eventually hear parts of the Blackfeet culture at work. After giving some time to reading about the Blackfeet, making their acquaintance, and learning some of their ways through observing and being with them, I came to a somewhat better understanding of Ms. Mina Running Eagle, and of what she was "up against" in her university course in public communication. Her exclamation of "I can't do that!," now over 16 years old, carries enduring meanings, and with the passing of time assumes newer meanings for me.

In this essay, I hope to show how I came to some understanding of Mina's exclamation by exploring the cultural forms of communication surrounding this required university course. By reflecting in this essay upon this event with Ms. Running Eagle, and similar others, I will demonstrate a complexity of cultural features that are involved in these and similar communicative events, and thus suggest what reflecting upon them can contribute to our critical understanding and practice of communication. I hope readers' teaching and understanding of communication will benefit, as mine has, by reflecting upon the use of diverse cultural forms of communication in settings of education, and in other human institutions.

Blackfeet "Communication"[2]

My grandparents taught me: The people lived in harmony with nature. The animals were able to speak. Their understanding of communication was far more advanced than from today's standards.   —Leon Rising Wolf

Some Blackfeet people, like Leon Rising Wolf, upon some occasions, use a cultural model of "communication" that presumes, *sui generis*, a patterned way of living. A primary mode of this "communication," from the Blackfeet view, is what might be called a "deeply communicative silence," a listener active form of non-verbal co-presence in which all is presumably interconnected. Mr. Leon Rising Wolf, a Blackfeet "blood" (i.e., a full-blooded Blackfeet) introduced that form of "communication" above, as something he was taught by his "grandparents," and discussed it further in this way: you are "able to communicate spiritually and physically . . . you are in tune with something long enough, to a point that you know it inside-out." His main examples of this cultural form consisted of detailed descriptions of "communicating with animals and spirits," "because when you're able to communicate with the animals [and spirits], you actually live that life, and you try to live that life every day."

This Blackfeet model of "communication," when realized, involves a scene of "harmony," of silently connective co-presence, a nonlinguistic togetherness in which one is knowingly integral to and communing with the actual persons, animals, spirits, and things with which one dwells. This is both an ideal for "communication" that is especially apparent in some special Blackfeet ceremonies (e.g., sweat lodge rituals), and, it is a desirable condition of "every day" communicative action. For this kind of "communication" to be forceful in social living, it presumes (and thus recreates) an unspoken consensus of interconnection that is largely non-verbal and non-linguistic, yet shared and publicly accessible, if one just listens.

This cultural model of "communication" creates a special significance for nonlinguistic channels of messages, and an important duty for communicants as listeners. Participants in this communication must therefore become active *listeners*, and observers of that which they are already a part. Mr. Rising Wolf described this ever-watchful form of "communication" in this way.

It's the hardest thing to concentrate on
    what you really believe in
It's the hardest thing to listen
It's one of the hardest things I think human
    beings have
    is to listen

And actually listen and hear what they listen to
    Not listen and then make up their own mind
        of what they heard
    Which is pretty common today
But to actually listen.
    And you start hearing the spirits talking
    And they communicate with people like
        Bigfoot, the eagle,
        elk, deer, the rocks, water

When these spirits come in
    you can feel, or
    you can hear those spirits. And
    you can feel them doing things to you.
Say if an eagle came in
    you could feel the breeze of that wing as he
        flies by
    you can feel it when he comes and puts his
        head by you
Same with an animal that has hair
    you can feel the hair
    you can feel the difference in hair too
        if you're born in the mountains
            been around mountains
            been around animals
    you've always touched the animals, so
    you can tell the difference
    you can close your eyes and
    you can almost say
        this is a dog
        this is a deer

        this is an elk
So you can tell that
    in the ceremonies.

By going through those there
    it rejuvenates your spiritual, spirituality
        and your rebirth of your confidence in
            who you are
        and that it's still alive and strong
        and no matter how far back East in
            some city
    you might be
  you know that nature and the
        communication
        between the animals and man is still
          there.
    it makes you feel spiritually strong
        to the point that you just want
        to jump with cheer and joy.

And you go back to your city life with that
    energy.

Mr. Rising Wolf's words point to a dimension of experience that is itself not a verbal event, but a real spiritual and physical event in which a person can (and should) participate, in which the meanings of interconnective living are constantly being re-created, if one listens and observes properly. This is a most valued event, a scene of Blackfeet "communication," that can be sought and realized not primarily through verbal interaction, but through actively listening amidst a silent co-presence.[3]

This form of communication can be alluded to with a rather quick verbal ellipsis. A middle-aged Blackfeet male, Mr. Perry Weasel, invoked this cultural form of "communication" with these few words, as he told me about his grandfather: "He was a superb communicator," then later, "he very rarely verbally talked, but there was just always a sense of knowing. His communication had a great effect on me as a child." The grandfather embodied and taught "superb" Blackfeet communication, not mainly through his words, but with a nonlinguistic "sense of knowing."

Using—what I now understand to be—this mode of communication, a Blackfeet boy gave what one fellow student called a "mesmerizing" seven minute public communication (i.e., a "public speech"). His presentation consisted of actively and artfully maneuvering "nunchakus" for his "speech." The only verbal portion of his "speech" consisted of only three words, spoken once about midway through the presentation (i.e., "like an eagle").

In these comments and actions, a primary mode of Blackfeet communication is being culturally invoked, and signified. It involves a kind of listener active, participant co-presence within shared activities, with each activity (e.g., Leon Rising Wolf's words, Perry Weasel's grandfather, the nonverbal "speech") demonstrating a kind of Blackfeet nonlinguistic "communication." Through this mode, the Blackfeet are saying something about people being already connected (or seeking a holistic connectedness), about people, spirits—and ancestors—being an inherent part of this grand picture, about natural features and animals being figured into this interconnected realm, with all of this providing a cultural scene of Blackfeet "communication." A primary mode of some Blackfeet communication is thus to "communicate spiritually and physically" through a listener-active silence with a cultural premise (a belief and value) of this mode being the inheritance of a holistic world of intricate interconnections.

This means of communicative living is difficult for Blackfeet to sustain in some institutional settings, yet it is also a means of coping with that very difficulty. As Leon Rising Wolf puts it:

After I finish school here I go back [home, to the
        reservation]
    to regenerate my knowledge
    to regenerate my spiritual beliefs
        myself
    by going to the sweats and start communi-
        cating again
        with the animals and the way of life
            around you
    the frustration, the turmoil, the confusion
        of everything is gone

Y'know, you've got a clear mind and a clean body
    you can think
    you can see a lot better
    you can actually see around corners
    you can actually feel things happen
        when they actually happen

So today I use my Indian ways to help me
    communicate
    in the Whiteman's world and travel
        through it.

While "school" had created "frustration," "turmoil," and "confusion," "communicating" the Blackfeet way enabled Mr. Rising Wolf to "think," "see," and "feel" "a lot better," to the point that he could "see around corners." By tuning into the nonlinguistic "way of life around" him, he was able both to "regenerate" his "knowledge" and "beliefs," and to "travel through" "the Whiteman's world."

For Blackfeet people who hold to this primary mode of connective co-presence, verbal "speaking" and "speaking in public" assumes a secondary status or mode. To "speak" in public, literally to say words while in the presence of many others, is an important skill for some in the tribe to master. In fact, speaking well is a valued art, as we will see shortly. But it is also risky as a social action. To speak publicly is to risk severing or tearing the actual or preferred interconnections among people, and to risk rippling the communal waters from which every member of the tribe draws sustenance. Part of the risk also results from stepping into a very weighty social position: it is to be one who can and should take such a performative risk; it is to be one who has been apprenticed in the proper form for this public, verbal action; it is to be one who is known by the community to be so apprenticed and so skilled; it is to be one whose speaking others can trust, for to speak is to carry (not necessarily only positive) repercussions for the community and the interconnected world. "Speaking in public" is thus to activate a secondary mode of communication that is risky both as a form of social action and weighty as to its social position.

For Blackfeet people, the social position associated with speaking in public is most typically, but not exclusively, an elder male.[4] As noted, to be one who can so speak is to be one of the proper social rank including one who has been tutored for years in proper public speaking. The risk of speaking, however, is magnified when in the presence of certain audience members, especially when with "outsiders" and "elders." Mr. Jon

Moore, a professional, highly educated (i.e., Ph.D.) middle-aged Blackfeet male who "enjoys speaking to kids," discussed the special context created when "older people" are in his audience: "I don't like to talk in front of older people. Subconsciously, I get a feeling of inadequacy, not up to par with everyone else, fear that you might tread on waters you shouldn't tread on because you're not as experienced as someone in the crowd." To do so is, for Mr. Moore, to insinuate yourself into a place where you do not quite fully belong. Presumably, those best equipped to speak are those who have been a part of this world the longest, are properly "in tune" with it, and have been properly trained to speak about it. As another Blackfeet put it: "If you speak out, you subject yourself to criticism," with this criticism coming most likely from those deemed most knowledgeable and skilled at public speaking, the elders of the tribe.

To speak, then, implies that one is presuming a particular social position, but further, that one is conducting a weighty social action. Why? Because the act itself involves pulling something out of the interconnected realm and giving it verbal attention. This is intrinsically a risky action, in that what one extricates from the interconnected realm is potentially (through the interconnective premise) a part of everyone's shared world, and that speaking about it invokes a knowledge that is the special province of "the elders." Speaking then presumes that one has stepped into a revered social position, that one has command of knowledge requisite to that social position, that one has the exercised ability to indeed speak about this in the presence of the present others, and that what one is verbalizing might—in varying degrees—be already known to everyone present.[5]

Those best equipped for public speaking are also those most socially interconnected (i.e., the elders). As an elder, one incurs the obligation to embody and transmit communal ways, and, when appropriate, to speak for other members of the community. This is an important ability because "speaking for others" in this way is a way of properly vocalizing the concerns of others in some communal affairs. That Blackfeet are prominently members of the familial community is evident with the wide use of a popular form of address— "nixokoawa," or "my relations"—which expresses

this presumed collective membership, and indicates possible access of each to the others, including the elders who can speak for them. Important to emphasize here is that the elder, in the performance as a vocalizer for others, is speaking not just for himself or herself but is speaking carefully and artfully as a member of an already inter-related community. The basic premise for such speaking is the inter-related whole of which each is an integral part. The specific focal concern being expressed by the individual who is speaking thus plays the concerns of individuals within this largely familial and communal premise. Through this process of elders being vocalizers for and with others, all active members of the interconnected Blackfeet people—including all others who are not elders—are presumably involved in communal, or tribal affairs, whether being the explicit vocalizer or not.[6]

These modes of Blackfeet "communication" rely upon, and in turn recreate deeply held cultural values. Some of these are the nurturing of the tribal heritage and natural geography, which are especially associated with tribal ancestors (especially "grandparents"), events (e.g., "traditional encampments," sweat lodge ceremonies), and the unspoken system of interconnections that precedes and encompasses any one sentient being, thing, or event. Related values involve modesty (deferring to the difference of each other, and a reverence for the whole) and stability (continuity of belief and value across time) with particular tribal members deemed a small and relatively unimportant part of this rather durable and holistic, "spiritual and physical" picture. Within this communal scene, persons and relations are erected upon a valuing of, and respect for social difference, with the society, and public speaking itself being at times a performance of social differences based upon individual autonomy, age, and gender.

In summary, Blackfeet "communication" is designed upon a primary mode of listener-active silence and its associated premise of interconnectedness. Figured upon this premise, the secondary mode of verbal speaking in public is deemed risky as a social action (because it might violate the presumed interconnectedness), and presumptuous as to social position (in that one steps into a highly respected position presuming one can so act by speaking). The secondary mode of verbal speaking relies upon and invokes social positions of difference with elder males being the traditional public vocalizers. These modes of communication and the cultural life they express reflect a valuing of heritage, nature, modesty, stability, and respect for differences in social positions.

"The Whiteman's Communication"

The alternate model of communication that Mina Running Eagle had contacted in her course in public communication could be called a "whiteman" or "white people's" model, this being the way it is characterized by the Blackfeet. Note that here, with this cultural model, the primary mode of communication is not a listener-active silence, but verbal speaking. The "white people's" primary mode of action is verbal and is based at least partly upon these "other" cultural premises: Speaking makes something public that was heretofore private, personal, or internal; Speaking helps create (or construct) social connections among those who were presumably different or separate; and, Connecting through speech is the principal way a society is made, and made to work. From the "white people's" view, the primary mode of communication is verbal speaking, with this mode being important for the actual "constructions" of personal, social, and societal life (Carbaugh, 1988).

A secondary mode of communication in the "white people's" system is silence. Communicative silence is figured upon the primary mode of verbal speaking and its premises. Silence plays upon the primary mode, however, by risking its negation, or by signaling the absence of the very premises that are presumably being activated in "white people's" actions of verbal speaking. Silence as a communicative action can mean, to "white people," a negation of one's personal being (as in "the silent treatment"), a failure to "connect" with others in "relationship," and a sign that social institutions have been ruptured or broken or corrupted (e.g., "a conspiracy of silence"). Without speaking, and with silence, one can hear

(or feel) being amplified not an interconnectedness as among the Blackfeet, but a separateness, and disconnectedness that is present between presumably different individuals or peoples. Silence, then, is a prominent way to accentuate the different, separate, and even disconnected states of affairs which are so often presumed as a basis for many public American (i.e., multicultural) events and scenes.

For the Anglo speaker, the primary mode of verbal speaking is associated not with a special role of "elder," but with the prominent and common social position of "citizen." Speaking in public, as a political and legal (i.e., constitutional) matter, is a performative possibility for everyone. The action of speaking in public is an essential part of being a citizen, and this action is codified and cultivated in the nation's legal codes. As a citizen, one is entitled to "speak in public," and given this "right," one can (and should) exercise it—and permit it to be exercised—rather "freely." The role of "citizen," from the vantage point of the primary mode of speaking, then, is not erected fundamentally upon social differences between the members of the society, but is erected upon a political premise of commonality among all members of the nation of the United States of America.

Because speaking is available to all citizens, and because it can be used to construct personal lives and social organization, one can use speaking as a means both to gain access into society, and to better one's place within that society. This Anglo belief—and the attendant, deeply felt necessities for construction and progress—it is crucial to recognize, is not a natural state of human beings, but is a belief that has been *created*, partly through this cultural conception of speaking. Further, it is being actively (re)created each time the political position of "citizen" is being connected with the primary expectation for verbal participation, and all of the typical cultural premises associated with that expectation (i.e., verbal participation as the necessary means of constructing, and bettering individual, social, and socio-political life). Some of the values associated with this belief system are upward mobility (that one can and should do better than one's current lot in life), change (that one should be different or "grow" beyond one's present state or lot in life), and progress (that movement and change is necessary for betterment and improvement). These values are often operationalized at a personal level, leading "the whiteman" to articulate and assert the values of change and uniqueness (that individuals are psychologically different, and should aspire to become better and different as a person).

The "white person's communication," then, relies upon a primary mode of oral speaking, with this being the means through which personal, social, and socio-political life is "constructed." The secondary mode of silence plays upon this primary mode and is a prominent way of signifying the absence of, or negating the possibility for personal, social, and socio-political life. The quintessential social position associated with verbal speaking in public is the role of "citizen" which is erected upon a common political model of "individual rights" among the nation's members. Anglo "communication," designed this way, reflects and recreates beliefs about the separateness of individuals as well as the optimism of constructing a personal yet communal life, while valuing upward mobility, change, progress, and uniqueness.

Intercultural Dynamics in the Classroom

With the benefit of these different cultural understandings of communication, we might now better understand Ms. Mina Running Eagle's comments, and the larger situation in which she found herself. What was she saying, when she said, "I can't do that!" What exactly was it that she couldn't do?

TABLE 1   Summary of Blackfeet and "Whiteman's" models of communication in a classroom setting

	Blackfeet	"Whiteman"
Primary Mode:	Silence →	Speaking →
Cultural Premise:	Listener-active, Interconnected	Speaker-active, Constructive
Secondary Mode:	Verbal Speaking→	Silence →
Cultural Premise:	Risky, Rupture	Division
Social Position:	Differences by gender and age	Commonality, equality
Typical Speaker:	Elder Male	Citizen
Cultural Persona:	Relational Connection	Unique individual
Values:	Nature, heritage, modesty, stability	Upward mobility, change, progress

The general, "whitepeople's" logic of the classroom assignment to which Mina responded could be put this way: As a citizen of this country, you will be required to speak in public, and you yourself can benefit from so speaking. Thus, learning to speak in public is essential to your general liberal arts education. In this class, the first assignment requires you to speak for about 5–7 minutes. You will verbally inform the class about a topic of your choice, one that is important to you, but also one that is important to this class, or this community today. In your speaking, you will not only display what you know about the topic, but also you will help construct a sense of that topic for your audience. This was the task before her.

From Mina's point-of-view, she had a different, or additional cultural frame-of-reference which competed for her allegiance, and with which she reacted to the assignment. Perhaps this, her interpretation, reflected—as another Blackfeet put it—a deeply "subconscious," "physical and spiritual" worldview or ethos. From this, Mina's view, the assignment was creating a social position of "public speaker" which was foreign to her and her place in her communal ways. Incoherent social expectations were being created for her as the assignment asked her, a young female adult, in effect, to speak publicly, and thus to step into the traditional position of being an elder male. With regard to the age dimension of this speaking role, she was too young and had no experience or training or at this point even desire to become an elder who would or could so speak. With regard to the gender dimension of this speaking role, she had of course no real physical or cultural experience. Public actions of speaking would (and should) come, if at all, much later in her developmental and cultural scheme of things. In effect, the course was addressing her as one who must perform in a social position that she respectfully reserved for "elders," especially "elder males."

With regard to her "communication" activities, she had been watching and "listening" carefully in class. She knew she was being asked to perform verbally (in her secondary mode), and she also knew that her verbal performance was to be witnessed by an audience that included two types of people—"whitepeople" and an older male teacher—cultural *persona* that were culturally salient to her, and to whom she felt public speaking was deeply inappropriate. To speak to this public was, to her, both inappropriate and incredible. From her cultural frame of reference, this presented a real problem, for she was being required to "talk" in public, to do so to people who were different and knew more than her, and further to do so in a scene which to her was very disconnected from her past, thus removing traditional sources of knowledge she had been taught to recognize and use. Further, she was being asked to perform through a communicative mode that was secondary to her. This kind of communication, itself, even for an elder male, is risky. To act this way, at so young an age, as a female, to this group of "whitepeople" including an older man, from whom she was culturally disconnected, all of this was nearly incomprehensible and dearly anxiety provoking for her. As a middle-aged, very successful, public *male* Blackfeet figure put it: "when I was younger, I used to get sick when I'd have to speak." Imagine how Mina felt.

We could summarize the sense of confusion and violation that the assignment created for Mina by formulating at least these conflicting, cultural messages: (1) About what was deemed proper in a learning environment: Mina was caught between Blackfeet demands to be a respectful listening student and "the whitepeople's" expectation that she be a verbally active student; (2) About what was deemed sensible as social organization: She was caught between her Black-

feet status as a young adult female and "Whitepeople's" expectations that treated her as a "citizen," with this role of "citizen" placing her incredibly, from her Blackfeet view, in the position of a male elder; (3) About "communication": She was caught between Blackfeet demands to utilize the primary, proper connective silence rather than the "whitepeople's" expectations to utilize, what was to her, a secondary, presumptuous verbal performance; (4) About attitudes toward the audience: She was caught between her Blackfeet heritage that taught her to respect differences in people based on age and gender and thus remain observant, rather than enact the "whitepeople's" citizen role and speak out; and (5) About the values that should be operative in this scene: Mina felt both the Blackfeet imperative to exercise proper modesty and respect for self, scene, and others, and the "whitepeople's" apparent requirement to exercise a productive verbal efficacy. Because she was being asked (required) to be, what she considered to be, inappropriately verbally active, incredibly an elder role, improperly speaking to an audience she did not know but whom she knew included "whitepeople" and a male teacher she wanted to respect, and because she thought the assignment required her to be not only rude but someone whom she was not and could not be, she exclaimed: "I can't do that!"

Beyond Mina's particular position, we could summarize the generally operative intercultural dynamics in this classroom in this way: In public speaking, "whiteman's" model presumes a common role of citizen, and a primary mode of speaking, which is erected upon beliefs about the separateness of individuals and thus the necessity to verbally construct life. Such "constructions" are often guided by the values of upward mobility, change, and progress. From the Blackfeet point-of-view, setting the educational scene in this way puts undue emphasis upon a secondary mode of communication (i.e., verbal activity), and strips the social scene of its deepest resources (i.e., the interconnected cosmos), its proper persona (i.e., elders), and its most valued features (i.e., of heritage, modesty, and respect for differences in gender and age). Entirely supplanted in this scene is the more primary Blackfeet mode of traditional communication (which to "whitepeople" can symbolize not affirmation and holism but negation and division) and the proper beliefs about persons, social positions, tribal living, and values associated with these.

Culturally Situated, Critical Reflections

In the contemporary world that we [Native Americans] deal with, we have an understanding of all the other religions, different types of language and cultures. Then when we try to communicate, say, with the people around us, or the people we're working with, it's really hard to do because (pause) of a lack of understanding of other Ind- of other people. Where a white person, wh- I don't know. (long pause) a confusion will really set in because white people don't understand the Native American.

—Leon Rising Wolf

What is an ethnographer's responsibility when confronted with situations like these, as in some scenes of education when a female American Indian student exclaims, "I can't do that!"? Or, when a male American Indian student gives a seven minute "speech" of three spoken words? Or, similarly, when Blackfeet males come to one's office and "speak for" a Blackfeet female?

I think we should, first of all, educate ourselves about such moments of communication, and be sure we recognize if, and when, and how, there are cultures at work in them. For each educational context, and for each peopled place, there will be cultural views of communication operating. Perhaps for some, a verbal channel is deemed valuable and very constructive; it is used as a way for each to exercise fundamental rights of each human being. Teaching and learning this channel is highly valued by them, for it can carry great force in their common political life. Failing to engage the verbal channel can lead, from this vantage point, to missed opportunities, continued oppression, even social disorganization. For others, from another view, a nonverbal channel is deemed valuable and interconnective; it is a way

of inhabiting an already inhabited world. Teaching and learning this channel is highly valued, for it keeps one "in tune" with "physical and spiritual" life. Failing to learn and exercise the nonverbal channel can lead, as some Blackfeet have said, to "elimination," "confusion and turmoil." As teachers, researchers, and citizens, we should be vigilant and cautious when the former "white" view requires the Blackfeet to speak up verbally and be heard, even (especially?) under the guise of "participatory democracy," for the demand itself supplants that which it seeks to understand and include. From the other angle of vision, if the Blackfeet were to make a demand, it might be for us to watch and listen, to be respectful and modest of that which we are all a part, especially when in the presence of something to which we are not yet attuned, like a deep cultural difference. The latter suggestion seems forcefully pertinent today, because it is too often "talked over," especially when our expectations are built upon narrow conceptions of "communication" and "democracy," with the accompanying imperative that all voices speak-up and be heard.

Ethnographic studies of intercultural communication can help us understand how different cultural orientations relate to practices of living like these, in and out of the classroom. They can help us understand the complexity and depth of perplexity created in some intercultural encounters, as when one sees great value in speaking up, participating and being heard, while the other sees value in remaining quiet, for so much goes (and should go) without saying. Knowledge as this is necessary if we are to understand, and critically reflect upon intercultural relations of each with the other.

In situations of education like the ones between the "White" teacher and the Blackfeet students, we must get to know better what our students are doing when they communicate. We must know who we, as teachers, are teaching, and the depth (when there is depth) of what we, therefore, are dealing with as we teach. In the process, we can come to know better what we are doing as teachers, only as we understand better what we are attempting to "undo" in our students. Only by knowing what we are attempting to un-do, can we better appreciate what our brand of education (and communication) is doing.

In turn, we must reflect upon what we, ourselves, are presuming as we teach, such as the beliefs and values we presume about speaking and learning. In time, we can then come to know better what at least some of our students are up against.

As with Mina and her teacher, so too for others can the paths of cultural reflection lead to mysterious places, including a critical distance from one's own familiar ways. By taking some time to walk and watch with each other, then, perhaps, we can design our actions—theories, practices, tools—with the intelligence of both in mind, knowingly creating our lives within the variety of available cultural views, helping each along our various ways. Proceeding in this way, giving each its proper due, suggests diagnosing our social ills, and designing elegant solutions for them, not by distributing some general critical manual for proper social and cultural and communicative conduct, but by carefully exploring the actual worlds of people and practices in particular places. So placed, situated in scenes of actual living, within cultural and communicative processes, we can then remain vigilantly watchful and cautious, so we do not—by championing our own way—mindlessly "eliminate" that which we failed to understand.

In the wake of the French Revolution, Vicomte de Chateaubriand expressed a similar thought when reflecting upon what others considered to be the perhaps quaint or obsolete mysteries of their day: "There is nothing beautiful, pleasing, or grand in life, but that which is more or less mysterious. The most wonderful sentiments are those which produce impressions difficult to be explained. . . . It is a pitiful mode of reasoning to reject whatever we cannot comprehend." Perhaps Leon Rising Wolf opens the door to a similar, under-appreciated "beautiful, pleasing, or grand" mystery with his comments about "the communication between the animals and man," since communicating this Blackfeet way can "make you spiritually strong to the point that you just want to jump with cheer and joy." Failing to learn from these "difficult to be explained" impressions, from

the delightful cultural mysteries others' lives present for our own, would be pitiful indeed.

NOTES

1. The selection of name for these people is not without some complication. The people of concern here are one of "the Blackfoot Confederacy" that consists of five tribes: the North Blackfoot, the Bloods, The North and the South Piegans and the Small Robes, the latter being exterminated by small-pox and warfare. What were the South Piegans are now called the Blackfeet, referring to the only tribe located in Montana, the others being in Canada. However, this version of history is written in English, and stands rather uneasily beside one inscribed in the Blackfoot or "Siksika" language. According to a Blackfeet: "In the Blackfoot language, the term Blackfeet is seldom, if ever, used to describe the American tribe. The name Blackfeet is an exclusively English term. The Blackfoot language name of the tribe is Amskapi Pikuni, or South Piegans. Pikuni derives from an old form meaning, 'Spotted Robes'" (Darrell Robes Kipp, 1993, p. 5). Because Robes Kipp goes on to use "Blackfeet" in his English writings, because this usage was adopted by my informants, and because this is the typical way of referring to these people in English, I select this usage. The Blackfeet reservation consists of four different governmental districts: Browning, Heart Butte, Seville, and Old Agency. Most of my consultants and observations are centered in Browning, with a few from Heart Butte.

2. The cultural models of communication summarized here are based upon earlier works with the Blackfeet (i.e., Carbaugh, 1993) and other Americans (e.g., Carbaugh, 1988). The larger project of which this essay is a part involves additional chapters, one exploring Blackfeet views of "education," another a comparative analysis of Native American peoples' views of speaking, teaching, and learning, and a third that explores the implications of these views for a communication theory of language, culture, thought, and reality. Following the Blackfeet, I use the terms "Whiteman" and "White people" as a cultural term to characterize prominent patterns in America today. Following Philips (1983, p. 16), I also use the term Anglo as a way of referring to traditions

of communication that derive from an English heritage (see also Philips, 1983, p. 16). There is no easy way to refer to these patterns, yet perhaps they are best identified as "prominent American" in that they are prominent in many scenes of America today, and are thus used by—or expected of—people with various heritages (racial, ethnic, or cultural). Exactly how such patterns play into these various scenes is an ongoing topic of my own research.

3. Mr. Rising Wolf's story is of course a verbal narration. What it narrates, however, or points to, is a kind of cultural "communication" that is not itself verbal. The event he narrates is deeply communicative but it is not itself a linguistic or verbal event. It is a "spiritual and physical" connection among things, beings. That it takes linguistic communication or a verbal narrative to describe that non-linguistic event, should not imply that the event being narrated, itself, is linguistic or verbal. This further underlines the importance of learning this kind of "communication" through watching, listening, and observing, through direct involvement in it, rather than through a secondary verbal discussion about it.

The crucial role of "listening" is apparent in a recent reflection upon the Cultural Survival group's State of the People Tour, a tour designed to educate audiences of violations in indigenous groups' rights around the world. In summarizing the tour, from "an indigenous person's point-of-view," Marchell Wesaw (1994, p. 1) wrote: "Each solution, if it is to be an effective solution, must come from a finely tuned listening. Indigenous communities know what is best for themselves."

4. The skill of speaking well, its association with elder males, and its use in disputes has deep historical roots in Blackfeet culture. One historian of the Blackfeet, when writing about the Northern Plains Indians during the late 17th century noted as much: Each band was led by a chief selected for his generosity, bravery and ability to speak well. Chiefs decided band movements and resolved internal disputes" (Bryan, 1985, p. 56).

Speaking in public however is just one activity within a whole cultural system of practice. That system, as a way of living, according to Beatrice Medicine (1994) derives from an equitable gender arrangement. She discusses American Indians prior to contacting the "Whiteman": "In most precontact societies, native women shared equally with men in so-

cial, economic, and ritual roles. Most ethnographic accounts (for the Plains culture area) emphasize the dynamic, dyadic interplay of both genders in the ongoing enterprise that allows indigenous societies to exist" (Medicine, 1994, p. 67). She goes on to review some of the deleterious consequences to indigenous people of contacting the "Whiteman's" educational (see below) and legal systems. She concludes somewhat optimistically by noting that now, over one third of the "seven hundred American Indian and Alaska Native lawyers" educated since the 1970's are women. Whether and how these changes—adaptations to the "Whiteman's" world—pervade traditional Indian modes of communication, and the resulting conceptions and arrangements of gender roles in American Indian societies, needs investigated. For example, in 1985, Myrna Galbreath, became "one of the few Blackfeet women to be elected to a tribal leadership position" (Bryan, 1985, p. 71). Whether Blackfeet (and other peoples) deem this event to be culturally significant and if so, how so, needs further attention, especially focusing on the role of communication in executing such a position (e.g., as a woman in an elected position of tribal leadership).

5. The possible exception to this is a speech about "oneself." A Blackfeet consultant explained that the "easiest speech to give is a speech about oneself." Presumably such a speech lays no claims to knowledge beyond oneself and is thus less featured in, but perhaps no less a part of the interconnected realm. The relation between Blackfeet models of person, "self," verbal speaking, and the listener active realm of "communicating with the animals and life around you," warrants much further attention. See Percy Bullchild (1985).

6. The importance and prominence of this elder speaking role is apparent in an advertisement for "The second annual Blackfeet Community College Traditional Encampment." Its first words are: "Join the elders and Blackfeet Community College for the second annual encampment. The elders will share knowledge and wisdom in the following areas: approaching an elder for assistance or knowledge . . . story telling by elders and traditional people." From the "Official publication for the town of Browning and the Blackfeet Reservation," *Glacier Reporter,* July 6, 1989, p. 8.

Author's note: I express deep thanks to the Blackfeet people who gave me the gift of their time and words. Parts of this essay were presented at the Ethnography of Communication Conference in Portland, Oregon, August, 1992; at a forum on Discursive Psychology, Oxford, England, October, 1992; at the Applied Linguistics Conference on the Intercultural Communicator, Tampere, Finland, November, 1992; at the Institute for Psychology, Innsbruck, Austria, March, 1993; and at the University of Massachusetts Conference on Ethnography and Qualitative Research in Education, June, 1994.

REFERENCES

Basso, K. (1990). "To give up on words": Silence in Western Apache culture. In D. Carbaugh (Ed.), *Cultural communication and intercultural contact* (pp. 303–320). Hillsdale, NJ: Lawrence Erlbaum Associates, Inc.

Berry, W. (1990). *What are people for?* San Francisco: North Point Press.

Bryan, W., Jr. (1985). *Montana's Indians: Yesterday and today.* Helena: Montana Magazine, Inc.

Bullchild, P. (1985). *The sun came down: The history of the world as my Blackfeet Elders told it.* San Francisco: Harper & Row.

Carbaugh, D. (1988). *Talking American.* Norwood, NJ: Ablex.

Carbaugh, D. (1990). The critical voice in ethnography of communication research. *Research on Language and Social Interaction, 23,* 262–282.

Carbaugh, D. (Ed.). (1990). *Cultural communication and intercultural contact.* Hillsdale, NJ: Lawrence Erlbaum Associates.

Carbaugh, D. (1993). Cultural pragmatics and intercultural competence, *The competent intercultural communicator: AFinLA yearbook 1993.* (Ed. by L. Lofman, L. Kurki-Suonio, S. Pellinen, and J. Lehtonen) *Publications de l'association Finlandaise de linguistique appliquee, 51,* 117–129.

Darnell, R. (1988). The implications of Cree interactional etiquette. In R. Darnell & M. Foster (Eds.), *Native North American interaction patterns* (pp. 69–77). Hull, Quebec: Canadian Museum of Civilization.

Deetz, S. (1992). *Democracy in an age of corporate colonization: Developments in communication and the politics of everyday life.* Albany: State University of New York Press.

Kipp, D. R. (June 1993). The Blackfeet: A Native American perspective," *Montana Magazine, 119,* 4–11.

Medicine, B. (Winter 1994). North American indigenous women and cultural domination. *Cultural Survival Quarterly, 17,* 66–69.

Philips, S. U. (1993). *The invisible culture: Communication in classroom and community on the Warm Springs Indian Reservation.* Prospect Heights, IL: Waveland.

Powell, R., & Collier, M. J. (1990). Public speaking instruction and cultural bias. *American Behavioral Scientist, 34,* 240–250.

Scollon, R., & Scollon, S. (1981). *Narrative, literacy, and face in interethnic communication.* Norwood, NJ: Ablex.

Sousa, A. (1994). *An "observation" of "participation": Interaction between Cheyenne Americans and Anglo-Americans.* Paper prepared for Communication 514: Social Uses of Language, University of Massachusetts, Amherst.

Weider, L., & Pratt, S. (1990). On being a recognizable Indian among Indians. In D. Carbaugh (Ed.), *Cultural communication and intercultural contact* (pp. 45–64). Hillsdale, NJ: Lawrence Erlbaum Associates, Inc.

Weider, L., & Pratt, S. (1993). The case of "saying a few words" and "talking for another" among the Osage people: "Public speaking" as an object of ethnography. *Research on Language and Social Interaction, 26,* 353–408.

Welch, J. (1987). *The death of Jim Loney.* New York: Penguin.

Wesaw, M. J. (Winter 1994). Mind over matter: Reflections on the State of the Peoples Tour. *Cultural Survival Quarterly, 17,* 1.

KEY TERMS

Blackfeet	public speaking
silence	Whiteman's model
communication style	

DISCUSSION QUESTIONS

1. How does listener-active silence as expressed by the Blackfeet differ from listening as experienced by most White people?

2. What are some similarities between the Black-feet and the Whiteman's model of communi-cation?

3. Donal Carbaugh used ethnographic research methods (observations, interviewing) in this study. What are other methods a researcher could use to investigate this same topic?

4. What are some communication strategies that White people might use in order to communicate effectively with Blackfeet people?

5. Can you think of other groups of students in U.S. college classrooms for whom public speaking may be a very unusual and difficult situation?

18
RITUAL AS PART OF EVERYDAY LIFE

BRADFORD "J" HALL

Many different assumptions underlie the study of intercultural communication. Perhaps one of the most basic is the idea of differences themselves. When we discuss the idea of communication across various cultures we assume that there will be at least some differences in dress, manners, values, gestures, and so on. After all, if there were no differences, the study of intercultural communication would be meaningless. However, this focus on differences can at times distract us from seeing that there are also many similarities across cultures. It is these similarities that make understanding differences possible, both in terms of scholarly study and daily practice. This essay attempts to detail and describe one form of similarity, ritual.

I maintain that ritual is a universal form of communication and that examples of ritual may be found in every cultural group or community. Ritual is a communication activity whose universal nature at the process level allows us to discover cultural differences in content (Philipsen, 1987). In this introduction to the concept of ritual and its manifestation in everyday life, I deal with three basic concerns about rituals. First, I try to explain what a ritual is by using common impressions about what constitutes a ritual as a seed from which a fuller, more useful understanding of the nature of rituals may be produced. Second, I briefly consider how and where individuals might discover rituals in their everyday lives and in the lives of others. Finally, I consider the value of rituals in terms of what purpose they serve within a community and why we would be interested in studying them.

In understanding and identifying rituals within any given community, I follow the lead of Philipsen (1992), who posits ritual as "a structured sequence of actions the correct performance of which pays homage to a sacred object" (p. 133). As is often the case, this definition will be both more meaningful and more useful when considered in light of specific examples; therefore, I will give some examples before trying to elaborate on the definition itself. I begin the essay by looking at the concept of ritual as it is commonly viewed in the United States.

(Mis)Impressions About the Nature of Rituals

When the term "ritual" is mentioned in class, it typically evokes one or more of the following four images: (1) a form of communication that involves doing the same thing over and over; (2) communication that is essentially outdated and hypocritical, and meaningless; (3) something reserved for very specialized settings, such as religious institutions or secret organizations; and (4) something that is quite foreign to our daily lives or that is performed by others whom we perceive as being less sophisticated than ourselves. I use each of these impressions as a foil to help explain and illustrate how ritual is a part of a communal life across very distinct cultures, including your own.

The *first* notion, that ritual is simply the repetition of the same thing over and over, roughly corresponds with the "structured sequence of actions" part of the definition I presented earlier. However, viewing ritual as simply the same thing done over and over is potentially misleading. As with all of the four impressions to be considered, I will use an actual example of a ritual to help give a fuller understanding of ritual communication. To begin with I will use Chen's (1990/1991) example of the *keh chee* ritual, an exchange between host and guest at a Chinese dinner table:

1. Host: Eat more? Come on: don't be "keh chee." . . . Have more food, please have more. . . .

2. Guest: No, thanks, I've eaten a lot already, really, thank you: I can't eat any more. . . .

3. Host: Come on, more, just a bit more. You're the most important guest tonight. . . . So "keh chee". . . . How come eat so little?

4. Guest: No, it's enough, really, really . . . I'm not being "keh chee"; eat more yourself. (rotating the Lazy Susan back so that the new dish is facing the host)

5. Host: (with enthusiasm): Come on, don't be "keh chee," you can afford to eat more. . . . You ate too little. Just a bit more. . . . (rotating the Lazy Susan again)

6. Guest: Alright, just a bit more. . . . Thank you: too much food, so "keh chee." (p. 109)

Keh chee may be translated as "guest spirit." Both host and guest may be said to have guest spirit. The guest is *keh chee* in that he or she is polite and modest about food consumption. The host has *keh chee* because he or she has provided an abundance of food. In fact, Chen notes that a successful dinner party is marked by both an abundance of food and a noisy, boisterous atmosphere. Consistent with my initial definition, the *keh chee* ritual itself, just one part of the overall dinner interaction, is marked by a structured sequence of communicative actions or moves. The first move is made by the host, who offers the guest more food. The guest in turn declines

this offer so as not to look like a "hungry pig." The host then challenges the guest's declination by finding some excuse for the guest to eat, such as "You're so skinny, you ought to eat some more" (Chen, 1990/1991, p. 125). The fourth and final move is the guest submitting to the host's offer and accepting more food. Thus, the structured sequence of actions is offer, decline, challenge, and submit. The second and third actions may be repeated before the fourth one is engaged in. This structured sequence, in accordance with the impression noted earlier, is repetitive in nature. However, this repetition is in regard to the type of communication, not in the sense of the same words being spoken over and over. There is room for great creativity by both guest and host. Indeed, a sign of a good host is the ability to create excuses for the guest to eat more.

It has been argued that for the Chinese, sincerity has more to do with correctly performing social duties than with being "true" to one's inner self, as is typical in the West (Stover & Stover, 1976). Chen's (1990/1991) discussion of *keh chee* ritual illustrates this very point, for to correctly engage in the ritual, guests must at some point deny their personal feelings. If they really want more food, they must still initially decline; and if they really do not want any more, they must still accept more if the ritual is going to be played out correctly. Thus, Chinese understanding of sincerity may be said to be both reflected and constituted within this particular ritual.

The *second* impression to be considered is often an extension of the idea that ritual is viewed as a mindless routine. Ritual is thus taken to be relatively meaningless or even hypocritical. A comment such as "Oh, it's just a ritual" implies that one should not take it seriously, that it is just something done for the sake of appearances. The understanding of ritual aimed at in this essay is in marked contrast to such an idea. Research from another part of the world provides an example of how this second impression distorts the concept of ritual as discussed here. Fitch (1990/1991) takes a close look at cultural communication within Colombia, specifically detailing something she calls the *salsipuede* ritual.

An example of this ritual is recorded by Fitch (1990/1991) during a wedding reception held in the home of H1 and H2. Fitch provides the

Spanish version and the English translation, but for the sake of space, I have adapted it to include only the English version:

1. G: I'm leaving.

2. H1:   You're leaving? Why?

3. G: The little card [wedding invitation] said very clearly that [the reception would last] from 7 to 10 and now it's 10:30.

4. H2:   But so <u>what</u>, until five thirty (G starts to chuckle) in the morning I'll be here=

5. G: =But I have to <u>go</u>=

6. H1:   =Hmf, that you have to go. And <u>why</u>.

7. G: Because I live far away

8. H2:   (H2 cuts in on top of G) But that doesn't <u>matt</u>er

9. H1:   Hmf. Says he's going. Just like (G starts to laugh again) that I'm going.

10. G: But it's that I have to go catch a <u>bus</u>=

11. H2:   =No, no, later we'll take you

12. H1:   (talking over H2) Have another little drink brother.

13. H2:   or you can go with Alberto who lives out there and has a car.

G finally agrees and stays at the party another hour.

Fitch notes that given the tenacity with which H1 and H2 consistently deny G's attempts to leave, one might believe that they know G well and particularly desire his company. However, they have only just met briefly earlier in the evening and in fact spent very little, if any, time talking with G through the rest of the time he spent at the party after agreeing to stay. In spite of the pressure to stay and the lack of interaction after the pressure has succeeded, Fitch notes that the atmosphere stays light and friendly throughout this interaction and the evening in general.

Such an exchange could be very frustrating to someone from the United States. In fact, given Basso's (1979) description of norms for leave-taking among the Western Apache, the exchange could be seen as extremely rude. So how does one make sense of this interaction? Through a process of ethnographic observation and interviews, Fitch

found that Colombian hosts inevitably performed what she came to call the *salsipuede* (or "leave if you can") ritual. The structured sequence of acts in this ritual includes an announced intention to leave, a request for an account of why that person must leave, an account or explanation, a denial of the legitimacy of that account and a proposed alternative that would allow the guest to stay, and finally an agreement to stay. As with the *keh chee* ritual, some of the moves, such as the account or explanation move and denial of that account's legitimacy move, may be repeated before getting to the final agreement to stay.

So, does the fact that the hosts did not seem to pay that much attention to G afterward mean that their actions were hypocritical and meaningless? No, but to better understand this we need to return to the latter part of the definition noted earlier—that when these structured actions are performed correctly, they pay homage to some sacred object. The sacred object referenced in this definition may be something of a religious nature, but it may also be any item or ideal that is highly valued within the community in which the ritual is relevant. In other words, if the people involved in the interaction follow the steps of the ritual correctly, some ideal or cultural good is reinforced and explicitly or implicitly honored.

Fitch (1990/1991) explains that the sacred object or ideal to which the *salsipuede* ritual is paying homage is the *vínculo*, or relationship formed and celebrated during the event. Colombians see this relationship or interpersonal bond as a crucial part of defining who a person is. It is not the individual (or his or her desire to leave a party) that is so important here, but the connection that is formed and maintained in that situation. Fitch argues that the development and recognition of these interpersonal bonds or contacts is an important part of effectively engaging in virtually all facets of Colombian society. The point of the ritual is not that the individual's unique presence is strongly desired as much as it is that the bond created or reflected by his or her attendance at this social event (for which the host is at least in part responsible) is honored by communication that encourages a continued mutual presence.

The *keh chee* ritual discussed earlier also paid homage to a cultural ideal. Chen (1990/1991) discusses this object in terms of the generosity of the other person. The host recognizes the generosity of the guest by assuming that the food is declined out of guest spirit, whereas the guest honors the generosity of the host by eventually eating and acknowledging the host's excellent meal, thus establishing the competence of the host in fulfilling that social role. Chen argues that this positive image or "face" for the host is the primary object to which homage is paid in the ritual.

Perhaps the meaningfulness of these rituals is best grasped when considering the consequences of not performing them correctly. Fitch (1990/1991) reports that the few violations of this ritual (such as someone actually leaving directly) were considered to be either rude or incompetent. A guest who just leaves without saying good-bye or leaves in spite of the host's efforts to get him or her to stay for a little while longer, or a host who simply says, "Nice you could come, see you later," would face very negative social repercussions. Therefore, although these rituals are done routinely and often quickly, they are not meaningless. It is certainly possible for a person to fulfill his or her part of a ritual while privately preferring not to, but the real desire to build and maintain certain images and relationships makes the individual's enactment sincere at a deeper level.

The *third* impression to be considered is that ritual is something reserved for very specialized settings, such as religious institutions or secret organizations. The examples of *keh chee* and *salsipuede* may, in part, lend credence to such an idea, for these rituals are done only in certain social settings. One does not engage in the *keh chee* every time one eats dinner, nor does one engage in the *salsipuede* ritual every time one parts from another person. In addition, virtually all religions have meetings or activities of some form that involve set steps that when followed properly pay homage to some form of divinity, and many organizations have secret rites that would also fit the concept of ritual. However, as with the first assumption, although this assumption may be correct in some ways, taken simply at face value it distorts and unnecessarily restricts the notion of ritual discussed here.

Rituals can be and often are part of the mundane, everyday interactions of life. For ex-

ample, three female Japanese students who were studying in the United States were seated at a table sharing lunch when the following exchange (translated from the original Japanese) occurred between two of the women:

1. A: I want you to help to organize my ⌈essay
2. B: No!
3.   (laugh) I am not a person who can give you
4.   advice because I haven't passed the English
5.   Proficiency Exam yet
6. A: (laugh) But, you are taking one of English
7.   classes, aren't you? English ⌈class!
8. B: No! It has
9.   nothing to do with my ability to write
10.   English I am doing a terrible job in the
11.   the class and (pause) I usually have to
12.   spend three days for writing an essay like
13.   this (laugh)
14. A: Come on! I have to submit this essay by
15.   tomorrow I don't have time
16. B: You are so coercive! (laugh) ((serves as notice that the request will be granted))

This conversation is an example of what Hall and Noguchi (1995) term the *kenson* ritual. *Kenson* is a Japanese term that may be translated as modesty. However, there are some subtle but significant differences. For example, although both modesty and *kenson* involve a discounting of one's personal abilities, modesty functions more as a shield against negative attributions directed toward the individual, whereas *kenson* is more of a social glue that maintains the status quo of a relationship. One may cover oneself with clothes and be said to dress with modesty, but one can never be said to dress with *kenson;* such an idea is nonsensical.

Hall and Noguchi (1995) explain that ritualized *kenson* involves four basic steps: (1) highlighting of another's ability, (2) denial, (3) reassertion, and (4) indirect acceptance. By engaging in these four steps, homage is subtly paid to the status quo of the relationship. In the example of the two students, a relatively equal relationship exists between the women, although all at the table know that B is better at English than is A. However, B is aware of the implied compliment in A's request, and in order to avoid putting herself in a higher position than A, B engages in ritualized *kenson*. As with the *keh chee* and *salsipuede* rituals, the middle steps of the *kenson* example are repeated before going to the final step, but this is not necessary.

As with other rituals, however, if these steps were not followed correctly, negative social implications would arise. For example, if B just said, "Sure, I'd be glad to help," she would come across as somewhat pompous. Even if she spoke modestly (by American standards), saying, "Well, I'm not that great, but I'll try," she would be seen as expressing only reluctance, not *kenson*. In addition, if A had accepted B's first refusal, she would have been seen as insensitive and would have put B in the awkward spot of seeming to be uncooperative. The *kenson* ritual requires both persons' proper participation.

Finally, and most important for the purposes of this essay, this ritual was done spontaneously, over just a matter of seconds in a very everyday sort of setting. The young women were simply having an informal lunch together, a frequent and mundane activity. It is very unlikely that either of them even thought about *kenson* in an explicit way while they were engaged in it. It was simply an everyday sort of interaction that is recognizable as a ritual only after careful analysis.

This point brings us to the *fourth* and final assumption to be considered in this essay, the notion that ritual is something that is quite foreign to our daily lives or is performed by people whom we perceive as being less sophisticated than ourselves. No doubt, examples of ritual can be found in other communities besides our own. In fact, these are often easier to notice because, as with the *kenson* example, many of our own rituals seem so natural and spontaneous that we never see them as such, although we always know when something has gone wrong in their performance. Even then we don't typically think something like

"Oh, he violated the *salsipuede* ritual"; we just know that "he" is rude or has some other negative characteristic.

However, if we assume that we (whatever "we" that is) are somehow above rituals, we make a serious misjudgment. To help illustrate this point, let me explain a ritual that is common in the United States (and among college-educated people) and, as with the other rituals noted previously, is engaged in without consciously being aware that it is even a ritual. The ritual I speak of is the "communication" ritual (Katriel & Philipsen, 1981). Violations of this ritual are often revealed in such statements as "What we need is communication" or "There is a lack of communication here."

Katriel and Philipsen (1981) identify four communicative moves in the communication ritual that must be followed in order to be able to say that some people really communicated. The first move is to raise some sort of issue or concern upon which a person may take a stand. The second move involves acknowledging the legitimacy of that concern or issue as worth attending to. Third, there is a sharing of ideas on that issue or concern from either the participants or just the initiator. The fourth and final move must in some way express the idea that "I'm okay, you're okay." This expression may be explicit or implicit. When this ritual is performed correctly, it pays homage to the inherent worth of each individual.

This is a ritual with which I suspect many of you will be familiar, even if you have never thought of it as a ritual. A clue to whether or not you share an understanding of this ritual is how you would react to violations. For example, suppose a wife says to her husband, "I'm worried about Johnny. He got in another fight today at school," and the husband responds with "Not now, I'm in the middle of my show." Many would feel that there is a lack of communication. If this scene were typical of the husband and wife's interaction as a whole, there is a good chance that the feeling of a lack of communication would be even stronger and would likely include some negative connotations toward the husband or wife. Such attributions use a very culturally biased view of "communication." After all, meanings were passed across people, communication did in fact occur in what may be argued to be a very forceful manner. Furthermore, if the talk ended with the individuals blaming each other and so forth, it is likely that many would say there had been a "communication breakdown," even though communication in a more universal sense was going on in a very active manner. The problem is that when people don't follow the communication ritual, they are viewed from a certain cultural viewpoint as not really having communicated. Many people who might feel that they don't believe in or participate in rituals get quite offended when someone else refuses to perform the "communication ritual" properly.

Recognizing Rituals Around Us

You may be asking, how can I recognize and understand rituals? Although a full answer to this question is beyond the scope of this essay, here are a couple of suggestions. One, look for rituals around important social events. Trice and Beyer (1984) identified six events that often take place within some form of organization (business, political, religious, government, education, volunteer, family, and so forth). These events include rites of passage, degradation, enhancement, integration, and termination. All of these events center around those times when a person's social role, identity, status, or power level is changed. The change may be for the better or the worse, but regardless of the direction of the change, the social relationships are altered and highlighted. Thus, one way to begin to look for rituals is to identify set times that involve some kind of relational change. This identification of recognized social change may be approached through such questions as Do these changes follow a certain pattern? and What sort of values are being honored, directly or indirectly, by change?

Not all rituals involve a relational *change;* indeed, most of the examples given so far in this essay involve more of a confirmation and recognition of existing relationships than a perceived change in a relationship. Another way to start to notice rituals is to ask yourself what you say just

because you and someone else are friends, brothers, sisters, classmates, or any other social role relationship you may consider. Although the exact content may change, do you say the same types of things in a similar order in similar places? Do others in your community say similar sorts of things when acting in those social roles? What do you think you get out of these exchanges? Why do you engage in them? Try to go beyond the initial surface explanations. If the pattern you discover is culturally significant, you can expect that violations of the pattern will be disturbing to one or more of those involved in the interaction.

A third way to discover often-taken-for-granted rituals is to observe when you or someone else makes negative attributions about other people. What expectations were violated that led to the negative feelings? Perhaps the other person was not following the proper form or steps of an unspoken and culturally assumed ritual. This is opposite to the previous approach, in that you use the negative attributions as a signal of where to look instead of as a piece of evidence to support your claim that a certain type of interaction is ritualistic. Remember, many rituals are often not really seen as rituals and bring no attention to themselves except when their proper enactment is violated. Thus, frustrations with others may provide one possible pathway to tracking down a common ritual that would otherwise have been missed because people seemed to just be acting normal.

The Worth of Rituals

One question that often comes up in a discussion of ritual is, Why don't people just be open and get to the point? If I want more food, I should just say so, and I should be just as open if I don't want more food. Rituals may seem very inefficient, a sort of cultural fluff that would be better put behind us. I will try to illustrate the importance of rituals by reviewing one I learned and participated in while still a youth (also discussed in Hall, 1996). When I was very young, we moved across the country to within walking distance of my mother's parents' home. Around the age of 7 or 8,

I started helping out around my grandparents' place by mowing, weeding, and doing other yard work. After one of these initial efforts, my grandmother gave me some money for my help. Quite excited about this turn of events, I told my mother about the money, but she was not as excited as I. "Didn't you tell her no?" she asked. My uncomfortable silence was answer enough. She then tried to explain to me about fixed income and helping out just because we were family, and that I should not be taking my grandparents' money for helping.

So, after the next time I helped out and was offered money, I told my grandmother, "No thanks, I was just happy to help out." My grandmother insisted on paying me. Finally, after going back and forth a bit, she stuffed the money into my pocket and told me to get an ice cream or something. Worried that my mother would find out (she always seemed to), I told her what had happened. Instead of being upset, she noted that at least I had tried. I quickly learned that if I communicated in the right way, said no at first and indicated that I just wanted to help out, it was okay to get the money (which I wanted), but that if I did not communicate appropriately, the same activity—taking the money—was not acceptable.

Some might assume that what I was learning was how to manipulate people and that it would have been better if I had just taken the money without the ritual. I would disagree with this because as time went on I found myself *wanting* to help out without being paid, and at certain times I could accomplish this by doing the act secretly or leaving before the ritual could be enacted, for once the ritual was started, a violation never created the same good feelings. This development of the right "feelings" was an important part of my cultural education. It was part of the development of my cultural competence; I was being taught about important values within my community, such as respect and gratitude. Rituals may seem to be very ineffective ways to accomplish certain immediate tasks, but what is sometimes forgotten is that the primary tasks being accomplished are to affirm and reaffirm certain types of relationships and teach values that are important in a particular cultural community.

Rituals are a vital part of any community not only because they teach people what is good, providing, as noted before, a way to create and maintain important social relationships, but rituals also serve a cohesive function for the larger community in general. With all the rituals noted thus far, people who are engaged in them do not consciously think, "I am engaging in a ritual." Yet they still routinely follow structured series of acts, the correct performance of which pays homage to some cultural good or ideal. So, even though certain aspects of the content may vary and there is a sense of spontaneity, if someone violates the proper form, it is immediately noted and has negative implications for the social standing of the violator. In this way rituals work to bind communities of people together, even in very individualistic cultures.

Knuf (1993) argues that rituals are the ultimate expression of an individual to the group. From an individualistic perspective such an idea may be upsetting, however much of our individual identity is inescapably tied up with our group memberships (family, work, religious, political, ethnic, etc.), thus creating a genuine need to engage in communication in which we learn community values and establish and maintain community ties. Although ritual is only one of many important forms of communication, it does help fill those teaching and bonding needs that exist within any community. Recognizing and understanding these rituals within our own and other communities provides one way to better appreciate and understand that which is significant in all cultures.

REFERENCES

Basso, K. H. (1979). *Portraits of "The Whiteman": Linguistic play and cultural symbols among the Western Apache*. Cambridge: Cambridge University Press.

Chen, V. (1990/1991). *Mien Tze* at the Chinese dinner table: A study of interactional accomplishment of face. *Research on Language and Social Interaction, 24,* 109–140.

Fitch, K. (1990/1991). A ritual for attempting leave-taking in Colombia. *Research on Language and Social Interaction, 24,* 209–224.

Hall, B. J. (1996). Culture, ethics and communication. In F. Casmir (Ed.), *Ethics in international communication.* Hillsdale, NJ: Lawrence Erlbaum Associates.

Hall, B. J., & Noguchi, M. (1995). Engaging in *kenson:* An extended case study of one form of "common" sense. *Human Relations, 48,* 1129–1147.

Katriel, T., & Philipsen, G. (1981). "What we need is communication": "Communication" as a cultural category in some American speech. *Communication Monographs, 48,* 302–317.

Knuf, J. (1993). "Ritual" in organizational culture theory: Some theoretical reflections and a plea for greater terminological rigor. In S. A. Deetz (Ed.), *Communication yearbook, vol. 16* (pp. 61–103). Newbury Park, CA: Sage.

Philipsen, G. (1987). The prospect for cultural communication. In D. L. Kincaid (Ed.), *Communication theory: Eastern and Western perspectives* (pp. 245–254). San Diego, CA: Academic Press.

Philipsen, G. (1992). *Speaking culturally: Exploration in social communication.* Albany: State University of New York.

Stover, L. E., & Stover, T. K. (1976). *China: An anthropological perspective.* Pacific Palisades, CA: Goodyear Publishing Company.

Trice, H., & Beyer, J. (1984). Studying organizational cultures through rites and ceremonials. *Academy of Management Review, 9,* 663–669.

KEY TERMS

culture	maintaining community
everyday talk	membership
ritual	

DISCUSSION QUESTIONS

1. Hall describes four typical reactions to the concept of ritual. How do these compare with your own impression of ritual before reading this essay?
2. Hall describes three ways to identify rituals within your own community. What are some of the rituals you can identify?
3. Hall argues that rituals teach and reaffirm important cultural values. What specific values are being taught in your community through the enactment of the rituals you identified in the previous question?
4. What unintended social consequences may stem from ignorance of everyday rituals? What social attributions might you make about someone who violates some of the rituals existing within your community?
5. Do you believe that rituals are truly a universal form of communication? Would our lives be better if we could eliminate rituals? Why or why not?

19
A RITUAL FOR ATTEMPTING LEAVE-TAKING IN COLOMBIA

KRISTINE FITCH

Today's urban Colombians live in an interpersonal world centered on connectedness and relationships. Persons are, according to Colombians, first and foremost sets of bonds (*vínculos*) to other people. This world view contrasts sharply with North Americans', which focuses primarily on individuality and freedom of choice (e.g., Carbaugh, 1988; Slater, 1970; Bellah et al., 1985). The pervasiveness and power of this Colombian idiom of human union can be heard in countless instances of interpersonal discourse.[1] For example, confidence is often expressed in the importance of influential "connections," through whom persons may expect to transcend virtually any law or institutional regulation to achieve a goal. In a related vein, Colombians devote significant attention to development of relationships with service providers with whom they must deal on a regular basis, such as auto mechanics, hair stylists and shopkeepers. They explain the investment of time and energy involved in forming such connections as a preference for service *relationships* over service *encounters*. That is, they believe that business should ideally be conducted with persons one has an established relationship with, rather than with strangers.

A final illustration of the importance Colombians attach to connectedness is the frequency with which the desirability of developing romantic relationships is commented upon in terms of the group memberships of the potential partners. Individual dispositions are rarely talked about as significant determiners of whether a relationship is likely to "work out." Instead, the compatibility of each individual's important relational circles is discussed: Their social and occupational parity, their regional origin, their political affiliation, etc. Assertions are frequently made to the effect that, if those networks were sufficiently similar, any individual discord could be resolved. If they were not, tremendous difficulty would befall the couple regardless of how well the two of them might get along. For that reason, unions considered undesirable by friends or family members are verbally discouraged, and more direct intervention to disrupt the relationship is commonplace.

These examples illustrate the point of Colombian connectedness in a way which is consistent with much traditional ethnographic practice. But the mission of Michael Moerman's *Talking Culture* (1988) is to lessen reliance on reasoning from this kind of data, drawn from interviews and/or the researcher's field notes. The examples given above would not, in his view, constitute sufficient evidence for a claim about Colombian interpersonal ideology. Moerman urges, instead, that ethnographers draw on everyday conversation, produced spontaneously and recorded (presumably) unobtrusively. Examination of the sequential organization of such conversation would enable a closer view of the culture, less distorted by the ethnographer's own cultural understanding of the nature of the world and of persons. Conversation analysis as a centerpiece of ethnographic method provides a way to ground cultural claims in recordings and transcriptions which are "'out there' on the page for analyst and reader to encounter, cite, be responsible to, and make sense of according to explicit conversation analytic procedures" (Moerman, 1988, p. 33).

This paper follows Moerman's lead by presenting a conversational enactment of a leave-taking ritual which is, I will argue, an archetype for Colombian spoken life in a sense similar to the way that *dugri* speech expresses an essential element of Israeli *sabra* culture (Katriel, 1986). It is drawn from audiotaped, naturally-occurring conversation recorded in Colombia in 1987. The purpose of analyzing this conversation is both to describe a conversational sequence which performs a symbolic activity among Colombians during leave-taking from social gatherings, and to elucidate what ethnographic information may (and may not) emerge from conversation analysis. Beyond celebrating the importance of Moerman's proposal for the practice of conversation analysis in ethnography, I hope to demonstrate that in this speech pattern, an interpersonal ideology is revealed which revolves around the crucial importance of human connectedness, over and above individual desires.

Taking Leave

The participants in this conversation are two brothers of the bride, hosts (H1, H2) at a wedding reception held in their home, and a friend of the groom who is a guest (G) at the reception. The three have spoken only briefly, if at all, earlier in the evening.

1 G:	Me voy.	I'm leaving.
2 H1:	¿Se va? ¿Por qué?	You're leaving? Why?
3 G:	La tarjetica decía muy <u>claramente</u> que de 7 a 10 y ya son las 10:30.	The little card [wedding invitation] said very <u>clear</u>ly that [the reception would last] from 7 to 10 and now it's 10:30.

4 H2: Pero que va, yo   But so what, until
          hasta las cinco y
          media de la mañana   five thirty in the morning
          [   ]   [   ]
5 G: heh heh heh   heh heh heh

6 H2: estoy aquí=   I'll be here=

7 G: =Pero me tengo   =But I have to go=
          que ir=

8 H1: =Hmf, que se   =Hmf, that you have
          tiene que ir. Y por   to go. And why.
          que.

9 G: Porque vivo   Because I live
          le jos   far away
          [   ]   [   ]
10 H2:   Pero   But that
          no impor::ta   doesn't matter

11 H1: Hmf. Dizque me   Hmf. Says he's going.
          voy. Asi no   Just like that, I'm going
          má s, me voy   [
          [   ]   heh heh
12 G: heh heh   ha ha ha ha
          ha ha ha ha   (.3)
          (.3)
          Pero es que tengo   But it's that I have to go
          que salir a coger   catch a bus=
          bus=

13 H2: =No, no, luego le   =No, no, later
          lle vamos   we'll take you
          [   ]   [   ]
14 H1:   To:me se   Ha:ve
          otro traguito   another little drink
          mano   brother
          [   ]   [   ]
15 H2: o se va   or you can go with
          con Alberto   Alberto who lives out
          que vive por alla y   there and has a car . . .
          tiene carro . . .

This conversation begins with G initiating leave-taking. His intention is questioned. He responds, and the response is challenged. He repeats his intention, which is questioned again; offers another account, which is denied; and offers another, different account, which is also denied. Much like Moerman's example (1988, p. 23; transcript p. 127), the participants in this episode are divided into two "teams." G is a guest, whose expressed intention is to leave the party. H1 and H2 are hosts, whose apparent intention is to keep G at the party awhile longer. H1 and H2 were successful in this aim; G stayed at the party for another hour.

From the tenacity with which H1 and H2 deny G's reasons for needing to leave, and the number of alternatives to his leaving that they propose, it might seem as though they particularly enjoy or desire his company. But the fact is that, because G is a friend of the groom rather than the bride (their sister), they have met him only briefly earlier in the reception, if at all. They persistently ask, "Why?" when G announces that he must leave:

1 G: Me\ voy.   I'm leaving.
2 H1: ¿Se va? ¿Por qué?   You're leaving? Why?
       .   .
     .   .
   .   .
     .   .

7 G: =Pero me tengo   =But I have to go=
          qui ir=
8 H1: =Hmf, que se   =Hmf, that you have
          tiene que ir. Y   to go. And why.
          por que.

Additionally, they negate the accounts he offers for why leave-taking is appropriate at that moment:

3 G: La tarjetica decía   The little card [wedding
          muy claramente   invitation] said very
          que de 7 a 10 ya   clearly that [the reception
          son las 10:30.   would last] from 7 to 10
                                  and now it's 10:30.

4 H2: Pero que va, yo   But so what, until five
          hasta las cinco y   thirty in the morning
          media de la
          mañana

6 H2: estoy aquí=   I'll be here=

H2 even mimics G's announced intention, by repeating in his dismissal of G's excuse the intonation with which the excuse was offered:

9 G: Porque vivo   Because I live
          le jos   far away
          [   ]   [   ]
10 H2:   Per o   But that
          no impor::ta   doesn't matter

Although G has reminded them that the invitation said the reception was expected to last from 7 to

10 p.m. and that it is now well past 10, H2's mimicry suggests that leave-taking at that moment is a ludicrous action, which may even be an affront to the hosts.

Despite the frequency of vigorous negation and denial, the sequence does not evoke a confrontive or tense atmosphere. G laughs in turns 5 and 12 as his accounts are denied. On both occasions his laughter is preemptive, suggesting that he sensed the point that was about to be made and was amused by it.

A noteworthy feature of this conversation is that there are few pauses, and considerable overlap and latching. The two "teams" seem to be working closely together to bring something off. Because G's oft-repeated intention is to leave the gathering, that "something" seems akin to terminal exchanges that close conversations generally (Schegloff & Sacks, 1984). Schegloff and Sacks point out that some types of conversational tasks require particularly close ordering of utterances, to assure that a desired successive utterance type is eventually produced. Encounters and closings, they argue, are such tasks.

The transcribed fragment is not, however, the termination of an ongoing conversation. It is virtually the *entire* conversation, preceded only by eye contact between G and the brothers and followed by trailing-off attempts from H1 to secure "another little drink" for the guest.

Additionally, H1 and H2's comments on G's intention, and their refusals of his accounts, challenge G's competence to decide when to leave. Their challenges range from very general ("But that doesn't matter," turn 10) to specific ("you can go with Alberto who lives out there," turn 15, when in fact H1 and H2 have no way of knowing where G lives). In Labov and Fanshel's (1977) terms, they deny G's readiness to leave as being an A event (one that can only be known by the speaker, as opposed to B events, which may be known by both speaker and hearer). By hinting that leave-taking at that moment would be offensive, H1 and H2 reframe G's departure from something that affects primarily, or only, himself into an action which has an impact on them as well. If he follows through on his announced intention, he will insult/hurt/deprive them of something they are willing to engage in verbal battle to preserve.

The two teams seem to be engaging in a sequence which has, as its logical ultimate objective, the guest's departure. Why, then, are apparently strenuous objections offered to his going?

A candidate answer to that question is that this leave-taking is an instance of a conversational routine, similar to the telephone openings described by Hopper (1989). That is, it could be that the hosts respond to announced intentions to depart with objections because that expectation has arisen through years and generations of Colombians interacting. This kind of leave-taking has become so habitual that it is only remarkable in its absence.

There is no question that this episode fits neatly into grooves worn deep into Colombian social interaction. The pattern of:

1. G announces intention
2. H1 or H2 asks for account
3. G gives account
4. H1 or H2 denies account and/or offers alternative

is repeated twice (turns 1–6 and 7–10). A partial third repetition occurs in turns 12–15 as G recycles step 3 and again receives step 4 in response, this time from H1 and H2 almost in chorus. As noted earlier, the exchange is produced rapidly, almost without pause. There is a finely tuned syncopation of turns here. Even though the participants have not met, they seem to experience little difficulty coordinating the steps of a leavetaking sequence. They have never "talked" this route before; or have they?

Examination of 11 leavetaking episodes, transcribed from tape recordings or written down from memory, shows a consistent pattern of exchange. The pattern is close to the one identified in the conversation transcribed above:

1. Guest(s) announce intentions to leave, sometimes thanking host(s) for invitation.
2. Host asks why guest is proposing to leave and protests timing of departure (it's early yet, you just got here, your companion is still having fun).
3. Guest repeats intention to leave and/or offers account for needing to leave.

4. Host rejects account and/or suggests alternative (wait until this song is over and we'll call you a taxi; have one more drink; ten minutes and X will go with you or take you home, etc.)

In slots 2 and 4, hosts have a third option, which is to introduce a new topic, suggesting that departure is inappropriate until the new conversational business is concluded. In those cases, the guests' announcements that they are leaving act as possible pre-closings (Schegloff & Sacks, 1984). That is, they offer an opportunity for closing (in this case leavetaking) which may be taken as opportunities to bring up an "unmentioned mentionable." As Schegloff and Sacks point out,

> The opening that a possible pre-closing makes for an unmentioned mentionable may thus result in much more ensuing talk than the initial mentionable that is inserted; for that may provide the occasion for the "natural occurrence" of someone else's mentionables in a fitted manner. It is thus not negative evidence for the status of (such utterances) as possible pre-closings that extensive conversational developments may follow them. (1984, p. 80)

This type of exchange is repeated with minor variations, perhaps several times, until someone changes the subject or engages the guest or host in some other activity. Leavetaking occurs after some time has elapsed after the initial attempt, and three or more exchanges of this type often precede departure. The fact that so many instances of leavetaking followed a similar sequence of assertion/denial suggests that an identifiable closing exchange sequence exists among Colombians.

Of the 11 recorded instances, on only two occasions did the guests actually leave after the first performance of the *salsipuede* ritual. I also observed or was told about three occasions when guests left social gatherings without engaging in the ritual at all. Both actions (leaving after the first round of goodbyes, and leaving without saying goodbye) were evaluated as rude or incompetent, i.e., deficient performances of the act of leavetaking.

This leavetaking episode thus reflects a structure similar to that claimed as universal to conversational closings by Schegloff and Sacks. It is so familiar to the participants precisely because it follows a routine that all of them, as competent members of the interpersonal world, have engaged in countless times before.

More importantly than the conversational problem of drawing interaction to a close, however, a task central to Colombian interpersonal ideology is performed here. Much in the way that *dugri* speech celebrates *sabra* toughness through straightforward communication among Israelis (Katriel, 1986); this sequence constitutes "connection" talk among Colombians. Exploration of the task performed, and discovery of its cultural significance, are elucidations which must go outside of any naturally occurring conversation or collection of instances. That inquiry, in other words, requires examination of the cultural context in which the interaction took place.

The Communication Ritual of "*Salsipuede*"

Colombians, and probably other Latin Americans[2] engage in the kind of conversational exchange exemplified by the instance reported here virtually every time they depart from a social gathering. The purpose does not seem to be to thank the host. Often (as in this conversation) no word of thanks is uttered in the course of the interaction. This type of exchange is confined to social gatherings; it does not occur after business meetings, at the end of telephone conversations, or when family members leave for work in the morning. The native term for the action performed is "*despedirse*," to say goodbye. Saying goodbye requires two teams of at least one person each, representing the host(s) or organizer(s) of the event and the guest(s) or attender(s). Although the exchange presented earlier was a good-natured series of contradictions and denials, the sequence itself is not merely a pro forma pre-sequence to taking leave. I tried countless times, with utmost sincerity and determination, to leave social gatherings at what seemed to me to be reasonable hours, and found it often was impossible to actually escape until much later than I wanted. Colombians tell with rueful laughter of similar experiences, so that it was not merely a marker of non-native incompetence that I was unable to break away sooner.

My initial reactions on such occasions were anger and confusion. Hosts and organizers seemed quite comfortable denying my own and my companions' experience of the moment (e.g., I'm tired, I've had enough of your company, it's a long way home) to insist we stay longer. I was puzzled about why they did so when they hardly knew me/us. In the case above, the hosts had not said two words to G during the course of the gathering, but then vehemently opposed his leavetaking. Confusion about this eventually motivated me to carry a tape recorder to several social events (including this wedding reception) and turn it on as I was about to leave.

Through interviews with Colombians, I came to understand that the worst thing that could happen at any social gathering, regardless of how well hosts and guests might or might not know one another (or like each other) was taking leave without engaging in the kind of conversational sequence presented earlier. The American pattern of

GUEST: Well, we must be going.

HOST: Oh, so soon? Well, thanks for coming.

would be a sign in Colombia of boredom, even antagonism, on the part of the host. Having observed on numerous occasions the sequential pattern in the transcript above of the guest's "departure" from the wedding reception, I came to call it the "*salsipuede*" (leave if you can) ritual. The term *salsipuede* is drawn from a popular dance tune from the 1970s, in which "Salsipuede" is the name of a most agreeable, friendly small town. The general flavor is one of nostalgia, as if the singer had departed with difficulty, and with many fond memories of wonderful times spent there. The term struck me as appropriate, because guests' attempts to pull themselves away from parties met with such resistance from their hosts. From their end, guests seemed to accompany their expressed desires to leave with an apparent willingness to stay, as though the ambience of the party exerted an attraction far stronger than their needs to get up the next morning.

Presented with the term "*salsipuede,*" Colombians immediately recognized the kind of leavetaking behavior it connoted. Nonetheless, *salsi-*

puede is an ethnographer's borrowing, not a native term for a commonplace interactional event. The *lack* of a native term does not, however, in itself call into question the cultural significance of the action. Katriel and Philipsen (1981), for example, describe "communication" as a cultural ritual among certain Americans, proposing that essential features of American interpersonal life are captured in the term "communication." When their subjects described the episodic sequence of "communication," however, they referred to the action with different native phrases such as "sit down and talk," "work out problems," or "discuss our relationship" (1981, p. 310). Although they used different words to refer to the events than did the ethnographers, the subjects had identifiable expectations for the ritual of "communication." In a similar sense, Colombians shared expectations for leavetaking episodes at parties that reflected common beliefs about relationships, even though they did not attend to those episodes so consciously that a specialized term had evolved to describe them.

The episode presented earlier may, like "communication" among Americans, appropriately be described as a ritual for several reasons. First, the moves which constituted the speech event of announcing intentions to leave, and having those intentions met with spirited opposition, were performed in similar ways on 11 occasions detailed in my fieldnotes, three of which were also captured on audiotape. This repetitive quality suggests that whatever function is performed by the exchange, it is a function recognized by most or all Colombians and performed in similar ways across dissimilar contexts.

Another reason that the term "ritual" seems appropriate to the event described earlier is its close fit with Philipsen's (1987, p. 250) definition of ritual as a form of cultural communication: A "structured sequence of symbolic acts, the correct performance of which constitutes homage to a sacred object." The moves which constitute the *salsipuede* ritual may be viewed as symbolic in that they take place in roughly the same manner and intensity regardless of the nature of the relationship between participants. That is, hosts are expected to vigorously oppose guests' departure from social events whether or not they have a sincere interest in the guests' remaining. Even when hosts and guests barely know one another and have not interacted during the course of the event, as was the case in the conversation transcribed here, a relationally significant moment is botched if the *salsipuede* ritual is not performed when the guests first attempt to depart.

The sacred object to which tribute is paid by this ritual is the *vínculo:* the relationship formed, symbolically or concretely, during the social event. When Colombians share a meal, a drink, an evening of song and poetry, or an afternoon of sandlot soccer, an interpersonal bond forms between the participants. The native term for such a bond is *"vínculo"* (literally: tie), a central symbol in the Colombian ideology of personal identity. Persons are, according to Colombians, first and foremost conjunctions of ties to other people. Beyond their individual uniqueness, persons are much more crucially defined by to whom, and how profoundly, they are connected to others. It follows that individuals (or pairs of individuals) are not supposed to leave a social event simply because they, *as* individuals, are ready to go. Some affirmation that a relationship has been formed or maintained must occur, and that affirmation may be accomplished by denying guests' needs or even rights to leave.

In this context, social events take on a much greater importance for Colombians than they do for North Americans. Many occasions commemorated by Americans with phone calls or a card, such as Mother's Day and anniversaries, are celebrated with social gatherings by Colombians. Social events in Colombia are, from my observation, rarely only half-social (such as working lunches or gatherings convened for purposes of "networking"), nor are guest/host roles ever ambiguated (as with potluck meals, progressive dinners, bring-your-own-bottle or no-host cocktail hours). When Colombians socialize, they do so lavishly, relative to the socioeconomic status and age of the hosts. Social events are significant because of the sacredness of the *vínculos* (interpersonal ties) that are formed and maintained in that context. The importance of those bonds is reaffirmed in the *salsipuede* ritual.

Interpersonal bonds are important for all of the reasons suggested at the beginning of this essay. Through contacts with appropriately powerful others, one may transcend institutional regula-

tions to achieve almost any goal. Everyday tasks of life are accomplished far more quickly and reliably if one has developed a *vínculo* with the service provider. One's choices about the future, including friends and spouse, will affect those persons with whom strong *vínculos* already exist, so that comment and even intervention in those decisions is to be expected from the other parties.

NOTES

1. The data on which this essay is based are reported more fully in Fitch (1989), drawn from ten months' fieldwork in Bogotá, Colombia in 1987.

2. I have not encountered data on interpersonal communication patterns in other Latin American countries that would allow for a systematic comparison. The similarities of history and tradition among Colombia and its close neighbors, such as Ecuador, Venezuela and certainly Panama, are so extensive that I am sure the pattern and beliefs I describe here are not unique to Colombians. Yet it seems appropriate to describe this as a "Colombian ritual" because all of the data were collected in Colombia, among Colombians; and because of the current lack of data that would allow for comparison with other countries in the region.

REFERENCES

Bellah, R., Madsen, R., Sullivan, W., Swidler, A., & Tipton, S. (1985). *Habits of the heart: Individualism and commitment in American life.* Berkeley: University of California Press.

Carbaugh, D. (1988). *Talking American: Cultural discourses on Donahue.* Norwood, NJ: Ablex.

Fitch, K. (1989). Communicative enactment of interpersonal ideology: Personal address in urban Colombian society. Unpublished Ph.D. dissertation, University of Washington, Seattle.

Hopper, R. (1989). Speech in telephone openings: Emergent interaction vs. routines. *Western Journal of Speech Communication, 53,* 178–194.

Katriel, T. (1986). *Talking straight:* "Dugri" *speech in Israeli Sabra culture.* Cambridge: Cambridge University Press.

Katriel, T., & Philipsen, G. (1981). "What we need is communication": "Communication" as a cultural category in some American speech. *Communication Monographs, 48,* 301–317.

Labov, W., & Fanshel, D. (1977). *Therapeutic discourse: Psychotherapy as conversation.* New York: Academic Press.

Philipsen, G. (1987). The prospect for cultural communication. In L. Kinkaid (Ed.), *Communication theory: Eastern and Western perspectives* (pp. 245–254). New York: Academic Press.

Schegloff, E. A., & Sacks, H. (1984). Opening up closings. In J. Baugh & J. Scherzer (Eds.), *Language in use* (pp. 69–99). Englewood Cliffs, NJ: Prentice-Hall.

Slater, P. (1970). *The pursuit of loneliness.* Boston: Beacon Press.

KEY TERMS

leavetaking   social relationships
ethnography   Colombia

DISCUSSION QUESTIONS

1. How does this *"salsipuede"* leavetaking ritual in Colombia reflect an important Colombian cultural value?

2. What leavetaking rituals do you and your friends engage in? Do these rituals vary from context to context (social vs. task)?

3. To what extent does Fitch's characterization of the typical North American leavetaking ritual hold true for all cultural groups in the United States?

4. Why is *"salsipuede"* leavetaking in Colombia described as a "communication *ritual*"?

5. How might a critical researcher approach this study of communication rituals?

20

WHEN OUTSIDERS ENCOUNTER INSIDERS IN SPEAKING: OPPRESSED COLLECTIVES ON THE DEFENSIVE

DETINE L. BOWERS

Many whites treat a militant speech—not action, mind you, but a speech, a presentation of rhetoric in public—like a revolutionary conspiracy. When even a small group of blacks gather for some purpose other than a card party, whites get upset.   —Bell, 1992, p. 67

Oppressed populations such as African Americans are forced into defensive postures, constantly identifying ourselves and justifying our

Author's Note: This essay is an adaptation of a speech delivered at the "Women and the First Amendment" forum at Radford University, Radford, Virginia, October 1993. I am grateful to Barry Brummett and Wayne Hensley for their reading of a draft of this essay.

place in society. Our task is an ongoing attempt to argue for our right to equality and our right to speak before getting on with our particular policy claim—that is, when we can make the policy claim. Such claims are usually left untackled because matters of collective definition take precedence. The predetermined condition for speech, one that accepts voices of the oppressed only on the definitional terms of the power structure, reminds the public that oppressed collectives, "groups that have goals that transcend the ending of discrimination against their members," are actually struggling to be like our oppressors (Sanders, 1991, p. 369). Such a condition results from a hierarchy of voices that claim the high ground on rationality and reason to justify actions in a civilized society—a society that expects univocal responses from oppressed collectives to inherently repressive claims and rhetorical agendas. This dominance is manifest in a Eurocentric rhetorical condition. Asante's (1987) definition of the rhetorical condition is "the structure and power pattern, assumed or imposed, during a rhetorical situation by society" (p. 22). Characteristics of a condition of hierarchical discourse include "control over the rhetorical territory through definition . . . and the stifling of opposing discourse" (p. 22). Such control ultimately includes the domination of rhetorical agendas as evidenced in television programs and in the interpretation of law. The rhetorical condition is structurally embedded in media and legal institutions.

My goal in this essay is not merely to join the perceived gloom and doom of marginalized voices demanding access to institutional media for public discourse (e.g., feminists, African Americans, Latinos) but to explore some of the reasons for rhetorical deadlock for oppressed populations even when there is access to public discourse channels. My aim is to demonstrate the inherent cost of individuals and groups representing oppressed collectives freely speaking and speaking freely. I contend that oppressed collectives must stop letting institutional structures set the rhetorical agenda, and should use institutional structures more effectively. This work is about how the rhetorical agenda of the media, as a free speech channel, harms oppressed spokespersons and how those spokespersons can exercise proactive strategies to empower themselves. The media, the law, and other institutions subvert the rhetoric of oppressed collectives by creating ambiguity in the discourse. As participants in institutional strategies, collectives spend excessive time satisfying the remedial needs of journalists and lawmakers who focus on *who* we are rather than offer an opportunity to explain our program. To understand how ambiguity is created, we must next confront the current controversy over the First Amendment.

Catherine MacKinnon, a radical feminist, and Derrick Bell and Patricia Williams, critical race theorists, pinpoint the dominance of the rhetorical agenda in legal decision making that goes on

daily, especially in the case of the First Amendment (Bell, 1992; MacKinnon, 1987; Williams, 1991). An inherent structural problem for oppressed collectives is that judicial decision making is a political process that might enforce the persuasion principle in one instance and not do so in another. The persuasion principle, a fundamental principle of the First Amendment, tells us that "government may not suppress speech on the ground that the speech is likely to persuade people to do something the government considers harmful" (Strauss, 1991, p. 335). But, according to MacKinnon and others, the First Amendment is harm-based law, not a content-based law, because it can silence an oppressed collective such as women (MacKinnon, 1987, p. 207). Judgment regarding First Amendment interpretation is then based on the court's view of what is rational and reasonable at the time, and it protects the interest that the establishment deems important even though members of the establishment *say* that is not the case. The history of First Amendment decision making shows this to be true in cases where prior interpretations were ignored over prevailing opinion (Kairys, 1982).

Given this rhetorical agenda of the dominant structure, efforts to change that agenda by creating more diversity about First Amendment interpretations and decisions is not a place for oppressed populations to concentrate protest rhetoric. A short-term victory when it comes to legislating against freedom of expression, even those biased views of what it should be, does not get anyone far. To silence some expressions because they are harmful or irrational about particular collectives does little to alter massive repressive attitudes about that collective. Focusing voices on denying access to pornographic images may not necessarily alter attitudes that associate women's images with sex and constitute a long-term risk. Long before media images were in vogue—for example, in the age of Thomas Jefferson and, later, Angelina Grimke—women's behavior was linked to sexual promiscuity and immorality, as when women who publicly protested against slavery were associated with sexual promiscuity. Why would banning sexual suggestion through pornography change attitudes now? Further, reprimanding prior acts (motives) that lead to hate speech on college campuses— acts aimed to punish students who yell, write obscenities, or promulgate, in any way, insensitivities toward a particular victim—risks backlash, a reversal of the problem. The core of rhetorical problems for oppressed collectives lies not so much in institutional permissions of freedom of expression at the expense of the civil liberties of someone else. Nor is the root in lack of access to the media or other channels for public discourse, for the actual mechanisms and opportunities to cash in on them exist.

Rhetorical Condition: Structure and Resistance

The individual right to hear or see what one person or participant in a collective deems offensive behavior is at the same time an opportunity to voice objections to that behavior. Whereas members of oppressed collectives may be conditioned to accept many offensive behaviors, those who are not so conditioned must use communication channels open to them to object to oppressive behaviors and rhetorical agendas such as those of the media.

Asante explains that the rhetorical condition is rule oriented and is governed by the dictates of the dominant discourse in a society. In *The Afrocentric Idea*, Asante (1987) writes,

> There are three characteristics for a condition of hierarchical discourse: control over the rhetorical territory through definition, establishment of a self-perpetuating initiation or rite de passage, and the stifling of opposing discourse. These characteristics may be seen in the rhetoric of domination. One way to create ambiguity is to redefine established terms in such a manner that the original meaning is lost. Wherever ambiguity exists, the established order is able to occupy the ground of clarity by contending that ambiguity did not exist prior to the rise of the opposition, although the established order may have participated in creating the ambiguous situation. In this manner, the established order can undercut the opposition and manipulate the pattern of communication for its own effect. By defining not only the terms of discussion but also the grounds upon which the discussion will be waged, the established order concentrates power in its own hands. (p. 22)

The dominant power structure sets not only the language rules but the ground rules for which the language functions. It uses a creative range of strategies to stifle voices of the oppressed. Being cognizant of such subversive rhetorical agendas can reverse those conditions. The media attempts to subvert the rhetoric of oppressed collectives through setting agendas that create ambiguity in discourse of collectives through television, newspapers, magazines, and a range of other media. Media efforts often damage the credibility of individual members of collectives before we speak. In establishing strategies for countering these rhetorical agendas, oppressed collectives can alter the structural conditions for our discourse by challenging the condition in which we participate. This can be done by pointing out stifling agendas to the general public.

Although oppressed collectives may argue that breaking the chain of oppression requires shaking up the establishment's exclusive laws through counterrhetorical strategies directed at the lawmakers, we have been misguided about the full range of target audiences and strategies to capture them. In other words, there has been confusion about emphasis—who collectives should persuade that what is advocated is right. It is true that legal institutions that serve the public need to be shaken—and, over the past 30 years, civil rights movement spokespersons have done that. That was the purpose of the counterprotest rhetoric that shook the fundamental constructs of rational discourse by invoking another kind of logic, one common to oppressed collectives (Gresson, 1977). The opportunity exists under the First Amendment whatever the interpretation and whether one views laws as harm-based or not. To take such a stand is not necessarily to accept the "marketplace of ideas" concept that has no standards for what constitutes a perfect set of conditions that allow fair competition in a public marketplace of free-flowing ideas (Strauss, 1991, pp. 348–349). Further, there are not enough sensitized oppressed people in any one collective who can answer all the repressive dominant rhetorical agendas that confront us daily, and, in many cases, there are political reasons why we cannot. But the marketplace is a place where oppressed populations can provide more evidence of *collective strategies*—a place where we can create counterstructural conditions for the rhetorical condition in which we are forced. The remainder of this essay explores contexts for altering the conditions.

Although shaking multiple establishments through protest rhetoric must continue to be a part of protest life, it is becoming increasingly apparent that strategies for winning long-term gains must be targeted at the public mind through more discourse aimed to disclose manipulative rhetorical agendas. The public mind is being shaped by that percentage of those who represent oppressed populations, those who gain access to public discourse channels such as organization heads and spokespersons, professors, and media staff.

The most important question for the oppressed now is, What constitutes a rhetorical agenda of dominance? What prohibits listening to arguments? One strategy that underlies the creation of ambiguous discourse of oppressed collectives is to feed on the public's faulty reasoning. Bell (1992), in *Faces at the Bottom of the Well: The Permanence of Racism*, reveals four crucial "rules of racial standing" regarding society's premises about Blacks as institutions set rhetorical agendas:

1. No matter their experience or expertise, blacks' statements involving race are deemed "special pleading" and thus not entitled to serious consideration. (p. 111)
2. [There is] a widespread assumption that blacks, unlike whites, cannot be objective on racial issues and will favor their own no matter what. (p. 113)
3. Statements of one black who publicly disparages or criticizes other blacks who speak or act in ways that upset whites are granted "enhanced standing" even when the speaker has no special expertise or experience in the subject he or she is criticizing. (p. 114)
4. When a black person or group makes a statement or takes an action that the white com-

munity or vocal components thereof deem "outrageous," the latter will actively recruit blacks willing to refute the statement or condemn the action. (p. 118)

The first two are faulty premises that institutions and individuals buy into. The second two are actual strategies of institutions and individuals to manipulate the condition for the discourse.

From talk shows to headlines, these "rules of racial standing" create the rhetorical condition for oppressed collectives. The institution perpetuates false images of speakers and incites false premises about the oppressed for the consuming public. These rules are important because they inhibit listening to those speakers who attempt to eradicate negative images and they inhibit the voluntary process of absorbing public discourse content.

Divide and Conquer Strategies: Fostering Ambiguity

Now consider media manipulation that perpetuates faulty premises when it comes to a particular oppressed collective. Widely watched television programs create ambiguity within the discourse of oppressed collectives. For instance, the June 2, 1991, ABC program *This Week With David Brinkley* focused on impending civil rights legislation, and Brinkley's guests included three African American spokespersons: Shelby Steele, professor of English at San Jose State University; Benjamin Hooks, the executive director of the National Association for the Advancement of Colored People at that time; and Don Edwards of the Civil Rights Commission. The usual program format is a news update from Brinkley, a brief background report on the issue to be discussed on the program, followed by the appearance of each guest presented separately. Three panelists—George Will, Sam Donaldson, and Brinkley—interview each guest. On that particular Sunday, as has been the case when other African Americans have appeared on the program, two of the guests were allowed to speak during a single segment. Hooks and Steele were at separate remote locations and ended up engaging in feuding that turned into babble on commercial television while Will, Donaldson, and Brinkley just watched the brawl. At that time, this particular program structure was seldom used for other guests. Brinkley, Donaldson, and Will just smiled through the incendiary format ABC had orchestrated. But also at fault were the guests, who played into media hands by saluting to unethical establishment arguments using ad hominem to "win" their (dis)respective arguments. They fell into the trap of participating in the "enhanced standing" trap that Bell (1992) outlines, statements from a Black "who publicly disparages or criticizes other blacks who are speaking or acting in ways that upset whites," and divide-and-conquer techniques (p. 114). The deck was stacked by the very nature of the structure. Hooks, Steele, and Edwards could have averted such a rhetorical agenda by agreeing in advance on an acceptable one. Then they could have held the interviewers responsible for that agenda by refusing, on the air, to participate in this rhetorical agenda by revealing the common premise that oppressed collectives ought to be univocal.

On a November 13, 1992, CNN *Crier and Company* program, three African American women—Julia Hare, renowned educational psychologist; Ezola Foster, president of Black Americans for Family Values; and Pearl Cleage, playwright and writer-in-residence at Spellman—were special guests for a segment about Spike Lee's *Malcolm X*. Foster argued that Malcolm X was "nothing more than a petty thief, a little hoodlum that went to prison and became a Muslim, and all of a sudden he became a hero. Unfortunately, this is the kind of heroes we're giving to our young people. Our young children do not need to see gangsters as heroes or role models for them." Foster engaged in hasty generalizations and ad hominem attack; she shot Malcolm X with more verbal bullets than his body had received physical bullets using acceptable, although defective and unethical, arguments to win. This shows that members of collectives should be careful about who we make our beds with, and Foster's selling out to the right and an ideal of family values to gain enhanced standing in public discourse damaged African American values in the public eye. Sleeping with the enemy in public intercourse keeps collectives speaking against ourselves in ways that harm collective in-

terest most. Again, each participant must question the rhetorical agenda of the media and determine the likely positions of the other program guests before going on the air.

Other media programs such as talk shows have a field day with squabbling from a range of feminist voices. Members of collectives cannot afford to consciously put the collective in the position of speaking against self in public discourse for the sake of getting press coverage for the issues or self. These members must demand more control over collective presentation, refuse to participate, or require a situation that schools the audience about the range of diverse voices on the issue. How many groups or individuals representing the marginalized ensure that there are image watchdogs aimed to monitor media coverage of "internal affairs" that help shape and mold public perception of the collective? Groups and individual members are responsible for presenting not only voices that will be heard but also voices that will be listened to, and someone needs to work toward battling against establishment control over public opinion about members. Until the groups and individuals stop pandering to institutional agendas and start defining them, pointing out faulty premises that underlie these rhetorical agendas, discourse of the oppressed will continue to be empty. In addition, members will be repetitious, caught in a never-ending cycle, shouting to be heard rather than listened to as we stay on the defensive.

If collective members question why oppressed collectives have to be univocal in the eyes of the public, then we are on the right track for eradicating the problem. If members talk about how ludicrous it is for anyone to expect univocal marginalized groups within oppressed collectives, then we are on the right track. But many are buying into faulty premises about collectives, even those who are members of them. Members must bring arguments against institutional agendas, even those of the media, into public forums as we challenge the very channels we use.

Ambiguity within the ranks of the oppressed operating as collectives or within full-blown social movements plays itself out in public discourse in extremely damaging ways, and, unfortunately, few from within the collectives have monitored the perceptions created by these voices—blatant voices of disagreement in the eyes of the public. The varied interpretations of those voices created by the establishment and the oppressed who learn to play the game perpetuate the problem because the oppressed adopt establishment strategies—the very ones they claim are irrational and exclusive—to win without critiquing them and even flaunt the choice to participate in such strategies or structural setups.

Credibility and the Rhetorical Condition

Oppressed collectives' arguments on policy are squelched before they even assert them. The media's treatment of Lani Guinier, a law professor at the University of Pennsylvania and President Clinton's nominee for assistant attorney general at the Justice Department, is a classic example of structural strategies that silence African Americans by destroying credibility. The media labeled Guinier "welfare queen" and "quota queen" before she was officially nominated for the position or heard. In the aftermath of the bruhaha, Guinier (1993) expressed dismay over the ways in which she was quelled when she encountered the structures that had introduced her to the public. There was little opportunity to defend her position. Guinier, like many others, was forced into defining her identity after questions about her compatibility with the president's policies were raised.

Individuals within a collective gain enhanced standing through a polarizing voice about the collective. The media reward rhetorical polarization among oppressed collectives. As Guinier (1993) points out, one Black female scholar wrote a derogatory op-ed piece about Guinier for the *New York Times* without having reviewed the allegedly controversial work. Later, the author admitted that there was little sense to what she had written.

The criticism leveled against Toni Morrison's winning the Nobel Prize for literature that came from African American peers such as authors Stanley Crouch and Charles Johnson is another example. Scores of commentaries came from noted Black men willing to gain enhanced standing and profit from speaking out against a "sister." For example, Johnson referred to the act of awarding Morrison the prize as "a triumph of political correctness." Was it impossible to say, "It is about time"? Was it necessary to make a polarizing comment publicly?

Consider William Raspberry's column titled, "Finding What You Look For." Raspberry obviously views his work as a contribution to the discussion of problems within the African American community. The column referenced is about racial discrimination. Raspberry's (1993) recommendation is for African Americans to focus on garnering economic and educational empowerment rather than on identifying incidents of racial discrimination. The commentary included a quote from John Shipley Butler, a professor at the University of Texas at Austin, who emphasized the need to focus on business and opportunity rather than rights and victimization.

Oppressed collectives often are forced into adopting defensive strategies in which we must assert our rights. We are constantly asked to define ourselves and establish our credibility before we can reveal any facts, policies, or prescriptions. It is extremely difficult to stay balanced with a focus on business and opportunities. Meanwhile, the establishment relegates oppressed collectives to obscurity and insignificance by misstating, misspelling, or exaggerating facts about us as we are introduced on the air or in publications. Another example of the rhetorical condition of dominance that keeps African Americans on the defensive is the location of public forums and conferences that feature oppressed collectives. They sometimes are held in the least appealing location or moved around so that there is ambiguity about location and time—a sure way to lose an audience. Another example is the naming of a person's racial identity within a news story when race has nothing to do with the story. How many times was Colin Powell referred to as the "Black" or "African American" joint chiefs of staff or general in the media?

Often, imminent scholars or celebrities are placed last on a television program or are invited to speak only about rights issues when their expertise is in another area. The media seeks to discover "opinion, feeling, and attitude" about experience rather than perspective, the affective position rather than the reasoned one. The ground of argument is focused on attitudes about rights. Substantive issues, such as economic and social strategies, of marginalized populations are rarely discussed in the mainstream media. Such issues are not deemed newsworthy. Accusations of discrimination or racial intolerance are news. In sum, oppressed collectives are treated as object rather than subject. Oppressed populations are treated as human commodities, bought and sold on public demand, and given token status when deemed appropriate.

So where do oppressed collectives go from here? How can we reverse the rhetorical condition, the structural dominance pervasive in our lives?

Public behavior changes will come with public mind changes, and it is at the level of the potential public listener that collectives must fight through public discourse. Those marginalized individuals who are determined to have access to communicative channels at public forums or through the media must work toward using such channels more effectively. How do the oppressed work toward persuading the public and capturing listeners?

First, alert the public about the "multiple voices" among African Americans, women, and other oppressed collectives in ways that encourage support despite differences over solutions.

Second, avoid pandering to the whims of the media by determining appropriate times to speak and to be silent because silence can be a rhetorical strategy. Raise questions about rhetorical agendas of dominant institutions and how they participate in weakening collective arguments while acknowledging that we live by discourse rules determined by a rhetorical condition of racist, paternalistic forces and that collectives must avoid substituting bad rhetoric with bad rhetoric and bad tactics with bad tactics. Collectives cannot take on the discourse of the oppressor for the sake of winning. We must challenge it at every front.

Third, question rather than accept unethical uses of argument such as ad hominem attack; do not use these tactics just because they are currently the "name of the political game" and foster

enhanced standing while attempting to win. Why do oppressed groups and individuals who represent us have to win against each other? Many have discovered that "loudness" and public fights bring attention to a particular issue within a group affiliation and engage in it for the sake of refutation. If social collectives can agree that the premise of univocal voices for us is false, then harmonize with that claim. Groups do not have to agree on everything on a political agenda to offer something unifying to the public about who we are and who we represent, but we must agree on a collective agenda. The cost is too great to long-term identity when we settle for reckless tactics to ensure that one version of African American culture or feminism wins social conversion. The cost may be "aversion" and "reversion" from the public.

Fourth, alert individuals to argumentative strategies that allow differences of opinion while deemphasizing differences and stressing commonalities. Clearly, one person or group cannot represent all people who are African American or all people who are women; however, the public expects univocal oppressed groups, assuming that anyone who fits the general definition functions like all others in that category—a faulty premise.

Fifth, create a more inclusive agenda that attacks those subliminal messages that come out of an establishment that reasons that divide and conquer works for oppressed collectives; go beyond the self-help discourse of fighting revolutions within our collectives. The next step is to move toward critiquing professionals and African American and feminist leaders who are catering to "macho discourse"—the "macho media machinery"—and recognize it as machinery to avoid falling into the establishment pit. Friedan's (1992) challenge to move beyond playing the role of victim and mobilizing new priorities that address polarization is on target. Guinier did the right thing following the 1993 media bashing incident when she took her concerns about the responsibility of the media to Black journalists at the National Association of Black Journalists in the summer of 1993. Another strategy might have been to bring the issue of media bashing to the attention of the public in a more forceful way by using the media themselves as an agency for a reflexive dialogue. There frequently are opportunities to make the media themselves news. For the industry, news is news because most Americans will not turn off their television sets even when the media are criticized. It is now the name of the game. That should have been the responsibility of organizations representing oppressed collectives. There was no coordinated defense.

Until groups representing oppressed collectives operate at the higher levels of discussion, offering more internal rhetorical strategies and informing the public about the many structural constraints and manipulations of public discourse, the arena of issues that stifle credibility, members remain lone voices in the wilderness contributing to a repetitious discourse while there is low credibility with the public where establishment voices continue to shape opinion. Credibility comes not by simply speaking eloquently but by discerning when, where, how, and with whom voices will be listened to, not just heard. There is an urgent need for some individuals to move beyond being starstruck in that abstract and imperfect marketplace of ideas so as to collectively develop better strategies for living.

REFERENCES

Asante, M. K. (1987). *The Afrocentric idea.* Philadelphia: Temple University Press.

Bell, D. (1992). *Faces at the bottom of the well: The permanence of racism.* New York: Basic Books.

Friedan, B. (1992, March 9). The war against feminism. *Time*, pp. 50–57.

Gresson, A. D. (1977). Minority epistemology and the rhetoric of creation. *Philosophy and Rhetoric, 10*, 244–262.

Guinier, L. (1993, November/December). A challenge to journalists on racial dialogue. *Extra*, pp. 7–9.

Kairys, D. (1982). Freedom of speech. In D. Kairys (Ed.), *The politics of law: A progressive critique* (pp. 240–271). New York: Pantheon.

MacKinnon, C. (1987). *Feminism unmodified: Discourses on life and law.* Cambridge, MA: Harvard University Press.

Raspberry, W. (1993, September 3). Finding what you look for [column]. *Washington Post.*

Sanders, D. (1991). Collective rights. *Human Rights Quarterly 3*, 368–386.

Strauss, D. (1991). Persuasion, autonomy, and freedom of expression. *Columbia Law Review, 91*, 334–371.

Williams, P. (1991). *The alchemy of race and rights.* Cambridge, MA: Harvard University Press.

KEY TERMS

oppressed collectives	discourse
rhetoric	media
race	

DISCUSSION QUESTIONS

1. Bowers is speaking primarily about African American groups. Can you identify other oppressed collectives to whom Bell's "rules of racial standing" might apply?
2. How do recent media examples (e.g., discussions about Oakland School Board and Ebonics issue) support Bowers's description of rhetorical rules imposed on oppressed collectives?
3. Bowers speaks from a critical perspective. How might a social science researcher investigate this same topic? How might an ethnographer of communication approach this topic?
4. What does Bowers mean by "If collective members question why oppressed collectives have to be univocal in the eyes of the public, then we are on the right track for eradicating the problem"?

PART FIVE

CULTURAL
SPACES
AND
NONVERBAL
COMMUNICATION

Part Five focuses on nonverbal aspects of intercultural communication. National cultures are often diverse and heterogeneous, and within cultures, there are many different norms and rules about how to communicate—norms and rules that are largely influenced by nonverbal cultural contexts or spaces.

Consider these questions as you read the articles in this part:

How do cultural spaces and contexts influence your verbal and nonverbal behavior?

How does communication create and maintain cultural spaces?

How much does nonverbal communication vary with cultural group membership (gender, age, ethnicity, nationality)?

What role does power play in nonverbal communication and cultural practices?

These cultural spaces and their respective communication norms often act to construct boundaries that can reinforce ingroup-outgroup dichotomies. Within these spaces, cultural groups develop and share communication practices that can sustain cultural identity and strengthen

195

ingroup unity. Simultaneously, however, these same culturally situated communication norms and rules can prevent intergroup interaction. As we move into cultural spaces that have unique communication norms, we can easily find ourselves relegated to the fringes of that community, hampered by our lack of familiarity with these norms.

The essays in this part discuss cultural spaces and practices both as static, cultural, and consistent across contexts, *and* as dynamic, emerging, and contested. They reveal how cultural practices may not only strengthen a community but also have competing and contradictory meanings in these cultural locations. The first three readings search for consistent shared meanings in cultural practices that may vary from culture to culture. The final essay emphasizes competing meanings of cultural practices.

In a classic essay, "Key Concepts: Underlying Structures of Culture," Edward T. Hall and Mildred Reed Hall describe cultural spaces and practices of various national groups. The authors identify broad cultural (national) differences in patterns of nonverbal communication based on E. T. Hall's earlier anthropological studies. They focus specifically on high-low context information, use of personal space, and monochronic-polychronic approaches to time. These distinctions have been used by many social science researchers to predict and explain related communication behaviors. Please note that although they discuss a kind of *contextual* information (high-low), they assume that nonverbal behavior is consistent across most contexts within national cultures—that is, the focus on high-low context information should not be confused with an emphasis on the importance of context in communication studies.

Min-Sun Kim's "A Comparative Analysis of Nonverbal Expressions as Portrayed by Korean and American Print-Media Advertising" is a good example of objective cross-cultural social science research. Based on research similar to that of E. T. Hall, Kim predicts (and finds) differences between nonverbal behaviors portrayed in magazine advertising in the United States and Korea—in facial expressions, hand and arm gestures, degree of body exposure, tactile communication and male-female communication. Note that Kim, like E. T. Hall, is interested in broad cultural differences in nonverbal communication that are assumed consistent across many contexts.

Gerry Philipsen, in "Places for Speaking in Teamsterville," describes the cultural practices of a very specific community—a working-class White neighborhood near Chicago. In this classic ethnographic (interpretive) study, Philipsen analyzes contextual rules for speaking in various locations in the community—the neighborhood, the street, the corner, and the front porch. His conclusions about the connections between perceptions of the world and cultural senses of place are based on months of participant observation and involvement in this community. Note that although his research is participatory and somewhat subjective, his style of reporting is rather objective.

The final essay in this unit takes a very different approach—emphasizing multiple and competing meanings for cultural practices. Using a critical-interpretive framework in "Warriors, Wampum, Gaming, and Glitter: Foxwoods Casino and the Re-Presentation of (Post)Modern Native Identity," Leda M. Cooks analyzes photographs and other cultural artifacts in a Native American gambling casino in Connecticut. She takes issue with E. T. Hall's broad generalizations about cultural space and practices. Noting the importance of historical background, she points out the disjunction of the cultural spaces of this casino: Images of the warrior-savage are prominently displayed (e.g., cocktail servers wearing loincloths and feathers) along with a museumlike collection of tribal artifacts. Her analysis shows the contradictory readings that could be given about contemporary Native American culture.

21
KEY CONCEPTS: UNDERLYING STRUCTURES OF CULTURE

EDWARD T. HALL / MILDRED REED HALL

Culture Is Communication

In physics today, so far as we know, the galaxies that one studies are all controlled by the same laws. This is not entirely true of the worlds created by humans. Each cultural world operates according to its own internal dynamic, its own principles, and its own laws—written and unwritten. Even time and space are unique to each culture. There are, however, some common threads that run through all cultures.

It is possible to say that the world of communication can be divided into three parts: *words, material things,* and *behavior.* Words are the medium of business, politics, and diplomacy. Material things are usually indicators of status and power. Behavior provides feedback on how other people feel and includes techniques for avoiding confrontation.

By studying these three parts of the communication process in our own and other cultures, we can come to recognize and understand a vast unexplored region of human behavior that exists outside the range of people's conscious awareness, a "silent language" that is usually conveyed unconsciously (see Edward T. Hall's *The Silent Language*). This silent language includes a broad range of evolutionary concepts, practices, and solutions to problems which have their roots not in the lofty ideas of philosophers but in the shared experiences of ordinary people. In the words of the director of a project on cross-cultural relations, understanding the silent language "provides insights into *the underlying principles that shape our lives."* These underlying principles are not only inherently interesting but eminently practical. The readers of this book, whether they be German, French, American, or from other countries, should find these principles useful at home and abroad.

Culture can be likened to a giant, extraordinarily complex, subtle computer. Its programs guide the actions and responses of human beings in every walk of life. This process requires attention to everything people do to survive, advance in the world, and gain satisfaction from life. Furthermore, cultural programs will not work if crucial steps are omitted, which happens when people unconsciously apply their own rules to another system.

During the three years we worked on this book, we had to learn two different programs for our office computer. The first was quite simple, but mastery did require paying close attention to every detail and several weeks of practice. The second was a much more complex program that required weeks of intensive practice, hours of tutoring, and days of depression and frustration when "the darn thing didn't work." Learning a new cultural program is infinitely more complicated and requires years of practice, yet there are many similarities in the learning process.

Cultural communications are deeper and more complex than spoken or written messages. *The essence of effective cross-cultural communication has more to do with releasing the right responses than with sending the "right" messages.* We offer here some conceptual tools to help our readers decipher the complex, unspoken rules of each culture.

Fast and Slow Messages: Finding the Appropriate Speed

The speed with which a particular message can be decoded and acted on is an important characteristic of human communication. There are fast and slow messages. A headline or cartoon, for example, is fast; the meaning that one extracts from books or art is slow. A fast message sent to people who are geared to a slow format will usually miss the target. While the content of the wrong-speed message may be understandable, it won't be received by someone accustomed to or expecting a different speed. The problem is that few people are aware that information can be sent at different speeds.

Examples of Fast and Slow Messages

Fast Messages	Slow Messages
Prose	Poetry
Headlines	Books
A communique	An ambassador
Propaganda	Art
Cartoons	Etchings
TV commercials	TV documentary
Television	Print
Easy familiarity	Deep relationships
Manners	Culture

Almost everything in life can be placed somewhere along the fast/slow message-speed spectrum. Such things as diplomacy, research, writing books, and creating art are accomplished in the slow mode. Buddha, Confucius, Shakespeare, Goethe, and Rembrandt all produced messages that human beings are still deciphering hundreds of years after the fact. Language is a very slow message; after 4,000 years, human beings are just beginning to discover what language is all about. The same can be said of culture, which incorporates multiple styles of "languages" that only release messages to those who are willing to spend the time to understand them.

In essence a person is a slow message; it takes time to get to know someone well. The message is, of course, slower in some cultures than in others. In the United States it is not too difficult to get to know people quickly in a relatively superficial way, which is all that most Americans want. Foreigners have often commented on how "unbelievably friendly" the Americans are. However, when Edward T. Hall studied the subject for the U.S. State Department, he discovered a worldwide complaint about Americans: they seem capable of forming only one kind of friendship—the informal, superficial kind that does not involve an exchange of deep confidences.

Conversely, in Europe personal relationships and friendships are highly valued and tend to take a long time to solidify. This is largely a function of the long-lasting, well-established networks of friends and relationships—particularly among the French—that one finds in Europe. Although there are exceptions, as a rule it will take Americans longer than they expect to really get to know Europeans. It is difficult, and at times may even be impossible, for a foreigner to break into these networks. Nevertheless, many businesspeople have found it expedient to take the time and make the effort to develop genuine friends among their business associates.

High and Low Context: How Much Information Is Enough?

Context is the information that surrounds an event; it is inextricably bound up with the meaning of that event. The elements that combine to produce a given meaning—events and context—are in different proportions depending on the culture. The cultures of the world can be compared on a scale from high to low context.

> A high context (HC) communication or message is one in which *most* of the information is already in the person, while very little is in the coded, explicit, transmitted part of the message. A low context (LC) communication is just the opposite; i.e., the mass of the information is vested in the explicit code. Twins who have grown up together can and do communicate more economically (HC) than two lawyers in a courtroom during a trial (LC), a mathematician programming a computer, two politicians drafting legislation, two administrators writing a regulation. (Edward T. Hall, 1976)

Japanese, Arabs, and Mediterranean peoples, who have extensive information networks among family, friends, colleagues, and clients and who are involved in close personal relationships, are high-context. As a result, for most normal transactions in daily life they do not require, nor do they expect, much in-depth, background information. This is because they keep themselves informed about everything having to do with the people who are important in their lives. Low-context people include Americans, Germans, Swiss, Scandinavians, and other northern Europeans; they compartmentalize their personal relationships, their work, and many aspects of day-to-day life. Consequently, each time they interact with others they need detailed background information. The French are much higher on the context scale than either the Germans or the Americans. This difference can affect virtually every situation and every relationship in which the members of these two opposite traditions find themselves.

Within each culture, of course, there are specific individual differences in the need for contexting—the process of filling in background data. But it is helpful to know whether the culture of a particular country falls on the high or low side of the scale since every person is influenced by the level of context.

Contexting performs multiple functions. For example, any shift in the level of context is a communication. The shift can be up the scale, indicating a warming of the relationship, or down the scale (lowering the context), communicating coolness or displeasure—signaling something has gone wrong with a relationship. In the United States the boss might communicate annoyance to an assistant when he shifts from the high-context, familiar form of address to the low-context, formal form of address. When this happens the boss is telling the subordinate in no uncertain terms that she or he has stepped out of line and incurred disfavor. In Japan moving the direction of the context is a source of daily feedback as to how things are going. The day starts with the use of honorifics, formal forms of address attached to each name. If things are going well the honorifics are dropped as the day progresses. First-naming in the United States is an artificial attempt at high-contexting; it tends to offend Europeans, who view the use of first names as acceptable only between close friends and family. With Europeans, one is always safe using a formal form of address,

waiting for the other person to indicate when familiarity is acceptable.

Like their near relations the Germans, many Anglo-Americans (mostly those of northern European heritage) are not only low-context but they also lack extensive, well-developed information networks. American networks are limited in scope and development compared to those of the French, the Spanish, the Italians, and the Japanese. What follows from this is that Americans, unless they are very unsophisticated, will feel the need for contexting, for detailed background information, any time they are asked to make a decision or to do something. The American approach to life is quite segmented and focused on discrete, compartmentalized information; Americans need to know what is going to be in what compartment before they commit themselves. We experienced this in Japan when we were asked on short notice to provide names of well-placed Japanese and Americans to be participants in a small conference. Like most prudent Americans, we were reluctant to provide names until we knew what the conference was about and what the individuals recommended would be expected to do. This seemed logical and reasonable enough to us. Nevertheless, our reluctance was read as obstructionist by our Japanese colleagues and friends responsible for the conference. In Japan the mere presence of certain individuals endows the group and its activities with authority and status, which is far more important than the topic of the conference. It is characteristic of high-context, high-information societies that attendance at functions is as much a matter of the prestige associated with the function as anything else. This in turn means that, quite frequently, invitations to high-level meetings and conferences will be issued on short notice. It is taken for granted that those invited will eschew all previous commitments if the meeting is important enough. As a general rule Americans place greater importance on how long ago a commitment was made, on the agenda, and on the relevance of the expertise of different individuals to the agenda. (For an in-depth discussion of the Japanese, we refer the reader to the authors' *Hidden Differences: Doing Business with the Japanese,* in the reading list.)

Another example of the contrast between how

high- and low-context systems work is this: consider a top American executive working in an office and receiving a normal quota of visitors, usually one at a time. Most of the information that is relevant to the job originates from the few people the executive sees in the course of the day, as well as from what she or he reads. This is why the advisors and support personnel who surround the presidents of American enterprises (as well as the president of the United States) are so important. They and they alone control the content and the flow of organizational information to the chief executive.

Contrast this with the office of virtually any business executive in a high-context country such as France or Japan, where information flows freely and from all sides. Not only are people constantly coming and going, both seeking and giving information, but the entire form and function of the organization is centered on gathering, processing, and disseminating information. Everyone stays informed about every aspect of the business and knows who is best informed on what subjects.

In Germany almost everything is low-context and compartmentalized. The executive office is both a refuge and a screen—a refuge for the boss from the distractions of day-to-day office interactions and a screen for the employees from continual supervision. Information communicated in the office is not shared except with a select few—the exact antithesis of the high-information cultures.

High-context people are apt to become impatient and irritated when low-context people insist on giving them information they don't need. Conversely, low-context people are at a loss when high-context people do not provide *enough* information. One of the great communications challenges in life is to find the appropriate level of contexting needed in each situation. Too much information leads people to feel they are being talked down to; too little information can mystify them or make them feel left out. Ordinarily, people make these adjustments automatically in their own country, but in other countries their messages frequently miss the target.

The other side of the coin when considering context level is the apparent paradox that high-context people, such as the French, want to see *everything* when evaluating a *new* enterprise to which they have not been contexted. Annual reports or tax returns are not enough. Furthermore, they will keep asking until they get the information they want. Being high context, the French are driven to make their own synthesis of the meanings of the figures. Unlike Americans, they feel uncomfortable with someone else's synthesis, someone else's "bottom line."

Space

Every living thing has a visible physical boundary—its skin—separating it from its external environment. This visible boundary is surrounded by a series of invisible boundaries that are more difficult to define but are just as real. These other boundaries begin with the individual's personal space and terminate with her or his "territory."

Territoriality

Territoriality, an innate characteristic whose roots lie hundreds of millions of years in the past, is the act of laying claim to and defending a territory and is a vital link in the chain of events necessary for survival. In humans territoriality is highly developed and strongly influenced by culture. It is particularly well developed in the Germans and the Americans. Americans tend to establish places that they label "mine"—a cook's feeling about a kitchen or a child's view of her or his bedroom. In Germany this same feeling of territoriality is commonly extended to all possessions, including the automobile. If a German's car is touched, it is as though the individual himself has been touched.

Space also communicates power. A corner office suite in the United States is conventionally occupied by "the brass," and a private office in any location has more status than a desk in the open without walls. In both German and American business, the top floors are reserved for high-ranking officials and executives. In contrast, important French officials occupy a position in the *middle,* surrounded by subordinates; the emphasis there is on occupying the central position in an information network, where one can stay informed and can control what is happening.

Personal Space

Personal space is another form of territory. Each person has around him an invisible bubble of space which expands and contracts depending on a number of things: the relationship to the people nearby, the person's emotional state, cultural background, and the activity being performed. Few people are allowed to penetrate this bit of mobile territory and then only for short periods of time. Changes in the bubble brought about by cramped quarters or crowding cause people to feel uncomfortable or aggressive. In northern Europe, the bubbles are quite large and people keep their distance. In southern France, Italy, Greece, and Spain, the bubbles get smaller and smaller so that the distance that is perceived as intimate in the north overlaps normal conversational distance in the south, all of which means that Mediterranean Europeans "get too close" to the Germans, the Scandinavians, the English, and those Americans of northern European ancestry. In northern Europe one does not touch others. Even the brushing of the overcoat sleeve used to elicit an apology.

The Multisensory Spatial Experience

Few people realize that space is perceived by *all* the senses, not by vision alone. Auditory space is perceived by the ears, thermal space by the skin, kinesthetic space by the muscles, and olfactory space by the nose. As one might imagine, there are great cultural differences in the programming of the senses. Americans to some extent and Germans to a greater extent rely heavily on auditory screening, particularly when they want to concentrate. High-context people reject auditory screening and thrive on being open to interruptions and in tune with what goes on around them. Hence, in French and Italian cities one is periodically and intrusively bombarded by noise.

Unconscious Reactions to Spatial Differences

Spatial changes give tone to communication, accent it, and at times even override the spoken word. As people interact, the flow and shift of distance between them is integral to the communication process. For example, if a stranger does not maintain "normal" conversational distance and gets too close, our reaction is automatic—we feel uncomfortable, sometimes even offended or threatened and we back up.

Human beings in the course of a lifetime incorporate literally hundreds of spatial cues. They imbibe the significance of these cues like mother's milk, in the context of their own culture. Just as a fragrance will trigger a memory, these cues and their associated behaviors release unconscious responses, regulating the tone, tempo, and mood of human transactions.

Since most people don't think about personal distance as something that is culturally patterned, foreign spatial cues are almost inevitably misinterpreted. This can lead to bad feelings which are then projected onto the people from the other culture in a most personal way. When a foreigner appears aggressive and pushy, or remote and cold, it may mean only that her or his personal distance is different from yours.

Americans have strong feelings about proximity and the attendant rights, responsibilities, and obligations associated with being a neighbor. Neighbors should be friendly and agreeable, cut their lawns, keep their places up, and do their bit for the neighborhood. By contrast, in France and Germany, simply sharing adjacent houses does not necessarily mean that people will interact with each other, particularly if they have not met socially. Proximity requires different behavior in other cultures.

Time

Life on earth evolved in response to the cycles of day and night and the ebb and flow of the tides. As humans evolved, a multiplicity of internal biological clocks also developed. These biological clocks now regulate most of the physiological functions of our bodies. It is not surprising, therefore, that human concepts of time grew out of the natural rhythms associated with daily, monthly, and annual cycles. From the beginning humans have been tied to growing seasons and were dependent on the forces and rhythms of nature.

Out of this background two time systems evolved—one as an expression of our biological clocks, the other of the solar, lunar, and annual cycles. These systems will be described under the headings "Time as Structure" and "Time as Communication." In the sections that follow we restrict ourselves to those manifestations of time that have proved to be stumbling blocks at the cultural interface.

Monochronic and Polychronic Time

There are many kinds of time systems in the world, but two are most important to international business. We call them monochronic and polychronic time. Monochronic time means paying attention to and doing only one thing at a time. Polychronic time means being involved with many things at once. Like oil and water, the two systems do not mix.

In monochronic cultures, time is experienced and used in a linear way—comparable to a road extending from the past into the future. Monochronic time is divided quite naturally into segments; it is scheduled and compartmentalized, making it possible for a person to concentrate on one thing at a time. In a monochronic system, the schedule may take priority above all else and be treated as sacred and unalterable.

Monochronic time is perceived as being almost *tangible:* people talk about it as though it were money, as something that can be "spent," "saved," "wasted," and "lost." It is also used as a classification system for ordering life and setting priorities: "I don't have time to see him." Because monochronic time concentrates on one thing at a time, people who are governed by it don't like to be interrupted. Monochronic time seals people off from one another and, as a result, intensifies some relationships while shortchanging others. Time becomes a room which some people are allowed to enter, while others are excluded.

Monochronic time dominates most business in the United States. While Americans perceive it as almost in the air they breathe, it is nevertheless a learned product of northern European culture and is therefore arbitrary and imposed. Monochronic time is an artifact of the industrial revolution in England; factory life required the labor force to be on hand and in place at an appointed hour. In spite of the fact that it is *learned,* monochronic time now appears to be natural and logical because the great majority of Americans grew up in monochronic time systems with whistles and bells counting off the hours.

Other Western cultures—Switzerland, Germany, and Scandinavia in particular—are dominated by the iron hand of monochronic time as well. German and Swiss cultures represent classic examples of monochronic time. Still, monochronic time is not natural time; in fact, it seems to violate many of humanity's innate rhythms.

In almost every respect, polychronic systems are the antithesis of monochronic systems. Polychronic time is characterized by the simultaneous occurrence of many things and by a *great involvement with people.* There is more emphasis on completing human transactions than on holding to schedules. For example, two polychronic Latins conversing on a street corner would likely opt to be late for their next appointment rather than abruptly terminate the conversation before its natural conclusion. Polychronic time is experienced as much less tangible than monochronic time and can better be compared to a single point than to a road.

Proper understanding of the difference between the monochronic and polychronic time systems will be helpful in dealing with the time-flexible Mediterranean peoples. While the generalizations listed below do not apply equally to all cultures, they will help convey a pattern:

Monochronic People	*Polychronic People*
do one thing at a time	do many things at once
concentrate on the job	are highly distractible and subject to interruptions

Monochronic People	Polychronic People
take time commitments (deadlines, schedules) seriously	consider time commitments an objective to be achieved, if possible
are low-context and need information	are high-context and already have information
are committed to the job	are committed to people and human relationships
adhere religiously to plans	change plans often and easily
are concerned about not disturbing others; follow rules of privacy and consideration	are more concerned with those who are closely related (family, friends, close business associates) than with privacy
show great respect for private property; seldom borrow or lend	borrow and lend things often and easily
emphasize promptness	base promptness on the relationship
are accustomed to short-term relationships	have strong tendency to build lifetime relationships

The Relation Between Time and Space

In monochronic time cultures the emphasis is on the compartmentalization of functions and people. Private offices are soundproof if possible. In polychronic Mediterranean cultures, business offices often have large reception areas where people can wait. Company or government officials may even transact their business by moving about in the reception area, stopping to confer with this group and that one until everyone has been attended to.

Polychronic people feel that private space disrupts the flow of information by shutting people off from one another. In polychronic systems, appointments mean very little and may be shifted around even at the last minute to accommodate someone more important in an individual's hierarchy of family, friends, or associates. Some polychronic people (such as Latin Americans and Arabs) give precedence to their large circle of family members over any business obligation. Polychronic people also have many close friends and good clients with whom they spend a great deal of time. The close links to clients or customers creates a reciprocal feeling of obligation and a mutual desire to be helpful.

Polychronic Time and Information

Polychronic people live in a sea of information. They feel they must be up to the minute about everything and everybody, be it business or personal, and they seldom subordinate personal relationships to the exigencies of schedules or budgets.

It is impossible to know how many millions of dollars have been lost in international business because monochronic and polychronic people do not understand each other or even realize that two such different time systems exist. The following example illustrates how difficult it is for these two types to relate:

> A French salesman working for a French company that had recently been bought by Americans found himself with a new American manager who expected instant results and higher profits immediately. Because of the emphasis on personal relationships, it frequently takes years to develop customers in polychronic France, and, in family-owned firms, relationships with customers may span generations. The American manager, not understanding this, ordered the salesman to develop new customers within three months. The salesman knew this was impossible and had to resign, asserting his legal right to take with him all the loyal customers he had developed over the years. Neither side understood what had happened.

These two opposing views of time and personal relationships often show up during business meetings. In French meetings the information flow is high, and one is expected to read other people's thoughts, intuit the state of their business, and even garner indirectly what government regulations are in the offing. For the French and other polychronic/high-context people, a tight, fixed agenda can be an encumbrance, even an insult to one's intelligence. Most, if not all, of those present have a pretty good idea of what will be discussed beforehand. The purpose of the meeting is to create consensus. A rigid agenda and consensus represent opposite goals and do not mix. *The importance of this basic dichotomy cannot be overemphasized.*

• • •

SELECTED REFERENCES

Hall, E. T. (1959). *The silent language.* Garden City, NY: Doubleday.

Hall, E. T. (1976). *Beyond culture.* Garden City, NY: Doubleday Anchor Books.

Hall, E. T. (1987). *Hidden differences: Doing business with the Japanese.* Garden City, NJ: Anchor Press/Doubleday.

KEY TERMS

high context	monochronic
low context	time
polychronic	space

DISCUSSION QUESTIONS

1. What kind of misunderstandings could occur between high- and low-context people?
2. What are some suggestions you might give to people who work together who have different orientations to time?
3. What are some common English sayings that reflect a monochronic time orientation (e.g., time is money, a stitch in time saves nine)?
4. What advice would you give French international students about time management at a U.S. university?
5. Would you characterize your communication with people whom you've known for a long time as more low-context or more high-context?

22

A COMPARATIVE ANALYSIS OF NONVERBAL EXPRESSIONS AS PORTRAYED BY KOREAN AND AMERICAN PRINT-MEDIA ADVERTISING

MIN-SUN KIM

Relationship Between Advertising and Culture

• • •

A persistent debate continues about whether advertising in non-Western countries reflects primarily the indigenous culture or Western culture. It is the purpose of this study to shed further light on this issue.

Nonverbal Expressions as Cultural Context

Print advertising usually consists of verbal and nonverbal messages. According to Millum (1975, p. 24) nonverbal messages are clear at a glance, facilitate conscious recall, and carry subconscious messages most effectively. Research has strongly suggested that major cultural differences are invested in nonverbal behaviors, because they are basic *core* values that are slow to change. Eisenberg and Smith (1971) argued that, as the symbols of language are structured into tight patterns, a *grammar* of nonverbal body language comes into being. Every culture has its specific set of *display rules* as to how and when its members may express themselves (Ekman, 1973). For instance, *boundary* is an important concept relating to people's mode of behavior. It refers to the way that people in a given culture cognitively divide up their worlds into separate areas. Cultures define boundaries temporally (days, microseconds), geographically (states, cities), and in terms of personal space (Arabs stand close to converse, whereas Americans stand three to four feet apart). Boundaries can be rigid (India's caste system) or flexible (America's egalitarian society) (cf., Durgee, 1986, p. 38). Watson and Graves (1966) found that Arabs confront each other more directly when conversing than do Americans, sitting closer to each other, and looking each other more squarely in the eye. Likewise, traditional Japanese culture requires two individuals to stand no closer than the distance permitting the customary bow (Kunihiro, 1980).

Nonverbal expressions of advertising models such as gestures, facial expressions, and postures are symbolic representations of cultural values. Goffman (1979) specifically examined ways in which men and women are pictured in advertisements. He found that women smile more often and more expansively than do men; and, similarly, men tend to be located at higher levels than women, symbolically confirming sexual stereotypes. Expression is considered to be socially learned and socially patterned. We take for granted our own modes of expression until we see them compared to those of another culture (i.e., nationality, ethnicity, or gender). Insights into the American mode of advertising expression and the fundamental cultural values by which the mode is influenced can be obtained by comparing American advertising to that of another culture.

Framework of the Study

The disagreement among researchers regarding the relationship between advertising and culture might be traced to the lack of a clear definition of *societal culture*. Most studies (Madden, Cabellero, & Matsukubo, 1986; Norman, 1965; Singh & Huang, 1962; Unwin, 1974) concentrate on differences and consistencies in the form of advertising expression—format, creative style, and information level—across cultures. Rarely is the relationship between advertising and culture studied in depth. For a fundamental understanding of the issue, a clear identification of the major values of a culture is essential, followed by a comparison of those values with the cultural content of advertising.

The importance of visual images in advertisements as a cultural parameter has not been studied comprehensively. It is through the influence of culture that people learn to communicate nonverbally. Cultures differ in their manner of encoding nonverbal messages. The culturally defined nonverbal patterns of communication, therefore, constitute indispensable parameters for analyzing culture. Some studies (e.g., Choe et al., 1986) have dealt with facial expressions in advertising, but few have focused on such pictorial displays as gestures, degree of body exposure, tactile communication, and eye behavior.

This study seeks to determine (a) whether nonverbal expressions of models in Korean and American advertising are related to their cultural orientation, (b) whether nonverbal expressions in advertising are influenced by the gender of the models and the products being advertised, (c) the possible influence of product categories on nonverbal expressions of both Korean and American advertising models, and (d) how far, if at all, Korean advertising values have converged with those of the West.

Communication Patterns of Korean and American Culture

Although generalizations about entire cultures and their communication patterns are difficult and dangerous to make, nonetheless, it is possible to observe and report cultural differences. The ways Koreans and Americans communicate are based mostly on their basic philosophies. Korean perception of communication is anchored in

Buddhist philosophy, which is characterized by the inarticulate or prelinguistic process of the mind (Yum, 1987): Truth must be gained without trying and in every spoken truth the unspoken has the last word; words are approximations, sometimes helpful, sometimes misleading (Oliver, 1962, p. 143). In Western culture, however, people believe that words do, in fact, mean what they say. Aristotle insisted that clarity is the first virtue of good style (Oliver, 1962, pp. 142–143).

• • •

. . . For purposes of this study, we limit the nonverbal aspects of culture mainly to facial expressions, hand and arm gestures, tactile communication, degree of body exposure, and communication between the sexes.

Facial Expressions

Everyday experience suggests that smiling is one of the most common nonverbal signals used for communication among humans. According to Ekman and Friesen (1971, pp. 124–129), happiness, generally indicated by a smile, is one of six human emotions said to be universally present and understood. Whereas a smile of happiness may be a universal expression, cultural, contextual, and personal influences can affect its meaning and frequency, as well as degree of expansiveness. Research has shown that general cultural rules about smiling (for example, frequency and expansiveness) are learned, and are significant in social interaction (Morse, 1982; Kraut & Johnston, 1979). Traditionally, Koreans are trained not to show their emotions. Because nonverbal expressions are associated mostly with the projection of emotional states, Koreans tend to avoid expressive nonverbal actions. Most Koreans do not, even in joyous humor, shout, laugh loudly, clap hands, jump up and down, tap the shoulders, embrace, or dance. Koreans who are angry try not to express their anger outwardly (Yim, 1970, p. 214). Among strangers, neutrality of expression is the rule in Korean culture. Adults, especially men, are not expected to smile frequently; it is a sign of weakness.

Hand and Arm Gestures

Hand and arm movement is another form of culture-specific expression. Clearly, there are differences among cultural groups as to what are considered appropriate frequency and style of hand and arm gestures. Whereas some people gesture broadly and often, others do so narrowly and seldom (Eisenberg et al., 1971, p. 100). A study of Waxer (1985), comparing nonverbal displays of emotion in American and Canadian television game show contestants, showed that American females use their hands more than do the Canadian females. In the Eastern view, adults who use many gestures when they speak are thought to be childish, because repression of overt bodily expression connotes self-control (Ramsey, 1984, p. 148). On the other hand, Western culture is likely to use strong expressive gestures to convey messages. One's ability to communicate is measured by his or her verbal and nonverbal expressive skills. These differences are assumed to be carried into nonverbal expressions used in print-media advertising illustrations.

Touching

Tactile communication is an important nonverbal expression that defines and differentiates cultural values. It is measured by the degree and extent of touch employed by people in the process of communicating with each other (Watson & Graves, 1966). Different cultures attach different meanings to distance and touch, consequently displaying different amounts and kinds of spatial behavior. Like Hedieger (1961), who divides animal species into *contact type* and *distant type*, Hall (1963, p. 1005) deals with *contact* and *non-contact* cultures. In contact culture, touch is common and acceptable as part of everyday life. Consequently, social members in that culture interact more closely with one another and touch one another more than do members of the noncontact group. The contact group is composed of Arabs, Latin Americans, and Southern Europeans; Asians, Indians, Pakistanis, and Northern Europeans make up the noncontact group.

Southeast Asians do not ordinarily touch during a conversation, especially one between opposite sexes, because many Asian cultures adhere to norms that forbid public display of affection and intimacy. Pares (1985) offered her impressions on the relationship between sexes:

> Contact between the two groups (men and women) seems to be slight: communication, be it serious or light-hearted, is confined to the immediate circle who, almost invariably, are of the same sex. To a Korean this doubtless seems proper and normal, but to a Westerner . . . the apparent indifference of sexes to each other can be somewhat disturbing. (p. 38)

One of the five harmonies of Confucian philosophy, the division of sexes still affects relationships between men and women. Even in modern times, embracing and kissing in public, winking at others, or engaging in intimate touch are regarded as uncivil (Yim, 1970).

Eye Behavior

The adage "eyes are the window of the soul" reflects the importance of eyes as a gauge of emotion (Watson, 1970, p. 48). Gaze, or visual behavior, refers to an individual's looking behavior, which may or may not be directed at another person. Mutual gaze refers to two interactants looking at each other, usually in the region of the face (Knapp, 1978, p. 276). Eye behavior also varies according to social norms. Hall (1963, p. 1012) mentioned some cross-cultural differences in eye contact. Navahos, for instance, are taught not to gaze directly at another person during a conversation. Watson (1970) performed the most extensive study of cultural differences in gaze. Subject dyads consisting of foreign students were observed conversing in their native language. A coding system for gaze behavior showed that Arabs, Latin Americans, and Southern Europeans focused their gaze on the eyes or face of their conversational partner. In contrast, Asians, Indians, Pakistanis, and Northern Europeans tended to show *peripheral gaze* (indirect gaze, oriented toward the other without looking directly at the face or eyes) or no gaze at all. Interestingly, no relationship has been found between gaze behavior and time spent overseas, suggesting that gaze patterns are unlikely to change with environmental social influence.

The Confucian tenet of division of the sexes is symbolically represented in Koreans' perception of direct eye contact among people of different ages or sex. In Korea, direct eye contact among unequals connotes competition, constituting an inappropriate form of behavior. On the other hand, Americans expect direct eye contact when they talk to each other. Many Americans think a person who shuns eye contact is shy or lacking in self-confidence.

Clothing and Degree of Body Exposure

The forms of nonverbal expressions discussed so far, such as facial expressions, hand and arm gestures, and tactile communication, involve bodily movements. Not all nonverbal communication is carried out with such signals. Cultural norms and values are also projected through style of dress. The way one dresses may represent "deep-seated psychic intentions" (Eisenberg & Smith, 1971, p. 105). Dress style hints at our self-image and the image we seek to project to others. Clothing is an important nonverbal parameter in conveying messages. The Japanese, whose culture is based upon group-centered identification, are notorious for uniformity in clothing: the stereotypical *salaryman* (businessman) wears a dark suit, dark tie, shiny black shoes, and company lapel pin. Japanese tourists baffle their foreign hosts with their uniformity in dress, buying habits, and group spirit, doing everything together in the same way (Condon & Yousef, 1975, p. 138).

The degree of body exposure in dress styles indicates some values of a cultural group. Each culture has its own understanding of which parts of the body may be exposed or should be covered, and of the significance of bodily display to social acceptance (Pares, 1985, p. 56). Because degree of body exposure is related to the function of clothes in matters of propriety and attraction, cultural norms and values in relationships between people determine the parts and degree of body exposure of societal members. In traditional Oriental philosophy, people have their place in nature as well as in society. Indeed, their social roles are as important as their roles as individuals. Manner, dress, etiquette, and behavior all assume considerable significance. The desire for propriety and the interest in social appearance have produced a tradition of the clothed, rather than unclothed, treatment of the human form in Korea (Pares, 1985, pp. 57–59).

In contrast, Americans have a higher tolerance for body exposure than Koreans. For instance, bared shoulders, legs, and backs are acceptable. However, American tolerance for body exposure is not uniform. The fundamental attitudes in Western Christian society toward nudity, shaped by its equation with sinfulness and by the Greco-Roman appreciation of the human form as the measure of nature, have engendered a tension and vitality that go far in explaining the Western preoccupation with the nude form (Pares, 1985, p. 57).

Although social rules governing nonverbal expressions in Korea are changing as a result of close and frequent contact with foreign countries, particularly the United States, the foundations of traditional values that gave rise to display rules remain.

• • •

Methodology

The research design used in this study was content analysis, which involves critical analysis of the advertising illustrations in terms of the parameters previously defined. In accordance with this technique, the study analyzes the manifest nonverbal parameters portrayed in Korean and American advertising illustrations.

• • •

To make advertisements comparable across cultures and to obtain a wide range in readership, two general interest magazines and one women's magazine published in each of the two countries were selected. The magazines targeted for the general audience were *Time* and *Newsweek* (American), and *Shin-Dong-Ah* and *Wol-Gan-Choson* (Korean). The two women's magazines were *Good Housekeeping* (American) and *Yeo-*

Sung-Jung-Ang (Korean). The magazines dated from January 1985 through December 1986.

• • •

The magazines used in this study were weeklies and monthlies. For the weekly magazines, the following issues were selected: (1) the first weeks' issues of January, May, and September; (2) the second weeks' issues of February, June, and October; (3) the third weeks' issues of March, July, and November; and (4) the fourth weeks' issues of April, August, and December. For the monthly magazines, every other month's issues were included. The procedure used in sampling the weekly and monthly magazines was designed to minimize any weekly or seasonal variations that might affect advertising content. This sampling procedure yielded 118 issues (May 1986 and September 1986 were not available for *Yeo-Sung-Jung-Ang*).

• • •

The criteria for selecting advertising illustrations were as follows:

1. Only full-page or double-page ads were used. Such illustrations can clearly portray nonverbal expressions and are easier to analyze than smaller ones.

2. Only advertisements that contained both adult males and females as main characters were included, because such ads portray real-life social interaction, showing the cultural value orientations of a given society more readily than single-sex ads. Family scenes with children were excluded.

A total of 400 ads from the six magazines were analyzed to provide a clear picture of nonverbal expressions presented and were considered to be an adequate number to satisfy the objectives of the study.

Operational Definition
of Nonverbal Expressions

Five nonverbal parameters were selected because they were considered to describe fully and to differentiate nonverbal expressions in advertising illustrations of the magazines. Categories of these parameters range from very conservative to highly expressive.

Facial Expressions   Facial expression was measured through categories of smiling, which were derived primarily from Kraut's and Johnston's (1979, p. 1542) smiling feature classification: (1) neutral face or blank expression (very conservative), wherein the mouth is relaxed; (2) hint-of-smile (conservative), which is characterized by corners of the mouth being turned up with the lips together, or the mouth being relaxed with lips slightly parted; (3) half-smile (expressive), wherein corners of the mouth are turned up and lips are parted to show teeth; and (4) full-smile (highly expressive), in which corners of the mouth are turned up and upper and lower teeth are parted.

Hand and Arm Gestures   Hand and arm gestures were classified as (1) nonuse (very conservative), wherein arms and hands are held downward, or wrists are raised; (2) narrow use (conservative), wherein movements of hands are limited to below the elbow area; (3) mild use (expressive), in which hands are raised above the elbow but below the shoulder line; and (4) broad use (highly expressive), in which hands are raised above the shoulder line.

Degree of Body Exposure   This category provides for the degree and kind of body exposure, including (1) nonexposure (very conservative), describing the models who show only face, neck, hands, lower arms, and areas below the knee; (2) slight-exposure (conservative), which includes exposure of the upper arm, knee, and cleavage; (3) half-exposure (expressive), describing models who expose their thighs and shoulders; and (4) full-exposure (highly expressive), showing chest, belly, back, or total nudity.

Tactile Communication   Tactile communication was measured by the degree of touching between male and female models: (1) nontouch (very conservative), which does not involve any type of bodily contact; (2) shoulder-to-shoulder touch (conservative), wherein models stand side-by-side touching each other's shoulder; (3) moderate touch (expressive), wherein models are shown holding hands, shaking hands, touching a shoulder by hand, locking arms, patting on the back, and touching chest-to-shoulder; and (4) intimate touch (highly expressive), which includes embracing, face-to-face hugging, hugging from the back, caressing, face-to-face touching, and kissing.

Communication Between the Sexes Through Eye Behavior   The analysis of communication between men and women was based upon the type of visual contact between them: (1) noncommunicative (very conservative), wherein models do not gaze at each other, rather they look down or gaze into space; (2) indirectly communicative (conservative), in which models look at a third object, having the other person within the field of vision; (3) one-way communicative (expressive) defined as only one—either male or female—model gazing at the other; and (4) highly communicative (highly expressive), in which both male and female models focus directly on each other's eyes.

Product Categories

In addition to these nonverbal parameters, the types of products advertised were also coded. It was assumed that the types of products might induce a different degree of nonverbal expression in advertising illustrations. Product categories were classified into primary goods and secondary goods. The criterion for the classification was how basic were the needs those products served. Primary goods include clothes, food, and household goods such as televisions, refrigerators, furniture, and telephones. Secondary goods include cosmetics, jewelry, beer, liquor, cigarettes, and services such as banking, insurance, resorts, hotels, and transportation.

• • •

Discussion of Findings

Relationship Between Nonverbal Expressions and Cultural Orientation

. . . A significant relationship between nonverbal expressions shown by advertising models and their cultural orientations was found to exist. The findings generally support the expectation that Korean models use more conservative, traditional modes of nonverbal expression than do the American models. On the other hand, the American models reflect their open cultural values, showing more expansive nonverbal expressions than do the Korean models.

Hypothesis 1.1   A significant difference in the frequencies of facial expressions between the American and Korean models was noted. . . . the greatest difference between the two cultural groups was in the full-smile category (highly expressive). . . . The general pattern shows that Korean models were less expansive in facial expressions than their American counterparts.

Hypothesis 1.2   Analysis of the relationship between hand and arm gestures and culture . . . shows . . . differences in the hand and arm gestures between the American and Korean advertising models were striking, with the majority of the American models showing wide, open hand use, while the Korean models remained passive, rarely using exaggerated hand or arm gestures (most of the Korean models with broad hand usage were teenagers).

Hypothesis 1.3   The results of the analysis of the degree of body exposure . . . illustrate that the American models showed a greater degree of body exposure than the Korean models. . . . American models scored fairly high percentages of body exposure in all three categories: slight-, half-, and full-exposure (19.3% combined). On the other hand, only 10.4% of the total Korean models were classified under these three categories.

Hypothesis 1.4   This hypothesis was analyzed through the type of touch that occurred between male and female models. . . . there is a strong relationship between the degree of expression in the touching behavior of Korean and American couples shown in ads and their cultural orientation. . . . Overall 58.3% of the 181 Korean couples were depicted as not involved in any type of bodily contact (nontouch/very conservative), while only 45.9% of the American couples were thus

shown. Among other categories, American advertising models showed fairly high percentages . . . in the intimate touch (highly expressive) category as contrasted with relatively low percentages . . . among Korean models. American models showed more intimate and closer bodily contact than Korean models; touching by Korean models tended to be limited to hand contact.

Hypothesis 1.5   Degree of nonverbal expression through communication between the sexes was analyzed through eye behavior between males and females shown in advertising illustrations. The findings . . . illustrate that advertising does reflect the cultural orientations of the two countries. . . . Thirty-two percent of the American couples were classified in the highly communicative category (highly expressive—couples looking at each other), compared to only 13.9% of the Korean models in that category. On the other hand, more Korean couples . . . were classified in the noncommunicative category (couples not looking at each other) than were their American counterparts. . . .

Relationship Between Nonverbal Expressions and Gender of Models Within Cultural Groups

The relationship between nonverbal expressions and gender was analyzed on the first three parameters; namely, facial expressions, hand and arm gestures, and degree of body exposure. The results of the analysis yield strong support for gender differences in nonverbal expressions within cultural group, except for hand and arm gestures as shown by American models.

Hypothesis 2.1   In comparing facial expressions between Korean male and female models . . . , more Korean females fell into half-smile (expressive) and full-smile (highly expressive) categories than did their male counterparts. On the other hand, male models portrayed neutral faces . . . more often than did females. . . .

American female models also had higher percentages in half-smile (expressive) and full-smile (highly expressive) categories than did American male models. . . . The results of this analysis demonstrate that facial expressions of advertising models depend upon the gender of the models in each culture. . . .

Hypothesis 2.2 . . . Korean female models were more conservative in hand use than Korean male models (44.8% vs. 31.4%). Examined in more detail, Korean males were depicted more frequently with broad use of their hands . . . than were the Korean female group. . . . In the case of American advertising models . . . , interestingly enough, the American female models exhibited a far higher percentage of broad use . . . than did their male counterparts. . . .

Hypothesis 2.3 . . . Korean female models exposed their bodies more frequently than did Korean male models in all three exposure categories (slight-, half-, and full-exposure). . . . There were also highly significant differences between American male and female models and degree of body exposure. . . . the American female models show relatively higher percentages in all three exposure categories (slight-, half-, and full-exposure) than do male models. . . .

Relationship Between Nonverbal Expressions and Product Categories Within Cultural Groups

The results of the comparison between product categories and nonverbal expressions shown by Korean advertising models demonstrate that only female facial expressions, female hand and arm use, and communication between the sexes were dependent upon the types of products advertised. . . . None of the other nonverbal parameters yields strong differences across primary and secondary products. In terms of facial expression, . . . Korean female models showed a higher score (13.5%) in the full-smile classification for primary goods such as clothes and food, while only 7.1% for secondary goods. . . . As to hand and arm use, Korean female models showed far more broad use . . . in primary goods than in secondary goods. . . .

In the case of American advertising models, only facial expression was dependent upon the product categories advertised among five nonverbal parameters. . . . The most striking difference

in male facial expression across product categories was found in the full-smile classification, where American male models scored 31.3% for primary goods ads, but only 9.8% for secondary goods. . . . It was also found that the female models followed almost the same trend as their male counterparts: more full-smile classifications in primary goods ads, and more neutral face classifications in secondary goods. All the other parameters, such as hand and arm use, degree of body exposure, touch, and communication between the sexes, yielded no significant relationship between product categories advertised and models' nonverbal expressions.

In sum, among the five nonverbal parameters, only that of facial expression was dependent upon the product categories advertised in both American and Korean advertising models: regardless of culture, more models fit the full-smile classification in primary goods ads and the neutral face classification in secondary goods ads.

Discussion

It was found that the five nonverbal expressions were important cultural parameters, which served as determinants of the different cultural orientations in Korea and America. The cultural parameters effectively describe and differentiate nonverbal expressions between Korean and American models. The findings show that nonverbal messages transmitted by models in Korean and American magazine advertisements are generally reflective of their cultural orientations. Korean models tended to smile less frequently, use their hands and arms less frequently, and expose their bodies less frequently than did American models, thus reflecting each culture. Male and female models in American advertising tended to touch each other more frequently and look at each other more frequently than their counterparts in Korean magazines.

Regarding gender differences, female models in both countries smiled more and exposed their bodies more frequently than did their male counterparts. These findings conform to the social norms of both societies. As far as these two cultural parameters are concerned, gender differences seem to be similar regardless of the cultural setting. In terms of hand and arm use, Korean female models showed less expressive hand gestures than their male counterparts, as was expected. For American models, however, the trend was the opposite: female models showed a far higher percentage of broad use of hand and arm gestures than did males. These findings somewhat limit cross-cultural generalizations or stereotypes of males using relaxed gestures (open, expansive, and frequent use of arms) and females using tense hand gestures (narrow and infrequent use of arms).

Another important finding is that facial expressions vary across product categories in both Korean and American advertising illustrations. Different products may require different degrees of facial expression, because models in both countries had more full-smile classification in primary goods ads and more neutral face classification in secondary goods ads. For primary goods, models try to show product satisfaction through smiling expressions, while for secondary products they strive to create a mood that does not necessarily require a full smile.

Theoretical Implications

The foregoing literature has revealed that there are three basic arguments about the relationship between culture and advertising. The first begins with the premise that advertising primarily reflects the unique indigenous culture, be it Western or non-Western. To prove this argument, the cultural content of advertising in Korea should contain primarily Korean elements of expression, and, likewise, in America, American elements. Consistent with this position, nonverbal expressions shown by models in Korean and American magazine advertisements were found to be highly related to their cultural orientations. Korean models tend to be more conservative than expressive in nonverbal modes, such as facial expression, body exposure, touch, hand and arm gestures, and eye behavior, than do American models.

The second position declares that advertising in non-Western countries is not a product of those cultures, but is primarily Western in character. This position is clearly negated by the results of the study. The findings obtained in the content analysis show that Korean advertising primarily reflects its own cultural values rather than Western values, at least in the context of nonverbal expressions.

The third position asserts that advertising in non-Western countries does not reflect solely the indigenous cultures, but a mixture of those cultures with some selected Western cultural traits. These researchers have reported the trend of countries to move toward a global, predominantly Western culture. This position is not consistent with the current data. Nonverbal expressions shown by Korean advertising models still basically reflect their indigenous cultural traits.

To summarize, the results of this study are consistent with the first position, which claims that advertising reflects primarily the indigenous culture, be it Western or non-Western. The strong relationship between advertising and cultural orientation observed in the present study may be due, in part, to the focus on nonverbal behaviors, which are fundamental core values that are hard to change. People's unconscious nonverbal cues are truer than their conscious verbal cues. Thus, nonverbal cues may constitute deeply hidden messages that are less susceptible to foreign influence. Advertising and culture can have a symbiotic relationship in the sense that culture influences advertising, which, in turn, engenders a way of life that becomes a part of that culture (cf. Marquez, 1973). Future research should examine how, with increasing interdependence among nations, nonverbal expressions shown in advertising change over time.

The major concern of this research is the cultural aspect of advertising. Advertising has an overt function—to sell things; however, the inner structures of advertising communication bear important cultural meanings and connotations that must be uncovered in order to make clear the full meaning of advertising messages. In the United States, the study of advertising communication has occurred mostly within a paradigm shaped primarily by the interests of the business community and defined as *consumer behavior* (Schultze, 1981, p. 371). This paradigm emphasizes consumer demographics and advertising appeals. Advertising communication should be studied in a broader cultural context in order to improve our understanding of international advertising.

Practical Implications

International marketers are often faced with the problem of whether, and to what extent, they should alter their advertising messages from one country to another (see Britt, 1974; Hornick, 1980; Munson & McIntyre, 1979; Ricks, Arpan, & Fu, 1974; Whitelock & Chung, 1989). Multinational companies that market their products on a worldwide basis are faced with the decision of whether to standardize their messages across countries, or to individualize their messages in each country. Traditionally, it has been more or less accepted that nationalistic differences prevented the use of similar copy and themes on a multinational level (Ryans, 1969). However, the apparent success of various companies, including Coca-Cola and Exxon, with its "Tiger" campaign, along with the benefits of using a standardized approach, are leading other companies to examine the feasibility of universal advertising themes (see Whitelock & Chung, 1989). Advertising standardization is not a simplistic concept and should be considered in terms of degree of uniformity rather than in absolute terms (see Peebles, Ryans, & Vernon, 1978). In general, however, the findings suggest limitations to the universal approach to advertising, because significant differences in nonverbal expressions exist between nations. One may suspect that a foreign model would be permitted to violate local norms; however, use of foreign models in Korean advertising was almost nonexistent. Overall, the current findings suggest that expressive nonverbal cues shown by American advertising models may be less effective in Korea because their appeal runs counter to Korean cultural values.

In the past, language was considered to be an important constraint to advertising standardization and posed the most difficult obstacle to universal standardization of advertising messages (Thackray, 1985). Incorrect translation of an advertisement into clumsy or embarrassing wording can cause adverse reactions (e.g., Nova means "no go" in Spanish). Similar problems often arise from failure to understand nonverbal idioms in a culture. Domestic success is no guarantee of predictable performance in a different environment (Ricks et al., 1974). Different nonverbal idioms may render many businesses' normal procedures inapplicable or untransferable.

There seems to be little doubt that culture plays an important role in the perception and use of advertising. Certain fundamental differences across cultures make imperative the use of sensitized advertising appeals when advertising abroad. Ricks et al. (1974) found that most international advertising blunders occur because of a failure to understand the foreign culture and its social norms. The importance of having an adequate cultural sensitivity on the part of advertising practitioners involved in international operations may be the major determinant in the success of an international business venture. It is particularly cogent for them to scrutinize and choose the correct cultural expectations in which advertising will appear. Only when the cultural rules of different cultural groups are identified will advertisers be able to get across their messages, reach the hearts and minds of the targeted group, and successfully promote their products in a foreign market.

REFERENCES

Britt, S. H. (1974). Standardizing marketing for the international market. *Columbia Journal of World Business, 9*, 39–45.

Choe, J.-H., Wilcox, G. B., & Hardy, A. P. (1986). Facial expressions in magazine advertisements: A cross-cultural comparison. *Journalism Quarterly, 63*(1), 122–126, 166.

Condon, J. C., & Yousef, F. (1975). *An introduction to intercultural communication.* New York: Bobbs-Merrill.

Durgee, J. F. (1986). Richer findings from qualitative research. *Journal of Advertising Research, 26*(4), 36–44.

Eisenberg, A. M., & Smith, R., Jr. (1971). *Nonverbal communication.* New York: Bobbs-Merrill.

Ekman, P. (1973). Cross-cultural studies of facial expression. In P. Ekman (Ed.), *Darwin and facial expression: A century of research in review.* New York: Academic Press.

Ekman, P., & Friesen, W. V. (1971). Constants across cultures in the face and emotion. *Journal of Personality and Social Psychology, 17*(2), 124–129.

Goffman, E. (1979). *Gender advertisements.* Cambridge, MA: Harvard University Press.

Hall, E. T. (1963). A system for the notation of proxemic behavior. *American Anthropologist, 65,* 1003–1026.

Hall, P. M., & Hewitt, J. P. (1973). The quasi-theory of communication and the management of dissent. In M. H. Prosser (Ed.), *Intercommunication among nations and peoples* (pp. 530–540). New York: Harper & Row.

Hediger, H. (1961). The evolution of territorial behavior. In S. L. Washburn (Ed.), *Social life of early man* (pp. 34–57). Chicago: Aldine.

Hornick, J. (1980). Comparative evaluation of international versus national advertising strategies. *Columbia Journal of World Business, 21,* 9–17.

Knapp, M. L. (1978). *Nonverbal communication in human interaction.* New York: Holt, Rinehart & Winston.

Kraut, R. S., & Johnston, R. E. (1979). Social and emotional messages of smiling: An ethological approach. *Journal of Personality and Social Psychology, 37,* 1539–1553.

Kunihiro, T. (1980). Personality structure and communication behavior: A comparison of Japanese and Americans. In W. von Raffler-Engel (Ed.), *Aspects of nonverbal communication.* Lisse, Swets, and Zeitlinger.

Madden, C. S., Cabellero, M. J., & Matsukubo, S. (1986). Analysis of information content in U.S. and Japanese magazine advertising. *Journal of Advertising, 15,* 38–45.

Marquez, F. T. (1973). *A comparative analysis of culture and the cultural content of print-media advertising in the Philippines and Thailand.* Unpublished doctoral dissertation, The University of Wisconsin, Madison.

Millum, T. (1975). *Images of women: Advertising in women's magazines.* Savage, MD: Rowman & Littlefield.

Morse, C. (1982). College yearbook picture: More females smile than males. *Journal of Psychology, 110,* 3–6.

Munson, J. M., & McIntyre, S. M. (1979). Developing practical procedures for the measurement of personal values in cross-cultural marketing. *Journal of Marketing Research, 16*(1), 48–52.

Norman, G. R. (1965). *Advertising as a reflection of national character in the United States and Great Britain.* Unpublished master's thesis, The Pennsylvania State University, University Park, PA.

Oliver, R. T. (1962). *Communication and culture: The problem of penetrating national and cultural boundaries.* Springfield, IL: Charles C. Thomas.

Pares, S. (1985). *Crosscurrents: Korean Western culture in contrast.* Seoul, South Korea: Seoul International Publishing House.

Peebles, D. M., Ryans, J. K., & Vernon, I. R. (1978). Coordinating international advertising. *Journal of Marketing, 42,* 28–34.

Ramsey, S. (1984). Double vision: Nonverbal behavior East and West. In A. Wolfgang (Ed.), *Nonverbal behavior: Perspectives, applications, intercultural insights* (pp. 139–167). New York: C. J. Hogrefe.

Ricks, D. A., Arpan, J. S., & Fu, M. Y. (1974). Pitfalls in advertising overseas. *Journal of Advertising Research, 14,* 47–51.

Ryans, J. K. (1969). Is it too soon to put a tiger in every tank? *Columbia Journal of World Business, 4,* 69–75.

Schultze, Q. J. (1981). Advertising, culture, and economic interest. *Communication Research, 8,* 371–384.

Singh, P. N., & Huang, S. (1962). Some sociocultural and psychological determinants of advertising in India: A comparative study. *Journal of Social Psychology, 57,* 113–121.

Thackray, J. (1985, November). Much ado about global advertising. *Newsweek:* Special Marketing Section.

Unwin, S. J. F. (1974). How culture affects advertising expression and communication style. *Journal of Advertising, 3*(2), 24–27.

Watson, O. M. (1970). *Proxemic behavior: A cross-cultural study.* Hawthorne, NY: Mouton de Gruyter.

Watson, O. M., & Graves, T. D. (1966). Quantitative research in proxemic behavior. *American Anthropologist, 68,* 971–985.

Waxer, P. H. (1985). Video ethology: Television as a data base for cross-cultural studies in nonverbal displays. *Journal of Nonverbal Behavior, 9*(2), 111–120.

Whitelock, J., & Chung, D. (1989). Cross-cultural advertising: An empirical study. *International Journal of Advertising, 8,* 291–310.

Yim, S.-C. (1970). Customs and folklore. In S.-S. Lee et al. (Eds.), *Korean studies today: Development and state of the field* (pp. 199–220). Seoul National University: Institute of Asian Studies.

Yum, J. O. (1987). Korean philosophy and communication. In D. Kincaid (Ed.), *Communication theory: Eastern and Western perspectives.* New York: Academic Press.

KEY TERMS

cross-cultural comparisons advertising

Korea
nonverbal communication

DISCUSSION QUESTIONS

1. How do the philosophy and religious beliefs in Korea influence nonverbal behavior? Do you think religious beliefs in America influence nonverbal behavior?
2. Kim investigated the effects of nationality and gender on nonverbal behavior. What are other factors that may influence nonverbal behavior?
3. Based on Kim's findings, how would television advertising in Korea differ from television advertising in the United States?
4. How might a critical researcher conduct a study of print advertising in Korea and the United States?
5. How might Kim's findings be different if the analyzed advertisements were from different magazines (e.g., *Ebony, Rolling Stone*)?

23
PLACES FOR SPEAKING IN TEAMSTERVILLE

GERRY PHILIPSEN

The significance of speaking as a domain within a culture varies across speech communities. Not only do bearers of different cultures speak differently one from another but, more importantly, they hold different assumptions about the value, purposes, and significance of speaking as a mode of human experience. Like religion, politics, and law, so speech, the principal medium of creating meanings in social interaction, itself holds different meanings for the various peoples whose views of the world afford it a place.

This essay reports in part the meanings which speech has in a community I labeled Teamsterville. It builds upon a previous essay[1] by developing further my answers to two questions: When the people of Teamsterville look out on the world

or conjure up some image of it, what does the world look like to them, and what do they envision as the place of speaking within it? Does Teamsterville's view of the situated appropriateness of speaking implicate something about the meaning and significance of speaking to its people? Answers to such questions, in this study and others like it, provide the descriptive materials from which to construct a theory of the place of speaking in cultures.

Attention to at least the most salient and accessible features of Teamsterville's outlook on speaking was facilitated by using Hymes' schema of components of speech events.[2] The idea behind

[1] Gerry Philipsen, "Speaking 'Like a Man' in Teamsterville: Culture Patterns of Role Enactment in an Urban Neighborhood," *QJS,* 61 (1975), 13–22.

[2] Dell Hymes, "Models of the Interaction of Language and Social Life," in *Directions in Sociolinguistics: The Ethnography of Communication,* ed. John J. Gumprez and Dell Hymes (New York: Holt, Rinehart, and Winston, 1972), see particularly pp. 58–71.

using schematic components such as "partici-pants," "topic," or "setting" is that they are, singly or in combinations, devices for discovering native interpretations about speaking. The assumption is that since natives use such conceptual devices as frames, places, or features for discovering and ordering cultural interpretations about speaking, the investigator can use these devices to accom-plish roughly the same thing, albeit for different purposes. For example, a number of studies show that much of a person's culture—his shared, tacit knowledge—is organized in terms of social iden-tities,[3] and other work suggests that components such as topic and setting also serve as organizing features in cultural world views.[4]

Previously I used one of these situational fea-tures in reporting on how Teamstervillers view the place of speaking in social life. That report focused on the native view of *who* may appropri-ately use speech and in what situations. That view is very sensitive to speaking as an instrument for creating social meaning by virtue of either using it or refraining from its use in the context of specific social identity relationships. For example, when a Teamsterville boy talks brashly to a man, the boy implicitly violates a social boundary. For the man to respond with talk implicitly confirms that the boundary is weak; in contrast, nonverbal threats or physical retaliation reestablish the so-cial boundary by warning the boy to "keep his place" and by affirming the man's place in the so-cial hierarchy. In this view of the personae who dwell in the world and of the activities by which they most convincingly enact specific roles, speech is located both situationally and functionally.

A Teamsterville outlook on settings or locales also informs native understandings about speak-ing as a situated mode of social activity. In addi-tion to the personae which the culture marks for speaking "parts," the culture also marks particu-lar scenes for occasions of talk. There are no labeled conversation areas or orators' arenas in the community, but its world view includes so-cial boundaries, scenes, and scenes within scenes which refer to everyday stages upon which a par-ticular kind of dramatic action may unfold. The native view of settings, and of the activities they most appropriately realize specifies, among other things, places for speaking, and in turn that spec-ification permits an inference about the place of speaking in Teamsterville.

"Place" is used here in several senses but each contains various ideas of location, such as a posi-tion in a social hierarchy, a physical setting, or the niche which is properly occupied by a thing, per-son, or idea. In the latter sense one speaks not only of things but also of people and ideas as hav-ing a place "in the scheme of things." A place can also be regarded as a perspective from which one discovers or explores a subject by the use of men-tal images. "Place," then, may simultaneously sug-gest notions of social, physical, perceptual, and heuristic location.

The phrase, "places for speaking in Teamster-ville," uses each of these senses of the word "place." Although this paper locates speaking in social and physical space, primarily it locates speech in the community's culture. Teamsterville's outlook on the occasioned uses of speaking sug-gests that a sense of place—at once both hierar-chical and physical—is a "major unifying per-ception"[5] in its cultural world view; a perception which creates shades of meaning and inter-pretation regarding speech as an instrument of communication and social life. Accordingly, two features of place, personae and scene, are per-spectives which have special relevance for ex-ploring Teamsterville's images of the world, and for thereby discovering where its people locate speech in their cultural scheme of things.

Four Teamsterville place concepts form a simple taxonomy of culturally defined places for speaking. Each is labeled by a native place term, and is defined in terms of the kind of setting to which it refers, the personae whose presence in it create a scene, and how the scene-personae configuration creates an occasion for talk. Scene, personae, and talk thus are interwoven aspects of

[3] Roger M. Keesing, "Toward a Model of Role Analysis," in *A Handbook of Method in Cultural Anthropology*, ed. Raoul Naroll and Ronald Cohen (Garden City, New York: The Natural History Press, 1970), pp. 423–453.

[4] See Susan U. Philips, "Acquisition of Rules for Ap-propriate Speech Usage," *Georgetown University Monograph Series on Languages and Linguistics*, 2 (1970), 77–94.

[5] The phrase is from Walter J. Ong, "World as View and World as Event," *American Anthropologist*, 71 (1969), p. 635.

the design I use in reporting Teamsterville places for speaking, "the neighborhood," "the street," "the corner," and "the porch."

Places for Speaking

A sense of neighborhood has a deep and compelling significance to the dwellers of Teamsterville. The sociospatial boundaries which residents perceive as "the neighborhood" make up the largest region within which it is considered most appropriate and in which it is most "natural" to engage in talk, and the residents think of these boundaries as co-extensive with a particular style of speaking which is characteristic of the community and to which its residents should conform. Definitions of neighborhood as scene, then, relate to native judgments about when to talk and ways of speaking, and both kinds of judgment are linked to a native view of place.

Every resident readily and emphatically identifies "the neighborhood" and defines it very insistently in terms of specific streets and blocks. Residents are equally insistent that they "know everybody around here," i.e., within the boundaries they perceive. Field observation and questioning of informants reveal that the boundaries reported vary considerably from person to person, and that the "we know everybody" assertion is not literally true. But the very specific definition and the insistent assertion suggest that a resident defines "the neighborhood" by reference both to physical setting ("around here") and to the particular people who make up his network of friends, associates, and acquaintances ("everybody") within it.

The physical boundaries of the neighborhood frame a scene for sociable interaction. For most residents these boundaries are the outer perimeter beyond which they do not socialize. In the course of my interviews of them, few Teamsterville men or women reported that they had participated in social events during the previous year with anyone who lives more than ten blocks from their home. Their reports of speaking practices, which observation confirmed in most cases, indicate a pattern of overt behavior, but what is more important here is that the reports suggest a lo-cal preference for talking within, not without, the perceived physical boundaries. Teamstervillers view the physical neighborhood as the largest scene within which talk is appropriately a focus of activity.

Within the physical neighborhood a Teamsterviller can be in the presence of people whom he defines as intruding into his social world. The physical boundaries are therefore supplemented by social boundaries which define "everybody"—the roster from which may be drawn appropriate personae for talk. Specifically, the ethnicity and residence of a potential interlocutor—his social and physical place—are salient variables in decisions to mark an occasion as appropriate for speaking. A visitor to the neighborhood, if he is so bold as to intrude into semiprivate regions (which include, among other places, "the street"), must be placed by the resident in terms of ethnicity and residence before a conversation can comfortably proceed. Once a stranger is so located, talk might be relatively free, depending on the kind of person he is. "The hillbillies" and "the Mexicans" live within the neighborhood boundaries but do not, in the eyes of the long-term white residents, really "belong" there. These groups should, in the view of the people I studied, "keep in their place" by living elsewhere and socializing among themselves. They are not, as a rule, appropriate partners for talk. Finally, there are those people who live in the neighborhood and whose ethnicity fits one of the traditional categories but whose ethnicity is different from one's own. Germans, Italians, Poles, and Lithuanians, among others, now talk to each other, but in the past these neighborhood groups had been relatively isolated from each other physically and socially, and there is still a sharp sense of difference between them. These persons include some people in the other groups in the term, "everybody," yet they still can visualize an image of "the neighborhood" as people of like ethnicity sharing a street or block, and it is that scene in which talk most appropriately and naturally has its place.

The unusually strong relationship of social to physical place is no accident. In the nineteenth century Teamsterville's first residents established tightly segregated patterns of residence and association along ethnic lines. The residents, who were new or relatively new immigrants, settled in row houses on a block or street peopled by their countrymen, and ethnicity was a pervasive determinant of interaction, association, and residence. Today the patterns born of ethnicity are altered but not totally replaced. Even though a person's street address is no longer a perfect guide to his ethnicity, many streets and blocks are still associated with a particular ethnic group. Parents still forbid their children to play in a particular place because it is an "Italian [Polish, etc.] block." Ethnicity and locality thus are at least partially interchangeable as organizing devices, criteria by which the Teamsterville resident selects from among the many social experiences available to him those which appropriately call forth speaking as a mode of activity.[6]

In addition to locating occasions of speaking within the boundaries of "the neighborhood," Teamstervillers also locate on a scale of social worth the style of speaking they associate with the neighborhood. Awareness of their own speaking style as one distinct from others is reflected in their readily reported assessment, consistent across informants, that their speech is inferior to the Standard English of middle class people, e.g., people who live on "the north side" (of Chicago), but superior to the speech of, respectively, "hillbillies," "Mexicans," and "Negroes." They respect and resent the speech of people who have a better control of Standard English than they do, are insecure about their own speech outside of neighborhood contexts, and find reassurance in what they perceive to be the deficiencies of "Negro" speech. Thus Teamsterville judgments of locale, socioeconomic standing, and conformity to accepted standards of speaking are correlated—Teamstervillers see themselves as being sandwiched between the richer, linguistically superior whites of the north side of town and the poorer, linguistically inferior blacks who live to the south of Teamsterville.

Awareness of a linguistic norm and the concurrent belief that one's own speech is substandard can create what Labov calls "linguistic insecurity."[7] This in turn can lead to attempts at correction, even hypercorrection, the practice of speaking so carefully as to betray a deliberate attempt at compensation. Teamstervillers do not attempt or value correction or hypercorrection, and cultural interpretations linking speech behavior with native attitudes about social and physical place may account for suppression of attempts at change. On the one hand, the awareness of a linguistic norm that Teamstervillers do not measure up to serves to heighten a positive affective awareness of community patterns, providing a kind of unity in adversity, in which the local deviation from Standard English functions as a defining attribute of membership in "everybody around here." On the other hand, a resident who changes his speech to be more like Standard English is seen as symbolically attempting to leave the neighborhood. His deviation from local usage is interpreted as an inappropriate assertion of upward mobility, an assertion which is, like other attempts at rising in the world, resented by those who do not make such efforts. One informant revealed a significant Teamsterville image when he described the neighborhood as a big crawfish barrel from which everyone tries to crawl out and in which everyone resents those few who succeed in reaching the top.

Teamstervillers believe that in order to maintain their status as one of the "everybody" they should not significantly modify their speaking style so as to deviate from local patterns. Changes in speech are easily noticed, so speech is therefore a means by which a person can signal his desire either to move upward on the social scale or to affirm his commitment to the norms of his present group. Teamsterville reactions to two prominent people provide a neat illustration of this dual possibility. Speech style is a principal factor verbalized in positive evaluations by Teamsterville teenagers of the television program "All in the Family," based on the lives of a New York City

---

[6]For other treatments of neighborhoods much like Teamsterville as "urban villages," see Herbert I. Gans *The Urban Villagers: Group and Class in the Life of Italian-Americans* (New York: The Free Press, 1962); Gerald D. Suttles, *The Social Order of the Slum: Ethnicity and Territory in the Inner City* (Chicago: Univ. of Chicago Press, 1968).

---

[7]William Labov, *The Social Stratification of English in New York City* (Washington, D.C.: Center for Applied Linguistics, 1966), p. 477.

family which lives in a neighborhood much like Teamsterville. The day after Jean Stapleton won an Emmy award for her performances on the show, a group of Teamsterville girls expressed their strong approval of the show and the award. They were, however, keenly disappointed to learn that in real life Jean Stapleton talks differently from the character she portrays on television, i.e., she sounds "real sophisticated." On the other hand, a Teamsterville resident can succeed in the eyes of the world and yet not be resented by his neighbors. I asked one informant why it is that a particular local politician could be so successful and still enjoy the almost reverent adoration of his Teamsterville neighbors. The informant replied, in a tape recorded interview, "Well, see, he doesn't scare anybody because he speaks lousy English. I mean he has rotten pronunciation. And he has, y'know, he murders the American language, the way most of us do, so we know he's one of us, he's just like us."[8]

A college student, responding to a question about his own speech, spoke for himself and other Teamsterville residents when he said that he feels insecure in a university or other "middle class" setting because he grew up in an "illiterate, poor neighborhood." The informant said he is reluctant to change his speaking habits because that would alienate him from his friends in the neighborhood. Few residents face the dilemma articulated by the informant, for they live their lives amidst friends and neighbors who constitute the network of people known as "the neighborhood," and among these people speech is viewed as a resource for signaling one's similarity to his friends and for confirming his loyalty to them and their shared values. Thus it is that a Teamsterviller's sense of neighborhood is a lens through which he locates speech, socially, physically, and hierarchically.

"The neighborhood" is the most macroscopic concept which Teamstervillers use to distinguish places in general from places for speaking. They supplement their view of places for speaking with several other place concepts which "the neighborhood" subsumes. The most important supplementary concept is "the street," which as physical location refers to all outdoor areas in the neighborhood, but particularly to streets, sidewalks, and porches. "Everybody" participates in street life. A street is, however, considered primarily a man's rather than a woman's territory. Men spend more time in the street and have access to more of it than women do. It is used as a general setting for sociability among neighborhood residents. Although it legally is public territory, residents do not treat it merely as such; street territory as physical setting can be a scene in Teamsterville because people actively socialize there, and outsiders who walk or drive on sidewalks or streets often are felt to be intruding on at least semi-private territory.

The nature of front porches, the physical design of the neighborhood, and the density of population facilitate the use of the street as a social setting. Porches are open and in most cases flush to the ground; they are small, usually about six feet square. One porch is near enough to another that neighbors can converse and at the least are mutually visible. People socialize in front of, not behind, their houses; they visit on front porches but not on back porches, perhaps because the latter look out on alleys and hold garbage cans. There are few back or side yards. A typical street has twenty-four buildings on one side (with a very small space between each building), each building has two or three flats (one flat per story), and flats house an average of 3.4 people. On one side of a typical block, then, there are about 160 people who are potential users of that block's porches, sidewalk, and street. There are about seven to ten people available for interaction in and around each front porch stoop.

An upper middle class suburb contiguous to the northern boundary of Chicago is an instructive contrast to Teamsterville. There friends visit inside houses or in back yards where there is a patio, a large fenced yard, and a garden. Visitors are usually from outside a ten block radius. Only one family lives in each building, with an average of 2.95 people per household. A resident can enter

---

[8] The same politician mentioned by the informant once sought, upon the recommendation of a political advisor, to undertake speech lessons from a professor of speech at Northwestern University. At the end of the first lesson, the politician said, "I'm sorry, Doc, if I talked the way you want me to they'd laugh me out of the neighborhood." I am indebted to Glen E. Mills for this information.

his home by driving in the alley to his garage and walking from the garage door to enter the house by the back door, without exposure to his neighbors. Adults do not socialize in front yards, and certainly not on front porches. In short, there are relatively few residents per block and they preserve privacy and avoidance patterns.[9]

It is as part of the general physical layout that the street can be understood to be a significant setting in Teamsterville. Sociable speech is conducted in a relatively public region, the street, where people are available to each other because of the physical design of the community. Add to this the facts of population density and the relative absence of air conditioning, and one can picture people spilling out in the street in summer. When outdoors, people frequently congregate at porches and corners, and Teamstervillers share a view of what personae and what speech activity are appropriate to those two places.

"The corner" is an outdoor setting, at or near a street corner, which a particular group of boys marks as its regular meeting place and as its "turf," which is to say that a corner is the territory of boys or young men who are long-time friends and associates. For some men the neighborhood tavern becomes a surrogate for a street corner, so "corner personae" can include men of all ages beyond early adolescence with the scene shifting from corner to tavern in early adulthood. "The corner" in the broad sense is the principal scene where members of a group of males converse. Group members promote extensive sociability among themselves and define sharp boundaries between themselves and non-members. Accordingly, talk is an appropriate focus of activity "on the corner," but not elsewhere, and talk has value as social currency among corner personae but not with others.

A particular corner has social significance for a Teamsterville boy not only because that corner is where the boy's most important social activity occurs, or where he meets the group with which he has deep feelings of loyalty and identification, but also because there is more than a casual association of scene with personae. Youths express

their group membership in terms of place references: they describe themselves as "Wallace [Street] Boys," "The Spirits of 32nd [Street]," "the 33rds," etc. They write the street name on their clothing, and they paint the street name on neighborhood buildings.[10] Accordingly, where a boy "hangs" influences how others see him and how he sees himself—it is a significant attribute of his persona. A boy feels at home, in the "right place," at his corner, and that has special significance in a neighborhood in which "keeping your place" both physically and hierarchically is an extremely compelling *topos*. Thus one boy summarized the corner's significance to him in saying, "Where you hang is your turf—you won it and it's yours."

One corner boy said that his group did not allow Mexicans to enter its turf but that others could pass through without incident. The boy's group does not define Mexicans as part of "the neighborhood," even though Mexicans live within the physical boundaries. This illustrates that a stranger's entry into another group's turf is considered a challenge to the claimants' control of their territory. Frequently such an intrusion prompts a fight. On the other hand, if a boy enters the turf of people he knows, even if he does not "belong" there, he is allowed safe passage because he is part of "everybody" around there. Thus, to walk only where one is known ensures peaceful relations even with unfriendly groups. Because the presence of a stranger in alien territory can lead to fighting, residents value both staying where one "belongs" and knowing everybody.

Where a boy "hangs" is not only his turf but is also the social context he marks as most appropriate to speaking occasions, and this association of speech with a particular context has significance for understanding the Teamsterville boy's outlook on speaking. At the corner, the boy acquires a highly developed appreciation for loyalty to and familiarity with his identity-matched fellows, and an equally sharp sense of the importance of the social and physical boundaries which insulate his

[9] Demographic data are from Evelyn Kitagawa and Karl Taeuber, *Local Community Fact Book, 1960* (Chicago: Univ. of Chicago Press, 1963).

[10] The use of public walls for culturally significant writings is, of course, not new. For an interesting example of another contemporary setting, see Herbert Kohl, "Names, Graffiti, and Culture," in *Rappin' and Stylin' Out: Communication in Urban Black America*, ed. Thomas Kochman (Urbana: Univ. of Illinois Press, 1972), pp. 109–133.

group from outsiders. The corner boy's place for speaking is therefore relatively impermeable by interlocutors who do not share his background of meanings and experiences; and, on the other hand, the boy sees the world outside his place as a context not appropriate to activity which has speech as its focus. A consequence is a heightened appreciation for speech which (1) by its form emphasizes the boy's similarity to others in his group and sets him apart from those outside, and (2) is highly dependent for its meanings upon a context of shared experience. In short, the cultural meanings attached to places for speaking imply a preference for what Bernstein calls a "restricted" mode of speaking (in which the speaker does not make verbally explicit his meanings and in which speech does not serve as a mode for expressing the personal uniqueness of the speaker), and a relative de-emphasis of what he calls speaking in the "elaborated" mode (speaking which is verbally explicit and which serves to make public the unique motives, feelings, ideas, etc., of the speaker).[11]

Since women are denied full use of the street, they use front porches. The front porch of a house is not exclusively a woman's territory, but it has special significance for the Teamsterville woman. Although the street is in general a setting for sociability, not every means of participation in street life is sanctioned for women. In the local view, the woman's place is in the kitchen and the home, the man's in the street and the outside; and Teamsterville men and boys report neighborhood boundaries which are more extensive than those reported by girls and women. The negative sanction on certain types of female street interaction is reflected in patterns of child rearing. Girls are not allowed outside of the home without permission. They are carefully supervised and must account for their whereabouts at all times. Teamstervillers believe that strict control in raising a girl is the only alternative to overpermissiveness, which brings many negative sanctions. How, then,

is a woman or young girl to participate in the social life of the neighborhood? The front porch serves as a link between street and home, as a place in which a Teamsterville woman can appropriately participate in social life. An adult woman, who has lived in Teamsterville all her life, reported that in winter she hardly sees anyone, but "in summer the whole block opens up" and everyone congregates on or around front porches.

"The porch" is a place at or near the front porch of a house, the physical porch usually being only a stoop or a few steps. "Everybody" uses the porch. It is a principal setting for sociability, particularly for young children and for women of all ages. Its use also facilitates a person's entry into neighborhood life, serving as a link between home and street. Although I had previously been aware of the front porch as a gathering place, and had participated in front porch conversation, its deep cultural significance first became apparent to me by accident. I asked an informant about who is and who is not socially active in the neighborhood, as a way of eliciting the characteristics of socially accepted people. The informant mentioned an attorney who was minimally accepted but not active in the round of block sociability. After several minutes of persistent but unproductive questioning about how the man could become more socially active if he so wanted, the informant answered with a note of exasperation and finality that the man could never be fully accepted because he did not have a porch. Later work with other informants indicates that the front porch is used for extending invitations to talk and as a place for launching one's own participation in neighborhood social life. The consequences of having a front porch might appear negligible. However, an understanding of the function of the front porch in Teamsterville suggests ways of introducing oneself in the neighborhood, of initiating sociability, and of receiving such initiations from others.

Fieldwork as Intercultural Communication

When a person seeks to understand speech behavior in a community whose culture is alien to him, the possibility of misunderstanding is high. Upon

[11] Basil Bernstein, "Social Class, Language, and Socialization," in *Language and Social Context*, ed. Pier Paoli Giglioli (Harmondsworth, Middlesex, England: Penguin Books, 1972), pp. 173–78. For the classic treatment of corner groups in a white, working class neighborhood, see William Foote Whyte, *Street Corner Society: The Social Structure of an Italian Slum* (Chicago: Univ. of Chicago Press, 1943).

hearing that I was studying "Communication in Teamsterville," a middle class visitor to the neighborhood remarked, "There is no communication in Teamsterville," for this outsider believed that because he heard little talk where he expected it, there was none. Richard Sennett, a student of middle class mores and manners, wrote that when middle class people want to feel they are socializing in a warm, personal way they seek out "intimate and small places, the most powerful being their own homes."[12] Real entertaining is sheltered by the house walls and limited to those invited within. Teamsterville's taxonomy of places for speaking suggests a very different model from that of middle class or white collar America: Teamstervillers have a strong appreciation for sociability in such "public" places as neighborhood, street, corner, and porch. Indeed, these are the kinds of places for speaking they value most. An implication is that one should discover where people talk in order to acquire anything but a culture-bound understanding of a people's speech behavior.

Teamsterville's criterion for marking a place for speech is different from that of some other communities. An upper middle class living room is a place for talk, and men and women, adults and children, are appropriate personae for conversation there. Even relative strangers can be welcome; note that a host is anxious if a visitor does not participate in the round of talk and often a host deliberately encourages a reticent guest to speak. In Teamsterville, by contrast, the living room is not popular as a setting for talk. Rather, settings are popular which exclude those of different sex or social position and where outsiders would not be present to participate. In Teamsterville it is the presence of such identity-matched personae in a location traditionally set aside for sociability among them, to the exclusion of others, that marks a place for speaking. The search, then, should not end with the discovery of speaking locations but should uncover what, in the native view, makes a place fitting for talk.

In the present study the question of places invariably became, upon analysis, one of personae

and of the scenes most appropriate for gatherings of particular personae. In other words, talk is not a focus of activity merely because of the setting. A gathering of Mexican and Italian boys on the same corner is an occasion for careful visual scrutiny as one group quietly passes through the other's turf, but to make it an occasion for talk would be to invite trouble. Similarly when an outsider walks into a corner tavern he changes the occasion from one of loud frequent talk to one of near-perfect silence. On the other hand, a person comes to have a particular persona through participating in activity which is inextricably bound up with particular locales. One becomes part of the "everybody" by being from "around here." An adolescent girl can be excluded from the round of talk because she lives a block away from other participants in a conversation. A boy becomes a corner boy because he spends time on a corner and "his" corner is, to him and others, a significant aspect of his persona. The two schematic components, scenes and personae, were not in this study discretely separable. The outsider who uses situational components heuristically, as means for discovering a pattern in native judgments about talk, should be prepared to find that in accounting for cultural data in any given case, the components are interdependent.

Teamsterville data suggest that the major settings and occasions a people mark for speaking are important to understanding a culture pattern of speaking. It would, for example, be difficult to discern the significance of the front porch to Teamsterville ways of speaking if the investigator could not see its use and meaning as part of a larger pattern of setting and speech behavior in the community, a pattern which interrelates concepts of neighborhood, street, corner, and porch. Furthermore, discovering that pattern enables an investigator to explain symbolic behavior other than speaking which might otherwise be inexplicable. For example, Teamsterville place concepts were helpful to me in explaining one neighborhood practice which at first struck me as quite puzzling, the display of bowling trophies in funeral parlor windows.

A Teamsterville funeral parlor is, like a Teamsterville tavern, not so much an impersonal public setting as it is an intimate, familiar, private

---

[12] Richard Sennett, *The Uses of Disorder: Personal Identity and City Life* (New York: Vintage Books, 1970), p. 76.

setting. It is not the setting for a brief service followed almost immediately by a trip to the cemetery; rather, there is a wake, which is attended by many people throughout the day and evening. A family chooses a funeral parlor along socially patterned lines, following the preference of their social circle within their parish. The funeral parlor owner is, in many cases, a resident of the neighborhood, a person who is an acquaintance, if not a social intimate, of the mourners. Thus the funeral parlor is a place for the meeting of friends and relatives as well as for the expression of sympathy.

For the funeral parlor, symbolic participation in the life of the street is an important rhetorical strategy, one aim of which is to create a scene appropriate to the funeral parlor's activities, and the display of a bowling trophy is a tactic in this strategy. The trophy faces *into the street*, not into the building, as is true of the small military figures which were, at the time of the research, displayed in many Teamsterville homes which had a family member in the military service. The funeral parlor businessmen and the residents display the trophies to people in the street, the front window serving not only as a boundary marker but also as a channel through which to announce locally-valued information, and through which to participate in the life of the street, a life whose focus is the expression of solidarity and of interaction with a close-knit peer group.

A bowling trophy in the window of a funeral parlor creates an effect which is wholly consonant with local patterns of symbolic expression of neighborhood solidarity. It is significant to local passersby. It communicates that the displayer values a popular peer group activity in the neighborhood, bowling, and that the displayer is therefore very much a part of neighborhood life. A bowling trophy in the window symbolically links the inside region of the funeral parlor with the outside regions of street and corner and thus serves the rhetorical end of creating an impression that the funeral parlor is an appropriate place for its principal activity, meetings at which friends express solidarity and support. So viewed, as symbolic participation in neighborhood street life, the bowling trophy in the window is neither tasteless indelicacy nor queer custom but a fitting dis-

play in its context. In order to see it thus, one must use the Teamsterville perspective on places for speaking.

Conclusions

When Teamstervillers look out on the world their perception of it is shaped by a finely developed sense of place. They see boundaries, social and physical, where others do not, and this vision serves as a major unifying perception in their world view. The centrality of place in the cultural outlook is reflected in a strong concern for locating people in social-physical space; in a view of places as locales whose boundaries rightly enclose and shelter some people and deny entry to others; and in a pervasive concern that oneself and others know and stay in the proper place both hierarchically and physically.

Speech, of course, is an object of that world view, and speaking as a mode of human experience takes on a culturally distinctive meaning when viewed from Teamsterville's perspective. Speaking is a focus of activity in social relationships and in physical settings which have sharp boundaries that insulate the participants from interaction with those not matched to the relevant identity attributes. Speech is seen as an instrument of sociability with one's fellows, as a medium for asserting communal ties and loyalty to a group, and serves—by its use or disuse, or by the particular manner of its use—to signal that one knows one's place in the world.

One feature of "place" in Teamsterville is the settings in which the world view locates speaking. These settings are significant not merely as physical locations, as the blocks and boundaries which define a neighborhood, as particular streets, or as the corners and porches which dot the streets. The world view associates these places with certain people and thus "imbues the landscape with social meaning."[13] These are the scenes in which speaking has a place in Teamsterville life, and these scene-personae configurations, because of

---

[13] Philip K. Bock, *Modern Cultural Anthropology: An Introduction* (1969; rpt. New York: Alfred A. Knopf, 1974), p. 175.

the kinds of talk they invite, create for the resident of the community a cultural awareness of speaking. Thus by attending to the settings the community marks for talk, one can discover a lens through which to see not only the community's places for speaking but also the particular way in which its people understand that, in human affairs, talk has its place.

KEY TERMS

social identity   speech
neighborhood   ethnicity

DISCUSSION QUESTIONS

1. Philipsen describes how speaking serves cultural ends in Teamsterville. Can you think of other contexts in which speaking serves cultural ends?

2. Philipsen suggests that we know little about the cultural values placed upon speaking in contemporary America. What other cultural spaces would you explore to find these cultural differences?

3. Philipsen's essay helps us understand that there are many different ways of speaking in the United States. If we are so diverse, is there a recognizable or identifiable U.S. American way of communicating? Who "owns" this type of communication?

4. What does Philipsen's essay suggest about how language helps create cultural spaces and cultural boundaries? Can we learn to speak in culturally appropriate ways in order to gain access to and acceptance in cultural communities?

5. What does Philipsen's essay tell us about the role of class in culture? of race and ethnicity? of gender? of age?

24

WARRIORS, WAMPUM, GAMING, AND GLITTER: FOXWOODS CASINO AND THE RE-PRESENTATION OF (POST)MODERN NATIVE IDENTITY

LEDA M. COOKS

Framed against a clear sky, the lone tree on a prominent knoll represents Mashantucket, the "much-wooded land" where the Pequots hunted and kept alive their identity as an independent people. . . . The fox stands as a reminder that the Pequots are known as "the fox people."
—Promotional pamphlet for Foxwoods Casino

The promotional pamphlets and commercials advertising the Foxwoods Casino in Ledyard, Connecticut, use the slogan "Gaming In Its Natural State." "Gaming" in this instance means gambling: slot machines, roulette tables, bingo, Bacca-

rat, Keno, racing, Blackjack, craps, and Pai Gow poker. In other contexts, gaming is often the verb used to describe the activity of hunting, the activity that once provided the Pequots with sustenance and survival on this very land. Thus, gaming here takes on several meanings that are of great importance in understanding both the history of the Pequots and the complex cultural spaces that make up Foxwoods Casino.

The irony of their present wealth, acquired through casino gaming as opposed to the gaming that provided their livelihood for thousands of years, is not lost on the Pequots. However, the fact that Foxwoods is the wealthiest and the largest casino in the world has little to do with the luck and chance often associated with gambling. The Pequots are, first and foremost, survivors. They lost almost all of their land and their people and have fought for centuries to get it back.

Understanding the meaning and importance of land in Pequot history is essential to comprehension of the complex cultural symbols that went into the design and structure of the casino. In one enormous space—including two hotels, a shopping mall, both a smoking and a nonsmoking casino, several restaurants, a bingo parlor that seats 3,200, a cinetropolis (city of specialty theaters)—are representations of indigenous culture, imperialistic images of the warrior-savage, and re-creations of colonial New England. These images (and others discussed throughout this essay) point to the complexities of a postmodern Native identity: romanticized and racialized, neither oppressive nor empowering, but negotiated in certain moments and in ways that have served to make the Pequots wealthy. And, along with this wealth, to make them arguably the most (in)visible tribe in the world.

This chapter examines the cultural spaces where the multiple notions of gaming come together to signify the complexity of Native identities.[1] In the process, it seeks to raise the issues complicating traditional notions of a unidimensional and static cultural space. Traditional representations of marginalized or indigenous cultural space fail to recognize the complexities of dynamics that racialize, ethnicize, or romanticize identities for consumption of the dominant culture. Space itself is thus a social construction that reflects the dynamics of power in cultural stories.

This chapter examines the junctures at which diverse stories about cultural space come together. In doing so, it suggests movement from a functionalist perspective of space toward a more complex understanding of the spaces in which cultural meanings are created. Borrowing from social constructionist and critical perspectives, the chapter examines the negotiation of dominant and marginalized identities at work in particular works of art, architecture, statues, and the tribal mascot. It does this by interweaving dominant cultural stories about the history of the Pequots and notions about their indigenous identity with representations of such at work in the particular artifacts and spaces of the casino.

To begin to understand the interplay among spaces, symbols, and stories about cultural identity, we should first assess the overall layout of the casino and the placement of walls, windows, lighting, shops, casinos, restaurants, bingo parlors, and so forth within it. The casino is located several miles into the reservation and sits isolated from residential or commercial areas. Only one two-lane road leads to and from the casino, and this approach provides visitors with a view of a giant self-contained city—almost spaceship-like in structure. As you enter Foxwoods, you enter into a world that easily overwhelms the senses: bright neon lights, clanging bells, masses of people everywhere. The gaming rooms are primarily lit by the neon of the slot machines; the low ceilings provide little overhead lighting and there are no windows. This lack of overhead lighting in the immense gaming rooms makes them seem to go on forever. All of these structural arrangements (along with the absence of clocks) combine to produce an effect of timelessness well known among casino designers. Many people interviewed at Foxwoods for this study reported feeling as though they had lost track of the passage of time while in the casino area.[2] Although Foxwoods promoters often remark that it is one of the only casinos that has windows, the windows are located in the mall area of the casino, not in the gambling areas. The effect of such spatial design is both to create the effect of escaping time and to keep the senses so overwhelmed with the high-pitched and high-paced world of fantasy (and addiction) that real-world concerns become irrelevant.

The mall area of Foxwoods, while totally enclosed, is designed to create the effect of being outside (the man-made "natural state" of gaming). The ceilings are very high, and atriums throughout the mall display artificial and real plants hanging from wrought iron archways and planters along the walls. The iron arches and other fixtures are painted aquamarine and mauve—colors that signify the Pequot tribe. Large disks with designs of vines and flowers painted on them hang from the iron bars. On the other side of the mall are false storefronts that give the impression that one is walking through a small town in colonial New England. One of the false fronts looks like an old fire station, another a lithograph shop, and yet another—in an interesting re-creation of local colonial history—the "Mashantucket Town Hall." Behind the other false fronts of colonial houses are expensive specialty stores that sell dominant cultural representations of Native Americans (fringe-and-moccasin-wearing plastic dolls for $400) or artifacts that have been appropriated and commercialized as indicative of all tribes, regardless of their origin. Leather jackets with fringe, jackets with colorful Navajo designs, moccasins, wind catchers, blankets, and wood flutes are sold along with imported clothing from Third World countries in South America, Africa, and Asia.

Above these specialty boutiques are Disney-like displays of colonial U.S. history. These animated and mechanized figures act out scenes from 17th-century coastal New England: In one a wife chastises her husband for staying out all night; in another a captain asks passersby to sign up on his whaling ship; in another a young woman talks with her father. The irony of these scenes is, of course, that they represent certain symbols that are active in dominant cultural stories of New England history. All the figures are White, all are dressed in colonial garb, and none tell us anything about the oppression suffered by the tribe on whose land we stand. These animated "historical displays" are at odds with the other cultural "decor" of Foxwoods—the Hollywood and commercialized representations of Native Americans, the Vegas-style casinos and gaming rooms, and the high-tech cinetropolis/virtual reality area.

At the center of the mall area is a warrior statue that serves as its focal point. The warrior is made of glass that glows and changes colors. Aiming a bow toward the sky (or in this case the roof of the atrium), he stands amid fountains of water. He speaks every hour on the hour as thunder claps, lasers shoot from his bow, and water shoots out of the fountains. Statues of Native American warriors, women, and children are scattered throughout the casino—but none are in positions of prominence and certainly none are as large or as grandiose as the glass statue. These statues are of Indians far removed from the Pequot tribe. None have the facial structure, hair, or skin that are indicative of the Mashantuckets, and many of the costumes are representative of Plains warriors.

Near the statues, walking in and out of the restaurants, lounge, and gaming areas are other pseudo-Pequots. These "Indians" are cocktail servers (White women) in Native costume. They are wearing low-cut tops and mini-loincloths and have headbands and feathers in their hair. Although they are not statues, these women are perhaps equally objectified. They are moving mannequins, adornments to the farce of representation. These symbols play to the stories, colonial and colonized, of warriors frozen in time—warriors with feathers in their hair, who wear loincloths and live in tepees—of women who remain colonized by historical stories in which they are not actors but objects of men's actions.

Although the casino could arguably be said to represent more about gambling culture than Pequot culture, it stands on Pequot land and is filled with representations (Hollywood, Disney, and otherwise) of Native American peoples and artifacts. What, then, about these spaces can lend further insight into the numerous and seemingly contradictory meanings that inhabit this cultural space?

As mentioned previously, traditional theories about cultural space are useful as a frame for understanding the varying functions of space; however, they are limited in that they cannot account for the dynamics of social interaction, which constantly (re)create the variety of cultural meanings active here. In other words, space and culture are created through language, through the stories people tell about what they mean and thus who they are. There are numerous possibilities for cultural stories, depending on who is telling the stories, where the stories are being told, who the audience is for these stories, and the time in which the storytelling takes place (at what historical juncture). What becomes important then are the ways cultural spaces are (re)created through language and the narrative construction of history.

The following section looks at the space of the casino from the standpoint of the social construction of stories around gaming.

Space and Gaming as a Social Construction

This section tells three stories of gaming that both reflect and deflect the cultural spaces of the casino. Language or, more specifically, a word such as gaming refuses a closed interpretation, a single meaning that is complete in and of itself. Thus, the word gaming as used by the Pequots to advertise Foxwoods Casino (Gaming In Its Natural State), draws meaning from the past history of the Pequots as hunters and survivors, even as it points us toward other referents—gaming as gambling or as identity at play (in images and cultural signifiers that represent and negate the Native American identity). Each reading points to the difficulty of directly representing cultural identity through space in a society where spaces no longer signify cultural locations.

Gaming: Wampum and Warriors

The stories of the past are always present in cultural spaces. Archeological evidence suggests that Pequot culture dates back thousands of years; however, the earliest European account of the tribe dates back to 1614, when a Dutch explorer reported the presence of the tribe. At that point the Pequots were already heavily involved in the production of wampum, the currency for trading in the fur industry.[3] Because of their ideal location (the Pequots controlled the area from Long Island Sound to the lower Connecticut River) and their reputation as the main producers of wampum in the area, the Pequots were targeted by the English and Dutch colonists. In 1637 the settlers invaded the Pequots, burning their villages, killing their leader, and killing or enslaving most of the population. Throughout the 17th and 18th centuries, the Pequots were granted small parcels of forest and swampland (from 500 to 1,000 acres), which were always repossessed by colonists who wanted the land for farming. In 1667 the Pequots were awarded the dubious distinction of being the first

Native reservation in the English Colonies and received 3,000 acres of primarily rock and swampland.[4] They refused to move from their coastal home near present-day Noank until 1712, when the town of Groton legislated their land for the English colonists. At that time the Pequots were forced to move to the Ledyard Reservation—to the land where they are today.

By the late 18th century, their 3,000 acres had dwindled to approximately 300 and the Pequots, having been once again dispossessed of their land, were widely dispersed throughout New England. Some were sold into slavery in the West Indies; others were indentured to their English conquerors; some worked on whaling ships and still others worked on mills and farms.[5] By the 1960s the few acres (approximately 213) of remaining reservation land were maintained by two female tribal elders who used their guns and their settlement deeds to resist territorial encroachment from the state as well as from the local hunters. In 1973 Richard (Skip) Hayward took over as the leader (chair) of the newly created tribal council. Under his leadership, the tribe has received federal recognition and progressed from selling maple syrup to running bingo games, and it now owns the largest casino in the world. The tribe now offers extensive social and health services for its members and invests in local communities through charitable donations. In the late 1980s the tribe established the Mashantucket Pequot Archeological Project, which has functioned to locate and recover lost graves and artifacts and, in the process, document land since lost to the state government.[6]

Even as they were forced to assimilate into local communities to survive, the Pequots fought to hang on to their cultural values and traditions. Perhaps it is because of their struggle for centuries to retain their tribal lands that the concepts of land and survival continue to be central values in Pequot culture. According to many historians, archeologists, and anthropologists working with the Pequot community on the museum, casino, and projects such as land reclamation, the genocide of 1637 is still very much a part of the present Pequot cultural story. Hauptman (1990) goes so far as to note that "[t]he ways in which the Pequots, who are always conscious of the War of

1637, commemorate this tragedy, interact with both their Indian and non-Indian neighbors and build the modern day community are similar to other experiences after genocide" (p. 71). Hauptman further comments that the geographical location of the Pequot Reservation—only 10 miles from the Mystic Fort site of the 1637 massacre—and the nearby Mohegan and Narragansett tribes who, along with the British, "enslaved and nearly annihilated them in the seventeenth century" (p. 77), serve as a constant physical reminder of a tragic past.

The Connection Between History, Identity, and Cultural Space

Cultural spaces are infused with the past, markers of identity that are creative and created through historical events and experiences. Comparing Native and western European notions of history, Deloria (1994) comments that

> American Indians hold their lands—places— as having the highest possible meaning, and all their statements are made with this reference point in mind. Immigrants review the movement of their ancestors across the continent as the steady progression of basically good events and experiences, thereby placing history—time—in the best possible light. When one group is concerned with the philosophical problem of space and the other with the philosophical problem of time, then the statements of either group do not make much sense when transferred from one context to the other without the proper consideration of what is taking place. (pp. 62–63)

The experience of tragedy and the struggle to reclaim their land and, in doing so, their existence, are part of the contemporary spaces of the Pequots. While many non-native peoples talk about the reservation as land "granted" the Mashantuckets, the Pequots are quick to point out that the tribe received a land "settlement" and not a land "grant." The difference between the two words, while seemingly trivial to an outsider, is of great significance to the Pequots. The phrase "land grant" ignores the fact that the Pequots were the original settlers of coastal Connecticut, forced off their land through invasion and legislation, and assumes that the land was donated as a social service by the U.S. government. Here again, cultural space and representation are intimately connected with language. Who employs the words and phrases that characterize ownership of this space shape the ways in which a culture is legitimized or marginalized. As such, the casino is a location invested with historical and cultural meanings that represent the (in)visibility of the Pequot people.

The Warrior

The Pequots call themselves the fox people, and history shows that they were skilled hunters and warriors. They were known by surrounding tribes and traders as a fiercely aggressive and independent people. Today the notion of the warrior is very much a part of Pequot identity, although some confusion exists about what it means to embody that idea. As Kate Abril (1996) described it,

> there are warriors. And warriors aren't just soldiers. They are people trying to do the right thing—which oftentimes gets confused even by the warriors. But then it can be with any missionary too. It gets too focused on principle rather than on relationships . . . on accumulation versus giving away—those are often contradictory ideas that get Indians in trouble. . . .[7]

This notion of Mashantucket history—that the Pequots were warriors and hunters—is perhaps represented to visitors in the giant warrior statue that is the focal point of the mall area of the casino. Although such representations harken back to the early Hollywood stereotypes of Indians-with-feathers-in-their-hair-who-live-in-tepees, they are an effective way of making visitors aware of whose land they are on as they gamble. But the irony of the warrior statue is that it plays into the racism that continues to plague the modern-day Pequots, for not only are they most definitely not loin-clothed warriors living in tepees, their skin color is not representative of the dominant Indian stereotype.[8] The warrior statue serves to make visible a powerful image of the tribe that conforms to the stereotype of the dominant culture while it perpetuates the Pequots' invisibility.

It [the excavation of the mass graves] became a powerful experience. The artifacts and

everything that was buried with them were so gorgeous. . . . And I can remember Loretta, Skip's aunt, looking at them. And she's a real tough old lady. She had tears in her eyes and she said, "And they call us savages. How could savages make anything that beautiful?" And they were beautiful. Like something out of Egypt.
—*Interview with Kate Abril, past museum coordinator and PR director for Mashantucket Pequots, September 4, 1996*

Wampum and Other Artifacts   One of the driving forces in the design of the casino was the historical significance of wampum, Pequot basketry, and the tribal artifacts uncovered in burial sites around Connecticut. The aquamarine and mauve colors throughout the casino came from the colorful costumes and artifacts unearthed in the excavations of the Long Pond and other digs in the late 1980s. The shell design that signifies wampum can be seen in various areas of the mall, and representations of Native artifacts are scattered throughout the atrium and waterfall area. Until recently, Foxwoods contained the largest collection of Native artifacts in New England.[9] However, the designs and artifacts that represent Pequot and Native American history are located away from the gaming and other entertainment areas and are not easily accessible to visitors. The artworks display price tags and names of artists but give no information about origin or cultural significance.

The centrality accorded to the more gaudy Indian stereotypes is neither an accident nor the design of some architect unfamiliar with Pequot culture. All of the design work in the casino was discussed in tribal council meetings and had to pass council in order to be approved. The meetings were often 5 or 6 hours long and were in most cases a formality, but according to one source, they produced a sense that the tribe was involved collectively in the building of the casino:

Everyone was complaining about the long hours and the meetings, and all the kids were getting into trouble because the parents weren't around as much. But on the whole it was exciting. Walking through the casino and seeing the building . . .[10]

The importance of the tribe's involvement in both the excavations and the design of the casino is that they were part of a larger process of re-creating and re-presenting Pequot identity to the dominant culture. As part of the process of legitimizing the tribe to gain federal recognition and status, and as part of the survival (often in very physical terms) of a culture, gaming takes on the meaning of the Pequot as hunter, as warrior, and, most important, as survivor.

Gaming as Gambling: A New Version of an Old Game

Gambling has a long history among Native Americans and is associated with spiritual and ritual traditions. Numerous Native American tribes played dice games long before European settlers arrived, but the games had different meanings and functioned quite differently than they do today. Pasquaretta (1994) observes that "unlike Euro-American games of chance which function as secular rituals and foster acquisitiveness, individual competition and greed, traditional Native American games of chance are sacred rituals that foster personal sacrifice, group competition and generosity" (p. 698). Most early games of chance were offerings to the gods and helped to enhance community with singing and good-natured joking. As Mourning Dove comments: "All gambling required good sportsmanship. It was shameful for poor losers to grieve. They would get no sympathy."[11] Although scholars such as Vizenor and Pasquaretta argue that perhaps the contrast between the high-stakes Vegas-style gambling that promotes materialism and competitiveness and the early games that promoted community signals the last phase of Native American assimilation, the Foxwoods Casino can be seen as a business venture that functions to support institutions and communities that have revitalized Pequot culture.

Still, the gambling story is more complex than simply indigenous forms of gambling (and thus indigenous culture) lost to the competitive and greedy world of contemporary casinos. The conceptualization and design of the casino reflect both the big business of gambling addiction and the big business of exoticizing culture. Designers and architects involved in the building of the casino went to Las Vegas and to Epcot Center for inspiration, and one source who worked closely with the tribe observed that the casino reflected Hayward (the tribe's leader): "One side of his family is Mashantucket Pequot and the other D.A.R. [Daughters of the American Revolution]. This was Skip's vision."

Addiction as Big Business   Since its opening day over 4 years ago, the casino has never shut down. It remains open to gambling 24 hours a day, 7 days a week. The state of Connecticut requires that 1-800-gambling posters and pamphlets (for gambling addiction support groups) be displayed prominently in front of each of the slot rooms. Next to the signs are automatic teller machines that take credit cards. "Wampum clubs" located near the entrance to the gaming rooms offer credit. Although seemingly contradictory on the surface, the message is consistent with other messages surrounding success and addiction in a late capitalistic society. Advertising creates and then supports a culture of excess; then social and governmental institutions offer support services for the unfortunate addicted. The message is that money can buy you everything—success, good looks, good health, and, at Foxwoods, even culture.

Certainly, the Pequot tribe has grown wealthy from their venture into the industry. Yet economic wealth and cultural wealth take on vastly different meanings in terms of (re)creating cultural traditions and of assimilating into the dominant society. The dominant culture as well as other tribes in the northeastern United States see Pequot identity as being most closely associated with gambling and wealth. In the media, issues around gambling and around the plight of Native Americans in the United States most certainly invoke the Pequots. The Mashantuckets have been hired as consultants to tribes and corporations building casinos around the world. The tribe was featured on the popular prime-time news show *60 Minutes* and in cover stories in *Money* and *Fortune* magazines. Local and national news stories on Native Americans and casinos highlight the controversy around gambling in general: Gaming is the big business of addiction. All view Indian culture from a dominant perspective that highlights the

ethics of gambling and the impact on local communities over stories about tribal survival and the decimation of tribal culture. Another frequent focus of news stories is the use and abuse of blood quantum as a marker of Indianness and a ticket to free land and health care.

These stories contribute to the contemporary narrative of Native American gaming from a dominant cultural perspective. Because "recognizable Indians" (i.e., those who wear loincloths and have feathers in their hair) no longer pose a threat to White settlers—and Native identity is developed scientifically through the measurement of blood—popular culture needs a new signifier for a different kind of savage. The success of tribal casinos has given rise to images of the new Indian who feeds off the addictions of the poor and the socially disadvantaged.

Gaming as Socioacupuncture[12]: The Space of Imagination

The final story of gaming is that of the Pequots as players in a carnival of ironic and contradictory images of Native identity. The giant glass warrior with his bow raised to the sky rotates on the stage. Thunder claps and he changes colors; he speaks, although his voice is lost amid the din of clanging slot machines. Cocktail waitresses with feathers in their hair and dressed in sexy pseudo-loincloths serve beverages to clientele who gamble in a fantasyland of money. Venders throughout the casino sell Pequot Reservation t-shirts and sweatshirts along with key chains and other souvenirs of a visit to the exotic space of Pequot land.

Revisiting the Mall   Geographic space as representative of both culture and history becomes irrelevant in the space of imagination. Any customer at Foxwoods with enough money—or credit—can buy the spaces of history and culture. The Pequots as capitalist entrepreneurs contribute to the decimation of local cultures in favor of the global Indian—the universal savage—through the marketing of this representation. A consumer buying Native art buys it because of its decorative function as an exotic artifact. Certainly, reproductions of artifacts are marketed for this function: The Indian doll for $400 is made in

China, the leather jackets with fringe on them (certainly a Hollywood creation) now represent all Native American cultures divorced from the historical spaces they inhabit. The mall is the new global cultural space. Indeed, even the mall specialty stores located in the casino on the Pequot Reservation contain artifacts that represent other Native cultures as their own. All cultural spaces can be collapsed for the purposes of buying and selling—and what is exotically primitive to the colonizers are now the artifacts of the colonized.

Reconfiguring Time and Space as Native Culture   Much like the clockless, timeless space of the casino, the history of Native peoples has been characterized by space, not time. Tune Browne, speaking at a conference on tribal identities at U.C. Berkeley, noted that the photographer who captured his image in Native "costume,"

> removed the clock, colonized the culture games and denied us our time in the world . . . [the photographer] paid us for our poses; it was hot then, but he wanted us to wear leathers to create the appearance of a traditional scene, his idea of the past. . . . We never saw the photographs then and never thought that it would make a difference in the world of dreams, that we would become *his* images. (cited in Vizenor, 1990, p. 90)

That these images of the past, snapshots created to capture the time of the space of Native history and identity, have become part of national memory merely validates dominant images of Native identity. To legitimize themselves as "real" Indians to the governments and people that captured their land and their culture, Native Americans had to reinvent themselves as the images created and contained in photographic images. The Pequots are by no means exempt from this game of "playing Indian." The images that they construct to represent Indianness are satirical, not shameful. The irony is not lost in translation; it is part of a (re)created tribal identity, an identity that cannot be divorced from a history of domination and the current circumstances that dictate their legitimacy as marginalized peoples.

Browne (cited in Vizenor, 1990) explains that satire is "not social ridicule as a form of social control . . . but satire from magical connections with the oral tradition . . ." (p. 91). Satire is socioacupuncture, a process that puts the "facts" of Native identity and existence into play:

> Socioacupuncture reverses the documents, deflates data, dissolves historical time, releases the pressure in captured images, and exposes the pale inventors of the tribes. . . . Lyman tells us that [the photographer] set out to construct a "photographic monument to a vanishing race." Not so, it was the photographer who would have vanished without our images to take as captured families. (p. 91)

Gaming at Foxwoods is definitive of socioacupuncture; the images validate the White imagination while the Pequots work behind the scenes. The Pequots are the ultimate marketers of a global culture; all cultural spaces meld into one Mall Mecca where they are sold as souvenirs. Here, displaced and marginalized people sell "exotic" artifacts to those who long to be diasporic peoples, to be marginalized because it isn't trendy to be mainstream.

Here, also, perhaps Native peoples work to imagine different possibilities, to conceive of identities not completely captured and defined by White words and White science. As N. Scott Momaday said: "We are what we imagine. . . . Our very existence consists in our imagination of ourselves. . . . The greatest tragedy that can befall us is to go unimagined" (cited in Vizenor, 1990, p. 96).

Conclusion

This essay has sought to examine the space of culture as a social construction. Although the functions and uses of space in Foxwoods Casino were discussed in descriptive terms, to more fully comprehend the complexities of identities as they are bound to the spaces of culture, the notion of space as a social and cultural construction was examined through three narratives about gaming. From these narratives of warriors, wampum, land, survival, gambling, irony, and contradiction we can see that the meaning of space emerges in and through its interpretation. The notable difference in understanding cultural space from this vantage point is that space and culture cannot function apart from the language we use to construct it. Thus, communication is central to the process of cultural interpretation.

What also becomes important in this analysis is the role that power plays in the dynamics of interpretation. The viewpoint espoused in this essay indicates White/dominant culture and cultural spaces even as it points to other ways of knowing and thinking about space as history and identity. Cultural space includes the negotiated places where imperialist and colonized stories are in conflict *with* and determinate *of* the indigenous and creative knowledges that characterize modern Pequot identities. The fox people play games; they set up uneasy coalitions of power. They are the new warriors, with a new kind of dice game and wampum made in Malaysia.

NOTES

1. I use the plural form of identity to connote the idea that identities themselves are social constructions and thus cannot be separated from the social context in which they are "identified." It follows then that communication (both verbal and nonverbal) is central to any understanding of culture and cultural space.

2. Fifteen people were interviewed in the mall area of the casino. They were asked whether this was their first time at the casino, where they came from, and what their reactions were to the general atmosphere of the gaming rooms and the mall area. They were also asked what they knew of the Pequots and whether they had seen the statue and other artifacts around the casino.

3. Wampum are small tubular columella beads that are woven into chains, bracelets, necklaces, and belts. White and purple wampum beads came from grinding down the inner pillars or columellas of rare northern whelks (white) or hard-shell clams (purple). The use of wampum as currency has a long history among the coastal Indian tribes that predates the arrival of European explorers. The Europeans (Dutch, British, Portuguese, and French) discovered the value of the beads through the process of fur trading; the Iroquois were said to value wampum

more than any of the other valuables the traders could produce (Ceci, 1990).

4. Silberman, 1991, 35.

5. De Forest, 1964, 423–425.

6. Silberman, 1991, 36.

7. Interview 1. Teacher of Native American Studies at Mohegan Community College.

8. The fact that many Pequots appear "darker" than the stereotypical Native American is a significant dynamic in their history and current identity that is not addressed in academic discussions of culture. As their wealth and visibility through business ventures increases, so too does the racism and imperialist sensibility with which people mark them as neither White nor Indian, neither conqueror nor "legitimately" conquered.

9. The new Mashantucket Pequot Museum is currently under construction.

10. Interview with Kate Abril, September 1, 1996.

11. Mourning Dove, 1990, 102–103.

12. The inspiration for the concept of socio-acupuncture, according to Edward Vizenor (1990), is Tune Browne, who "never wore beads or feathers or a wristwatch; he never paid much attention to time or to his image until he became an independent candidate for alderman" (p. 88).

REFERENCES

Abril, K. (Sept. 4, 1996). Personal interview.

Ceci, L. (1990). Native wampum as a peripheral resource in the seventeenth-century world-system. In L. M. Hauptman & J. D. Wherry (Eds.), *The Pequots in southern New England: The fall and rise of an American Indian nation.* Norman: University of Oklahoma Press.

De Forest, J. W. (1964). *History of the Indians of Connecticut from the earliest known period to 1850.* Hamden, CT: Anchor Books.

Deloria, V. (1994). *God is red: A native view of religion.* Golden, CO: Fulcrum Publishing.

Hauptman, L. M. (1990). The Pequot war and its legacies. In L. M. Hauptman & J. D. Wherry (Eds.), *The Pequots in southern New England: The fall and rise of an American Indian nation* (pp. 69–80). Norman: University of Oklahoma Press.

Mourning Dove. (1990). *Mourning Dove: A Salishan*

autobiography (J. Miller, Ed.). Lincoln: University of Nebraska Press.

Pasquaretta, P. (1994). On the Indianness of bingo: Gambling and the Native American community. *Critical Inquiry, 20,* 694–714.

Silberman, N. A. (1991). Pequot country. *Archeology, 44,* 34–39.

Vizenor, E. (1990). *Crossbloods: Bone courts, bingo and other reports.* Minneapolis: University of Minnesota Press.

KEY TERMS

gaming	culture
Native	casino
Pequot	gambling
space	

DISCUSSION QUESTIONS

1. What is the relationship between symbols and stories? Who participates in symbol creation?

2. Who are the storytellers in this essay? Who are the audiences? Does anyone "own" a particular cultural story?

3. The author makes the point that spaces cannot directly represent cultural identities. Do you agree or disagree? Are there some spaces that might signify cultural locales? If so, where?

4. What, in Cooks's view, can language tell us about the naming of cultural identities and spaces?

5. From the quotes from Tune Browne, what role do you think photography has played in establishing a cultural identity and cultural space for Native peoples?

6. What symbols stand out to you in each of the three stories told in this essay? Do you think that these are important symbols to the Pequots? Why or why not?

PART SIX

POPULAR CULTURE AND INTERCULTURAL COMMUNICATION

The essays in this part emphasize the place of popular culture in understanding intercultural communication. Popular culture, from movies and television shows to sports and music, can be an important arena for intercultural interaction. In our personal lives we engage with popular culture on a daily basis. In fact, in many industrialized societies, there is almost no escape from the influence of popular culture. Although we can negotiate our consumption of some popular culture, by refusing to watch particular television programs or films, or simply by not buying and reading certain magazines or newspapers, we cannot entirely avoid popular culture. From advertisements to music to sports, popular culture surrounds us.

The ubiquity of popular culture means that as we think about cultural interactions, we must consider the ways in which our knowledge and perception of other groups is shaped by popular culture. One concern for intercultural communication, then, is how cultural groups are portrayed in popular culture. Popular culture plays a role in what we know about cultural groups. Representations of the United States in other countries, for example, may influence social attitudes about U.S. citizens. We can also remember news coverage of the L.A. riots or the Gulf War and the emotions raised by these portrayals.

The increasing heterogeneity of societies and the growing global village have also meant that popular culture must respond to the many differences in cultural groups. Witness, for example, the rise in popularity of Latino music or the many magazines targeted at particular audiences. Our exposure to and consumption of diverse "texts" can provide us with multiple perspectives. What we learn about a Gay Rights parade may depend on what information source we utilize.

As scholars have recognized the many ways in which we are affected by popular culture, they have also begun to investigate how different cultural groups respond to popular culture. Much research is devoted to describing the stereotypes of cultural groups that circulate in popular culture, but there is also interest in understanding how cultural groups use "texts" to question social meanings. Differences in gender, class, race, ethnicity, and sexuality affect our understanding of and use of popular culture. In these interactions, popular culture can be a means for the creation of cultural identity through participation in particular types of popular culture. Through identification with certain cultural forms, many people engage in the construction of personal and social identities.

Finally, popular culture can offer models of effective and problematic interaction. Through the imagined worlds of television and film, we can envision cultural interaction and learn from the successes and failures we see. Science fiction, for example, often builds worlds in which individuals must confront drastic differences. Popular movies, such as *Independence Day,* can play on fears of immigration and of "aliens." As we watch intercultural communication occurring in popular culture, we can build our knowledge bases for how to communicate across cultures.

Consider these questions as you read the articles in this part:

How have you and other members of your cultural groups been represented in popular culture?

Are there differences in how your cultural group(s) and other cultural groups are depicted in popular culture?

What popular culture is widely consumed by members of your cultural groups? What do members of your cultural groups resist consuming?

What is the role of power in popular culture and intercultural communication?

The essays that follow investigate the cultural implications of popular culture, showing how it can be instrumental in shaping images of racial and ethnic groups and how it can contribute to the invisibility of particular groups. The essays also help us understand how we can use popular culture to think about interpersonal, social, and even international intercultural relations. We learn about film, television, newspapers, and music in this section. The authors rely on both interpretive and critical approaches in their analyses. The method used is textual analysis.

Angharad N. Valdivia, in "Big Hair and Bigger Hoops: Rosie Perez Goes to Hollywood," explores the Latina actress Rosie Perez. Using critical theory, Valdivia explains how Perez's films and interviews contribute to the creation of an image of Latinas as loud, working class, and heavily accented. Although Perez has been typecast throughout her professional career, Valdivia reminds readers that Perez is one of the few Latinas who has been welcomed by Hollywood. This raises an important question: Is it better to be absent in media or to be limited to a particular representation?

Questions of representation are also central in Janis L. King's essay, "Cultural Differences in the Perceptions of Sports Mascots." King addresses an issue that has plagued, perplexed, and confused many—Is the use of Native Americans as sports mascots problematic? King follows a campaign to end this use and analyzes the persuasive strategies and their effectiveness for different audiences. Using rhetorical analysis, King describes various strategies: trying to educate non-Indians about these racist practices and the disrespect shown by imitating and appropriating Native religious and cultural practices. She is then able to explain why the campaign ultimately failed. She identifies the role of power, especially that power held by team owners and fans, as central in the continued use of Native Americans as mascots.

From these essays we move to television. Ellen Seiter, in her essay "Different Children, Different Dreams: Racial Representations in Advertising," looks at issues of representation in advertising. Seiter argues that U.S. advertising, and especially advertisements with children, perpetuate notions of racial divisions by emphasizing White-Other differences in ads. She uses theories on Whiteness to look at how Whiteness is constructed as normal and as tied to the American dream, while non-Whites are marked as "different." She concludes that more attention should be given to the ideological underpinnings of representations of race and ethnicity in advertising.

Rona Tamiko Halualani, in *"Seeing Through the Screen:* A Struggle of 'Culture,'" also contributes to the discussion of representation. For Halualani, however, the question of representation shifts. Halualani, a Japanese Hawaiian English woman, recalls her childhood use of television and her recognition that she was absent in much of what she watched. She shows how media messages present and reinforce certain cultural images and meanings (e.g., Hawaii as a paradise to be experienced by White tourists), and how these meanings contrasted with her own experience as a Japanese Hawaiian. She argues that it is useful to interrogate, to question interpretations of media, to look for power relations, to not be satisfied with simple, dichotomous meanings for culture. She then explores the tensions in representations by identifying the intersections between culture and ideology. To demonstrate these tensions, Halualani includes a narrative performance of her "struggle of culture" and uses this performance to critique popular notions of "American" culture.

In *"Space Traders,* Media Criticism, and the Interpositional Strategy," Dwight E. Brooks uses the HBO program *Space Traders* to investigate the role of power in intercultural interactions. He emphasizes the tensions that occur not only between cultural groups, but within them. His analysis shows how race and class can lead to conflicting goals and potentially divide cultural groups. He then develops a theory of interpositionality as a response. Brooks argues that we can negotiate intercultural relations by looking at cultural identity as in between.

The final essay in this section focuses on international concerns about representation. Michel Dion, in "Madonna in the French Press," looks at French responses to pop music icon Madonna. His essay shows how culture influences the reception of celebrities. Surveying about 800 French press articles on Madonna, Dion attempts to understand how and why she was praised and attacked. He situates his interpretation of Madonna's reception by the French press within historical and religious constructions of "woman" in European culture.

25
BIG HAIR AND BIGGER HOOPS: ROSIE PEREZ GOES TO HOLLYWOOD

ANGHARAD N. VALDIVIA

Introduction

In the wide-ranging debate about multiculturalism, one of the component strategies is the representation of people from the heterogeneous populations within the United States. In this study I seek to examine the presence of minorities on the Hollywood screen. Rosie Perez presents us with an ideal case study of the issues of representation politics because she simultaneously demonstrates that some Latina women can get into Hollywood and that once there, they are stereotyped. It is important to underscore, however, that Hollywood is not opening its arms to hoards of Latina actresses—Rosie seems to be the only one to have achieved significant crossover success, although others have appeared in the very occasional Latino movie (Amador, 1988; Corliss, 1988). Thus it is more important to ask in what kinds of roles is Rosie cast and what is it about Rosie that enabled her, as agent, and made her, as object, to be one of the token Latina actresses in Hollywood today.

Theoretical Background

To understand the phenomenon of Rosie Perez we must examine the theoretical traditions whose disparate roots meet in Rosie's body, as it were. To begin with, traditional, mainstream feminist scholarship yields a finding of symbolic annihilation (Tuchman, Daniels, & Benet, 1978) whose two components are that women and minorities are underrepresented in media content and that when they are represented, they are marginalized, trivialized, or victimized. Additionally, women of color are less represented than White women and men of color. Furthermore, we find that when

women of color appear, they are more likely to be African American than Latina, Native American, or Asian. To sum up, Latina women are not frequently portrayed in mainstream popular culture, although as Hadley-García (1990) claims, they are represented "more sympathetically" than Latinos (p. 161). The "sympathetic" label may well be the result of the passive portrayal of women in general, which would render active male Latinos more threatening.

Portrayal is necessary but not sufficient. For example, Latinas/os may be played by Anglo protagonists (Hadley-García, 1990), thus preempting employment of culturally diverse actors. It is especially easy to cast brunettes as Latinas, and, in fact, Merisa Tomei, one of Rosie's contemporaries, has played such a role several times. Another way in which Hollywood deals with people of color is through total absence. For example, other than an occasional appearance in any number of cowboy-and-Indian movies and in Disney's recent *Pocahontas*, Native American or First Nation women are nearly absent from mainstream films. A third form of representation is through stereotypical portrayals that ignore the multiplicity of experiences and contributions by a heterogeneous group of people such as Latinos in the United States. For the fact is that Latinos come from a variety of backgrounds. Even those of the same country of origin may not share race class, racial, ethnic, religious, or language characteristics. Consequently, the Latino portrayal of the stereotypical inner-city Mexican or Puerto Rican who is violent, inept, or drug-addicted (or any combination of these) tokenizes and effaces a diverse group of people (Amador, 1988; Siegel, 1995).

Latinas are portrayed in a limited number of roles; some, such as the maid and the welfare mother, overlap with African American female images. We also get the sexually-out-of-control and utterly colorful spitfire, an image quite specific to Latinas. A large component of this image is sexually suggestive dancing. In addition, Latina women in Hollywood film almost always have thick, unshakable, often humorous, and self-deprecating accents, most extremely portrayed by Charo though dating back to Carmen Miranda[1] and others. This despite the fact that many Latina women in the United States speak English as their first language. In large part the endurance of the accent in the stereotypes stems from the mistaken characterization of all Latinos as recent and, quite often, illegal immigrants.

Portrayal, then, is not the entire answer or strategy from a multiculturalist position (Shohat & Stam, 1994). From another tradition in media studies, we pose questions about individual agency within organizations with deeply imbedded rules and conventions that are in turn part of institutions with historically rooted norms and values (Cantor, 1989; McQuail, 1987; and Van Zoonen, 1994). Without precluding individual initiative and creativity, media workers face a number of limits and constraints in the workplace. This finding relates to the above issues of representation in that although individual actors may be of a particular ethnic or racial background, this by itself does not mean that they will be powerful enough to demand a sensitive portrayal, whatever this may be. Quite often, actors are told that they are not Black or Latino enough—that is, according to stereotypes that have become paradigmatic in producers' minds. Also, not all actors of a particular ethnic or racial background will necessarily want to deviate from stereotype or acknowledge that there are stereotypes altogether!

From an activist standpoint based on historically grounded theory, the issue becomes one of representation with sensitivity. With underrepresentation we have the issue that a limited number of images bear the burden of representing all of that group. The burden of underrepresentation results in major demands being placed on that one or those few images. Witness the large literature and debate concerning the *Cosby Show* precisely because so few well-adjusted, affluent, and nuclear African American families had been on U.S. television. Thus the democratization strategy should focus on more texts and representations produced by a broad spectrum of sources. In sum, based on the past 30 years of activism inspired by both Civil Rights and women's movements, we have learned that textual strategies or increased representations by themselves have to be supplemented and complemented by production strategies, an increased playing field of producers who speak for an expanded spectrum of participants in our multicultural reality.

In conclusion, when we study representation we find that more socially and culturally powerful groups, although they may not necessarily be the numerical majority, receive more and better representation in terms of variety and depth. This is why representation remains one of the important arenas of struggle within multicultural politics. Increasing and changing representations can be an indicator both of the relative valuation at large and of a more democratic production process of our popular culture. The repetition of old stereotypes, conversely, suggests that despite the growing number of Latinos in the United States, both our value and our cultural power remain lower than our proportion of the population would seem to indicate.

Method

Following this theoretical trajectory, we will examine Rosie's roles. Textual analyses of her films will be discussed beyond whether she portrays a primary or secondary character. Of relevance will be her attire, talents, occupation, life goals, intensity of personality, and language skills. Media theory suggests that representation—that is, the portrayal of different groups and individuals in popular culture—does not directly reflect reality but speaks to issues of power and value within our culture. Furthermore, multicultural scholars suggest that meaning is made only in relation (Shohat, 1991b), so that, for example, a portrayal of a White middle-class woman resonates because there is a working-class Latina acting differently and vice versa. The following section will highlight issues of gender and class as suggested by relational representation.

Textual Musings

Rosie Perez made her video debut as a dancer and choreographer in *Soul Train* and later as one of the Fly Girls in the Fox network's *In Living Color*. From there she appeared in Spike Lee's *Do the Right Thing* after he reportedly saw her dancing atop a sound speaker in an L.A. club. Although she has appeared in other movies, this analysis focuses only on *Do the Right Thing, Fearless, White Men Can't Jump, Untamed Heart,* and *It Could Happen to You.*[2]

There are many more patterns than exceptions and singularities in her portrayals. To begin with, she plays a supporting role in all of the movies. In *Do the Right Thing,* Spike Lee foregrounds the interracial struggles between an Italian family and the African American community within which the Italian restaurant resides. There are also Latinos in this community. Rosie plays Mookie's (Spike Lee) girlfriend, Tina, the mother of their child. The opening scene features her gyrating her body to the tune of Public Enemy's "Fight the Power." In fact, much of the portrayal of Latinos in this film revolves around music and music struggles—the lengthiest one being a standoff between loud rap and salsa. One could say that Latinos provide a background of cultural contestation over musical and cultural terrain, whereas the Italian and African American struggle is over the material and physical terrain of the ghetto. Nevertheless, the struggle is primarily in the masculine domain of the public sphere of work in the restaurant and in the streets. Rosie stays at home, as the mother in the private sphere. Most of her interactions and appearances take place in the bedroom or elsewhere in the home. In substance, these scenes concern issues of relationship and parenting, classic female-gendered issues in feminine spaces.

In both *It Could Happen to You* and *Untamed Heart*, Rosie plays a supporting role as well. In *It Could Happen* she is the wife (and then ex-wife) of the Nicholas Cage character, secondary to

his budding romance with leading lady Bridget Fonda. In *Untamed Heart* she is the girlfriend and co-worker of Merisa Tomei's leading lady role. In both of these movies the leading ladies represent wholesomeness and goodness while Rosie serves as the less pure foil that allows these leading ladies to stand out as the deserving ones.

In *White Men Can't Jump* she is also the other woman, but with a gender and racial twist. She plays Woody Harrelson's girlfriend in a movie that is a classic buddy film with a biracial twist: Woody's buddy, Wesley Snipes, is African American. Rosie plays the woman who eventually skates out of their lives as Woody and Wesley remain together hustling the urban basketball courts of L.A. In *Fearless* Rosie plays the catatonic crash survivor who is rescued from despair by Jeff Bridges. In both *White Men* and *Fearless* she does not enter the dialogue until the movie has foregrounded the male character's quest for self for nearly 20 minutes!

In addition to her typecasting as a supporting actress, Rosie plays a working-class woman in all of these films. As such, she is engaged in a representative range of working-class occupations, including waitress, hairdresser, housewife, and wannabe *Jeopardy* contestant. This latter role, although unusual, is typical in that it highlights more of a working-class version of success. For example, Rosie is not studying for the M-CATS (medical school entrance exams) and is doubtful that her knowledge is generalizable to anything other than the *Jeopardy* game show. She prepares for her quest by studying trivia: This turns out to be a successful strategy because she wins when answering all five questions in the "Foods that start with the letter Q" category. In none of her roles does she possess degrees of higher education, but she is very street savvy, especially when it comes to romance and men, the exception being *Fearless*, where Jeff Bridges saves her from despair.

Her ethnicity—which, judging from her accent, is Puerto Rican—is collapsed with working-class status in an inextricable manner. She is at once Latina because she is working class and is working class because she is Latina. Her class and ethnic status are illustrated by her dress, demeanor, and juxtaposition with the White leading ladies who are or become the leading ladies in the leading males' lives.

In terms of dress, the operative style begins with hoops and is complemented by big hair. In *White Men* hoops come in all different colors, but they are always big. In *Fearless* she begins with little hearts, but as she recovers, she is back to large gold or silver hoops. Even as a waitress in *Untamed Heart*, she wears hoops, sporting a pair of black ones for the funeral scene. Hair is also a big indicator of class and ethnicity.[3] Big hair goes with the big hoops. Rosie's curls are coiffed up and her bangs are tall, especially when compared to the hair of the other women in the films, including the blonde and straight page boy cut of Bridget Fonda, or the stylishly short brunette look of Isabella Rosellini, and the short ponytail do of Merisa Tomei. Even Wesley Snipe's wife in *White Men*, though African American, has straighter and smaller hair than Rosie. In effect, Rosie sports "mall chick hair," a slang term that captures the essence of working-class femininity and is more often than not deployed on the bodies of Latina women.

Thus even when juxtaposed to White working-class women, Rosie's style sets her apart as "other." Her clothes are brighter and tighter than those of her working-class counterparts. The juxtaposition is all the more salient when she plays opposite an upper-middle-class woman such as the character played by Isabella Rosellini in *Fearless*. Toward the end of the film when Isabella tells Rosie to lay off her man, we have a classic juxtaposition: the upper-middle-class White European woman, at home in her upscale surroundings, wearing an expensive ensemble in rich but subdued green, small yet expensive jewelry, the natural look in makeup, and, of course, small hair, opposite Rosie's big, curly hair, large hoop earrings, low-cut turquoise leotard, short tight skirt, and colorful ethnic-style cloth bomber jacket. To top it off, Isabella is smoking some sort of dark and thin cigarette, which she lights with an equally expensive-looking lighter. We have already been shown that Isabella is a classical ballet teacher with a hobby in small figurines, whereas we can only deduce that Rosie does not work and has no hobbies or activities other than her wifely duties, which have nearly ceased since the death of her child and her separation from her husband. Isabella is in her domain, and Rosie is clearly physically class trespassing as she is being simultaneously told to retreat from Isabella's other property, her man. Rosie retreats from both. In fact, other than the initial scene of Rosie crying in her bed, we often meet her on the street outside of her house, whereas we encounter Isabella at home or at her place of work. Thus we have inside spaces as a way of demarcating gender and class. In *Do the Right Thing* gender is established by keeping Rosie in and Spike out. In *Fearless* class is established by keeping Rosie out and Isabella in.

Demeanor-wise Rosie also portrays a lively person. One of the stereotypes of Latinas/os in general is their ability to dance. This is reinforced by the fact that Rosie was a dancer first and an actress second. So, it's only appropriate that she opens for *Do the Right Thing*, although she does not dance for the rest of the movie. In *Untamed Heart* she is shown dancing, even though her role in that movie is that of the co-worker in the diner. We get to see her dancing both at work, as she conveniently plays the jukebox when cleaning up, and at a disco, where she drags her non-dancing friend, played by leading lady Merisa Tomei. The director, however, claims that Rosie's dancing at the jukebox was her own improvisation (Millea, 1993). In *It Could Happen* she partly seduces the older tycoon by dancing. In all three movies she dances alone, which codes the dancing as something other than the classy pairings classically portrayed by the likes of Ginger Rogers and Fred Astaire.

In accordance to the tradition of both working-class women and women of color, Rosie is no fly on the wall in her relationships. In fact, her demeanor could be described as ranging from assertive to loud. Other than the catatonic role played in *Fearless*, she is a vocal partner. In *Do the Right Thing* she demands that Mookie come home more often, stay longer, and ask for higher wages and better working conditions. In *It Could Happen* she wants the full share of her husband's lottery winnings. In this particular movie her character is demanding to the point of extreme so that we as the audience are almost inevitably positioned to dislike her greedy posture, which of course is all the more salient when compared to that of her husband, angelically played by Nicholas Cage, or to the good other woman, played by Bridget Fonda. Finally, in *White Men*, though unemployed and devoted to the questionable quest of preparing for a highly unlikely appearance on *Jeopardy*, she still makes demands on her hustler partner and leaves him twice, the second time for good. As well, Rosie plays sexually active roles, demonstrating what Shohat (1991a) has documented as Hollywood's tendency to transfer sexuality onto the bodies of women of color so that White women can remain pure. Rosie is loud, Rosie is pushy, Rosie gets left behind for quieter, whiter, more subdued, less colorful women or for men.

This brings us to Rosie as a woman and partner. Her romantic liaisons are biracial, unfulfilling, and eventually unsuccessful. Furthermore, she is not shown to belong to a Latino community, but is alone or estranged. In *Do the Right Thing* she is paired off with Spike Lee, for whom she is a side attraction; in *It Could Happen* she is paired off to Nicholas Cage and leaves him for an older and presumably richer man, but at the movie's end she is left without money and without a man because it turns out she was just being used for the money (a little of "what goes around comes around"). Meanwhile, Cage ends up happily paired off to Bridget Fonda as they spread goodness throughout New York City. Similarly, in *White Men* Rosie begins as Woody Harrelson's girlfriend and eventually leaves him—but only after he repeatedly hustles their money away, even after all his debts are paid. Woody Harrelson is left pining after Rosie, but he is still pretty happy with his buddy Wesley Snipes as Rosie fades out. In *Untamed Heart* she is peripheral enough to the main plot that we can't really tell if she's got one steady boyfriend, but she does seem pretty close to her date in the one scene where we get to see her outside of the diner. Even in *Fearless* she breaks up with her husband yet also walks away from Jeff Bridges after her short talk with his wife, the ever-so-proper upper-middle-class Isabella Rosellini. As such, Rosie functions as a bridge (see Moraga & Anzaldúa, 1983) between White and African American people (*Do the Right Thing*); as a facilitator in the eventual happiness of White men with White women (*It Could Happen to You*, *Untamed Heart*, and *Fearless*); or as a link between two male buddies (*White Men*). In Hollywood film, Rosie provides a touristic detour in the lives of otherwise happy individuals.

Other possible areas of focus would include an analysis of reviews of Rosie's films and of her interviews. The former would add insight into popular reception of her films and persona. The latter might reveal some of Rosie's agency in the production of film and of the stereotypical Latina image that she so often portrays. While both of these topics would illuminate issues of the production of images and stereotypes, they are beyond the scope of this chapter.

Conclusions

Rosie Perez presents us with a compact case study into the politics of representation. As is usually the case, we have accessible information on the level of textual documents—that is, her films. We can conclude that Rosie is typecast. Whether because of her voice or her choice, she almost always plays a loud Puerto Rican. Second, it appears Hollywood is unable to envision a Latina with an accent as other than a working-class person. Rosie is always working class, even when she is not loud. Because she is and portrays a blend of ethnic and racial and class identities, she appears to pose a challenge to those who seek to represent both her in particular and Latina women in general.

We study the politics of representation to better understand the relative value of different groups and individuals in our society. That some groups are less often portrayed, according to their proportion of the general population, suggests to us that we or they are less valued and that we or they have less power to influence our or their own portrayal. The continuous and repetitive use of pejorative stereotypes suggests that those individuals or groups represent a threat of some form to mainstream culture. Rosie's salience positions her as one of the few Latina icons to which the general population is exposed. Her portrayal falls within the pattern of the way that Latina women have generally appeared in Hollywood film. As such, her presence is not necessarily an improvement. However, representation is an issue that has wider implications than just those of interpretive practices. Rosie's stereotypical roles have the potential of impacting larger social understandings of culture and difference. Popular culture, including film, is implicated in a process that helps us make meaning and sense of our world. It affects the way we think of ourselves and others. As long as nonhegemonic groups continue to be portrayed in negative ways, they continue to be less valued and their difference continues to be coded as negative and dangerous. Representation remains a very important site of struggle because the effects are not merely symbolic but quite material and crippling. For now, Rosie Perez is yet another woman in the very short line of Latina actresses in Hollywood who has been typecast into the stereotypical Latina role. We as an audience and as a heterogeneous culture await the availability of a broad spectrum of multicultural subjects to people the stories that Hollywood chooses to tell.

NOTES

1. In classic overdetermined casting, although Miranda spoke English fluently and flawlessly, she was made to have a thick accent on-screen to fit the U.S. audience's expectation of Latinas.

2. It was as a result of viewing *It Could Happen to You* that I began this project. I went to see the movie with a Latina friend, and we were astonished and greatly bothered by the role played by Rosie Perez.

3. Hair is highlighted in two very different movies—*Hairpiece* and *School Daze*. Hair is *the site* of struggle over issues of class and ethnicity within the dominant construction of femininity.

REFERENCES

Amador, O. G. (1988, July/August). Galanes latinos, lita y "La Bamba." *Americas, 40,* 2–9.

Cantor, M. G. (1989). Writing fiction as women's work. In R. R. Rush, & D. Allen (Ed.), *Communications at the crossroads: The gender gap connection* (1st ed., p. 316). Norwood, NJ: Ablex.

Corliss, R. (1988, July 11). Born in east L.A. *Time,* 66–67.

Hadley-García, G. (1990). *Hispanic Hollywood: The Latins in motion pictures.* New York: Citadel Press.

McQuail, D. (1987). *Mass Communication Theory: An introduction* (2nd ed.). Newbury Park, CA: Sage.

Millea, H. (1993, March). Behind the scenes: Wild at heart. *Premiere, 6,* 35.

Moraga, C., & Anzaldúa, G. (Eds.). (1983). *This bridge called my back: Writings by radical women of color* (2nd ed.). New York: Kitchen Table: Women of Color Press.

Shohat, E. (1991a). Gender and culture of empire: Toward a feminist ethnography of the cinema. *Quarterly Review of Film and Video, 13*(1–3), 45–84.

Shohat, E. (1991b). Ethnicities-in-relation: Toward a multicultural reading of American cinema. In L. D. Friedman (Ed.), *Unspeakable images: Ethnicity and the American cinema* (pp. 215–250). Urbana: University of Illinois Press.

Shohat, E., & Stam, R. (1994). *Unthinking Eurocentrism: Multiculturalism and the media* (1st ed.). New York: Routledge.

Siegel, G. (1995, May). Familia values. *Los Angeles,* 21.

Tuchman, G., Daniels, A. K., & Benet, J. (Eds.). (1978). *Hearth and home: Images of women in the mass media* (1st ed.). New York: Oxford University Press.

van Zoonen, L. (1994). *Feminist media studies.* London: Sage.

KEY TERMS

Latina

film

politics of
representation

symbolic annihilation

portrayal

DISCUSSION QUESTIONS

1. Valdivia argues that in mass media, women and minorities are marginalized, trivialized, or victimized. How does this happen? What are some examples of these problematic represen-

tations in the television shows and films with which you are familiar?

2. What does Valdivia mean when she says that for Latinas, "portrayal is necessary but not sufficient"? What happens when we have few examples of a particular group (e.g., Latinas), and those examples "bear the burden of representing all of that group"?

3. Using Valdivia's notion of the "politics of representation," think about how your cultural group has been depicted in mainstream mass media. Then, think about how your cultural group is de-

picted in non-mainstream mass media. Are there differences? What kind? What do they suggest about culture and the politics of representation?

4. Valdivia notes that the physical representation of Rosie Perez, with her big hair and big hoops, sends messages about class. What other meanings might be contained in some of the ways that Perez is represented?

5. Mass media has played and will likely continue to play an important role in the everyday life of all or many of us. In what ways can mass media improve intercultural relations?

26

CULTURAL DIFFERENCES IN THE PERCEPTIONS OF SPORTS MASCOTS: A RHETORICAL STUDY OF TIM GIAGO'S NEWSPAPER COLUMNS

JANIS L. KING

Every fall, two sporting activities, baseball's World Series and professional football, draw public attention. But it was not until the fall of 1991 that these received media coverage for something other than the actual games. With the Atlanta Braves reaching the World Series and the Washington Redskins' winning record came attention to their mascots.

Native Americans protested the use of names and rituals that ridiculed Native American traditions. One person who publicly voiced opposition was Tim Giago, the editor-in-chief and publisher of *Indian Country Today*. There are three purposes for studying Giago. The first is to discuss the strategies employed in arguing that sports teams should discontinue the use of words, mascots, dress, objects, caricatures, and actions that pertain to Native Americans. The debate about mascots and regalia is a continuing exigence. Native Americans again protested at the 1995 World Series when the Atlanta Braves and

Braves fans' infamous tomahawk chop, tom-toms, and turkey feathers met the Cleveland Indians and Chief Wahoo, with his huge nose and wide grin. Giago (1996) continues to write concerning Native Americans allowing their "proud name to be dragged through the mud" (p. A4). Second, this study seeks to analyze cross-cultural rhetoric that has many audiences—Native American and non–Native American. More rhetorical situations are developing that require one piece of persuasion to be designed for many cultures; consequently, differences in culture and perceptions need to be addressed. And third, this study illustrates the use of Smith and Lybarger's (1996) suggestions in reconstructing Bitzer's (1968, 1980) rhetorical situation.

In order to complete this discussion, 11 of Tim Giago's columns ("Notes From Indian Country") will be examined. These articles date from September 25, 1991, to August 11, 1993. All appeared in *Indian Country Today* (formerly *The*

Lakota Times), a weekly newspaper founded in July 1981, and were made available for syndication through the Knight-Ridder Tribune News Service. The text is not edited or changed based on the potential audience. It is estimated that at least 200 non-Indian newspapers reprint the columns each week, with the possibility of about 1,000 newspapers if all subscribing to the service did use their reprint option (A. Little Eagle, personal communication, December 9, 1996). As the 1991 World Series ended, Giago (1991c) wrote that his columns were developed to be "sound, intelligently made and educational" (p. A4). In addition, as a good editorial writer, he created a dialogue or debate that would make people want to comment.

A reconstructed model of a rhetorical situation will serve as the guide in discussing Giago's columns. In 1968, Lloyd Bitzer wrote about rhetorical situations in which the situation "calls the discourse into existence" (p. 2) and that consisted of three components: the exigence, "an imperfection marked by urgency" (p. 6) or reason to persuade; the rhetorical audience, "those persons who are capable of being influenced by discourse and of being mediators of change" (p. 8); and a set of constraints, "beliefs, attitudes, documents, facts, traditions, images, interests, motives" (p. 8). After several scholars critically responded to this initial discussion, Bitzer (1980) revised his original concept. But Smith and Lybarger (1996) believed that he still maintained a "bias against the social construction of reality" (p. 201) and that he did not acknowledge situations as a collection of perceptions that made the situation more subjective and less controlling than the objective, linear concept that Bitzer conceived. Smith and Lybarger employed some of Bitzer's revisions to extend the model of the rhetorical situation into the complex postmodern world. The reconstructed model then allowed for multiexigences that may be real as well as created by the rhetor; multiaudiences that may be capable of altering the situation though not necessarily in the same ways; and multiconstraints that develop from the many perceptions of the audiences. These multicomponents explained why a piece of rhetoric succeeds with one of the audiences but does not remove incongruity between the perceptions of the rhetor and those perceptions of another audience.

In each calendar year of this study, Tim Giago wrote about his exigences, his need to persuade. He (1991b) wrote:

> Isn't it amazing when things I have been writing about for years suddenly are given a national focus. . . . The media has centered its attention on whether the sham rituals and painted faces in the stands at Braves' baseball games border on racism. In our minds (Indians) it does, . . . (p. A4)

A week later, after being on a radio talk show, Giago (1991c) extended his discussion to answer the question, Why now?

> A common question was, "Why are Indians jumping on this issue all of a sudden when they haven't said anything all of these years?" The fact of the matter is, we have been saying something all of these years but no one was listening, . . . It all came to a head when the Atlanta Braves won the pennant and then went on to the World Series. Out of the woodwork, on national television, many of us saw for the first time the now infamous "tomahawk chop." (p. A4)

So why are Native Americans upset? Millions of television viewers in the United States as well as other countries are seeing non–Native Americans ridiculing and making light of Indian dress, songs and chants, dance, and sacred traditions.

A year later, Giago (1992a) simply stated: "Well, another football season has just begun and this is my annual column about mascots. The battle isn't so uphill anymore" (p. A4) because Indians' concerns are receiving national media coverage. And by February 4, 1993, he simply noted that "Indians as mascots has been an issue with most American Indians for many years. . . . It has just become public knowledge over the past two years when the national media finally focused on our complaints" (p. A4). Racism, ridiculing Indian religious and sacred traditions, and Indians as mascots provided the reasons for Giago's attempts to convince team owners and fans who did not (and still do not) see the use of Indian mascots as a problem. In addition, Giago had to address Native Americans who did not view the mascot issue as a problem or who were manufacturing and selling Indian regalia to the sports teams as well as Native Americans who supported Giago's position and were picketing at games. Consequently, his persuasive commentaries had to be developed with many audiences in mind.

The articles contained several arguments to convince fans and team owners to discontinue the use of Indian mascots and regalia. Giago's comments centered around two topics: discrimination based on and insensitive to skin color and insensitivity to religion. The primary strategy that he used in organizing and presenting these arguments was to educate individuals. Giago (1991a) provided examples of new team names to illustrate the offensiveness and unlikelihood of the use of stereotypes associated with different races and cultures:

> Just think of the pageantry the [San Francisco] Forty Niners could add to their half-time show if their team was the "Yellowskins." A mascot dressed as a mandarin could leap about the infield while the fans in the stands could paint their faces yellow, wear long pigtails, and attempt to sing ancient Oriental songs while bashing a giant gong. . . . "Redskin" fans see nothing wrong in waltzing about wearing feathers, toting imitation Pipestone pipes, beating miniature drums, sporting painted faces, and conducting themselves in other bizarre ways that insult the traditions, culture and spirituality of the First Americans. . . . Suppose the Washington Redskins . . . did change their names to "Blackskins." Would the fans in the stands feel comfortable painting their faces black, wearing Afro wigs and otherwise carrying out stereotypical activities that are supposedly characteristic of blacks? Not on your life. . . . (p. A4)

Giago (1991c) later continued the analogy when he discussed his participation on a radio talk show:

> One lady called and said she was a Cub Scout leader and she often has her Cubs dress up as Indians so they can get the feel of being a part of another culture. I asked her if she also had them paint their faces black, wear African attire,

and learn to say "B'wana." Utterly horrified she said, "Why of course not. That would be insulting to black people." (p. A4)

Giago's educational approach in showing that people would not dress up and act like other minorities should have made team owners and fans more sensitive to Indian concerns. If fans would not dress up as other minorities because it would be offensive, then the same should hold true for American Indians. But the persuasion did not succeed. Fans stuck turkey feathers in their hair and performed humorous versions of acts and gestures. Team owners did not change names or mascots. Giago, consequently, took a different approach in 1993.

Interpretation of words and symbols often creates problems cross-culturally because of differences in perceptions. In a column entitled "What's in a word? Racism," Giago (1993b) educated readers about the meaning of the word "redskin":

> The word "redskin" comes to us from the slang of the early, white hunters and trappers. When a bounty was placed upon Indians, the hunters and trappers brought in their grisly trophies of scalps, ears, scrotums, and the severed breasts of Indian women along with their other pelts. They would say, "Here's a beaver skin, raccoon skin, ermine skin and this here one's a redskin." (p. A4)

How many White fans would have a similar reaction to the term "whiteskins" if their ancestors had been hunted and skinned for money and for extermination? Giago wanted the fans to understand the history of the word "redskin" and the negative connotation the word has for American Indians.

If arguments pointing out racism and word etymology would not work, perhaps a plea and examples of a religious nature would make team owners and fans more understanding of Native American objections. Giago (1991b) called the various activities performed by a team mascot and the fans "sham rituals" and suggested that these performances were "direct attacks upon the spirituality (religion) of the Indian people" (p. A4). He then employed an analogy using the

New Orleans Saints as a way to show a comparison between religions:

> For instance, suppose Saints' fans decided to emulate Catholicism as part of their routine. What if they carried crosses, had a mascot dressed up like the Pope, spread ashes on their foreheads, and displayed enlarged replicas of the sacramental bread of Holy Communion while drinking from chalices filled with wine? (1991b, p. A4)

He referred to the Christian Bible and the proverb "Do unto others as you would have them do unto you." He (1991b) ended his comparison by asking "Would God-fearing Christians use sports mascots that would insult the Jewish people, Muslims, Buddhists, Shintoists, Hindus or any other minority religious group?" (p. A4). By referring to the religions of team owners and fans, Giago hoped to change people's perceptions so that consequently they would understand the reasons for Indians' objections to current practices of not only the Atlanta Braves and Washington Redskins, but also the Cleveland Indians and Kansas City Chiefs.

Giago (1993c) continued his religious comparison referring to the Fighting Irish of Notre Dame, the Celtics of Boston, and the San Diego Padres:

> The "Irish" were named from the inside by Jesuit priests who were themselves Irish. The Celtics were also named from within. The avid fans of these teams do not jump up and down in the stands pretending to be Irishmen or Celtics. They also do not insult the religion or the spirituality of the Irish or Celts. . . . No, the Padres' fans do not make fun of a religious order in supporting this team. They do not dress up as priests or use religious symbols and artifacts to enhance their mascot. . . . It's the things the fans do not do that makes the world of difference. (p. A4)

Giago (1993c) then completed the comparison when he reviewed the activities of fans for teams with Indian mascots:

> However, the fans do dress up like Indians, they do paint their faces in Day-glow paint and stick

turkey feathers in their hair. They do attempt to sing what they believe to be Indian war chants, and they do use a deadly weapon, the tomahawk, to make threatening gestures. (p. A4)

If fans do not do these acts for teams based on various religions and ethnic groups, then they should not perform acts based on American Indian religions.

By 1993 some university and college teams had changed their names and mascots to eliminate the use of Indian images and objects. But no professional team had made any effort. Giago published a letter that he had written to Ted Turner, the owner of the Atlanta Braves, in response to Turner's comments that he did not see any problems with the use of Indian clothing, objects, and chants. Giago (1993a) explained the meaning of a feather:

> At the end of the ceremony [Sun Dance], most of the other participants gave the boy [only 8 years old] an eagle feather. The eagle, a messenger between the people and *Wakan Tanka* (God), is sacred. Its feathers bestow honor and wearing its feathers on your head lifts your thoughts from the earth to a sacred place. . . . Feathers are given only at times of great honor—a graduation, a naming ceremony, after saving someone's life or after serving honorably in the defense of this nation. . . . We all know that the easiest way to destroy someone's pride in something is to make light of it, to belittle it, to insist that it is not important. Just as you and your fans insist that mimicking of Indians and Indian ways is only for sport and should not offend. (p. A4)

Giago used instruction about the meaning of the feather as a way to convince Turner and fans to make changes based on religion. This completed his strategy of illustrating racism, language and meanings, and religious ridicule.

Giago (1993d) summarized his arguments developed to convince non–Native Americans to change the mascots:

> American Indians are a living, breathing, vital race of people. One hundred years ago, when

colleges and high schools began to use Indians as mascots for their sporting teams, America as a whole believed Indians were about to become extinct. But that never happened. The original idea was to honor a dying race. (p. A4)

But this is no longer the case (Giago, 1996). Native Americans are here and many are offended by Indian mascots and by fans who ridicule Indians' beliefs, religions, and traditions.

Giago's messages were designed to use common beliefs and values (discrimination is bad; respect people's religions; do unto others) that could assist in readjusting team owners' and fans' perceptions and make the exigence real to them. Only when this audience perceived the mascots as a problem would change occur. But these people were not the only audiences that he had to address in his columns. Native Americans composed another element of the reading audience.

In the same articles Giago also educated Native American audiences. Native Americans who were protesting at the games already viewed the exigence as real and only needed Giago's ideas as further reinforcement that they were correct in their actions. Giago's comments served to unify and encourage them. But Giago needed a more pragmatic style when addressing the other two Native American audiences. One such group felt that the mascot issue was not a major concern and that there were far more serious problems to solve, such as drug and alcohol use, poverty, and suicide. The other Native American audience consisted of those who manufactured and sold cheap versions of Indian regalia and objects. Giago used religion, profiteering, and long-term effects on children in educating these groups.

On October 23, 1991, Giago called the various things that fans perform as imitation Indians "sham rituals" (p. A4), including "wearing of feathers, smoking of so-called peace pipes, beating of tom-toms, fake dances, horrendous attempts at singing Indian songs, the so-called war whoops, and the painted faces" (p. A4). He claimed that these actions were "direct attacks upon the spirituality (religion) of the Indian people" (p. A4). Religion and tradition are extremely important in Native American cultures, so reminding those who felt that there was no

problem about the religious significance served to change the perceptions of the uncommitted.

A week later Giago (1991c) wrote about the Eastern Cherokees who were manufacturing tomahawks for the Atlanta Braves. He noted that a group from the Eastern Cherokees had been on CNN and had discussed the money that they were making. Giago described this interview: "This little charade by the Eastern Cherokee was used by many white callers to support their ignorance and bigotry. Profiteering isn't peculiar to the white race" (p. A4). This line of argument was continued in an editorial entitled "We are humans, never mascots" (1991), which argued,

We must consider those Indian people who would profit at the expense of their own culture and spirituality by selling sacred artifacts to tourists or to professional sporting teams as traitors to their own kind. We can think of no other way to phrase this. . . . Surely there are other items these profiteers can sell that will not be used to degrade or insult us. (p. A4)

Giago's ("We are humans," 1991) last appeal concerned Princess Pale Moon, an imitation "Indian" who sings at Redskins games played in Washington, D.C., and fans' pre-game behavior. The editorial stated that Native Americans protesting outside of the stadium were being spat upon by both White and Black fans arriving at the game and that this action is "a situation all grassroots Indians should find intolerable" (p. A4). The final plea appeared at the end of the editorial: "We must stand together as Indian people to bring this disgraceful use of our heritage and our race to promote fun and games for black and white sports fans to an end. These racial slurs and insults must cease!" (p. A4). The editorial attempted to change perceptions of the two Native American audiences so that they would believe the exigence to be an imperfection that must be changed.

The following year Giago (1992a) referred to a petition presented to the federal government that was initiated by seven well-known and respected Native Americans. By using "experts," Giago attempted to convince other Native Americans that they, too, should support the elimination of Indians as mascots. A couple of the names on the petition (Vine Deloria, Jr., and Manley Begay, Jr.) would be known to some people who are not Native Americans, but all of the petitioners would be more credible to Indians. Giago wrote:

> "Those guys" took a look at seven Washington Redskin trademarks and said, "Whoa!" The old war horse Vine Deloria, a man active in Indian affairs for more than 30 years, saw a fly in the ointment. The federal government cannot issue federal trademark registrations on matters that are offensive or disparaging. . . . The petition found these trademark names to be "pejorative, derogatory, denigrating, offensive, scandalous, contemptuous, disreputable, disparaging and racist." (p. A4)

Giago (1993e) used an expert later when he discussed Native American Ben Nighthorse Campbell, a United States Senator from Colorado. Campbell attempted to get Jack Kent Cooke, owner of the Washington Redskins, to change the name of the team by introducing legislation concerning Cooke's desire for federal land for a new stadium and by comparing the name "Redskins" to "'prairie nigger'" (p. A4). Perhaps the use of experts' perceptions of the mascot issue would cause Native Americans to view the exigence in the same way.

In October, Giago (1992b) wrote a column in response to his appearance on the *Oprah Winfrey Show*. Giago suggested that selling products that demeaned Indians was affecting the self-esteem of Native American children. He concluded:

> There are always those Indians who are out of step with the majority. They call whenever I do a radio talk show and say, "I'm part Cherokee (or Chippewa, or Aztec) and I don't mind being a mascot." Every time this has happened, the caller has always admitted to having been raised in a totally white environment, never living on an Indian reservation, and having lost all touch with their heritage. And yet, these are the people the media turns to when pointing out that some Indians don't mind being used as mascots. (p. A4)

Giago clearly discredited these Native Americans as well as the media because these spokespersons have a White person's perception of the exigence rather than an Indian perception. It was hoped that Native Americans would change their perceptions of these spokespersons.

In addition, Giago (1993d) compared the Indian struggle over the mascot issue to the beginning of the Civil Rights movement in the 1950s and 1960s when Rosa Parks refused to give up her bus seat to a White person:

> Educating America has also included educating some of our own people. Indians, like any other ethnic group, can become conditioned to bending to the will of the majority. Please recall that it wasn't that long ago when white America was singing about the happy and contented "darkies" lolling about the little cabin floor. . . . The process of educating the non-Indian means educating some of our own people at times. (p. A4)

Giago concluded by reinforcing the need not only to educate Whites in general and team owners in particular but also to reach those Indians who were not supporting the protest.

Two questions need to be answered to evaluate Giago's columns: (1) Why use the strategy of education? and (2) Did Giago's strategy work in changing perceptions and eliminating Indian sports mascots?

First, the strategy of education allowed Giago to use one column to reach all audiences because the lack of knowledge about the demeaning and denigrating nature of the teams' mascots applied to the various reading audiences. Giago (1992a) wrote that "it has always been a matter of educating the masses. I've always believed that if white and black people knew why we objected to being used as mascots, they would understand" (p. A4). Giago believed that readers, once informed, would alter their beliefs and subsequently want to change patterns of behaviors.

Second, the educational strategy was an ideal choice because it allowed Giago to address the issue of Native Americans joining together to protest in a unified manner. To restore unity was very important because internal division created only confusion. If Native Americans did not see the mascots as a concern, why should non–Native

Americans perceive them as a problem? By reminding Native Americans about religious traditions, the meanings of the feather, songs, and drums, and by using respected Native Americans as support for his ideas, he forced these two non-supporting audiences to address and rethink their decisions.

The second question of importance to this discussion is whether Giago succeeded in his persuasion. All of the changes in the use of Indian mascots have been at the high school and university levels. Stanford University now has the cardinal as a mascot and St. Johns University is no longer referred to as the Redmen. But no professional sports team has made any attempt to change the names or items sold at the stadiums. Fans of these teams still dress as Indians and perform imitation rituals. Ignorance and a lack of understanding still prevail. The only indication of some success in reaching a team owner is with Ted Turner. One of Turner's cable networks produced several made-for-television movies about Indians of the past (Geronimo, the Iroquois Confederacy, and Crazy Horse) using Native American actors. The Braves, however, are still the Braves and the tomahawk chop is still part of fan ritual at games.

The educational strategy with team owners and fans who ultimately control the language and actions did not work. Why did pointing out racial insults, redefining terms, and an appeal to religious insensitivity fail? The answer is found in Smith and Lybarger's postmodern description of a rhetorical situation.

Smith and Lybarger (1996) identified two questions that come out of the complexity of multiple exigences and audiences and the resulting constraints as the rhetor attempts to achieve congruence with the many audiences: (1) "Is the speaker's assessment of an exigence the same as the audience's?" and (2) "Did the speaker make adjustments for differences with audience regarding the perception of and felt interest in an exigence?" (p. 210). Giago perceived the sports mascots as a problem but his non–Native American audience did not. Consequently, as Smith and Lybarger noted, Giago had to create an exigence for this group. He attempted this creation by pointing out (1) the discrimination in using Native Americans as mascots when Whites would never do such a thing with other ethnic or religious groups, (2) the religious ridicule associated with attire and actions, and (3) the meanings of certain names and actions. But Giago failed in this creation of an exigence because he did not make adjustments for the different perceptions and did not take into consideration the felt interests of the non-Indian audience. Native Americans raised in their tribal heritages, such as Giago, have different perceptions from non–Native Americans and even Native Americans raised in a White European-based culture. Native Americans with a strong heritage viewed fans' actions as ridiculous and almost sacrilegious, whereas non–Native Americans believed that these actions honored those who demonstrated courage and perseverance in the face of adversity and enemies. Giago did not deal with this "honor" perception; consequently, non–Native Americans, who believed that they were representing courageous behavior, did not change their perceptions, and thus would not see the exigence as real.

In addition, Giago ignored the felt interests of the non–Native American audience. He did mention African Americans and Asian Americans in one of the early columns and may have made the few fans of these racial groups more sensitive to the exigence, but team owners and the majority of the fans are White. And it is these individuals who have the power to eliminate the mascots, clothing, and actions. Giago did not provide any interests to which the owners and fans could relate. He did not address the financial factors, including profit losses, that team owners and players would incur by changing mascots and creating new artifacts to sell to fans. Most of the fans have not had their civil rights denied or ridiculed; therefore, they have no direct experience with discrimination or lack of recognition or both. These individuals, thus, are not able to transfer abstract beliefs and values to real-life felt interests. They have not experienced the same "life" and, consequently, do not have similar perceptions and worldviews. Those with the money (team owners) and those in the majority (White fans) are traditionally, in the American culture, the ones with the power to change the exigence. In this case, the exigence has no power for the non–Native Americans because it is not perceived. Giago did not deal with the interests of this group, which resulted in no changes in perceptions. The groups remained in a fragmented stage.

Based on this essay's study, there are a few suggestions for intercultural communication. First, rhetors must include factors that relate to the various audiences' perceptions and felt interests in order to create congruence with each group. Although the ideal would be to have distinct pieces of rhetoric for each audience, this is not practical in today's media coverage. Second, the education strategy should work well for others if various perceptions are included because it tends to make people less defensive. But information must be provided that appeals to the felt interests of all audiences. Third, rhetors must recognize which audiences truly have the power to make changes and then make the exigence "real" for these groups by modifying their perceptions and including their interests. If the rhetor's purpose is to modify or remove the exigence, the rhetor in a postmodern world must reach congruence with those who have societal power, a factor that Smith and Lybarger did not deal with specifically. Fourth, in many instances of intercultural persuasion, rhetors ignore, intentionally or unintentionally, the lack of agreement in perceptions. Rhetors of any race or culture involved in intercultural communication must deal with worldviews other than their own. To fail to recognize this means persuasion and communication will not succeed.

REFERENCES

Bitzer, L. F. (1968). The rhetorical situation. *Philosophy and Rhetoric, 1,* 1–14.

Bitzer, L. F. (1980). Functional communication: A situational perspective. In E. White (Ed.), *Rhetoric in transition: Studies in the nature and uses of rhetoric* (pp. 21–38). State College: Pennsylvania State University Press.

Giago, T. (1991a, September 25). Pigskin mascots: A seasonal insult. *The Lakota Times,* p. A4.

Giago, T. (1991b, October 23). Mascots, spirituality and insensitivity. *The Lakota Times,* p. A4.

Giago, T. (1991c, October 30). Ignorance adds insult to injury. *The Lakota Times,* p. A4.

Giago, T. (1992a, September 16). Keeping looking over your shoulders, you "R————s." *The Lakota Times,* p. A4.

Giago, T. (1992b, October 15). Tuning into an important topic on a talk show stage. *Indian Country Today,* p. A4.

Giago, T. (1993a, February 4). Waiting for reply from broadcaster Ted Turner. *Indian Country Today,* p. A4.

Giago, T. (1993b, March 10). What's in a word? Racism. *Indian Country Today,* p. A4.

Giago, T. (1993c, May 5). *Denver Post* still doesn't get it. *Indian Country Today,* p. A4.

Giago, T. (1993d, June 23). Pepsico stand against mascots is the right one baby—uh-huh! *Indian Country Today,* p. A4.

Giago, T. (1993e, August 11). Racist cartoons: We are not amused. *Indian Country Today,* p. A4.

Giago, T. (1996, December 16–23). Seminoles allow proud name to be dragged through the mud of Florida State football field. *Indian Country Today,* p. A4.

Smith, C. R., & Lybarger, S. (1996). Bitzer's model reconstructed. *Communication Quarterly, 44,* 197–213.

We are humans, never mascots. (1991, November 13). *The Lakota Times,* p. A4.

KEY TERMS

Native American	mascots
racism	sports
naming	exigence
rhetor	perception
rhetoric	felt interests

DISCUSSION QUESTIONS

1. King's essay suggests that one piece of rhetoric may have many audiences of different cultural backgrounds and with different concerns. What other rhetorical situations exist that involve such audiences?

2. King uses Giago's columns to illustrate how exigences may be real to one cultural group but must be created for another cultural group. Can you think of other social contexts or issues in which this creation must occur?

3. What suggestions for change would you give to Mr. Giago in order to make his columns more "real" for non–Native American audiences?

4. What does King's essay tell us about cultural perceptions? Can a person of one cultural background really understand the perceptions of a person from a different culture?

5. In King's essay, names and the various perceptions associated with the names cause conflict for those involved. Can you think of other intercultural situations, such as generational differences, in which naming may be one of the factors in the conflict?

27

DIFFERENT CHILDREN, DIFFERENT DREAMS: RACIAL REPRESENTATION IN ADVERTISING[1]

ELLEN SEITER

Advertisers like to use children—and not only in advertisements for toys and diapers. Babies are attention grabbers, they are especially good at catching the eyes of women consumers who so often constitute the target market. Perhaps most important for the cautious advertiser, children rarely offend. Picturing children allows advertisers to call up rich, cherished associations: nostalgia, love, the fullness of the future, the comfort of home, the pleasures of family life. The use of children is a way to suggest many of the values that advertisers routinely associate with their products: newness, innocence, energy, rejuvenation, mildness, happiness, protection. Increasingly, corporate image advertising draws on images of children to suggest kindness, responsibility, benevolence, and the ordinariness of their concerns.

• • •

Symbolic connotations aside, there is nothing innocent about the use of children in advertising. Each infant crawling across the screen carries a heavy load of ideological projections. The scene in a commercial for Luv's diapers of a blonde girl tempting a boy with an apple juice bottle is typical of the gender projections found in children's advertising. The regal infant, white-skinned and dressed in white, picnicking with mom and dad beside the tennis court, expresses "Cadillac style" and the assurance of lifetime affluence. Our common sense notions of childhood are tied up with ideas about social Darwinism, genetics, inheritance, nature vs. nurture. Children so often grow up to fulfill the status quo that the representation of children is especially good at "naturalizing" social relations, by making unequal destinies seem inevitable. After all, boys so often grow up to be boys. For the blonde blue-eyed laughing boy, advertisements project dreams of power and success. For the dancing, light-skinned Black girl no such future is ever envisioned.

• • •

Most families on series television are upper middle class; poor and working-class children appear to us only on news and tabloid shows, where their stories of victimization mark them off—as though members of another nation entirely, as of the Third World—from the beautiful, happy faces of the advertisements. Overall, people of color are usually represented through the frame of "problems," which is why they are seen more often on the news. Television so often portrays suffering children as Black and Hispanic that it has been hard for the white middle class in the 1980s to comprehend the fact that staggering numbers of mothers and children who live in poverty are white.

The Geography of Whiteness

Let me begin with a discussion of white babies in mass-market advertising and by calling attention to those advertisements where children of color never appear. Tessa Perkins has argued that you must look at stereotypes of dominant groups to understand the latent content of stereotypes of oppressed groups. Positive, laudatory stereotypes about white men, for example, may be as persistent as pejorative stereotypes of Black women. The association of reasoned authority with white men is as strong as the association of heightened sexuality with Black women. Positive stereotypes are as important as negative ones in defining the field of what the media communicate to us about race. As Hazel Carby has put it, "Stereotypes only appear to exist in isolation while actually depending on a nexus of figurations which can be explained only in relation to each other" (Carby, 1987, p. 20).

Dreams of a great and inevitable destiny begin at infancy for whites as seen in print advertising. Their preciousness is underscored by allusions to their future economic value. A Johnson advertisement shows a bare white buttocks under the headline, "One day this little bottom may sit on the board of directors. Today it needs Johnson's." (The girl's version of the advertisement reads "One day this soft hair may be colored and permed," across the forehead of a blonde, blue-eyed girl in extreme close up: a typical example of the strenuous gender identification of all children in advertisements.) "Power Play" reads the bold headline over a picture of a blonde, grimacing boy ruggedly dressed in flannel shirt, jeans and thermal undershirt; as he drives his *Power Wheels*. Playskool advertises "Alphie II My First Computer," with a picture of a red-haired boy, gazing directly into the camera, above the line "We've Got a Genius for Making Learning Fun." In a two-page advertisement for the Socrates "Educational Video System," a smiling blonde boy holds up his test with an A plus marked prominently in red, the oppo-

site page reads, "'Pay attention to the young and make them just as good as possible'—Socrates." The preoccupation with children's intelligence and achievement spills over into all product categories: "Kids are brighter than they used to be" promises Vivid bleach, above three fashionably dressed and smiling white kids.

• • •

One of the most common stereotypes of white infants and small children in advertising is the go-getter. The go-getter is not a stereotype available for the representation of Black children, who tend to be shown in advertising as passive observers of their white playmates. If Black children were pictured in the same aggressive postures used for white boys, the available stereotype with which they are likely to be associated by whites is the "pushy" Black or the hoodlum. Thus the same set of behaviors, descriptively speaking, can be negatively or positively evaluated in racial stereotypes.

When I began looking for children in commercials, I was struck by the remarkable stability of images of white children, how often blondes were cast in commercials, and how similar they all looked. It is because "a dominant group's position is relatively stable and unproblematic" that images of blonde children seem to have remained largely unchanged for a century (Perkins, 1979, p. 148). It is very difficult for whites to see how whiteness *as a norm* informs all media representation, "as if it is the natural, inevitable, ordinary way of being human," Richard Dyer explains (Dyer, 1988, p. 44).

> "White is not anything really, not an identity, not a particularizing quality, because it is everything—white is no color because it is all colors. This property of whiteness to be everything and nothing, is the source of its representational power . . ." (Dyer, 1988, p. 45).

This is why it is easy to pick out children of color in advertisements, but harder to see their absence in all-white commercials. The perspective of whiteness makes it impossible to see difference within minority groups. Overwhelmingly, advertisers use a single Black to signify "minority," while whites are portrayed as endlessly varied, individual, even quirky and idiosyncratic.[2] Advertisers utterly fail to register the tremendous range of differences *among* Hispanics, *among* Blacks, *among* Asians, *among* American Indians.

"The invisibility of whiteness," writes Richard Dyer, "masks whiteness itself as a category." One of the most opaque masks of whiteness is the code of "nostalgia." Norman Rockwell's illustrations made a comeback in 1989 commercials to sell breakfast cereal and station wagons, and they offer a good example of the representation of whiteness as innocence. Rockwell's work epitomizes many aspects of the nostalgic myth of America: small town, parents and children together, naughtiness in boys, flirtatiousness in girls, the institutions of school, church, Boy Scouts—everyone is white.

The classroom is a favorite location for the nostalgia motif. The set design—bathed in yellow light, flag in the front of the class and globe on the teacher's desk—places the classroom in a mythical and decidedly pre-integration past. This is made explicit in a US West commercial where the music classroom of the past (bathed in soft white light, resembling an illustration from Laura Ingalls Wilder's *Little House on the Prairie*) gives way to the "modern" classroom where the music teacher, an Asian woman, instructs via a video monitor. It is the white girl, center frame, who performs for the teacher. The Asian girl seated next to her listens silently, politely[3]. In a commercial for Eggo waffles, the classroom is visually the same as the room in the US West "flashback," and again every face is white. A boy gets up in front of the class to explain his "invention"—he has remodelled his toaster to prevent his brother from stealing his waffles—displaying the smartness and ingenuity of young white boys.

When television commercials are set in the home, in the domestic sphere, we can predict with certainty that only white children will be shown. Whenever commercials take place at the kitchen table, or on the front porch, whites are pictured alone. White children may be pictured with Black children playing in public (albeit in a restricted set of locations, as I shall describe below) but whenever the parents or grandparents are present, if the space is personal, intimate, familial, scenes are totally segregated by race. Children of color are orphaned on television commercials, excluded from the loving grasp of parents, restricted to token membership in a peer group, relegated to the status of "neighborhood kids" as Mattel named one of its multi-racial ensembles of dolls.

• • •

Exploration and Discovery

Commercials targeted directly at children, those shown during Saturday morning television, for example, differ in important ways from general-market commercials featuring children in the cast. Adults are only rarely present, and parents are subjected to various forms of rebellion—even humiliation. In a Cornflakes commercial, a red-haired girl sits at the kitchen table refusing to speak to her mother—she answers by holding up signs, "Yes" and "No" in a strategy to persuade her mother to let her eat grown-up cereal—Cornflakes. In another advertisement, a boy of six or seven sneaks up on his father quietly reading the paper on the porch, and snaps his picture (with a camera available through proof of purchase seals) at the very moment the father's toupee blows off.

• • •

. . . White boys are always cast as the adventurous, courageous "explorers"; while children of color are either excluded altogether, or are represented as passive, primitive, and ignorant. In a Nestle's Quik cartoon, two children in search of a schoolhouse, accompanied by a rabbit and polar bear as their guides, suffer an avalanche, then head into a diner for a spot of hot chocolate. A smiling Eskimo, so much a caricature that his eyes are drawn by straight lines, speechlessly and smilingly serves them. Silent, smiling, and in the background, this is the only Native American child I found on contemporary television commercials from 1988–1990. After drinking their Quik, the rabbit frightens the polar bear who runs through the wall of the igloo. The huge hole in the wall reveals to the now happy children that the school is within sight. In another version of the Quik advertisement, the scene is a space ship and all the child astronauts are white. The same is true of the junior explorers used for the "Dinosaur Hunt" for Chef-Boy-Ar-Dee and for the Chips-Ahoy "Expedition." In a mixture of horror and adventure genres, a group of children who are camped out in the "Fun Fruits Forest" tell ghost stories and "discover" Sunkist Fun fruits as skeletons and monsters jump out at them. One of the four children is a Black boy. He is once again seen only in long shot, our view of him partially obscured as he dances in the background.

Fanciful "exotic" adults populate live action advertisements also. In a Honeycomb commercial, the white children are visited by a magical strong man genie: a well-muscled shirtless Black man, turbanned, covered with jewelry. He is shot in extreme close up to emphasize his huge size, and he appears and disappears according to the children's whim. An inscrutable Asian man, "The Wisdom Tooth," recommends Crest toothpaste. An Indian man sings in English about potato chips baked by "Pequenos Keebleros," animated Keebler elves. In a commercial for trash bags, a group of aged American Indians watch over children dressed in scouting uniforms as they pick up trash on a hillside. In close up, the chief nods approvingly then literally "vanishes," optically dissolving from the picture. "Leave the land as you found it," is the voice over's message. Thus, minority adults are relegated to the roles of supernatural companions and helpers, playing roles very similar to those of animated animal figures. Their representations are fixed in "orientalist" fairy tales (Said, 1978). Again, we need only re-cast these advertisements with a middle aged white man in any of these parts to recognize the racial problematic implicit in these images.

Together on Saturday Morning

A spot that launched the Nabisco cookie, Teddy Grahams, typifies the representation of white and black children together. This commercial, in thirty and fifteen second versions, has had a great deal of air play, both on Saturday morning and in the "early fringe" weekday slots. It has been shown hundreds of times during many different time periods, during and outside of Saturday morning. Three adult-sized Teddy Bears sing a version of Elvis's "Teddy Bear" ("I wanna be your Teddy Graham"). They perform on a glittery stage, wearing fashion sunglasses and holding microphones. Three children join them on stage: a white boy and girl and a black boy. (The children syntagmatically represent the three varieties of teddy grahams, chocolate, vanilla and cinnamon). As the children pop up behind the white piano that one of the bear musicians plays, eat cookies, and crowd into the spotlight, the Black boy is partially obscured from view by the piano or nearly pushed out of the frame by the other kids.

This commercial exemplifies many of the rules which seem to govern the representation of children of color in Saturday morning commercials. First, they are always outnumbered by whites. Most often three children are pictured—two whites and one African-American (white boy in center, Black boy on left, white girl on right, as in the Teddy Grahams commercial). Children of color are pictured singly on commercials, if at all. The minority child is seen left screen—the least dynamic portion of the frame according to design theory. The Black child is not given a speaking part and is seen mainly in group shots with white children, only once alone and never in facial close up. Like most Black models, the boy has been directed to smile broadly and act clownish, manic. (Sadness, frustration, or complaint are the prerogatives of whites.) These rules govern the representation of children in commercials across a broad range of advertising styles and narratives.

Through casting, advertising glorifies white features, "good hair," light skin. Black feminists have described the oppressiveness of this beauty standard: to look as much like whites as possible. Toni Morrison has described a child's point of view in *The Bluest Eye* (Morrison, 1970). This tyranny of physical type is strongest in the representation of Black girls. When advertising the most feminine toys: baby dolls, modelling clay flowers, kitchens, toy commercials use white models. When girls are really being middle-class girls—wearing long hair and traditional, pastel dresses, playing with dolls and flowers—they are always *white* girls. This is an extension of the taboo against representing children of color in the domestic space. Commercials such as those for "Boucin' Babies" and "Fantastic Flower Basket" are typical of this genre. Merchandising as well as advertising excludes Black girls from the most strictly gender-coded types of play. An exception here is Mattel, which markets Black and Hispanic product lines extensively. In television commercials for a new "Style Magic," one African-American and two white girls appear together. Here the girls marvel over the voluptuous curly blonde hair of Barbie. It is unusual that the Black girl is given the largest speaking part, exclaiming over the fun of Barbie, enthusiastically describing her attributes. But the Black version of the doll is seen only in long shot, and is never admired or played with by the Black girl. In the final shot, the Black girl stands behind a seated white girl, fixing her hair.

• • •

Typically, advertisements express a hierarchy of race relations. White children are always the stars, African-American children the bit players. The superiority of white children is reinforced through visual composition and through gestural codes. Erving Goffman has noted how characters' "placement relative to one another will provide an index or mapping of their presumed *social* position relative to one another." (Goffman, 1976, p. 26) A four page advertisement for the Today's Kids series features four different pieces of play equipment: On the first page, five children of different ages direct their attention to various "activity centers" on the circular "Busy Center." Only the Black child has his back to the camera, his face turned away. On the second page girls play with the stove, the play phone, the vanity of the "Sweetheart Playhouse." Seven children appear, all of them white, with long curly hair. On the third page, the Merry-go-Round features three children playing. Again, it is the blonde children who smile and look directly into the ·camera, while the Black child has turned his head so that his face is completely out of view. Finally, on the last page, three boys play "All Star Basketball,"

and the Black boy is shown full face. His two white playmates are somewhat blurred as they go up for a shot but, they are twice the size and twice the age of the Black child.

• • •

Black children are routinely granted the authority of a privileged relation to sports and music. For example, Black children appear in nearly all the advertisements for infant sports shoes, thus emphasizing their presumably "inborn" athletic ability. A television commercial for Apple Jacks uses a rap soundtrack and a basketball game to envision the "teamwork" of whites and Blacks playing together. One of the Black boys makes the final slam dunk of the cereal box at the end: the only starring role repeatedly offered to Black boys. In a commercial for "Pocket Rockers," top-forty singles on miniature cassettes, a Black girl is given center stage, flanked by her white playmates as they dance down the street. Achievement in sports and in music are obviously a proud and valuable aspect of Black culture. But in advertising they are distorted because they appear not as aspects of culture but as innate, natural talents. They are the only arenas for achievement and ambition allowed Black children.

To understand the significance of this, we must return to the representation of white children. Cultivation of learning and creativity are the qualities advertisers associate with white children. It is especially significant that toy advertising that makes particular claims for developing creativity have only white actors. The commercial for Ohio Art's ZAKS (a lego-like building toy) features a rap soundtrack: but only whites play in the advertisements. The same is true of the new series of PlayDoh commercials. McDonald's has run a couple of Saturday morning advertisements where the link to the future is made explicit. In the first, "Report Card," a group of children is seen at school opening their report cards. The white children have a range of reactions—joy, excitement, fainting, grief. But the single Black boy is seen opening the card and rapidly closing it, in a quick shot in which his reaction is open to a variety of readings (shock? relief?). The kids then head off to McDonald's to recuperate. The Black boy joins them at the table, but he is seen only from the back in an over-the-shoulder-shot. A second advertisement, "Big Dreams," features a group of children discussing what they want to be when they grow up. A girl says, giggling, "I want to be a lawyer, or maybe a fashion designer." A song describes three of the dreams in flashback/ fantasies—to be a dancer, rock-n-roller, rodeo rider. When we cut back to the scene at the table, two Black girls are briefly shown, moving in and out of frame, slightly out of focus[4]. They are not given speaking parts. The range of possibilities discussed by the kids: from Aerospace engineer, to Electrocardiogramtechnologist, are the province of the white kids. "Tomorrow belongs to you," advertising tells white children over and over again.

· · ·

Advertising is one discourse that negotiates these contradictions; it must be seen as part of a complex of messages that children receive, along with school, religion, family, and so on.

· · ·

The search for "positive images" is limited by ideology, a set of relations which include hierarchies based in class and gender. The work of the Burrell agency certainly offers more desirable images of African-American children than those offered in white advertisements. But the efforts of minority agencies are circumscribed by ideology and by the worry over offending white audiences. In focusing on the family in these commercials, they both answer and replicate the dominant media construction of minorities as a "problem." Since the Moynihan report of the 1960s, the media have explained the problem with Blacks as deriving from the absence of the father and the female-headed household (the Black matriarch). As many Black sociologists and feminists have explained, this thesis, which has been remarkably durable as an ideological construct, denies the possibility that Black poverty is created through white economic privilege (hooks, 1981, pp. 51–86). The history of slavery, the grossly inferior public education system, and employment discrimination vanish and the Black family is the source of the problem. These commercials "answer" the negative Black images produced by

whites by picturing the Black middle-class family—with father present. But the terms of the representation are the same; we simply have the positive rather than the negative version of the stereotype. These issues have been heard in the debate over the *Cosby* show, the object of great suspicion (by white leftists) and wonder (by industry workers) because of its enormous popularity with whites and Blacks. While it has "normalized" the Black family, *Cosby* has been vigorously attacked for its upper-middle-classness, its materialism, its conspicuous consumption, its adoption of conventions from white family sitcoms (see Miller, 1988).

The Burrell commercials do what advertising does best: provide celebratory, utopian, unabashedly sentimental pictures of the family. They are important as an intervention, as an antidote, to the white advertising I have described here. But there is no such thing as a free lunch. The African-American community has had to badger McDonald's to purchase advertising time on Black-owned stations. Their huge profits are substantially due to Black consumers (and to Black employees). These "best" images of the Black family advertise a product indisputably dangerous to a community at risk of high blood pressure and heart disease.

· · ·

Postscript: Studying Stereotypes

· · ·

Many advertisers treat minority consumers no better than Columbus treated the Indians centuries ago. The comparison is apt because media audiences today are indeed, like the Indians, an economic colony, exploited and disregarded by a dominant group with little interest in their culture. The press and trade journals report that advertisers are paying increasing attention to minority audiences through target marketing. But when we consider advertising on network television and popular magazines it becomes clear that most advertising is for the general market, that is, for whites. To complain of stereotyping in advertising is to raise the two issues that Todorov discusses:

the hierarchical representation of characters in advertisements, in which whites are always favored, and the erasure of difference, the incessant reworking and repetition of white values, scenarios, beliefs, and images, ideology.

• • •

NOTES

1. This paper is based on a book chapter from *Sold Separately: Aspects of Children's Consumer Culture*. Winchester, MA, and London: Unwin Hyman, forthcoming.

2. Jews are an ideologically crucial exclusion here. Whiteness is Christian, usually WASP. One of the marks of anti-semitism is the obliteration of Jews from advertising images. Totally assimilated Jews do appear on some popular dramatic television shows, such as *LA Law* and *thirtysomething*.

3. Since the 1940s, Asians have been represented as a "Model Minority," a stereotype that is defined primarily by the fact that Asians are seen as different from and more desirable than African-Americans. Asian children usually conform to this model minority stereotype. Currently, the model minority stereotype seems to be undergoing a process of re-evaluation, and is now taking on the negative connotations of "drudge." The Asian student as drudge is seen as an "unfair" competitor with white college students (see Fong, 1989).

• • •

4. This imitation documentary style (handheld camera, imperfect framing, loss of focus) is frequently used to pan quickly past children of color. It is a way of signalling their presence, while "accidentally" passing them over.

• • •

REFERENCES

Carby, H. (1987). *Reconstructing Womanhood: The Emergence of the Afro-American Woman Novelist.* New York: Oxford.

Dyer, R. (1988). "White." *Screen 29*(4), 44–65.

Fong, C. (1989). "The Model Minority and Shifts in the Images of Chinese Americans, 1800–1930." Unpublished Ph.D. dissertation, University of Oregon.

Goffman, E. (1976). *Gender Advertisements.* New York: Harper and Row.

hooks, b. (1981). *Ain't I A Woman: Black Women and Feminism.* Boston: South End Press.

Marchand, R. (1985). *Advertising the American Dream.* Berkeley: University of California Press.

Miller, M. C. (1988). "Cosby Knows Best." *Boxed In.* Evanston: Northwestern University, pp. 69–78.

Morrison, T. (1970). *The Bluest Eye.* New York: Washington Square Press.

Perkins, T. E. (1979). "Rethinking Stereotypes." *Ideology and Cultural Production.* Eds. Michele Barrett, et al. New York: St. Martin's Press, pp. 135–159.

Said, E. (1978). *Orientalism.* London: Routledge & Kegan Paul.

Simpson, P., Ed. (1987). *Parents Talking Television.* London: Comedia.

Spivak, G. (1988). *In Other Worlds.* New York: Routledge.

Todorov, T. (1984). *The Conquest of America: The question of the other.* Trans. Richard Howard. New York: Harper and Row.

KEY TERMS

advertising	stereotypes
Whiteness	race relations
representation	

DISCUSSION QUESTIONS

1. What does Seiter mean by the "geography of Whiteness"? What other examples in popular culture contribute to this geography of Whiteness?

2. Seiter argues that Whiteness is invisible. In what ways is it invisible?

3. How does understanding the representations of Whiteness help us understand the representations of other ethnic groups?

4. Seiter argues that different characteristics are attributed in advertising to Whites and non-Whites. What are these different characteristics, and what are some possible implications of this differentiation for intercultural communication?

5. In what ways does advertising help us negotiate social meanings of race and ethnicity?

28
"SEEING THROUGH THE SCREEN": A STRUGGLE OF "CULTURE"

RONA TAMIKO HALUALANI

A solid black frame ignites with blaring static tones and fuzzy lines that move both horizontally and vertically. Suddenly, out from the right-hand corner, there is a space that clearly outlines the figure of a woman; you can begin to hear a distinct voice. The woman is standing amid a jet black backdrop as scattered lighting tints over her *ehu* ("reddish" in Hawaiian) hair. Dressed in a black turtleneck and jeans, she is facing the camera. As the woman lifts her head, the web of lights transforms into a bright spotlight, focused on her face. In a medium distance shot from the camera, the woman looks straight ahead, and then faintly smiles. She speaks.

I lived most of my childhood in front of the television. Aside from providing me with an activity while my older brothers were at school or out playing until sundown, I was utterly fascinated with the "tube." At age 7, I could "see" things that I knew I would never ever experience: faraway, exotic places, suspenseful drama that is always resolved at the end, and amusing, almost ridiculous characters. Religiously, I would watch those old Disney movies on TV, like The Shaggy D.A. *or* The Parent Trap. *You know, the ones where the kids get into this big predicament, and then by the end everything is figured out and they return to their safe, happy existence.*

Watching the domestic bliss and everyday ease of family shows such as The Brady Bunch *and* The Partridge Family *provided me with a false sense of what life is like, of what life in "American" society is like. Economic issues (e.g., jobs, housing) and interpersonal factors (e.g., meeting people, socializing in different places and spaces) never seemed to be too difficult for the children in those "variety" family shows. In fact, social life was apparently*

"seamless"; each thread smoothly flowing into another. Utter peace, happiness, and prosperity. Seemed so "real," only a "channel" away . . . And I would only see "me" in TV when I pushed in the ON/OFF button and the picture band closed in on a glossy greyish-brown frame, which revealed a faint reflection of my "face"; my eyes piercing the screen with hope and excitement . . .

In front of a televisual camera that cannot be seen, before lights that cannot be shunned, and before an audience that is only symbolically present, I narrate and perform my *struggle of culture;* a struggle of being "Asian Pacific American" in a totalistic "American" society, of being ethnically mixed in a world of categories and purities, and of being a mixed Japanese/Hawaiian/English woman in a patriarchal monoculture. I perform such a struggle as a counterdiscourse that re-presents how I and many other Asian Pacific Americans have been re-presented by popular media culture. I have and continue to live in a conflict between a "common American culture" that was produced and passed on to me (and the rest of society) and an "Asian Pacific culture" that I continually redefine and refashion for myself, according to my own experiences, needs, and circumstances.

This *struggle of culture* symbolizes the notion that culture is indeed *political;* that is, culture is the contested discursive terrain of meaning among various groups that occupy differently situated power positions (Fiske, 1987, 1992; Hall, 1980). Thus, culture is intimately linked with power; we are immersed in a struggle to define and attain "culture" and "identity" (as well as other social practices and meanings). Here, on such terrain, a dominant group (or the powerholders) (e.g., leading politicians, business executives, military/legal/law enforcement command, self-proclaimed "intellectuals") with a particular ideology or system of beliefs and thoughts holds the power to determine what "culture" is for society and what ends this "culture" will serve (Hall, 1980). As a result, the dominant few channel their power interests into the "culture industry" and manufacture, package, process, and reproduce a uniform, homogenized product known as "Culture" in television, film, music, and fashion (Fiske, 1987, 1992; Gitlin, 1994; Hall, 1980). Captured in many narrative forms, the Culture product resonates only of an American nation, a modern nation of a unified people with a shared, dignified history, a timeless past, and a promising future (Bhabha, 1990). This one culture carries seemingly guaranteed tenets such as freedom, individualism, mobility, success, and wealth to the subordinated "masses." Such politicized culture reigns supreme until a *struggle* occurs. The struggle surfaces when individuals and groups who have internalized their "common national culture" realize that their lived experiences are wholly incompatible with those embodied in the Culture. In turn, after numerous failed attempts to account for such inconsistencies, they resist the political culture they have consumed and reconstruct their identities, ideologies, and their "cultures." Thus, social groups and individuals fight for the right to define their own behavior, values, beliefs, experiences, identities, and voices in what I term the *struggle of culture,* or the clash between a Culture produced for us and a culture we continually redefine for ourselves.

In this paper, I argue and *perform* that culture moves beyond concrete artifacts with an *exotic, ethnic* flavor (e.g., tools, jewelry) and more than shared meaning-making activities among groups. Instead, culture encompasses the discursive meanings and practices that are assigned to objects and experiences. But the questions Who gets to do the assigning? and Why? become paramount. The answers to these questions vary among different groups and individuals, thereby spurring on a continual struggle of culture. Specifically, culture signifies a political discursive struggle between (1) dominant groups who reproduce their ideologies by generating and circulating

meanings-as-culture via media (e.g., television, film, music), which ultimately serves to establish and maintain their power positions, and (2) socially oppressed groups and individuals who reshape "culture" in terms of their oppositional experiences and identities and what they bring to the "screens," or the media.

In this essay, I interchangeably *discuss* and *enact* how culture, ideology, and narrative all relate to a political struggle for meaning. "Culture" symbolizes a battleground for groups with differing ideologies to struggle over the claim to create meaning, which, in turn, shapes and maintains a particular set of power relations. Narratives, or the tellings of experience, both enable and constrain the ideological control of culture. Interspersed throughout the analysis, I narrate how "culture" has been a painful and awakening political struggle throughout my life; how I struggle with being/not being "American" (the political Culture produced for me/us) and re-creating my own oppositional identities. I narrate and perform my struggle with the hopes that uniform, homogenized, American Culture can be both critiqued and contested and that all of us, on our own, can form/inform/re-form who we are, how we are to act and live, and what we are to believe.

The woman's voice can still be heard. She is sitting on a stool, looking directly into the camera and transfixing her eyes through the screen. She glances up.

It is still vivid in my mind; I can actually reach out and grasp the cold, hard edges of my "horror" from that day long ago. I was 7 at the time and very content with my daily television routine in the family room. That day, a friend was over and we had just flipped to an old black-and-white movie from the 1950s. The screen soon filled with images of fighter planes swarming the air; fire guns were blasting, and the film's piercing bullets and bombs echoed in my ears. Then, the pilots appeared before us. They looked different; actually, different from what I see on the other TV channels and yet not so different from my Sunday family dinners and New Year's parties. They had jet black hair, fair skin, and deep-set, slanted, dark brown eyes; they were Asian like me, like my family. Immediately following this frame, the camera scans two other pilots who were yelling in a craze, "The Japs are coming!! The Japs are coming!!" These men, donned in ornate U.S. military uniforms, appeared to be haoles *or Caucasian and wore fearful facial expressions. They ran, grabbing large guns and firing off as much ammunition as they could. On my side, my friend looked at me and asked, "What's a Jap?" "I don't know," I responded, both annoyed and afraid that I did not know how to answer her. She turned away and we continued to watch the rest of the film. On that day, silently entranced by the film, I felt both confused and a bit frightened of the images I had just seen; I feared these "Japs"; but, at the same time, I felt a strange closeness to the "Japs." It didn't seem so strange to me after all. I recognized that word in a comedy show I watched the other night and also from an encounter that had happened to my brother a couple of months ago when he was called a "traitor Jap." Who were those strangely familiar Asian pilot faces pasted to the screen, and why was I both drawn to and uneasy about them?*

A Framework of *Struggle:* Culture, Ideology, and Narrative

Intricately woven together, culture, ideology, narrative, and performance take part in the construction/re-construction of meaning to advance a particular power interest. *Culture* is the larger discursive template that individuals and groups with particular *ideologies* use to chisel out a specific way of living within a society that encompasses all the meanings of that social experience (Fiske, 1992). The chiseling occurs for several reasons: to massively produce a Culture product that sells and ensures dominant power relations, or to contest the popular definitions of Culture and redefine the meanings of social experience. Narrative constitutes the strategic mode through which a social order of meanings-as-culture can be constructed/extended or resisted. With different ideologies (and thus, different ways of being) and narratives, a struggle of "culture" among individuals and groups is inevitable.

In a medium distance shot from the camera, the woman looks straight ahead, and then smiles faintly. She continues to tell her story.

It never really hit me that I was "different" from other people until I was about 8. I remember watching reruns of That Girl *on TV. I, a scrawny kid with buck teeth, reddish hair, and eyes that took up most of my face, wanted to look exactly like Marlo Thomas—the flipped hairdo. I would try to brush my hair down and up in a curl every day just so that I could be like "That Girl." But, of course, the thickness and frizziness of my hair, hair from my Hawaiian heritage, never allowed for the "do." This routine would continue until my mother would yell, "Sista, time for school." Suddenly, I would drop the brush, unlock the door (I would be devastated if anyone found out!), and run to school. At school, everyone knew me as "girl with the really long and yet cool last name." I would smile when kids used to call my older brother, Michael, "H," short for "Halualani." I would just laugh when both teachers and students asked if I could dance hula or if I ate lots of pineapples and coconuts. After all, I was only 8. Life was carefree and fun.*

But it wasn't fun all the time. The woman looks down and up again. The camera slowly moves in to a close-up.

Every day, after school, my Baba *(the Japanese word for grandmother) and* Gigi *(the Japanese word for grandfather) used to pick me up and walk me about seven blocks away to my Japanese school class. For years, I had about 12-hour school days, split between my regular grade school and my Japanese school (a school my parents made me go to!). They'd drop me off, wave goodbye, and I would open up my* Hiragana *(Japanese characters) folder. Our* sensei *(the Japanese word for teacher) would begin class, as I happily sucked on my Astropop candy. But the lessons would always be suddenly interrupted by a bunch of mean kids who attended the school where our Japanese classes were held. They would throw rocks at the window. Racing by on their bikes, they would yell "Go home, you gooks!" or "Thanks for Pearl Harbor." Other times, the kids would throw food in the classroom. One time, a firecracker was thrown right in front of the* sensei; *thankfully, no one got hurt. And the good days were considered to be those when the kids would just stand in the windows and in an exaggerated fashion, slant their eyes at us.* (She shakes her head and sarcastically laughs.) ***That was a good day!!*** *During those days, I could faintly see the Japanese war pilots in the corner of my mind, looking at me. I felt that I knew them so well; that we had a type of kinship for they were produced/reproduced and I was being produced/shaped by dominant Culture, as in the media. Slowly, I began to realize how troubling that kinship was . . .* The lights fade to black. The woman slides off the stool and walks beyond what the camera can reveal.

Culture

The term "culture," as used in the phrase "cultural studies," is neither aesthetic nor humanist in emphasis, but *political.* [emphasis mine] (Fiske, 1992, p. 284)

Culture exceeds beyond surface ideals of form and beauty, the exotic and strange, and high/low civilization. Culture is not necessarily something we can see or reach out to touch. Rather, culture consists of the social meanings and practices and the discursive material (e.g., the discursive forms and practices, such as television, film, music, political discourses) that we use to create our identities, behavior, and worldviews. Such discourse (e.g., the language we use, the symbolic constructs that we invoke such as "progress" and "commitment," the representations and images that we copy) details how we should behave, what to think or believe, and who we are or should be. However, culture is not created in a vacuum; culture is deeply situated within a specific social context with an intact set of histories and power relations. Thus, culture is inexorably tied to the surrounding social, political, and economic structures. Culture, then, does not just immediately

surface; certain individuals, groups, and corporations *work hard* to designate what "culture" is to be and how that "culture" is to be used. Herein lies the struggle: Who ultimately has the power/privilege/right to define and reproduce "culture"? Who benefits from the creation of "culture"? Depending on the sociopolitical position that an individual or group occupies and the ideology that is espoused in such a position, the answers here will vary. Clearly, images of the serene lifestyle in the Disney movies and *That Girl* that I watched over and over again severely diverged from my everyday experience as a perceived "Jap" foreigner, thereby demonstrating a struggle between two images—one projected on a screen, the other enacted in everyday experience. Still a child, I did not understand the ongoing political struggle of Culture; it was just beginning to unfold before my eyes.

With a sudden flash of light, the woman dressed in black appears yet again. Her face is more somber than before. The camera is positioned on her right side as she speaks to the left side of the screen.

As I grew up, I found out that I (and my family) would be treated differently. It never really hit me until I saw the pain on my family's faces. Their pain became mine and mine became theirs. It was so different and conflicting with what I would see on those television family shows or Disney movies, in which the problem surfaced around a boy attracting a girl, a child getting into mischief with friends, or sibling rivalry. Those televisual experiences seemed so distant from mine; the nature of those televisual families revolved around communal harmony, financial security, and strong American values like independence, hard work, and equality.

The televisual family experience diverged from mine. For example, there was no financial security or communal harmony (social ease). One time when my mother and father came home, Mom was in a rage, crying and screaming at my father. I was only 12 at the time. (The woman looks directly into the camera. She pauses.) *I knew something was terribly wrong. Mom and Dad just came back from looking at a new house that we wanted to buy. With my two brothers and I, things were getting hectic in our old house. But what happened was, that last week, my father went to check out the place by himself. Mom was working at the hospital. Then, today, both my parents went to see the place. My father is Hawaiian English, but he passes for and looks just like his father: an Englishman . . . a haole (local pidgin for "Caucasian"/Hawaiian for "foreigner"). So, the real estate agent warmed up to Dad, but today, when he showed up with my mom, a very Japanese-looking woman with jet black hair, dark eyes, and ivory skin, the agent immediately hemmed and hawed. He said the house had been promised to someone else. Apparently, this wasn't the first time we had problems buying a house. We always encountered problems when we ate at restaurants or when we attended new schools.* (The woman is nervously shaken. Her eyes swell up with tears.) *The racism took its toll on my parents. They grew tougher. But, during those early years, I would hear my parents fighting and I would cry and cry, wondering why the world was so cruel.* Her head bobs down. She waves her hands down, motioning the director to fade the lights. The woman quickly jumps from her seat and exits. You can see the outlines of her hands wiping the tears from her face.

Ideology

Operating primarily within the discursive terrain of culture is ideology. Ideology is the sweeping hidden thread that *weaves* Culture, determining both its content and political end.

Ideology indeed shapes our lives (Thompson, 1990). When we engage in everyday interaction, we express our beliefs and views through the discussion of certain topics, through the words we use, and through the way we "choose" to present ourselves. To some degree, we locally inflect these "beliefs" and "views" to smoothly resonate with our experiences and identities (so that we may, in turn, believe that we invented and now own these systems of thought), but these "beliefs" and "views" are not products of our own creation. This is exactly the locus of the power of ideology. "Our" "beliefs" and "views" actually develop from larger (hidden) symbolic discourses, such as media culture, seeped in ideology and power; discourses that easily and cunningly create and re-produce gender relations, economic positions, racial hierarchies, and "appropriate" social issue stances (e.g., "equality" liberalism, political correctness, "agency," and "full participation"). But in social life, ideology and politics move in slippery, complex, and concealed ways. They are created and move both in larger societal structures—familiar social terrains such as the workplace, university, town meeting, and the home—and within our own "selfhoods" as we internalize already provided frameworks (e.g., as guided by language, religion, tradition) for looking at and interacting with the world—all without public realization/acknowledgment of its glaring, unnatural, contrived, and manufactured/packaging/refocusing/repackaging operation.

Ideology and politics are intertwined. The relationship between ideology and politics is not a simple, causal one. Instead, the ideological and the political both shape and reinforce one another. One way of conceptualizing ideology is as a system of beliefs or thoughts about personal experience, social action, and political practice, which works to create and maintain a specific set of power relations. More specifically, Thompson (1990) defines ideology as the continual process by which "meaning serves to establish and sustain relations of power that are systematically asymmetrical—relations of domination" (p. 7). Thus, ideology is "meaning in service of power," thereby allowing for the dominant creation of Culture (p. 7). Here dominant powerholders/forces (e.g., politicians, business "leaders," "intellectuals") occupy the strategically *in/visible* space to massively produce a "common and national culture" via the media, which permeates regional, socioeconomic, and political boundaries. Such a version abstracts and homogenizes vested meanings into a uniform/readily available/desirable Culture for the entire populace. *Culture as product* provides "the symbols, myths, and resources through which we constitute a common culture and through the appropriation of which we insert ourselves into this culture" (Kellner, 1995, p. 5). In this way, dominant norms, values, and practices are infused into a larger discourse (such as media) that guarantees communal unity and a sense of belonging and ownership, and promises financial prosperity. Many of us become attracted to the tenets of such a Culture, and we become loyal followers of an empty discourse. The ensuing widespread "faith" ultimately allows for dominant groups, or the "Culture producers" to establish and sustain asymmetrical power relations. Hence, Culture becomes a type of "common sense" or "regime of truth" that works to "speak, classify, name, and establish the dominant and relevant categories of knowledge" (Illouz, 1991, p. 233; see, e.g., Peck, 1994).

For example, in the Anglo Germanic capitalistic, patriarchal monoculture known as America, a national culture of Americanness has and continues to be reproduced with relative ease. Followers intake daily doses of talk of individualism, equality, freedom, agency, participation, and the American Dream, especially from the media, and believe that being "American" brings forth success and harmony. As a result, only the economic structures and the political incumbents that we support gain from our cultural consumption. Simply put, those housed within the status quo structure generate and circulate a Culture that will continually feed that very structure.

Thus, the "American (national) Culture" is dangerous in that it derives from a power-vested ideology that remains concealed and thus seals its immediate acceptance by people who, in turn, feel that they both *invented* and now *own* the Culture. Any change to the (or, our) Culture is deemed threatening, thereby safeguarding the dominant system.

A small light widens, making room for the woman in black to reappear. Her hair is brushed back. As her eyes meet the camera, she immediately looks down to the floor. Then, she speaks.

> *People always told me that I was too naive and trusting of people. I used to be that way. And it is because I have so much faith in others and in society in general. Or at least I did. It finally hit me late in college that I was not considered to be a part of American society or culture. I remember serving as a teaching assistant in many of my college courses in communication. You wouldn't believe the types of comments people would make to me.* (The light shines on the woman's face. She stands up and tilts her head. In a high-pitched voice, she resumes speaking.) *"I am so surprised you are doing so well as a communication major; I MEAN YOU SPEAK SO WELL!! With no accent."* (The light fades out to shadowed segments on the woman's face. She is sitting back on her stool.) *I couldn't believe people, I mean more than one, several actually, used to say things like that to me. My physical appearance provided others with immediate information about who I was and who I was not allowed to be. Someone else would say . . .* (The spotlight reappears.) *"It figures you're a TA, all Asians are the superbrains."* (The lights dim again.) *I never got used to these comments. In fact, every time I encountered someone who was immediately convinced that I dance hula because of my Hawaiian last name, or that I am "so different" in that I am very "assertive and confrontational" for an Asian woman, I became so angry. I couldn't believe what I was hearing. Where did I belong? Who could I identify with and talk about the way I see the world and all the different ways I see life? Everyone kept reminding me of and beating me over the head with how I did not belong and how "different" I was.* Then, she jumps from the stool and slowly walks away, leaving only shadowed lights in the corner. The lights create a reflection that is a web of orangish-grey hues.

The Ideological Struggle of Culture

But the political Culture that is created for us via media discourses is responsible for its own "undoing." In an American Culture that is supposed to be either equally benevolent toward all its "members" or socially neutral, many groups and individuals who are subjected underneath dominant forces experience and realize the incompatibilities of the Culture to which they have devoted their energies. For instance, immigrant families who travel from afar to chase the American Dream (a tenet of their new Culture—as exploited throughout literature, television shows, and films) confront possible deportation as a result of increasing xenophobic sentiment, anti-immigration campaigns devised by political candidates, and an entrenched color-caste system of inequalities. Or there is a fourth-generation Japanese American woman who is still referred to as an "Oriental Butterfly" and encounters vicious hate crimes such as car passengers yelling "Gook" and throwing rocks while she is walking to work. In these two cases, the individuals are not living the glory, hope, and success that are naturalized as immediate "truths" within American culture and, specifically, within American media/popular Culture. In fact, the physical essences (e.g., appearance, language acquisition, speech/accent) that are used to discriminate against these immigrants and this Japanese American woman are *safeguards* built into the American Culture that is consumed. As such, these safeguards protect and secure a purely Anglo Germanic capitalistic system undergirded by racialized and genderized inequalities. Thus, with such glaring disparities in the Culture, *ideological cracks* in the dominant system of meanings are revealed. At this point, a struggle is ignited.

Just as ideology operates to establish and sustain power relations, ideology (especially one that works against the status quo, larger sphere of control) can also contest and transform deeply entrenched views and create "alternative" and "resistive" modes of thought through social actions, interactions, and engagement with symbolic forms such as everyday language, sociopolitical discourses (e.g., "information," legislative issues, voting propositions), and media texts (e.g., media culture, music, television, film, fanship cultures). Community members, who see the Culture as a mere image, act and define themselves *against the grain* of the dominant system, thereby forging oppositional identities. Subsequently, this energy of resistance is used to protest against the political Culture that they have long held to be true. Subordinated individuals and groups contest the mass cultural product in several ways; they expose the Culture as pure myth that serves only a few, and/or they reconstruct, for themselves, the dis-

cursive meanings of their lived experiences and identities. Thus, new discourses and constructs of meaning are created by those with different social experiences and ways of thinking about/seeing/living the world. Dominantly produced Culture, therefore, can be redefined and reenacted by different ideological interests.[1]

The woman is still sitting on the stool. She motions the camera to move in on a close-up of her. Dissatisfied, she leaves the frame and repositions the camera herself. Popping back onto the stool, she tilts her head.

I would feel the tensions in so many of my interactions with people. "Oh, you're Hawaiian!! I've been to Hawaii. You know, on Hawaii Five-O *or in* South Pacific." *I would always correct them. "No, you don't know Hawai'i or what it means to be Hawaiian. You just know how Hawaii has been re-presented." The other person usually seems confused, smiles, and walks away. I am faced with that quite a bit. People feeling they know a culture through the* mirror *of television or film. Because the media are reflections of reality, right? Right? NO!! Mediated images are created for us, and we, lazy in our critical consciousness, accept and consume whatever is provided on the "shelf." So, when shows such as* The Byrds of Paradise, 2000 West Waikiki, *and* Magnum P.I. *come on the air, I feel the struggle of an image of Hawai'i as merely a paradise, a piece of land that can be colonized by others (via American televisual imperialism) against the restored image of Hawai'i as rich in cultural heritages, rich in a history marked by colonialist ventures and Hawaiian land dis/possession, and rich in social/political resistance by Hawaiians. I feel the struggle when I watch television and when I encounter others who have viewed dominant mediated discourses. The struggle moves from the screen to our minds to our personal interactions.*

I couldn't cope very well when situations like these occurred. So, I would tell my friends and acquaintances about the other images and meanings that they don't see on the screen—I gave them different accounts of what surrounds the "land" of Hawai'i: the people, beliefs, histories, and the struggles. I took them with me on my journey through the "screen"; on my journey to critically interrogate American Culture and cultural representations of others.

Narrative

Typically, when discussing "culture," we understand narratives as stories that symbolically capture the richness of different groups and voices. For example, from a social constructionist stance, González, Houston, and Chen (1994) stress that "the telling of experience constructs and informs about a culture and its participants" (p. xiv). However, it is this very assumption—that all stories directly "reflect" cultures—that resembles a type of ideological common sense. If all narratives are presumed to be the looking glasses of culture, then stories are akin to "truths," to experiential fact, and to a type of science of culture. Understood in this way, narratives become an ideological means to establish foundational knowledge as Culture.

As a form of ideology, narrative signifies a strategic process to establish/fix social control and disproportionate power relations. Stories and storytelling constitute discursive practices that *function* to construct the social reality and lived world of social actors (Langellier & Peterson, 1993; Mumby, 1993). The word "function" is key here; much energy is expended to devise "reality" for a group of people via narrativization. Thompson (1990) explains that such narrativization consists of "claims [that] are embedded in stories which recount the past and treat the present as part of a timeless and cherished tradition" (p. 61). So, the narrative strategy of tradition, for example, portrays social relations as unified within a community and shared history, so as to control such relations and keep them intact underneath the guises of group membership, "consensus," and the old adages "That's the way things have been done for years" and "That's the way things are."

With this in mind, narratives are not just mere re-presentations of "truth" or "reality." Narratives are strategic tools to construct the "social" and the "cultural" as seamless continuities. For instance, when narratives have been presented in certain contexts (e.g., organizations, private situations, classrooms), we often inquire about whether or not a story is real/true/nonfictional. This type of query captures yet again the ideological nature of narratives themselves; already-provided dichotomies of truth/nontruth, realness/falsity, and fiction/nonfiction disguise the extent to which these categories are determined by only a select few, thereby reinforcing dominant power relations behind the notions of "fact, truth, and nonfiction." Narrative forms that grate against dominant assumptions can easily be extinguished by labeling them as mere "fiction/fabrication." So, constructs that polarize narratives as being *real* or *not real* encourage both a lazy type of critical consciousness and a willing subordination in that individuals are urged to compare a story/experience with what occurs in the real context, thereby evading any issues of the hidden workings of power and ideology. Many times, our enveloping sociopolitical context is so laden with hidden ideologies and secured power interests that a narrative text/context dialectic actually becomes a magnification of dominant ideologies, thereby blinding a "critical eye." (Yes, the context is a larger ideological text with its own social codes, which problematizes comparing representations back to a context that is politically loaded in and of itself.) Thus, the important questions do not deal with the content of the narrative, but rather *where* and *why* a particular content is brought forth (e.g., Whose interest does a narrative serve? Who are we allowed to be and not to be?)

So, with this reconceptualization, narratives do more than just retell experiences; they are constructed by and construct their surrounding sociopolitical contexts. More specifically, stories emerge from a particular political structure in which groups are divided and located differently. According to Mumby (1987), "storytelling is not a simple representing of a pre-existing reality, but is rather a politically motivated production of a certain way of perceiving the world which privileges certain interests over others" (p. 114). Narratives, then, cannot be separated from larger discursive fields of power, social institutions, and subject-ivity (i.e., Who are constructed as the subjects and who are those-to-be-subjected?). And because of the interrelatedness of politics, a divided context, and narrative, there is an unequal distribution of storytelling rights among social groups. Dominant groups, for example, shape narratives that legitimate dominant forms of "reality" and discursively close the possibilities of identity and experience. Specifically, Langellier and Peterson (1993) argue that family storytelling practices oftentimes generate and reproduce specific meanings and relations of control such as "parents over children, males over females, and the white, middle-class family over alternative family structures" (p. 50).

Likewise, dominant groups create narratives of Culture, which privilege one version of meanings-as-experience and one that is (not surprisingly) aligned with prevailing practices and structures. One specific type of ideological narration in the dominant creation of Culture is that of the "modernist nation." As discussed by Homi Bhabha (1990), "nation as narration" is an ideological device used to establish and solidify unequal power relations among groups. Nation as narration is a system of representation that produces/manufactures a mythical Culture, which is characterized by one people and one time.

A narration of nation constructs the multifaceted character of individuals/groups as *one homogeneous, a priori people,* meaning that individuals are completely and totally unified within National Culture. The people of a nation, therefore, possess one uniform cultural identity. This National Culture is also characterized by a particular construction of time—*national time.* National time is a pure, mythical dimension of time and history as continuous, unified, and monumentalistic and completely without gaps or conflicts. The past is deemed as streamlined in terms of an accumulating (and harmonious) National character and pride, without social conquest, revolution, or disillusionment. Multiple identities and experiences are therefore purposively omitted, for they would threaten the construction of an "imagined community" (Gilroy, 1987). In the National Culture's imagined community, individuals come to identify with and adopt the political definition of "how they should be."

In terms of the sociopolitical context in the United States, a National Culture known as Americanness is generated. Within narratives of Americanness, the people are the "Americans" who value and live the notions of equality, liberty, democracy, and freedom. These "Americans" are bound together by the regional boundaries of the United States of America; they call themselves and one another "Americans"; they embrace consumerism, individualism, competition, and a hard-work ethic. Politicians refer to the masses as "fellow Americans." In the educational system, children are socialized to accept specific American tenets of the people: patriotic loyalty, citizenship, pride, and freedom. Specific events commemorating American independence and democratic participation are upheld. Thus, American Culture centers a unified and unwavering generic national character.

In terms of time, we know history to be "American history," or one that chronicles the pursuit of justice and independence by our founding fathers. Of course, the many ruptures within so-called American history, such as the colonialist ventures, civil wars/skirmishes, the burgeoning capitalist American patriarchy, and the increasing biological and institutional racism, are overlooked for the grandiose American victories against those who are beyond our national boundaries—England, France, Italy, Germany, Japan, China, and Korea. As a result, our sense of the past is distilled through dominant forces who work hard to create an undivided past that has progressed toward "continual freedom/justice."

Within the American space, Americans are "disciplined" to speak only of experiences and voices glorifying American freedom and the American Dream. "Discipline" results from controlling discursive practices (e.g., immigrant-chasing/attaining American fortune-stereotypes and mediated representations) that create a mythical reality of unbounded success, wealth, freedom, and opportunity for Americans. These freedom and success stories extend National Culture by reinforcing the supposed openness and workability of American social institutions for all, regardless of gender, ethnic background, occupation, regional origin, sexual identity, and age.

And this construction of Americanness carries built-in defense mechanisms against muted cries of social tyranny and oppression. With attacks on American Culture, national pride, character, and history are called forth to challenge the loyalty and devotion of a cultural member—that is, to speak out against America as a militaristic, religious, economic, and academic colonizer of other countries (e.g., Philippines, Mexico, Korea, Thailand, Vietnam) is to decry the ideals of democratic freedom/aid. To speak out against the huge xenophobic sentiment in the United States is to denounce the value of American citizenship. Furthermore, when a person charges that the American Dream is a hegemonic myth, she or he is deemed an embittered incompetent individual who is unwilling to work hard to attain the Dream. Therefore, through a narrative of an imagined, monolithic community in a continuous stream of time and plentiful space, specific dominant structures such as the global capitalistic economy and the partnership among State, Media, and Law are bolstered. National objects of knowledge, such as "Tradition," "People," "Culture," and "the State" are produced and, in turn, work for the willing (and manipulated) subordination of citizens (and noncitizens).

But, narrative-as-ideology can surely move beyond dominant power ploys; narrative is a shifting terrain of meaning that can destabilize, critique, and transform foundational knowledge and Culture as well. Here Bhabha (1990) offers us hope by arguing that a narration of National Culture is vulnerable to lived contingencies and shifting identities. The discourse of Nation re-presents the people as an image *and* as an *incomplete signification*. The margins holding up the National image reveal the in-between spaces of diverse identities, experiences, and meanings. Ultimately, individuals in the margins break free of the ruse known as National Culture and struggle to re-create their own cultures, or systems of meaning/discursive practices. This is not to say, then, that contestatory narratives are exempt from efforts of social control. (In fact, personal narratives now constitute a dominant co-optation strategy in which the individual/personal experience of equality and success is highlighted over broader social oppression. For instance, a person may reason that there is no racism because her or his past encounters did not "touch" upon any prejudices.) Every narrative derives from a specific political interest, and as such, each story/storytelling event needs

to be critically interrogated. Most especially, we need to critically explore how narratives help shape the struggle between National Culture and alternative cultural systems. In such a struggle, the dominant narratives of Nation *confront and grate* against margin-centered narratives from diverse voices. Hence, narratives both enable and constrain the ideological reproduction of Culture.

She reappears. This time, she is more at peace with her story. She turns to the camera.

> *I remember feeling powerless when I was a youth leader for an Asian community group. The kids were in high school and we were talking about identity and how it continually changes, as informed by our experiences and passions. So many of them shocked me. They kept telling me, "No, Rona. We are always going to be AMERICANS." And I asked them what it meant to be "American." They told me it meant being in a society that values freedom, equality, and opportunity for all. That the American Dream is possible and if people do not reach it, it is because they are not competent or are not skillful enough. Their persistence, their complete, unwavering belief in America shocked me. They believed Affirmative Action was unfair, especially to us Asians, who truly work hard and deserve to get a "piece of the pie." They poured their entire souls into this thing called Americanness. And I did not have the heart nor the soul to tell them that their beloved American society grants such freedom, equality, and opportunity to only a few on top, on top of everybody else. That under certain guaranteed freedoms, there always lie violent contradictions within the notions of "freedom" and "democracy."*

Culture, ideology, and narrative represent a chain of politically infused meanings that provokes a passionate struggle of culture. Culture is the contested territory of discursive meanings, raising questions such as Who defines "culture"? Of what does culture consist? and What will culture do? Using ideological tools such as narrative forms, different voices who live through particular ideologies provide conflicting answers and therefore clash and grind against one another. The struggle is intense and in a desperate attempt to adjust/direct the conflict, the groups involved reposition themselves differently. In my case, dominant forces such as the media and popular culture churn out their narratives of National Culture at an even faster rate and subsequently decry the loyalty and membership of my oppositional voice. On the other side, through my self-invented narratives/performances, I have fashioned a temporary counter-Culture voice that draws attention to my uniquely shifting identity, in the hope of stripping mass political Culture down to its mythical origin.

She appears one last time. She stands directly in front of the camera and smiles. Her name is Rona.

> I decided long ago to move through the screen—to create discussions about the struggle between Culture and self-inventions of culture-as-meaning. I would write, read, and critically interrogate all of the discourses before me. Especially the mediated/popular Culture discourses through which so many of us seem to identify or find pleasure. So that one day, we could revel in different types of structural relations, share different types of experiences/identities, and have dialogues about the complexities of meaning and culture.

Thus, throughout this discussion, I have performatively narrated my ongoing struggle of "culture"; my struggle that has involved how I first invoked the National American Culture that was fed to me via televisual/filmic discourse; how I then took note of the disparities in political American Culture from my own experiences that I brought to the screen; how I agonized over the entrenched struggle between an Americanness that was sold/provided to me and my own oppositional identities/experiences as an Asian Pacific American woman in the social world/in the academy; and how I began to break from Culture to re-make my own "culture," or meanings, that related to my moving experiences and insights. My family's ex-

periences and my encounters led me through a maze of anger and then transformation as I embark on a mission to re-locate cultures and meanings beyond provided and stagnant boundaries.

My counternarrative in this essay is one that somewhat resists/constrains dominant televisual/filmic narratives for I intervene in and re-occupy the space of the "screen" to tell my story, my experience, and my struggle in my own way. I re-position the camera. I choose the lighting, camera angles, and images. I decide when my name will be revealed. Although I change what is on a symbolic "screen," I encourage us to move and see through the screen; that is, to go beyond what is provided on the mere surface of discourse and critically engage with images/representations, looking for threads of struggle, clashing meanings, and mythical notions. In this way, our "seeing" through the screen ignites our passion(s) to interrogate the discourses that are provided to us via the media and to break/re-make the meanings of Culture, our National Identity, and what we think we believe. Indeed, there is hope for all of us; journey with me *through the screen* so that we may all continually shape a multitude of cultures.

REFERENCES

Bhabha, H. K. (1990). DissemiNation: Time, narrative, and the margins of the modern nation. In H. K. Bhabha (Ed.), *Nation and narration* (pp. 291–322). London: Routledge.

Fiske, J. (1987). *Television culture.* London: Routledge.

Fiske, J. (1992). British cultural studies and television. In R. C. Allen (Ed.), *Channels of discourse, reassembled* (pp. 284–326). Chapel Hill: University of North Carolina Press.

Gilroy, P. (1987). *There ain't no Black in the Union Jack.* London: Hutchinson.

Gitlin, T. (1994). Prime time ideology: The hegemonic process in television entertainment. In H. Newcomb (Ed.), *Television: The critical view* (pp. 516–536). New York: Oxford University Press.

González, A., Houston, M., & Chen, V. (1994). Introduction. In A. González, M. Houston, & V. Chen (Eds.), *Our voices: Essays in culture, ethnicity, and communication* (pp. xii–xxi). Los Angeles: Roxbury Publishing.

Hall, S. (1980). Encoding/decoding. In S. Hall, D. Hobson, A. Lowe, & P. Willis (Eds.), *Culture, media, language* (pp. 128–139). London: Hutchinson.

Hall, S. (1993). Culture, community, nation. *Cultural Studies, 7,* 349–363.

Illouz, E. (1991). Reason within passion: Love in women's magazines. *Critical Studies in Mass Communication, 8,* 231–248.

Kellner, D. (1995). Cultural studies, multiculturalism and media culture. In G. Dines & J. M. Humez (Eds.), *Gender, race and class in media* (pp. 5–17). Thousand Oaks, CA: Sage.

Langellier, K. M., & Peterson, E. E. (1993). Family storytelling as a strategy of social control. In D. Mumby (Ed.), *Narrative and social control: Critical perspectives* (pp. 49–76). Newbury Park, CA: Sage.

Mumby, D. (1987). The political function of narrative in organizations. *Communication Monographs, 54,* 113–127.

Mumby, D. (Ed.). (1993). *Narrative and social control: Critical perspectives.* Newbury Park, CA: Sage.

Peck, J. (1994). Talk about racism: Framing a popular discourse of race on Oprah Winfrey. *Cultural Critique, 5,* 89–126.

Thompson, J. B. (1990). *Ideology and modern culture.* Stanford, CA: Stanford University Press.

KEY TERMS

Culture   ideology
culture   nation
struggle of culture

DISCUSSION QUESTIONS

1. What does the author mean by "the struggle of culture"? Discuss in terms of defining culture in this intercultural communication course.

2. How does the media and popular society define "culture," "diversity," "race," and your own cultural or ethnic group? To what extent do you agree or disagree with these definitions? Whose definition carries more weight in society: yours or the media's? Why do you think this is the case?

3. Describe how the notions of culture, ideology, and struggle are implicitly illustrated in the author's scattered mini-narratives. How are these enacted?

4. Think of your own experiences with popular culture. How have representations of your culture and others' cultures influenced how you see yourself and others? Share with a partner.

5. What modes of resistance to degrading images of cultural groups exist within struggles of culture?

29

"SPACE TRADERS," MEDIA CRITICISM, AND THE INTERPOSITIONAL STRATEGY

DWIGHT E. BROOKS

Professor Gleason Golightly (Robert Guillaume) fights racial backlash in *Space Traders* (Hudlin & Hudlin, 1994), the lead segment in the Home Box Office (HBO) video anthology titled *Cosmic Slop*. Golightly, a high-ranking African American ad-

viser to the Republican U.S. president, confronts a dual form of backlash: a White backlash against African American "progress" and the perception that African Americans are subverting American peace and prosperity, and a Black backlash against

African Americans like Golightly who apparently have "sold out." As Golightly sets forth to fight this backlash, he proclaims, "Black people have been calling me an oreo ever since I was twelve; after tomorrow, they'll call me a hero."

As it is used here, backlash represents the process whereby individuals, cultural groups, or political organizations or all three institute repercussions against those who hold oppositional views or propose oppositional strategies for social change.[1] Backlash is one barrier to effective intercultural communication. Golightly's response to this type of backlash in *Space Traders* helps illustrate a communicative strategy that can be useful in fostering intercultural performances. Further, *Space Traders* provides a valuable text that can be used to address some of the racial tensions in our society.

The primary purpose of this chapter is to demonstrate the importance of media culture to our socially constructed identities by offering a textual analysis of *Space Traders* that both challenges common racial assumptions and illustrates the communicative strategy of interpositionality—the ability to construct dynamic cultural identities. After introducing you to the notion of media culture and to the critical approach known as oppositional African American cultural criticism, the essay analyzes the *Space Traders* text and outlines the interpositional strategy. After reading this essay, you should not only have an appreciation for the role of media criticism in your everyday life, but also be able to employ communicative strategies that enhance your intercultural communication.

We live in a media culture whereby mediated images and media texts and events help constitute the substance of our everyday lives. Beyond its role in our leisure time, our media culture is prominent in shaping our values, views, social behavior, and, most important, in the construction of our personal identities. According to Kellner (1995), media culture

> provides the materials out of which many people construct their sense of class, of ethnicity and race, of nationality, of sexuality, of "us" and "them." Media culture helps shape the prevalent view of the world and deepest values; it defines

what is considered good or bad, positive or negative, moral or evil. . . . Media culture provides the materials to create identities. . . . (p. 1)

Thus, our media culture provides resources that allow us to consider cultural identities by offering mediated texts that can be interpreted in ways that reveal how the construction of dynamic identities can facilitate effective intercultural communication.

This analysis of *Space Traders* utilizes Dyson's (1993) oppositional African American cultural criticism as an approach to media criticism. This is especially useful for analyzing *Space Traders* because it is based on three important principles: (1) That it be antiessentialist about Black racial and cultural identity; (2) while also acknowledging a wide range of American experiences (e.g., class and gender) that "influence its makeup, shape its expression, and challenge its existence" (p. xxi). In addition to keeping track of the effects of racism, an oppositional criticism describes how class and gender affect African American culture and develops strategies to underscore their importance as categories of social theory, criticism, and struggle. (3) Oppositional African American cultural criticism is public and receptive to critical insights from *all* quarters.

Most important to this analysis is the ability to resist essentialist representations. The notion of essentialism holds that cultures or races are composed of permanent, history-transcending characteristics. Appeals to racial or cultural essences must be replaced with expressions of the historical, social, and economic forces that produce and shape the social construction of race. In recognizing the diversity of influences on our experiences, we become more critical consumers of our media culture and free ourselves to explore various subject positions. In so doing, we engage in a politics of criticism that challenges those cultural assumptions that thwart intercultural understanding.

Although this essay uses an African American cultural approach to analyze *Space Traders*, any one of a number of other critical approaches, such as semiotic, feminist, ideological, and generic, could be employed. Of course, each approach is likely to produce an alternative set of interpretations. However, for most critics of media culture, the key is to understand how texts produce meaning and how various readers understand texts. What is most important to understand is that a media text such as *Space Traders* offers a multiplicity of meanings, or polysemy, and can be interpreted from a number of perspectives. Although *Space Traders* is explicit in encouraging you to think critically about your own cultural identities, a plethora of other media texts can be used in similar ways.

Space Traders

Space Traders was the first segment in the 1994 HBO trilogy *Cosmic Slop* and is part of HBO's Home Video series.[2] *Cosmic Slop* offers a unique televisual social commentary by incorporating comedy, serious drama, suspense, satire, and fantasy science fiction into its examination of class, religion, gender issues, and in the case of *Space Traders*, race. The 40-minute video of *Space Traders* is based on a short story by scholar Derrick Bell (1992), who sought to challenge the thinking of his law students and facilitate classroom discussion. *Space Traders* offers an engaging perspective on the United States' continuing struggle with race. The text's treatment of race builds from the premise that throughout American history, Blacks were sacrificed when it served the nation's interests. Bell's story is based on the assumption that racism is a permanent component of American life and emphasizes the urgency to move beyond the belief that time and the altruism of Americans will solve the country's racial problems. Although *Space Traders* makes intercultural communication problematic, as the following analysis reveals, it also provides opportunities to use the tensions in resourceful and positive ways.

Although *Space Traders* depicts the United States of America in the year 2000, much like our contemporary condition, the nation is burdened economically with a deficit, faces energy problems, suffers from severe environmental hazards, and of course continues to struggle with the issue of race. However, *all* of these social ills can be solved if the country surrenders its African Americans to the space traders. The American government is given 5 days to decide whether or not it will accept the space traders' offer. However, what happens on the fifth day is far less important than what is revealed about the country and Americans of all persuasions over the course of the 5 days. As the American government leaves the final decision to its citizens through a national telephone referendum, the text is organized around the responses to the trade offer from the country's government, its commercial culture industries, and its citizens—particularly its African Americans. As Black people mount traditional strategies of resistance in the form of rallies, sit-ins, and boycotts, American industry wages a massive campaign—largely through the media— to shape the consciousness of Americans.

In the *Space Traders* narrative, political, economic, and cultural themes converge to illustrate the belief that the core of this nation's problems are related to the presence of African Americans. First, the text reveals the tensions between political spin control and sound social policy, whereby spin control prevails. Instead of responding directly to the space traders' offer, the administration fails to consider the impact of the trade on its Black citizens and decides to leave the decision to the "will of the people." *Space Traders* exposes the government's support for the trade and highlights its attempt to shape the outcome. Conversely, Black people's efforts to block the trade consist of traditional political strategies that ultimately prove unsuccessful in defeating the referendum. Second, *Space Traders* addresses some of the economic dynamics of American capitalism and its ties to consumer culture and race. In this case, the video locates the social worth of African Americans to their commodification in the realms of entertainment and sports. Third, *Space Traders* explores race from an oppositional African American perspective that probes Black cultural and political experience. All in all, *Space Traders* explores the irresolute situation of Blacks in American society and discloses the limited political options at their disposal.[3]

Space Traders unmasks dominant racial assumptions in a scene that depicts a presidential cabinet meeting. Blacks are deemed expendable as soon as the president's chief of staff legitimates the space traders' offer by affirming the historical significance of bringing an end to poverty and pollution and providing cheap unlimited energy for every (remaining) American. The administration's support for the trade is revealed by the chief of staff's role as the president's "point" man on securing support for the referendum. The administration never gives serious consideration to the trade's impact on African Americans.

The sole woman in the meeting labels the propositions as "crazy," yet proceeds to note how welfare rolls would be cut 40% and that food stamps, Medicaid, and drug abuse programs would be "slashed." After one cabinet member asks the group to consider the possible downside to the offer, she argues that the guilt White people would feel for sending Blacks away would take a psychological toll that would substantially increase medical care costs. Her tacit support for the trade is revealed when she asks someone if he thinks the aliens will treat Black people any worse than "we" have. As a group, then, African Americans are of less consequence than Whites; as individuals, African Americans can rise above racial injustices, since structural forces are no longer relevant. Professor Golightly personifies the individual African American who has overcome racial injustice.

The sole African American participant in the meeting is the aforementioned Professor Golightly. When asked to offer his position, he offers a passionate argument against the trade: It cannot be passed off euphemistically as selective service because at its best, it is group banishment; at its worst, it is utter and complete extermination. Despite Golightly's position, the president, through his chief of staff, solicits Golightly's support for the referendum. Golightly is told that if the trade goes through, he can draw up a list of 100 Black families to be "smuggled" to England. Again, individual exemptions to group realities attempt to erase any serious consideration of powerful structural forces.

Space Traders' treatment of race via the discourse in the cabinet meeting reveals both elements of the dominant American racial ideology (and the limits to that ideology) and aspects of the contemporary debate over social policies such as welfare and affirmative action. This ideology, shared by many Whites and Blacks, is rooted in support of basic American values concerning in-

dividual initiative. Specifically, it holds that it is the moral fabric of individuals and not the social and economic structure of society that is at the core of most social problems. Despite his position against the trade, Golightly's discourse embraces themes consistent with this belief system that emphasizes the negative aspects of poverty and joblessness and welfare by focusing on individualistic and moral themes. Golightly's belief in the necessity of Black people functioning without the "crutches" of government represents how individualistic explanations for poverty are privileged over structural ones (lack of jobs, low wages, etc.): "I . . . still believe that Black people need to learn how to stand on their own two feet without the crutches of governmental legislation."

The administration's discourse on the trade offer is structured by its understanding of African Americans' relationship to government—largely its military and entitlement programs. Their concern over the decimation of the military is resolved by the prospect of creating weapons from an unlimited energy supply. In considering African Americans' relationship to entitlement programs, cabinet members rely upon the common-sense assumptions that often organize popular understanding of Black success and failure.[4] Among these assumptions is the belief that African Americans are more likely than Whites to be recipients of public assistance, to be drug users, and to favor and rely upon affirmative action programs. One scene in *Space Traders* uses a television talk show (*Betrice Berry*) to illustrate this type of common assumption that many Americans have about African Americans. A White woman states that because Black people are always complaining about their treatment here, she thinks that they would be "tickled pink" to get a *"free ride"* someplace else. A 1990 survey reported that 62% of non-Blacks believe that African Americans are more likely to "prefer to live off welfare" and less likely to "prefer to be self-supporting" (Terkel, 1992). However, as Wilson (1996) reminds us, fundamental assumptions about the nature of welfare and welfare families—that most are long-term recipients and that most are Black women with many children—are challenged by studies that analyze welfare data.

Another racial assumption depicted in *Space Traders* is that of the violent and disruptive nature of Black protest. African Americans are perceived as a threat not only to the country's prosperity, but also to the safety of Americans. As the chief of staff informs Golightly, "If this goes through, it's not going to be easy . . . some people might fight it—make the L.A. riots seem like a slumber party." In addition, gun sales to Blacks were halted as soon as the telephone referendum was announced. Governmental officials, unlike the Black people in *Space Traders*, fail to see the trade offer in the historical context of slavery. In fact, Golightly's claim that the trade amounts to genocide was rejected by every member of the cabinet.

Space Traders represents the African American opposition to the trade referendum within the context of the traditional (mainstream) African American Civil Rights movement. At a church rally, a Black minister connects the proposed trade to slavery by proclaiming that his people were brought here involuntarily, and "involuntarily is the only way they're gonna take me out!" Beyond signaling the centrality of the Black church to Black political struggle, the text interrogates the condition of Black leadership and its continued reliance on the same political allies and strategies that it traditionally has utilized in times of crisis. Black political struggle is mobilized by religious leaders (including Jews), and the Black church is depicted as the central venue for discussing and deciding upon the specific forms of resistance. However, the Black church becomes a barrier to the movement's pursuit of progressive social change because its (religious) leaders are caricatured as being preoccupied with offering the congregation a self-serving discourse.

Another impediment to successful political mobilization can be traced to the sexism prevalent within the Black church. In *Space Traders*, Black men are the primary leaders of the organized movement, and Black women are removed as central participants in the struggle. However, as Paula Giddings (1984) has shown, not only did Black women help launch and sustain the modern Civil Rights movement, but their specific role as women was not defined and their full leadership potential was lost amid "White feminism, Black power, social science, and poverty programs" (p. 350). *Space Traders'* treatment of Black political struggle makes it clear that petty divi-

sions, political posturing, and sexism within Black communities are detrimental to positive social change. The text also uses Professor Golightly to highlight the weak condition of Black leadership. When Golightly ponders whether or not to lobby on behalf of the administration, he tells his wife, "I'm not sure they'll need my help, Gail, given the state of Black leadership."

Space Traders depicts the White opposition to the trade by exposing their proclivity for certain aspects of Black popular culture. In this instance, American media culture and consumer culture converge in the narrative to promote and sell "difference." Black worth in American society is restricted to the realms of entertainment and sports. In a television infomercial, Casey Kasem asks, "Can you imagine a world without the blues, or jazz, or rock 'n' roll? That's where we'd be without the contributions of African Americans!" Kasem goes on to note that "You can forget about having another Dream Team again!" As is often the case in American consumer culture, images of African Americans such as Michael Jackson are used in the infomercial to expedite commercial communication between White people (Lury, 1996). Because Black worth to American society is commodified, life will not be as exciting because it cannot, in the words of bell hooks (1992), "eat the other":

> The commodification of Otherness has been so successful because it is offered as a new delight, more intense, more satisfying than normal ways of doing and feeling. Within commodity culture, ethnicity becomes spice, seasoning that can liven up the dull dish that is mainstream white culture. (p. 21)

Space Traders repeatedly calls attention to the importance of Black participation as consumers (never as producers) in America's consumer culture. In fact, the health and survival of American business and, in turn, of American society, are cast as dependent on continued Black participation in a system of commodity gratification. One scene depicts American capitalists lamenting the loss of profits caused by the cessation of Black consumption of such products as hard liquor, pork, (Kool and Newport brand) cigarettes, and athletic shoes. According to one capitalist, 15%

of "our" best consumers will be gone. Another businessman recognizes the tensions between race and class when he predicts a "revolution" when poor Whites find themselves at the bottom of America's social structure.

Despite this claim by the businessman, before poor Whites replace Blacks at the bottom of the social hierarchy, other minority groups such as Latinos would displace Blacks. According to Omi and Winant (1994), this has already occurred in some social contexts and is alluded to in *Space Traders* in a conversation between Gail Golightly and her daughter in which they debate if the trade will occur. By quoting her grandmother, who was a domestic servant to Whites, Mrs. Golightly tries to reassure her daughter by claiming that Whites cannot do without the presence of Blacks: "They may not like us, but they sure can't live without us." The daughter responds, "But, Mommy, Guatemalans clean their houses now." The scene ends with a quick cut to the Golightlys' own cleaning person—a Latina.

Space Traders also points to distinct Black cultural characteristics that persist over space and time. For example, race is depicted in terms of cultural identity, style, and language. In a humorous scene, Golightly's barber (comedian George Wallace) employs colorful language to express the significance of hair care to African Americans and to separate Blacks from other races: "Cause you know us Black folks, we don't like arriving nowhere all nappy-headed." In addition, scenes from the Black church include the verbal/artistic invention known as call and response. In this case, the verbal performances of those in the pulpit are shaped by a responsive audience that registers either expressive vocal support or silent rejection of the speaker's message. These aspects of the text are noted to underscore that even these distinct features of Black life are socially constructed and do not form the basis of Black racial or cultural essence.[5]

Space Traders also directs viewers' attention to fundamental tensions within African American cultural experience. For instance, the drama centers around the Golightly family—as in If you are Black and successful, you better "go lightly." In *Space Traders*, Black success, as personified by Golightly, leads to backlash when African Americans cast him as a "sellout" and ostracize him

from the Black community. In turn, Whites such as the president's chief of staff see Golightly as "uppity" and take measures to put him in his "place." In calling attention to the problematic nature of individual Black success and achievement, *Space Traders* uses Golightly to emphasize the need to create new identities.

Another tension within African American culture is revealed in *Space Traders* through a subtext of sibling conflict within the Golightly household. The major source of the conflict is the divergent ideas on race between the son and daughter. Golightly's daughter invokes the well-known Malcolm X expression to her father in response to the trade proposal: "Well, Dad, it looks like your chickens are finally coming home to roost." To which her older brother replies: "Look, little Miss Militant, give Dad a break. How was he supposed to know?" However, the most vivid representation of this intraracial conflict, and certainly a major issue of contention among many African Americans, is the male son's romantic involvement with a (blonde) White woman who is always present in the Golightly household. Although this woman never utters a word, her acceptance in the Golightly family household is revealed when she joins the family when they believe they are being "smuggled" to England.[6]

Space Traders also deals with skin color, which is a key marker of race. Specifically, the text uncovers the paradox of skin color and demonstrates that once again, Blacks with lighter skin tones will receive favored treatment in American society. The space traders' request for America's Black citizens was specified in terms of physiological difference—the amount of melanin in their skin. Even Golightly's wife (Gail) has trouble explaining to her daughter why she purchased (in her words, "the last jar on the shelf") skin whitener for her family. In this way, *Space Traders* alludes to the legacy of using products that claim to alter one's skin tone and suggests through Gail Golightly's unsuccessful attempt to darken her skin (to remain with her family) that although skin color can be altered temporarily, it is a permanent marker of race.

Space Traders' treatment of the color prejudices of African Americans—or what some label as "the color complex"[7]—is revealed in a scene that depicts a television news interview between two Black men. The purpose of the interview is to demonstrate how the amount of melanin in Black people's skin corresponds to complexion. The Black male anchor is disgusted upon learning from the considerably lighter-skinned (and obviously amused) physician that the doctor's complexion would exempt him from the trade.[8] In this case, the difference between being Black and non-Black is depicted as a question of physiology, and the political significance of racism is replaced by a concern for an "authentic" Black. Equally important, skin color prejudice, like any kind of prejudice, creates systems of privilege as well as oppression (Russell, Wilson, & Hall, 1992). Yet the central problem in *Space Traders* is Golightly's response to the racial backlash that he faces.

Golightly as Interposer

In asking Golightly to lobby on behalf of the trade, the president deduces that most African Americans will be opposed to the trade and hopes that one of their own can help persuade them. As we have seen, Golightly is not your "typical" African American: In addition to his status as a die-hard Republican, the text presents us with several images that suggest that he is not part of the mainstream African American community—he has seats on the board of directors of Fortune 500 companies and is a member of a historically White college fraternity.

Golightly faces a difficult choice: Should he go along with the request and, perhaps, gain true acceptance in the White community that he has worked so hard to enter, or will he (re)establish ties to the mainstream African American community that, like it or not, he can never really leave behind? Although Golightly is tormented by memories of a lifelong perception of being an "oreo," he does not desire to break away completely from African Americans and their concerns. As his performances in both the cabinet meeting and the church rally demonstrate, Golightly does not wish to be bound up in the essentializing projects in either community.

It is useful to see Golightly as an interposer, or one who seeks to maintain distance from the Other (Jacobs, 1994). When with their "home"

group (in this case, African Americans), interposers attempt to demonstrate that although they have appropriated cultural or political elements from a foreign "host" group (here, White society), their social identities are still tied to and driven by concerns for the home group's well-being. When with the foreign host group, interposers try to critique and expand the perception of the home group on a variety of levels. In short, the interposer moves back and forth between the two communities in a quest to facilitate the construction of antiessentialist identities for members of both communities.

In terms of intercultural communication, interpositionality can be defined as *the strategic communicative performance of distance from the Other*. An interposer, then, (1) is concerned with reception of multiple communities, (2) has a multifaceted identity that is always in the process of formation, and (3) works to improve intercultural communication by bridging the gaps between cultures. Interposers distance themselves from essentializing and totalizing cultural forces and, in essence, try to become critical social agents:

> Living as a critical social agent means knowing how to live contingently and provisionally without the certainty of knowing the truth, yet at the same time with the courage to take a stand on issues of human suffering, domination, and oppression. (McLaren, 1995, p. 15)

Golightly decides to fight against the trade by calling a meeting of America's leading capitalists to remind them that they will undergo excessive profit losses when 15% of their best consumers disappear overnight. They decide to launch "the most massive ad campaign this country has ever seen" in order to convince the country that African Americans are an integral component of American society. However, to shape the sensibilities of Americans, America's "captains of consciousness" utilize the very stereotypes that work to help constrain access/recognition of African Americans to the spheres of entertainment and athletics.

In this situation, Golightly is not an effective interposer: Rather than seeking to problematize the perception of African Americans (by Whites and non-Whites), he is complicit in the use of stereotypes to paint a false ideal. If he desires to truly follow an antiessentialist strategy, he must contribute to the dismantling of easy generalizations. Instead, when his wife asks why the campaign can't also seek to highlight the accomplishments of scientists, politicians, and academics, Golightly replies, "It's what the people want."

The successful interposer should work to question the principal assumptions undergirding the racial backlash. While struggling with a backlash flowing from White-controlled society, African American interposers must also struggle with a Black "backlash," in which they must continually defend their perspectives against charges that they have "sold out." Golightly epitomizes this dual struggle when he visits a meeting of Black religious leaders and tries to convince them that "a people without power must use cunning and guile." He convincingly outlines the major motivations for racism and proposes a strategy designed to produce a rejection of the traders' proposition. His plan is rejected when one of the leaders reminds the audience that such "TOM-foolery" cannot be trusted and that only tried-and-true methods of resistance can succeed. Golightly's interpositional performance faces insurmountable odds in the face of backlash given his extreme estrangement from the African American mainstream. Those interposers who do, however, maintain some organic links to their home communities will fare better than Golightly, as they have more than a one-shot effort to problematize taken-for-granted assumptions.

Conclusion

The interpositional strategy can be performed by explicitly challenging taken-for-granted cultural assumptions, creating dynamic identities, and forging new unions. Interpositional strategies can be developed with critical engagement with media culture and criticism of media texts. This analysis of *Space Traders* challenged racial assumptions and fostered insight into, among other things, progressive positions on African American political ideology and cultural practices. Interposers realize that the meaning of "progressive" depends on context: They must be prepared to an-

alyze the sociocultural environment and seek to create identities that enhance the ability of all individuals to lead free and productive lives. The interpositional strategy is accomplished by following the lead of Cornel West (1990) and staying "attuned to the best of what the mainstream has to offer—its paradigms, viewpoints and methods—yet maintain[ing] a grounding in affirming and enabling subcultures of criticism" (p. 33). The overarching goal of the interposer is the creation of nonessentialist identities that produce communication with others from a wider range of traditions and experiences.

In conclusion, interpositionality begins with assuming a more critical posture to our increasingly mediated social world. The interpositional strategy demonstrates that the self as a historical and cultural construction is shaped in complex, related, and multiple ways through its interaction with both multiple and diverse communities and mediated sources. To that end, interposers rethink the meaning of collective by conceiving of new forms of community and assuming multiple identities. Successful interposers resist attempts at blind conformity from both within and without by creating identities that are continually refined. These types of intercultural strategies pose certain challenges and risks and may not always be successful. Yet because our media culture provides a plethora of texts that can be read from a number of subject positions, we encourage you to seek other relevant texts, critically analyze them, and create dynamic identities.[9] In short, not only can media texts be useful in identifying and developing successful intercultural communicative strategies, but the general strategy of creating distance from essentialized representations can be used by everyone, albeit in different ways.

NOTES

1. Susan Faludi's (1991) book details the backlash against feminism.

2. The *Cosmic Slop* video can be rented from video stores.

3. Kellner (1995) makes a similar argument regarding the films of Spike Lee.

4. Gray (1989) provides an excellent discussion of television's representations of Black middle-class

success and urban under-class failure.

5. Dyson (1993) also points to the call and response to call attention to the socially constructed nature of Black cultural experience.

6. Golightly's efforts to rally support against the trade apparently prevented him and his family from going to England. In fact, in a scene reminiscent of representations of the system of slavery in America, Golightly's wife was separated physically from the family (because of her light skin).

7. Russell, Wilson, and Hall (1992) provide an excellent examination of the color complex among African Americans.

8. The doctor, Erik Fanon, goes out of his way to correct the anchor's pronunciation of his name in an obvious allusion to Frantz Fanon, who has written on Black internalization of White standards.

9. Two other media texts that are extremely useful in this context are Sut Jhally's (1996) *Race, the floating signifier* and Marlon Riggs's (1995) documentary *Black is . . . Black ain't,* which deals explicitly with Black identity.

REFERENCES

Bell, D. (1992). The space traders. In D. Benn, *Faces at the bottom of the well: The permanence of racism* (pp. 158–194). New York: Basic Books.

Dyson, M. (1993). *Reflecting Black: African-American cultural criticism.* Minneapolis: University of Minnesota Press.

Faludi, S. (1991). *Backlash: The undeclared war against American women.* New York: Anchor Books.

Giddings, P. (1984). *When and where I enter: The impact of Black women on race and sex in America.* New York: Bantam Books.

Gray, H. (1989). Television, Black Americans and the American dream. *Critical Studies in Mass Communication, 6,*(4), 376–386.

hooks, b. (1992). *Black looks.* Boston: South End Press.

Hudlin, R., & Hudlin, W. (Producers). (1994). *Space Traders* (R. Hudlin, Director). In *Cosmic Slop.* New York: Home Box Office.

Jacobs, W. (1994). Off the margin: The interpositional stranger. *Symploke 2*(2), 177–194.

Jhally, S. (Producer/Director). (1996). *Race, the floating signifier* [videotape]. (Available from the Media Education Foundation, 26 Center Street, Northampton, MA 01060)

Kellner, D. (1995). *Media culture.* New York: Routledge.

Lury, C. (1996). *Consumer culture.* New Brunswick, NJ: Rutgers University Press.

McLaren, P. (1995). *Critical pedagogy and predatory culture.* New York: Routledge.

Omi, M., & Winant, H. (1994). *Racial formation in the United States* (2d ed.). New York: Routledge.

Riggs, M. (Producer/Director). (1995). *Black is . . . Black ain't* [film]. (Available from California Newsreel, 149 Ninth Street / 420, San Francisco, CA 94103)

Russell, K., Wilson, M., & Hall, R. (1992). *The color complex: The politics of skin color among African Americans.* New York: Anchor Books.

Terkel, S. (1992). *Race: How Blacks and Whites think and feel about the American obsession.* New York: Anchor Books.

West, C. (1990). The new cultural politics of difference. In R. Ferguson et al. (Eds.), *Out there: Marginalization and contemporary cultures* (pp. 19–36). Cambridge, MA: MIT Press.

Wilson, W. J. (1996). *When work disappears: The world of the new urban poor.* New York: Alfred A. Knopf.

KEY TERMS

African Americans	interpositionality
Blacks	interposer
backlash	media culture
essentialism	polysemy
essentialist	polysemic
essences	race
interpositional	*Space Traders*

DISCUSSION QUESTIONS

1. Each American citizen was given one vote on the space traders' proposal to take America's African American citizens in exchange for solving all of the country's social problems. How would *you* vote on the referendum and why would you vote this way?

2. If this vote was held in America today, what do you believe the outcome would be? Why would you expect Americans to vote this way? In what

ways (if any) do you think the fact that the *private* nature of voting in America influenced the outcome of the vote?

3. (A) If you are not an African American, imagine that you are an African American. Would you be willing to accept the space traders' offer? Why or why not? (B) If you are an African American, assume the race of a non–African American. Would you be willing to accept the space traders' offer? Why or why not?

4. What did you like most about *Space Traders*? What did you like least about *Space Traders*?

5. In what way(s) does your own analysis or interpretation of *Space Traders* differ from the reading offered in this essay? In what way(s) is it similar?

6. Before reading this chapter, would any of your communicative behaviors have been consistent with the interpositional strategy? Explain. What were the results of these behaviors?

7. Discuss the pros and cons of the interpositional strategy.

30
MADONNA IN THE FRENCH PRESS

MICHEL DION[1] (TRANSLATED BY T. K. NAKAYAMA)

In 1992 and 1993 Madonna published a book of nude photos, *Sex*, released a compact disc, *Erotica*, and played in three films: *A League of Their Own*, directed by Penny Marshall; *Body of Evidence*, directed by Uli Edel; and *Snake Eyes*, directed by Abel Ferrara. This last film, presented at the 1993 Venice and Deauville Film Festivals, was produced by Maverick ("nonconformist") films, which Madonna created and heads. She undertook a world tour with the spectacle *The Girlie Show*, an extension of *Sex* and *Erotica*. She also participated in a number of television programs, three of which were in France: an interview on TF1 with Anne Sinclair in "7/7," which, on that day in October 1992, achieved a record audience of 9.5 million viewers; an amusing piece in a Christophe Dechavanne television program, on TF1 of course; and an interview with Isabelle

[1] I thank Mesdames Marie-Noelle Bas-Rousselot, press agent for *Sex;* Marie-Claude Castendet, press agent at WEA Music; A.M.L.F. company for *Body of Evidence;* Messieurs Frey, Dangol, Kinémastar for *Snake Eyes* who allowed me to use their press reviews. I also thank Monsieur Birnbaum, French editor of *Sex* who helped me in this work.

Giordano about the cinema on Canal + in February and March 1993.

I have counted some 800 articles on or about Madonna (about 600 concern *Sex* and *Body of Evidence*) in the French press during this period when so much was spoken about her; the exception was the Catholic press, which remained silent or nearly so. The cinema career of Madonna began in 1979 with her playing the principal female role in *A Certain Sacrifice*, a film by S. J. Lewicky, which was not released until 1985, without his agreement. She was 21 years old. In this film of the New York underground, which follows the cinematic style of J. L. Godard and J. Cassavetes, Madonna plays her own story: She seeks something to eat in the streets of New York in order to survive, and she hopes for fame. The filmmaker A. Ferrara, at that time a young musician in various New York rock groups, became acquainted with Madonna (*Paris-Match*, 14 October 1993):

> We were obscure unknowns. We hung out together in the cool places, the clubs, the fashionable restaurants, in the hopes of infiltrating into

this milieu. I had barely begun to get my head above water, but Madonna! What a path she cut! What a star! It's incredible to see how this girl left from the bottom of Michigan . . . overcoming hard blows . . . But she had the spirit to assert herself in a world of guys.

Ferrara also revealed, always in remarks that are attributed to her: "You know why she is so right and so moving in this scene [of rape in *Snake Eyes*]? Because that's her story. She has never told it to anyone." Already, in *A Certain Sacrifice*, she was raped, the day before her marriage, in the restroom of a bar. For her revenge, her future husband and a band of friends set out on a hunt to find the rapist. Captured, he is put to death in the course of a reckless evening of rock, according to a singing/dancing ritual that I am calling a rock ritual.

Madonna released her first record in 1983, and in 1985 she played in two films, *Vision Quest* by Harold Becker, in which she only sang, and *Desperately Seeking Susan* by Susan Seidelman. Presented at the Cannes Film Festival, this latter film would be a success and make her known. In 1988, and parallel with her film career, she played on Broadway in a scene in a David Mamet (author of *Oleanna*, which played in Paris in 1994) play, *Speed the Plow*, produced by Gregory Mosher. Her acting was praised by the critics (Andersen, 1992; Bego, 1992; Thompson, 1991; UGC Vidéo, 1991, 1993).

Madonna's art is, above all, action. As a dancer, she possesses "the art of moving the human body according to a certain agreement between space and time" (Christout, 1993, p. 36). Dance is often considered the firstborn of the arts "as it obeys an irresistible drive, satisfying as much artistic sense as nervous or muscular exaltation" (Christout, p. 36). Until Isadora Duncan broke all the rules at the beginning of this century for women in dance, dance was also the only means that women were allowed to express themselves with their bodies, as men found pleasure in their doing so (Duby & Perrot, 1991; Lever, 1987).

Like all female dancers of this century, Madonna is an heir of Isadora Duncan. And how can we not notice here: Camille Claudel, in whose image Rodin created "aimée," one of the most beautiful works, as he would have really wanted to "love" Isadora. It is said that she could only pose and dance for him, because her family and her brother Paul had her locked up because of her "madness." Twentieth-century women have faced these contradictions between how they are seen and how they present themselves. The problem of women's representations is fundamental to women's history. Women are enclosed in the images that men construct of them, that men impose as being the norm; what theologians, who made and always wanted to be in control of ideas, call "nature." But women have succeeded in challenging these notions, and until these notions are destroyed, the battle goes around and around and is relentlessly undertaken (Faludi, 1991). With social exclusions in all societies, the wars of ethnic identity that bloody Europe, the fall of communism, and the death of our utopias, this problem—too little studied and often obscured—is probably one of the major aspects of the crisis of the contemporary world. As in ethnic wars, no one controls the situation any longer, and the representations of women, which are in a continual process of being created and undone, collide with these other representations. Having taken the form that we recognize today as feudal Catholic Europe at the end of the Middle Ages, the churches found that their power over the sexuality of both women and men was shaken up.

I define the art of Madonna as being a production of herself as much as a work of art and an erotic center dancing between "sex" and "gender." This art of self-exposition, of overexposition, is organized around three axes: transgressions of the sexual, racial, and religious orders. I will say nothing about the first two, which are studied in the United States by C. R. Schwichtenberg (1994) and T. K. Nakayama (1994), but will address myself only to the third, the religious transgression.

I. A Non-Christian Image of Woman

Madonna, of Italian Catholic origin and raised by her father to be religious, professes "personal" religious convictions and transgresses institutionalized Christianity, particularly Catholicism. In referring to the style of the pendential door representing the crucified Christ, she declared in 1983 that "a naked man on a cross is erotic."

French commentators, with few exceptions (the weekly *Le Point* editorial by M. Imbert, "A propos de Madonna" [17 October 1992] and, in a smaller way, *VSD*), are as interested in religious transgressions as in sexual and racial transgressions. Thus, what is the Christian image of woman today? Where do we find it? The five volumes cited in *Histoire des femmes en Occident* carry numerous elements in answering these two questions and inspire my problem.

A. As far as one could go back in the history of women, which barely begins to be written in the 20th century, it appears that in all times and still today, even if there are some contrary tendencies made evident, women are constituted by "the look that men impose on them" (Klapisch-Zuber, 1991). This essential notion should probably be worked on and theorized much more today, specifically for the analysis of the (non) constitution of women by religions and by political parties in France and elsewhere (Fraisse, 1994).

B. The question of the constitution of women by religions is immediately made clear by: the invention by theologians in the 12th century of Mary Magdalene, repentant sinner (Dalarun, 1991) and indispensable bridge between "the mother" (Mary), model of the perfect woman that no other "real" woman could hope to attain, and the "whore" (Eve), by which evil (and the male [homonyms in French, trans. note]) comes. This triad that establishes three poles between which every woman "naturally" oscillates is always at the base of images of contemporary women of the West. In response to "Where is today's Christian image of woman?" I can answer that it is everywhere. For example, it is at the root of a French film by Jean Eustache, *La maman et la putain* [The mother and the whore], produced in 1973, which recounts, in the style of news reporting in post-1968 France, the story of two girls and a guy who plays between them. Film historians generally consider this film as a "cult" film and as a "turning point" between pre- and post-1968 films. This Christian image of woman is also at the base of the religious education of Madonna, who would one day declare: "When I was young, my

grandmother begged me not to frequent men, to love Jesus and to be a good girl. I grew up with two images of woman: the virgin and the whore. It's a little frightening" (*VSD*, 8–11 October 1992).

Here I rely on an article by J. Dalarun that recounts the invention of Mary Magdalene. In a society already doubly shaken to its core by the "grand schism" and the foundation of a Christian church in the East at Byzantium in 1054, and by the reasons for the crisis of feudalism and the subsequent appearance of courtly love, which pitted knightly culture against that of scholarly culture, it became urgent for the church to control reproduction in human societies that gave the appearance of beginning to drift away from church teachings. "Convinced that what we today call 'reality' is only the projection of an Idea of woman, who would know better not to reveal herself except in the figures issuing from these texts (l'Ecriture, M.D.), where lay the Revelation of everything else," the Catholic church constructs an imaginary Mary Magdalene to set off three women of the Gospel: "the pardoned and loved sinner" (Luke 7:36–50); "Mary called Magdalene" (Luke 8:2); Mary of Bethany, sister of Martha and Lazarus (John 12:1–8) (*La bible de Jérusalem*, 1975).

This invention of a Mary Magdalene in the Catholic church is one of the elements of its strategy to take control of the sexes, along with the battles to impose celibacy on priests and to impose holy marriage on princes. It is contemporary with the invention of Purgatory and has the same objective: to open the way to redemption. None of these inventions exist in the Orthodox church, which will attain these objectives through other means, as expressed in a different theology and in relation to different political situations.

The little that I have said about Madonna's art is sufficient to demonstrate where the image of woman disengages itself and, often shocking, diverges from the Christian model and the Catholic triad of Mary/Eve/Mary Magdalene, making her art "stand out." As it "stands out," it prolongs, along with the oppositions and controversies that I've highlighted earlier, the battles of women and ethnic minorities against their oppression. In the same way that she mixes and conflates sexual differences and overturns them, she mixes and overturns ethnic differences so well that we end up by no longer knowing, as Jean Baudrillard (1994) has remarked in relation to sexual differences, who and where the Other is located.

Madonna doesn't pretend to be a militant feminist, but she affirms a woman's perspective, as evidenced in several extracts from the television program *7/7:* "In the United States, women are considered second-class citizens. They still have a long road to travel. . . . I have nothing against men in particular; my fight is against ignorance in general, which leads to fear and then violence. . . . If I were a man, my style would certainly be considered less provoking." She has also declared, and it seems to me, what must be retained for the analysis of what is written about her in the French press: "What I do is political, not in the traditional meaning of the term, but what I say is revolutionary, in America in any case."

II. A Press Enraptured

For a book of nude photos, the launching of *Sex* is probably the largest commercial and publicity operation event mounted to date: 750,000 copies of the work—25,000 in France—were launched the same day on the Western market after a publicity campaign . . . that was secret about the content of the book. At the start, a black-and-white postcard showing her face, with eyes closed and at the peak of ecstasy, was sent to 150 newspapers. This postcard announced on the back in red letters, "*Sex*, the explosive book of Madonna," and gave the appearance date of the book. The work itself was already sent to 15 journalists, who could talk about it but were asked not to show it publicly (interviews with Mesdames Bas-Rousselot and Castendet, press agents). There was also, these press agents tell me, a rush of interest:

> The editors-in-chief of the newspapers brushed up the red carpet when one came to speak to them about Madonna; someone in charge of a radio show even said that Madonna did more than Sarajevo in ratings according to l'Audimat.

A first question, to which I reserve my answer, emerges: Why did the press, which declared itself unanimously shocked by this exceptional public-

ity campaign, to paraphrase one of my speakers, "unroll the red carpet" and assure its success?

A. The launching of *Sex* was clearly a media event. For my analysis, I have gathered the articles that made and created this event and have classified them under three topics: general information on the star, information on her stay in France, and editorials. I will say little here about articles in the first two categories. Star newspapers that give some information, true or false, on the lives of stars are part of the first group. With some exceptions, they do not take part in the "provocations" of Madonna and wonder only "how far will she go in scandal?" Those of the second group, recovered from press agencies, appeared quasi-identical but under different signatures, in almost all the newspapers. In a uniform manner and in a tone that tries to be "neutral" and "objective," they recount the comings and goings of the star. Furthermore, they summarize her public statements and, although further analysis would be needed, "suggest" what should be thought about those statements. A number of articles on her appearance on the program *7/7* begin thus: "Georges Bataille, George Bush, Eros, Thanatos, the battle against discrimination . . . Madonna proved once again that she doesn't hesitate to speak her mind" (*La Presse de la Manche*, 11 October 1992). Finally, there are the editorials to which I return and analyze. I have classified them, and the newspapers in which they were published, into two categories, "favorable overall" and "hostile overall," as there isn't any middle ground.

Being "favorable overall": *Le Figaro, France Soir, Le Parisien Libéré, Le Quotidien, Le Journal du Dimanche, L'Evènement du Jeudi, Le Point, VSD,* and *Paris-Match.*

Being "hostile overall": (not including the Catholic newspapers already cited) *Le Monde, Libération, L'Humanité, Le nouvel Observateur, L'Express, Globe Hebdo,* so-called satirical newspapers (*Le Canard Enchaîné, Hérisson, La Grosse Bertha, Charlie-Hebdo*), and the extreme right press.

Elle doesn't enter into this classification. In the issue that published some exclusive extracts from *Sex* (12 October 1992), two journalists expressed, in parallel columns, two opposed editorials, one favorable, the other hostile.

There are four themes, pondered differently according to "favorable overall" or "hostile overall" opinions, that intersect and frame all the arguments: business and money; scandal and provocation; if *Sex* scandalizes the puritan Americans, could it scandalize France?; the "mysteries" of eroticism and the star. The gender of the authors of these articles didn't impact or barely appeared to impact the opinions.

A1. The "overall favorable" newspapers, often close to those of the star-system, distinguish themselves from the "overall hostile" in that they do not share in the war against the star and her artistic work, which, in general, they do not speak about or barely speak about: They "accompany" the event, skipping over "money," "scandal," "provocation." The most interesting case is *Le Figaro*: "Madame Figaro" on 10 October 1992 published a very severe article against Madonna, but some opinions much more nuanced and "overall favorable" are expressed in three other articles (7, 12, and 20 October 1992). Is it an accident, or was there a specific opinion of the newspaper for readers of "Madame Figaro"? Be that as it may in this particular case, the constructions of images of Madonna that these newspaper readers have would be interesting to study, and would be valuable for star-system newspapers. Would they be "overall favorable"? Would there be research on correlations between these images and those that the newspapers reflect/construct?

A2. An article appeared in *Le Monde* on 23 October 1992 that synthesized those of the "overall hostile" press. *Sex* is generally appreciated as doubly scandalous, due to its advertising promotion, a "multimedia blitzkrieg" (underlined in the original, M.D.), and because to its content, which doesn't merit such a promotion. "The scandal will only exist in the eyes of the scandalized." Also mocking the "conscientious work of Madonna, . . . concentrated on her liberating mission" and of whom the texts "oscillate between banality of the messenger of erotica and an adolescent blunder sometimes moving." The article is entitled, "Eros and capitalization. Madonna practices the monoculture of sex: good profits, poor quality."

One of the other of these critiques to which is added the loss of the "magic," the loss of the "mystery" of eroticism, reappears in all the newspapers of this group, expressed in different forms and different ideologies. The pens of violence to denounce "a 'sinner' of the disco who merchandises her libido as others of the shady arenas" (*L'Humanité*, 7 October 1992) reemerge in this newspaper, but also in *L'Express* (15 October 1992), and in the newspapers called satirical and in *Rivarol* (16 October 1992), which called for the resignation of then-minister M. Strauss-Kahn as "guilty," along with others, as the husband of "Haine Sinclair," who had invited Madonna to her television program 7/7.

The few Catholic newspapers that spoke about Madonna were very harsh: *Témoignage Chrétien* of 10 October 1992 was indignant about her invitation to the program 7/7; *Télérama* of 21 October 1992 spoke of her with contempt; and *La Croix Magazine Nord/Pas-de-Calais* of 16 October 1992 set Madonna in opposition to actress Audrey Hepburn, who was shown going to "the exclusive service of Unicef." The Catholic points of view, expressed in these newspapers from the provinces, are of the same type, up to a quasi-integrity, in *Vie Nouvelle*, Chambéry (6 November 1992), that called M. Imbert to account for his editorial cited in *Le Point* in which he considered Madonna as a "symbol," a "phenomenon of society" that causes reflection.

The organization "Avenir de la culture," which claims to defend "Western and European cultural heritage," had protested earlier in 1988 the opening of Martin Scorsese's film *The Last Temptation of Christ* and now brought legal action, that it lost, against Madonna for appropriating "the name generally given to the Virgin Mary" and against the editor of *Sex*, Monsieur Birnbaum. In addition, M. Birnbaum received a flood of letters containing anti-Semitic threats of death and injuries. In March 1993, *MarieFrance* published a sample of these. Finally, some individuals, calling themselves members of the association "Honneur de la Police," tried to intimidate bookstores to stop them from selling the book. With the exception of *VSD*, 10 December 1992; the Seine-et-Marne edition of *Parisien*, 2 December 1992; and *La République de Seine-et-Marne*, 30 November 1992, which reported the lawsuit in Fontainebleau against the editor of *Sex*, the press spoke little about these attacks. This silence was regretted by M. Birnbaum in a press release that announced the second printing of the work at the end of December 1992. The first printing sold out within several hours.

B. There is little to say about the articles focusing on *Body of Evidence*, several months later, executed in near unanimity by criticism with arguments taken from . . . the *New York Times* (17 January 1993) that are often used: "Madonna is a marketing genius," "it's [the film] a hoot," and "Madonna's best role remains Madonna." The most negative articles appeared in *Première* (March 1993), a monthly movie magazine, which juxtaposed on one of its covers Isabelle Adjani and Madonna: "Finally Adjani! She stars in a film"; "Enough Madonna! She exhibits herself." Two journalists, one from *L'Express* cited earlier, invoke some rather racist remarks against the director of the film, Uli Edel, who is of German origin: "with completely German tact," "with a completely Teutonic touch." A much more rare exception appeared in another monthly cinema magazine, *Studio* (March 1993), which is much more measured and judges the film as "honestly produced"; it also said of Madonna that she "played her role with as much diligence as humility, and showed herself quite convincing."

Edel shot two notable films: *Moi, Christianne F.* (1980) recounts the hell of drugs and prostitution for an adolescent; *Last Exit to Brooklyn* (1989) is a political-sexual critique of the 1950s United States. *Body of Evidence* is written in this style. Edel uses the cinematic image as a boxer might use his fist (for example, in *Last Exit*, there is a group rape scene of a young girl by drunk dock workers). In *Body*, he works the ambiguity of a woman who is in control of her own body, who plays with it and in it as she wants, but who is also a criminal. In order to better decry it, the press compared this film to *Basic Instinct* (1992) by Paul Verhoeven, which is the exact opposite of *Body* and confronts, with elegance, the masculine fantasme of women "eaters" of men.

C. The few articles caused by *The Girlie Show*, which filled Bercy [an arena in Paris, trans. note] three days in a row, revealed the same classifications as those proposed for *Sex*. This spectacle

that *Le Figaro* (30 September 1993) judged "more a good child than shocking" and the *New York Times* (16 October 1993) "acceptable" ("back to palatability for Madonna") invoked the ire of the Latin American churches. In Brazil, for example, where I was researching an Afro Brazilian religion when Madonna came there, the spectacle was forbidden to those under 14 years old. Cardinal Arns of São Paulo announced that he was irritated (*irritado*) by Madonna, the star who asked that the crucifix be removed during her show by the workers at Morumbi Stadium (*O Globo*, 3 November 1993). The archdiocese of Rio published a long document (*Jornal do Brasil*, 6 November 1993) to "alert Catholics and all persons of good will of the affront (*acinte*) that the public exhibition in our city by the North American artist known under the name Madonna represents." This alert was followed by an extremely negative condemnation of the spectacle.

D. *Snake Eyes* reconfigured these interpretations of Madonna. As in his earlier films, as well as his work with other filmmakers, such as Edel, Ferrara continued to put the "American Dream" under the scalpel, or more accurately, under the critical eye of his camera. In general, this film was well received by the critics, and the role of Madonna—a television star who searches for God to save her from a life of orgies and drugs that she led with her husband—was also commended. For example, *Libération* wrote that in this film, she is "a bizarre Marilyn of the 1990s" (11–12 September 1993) and *Télérama* read the film across a dialectic between "sin," "expiation," and the "pardon" and made a comparison to Rita Hayworth in *The Woman of Shanghai* (13 October 1993).

Conclusion

Interpreting Madonna's images in the press is difficult indeed, but one comment emerges that is certainly not unrelated to political life. *Le Figaro* (12 October 1992) called itself "reassured" in hearing that Madonna "advises children to 'make their dreams come true' whom she calls 'revolutionaries.'" In the newspapers of the left that kill these dreams, they create strong opposition; *L'Humanité-Dimanche* (15 October 1992) writes:

"Madonna, everything but revolutionary." These two examples show that the images that Madonna projects tap into the imaginary and that they confirm that the imaginary, which newspapers follow, are probably how "the red carpet" unrolls before *Sex*, "instituting" society (Castoriadis, 1975). The theologians of the 12th century understood this perfectly in inventing Mary Magdalene.

Sex was a best seller, but contrary to what is written, Madonna is taking risks, financial risks above all, in exploiting this "scandalous" vein. Although she was neither the author nor the producer of *Body of Evidence*, it was a commercial failure that could have negative repercussions on her personal artistic productions. On another level, along with Elizabeth Taylor, she was one of the first American stars to mobilize against AIDS and, in 1987, gave a concert in New York's Madison Square Garden to help in the battle against this epidemic that she calls "next to Hitler, the worst thing to happen in the twentieth century" (interview in *Vanity Fair* in 1990). As such, she remains faithful to her role as a star, in the way the star system has fixed this role forever. "The star," writes E. Morin (1957, p. 192), "participates in all of the entertainments of the world, leaning on all of its wretchedness, intervening constantly in his/her destiny." Do stars of today do it in the same way as those of yesterday? For the same reasons? Are their fans the same as those of stars of yesteryear? What becomes of the star system when the stars no longer want to be constructed by it? In this essay, I have proposed some elements in the answers to these questions.

REFERENCES

Andersen, C. (1992). *Madonna unauthorized*. New York: Bantam Doubleday.

Baudrillard, J. (1994). Madonna deconnection. In M. Dion (Ed.), *Madonna, Érotisme et pouvoir*. Paris: Éditions Kimé, pp. 29–33.

Bego, M. (1992). *Madonna blonde ambition*. New York: Harmony Books.

La Bible de Jérusalem. (1975). Paris: Desclée de Brouwer.

Castoriadis, C. (1975). *L'Institution imaginaire de la société*. Paris: Éditions du Seuil.

Christout, M. F. (1993). Danse. *Encyclopaedia universalis*. Corpus 7, pp. 36–38.

Dalarun, J. (1991). Regards de clercs. In C. Klapisch-Zuber (Ed.), *Histoire des femmes en Occident*. Vol. 2. Paris: Plon, pp. 31–54.

Duby, G., & Perrot, M. (Eds.). (1991). *Histoire des femmes en Occident*. Vols. 3, 4, 5. Paris: Plon.

Faludi, S. (1991). *Backlash: The undeclared war against American women*. New York: Crown Publishers.

Fraisse, G. (1994). Quand gouverner n'est pas représenter. *Esprit, 3–4*, 103–114.

Klapisch-Zuber, C. (1991). "Introduction." In C. Klapisch-Zuber (ed.), *Histoire des femmes en Occident*. Vol. 2. Paris: Plon, p. 567.

Lever, M. (1987). *Isadora, Roman d'une vie*. Paris: Presses de la Renaissance.

Madonna. (1992). *Sex*. New York: Warner. Paris: Vade Retro.

Morin, E. (1957). *Les stars*. Paris: Éditions du Seuil.

Nakayama, T. K. (1994). "Races, culture populaire et Madonna." In M. Dion (Ed.), *Madonna, Érotisme et pouvoir*. Paris: Éditions Kimé, pp. 20–28.

Schwichtenberg, C. R. (1994). Le pouvoir de féminin, les travestis et Madonna. In M. Dion (Ed.), *Madonna, Érotisme et pouvoir*. M. Dion & T. K. Nakayama (tr.). Paris: Éditions Kimé, pp. 10–19.

Thompson, D. (1991). *Madonna revealed: The unauthorized biography*. New York: Birch Lane Press.

UGC Vidéo. (1991). *La Véritable Histoire de Madonna*.

UGC Vidéo. (1993). *Madonna, une vie privée*.

KEY TERMS

religion	star system
Madonna	virgin
Mary Magdalene	whore

DISCUSSION QUESTIONS

1. How is the reception of Madonna in France and Brazil similar to and different from her reception in the United States?
2. What role does religion play in the ways that these images are interpreted?
3. How does the star system work today? What is the significance of the U.S. domination of popular culture in the way that the star system works internationally?

PART SEVEN

COMMUNICATION AND INTERCULTURAL TRANSITIONS

Intercultural communication often takes place when we go from our home environment to a host, or foreign, culture. Those who travel from one cultural location to another often have to adapt to these cultural transitions. Part Seven explores communication and identity in various intercultural transitions, including short-term international travel and work, readaptation to home contexts, long-term immigration and acculturation, and "passing" from one race or class to another.

Consider these questions as you read the articles in this part:

What cultural transitions have you experienced?

Is cultural adaptation more difficult for some people than others? Why?

Are some cultural contexts easier to adapt to than others?

How does communication facilitate or inhibit cultural adaptation?

How does power come into play in transitions?

Although communication and identity are central themes in all these readings, they reflect a range of different approaches to adaptation and transitions. For some scholars, cultural adaptation is a very linear,

taken-for-granted process that occurs mainly as individuals travel overseas. In contrast, others see acculturation as a dynamic, problematic
process that calls into question static notions of culture and raises questions of identity. For these scholars, adaptation can only be understood
by considerations of power in host environments.

The first three essays address communication of migrants in overseas contexts. First, Young Yun Kim in "Cross-Cultural Adaptation: An
Integrative Theory" outlines a systems approach to cultural adaptation.
She identifies three outcomes of cultural adaptation: psychological health,
functional fitness, and intercultural identity. She sees adaptation as a fairly
linear transformative process involving a stress-adaptation-growth cycle.
She emphasizes the important role of the *individual* stranger's (immigrant)
communication (with host culture and other ethnic nationals), but sees
ethnic communication in the long term as a *barrier* to successful adaptation. This theory has led to a great deal of objective social science research
identifying factors that predict successful and unsuccessful adaptation of
sojourners and immigrants.

Along the same line, Shelley L. Smith in "Identity and Intercultural
Communication Competence in Reentry" addresses the question of how
sojourners readapt to their home environment after spending time abroad.
She points out that reentry adaptation is both similar to and different from
overseas adaptation. An important issue in readapting is intercultural
identity development. Smith outlines a communication model for understanding reentry that highlights aspects of identity development.

In contrast, the next reading addresses adaptation issues for immigrants from a critical perspective. In "Translated Enactments: The Relational Configurations of the Asian Indian Immigrant Experience,"

Radha S. Hegde questions the traditional notion of culture as static, and of acculturation as a linear, taken-for-granted process. She suggests that in today's global world, many immigrant groups find that their cultural boundaries are blurred and that their sense of home and identity is confused. It no longer makes sense to refer to culture and cultural groups as homogeneous groups of individuals residing in one place. Her ethnographic study of Asian Indian immigrants stands in contrast to Y. Y. Kim's essay in that Hegde emphasizes the importance of maintaining relationships with other immigrants. She shows how these relationships provide a sense of grounding and identity while living "on the borders."

Also from a critical perspective, Dreama G. Moon looks at a very different type of transition—"passing" from a less powerful to a more powerful identity. In "Performed Identities: 'Passing' as an Inter/cultural Discourse," she describes the unique characteristics of passing. Unlike other transitions, passing is usually unidirectional, from less to more powerful positions; it can be both active and passive, and it is of long-term duration. She also discusses how passing calls into question fixed and "essential" notions of intercultural identity.

31

CROSS-CULTURAL ADAPTATION: AN INTEGRATIVE THEORY

YOUNG YUN KIM

Millions of people change homes each year, crossing cultural boundaries. Immigrants and refugees resettle in search of a new life, side-by-side with temporary sojourners finding employment overseas as artists, musicians, writers, accountants, teachers, and construction workers. Diplomats and other governmental agency employees, business managers, Peace Corps volunteers, researchers, professors, students, military personnel, and missionaries likewise carry out their work overseas for varying lengths of time. Individuals such as these are, indeed, contemporary pioneers venturing into an unfamiliar cultural terrain where the "business-as-usual" ways of doing things quickly lose their relevance. Even relatively short-term sojourners must be at least minimally concerned with building a healthy functional relationship to the host environment in a way similar to the native population. They confront their cross-cultural predicaments and engage in new learning for an improved "goodness-of-fit" to handle their daily transactions with a greater ease and heightened sense of efficacy. Accompanying this process is an increased self-awareness, which, in time, facilitates the development of an identity that reaches beyond the original cultural perimeters.

• • •

Organizing Principles: An Open-Systems Approach

The present theory is predicated on a set of "open-systems" assumptions about the nature of humans as adaptive living entities. . . .

Assumption 1: Humans have an inherent drive to adapt and grow. Adaptation is a fundamental life goal for humans, something that people do naturally and continually as they face the challenges from their environment (Slavin & Kriegman, 1992). The introduction of every new experience, particularly one that is drastic and disorienting, leads to transformation throughout one's life. From the first frustrations of early childhood to the later changes in life circumstances, people go through a series of graduated sink-or-swim situations. For the most part, such challenges are successfully handled by people without a complete breakdown in their internal system. . . .

Assumption 2: Adaptation to one's social environment occurs through communication. Adaptive changes in individuals continue as long as they are engaged in a given sociocultural environment with which they send (encoding) and receive (decoding) messages. In this process, communicators continually engage in generating "information output" to the environment as well as generating meaning for the "information input" or "feedback" internally (Geyer, 1980). . . . This also means that individual adaptation activities occur as long as one lives in a given social environment (Dance & Larson, 1976).

Assumption 3: Adaptation is a complex and dynamic process. Because the person and the environment coparticipate in the person's adaptation through a continual give-and-take, adaptation . . . consists of multiple dimensions and facets.

• • •

The Process of Cross-Cultural Adaptation

How, then, do strangers adapt to new cultural challenges? . . .

Deculturation and Acculturation

Throughout the socialization process, children become adapted to the fellow members of their cultural group, which, in turn, gives them their status and assigns to them their role in the life of the community. Culture, indeed, is imprinted in its members as a pattern of knowledge, attitudes, values, mind-sets, perceptions, and behaviors that permeate all life activities. The mere fact that children grow up to be cultural beings bears witness to the fundamental fact of human pliability and the pervasive role of culture in shaping individual behavior.

Upon entering a new and unfamiliar culture, strangers set in motion the process of enculturation all over again. But this time, they are faced with situations that deviate from the familiar and internalized original cultural script. . . .

The process of *learning* and acquiring the elements of the host culture is commonly called *acculturation* (Shibutani & Kwan, 1965). . . . As new learning occurs, *unlearning,* or *deculturation,* of at least some of the old cultural habits occurs—at least in the sense that new responses are adopted in situations that previously would have evoked old ones. The cost of acquiring something new is inevitably the "losing" of something old in much the same way as "being someone requires the forfeiture of being someone else" (Thayer, 1975, p. 240).

The Stress-Adaptation-Growth Dynamic

Because cross-cultural adaptation necessitates both acculturation (learning) and deculturation (unlearning), and because a stranger's cultural identity and attributes are placed against the backdrop of the systemic forces of the host culture, the cross-cultural experiences of newcomers are unsettling indeed. The experiences of acculturation and deculturation inevitably produce forms of temporary personality disintegration, or even breakdown in some extreme cases. As parts of their internal organization undergo small changes, the strangers are, at least temporarily, in a state of disequilibrium, which is manifested in many emotional "lows" of uncertainty, confusion, and anxiety.

. . . Such disruptive experiences of a person reflect *stress,* . . . Indeed, the challenges of handling daily activities are most severe during the initial phases, as has been shown in many culture shock studies. . . . Under stress, a so-called defense mechanism is activated in strangers to hold the internal structure in balance by some form of protective psychological maneuvering. They attempt to avoid or minimize the anticipated or actual "pain" of disequilibrium by selective attention, self-deception, denial, avoidance, and withdrawal as well as by hostility, cynicism, and compulsively altruistic behavior (Lazarus, 1966, p. 262).

Defensive (or protective) stress reactions such as these, however, are generally temporary and counterproductive to the strangers' effective functioning in the host environment. They must, and generally do, accompany *adaptation* responses as well. . . .

What follows the stress and adaptation responses is a subtle internal transformation of *growth.* The periods of stress will pass in time as the strangers work out new ways of handling problems through sources of strength in themselves and in their social environment. A crisis, once managed by the strangers, presents an opportunity for a strengthening of their coping abilities. The stress-adaptation experiences bring about change and growth—the creative responses to new circumstances. Over time, the stress-adaptation-growth dynamic plays out not in a smooth, linear progression but in a cyclic and continual "draw-back-to-leap" pattern similar to the movement of a wheel depicted in Figure 1. Each stressful experience is responded to by strangers with a "draw back," which then activates their adaptive energy to help them reorganize themselves and "leap forward." It presents a dialectic relationship between push and pull, or engagement and disengagement, in the psychological movements of strangers.

• • •

Intercultural Transformation

As strangers experience a progression of internal change, they are likely to undergo a set of identi-

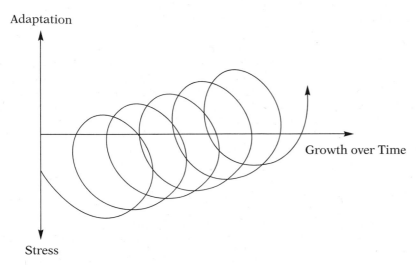

Adaptation

Growth over Time

Stress

FIGURE 1   *Stress-Adaptation-Growth Dynamics*

fiable transformations in their habitual patterns of cognitive, affective, and behavioral responses. Through the processes of deculturation and acculturation, some of the "old" cultural habits are replaced by new cultural habits. They acquire increasing proficiency in self-expression and in fulfilling their various social needs.

Three interrelated aspects of the strangers' intercultural transformation are specified in the present theory as the key outcomes of the cross-cultural adaptation process. The first aspect is an increased *functional fitness*. Through the repeated activities resulting in new cultural learning and internal reorganizing, strangers in time achieve an increasing "synchrony" (Hall, 1976; Y. Kim, 1993) between their internal responses and the external demands in the host environment. Successfully adapted strangers have accomplished a desired level of proficiency in communicating and developing a satisfactory relationship with the host society—particularly with those individuals and situations that are of direct relevance to their daily activities.

• • •

Closely associated with the increased functional fitness is increased *psychological health* in relation to their host environment. The psycho-logical health of strangers is directly linked to their ability to communicate and the accompanying functional fitness in the host society. . . .

The development of functional fitness and psychological health in strangers is likely to accompany an emergent *intercultural identity*. Adversarial cross-cultural experiences bring about the experiences of what Zaharna (1989) calls "self-shock," a "shake-up" of the strangers' sense of connection to their original cultural group and an accompanying growth. . . . In Adler's (1976) words, this emergent intercultural identity is based "not on 'belongingness' which implies either owning or being owned by a single culture, but on a style of self-consciousness that situates oneself neither totally *a part of* nor totally *apart from* a given culture" (p. 391).

The Structure of Cross-Cultural Adaptation

• • •

Personal Communication

The successful adaptation of strangers is realized only when their personal communication systems sufficiently overlap with those of the natives. The capacity of strangers to appropriately and effectively receive and process information (decoding) and to design and execute mental plans in initiating or responding to messages (encoding) is labeled here as *host communication competence.*

By definition, the strangers' host communication competence facilitates their cross-cultural adaptation process in a most direct and significant way. It serves as an instrumental, interpretive, and expressive means of coming to terms with the host environment. It enables strangers to develop their understanding of the way things are carried out in the host society and the way they themselves need to think, feel, and act in that environment. Until strangers have acquired a sufficient level of host communication competence, they are handicapped in their ability to meet their physical, psychological, and social needs and goals.

• • •

Social Communication

The strangers' host communication competence is directly and reciprocally associated with their participation in the interpersonal and mass communication activities of the host society. . . . [E]very host social communication event offers the stranger an opportunity for cultural learning.

Host-interpersonal communication, in particular, helps strangers to secure vital information and insight into the mind-sets and behaviors of the local people, thereby providing them with points of reference for a check and validation of their own behaviors. Most strangers in a new culture must begin to form a new set of relationships as they find themselves without an adequate support system when they are confronted with highly uncertain and stressful situations. The crucial importance of host interpersonal communication activities in facilitating cross-cultural adaptation has been acknowledged and demonstrated widely and repeatedly across the social sciences (Kim, 1986). In some cases, the degree of host interpersonal communication has been accepted as an indicator of cross-cultural adaptation itself (e.g., Gordon, 1973; Nagata, 1969; Spicer, 1968).

Similarly, *host mass communication* has been observed to facilitate the adaptation of strangers (Subervi-Velez, 1986). While the interpersonal channel of communication offers opportunities for more personalized and thus "meaningful" involvement with members of the host culture, mass communication channels help them participate in vicarious learning through "para-social interactions" with the host environment at large beyond the ordinary reaches of their daily lives (Horton & Wohl, 1979, p. 32). Compared with interpersonal communication activities, mediated communication activities may be governed by a lesser sense of mutual obligation and effort. Thus, while host mass communication renders less opportunity for feedback than do interpersonal communication situations where a quick exchange of information is maximal (Rogers, 1979; Schramm, 1979), it serves as an important source of cultural and language learning, particularly during early phases of the adaptation process when strangers have less direct access and less likelihood to succeed in communicating with the natives face-to-face.

In many countries today, most strangers' interpersonal and mass communication activities involve their coethnics or conationals and home cultural experiences as well. Whether we speak of British compounds in India, American military posts in West Germany, Puerto Rican barrios in New York City, Chinatown in Tokyo, or a Japanese student association in a Canadian university, ethnic communities provide strangers with access to their original cultural experiences. Many aliens have organized some form of mutual aid or self-help organizations that render assistance to those who need material, informational, emotional, and other forms of social support (DeCocq, 1976). In the case of many larger ethnic communities, mass media (including newspapers, radio stations, and television programs) perform various informational, educational, entertainment, and social services for their members.

These *ethnic interpersonal* and *mass communication systems* serve adaptation-facilitating functions for new immigrants and sojourners during the initial phase of their adaptation process (Kim, 1987). Because many strangers initially lack host communication competence and do not have access to resources to become self-reliant, they tend to seek and depend heavily on ethnic sources of informational, material, and emotional help and thereby compensate for the lack of support they are capable of obtaining from host nationals. Due to the relatively "easy" or stress-free communication experiences in dealing with their own ethnic individuals and media, in-traethnic communication experiences offer temporary refuge. In the case of certain temporary residents, such as American military personnel stationed overseas, their daily duties confine their social communication activities almost exclusively to other Americans at the military base.

Beyond the initial phase, however, ethnic social communication has been found to be important for group identity maintenance (Boekestijn, 1988) and negatively associated with adaptation into the host culture (J. Kim, 1980; Kim, 1976, 1977, 1980, 1986, 1989, 1990; Shah, 1991; Walker, 1993; Yang, 1988). Whether by choice or by circumstance, the strangers' heavy and prolonged reliance on coethnics sustains their original cultural identity and limits their opportunities to participate in the social communication activities of the host society (Burgess, 1978). Implied in this observation is that strangers cannot remain strongly ethnic in their communication activities and, at the same time, become highly adapted to the host cultural environment. They are likely to remain poor in their functional fitness in the host environment, which, in turn, hinders their intercultural transformation.

Environment

To the extent that strangers participate in the social (interpersonal, mass) communication activities of the host society, the host society exerts influence on their adaptation process. The nature of such influence, in turn, is shaped by the various characteristics of the host society and, for many, their social environment includes fellow coethnics as well.

Given the mixed nature of the environment in which many strangers find themselves, three environmental conditions are identified . . . as affect-ing the individual stranger's adaptation process: (1) host receptivity, (2) host conformity pressure, and (3) ethnic group strength. *Host receptivity* . . . refers to the degree to which a given environment is structurally and psychologically accessible and open to strangers. Different locations in a given society may offer different levels of receptivity toward different groups of strangers. For example, Canadian visitors arriving in a small town in the United States are likely to find a largely receptive host environment. On the other hand, the same small town may show less receptivity toward visitors from a lesser known and vastly different culture such as Turkey or Kenya.

Along with receptivity, *host conformity pressure* (Zajonc, 1952) varies as well across societies and communities. Here, *conformity pressure* refers to the extent to which the environment challenges strangers to adopt the normative patterns of the host culture and its communication system. In particular, the conformity pressure of a host environment is often reflected in the expectations the natives routinely have about how strangers should think and act. . . . Different host environments show different levels of tolerance to strangers and their ethnic/cultural characteristics. For example, heterogeneous and open host environments such as the United States generally tend to hold a more pluralistic political ideology concerning cultural/ethnic differences and thereby exert less pressure on strangers to change their habitual ways. Within the United States, ethnically heterogeneous metropolitan areas such as Los Angeles and Miami tend to demand less that strangers conform to the dominant Anglo-white cultural practices than do small, ethnically homogeneous rural towns. Further, even within a city, certain neighborhoods may be more homogeneous and thus expect more conformity from strangers.

The degree to which a given host environment exerts receptivity and conformity pressure on a stranger is closely influenced by *the strength of the stranger's ethnic group* relative to the host environment at large. . . . In the long run, however, a strong ethnic community is likely to exert stronger social pressure to conform to its own cultural practices and to maintain the strangers' ethnic group identity. This, in turn, discourages their participation in the host social communication activities that are necessary for their adaptation to the larger society. . . .

Predisposition

Along with the above-described host and ethnic environmental conditions, the process of cross-cultural adaptation is affected by the internal conditions of the strangers themselves prior to resettlement in the host society. . . .

First, strangers come to their new environment with differing levels of *preparedness,* that is, the mental, emotional, and motivational readiness to deal with the new cultural environment including understanding of the host language and culture. Affecting their preparedness are a wide range of formal and informal learning activities they may have had prior to moving to the host society. Included in such activities are the schooling and training in, and media exposure to, the host language and culture, and the direct and indirect experiences in dealing with members of the host society as well as the prior intercultural adaptation experiences in general. In addition, the strangers' preparedness is often influenced by the level of positive expectations toward the host society and of willingness to participate in it voluntarily. Voluntary, long-term immigrants, for example, are more likely to enter the host environment with a greater readiness for making adaptive changes in themselves compared with temporary sojourners who unwillingly relocate for reasons imposed on them.

Strangers also differ in cultural, racial, and linguistic backgrounds. The term *ethnicity* is used here as an inclusive term to refer to various characteristics of strangers pertaining to their distinctiveness as a people. As such, the Japanese sojourners and immigrants bring to a given host society common physical, linguistic, and cultural features that are different than, say, Mexicans or the French. Such ethnic characteristics play a crucial role in the cross-cultural adaptation process, as it affects the ease or difficulty with which the stranger is able to develop communication competence in a given host society and participate in its social communication activities. For instance,

many of the Japanese business executives in the United States are likely to face a lesser amount of host receptivity in overcoming their physical, linguistic, and cultural barriers than are their British counterparts. This suggests that strangers of different ethnic backgrounds embark on their cross-cultural journey with different levels of advantage or "handicap" (Phinney & Rosenthal, 1992, p. 145). . . .

Along with ethnic backgrounds, strangers enter a host environment with a set of more or less enduring *personality* traits. They begin the challenge of the new environment within the context of their existing personality, which serves as the basis upon which they pursue and internalize new experiences with varying degrees of success. Of particular interest to the present theory are those personality resources that would help facilitate the strangers' adaptation by enabling them to endure stressful challenges and to maximize new learning, both of which are essential to their intercultural transformation.

Openness is such a personality construct. . . . Openness minimizes resistance and maximizes a willingness to attend to new and changed circumstances. Openness further enables strangers to perceive and interpret various events and situations in the new environment as they occur with less rigid, ethnocentric judgments. . . . Also, the present meaning of openness includes the optimism and affirmative orientation in the strangers' basic outlook on life as well as their fundamental "self-trust" in the face of adverse circumstances. It is a dimension of personality that enables strangers to continually seek to acquire new cultural knowledge and to cultivate greater intellectual, emotional/aesthetic, and behavioral compatibility with the natives.

Strength is an additional personality trait that is vital to cross-cultural adaptation. Like openness, personality strength is a broad concept that represents a range of interrelated personality attributes such as resilience, risk-taking, hardiness, persistence, patience, elasticity, and resourcefulness. Personality strength thus means the inner quality that absorbs "shocks" from the environment and bounces back without being seriously damaged by them. Low levels of personality strength are seen in tendencies to be shy, fearful,

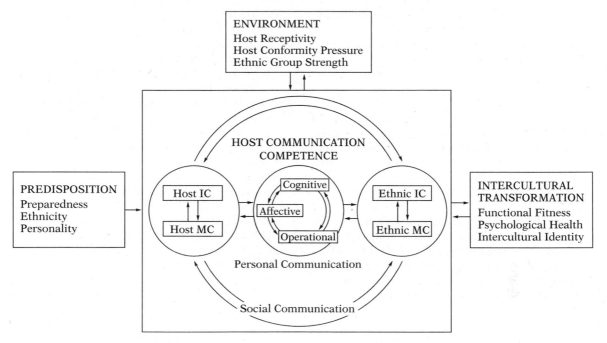

FIGURE 2   *A Communication Model of the Structure of Cross-Cultural Adaptation*
(NOTE: IC = interpersonal communication; MC = mass communication.)

and easily distressed by uncertain or stressful situations. On the other hand, individuals with high levels of personality strength tend to be stimulated by new challenges and remain effervescent and confident (Lifton, 1993).

The above two broad concepts, openness and strength, help define the strangers' overall personality predisposition to "push" themselves in their adaptation process. Strangers with greater openness and strength are less likely to succumb and more likely to take on the challenging situations in the host society. Their personality predisposition serves as an inner resource for working toward developing the host communication competence, so as to facilitate their own intercultural transformation and growth. A serious lack of openness and strength, on the other hand, would weaken their adaptive capacity and would serve as self-imposed psychological barriers against their own adaptation.

• • •

Conclusion

The present theory portrays cross-cultural adaptation as a collaborative effort, in which a stranger and the receiving environment are engaged in a joint venture [see Figure 2]. As such, one cannot overemphasize the important role that the host society can play to embrace the stranger and facilitate his or her adaptive effort. Ultimately, however, cross-cultural adaptation is, and must be, "the gift of the individuals" (Steele, 1990, p. 171). It is neither reasonable nor practical to expect any large population to significantly modify its own cultural habits with the sense of urgency that is required of a newcomer. The main power and responsibility for change has to reside in the stranger who, in the end, is responsible for his or her own psychological and social welfare.

Indeed, most strangers under most conditions appear to understand this reality and to accept their cross-cultural predicaments as part and parcel of living in an unfamiliar cultural milieu. They are not only willing but also able to make necessary self-corrections, recognizing that doing so is in their own self-interest (Cornell, 1988). Such is the case in the experiences of many of the former Peace Corps volunteers, diplomats, missionaries, and exchange students, not to mention the countless immigrants and refugees who have ventured through experiential territories seldom thought possible or even desirable. Their successful adaptation experiences are represented by Japanese American writer Jeanne Wakatsuki Houston (1981), who offers a personal intercultural transformation:

> Now I entertain according to how I feel that day. If my Japanese sensibility is stronger, I act accordingly and feel OK. If I feel like going all American, I can do that too and feel OK. I've come to accept the cultural hybrid of my personality and recognize it as a strength, not as a weakness.

Personal testimonials such as this bear witness to the remarkable human capacity to carry on life even under the conditions of an extreme cultural estrangement. Cross-cultural adaptation as depicted in this theory thus is not an extraordinary phenomenon that only exceptional individuals achieve. Rather, it is simply an incident of the normal human mutability manifesting itself in the work of ordinary people "stretching" themselves out of the old and familiar. In their individual stories, the present theory finally rests.

SELECTED REFERENCES

Adler, P. S. (1976). Beyond cultural identity: Reflections on cultural and multicultural man. In L. Samovar & R. Porter (Eds.), *Intercultural communication: A reader* (2nd ed., pp. 362–378). Belmont, CA: Wadsworth.

Boekestijn, C. (1988). Intercultural migration and the development of personal identity. *International Journal of Intercultural Relations, 12*(2), 83–105.

Burgess, M. (1978). The resurgence of ethnicity: Myth or reality? *Ethnic and Racial Studies, 1*(3), 265–285.

Cornell, S. (1988). *The return of the Natives: American Indian political resurgence.* New York: Oxford University Press.

Dance, F., & Larson, C. (1976). *The functions of human communication: A theoretical approach.* New York: Holt, Rinehart & Winston.

DeCocq, G. (1976). European and North American self-help movements: Some contrasts. In A. Katz & E. Bender (Eds.), *The strength in us: Self-help groups in the modern world* (pp. 202–208). New York: New Viewpoint.

Geyer, F. (1980). *Alienation theories: A general systems approach.* New York: Pergamon.

Gordon, M. (1973). Assimilation in America: Theory and reality. In P. Rose (Ed.), *The study of society* (pp. 350–365). New York: Random House.

Hall, E. T. (1976). *Beyond culture.* Garden City, NY: Anchor.

Horton, D., & Wohl, R. (1979). Mass communication and para-social interaction. In G. Gumpert & R. Cathcart (Eds.), *Inter/media: Interpersonal communication in a media world* (pp. 32–55). New York: Oxford University Press.

Houston, J. (1981, May). *Beyond Manzanar: A personal view on the Asian-American womanhood.* Audio-recording of a lecture delivered at Governors State University, University Park, IL.

Kim, J. (1980). Explaining acculturation in a communication framework: An empirical test. *Communication Monograph, 47*(3), 155–179.

Kim, Y. (1976). *Communication patterns of foreign immigrants in the process of acculturation: A survey among the Korean population in Chicago.* Unpublished doctoral dissertation, Northwestern University, Evanston, IL.

Kim, Y. (1977). Inter-ethnic and intra-ethnic communication: A study of Korean immigrants in Chicago. *International and Intercultural Communication Annual, 4*, 53–68.

Kim, Y. (1980). *Research project report on Indochinese refugees in Illinois: Vol. I. Introduction, summary and recommendations. Vol. 2. Methods and procedures. Vol. 3. Population characteristics and service needs. Vol. 4. Psychological, social and cultural adjustment of Indochinese refugees. Vol. 5. Survey of agencies serving Indochinese refugees* (Based on a grant from the Department of Health, Education and Welfare Region V, pp. 95–549). Chicago: Travelers Aid Society.

Kim, Y. (1986). Understanding the social context of intergroup communication: A personal network approach. In W. Gudykunst (Ed.), *Intergroup communication* (pp. 86–95). London: Edward Arnold.

Kim, Y. (1987). Facilitating immigrant adaptation: The role of communication and interpersonal ties. In T. Albrecht & M. Adelman (Eds.), *Communicating social support: Process in context* (pp. 192–211). Newbury Park, CA: Sage.

Kim, Y. (1989). Personal, social, and economic adaptation: The case of 1975–1979 arrivals in Illinois. In D. Haines (Ed.), *Refugees as immigrants: Survey research on Cambodians, Laotians, and Vietnamese in America* (pp. 86–104). Totowa, NJ: Rowman & Littlefield.

Kim, Y. (1990). Communication and adaptation of Asian Pacific refugees in the United States. *Journal of Pacific Rim Communication, 1,* 191–207.

Kim, Y. (1993, May). *Synchrony and intercultural communication competence.* Paper presented at the annual meeting of the International Communication Association, Washington, DC.

Lazarus, R. (1966). *Psychological stress and the coping process.* St. Louis, MO: McGraw-Hill.

Lifton, R. (1993). *The protean self: Human resilience in an age of fragmentation.* New York: Basic Books.

Nagata, K. (1969). *A statistical approach to the study of acculturation of an ethnic group based on communication oriented variables: The case of Japanese Americans in Chicago.* Unpublished doctoral dissertation, University of Illinois, Urbana-Champaign.

Phinney, J., & Rosenthal, D. (1992). Ethnic identity in adolescence: Process, context, and outcome. In G. Adams, T. Gullota, & R. Montemayer (Eds.), *Adolescent identity formation* (pp. 145–172). Newbury Park, CA: Sage.

Rogers, E. (1979). Mass media and interpersonal communication. In G. Gumpert & R. Cathcart (Eds.), *Inter/media: Interpersonal communication in a media world* (pp. 192–213). New York: Oxford University Press.

Schramm, W. (1979). Channels and audiences. In G. Gumpert & R. Cathcart (Eds.), *Inter/media: Interpersonal communication in a media world* (pp. 160–174). New York: Oxford University Press.

Shah, H. (1991). Communication and cross-cultural adaptation patterns among Asian Indians. *International Journal of Intercultural Relations, 15*(3), 311–321.

Shibutani, T., & Kwan, K. (1965). *Ethnic stratification: A comparative approach.* New York: Macmillan.

Slavin, M., & Kriegman, D. (1992). *The adaptive design of the human psyche.* New York: Guilford.

Spicer, E. (1968). Acculturation. In D. Sills (Ed.), *International encyclopedia of the social sciences* (pp. 21–27). New York: Macmillan.

Steele, S. (1990). *The content of our character: A new vision of race in America.* New York: St. Martin's.

Subervi-Velez, F. (1986). The mass media and ethnic assimilation and pluralism. *Communication Research, 13*(1), 71–96.

Thayer, L. (1975). Knowledge, order, and communication. In B. Rubin & J. Kim (Eds.), *General systems theory and human communication* (pp. 237–245). Rochelle Park, NJ: Hayden.

Walker, D. (1993, May). *The role of the mass media in the adaptation of Haitian immigrants in Miami.* Unpublished doctoral dissertation, Indiana University, Indianapolis.

Yang, S. (1988, June). *The role of mass media in immigrants' political socialization: A study of Korean immigrants in Northern California.* Unpublished doctoral dissertation, Stanford University, Stanford, CA.

Zaharna, R. (1989). Self-shock: The double-binding challenges of identity. *International Journal of Intercultural Relations, 13*(4), 501–525.

Zajonc, R. (1952). Aggressive attitude of the "stranger" as a function of conformity pressures. *Human Relations, 5,* 205–216.

KEY TERMS

adaptation	host environment
intercultural identity	interpersonal communication
stress	
growth	ethnic communication

DISCUSSION QUESTIONS

1. Why is cross-cultural adaptation so stressful?
2. Do you think it ever happens that sojourners do

not ultimately adapt and grow in cross-cultural transitions?

3. Can you identify groups of sojourners or migrants for whom cross-cultural adaptation is particularly difficult?

4. Do you think this theory would hold true for sojourners and migrants everywhere in the world? Why or why not?

5. What kinds of research methods might one use to gather information that would prove or disprove Kim's theory?

32
IDENTITY AND INTERCULTURAL COMMUNICATION COMPETENCE IN REENTRY

SHELLEY L. SMITH

Introduction

I was excited to see my family, my friends, eat certain foods that I hadn't been able to eat, and do activities that I hadn't been able to do. But terror was still underlying because I knew that I had changed a lot, that certain ideas and attitudes had changed, and that at times my reactions would be really different than what people would be expecting. I think that was the main source of my terror, knowing that I had changed and trying to figure out how I would fit back into the place that I had left. It was like I was a piece that had been taken out of a puzzle, but I was a different shape now and I didn't know whether I was going to be like an amoeba and just ooze back into it or if I was going to have to cut pieces of myself off and reapply them. That was the terror.

This U.S. student is describing how she felt before returning from study abroad. Her feelings of having changed and her expression of fear and confusion about how that change will affect her life at home are not unusual among sojourners who have lived, worked, and shared the lives of people in another culture.

This essay uses the "voices" of returnees to illustrate eight basic assumptions about (1) the rela-

tionships between identity change, cultural adaptation, and reentry; (2) how identity change makes communication between returnees and members of their home culture (at times) *intercultural;* and (3) the role identity plays in intercultural communication competence (ICCC). Finally, these issues and concerns are integrated into a single model of ICCC in reentry.

The discussion deals specifically with voluntary sojourners who have spent substantial time abroad and had meaningful interactions in their host culture. Their experiences are likely to be different from experiences of tourists, people who are isolated from their hosts (i.e., military personnel, guest workers in countries such as Saudi Arabia), and refugees. The term "abroad" is used to describe a significantly different culture, but it's quite possible to experience profound cultural difference without leaving the United States. A middle-class American who spent a lengthy period of time living on a Navaho reservation might experience changes as profound as one who lived for a time in Japan.

Assumptions About Reentry, Identity, and ICCC

1. *Reentry is a transition, and like all transitions it has potential for both pain and growth.*

These consequences are associated with identity change. Although "culture shock" used to be treated as a negative result of resistance to cultural adjustment, recent scholars have framed it as a normal part of culture learning—a "transition experience" qualitatively similar to any experience of fundamental, life-altering change, both painful and positive in its potential for intrapersonal growth. In fact, research shows that those who experience the greatest culture shock often achieve the most cultural effectiveness (Hawes & Kealey, 1989). The idea that culture shock is really deep learning places it at the heart of an intercultural experience. Grove and Torbijörn (1993) went so far as to suggest that "culture learning is possible only to the extent that one's frame of reference has had its tightly integrated and monolithic character disturbed" (p. 84). In addition, many scholars now believe that returning home (reentry) may have greater impact on the person than the initial experience in the foreign culture had (LaBrack, 1993). Returnees may feel "out of sync," no longer connected to those around them:

> I found it harder coming back than going, just because with going, I had everything to look forward to and . . . when I got back everything was just the same; nothing had changed; I felt like I had changed so much and everyone else had just stayed the same.

For others, the experience involves feelings akin to grief over leaving people behind:

> I remember being quite depressed because of what I had left . . . it eventually hit me and I began to realize that I had to leave everyone behind . . . I remember wanting to go back . . . to just be back there again . . .

> One guy . . . when I first got there, he was my interpreter, my translator, and my tour guide . . . he was my mother, my best friend, my boyfriend . . . he was everything to me . . . at least for a period of time. . . . and when I left him, it was really hard for me . . . like losing one of my limbs.

However, if the potential for adjustment difficulty in reentry is greater than the overseas adjustment, so is the potential for growth. Many people find that the difficulty of coming home helps them realize the importance of their experience abroad and inspires them to make significant changes in their lives and relationships.

2. *Reentry is the time when sojourners integrate their international experience with life in their home culture.* Reentry requires that returnees make a number of conscious and unconscious decisions about what aspects of their experience abroad will affect their lives and decisions at home. Recognizing precisely what has been learned and creatively applying that knowledge can be more or less difficult depending on the home culture's tolerance for deviation from the norm, the individual's psychological makeup, and the depth and breadth of the changes the person has undergone:

> You need to keep in mind how you're going to integrate that experience into your life . . . and understand that when you come home, what you did abroad is not over . . . it doesn't end right there . . . it keeps going and will go for the rest of your life as a part of you that is integrated into your being.

3. *Reentry differs from other cross-cultural transitions in the nature of the assumptions, expectations, and communication negotiations that are made regarding cultural identity.* Reentry differs from adaptation abroad in at least three ways: (1) *expectations* about the difficulty of the transition; (2) the unique aspects of returnees' *cognitive, behavioral,* and *affective change;* and (3) returnees' *awareness* of those changes (Martin, 1984). Although sojourners are likely to expect that they will need to adjust to the newness in the foreign environment, many return home expecting a comfortable sense of familiarity:

> I expected just to go home. . . . Everything would be the same. I knew that there will be some changes but I didn't expect that there would be this readjustment process to such a great extent.

Home can take on an idealistic quality where people, places, and events have stood still. Furthermore, family and friends are not likely to expect the returnee to have changed very much. The unrealistic quality of these expectations leaves both the returnees and their significant others unprepared for homecoming difficulties.

> I thought it would be a piece of cake. I thought, "I'm an American, this can't be easier. I know it takes a couple months of going, 'What?' And then it's fine." I went back to my original campus—same dorm room, same roommate, class schedule on a campus that I could draw maps of with my eyes closed, and everything was like it was when I left . . . not!

Sojourners may not immediately realize how much they have changed. As they adapted to the host culture, they felt more "normal," gaining positive reinforcement from those around them. The return home brings these changes into awareness by "forcing" comparisons to the home culture. This can mean facing once familiar surroundings and having them suddenly seem strange, or becoming aware of previously unconscious cultural patterns and expectations and of how they themselves have changed. The sojourner may feel critical of many things "American" that he or she previously accepted without question.

> The "hugest" thing that hits me all the time is our way of relating to each other socially in the US. There's a lot of focus on primary family relationships and there's not a lot of focus on extended family. You get all your needs met by a partner in a lot of cases . . . it's not spread out. Whereas in Senegal, there were all these different social relationships that were all important and also feelings of community. People don't talk to each other here . . . on the street, on the bus, whatever . . . everybody's focused on their own thing. . . . I think human beings need a lot more interaction than we're afforded in our busy schedules. I think that's really sad.

Reentry is also affected by the number of levels at which sojourners confront changes: (1) between the foreign and home environment, (2) in people and places at home (divorce, marriage, a new home, school, or job), and (3) within oneself. As a result, returnees can have multiple responses to a situation that alternate between predeparture, foreign, and postarrival perceptions (Adler,

1981). All of these changes can cause disorientation, frustration, confusion, or anger:

> . . . my parents were divorced and they both got in very serious relationships while I was gone . . . they both are now remarried. My dad remarried a couple months after I got home, but my mom . . . this man that she met moved in about three days before I got back . . . and I was really upset about it at the time. I was thinking, "I'm going to get home and everything is going to be different . . . there's going to be this guy there and I don't even know who he is and that is very uncharacteristic of my mother." I couldn't believe it.

4. *Identity change and identity negotiation are the keys to understanding ICCC in reentry.* If we recognize that living in another culture causes change, we can expect part of that change to be identity-altering. Insight into how identity influences judgment of communication competence is provided by Collier and Thomas's (1988) *Theory of Cultural Identity.* They suggest that identities are defined through interactions with others, and that *cultural identities* involve identification with and acceptance into groups with shared significant symbols, meanings, and rules for conduct. Culture, therefore, exists only to the degree that it has been internalized and is shared by individuals in a particular group.

Further, people have multiple cultural identities (based in ethnicity, gender, religion, race, occupation, etc.) that can emerge through and in an interaction. Because of this, *communication competence* is a dynamic phenomenon that changes with the identity that emerges in a particular situation. An interaction becomes intercultural if the cultural identities of the people involved differ greatly. *Intercultural communication competence,* therefore, is conduct that is appropriate and effective for both individuals.

Accepting that people bring multiple identities to an interaction, and that communication becomes intercultural when the people involved in an interaction adopt different cultural identities, helps us to see the intercultural nature of communication in reentry. The need to achieve identity satisfaction in relationships is a prime concern of many returnees. They will often discontinue friendships or romantic relationships if this process is unsuccessful and will develop new relationships that are more in tune with their new sense of self (Martin, 1986).

If cultural identity is tied to particular communication behaviors and returnees have acquired other cultural competencies and behaviors, it's reasonable to assume that at some time, the returnees' "intercultural" identities will emerge in interactions at home. Returnees may not be aware of the intercultural nature of this interaction, and it's likely to be a mystery to home culture members who do not share the returnees' international experience. With this identity confusion comes confusion in the ability to relate to others:

> In Taiwan, if I was talking to someone in his office I'd shake his hand and he'd show me the door. And I'd say, "No you don't need to show me to the door," but he'd show me to the door anyway. I was in a situation recently in a man's office here in Minneapolis and he was showing me the door and I said, . . . "Ahhh, you don't need to show me the door, I know my way out." He just stopped . . . I had to open the door myself. And I thought to myself, "What a rude guy! Where does he come off?" Then I thought, "But you told him . . ." But it still left a sour taste in my mouth.

Further, the inability of others to understand this identity confusion and returnees' needs to have their intercultural identity and experience validated adds to the "intercultural" nature of their interactions. It follows that communication behaviors adopted in any given interaction would be tied to how important the intercultural identity is in a given situation or relationship.

5. *Communication is central to the successful negotiation of a person's new (inter)cultural identity during reentry.* We know that effective communication and relationship formation plays an important role in sojourner adjustment abroad. Cross-cultural psychologist Nancy Adler (1981) found that "strong external support" (being able to make "a connection" with others regarding one's experiences abroad) also plays an important

role in successful reentry adjustment. Returnees frequently describe concerns about their inability to communicate experiences to family and friends. The richness of people, relationships, places, events, feelings, and physical sensations often seem largely inexpressible:

> The most frustrating thing for me was trying to communicate to people how something was; they just couldn't understand . . . they couldn't have an idea of what that was really like because they had never been there . . . they had never seen it . . . they had never tried it. And when you're trying to communicate to someone how something was, you really can't put it in words . . . you just can never get it as close to how you'd like them to understand it because they have just not a clue . . . they really don't.

> There are words . . . that are in my vocabulary now . . . that I cannot express to anyone who isn't Chinese or hasn't studied Chinese. . . .

Many also describe being unable to share things they *would* like to talk about because those at home are unable or unwilling to make the effort to listen to their stories about being abroad and their feelings, concerns, and confusion about reentry.

> Part of it too was that "Oh, how was your trip?" kind of question. People wanted a one-minute capsule—"It was great"—and they didn't want it to be, like, "Oh, well sometimes it was really hard to communicate"—They didn't want to hear all these things. I felt like, "God, no one really cares that I was away for so long and all these happened to me and I met all these people."

6. *If communication difficulties occur as a result of identity change brought on by internalizing different cultural values, social systems, and behaviors, it's important to realize that the person's entire* cognitive, behavioral, *and* affective *systems have been readjusted to accommodate those changes.* While abroad, the sojourner experiences a totally new environment and, with it, a loss of familiar external reinforcement. To adapt to this new environment, the sojourner makes *affective* (emotional and value adjustments), *behavioral*

(developing new verbal, nonverbal, and relational skills), and *cognitive* (knowledge and perceptual categories) changes (Kim, 1988). These changes are deeply interconnected, result from and are created through relationships and interaction in the host culture, and ultimately impact the sojourner's identity (Zaharna, 1989). As sojourners adapt, they integrate aspects of the host culture into their self-conception; identity becomes increasingly flexible and grows beyond the psychological boundaries of any one culture, and their sense of self changes from a single-culture identification to an increasingly *intercultural* one. There is no question that many returnees feel these changes deeply:

> I can't even imagine what my life would be like if I had never gone abroad. I think from the moment I left, there was no way to ever go back to what I was. Certain things I remember about myself that I know I'm not anymore . . . had I not gone away I would have continued along a different path. But my whole life now revolves around having been abroad.

> Going to Morocco was utterly life-changing. It completely changed who I was and who I hoped to be.

During reentry, this transformed identity and its accompanying perceptions and behaviors create a new set of adaptation issues. The sojourner has experienced complex changes that affect the whole person. Returnees can become "strangers" in their own culture. It's understandable, therefore, that readaptation and communication at home will at times involve concerns that impact the sojourner's identity.

7. *Because identity change is complex, identity restructuring during reentry is not easily accomplished. The integration of old and new knowledge, behaviors, feelings, and perspectives requires time and effort because all aspects of the internal and external environment must be considered.* Psychologist Diedre Kramer's (1986) model of adult cognitive development gives insight into the difficulty of integrating old and new knowledge and identities during reentry. She introduced the idea that

adult cognition centers on the development of relativistic and dialectic reasoning. *Relativistic* reasoning involves the awareness that "all things are in a state of flux, and our knowledge is influenced by the context in which we view reality. . . . Absolutes do not exist independently of the whole in which they are imbedded" (p. 280). Contradictions raised by this awareness can be accepted. *Dialectic* reasoning recognizes change as inherent in our knowledge of reality. It involves the ability to accept change as an evolutionary reconciliation of the tensions that result from the interaction and integration of opposites. This requires the capacity to see connections between knowledge events that at first appear incompatible. Kramer sees the development of these reasoning capacities as occurring most frequently in middle age (30 to 50).

Kramer's perspective provides a framework for discussing the increasing capacity for cognitive complexity, tolerance of ambiguity, and the intrapersonal growth and change so frequently described in the literature on impact of international experience. By transferring sojourners from one cultural context or "reality" to another, they may experience the acceleration of the natural patterns of cognitive development. The need first to recognize the existence of multiple cultural realities (relativistic) and then to integrate these seemingly unconnected elements into one's permanent definition of self (dialectic) adds credibility to the claims of so many study-abroad students that they feel they are more mature than their peers. The difficulty of this process was expressed by a returnee who said:

> I think the whole thing is as much about the two cultures as it's just about the single individual . . . and I went nuts trying to be two things in two places at the same time.

8. *The issues and dimensions of reentry are directly associated with the types of communication coping strategies returnees use to renegotiate their identities and relationships.* In the same way that intrapersonal change during reentry occurs on affective, behavioral, and cognitive levels, strategies identified for coping in adjustment occur on the

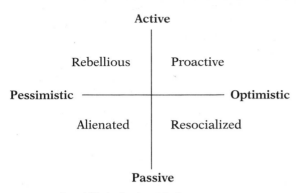

Active

Rebellious   Proactive

Pessimistic ─────────┼───────── Optimistic

Alienated   Resocialized

Passive

FIGURE 1   *Adler's Coping Modes*

same levels (Anderson, 1994). Nancy Adler (1981) also identified optimistic-pessimistic and active-passive dimensions that affect reentry. *Optimistic* modes cast reentry and the home culture in a positive light, whereas *pessimistic* modes view both as negative or problematic. *Active* modes focus on changing the environment to increase home culture fit; *passive* modes focus on internal change to achieve that fit. These dimensions intersect to describe four "coping modes" that returnees can adopt (Figure 1). The *resocialized* mode is passive and optimistic. Returnees in this mode fit easily back into their home environment, have little awareness of change, and have rewarding communication with those at home.

The *alienated* mode is passive and pessimistic. Returnees in this mode are largely unaware of the changes they have undergone. They feel alienated and out of place in their home environment but are unable to articulate why. They withdraw physically or emotionally or both and experience problematic communication with those around them. The *rebellious* mode is active and pessimistic. Returnees in this mode are acutely aware of changes, are critical of their culture, and seek actively to remake their home environment to accommodate their perspective. Their critical approach tends to alienate those around them. The *proactive* mode is active and optimistic. Returnees in this mode are aware of change, understand and creatively integrate their home and host country experiences in the self *and* the environment, and experience positive communication with others.

According to Adler, using a proactive style of coping maximizes potential for personal growth and continued learning:

> With my family . . . at first there seemed to be a real parent-kid struggle . . . the struggle of . . . child/parent separation . . . the child trying to define, "OK this is who I am" in front of the parent—which is different than what the parents expected. And after that struggle, . . . I'd see a respect . . . a respect for the fact that each is formed by our own experiences. . . . I had to be the instigator of some thoughts and theories into my family. I needed to explain that I had changed and the reasons that I changed and how I had changed. I was trying to look for a foundation to give them and say, "OK, here's what so and so says" or "this is what the research says," "this is what's going on with me."

The four coping *modes* identified by Adler can also be seen as communication *strategies* used by all returnees at one time or another. Given this, the *appropriate* and *effective* choice of communication coping strategies in reentry is a form of communication competence. If we also assume that these strategies are chosen because the returnee's intercultural or "other-cultural" identity has emerged in the interaction, it then becomes an instance of ICCC.

> There are times where people make such ignorant and biased comments and it makes me furious. In some situations, I don't really address anything because I know I won't be able to control my own frustrations (*passive*) and sometimes it's not just frustrations with that person but with the comment in general . . . where I know it's not just that one person who's thinking that but it's people all over the place who think like that and I think, "how am I going to make this person understand?" Because there are times when I think that ignorance is so great that my saying one thing isn't going to make any difference—people are going to interpret it in the wrong way and take it to fortify their own stereotypes or bias (*pessimistic*). So I just don't say anything; I just leave. Other times I try to

explain why a certain thing would be happening and look at the historical, social, economic, and cultural aspects of it . . . and I try to incorporate how the United States and its government and policies and ideals have directly influenced what happens in another country (*active*). So that's a battle—to educate people (*optimistic*).

Adapting a Model of ICCC to Reentry

So far, we have explored the connections between reentry and cross-cultural adjustment, reentry communication concerns, the impact of cultural adjustment on identity change, and how returnees cope with interactions when that intercultural identity is in play. The effort to integrate all of these issues and concerns into a single model brings us to one of the most comprehensive theories linking identity and ICCC to date: Cupach and Imahori's *Identity Management Theory* (1993).

Identity needs are said to vary along three interdependent dimensions:

♦ *Scope:* how many people potentially share the identity

♦ *Salience:* the importance of a particular identity in an interaction

♦ *Intensity:* the strength with which the identity is communicated

Variations in these dimensions are influenced by the relational, social, and cultural contexts in which an interaction occurs and the cultural identity (or identities) involved. From this perspective, competence includes one's ability to successfully negotiate mutually acceptable identities in an interaction.

Face needs vary along the dimensions of autonomy, acceptance, and respect:

♦ *Autonomy face* is the need for recognition as a unique individual who exists separate from cultural or group stereotypes. Those from more individualistic cultures such as the United States are normally considered to have high autonomy face needs and well-honed skills with regard to "taking care of yourself" (and the maintenance of those needs) in an interaction.

♦ *Acceptance face* is the need to be identified with and accepted into a broader community. Community or identity groups can be based in a wide variety of cultures. The more a culture values these relational concerns, the more important this dimension is likely to be.

♦ *Respect/Competence face* is the need to be recognized as having skills and abilities that allow one to meet necessary communication and relationship needs and expectations.

Dialectical tension exists between autonomy face needs and both acceptance and respect/competence face needs in identity and relationship negotiations. For example, our need to be recognized as individuals exists in opposition to the need to have our membership in a community acknowledged. Failure to balance the tension between these face needs can lead to stress as well as communication and relationship breakdown.

Because relationship phases are highly interdependent and cyclical, ICCC develops with and within the relationship. It influences the speed and effectiveness with which relationships move through the stages of *trial, enmeshment,* and *renegotiation.* To this end, interactions do not always need to be competent to result in relationship growth. For instance, people in intercultural relationships may inadvertently offend each other by violating the other's cultural rules. However, this "incompetent" behavior can help them identify important concerns that must be met if the relationship is to strengthen.

Dimensions of Reentry Communication

Identity is the link between the issues of adjustment and ICCC in transition. One does not simply "behave" differently in another culture; that behavior is identity-connected—we perceive our-selves *to be* as we are behaving. As a result, a core concern in any transition is an individual's changing identity. "Successful" (competent, satisfying, relationship-enhancing) communication is a key part of successful intercultural and reentry adaptation and adjustment. ICCC is a process of identity negotiation in which each person has multiple identities in an interaction.

With identity as the central concern, a *cultural* encounter becomes an *intercultural* encounter when the returnee's intercultural or other-cultural identity emerges. This is a *communication obstacle* if it creates a conflict in face needs (face dialectic) in the interaction. What happens in the interaction involves three dimensions: identity, relationship, and communication strategies. The path of this process, its dimensions, and the key concerns for each of these dimensions are illustrated in Figure 2 (p. 312).

Dimension I: Identity

The application of Cupach and Imahori's model shows how face needs and identity needs intersect in the reentry process. First, returnees could be expected to have strong issues associated with all dimensions of intercultural identity:

♦ *Scope* of the shared identity is extremely important to returnees. The need for a shared community (external support system) to understand and provide confirmation of the returnee's intercultural experience is critical to the successful integration of host and home identities. Many returnees seek out others with international or other-culture experience for that validation.

♦ The intercultural identity may be *salient* when the sojourner is in reentry transition. A degree of narcissistic self-focus is not only understandable but healthy when one is undergoing growth and change.

♦ For the same reason, the emotional nature of transition and adjustment will make the *intensity* of the returnee's identity focus in some situations quite strong.

Face Needs

♦ At some point, all returnees confront *autonomy* face needs as they decide how they will deal with the issue of "making their own place in the world" and struggle with the task of redefining their sense of identity.

♦ *Acceptance/fellowship* face needs revolve around the returnees' struggles with feelings of isolation, feeling that they are "going crazy" or that they are the only ones who have ever experienced this sense of alienation—especially if no one in their immediate support group has shared their intercultural experience.

♦ *Respect* and *competence* face needs involve desire to be acknowledged for and to use their other-cultural and intercultural expertise. Returnees may focus on helping other sojourners adjust to their home culture, seek out opportunities to use their languages and culture-specific expertise.

Returnees sometimes experience tension between competing face needs in the following ways:

♦ *Acceptance/Autonomy:* needs for identity integration and finding a way to use their unique talents and experience. Those needs are interdependent; one's identity cannot be separated from one's relational environment.

♦ *Competence/Autonomy:* Because competence would be interpreted differently by those in the home culture who have not shared the sojourner's international experience, the need to feel competent in their interactions would exist in opposition to this same need to do the necessary identity work.

♦ *Competence/Fellowship:* The need to be respected for the knowledge and skills that one has gained abroad would be in opposition to the need for establishing oneself back into a community.

Dimension II: Relationship Stages

Communicators confront relationship issues, shared meanings, and rules for dealing with

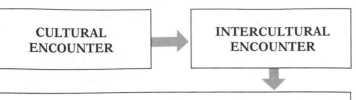

ENCOUNTER OBSTACLE

Conflict in a face dialectic

DIMENSION I: Identity

Intercultural Identity
- Scope
- Salience
- Intensity

Face Needs
- Autonomy
- Acceptance
- Respect

OVERCOME OBSTACLE

Identity negotiation through communication
strategies within a given relational context

DIMENSION II: Relationship negotiation
- Trial
- Enmeshment
- Renegotiation

DIMENSION III: Communication strategies
- Active or passive
- Optimistic or pessimistic
- Affective
- Behavioral
- Cognitive

ADAPTATION

Identity conflict resolution/Integration

FIGURE 2 *Dimensions in Reentry Communication*

conflict. The importance of this dimension during reentry should not be minimized. Many returnees need to have their intercultural identities acknowledged, understood, and confirmed in their relationships with significant others. This takes commitment and work to achieve. The degree of investment that participants have in the relationship will influence the strategies adopted. If existing relationships do not provide that confirmation, new relationships may be built.

♦ *Trial:* Returnees are likely to pursue new relationships with others who confirm their new intercultural identity.

♦ *Enmeshment:* Returnees are most likely to seek understanding from and be committed to continuing relationships that have reached this stage.

♦ *Renegotiation:* This involves the need to confirm the unique cultural identities of relationship partners. This is a key phase for many returnees who are deeply focused on redefining themselves in established relationships.

Dimension III: Communication Strategies

Returnees are faced with a number of difficult choices in negotiating their intercultural identity in reentry: (1) They can fit comfortably back into the home culture and essentially abandon their intercultural experience and identity (*resocialized*); (2) they can attempt to fit back into the home culture and deny their intercultural experience and identity but remain dissatisfied (*alienated*); (3) they can abandon old relationship networks and find new, supportive communities that share their international experience (*rebellious*); or (4) they can seek out new and creative ways to use their international experiences in the home culture (*proactive*). This includes the formation of new relationships based on common experience and the ability to maintain significant relationships with those who do not. Overcoming these identity conflicts requires making choices in communication strategies:

♦ *Active* strategies involve saying or doing something intended to get an active response or induce change.

♦ *Passive* strategies involve retreat, watching, waiting, "biding one's time," remaining silent. Nearly all returnees find that they need to "pick their battles" and make choices about when, where, and with whom they will take up the issue of their time spent abroad.

♦ *Optimistic* strategies involve a sense of positive, growth producing, or successful communication.

♦ *Pessimistic* strategies involve a sense of hopelessness, an inability to communicate feelings or ideas or to make changes in one's environment. This attitude can be read as defeatist or realistic depending on the circumstances.

Returnees may choose one concern over another or seek to integrate two or more. This is an interactive process that involves both partners and often includes negotiation and renegotiation over time. In addition, these strategies may be *affective, behavioral,* or *cognitive.*

The ideal outcome is resolution of the identity conflict through communication. Clearly, this is not always the case. When communication in these areas fails, returnees are faced with choosing between face needs; relationships may be abandoned, or identity needs may be submerged. Although these resolutions are relationship specific, they also represent a learning process that impacts the returnee's repertoire of reentry communication coping strategies (behavioral), the integration (or lack thereof) of the returnee's intercultural identity (affective), and his or her awareness of reentry issues and processes (cognitive).

ICCC in reentry, then, involves the management of interactions in which resolution of tension between face concerns is *appropriate* for the relationship and moves returnees closer to integrating their intercultural identities (*effective*).

Conclusion

Introducing reentry specifically into intercultural communication competence theory provides a set of guidelines for viewing the complexity of issues that face returnees as they renegotiate their sense of place and self in the home culture. As part of complex cultural and relational systems, they can have a wide variety of experiences. The implications of race, gender, relationship depth, life stage, home culture, and the pressures that those concerns place on how returnees deal with the dialectical concerns of self and community all have a place in this model.

REFERENCES

Adler, N. J. (1981). Reentry: Managing cross-cultural transitions. *Group and Organization Studies, 6,* 341–356.

Anderson, L. E. (1994). A new look at an old construct: Cross-cultural adaptation. *International Journal of Intercultural Relations, 18*(3), 293–328.

Collier, M. J., & Thomas, M. (1988). Identity in intercultural communication: An interpretive perspective. In Y. Y. Kim & W. B. Gudykunst (Eds.), *Theories in intercultural communication* (pp. 99–120). Newbury Park, CA: Sage.

Cupach, W. R., & Imahori, T. T. (1993). Identity management theory: Communication competence in intercultural episodes and relationships. In R. Wiseman & J. Koester (Eds.), *Intercultural communication competence* (pp. 193–218). Newbury Park, CA: Sage.

Grove, C., & Torbijörn, I. (1993). A new conceptualization of intercultural adjustment and the goals of training. In R. M. Paige (Ed.), *Education for the intercultural experience* (pp. 73–108). Yarmouth, ME: Intercultural Press.

Kealey, D. J. (1989). A study of cross-cultural effectiveness: Theoretical issues, practical applications. *International Journal of Intercultural Relations, 13,* 387–427.

Kim, Y. Y. (1988). *Communication and cross-cultural adaptation.* Philadelphia: Multilingual Matters.

Kramer, D. (1986). Relativistic and dialectic thought in three adult age groups. *Human Development, 29,* 280–290.

LaBrack, B. (1993). The missing linkage: The process of integrating orientation and reentry. In R. M. Paige (Ed.), *Education for the intercultural experience* (pp. 241–280). Yarmouth, ME: Intercultural Press.

Martin, J. N. (1984). The intercultural reentry: Conceptualizations and directions for future research. *International Journal of Intercultural Relations, 8,* 115–134.

Martin, J. N. (1986). Communication in the intercultural reentry: Student sojourners' perception of change in reentry relationships. *International Journal of Intercultural Relations, 10*(2), 1–22.

Ting-Toomey, S. (1993). Communication resourcefulness: An identity negotiation perspective. In R. Wiseman & J. Koester (Eds.), *Intercultural communication competence* (pp. 72–111). Newbury Park, CA: Sage.

Zaharna, R. S. (1989). Self shock: The double-binding challenge of identity. *International Journal of Intercultural Relations, 13,* 501–525.

KEY TERMS

identity	reentry
intercultural communication competence	adaptation

DISCUSSION QUESTIONS

1. What does the author believe to be at the root of intercultural adjustment? Do you agree?
2. What are the key differences between adaptation to another culture and the adaptation experienced during reentry?
3. The author suggests strong links between identity change, reentry adaptation, and communication competence. Do these connections make sense?
4. What other concerns might there be for returnees who have undergone profound identity changes because of time spent in another culture?
5. How might different cultural values and communication patterns affect how returnees would need to negotiate their return home? Why might it be important for them to "fit back in"?

33

TRANSLATED ENACTMENTS: THE RELATIONAL CONFIGURATIONS OF THE ASIAN INDIAN IMMIGRANT EXPERIENCE

RADHA S. HEGDE

"Migrants—borne-across humans—are metaphorical beings in their very essence; and migration, seen as a metaphor, is every-where around us. We all cross frontiers; in that sense, we are all migrant peoples."
(Rushdie, 1991, p. 278)

Migrants, as Rushdie suggests, cross far more than just national borders. In fact, the migrant experience is characterized by an oscillation between the past and present, the exterior world and the interior, the self and other. These tensions take on a complex and urgent turn in the lives of immigrants, who face a disruption in their sense of cultural coherence and continuity. A sense of loss and a desire to rebuild are frequently evoked by immigrants like myself from India. In the process of forging a new life on the borders, these 'borne-across' individuals redefine the very meaning of community, identity, and culture. The contestation of these taken-for-granted ideas takes place in the context of everyday interactions. This essay elaborates on the ways in which the realities of the Asian Indian[1] immigrant experience is constituted relationally.

Consider this weekend scenario in an Asian Indian immigrant home: The aroma of Indian cooking replete with cinnamon, cardamom, saffron, and ginger rises in the air as friends arrive. The colors of Indian saris stand out, making a statement of embodied difference. The afternoon warms up with an array of appetizers—a tantalizing multicultural spectacle ranging from salsa and chutney to tahini! The conversation also

spans a vast geographical and cultural terrain. We hear Raj commenting on the food: "You've really managed to get the taste of these samosas exactly as in India. It reminds me of eating hot samosas and chutney as a college kid in Delhi." "But we must watch the cholesterol," says Sunil. "Did you hear the rate of heart attack among Indian immigrants has gone up leaps and bounds? My cardiologist friends gave me this statistic. I tell you, it's all the tension in this country." When this morbid topic runs out, a suggestion for Indian music is made. "Any old-time music? I can't stand this new music from India." A raga, a classical melody, begins to waft melodiously and rather sonorously in the background. "So what is the election news in India? Do you get the ethnic channel on your cable network?" Some channel surfing finally yields the football game.

In another part of the house, Priya and Mohana are sharing their feelings about mothering—"It is so hard to parent in this bicultural world. I know my daughter thinks I don't understand her, and she is convinced I don't understand American life either." They share stories of sons and daughters, of workplace politics. Someone changes the subject to an ethnic event at the local Hindu temple—"Oh, by the way, did you hear about that Indian temple that was stoned?" A heated discussion ensues. Just then a new batch of samosas arrives from the kitchen, ready to be savored. There is a roar from the adjoining room. The football game gets intense. "American football is where the action is. What did you say, cricket? Can't take it anymore—just too long drawn out."

This scenario shows you how Asian Indian immigrants collapse cultural worlds even as they socialize and talk about seemingly mundane

---

[1] "Asian Indian" is a term used by the U.S. Census to refer to immigrants from South Asia—that is, India, Pakistan, Sri Lanka, Bangladesh, Nepal, and Bhutan.

things from food to raising children. Questions of change, the past, perception of difference by the world outside, and images of hybridity weave in and out of the conversation. The articulation of these issues arises directly from the critical location of these immigrants at the confluence of two cultures. A number of social questions and individual pressures arise from having to adapt to new norms while simultaneously adhering to older, more familiar ways. These experiences of new immigrants are marked by the multiple issues of race, class, gender, and varied historical positionings. The migrant experience is a very visible subject in the current context of increasing globalization and border-crossings (Bammer, 1994). This essay addresses the processes by which Asian Indians locate themselves and create meanings within the bicultural patterns of their ethnic lives.

Clustered in the large urban centers of the United States, Asian Indians represent a fast-growing and new Asian minority group. The major influx of immigrants from the Indian subcontinent came in the 1960s when changes in the immigration law made it possible for the entry of professionally trained people. Asian Indian immigrants represent the rich linguistic, religious, and cultural diversity of India and are very visible for their high levels of education and training in scientific and technological fields (Saran, 1985).

These immigrants actively maintain close connections with India and attempt to preserve Indian traditions by forming ethnic networks in their transplanted contexts (Fisher, 1980). In fact, there is quite a proliferation of Indian social organizations in the United States whose main mission is to promote traditional culture. Recently, there has also been an increase in the number of professional organizations, political groups that strive to provide a voice for the Asian Indian population, including organizations with a strong activist agenda.

Of Disruption and Reconstructions

In the process of traveling between worlds, migrants like the Asian Indians face disruptions in their historical roots, their language, and the so-

cial conventions they know and have practiced. Rushdie (1991), who writes with great sensitivity about the migrant sensibility, calls this the triple dislocation. The loss of the three most important parts of self-definition compels immigrants to find new ways of describing self. These disruptions are not just a passing phase or a cultural gap that will be filled in time. Rather, they continually arise and are reproduced in the communicative realities of migrant lives.

The tales of immigrants about their experiences in adopted worlds reveal how the triple dislocations acquire multiple forms. In my conversations with other immigrants from India, certain themes arise with an alarming regularity: a questioning about self, the meaning of immigrant existence, the uncertainty of the future. To immigrants who come from a culture where kinship and a sense of ancestry are important, the loss of historical roots is a deeply disturbing reality to confront. In this context, it is evident that the triple dislocation of roots, language, and societal connections that subsume the individuals and their relational world is not about to be remedied with a handbook on cultural dos and don'ts or a course in accent reduction. Acculturative change is not about exchanging or replacing behaviors. It is imperative to think of these ethnic transformations as a process and not as a simple, one-stop phenomenon. The dislocations identified by Rushdie permeate into the very core of existence—definitions of selfhood, communal bonds, the fabric of culture and what it means. These repercussions are not isolated, psychological reactions but are part of individual and collective migrant narratives that shape reality. The next section discusses the concepts of culture, self, and community and shows how they are interrelated and constituted in the everyday lives of Asian Indian immigrants.

Anchoring Culture

Culture has never been an easy concept to grapple with. Now with globalization, the spectrum of cultural forms has grown exponentially. An old church in Houston is renovated to be a Hindu temple. A street in Queens, New York, feels like and exudes the aura of Bombay. There are areas in Chicago, Cleveland, and Los Angeles where saris and curry make an authentic cultural statement. On August 15, a veil of Indianness covers New York's Times Square to celebrate Indian Independence Day. Each fall, South Street Seaport in New York City is transformed into an Indian *mela*, or festival, with crafts, art shows, music, and dances from India to celebrate Deepavali, the Hindu festival of lights. Through these experiences of food, music, and entertainment, it is possible to experience Indian culture as a collage. As a visitor from India told me in total surprise after being at one of these ethnic public gatherings, "You immigrants are more into 'Indian stuff' than we are in India." That "Indian stuff" is what migrants conjure up as ethnic culture.

What happens to culture when it loses its moorings, its connections to geographical space? Until recently, it has been taken for granted that each country or geographically defined space embodies its own distinctive culture. In a world of mobile communities and interconnectedness, this view of culture is highly problematic because it assumes culture to be a static and discrete category. In the context of Asian Indians, the distance between India and the United States collapses and the lines between here and there blur. As any ethnic neighborhood demonstrates, we now have transplanted or translated cultures. As Little Indias crop up side by side with Chinatowns and Little Italys, one can actually feel the unexpected fusion of culture and place. As Gupta and Ferguson (1992) write, "'cultures' and 'peoples' however persistent they may be, cease to be plausibly identifiable as spots on the map" (p. 10).

It is the fear of assimilation and total cultural absorption that drives Asian Indian immigrants, as it drove earlier groups of other immigrants, to passionately recreate their culture of origins. These hybrid cultures that emerge hold a precarious position and often face violent opposition. History offers many illustrations of immigrant groups surviving hostility and rejection— for example, the building of Hindu temples in New Jersey by Asian Indians has met fierce opposition from local communities who felt their environments had changed with the "invasion" of new immigrants. Neighborhoods that have changed in

character as a result of their new ethnic definitions have also aroused similar feelings. Hybrid cultures, therefore, are not always a romantic return to the homeland; they are also cultures that develop and survive as a form of collective resistance.

These experiences of ethnic communities call into question traditional notions of cultures as authentic and homogeneous. These immigrants, who are not only transplanted but translated, simultaneously inhabit the space of two cultures. In this process, they not only are transforming both cultures but at the same time are inventing a space of fusion and hybridity. Globalization and technological advances have so accelerated the interconnectedness of cultures that it seems archaic to think of cultures in any singular insular frameworks. As people are walking in and out of multiple cultural contexts, Chow's (1993) question seems timely: "Where have all the natives gone?" (p. 27). Extending this argument, one could ask, "Who is the authentic native?" What counts for authenticity in this contemporary age of globalization? The Asian Indian immigrants I meet consistently speak about their ambivalence, of being partially at home in two cultures and feeling part of none. What is it then to be an Indian in India and an Asian Indian in the United States?

Simplistic notions of culture have directed our attention to details such as clothing, food, and rituals. Although this total lifestyle view of culture is an important aspect, it is at best superficial. To understand the construction of hybrid cultures, we need to critically revisit the descriptive approach to the study of culture. Is it still a wrap that is superimposed on a community? Do Asian Indians form ethnic organizations only to take shelter under this remembered cultural rubric of the past? Why is it one hears of hybrid musical forms developing, such as Bhangra music among the Asian Indian diaspora that fuses the rhythms of traditional Indian folk music and rock? I am suggesting that we begin to think of cultures, particularly in this context of transitional movements, from the point of view of the processes through which communities render themselves distinct. You can study Indian culture in Delhi or in Queens, New York—which one constitutes the real "Indian stuff"? Cultures and natives travel in and out of familiar frames. You cannot contain culture for very long, not even in a pithy textbook definition.

Locating Identities

In this world of intersections, migrants are irrevocably the products of several interlocking histories and cultures (Hall, 1992). Consider the Singh family from Punjab in northern India whose family migrated to California to work in the orchards in the early 1900s. Take the example of Dr. Chandra, a renowned scientist who emigrated from India in the early 1930s and could not find a place to live because of his color. Meet the more recently arrived Mr. and Mrs. Sethi who run a chain of motels in Alabama and Tennessee, or Mr. Chadda who pumps gas on the New Jersey turnpike and longs for his family left back in India. Consider the second generation Asian Indian student in an Ivy League college who is being pressured by her parents to study engineering. Then there is Neeta, the computer scientist from Bombay who works for a major corporation in San Francisco and battles the glass ceiling as an Indian woman. Here are people who have taken different paths and many turns to reach their particular locations. You can see in each case how the individual is located within multiple points of cultural intersections. It is but inevitable that the narratives of self undergo a significant transformation under these contexts of relocation.

The key question to ask at this juncture is the one articulated by Clifford (1988): "What does it mean at the end of the twentieth century, to speak . . . of a native land? What processes, rather than essences, are involved in present experiences of cultural identity?" (p. 275). Identities, like culture, can no longer be viewed as self-contained, fixed, and stable but rather are constituted with the process of communication (see Gergen, 1994). This fluid conceptualization of identity is particularly relevant for understanding migrants whose coordinates of identity are being repositioned by multiple cultural narratives.

In the multiple crossings encountered by migrants, identity becomes a very salient topic. Identity becomes an issue only when it is in crisis, "when something assumed to be fixed, coherent

and stable is displaced by the experience of doubt and uncertainty" (Mercer, 1990, p. 43). Identity is enacted and negotiated in the everyday world of relationships. Traveling between cultures, Asian Indian immigrants are defined and define themselves in shifting patterns of inclusion and exclusion. For example, my Asian Indian respondents tell me of how they squirm when they hear the words "you people" hurled about the ethnic group. They talk with pain about the sense of helplessness when confronted by violent racial slurs. In this way the external world provides a frightening push to migrants to engage with questions about their identity and place in the world.

There is an infinite and complicated process of identity construction that accompanies migration and movement between cultures. It seems to make sense to talk of identities in the plural, or of identities as being constantly invented and negotiated between the self and the external world. For example, as Asian Indians move between varying performative contexts, they develop narratives of self that combine the past and open up a trajectory for the future. These narratives evolve as a quest for self, a process of making meaning of life in the cultural in-between. Ethnic identities have to be seen as a production in which the scripting is contested, negotiated, and transformed from particular cultural and relational locations. There are multiple cultural communities with which one identifies. The sense of belonging being so fluid, immigrants show remarkable creativity in constructing new communities.

Translated Communities

The homeland is a very powerful symbolic anchor around which a sense of community is established for migrants. In a context of the triple dislocations mentioned earlier where culture and roots have lost their moorings, relationships to the homeland assume imaginative and powerful dimensions. Asian Indians build very strong ethnic bonds around points of commonality such as language and place of origin. The ethnic community becomes the new context of connections where an aura of distilled "Indianness" can be recreated.

In this process of forming new relationships within the community, Asian Indian immigrants have created a vast organizational infrastructure. There are religious institutions, temples, and cultural organizations all over the United States. Weekends for Asian Indians are typically crammed with ethnic activities. Dances, plays, religious ceremonies, musical events, and group celebrations of Indian festivals provide the opportunity for Asian Indians to mingle and socialize. These occasions provide an occasion for immigrants to wear special Indian clothes, speak an Indian language, and enjoy the sensuous thrill of India almost as a fantasy.

In a world where Asian Indians are continually aware of being the cultural "other," the need for establishing communal anchors is intense. The past offers the terrain on which to construct community, and solidarity is built around memories. The past acquires significance as a cultural anchor and a point of reference in the context of dislocation. Immigrants create surrogate communities where remembered dimensions of time and space are collapsed into the present. These ethnic communities survive to a large extent on nostalgia and reconnect to places that often have changed or disappeared in reality. The past assumes multiple forms and meanings in the conversations, activities, and rituals of Asian Indians.

These ethnic communities thrive on reviving a spirit of Indianness, an imagined authenticity of tradition. The social mores, rituals, and customs of the past are maintained with self-conscious discipline by many Asian Indians. "Unless we teach our practices to our children, who will? What will happen to them? Will they continue to be Indian at least in their outlook?" asked Nitin, a computer engineer who believes in exposing his children to "Indian ways." This usually means taking oftentimes reluctant youngsters to Indian gatherings, making them familiar with the norms and mores of interaction, and most of all, enforcing on the children a yardstick of Indian cultural propriety.

The home usually represents the untouched Indian cultural space. It is here that the mask can be let down and the social protocols of the outside world can be dismissed. Migrants tend to describe and bracket their lives in cultural binaries such as east/west, tradition/modernity, Ameri-can/Indian. Mona, who has faced the pressures of growing up in an immigrant home, raised this issue: "My parents use the term 'modern'—they say we have to remember our traditions, kids from India are getting too modern." Or hear Bala, a professor who has lived in the United States for over 20 years: "I expect my kids to wear Indian clothes when we go out to ethnic gatherings and guess what I saw in Delhi? My friend's children who have grown up in India are more Americanized, wearing jeans, dancing to Macarena . . . the whole bit." To migrants, tradition is freezing a memory of Indian culture and a way of life that in all probability has changed even in India.

The ethnic community provides the cultural repository to fuse the narrative disruptions that migrants face in their transplanted lives. The building of ethnic communities represents a retreat into a perceived unity, a quest to bring together individuals who have the seeming potential for establishing solidarity. There is a great deal of time and energy that goes into building and maintaining relational ties within the ethnic group. In order to get at some everyday accounts of community, I asked some Asian Indians to talk about friendships and why they needed Indian friends. Their comments were insightful. The two worlds, inter- and intraethnic, were treated as completely different domains. The interethnic world represented the relationships and associations of the workplace. In contrast, their Asian Indian friendships were characterized as more spontaneous because there was no fear of doing something culturally amiss. An Asian Indian woman told me emphatically, "Even though the Indians I mix with are so different from me, in America, we are just Indians and I need them." In this way, even real differences among Indians are overlooked for the common bond of cultural origins. There we have it, the triple dislocations of social norms, roots, and language being healed in a sense by the cohesive power of the ethnic community.

The reproduced community also gains an old-world flavor and charm of its own. The active involvement in each other's lives, a characteristic of older and more cohesive societies, makes a reappearance. For example, Venu, who cherished his privacy, complained about the Indian community: "There is too much gossip, they want to know everything about you and then it's all out in the open." His friend Vasu was quick to retort: "Indians are changing, too. They are becoming as private and individualistic as Americans are, don't you think? You can't just walk into an Indian home in the United States as you can in India without calling or announcing yourself. It's not the same anymore."

The need and definition of community does shift even as the metaphorical distance from "home" changes. What is home to a migrant? The word is elusive to define and tantalizing to pin down. As Mohanty (1993) wonders, "Is home a geographical space, a historical space, an emotional, sensory space?" (p. 352). For those who live on the borders, home is an imaginary construct that shifts between all these spaces. Much as the ethnic group tries to fix the cultures of their origin, what they recreate asserts its own character. The hybrid culture of the Asian Indian community has an individual energy and identity of its own. How do we as scholars of intercultural communication study these cultures that are continually reinventing themselves without fixing them in narrow definitional straitjackets? The next part of the essay deals with this question of representing the complexity of the experiences of people in transition.

Remapping the Frontier

"Modes of representation that legitimated a world of strict cultural separation, collective identities, and rigid boundaries seem hopelessly outdated as the urban landscape is being rewritten within new and shifting borders of identity, race and ethnicity" (Giroux, 1994, p. 40).

The realities of displaced people provoke the reevaluation of some very important social issues. The experiences of the Asian Indian immigrants that you met in this essay exemplify the complex processes by which identities and social participation are constructed. Immigrant lives are constituted at the confluence of multiple realities. Contradictions are synchronous with life on the borderlands. The boundaries between concepts such as rooting-uprooting, local-global, here-there, past-future, national-international blur and are resurrected almost instantaneously. Ambigu-

ity paves the "routes" of immigrants and their hyphenated lives—". . . the realm in-between where predetermined rules cannot fully apply" (Trinh, 1991, p. 157).

These large-scale demographic movements associated with globalization have challenged many traditional ideas regarding the acculturation of ethnic groups. Traditional models of immigrant behavior are based on the assumption of the self-defined autonomous individual who assimilated over time. This adaptation was considered to be dependent solely on individual behavior patterns. However, the process of culture and identity constructions is by no means so clearly linear and straightforward. Negotiations of ethnic identities do not take place in a neutral, value-free environment. We need to be sensitive to the fact that difference and identities are framed within a complex web of factors, deep-set perceptual biases, and power systems that dictate social hierarchies.

It is unrealistic to recreate the ethnic condition as one of eternal longing for origins or as transitory stage to assimilation. Ethnic identity and culture are far more than frozen spectacles of the past. They are about changes and the multiple ways in which immigrants connect themselves in a social world and articulate their difference. Identity, community, and culture are so intertwined that even setting up boundaries between these concepts seems artificial in the everyday practices of migrant life. So our models have to be more messy and get multidimensional. They need to capture more lines and circles to represent the complex experiences of immigrants.

The experiences of displacement provide a spectacle of human drama. The Asian Indian examples reveal that narratives of self and configurations of culture are products of social interchange and take many curious turns. For example, I was deeply struck when a friend told me, "I went to this old neighborhood back home near Bangalore and some man who runs a store asked me about my grandfather. Can you believe it? Who would ever associate me with my grandfather in this country?" After 20 some years in the United States, where he is bereft of spatial and historical coordinates, this simple episode was emotionally overpowering and empowering in the connections it provided.

It is important to point out that the community of Asian Indians has grown enormously since the 1960s, and it is difficult to generalize about the experiences of diverse groups of immigrants. For example, the lives of Sunil the computer scientist, Raj who works at the docks in Newark, and Shetty who runs the Indian grocery store in the Midwest are caught up in completely different rhythms. Or consider the lives of Asian Indian women whose realities are appropriated by the sexist structures of multiple cultures. The simultaneity of race and gender further complicate the narrative trajectories of self for many immigrant women (see Hegde, forthcoming). Generational differences also impact the construction of ethnic realities. The famous "What will happen to our tradition?" question provokes an important issue to study and ponder: How will cultures of hybridity get reconstituted over time?

The translated lives and relationships of Asian Indian immigrants provide an enactment of the complexity of not-belonging or belonging partially to a new environment. The hybrid culture of Asian Indians demonstrates the problem of viewing cultures as homogeneous and static. Ethnic identities are the products of interlocking cultures and complex forms of identification. The memories of the past and the ambivalence of the present and the uncertainty of the future are woven together in complex relational configurations. It is in the communicative realities of their everyday world that the intertwined meanings of self, community, and culture are constituted for Asian Indian immigrants.

REFERENCES

Bammer, A. (1994). *Displacements: Cultural identities in question.* Bloomington: Indiana University Press.

Chow, R. (1993). *Writing diaspora.* Bloomington: Indiana University Press.

Clifford, J. (1988). *The predicament of culture.* Cambridge, MA: Harvard University Press.

Fisher, M. P. (1980). *The Indians of New York City: A study of immigrants from India.* New Delhi: Heritage.

Gergen, K. J. (1994). *Realities and relationships: Soundings in social construction.* Cambridge, MA: Harvard University Press.

Giroux, H. A. (1994). Living dangerously: Identity politics and the new cultural racism. In H. A. Giroux & P. McLaren (Eds.), *Between borders: Pedagogy and the politics of cultural studies* (pp. 29–55). New York: Routledge.

Gupta, A., & Ferguson, J. (1992). Beyond culture: Space, identity, and the politics of difference. *Cultural Anthropology, 7*(1), 6–23.

Hall, S. (1992). New ethnicities. In J. Donald & A. Rattansi (Eds.), *Race, culture and difference* (pp. 252–260). Newbury Park, CA: Sage.

Hegde, R. S. (forthcoming). Swinging the trapeze: The negotiation of identity among Asian Indian immigrant women in the U.S. *International and Intercultural Communication Annual 21.* Newbury Park, CA: Sage.

Mercer, K. (1990). Welcome to the jungle: Identity and diversity in postmodern politics. In J. Rutherford (Ed.), *Identity, community, culture, difference* (pp. 43–71). London: Wishart.

Mohanty, C. T. (1993). Defining genealogies: Feminist reflections on being South Asian in North America. In Women of South Asian Descent Collective (Eds.), *Our feet walk to sky: Women of the South Asian diaspora* (pp. 351–358). San Francisco: Aunt Lute Books.

Rushdie, S. (1991). *Imaginary homelands.* New York: Penguin.

Saran, P. (1985). *The Asian Indian experience.* Cambridge, MA: Schenkman.

Trinh, T. M.-H. (1991). *When the moon waxes red.* New York: Routledge.

KEY TERMS

Asian Indian	community
migrants	culture
hybridity	displacement
identity	

DISCUSSION QUESTIONS

1. Select any urban landscape, trace its growth spatially and symbolically, and see how it has been reconfigured with new borders of race, identity, and ethnicity.
2. Hegde talks about the construction of hybrid cultural forms as being an expression of migrant cultures. Talk to members of an ethnic group from varying age groups and see how they construct the meaning of these cultural forms.

3. Hegde describes globalization as a very significant contemporary issue. In what way does it make an impact in your everyday life? Is globalization in fact collapsing the categories of local and global, of the here and there?

4. Hegde's essay seems to suggest that Asian Indians maintain two distinct relational worlds—the inter- and intraethnic. Talk to people from different ethnic groups and see if their friendships and socializing differ along ethnic lines.

5. How do experiences of racism and discrimination affect the sense of community in an ethnic group? Direct your comments around a specific issue or news event.

34
PERFORMED IDENTITIES: "PASSING" AS AN INTER/CULTURAL DISCOURSE

DREAMA G. MOON

She's heard the arguments, most astonishingly that, statistically, . . . the average white American is 6 percent black. Or, put another way, 95 percent of white Americans are 5 to 80 percent black. Her Aunt Tyler has told her stories about these whites researching their roots in the National Archives and finding they've got an African-American or two in the family, some becoming so hysterical they have to be carried out by paramedics. (Perry as cited in Piper, 1994, p. 66)

[T]he real is no longer what it used to be. . . . (Baudrillard, 1988, p. 171)

Intercultural communication as a field suffers from a lack of imagination in terms of the way in which the concept of identity is envisioned. All too often, cultural identity is equated with nationality. Essentialized notions of nationality tend to privilege dominant expressions of what constitutes national identity within a particular nation-state (i.e., the United States) (Moon, 1996a). Thus, what is conceived as "American" in the United States is often conflated with that which comprises *White* American culture. For example, Nakayama and Krizek (1995) found that a significant percentage of White college students surveyed nationally equated being White with being American. When you reflect on what it means to be an American, what face(s) come to mind?

Defining culture as nationality obscures a multiplicity of experiences and voices that are indeed American by freezing identity as if there is only one way that Americanness can be understood. Muhammad Ali carrying the Olympic Torch in Atlanta, Roseanne grabbing her crotch while singing "The Star Spangled Banner," Christopher Reeve delivering an opening address at the 1996 Democratic Convention about family values, RuPaul performing fashion model chic, and Hillary Clinton insisting that "It takes a village" are all examples of the varied ways in which Americanness may be enacted. Limiting the definition of cultural identity to merely one of the many social positions that individuals occupy in society is problematic. Freezing identities in this way makes for very dull scholarship—scholarship that is not particularly relevant to, or reflective of, the lives of ordinary people engaged in everyday practices within any society, scholarship that maintains "business as usual."

Rather than reinscribe the ways in which we are all too often slotted into nice, safe categories (i.e., White, American, male, Latina, middle class, heterosexual, etc.), intercultural communication inquiry might be enriched by study of the ways in which people *resist* such categorizations, how we frequently are able to "steal" a bit of privilege and fun for ourselves. *Passing* is one such tactic of resistance. In the place of discrete essences of "natural" identities, passing allows for "competing rules of recognition," rules that trouble the boundaries constructed between "us" and "them" (Robinson, 1994, p. 716). In this essay, I explore the usefulness of the notion of passing in helping us to rethink the issues of identity and adaptation in intercultural communication research.

Toward a Practice of Passing

> Some people try to minimize the contradictions and create an identity, a social identity and self-concept that de-emphasizes [the contradictions]. I honestly don't think that anyone who has ever been a poor kid ever, ever really forgets what it's like. But, you can de-emphasize that. You can literally take on the persona of the middle class. You can pass. Lots of people pass and that is an option. (Moon, 1996b)

Passing as a social practice has been explored in many contexts, although often such discussions focus on Black people who pass for White. A quick glance at both popular and academic literatures reveals that passing is a topic in writings as diverse as those that address bi- or multiracial persons who pass for one race or another; lower-class persons who pass as middle or even upper class; rich kids who occasionally pass for "ghetto" ones (lest we forget Vanilla Ice!); women who pass as men and men who pass as women; lesbians and gay men who pass as heterosexuals (do heterosexuals ever pass as gay?); women who through the use of cosmetics pass for "natural"; single women who pass for married ones; and married men who pass as single . . . the list goes on. Indeed, passing has even been institutionalized in some arenas, such as with preoperative transsexuals who must pass for the sex to which they are evolving for a period of time to "prove" that they are indeed prepared for the final step of sex reassignment. So it seems there's a whole lot of passing going on around us! In light of this, we might ask, exactly what is this thing called passing?

Although many agree that passing as a social phenomenon exists, as we might expect, there is not a unified perspective on exactly what passing is. Let's briefly review some of the definitions of passing offered in various academic literatures. First, Caughie (1992) suggests that passing involves disguise and deception, or pretending to be something one is not. In this view, the idea of an essential identity or a core inner self is retained although dressed up in new clothes. Conversely, Hitchcock (1994) sees passing as a form of cultural politics, a political strategy that disrupts the notion of identity as unified and static. Along similar lines, Tyler (1994) sees passing as "a politically viable response to oppression" (p. 212). She also claims that passing is a means of *disrupting* identity and troubling the homogeneity of our groups and of our identifications with one another. In other words, she suggests that the very *existence* of passing suggests that defining cultural groups and recognizing fellow members are not the straightforward acts we would like to believe them to be. Bradshaw (1992) defines passing as "an attempt to achieve acceptability by claiming membership in some desired group" (p. 79). She sees passing as an *adaptive* response, as a way of laying claim to privileges unfairly denied to certain groups of people. So in her view, passing allows one to obtain social and personal benefits that one is always already due. Daniel (1992) discusses passing in terms of shifting reference groups. In this scenario, one's membership group (i.e., a group to which one "really" belongs in terms of sex, race, class, and so forth) differs from one's reference group (i.e., a group that one admires, envies, models oneself after, values, or looks to for guidance). Thus, one may pass as a member of whichever reference group is currently operative in order to gain some privilege "entitled" to members of that group.

Tactical Debates

> In many cases, white [blues] musicians are motivated by admiration and envy for the black performers that they emulate. . . . [T]he blues as purveyed by whites appears unauthentic and deeply impoverished; further, it too often

represents an appropriation of black culture. . . . Finally, it can be economically crippling to black artists through loss of jobs and critical attention. (Garon, 1995, p. 57)

Whichever definition of passing you ascribe to, it is clear that passing as a social practice problematizes traditional ideas about identity and offers itself as an adaptive tactic, particularly for those socially situated in the margins of a society. The various definitions of passing discussed above have two things in common: all of them are tied up in the ongoing debates about identity, and all suggest that passing is a tactic of the marginalized. Let's take a closer look at these two ideas.

Disrupting Identity

The notion of identity has received much attention in the field of intercultural communication. Antiessentialists argue against the use of checklists in determining the group (i.e., racial, ethnic, gender, and so forth) memberships of research participants, claiming that they should instead be asked to provide their own labels, presumably ones that have meaning for them (Martin, Krizek, Nakayama, & Bradford, 1996). However, the majority of intercultural scholars operate out of the tradition of positivism and routinely use such checklists as indicators of social identity. The phenomenon of passing suggests that there is danger in viewing identity as being comprised of an essence that is presocial and unchanging, as checklist identity categories might lead us to believe. It might be more useful to think of identity as a habit rather than an essence. Identity-as-habit is an idea that allows both for the ingrainedness of habits (as anyone who has attempted to break a long-term habit can attest) and for the possibility of movement away from such habits, a movement that passing provides us. This more fluid notion of identity is illustrated in Tanno (1997), who charts her personal journey through/with a number of ethnic names and cultural understandings— Spanish, Mexican American, Latina, and Chicana.

The definitions of passing discussed earlier tend to disrupt received views of identity and call into question who we really are while enabling us to make connections between identity-as-habits and larger social relations. As Hitchcock (1994)

suggests, rather than doing away with the notion of identity, the phenomenon of passing highlights the *politics* of identity. In other words, passing draws attention to the preexisting social relations in which passers and nonpassers are embedded that facilitate deception in the first place.

Passing as an Underground Tactic

In order to better grasp passing as a "bottom-up" tactic, it is useful to distinguish it from the notion of *appropriation*. Social examples that involve members of socially privileged groups passing as members of less powerful groups are not uncommon. Vanilla Ice, a White rapper popular in the early 1990s, immediately comes to mind. He grew up in a class-privileged neighborhood near Dallas, Texas, but passed himself off as a "White Brother from the streets" in order to win and maintain a Black following for his music. Another example is the situation that developed in Oklahoma when monies for education, housing, and so forth became available through the Bureau of Indian Affairs for those who could "document" that they were of at least one-sixteenth Indian descent. Needless to say, many Whites suddenly became Indian. A third example is heterosexual men who sometimes cross-dress (i.e., pass as women). In these examples, members of socially privileged groups are able to retain their dominant positional status and attendant social power and privilege in most contexts of their lives, while securing personal and/or financial benefit by taking on the persona of the "other." To be sure, Vanilla Ice did not and does not live as a Black man in America, many Oklahoma Whites are perceived as Native American only in relation to the Bureau of Indian Affairs, and heterosexual male cross-dressers still suit up and show up at their offices every day as men.

Thus, we see that the issue of *power* is deeply implicated in the notions of passing and appropriation. John Pepper's (1982) autobiography makes this point rather clearly. In documenting his personal history of cross-dressing, Pepper claims that cross-dressing allowed him the "treat" of being in "the high white tower . . . while some other bloody fool slew the dragons" (p. 83). Pepper conveniently overlooks the fact that some women have been trying to climb *out* of the patriarchal ivory tower for decades! Conversely, in her biography of the male impersonator Vesta Tilley, Maitland (1986) argues that "for a man to impersonate a woman is for him to undertake, voluntarily, an act of self-humiliation, (unless he can make the woman sufficiently ridiculous for his identification with 'her' to be seen as absurd)" (p. 89). In a similar vein, Millet (1971) suggests that male cross-dressers enjoy the best of both worlds in that they become "better" than mere women because they are "women" with a penis!

Passing: An "Other/wise" Tactic

Passing . . . draws attention to the problem in the politics of identity, for passing accentuates what the masquerade must hide: the pre-existing social relations that facilitate disguise in the first place. (Hitchcock, 1994, p. 3)

Another useful way to think more about the idea of passing is to examine it in relation to popular concepts found in intercultural communication literature. As passers may be seen as *cultural travelers* or *sojourners* of a kind, the notion of *adaptation* is of particular interest. The adaptation literature generally conceptualizes sojourners as foreign nationals who are visiting or temporarily residing in another country. Although the impact of situational and social elements is noted, the majority of this literature deals with the issue of adaptation on the psychological level; thus the power relations implicated in the sojourning experience are deflected, and the onus for failing to adjust or adapt to the host culture is placed squarely on the shoulders of the individual sojourner. In addition, such scholarship often conceives the individual sojourner as an "essentialized other"—an "American," a "Japanese," and so forth, thus ignoring the multitude of other identity positions that the sojourner occupies (i.e., a poor White American lesbian).

In order to recover the social context of sojourning, a reconceptualized notion of adaptation is needed that allows for the possibility of conceiving adaptation in "other" terms. Lefebvre (1971) suggests such a direction. Lefebvre distinguishes between *compulsion* and *adaptation* by pointing out that the former is the strategy of

the powerful, whereas the latter is the tactic of the weak. He argues that those who adapt to circumstances not of their own choosing have overcome compulsion by absorbing and transforming it into something useful for themselves (i.e., "stealing" a bit of privilege or fun). In a similar vein, de Certeau (1984) suggests that everyday life is deeply implicated in adaptation, which he defines as "ways of using imposed systems" (p. 18). By drawing on the insights of Lefebvre and de Certeau, we are able to construct a view of sojourners as everyday intercultural travelers who find ways to make a way for themselves within social relations not of their own making. One way to do this is to deploy passing. A tactic of passing necessitates the recognition of the wider social relations within which one moves and one's "place" within them as well as the willingness to go beyond them.

Next, we will explore the notion of passing in more detail. We begin our discussion by exploring five characteristics that define the terrain of passing: unidirectionality, actionality, temporality, performative content, and tactical focus.

Unidirectionality

What is often naturalized in "passing" is the notion of classing-up: the idea that breaking dress codes—dressing up, dressing for success, etc.—is primarily a desire for upward mobility, in order to gain a room at the top. . . . it is clear that cross-dressing is more than an ambition for economic well-being: instead it suggests that specific forms of social order are deemed repressive and inadequate. (Hitchcock, 1994, p. 4)

As discussed earlier, passing is configured primarily as an underground tactic. Keeping in mind the discussion on appropriation, we see that the movement of passing is unidirectional, meaning that people generally seek to pass "up" rather than "down." In short, individuals who pass usually do so in order to take up positions that generally incur more social and material privileges in U.S. society, rather than ones that are viewed as inferior or less desirable. So for the most part, women are more likely to pass "up" as men, the lower class "up" to middle class, gay men and lesbians "up" as heterosexuals, and so on, in order to gain the privileges ascribed to those social positions or to avoid the penalties or lack of privilege associated with less powerful ones.

Actionality

"I'm gonna get you, you flatfaced chinaman." I want to tell her that I'm only half Japanese, but the words stick in my mouth. . . . Later, when I am thirteen, I bury my mother once and for all and decide to go Mexican. It makes a lot of sense. I am no longer Elena, I am now Elaina and I begin insisting that I am Mexican wherever I go. With my long black hair, my sun-darkened skin, and my new name, I can pass and I am safe. (Creef, 1990, pp. 82–83)

Another element pertinent to the concept of passing is that of actionality. Although many adaptive strategies, such as code-switching, are primarily *active* tactics (i.e., one actively chooses to take on the linguistic behavior of the "other"), passing manifests both active and passive varieties. For example, passing as an active strategy would involve situations such as those in which surgically altered 40-year-old women in 20-year-old bodies claim their daughters as "sisters" in order to be treated with the deference awarded to young females in U.S. society, or the case of some southerners and easterners who rid themselves of their indigenous (and unacceptable) accents and dialects to avoid negative stereotyping. Examples involving a more *passive* use of passing include situations in which lower-class people passing as upper class keep silent on issues such as where they went to undergraduate school and allow others to assume that they are "one of them." In short, active strategies involve a deliberate move to construct and present oneself as "other," whereas passive ones entail allowing others to "think what they will."

Temporality

"No one knew," said Kitty Oakes, the woman Billy Tipton married in 1960. The newspaper said Billy Tipton apparently began appearing as a man to improve her chances of success as a jazz musician. "He gave up everything," Ms. Oakes said. "There were certain rules and regulations in those days if you were going to be a musician." (cited in Wood, 1997, p. 29)

As an adaptive tactic, passing can be either continuous or discontinuous, temporary or permanent, process or event. Passing can range from being a momentary matter of convenience ("event"), such as when a Black person passes as White for an evening in order to enjoy an outing in a White space, to a whole way of life ("process") as in the case of jazz musician Billy Tipton, whose "true" sex went undiscovered (even by his/her own wife and adopted children) until his/her death. In addition, passing can also involve a *mixture* of continuity and discontinuity, of process and event. For instance, Navajos from a reservation might pass as "assimilated Indians" while they are away at college but participate in traditional ways of life when they return to the reservation. Or Blacks may utilize White English in their places of employment but use Black English at home.

Performative Content

"It's easy for a Negro to 'pass' for white" [Irene (a Black woman passing for white) says]. "But I don't think it would be so simple for a white person to 'pass' for coloured."
    "Never thought of that" [Hugh (a white man) remarks].
    "No, you wouldn't. Why would you?"
(Larsen, 1929/1986, p. 206)

Passing as an adaptive strategy tends to be wide-ranging, relying on a variety of performative behaviors. While much of the literature on passing has been written within the context of race (i.e., predominantly in relation to Blacks who pass as Whites), passing as an identity performance can and does occur in a broad range of contexts including race, gender/sex, social class, age, sexual orientation, and so forth. Although passing may include linguistic strategies such as code-switching, those who pass usually employ a wide range of nonverbal and verbal communicative behaviors, including the use of clothing and accessories, mannerisms, hairstyle, body language, fabricated personal histories, silence, and even surgical alteration. One such example is that of the female professor from a working-class background who not only takes on the academic jargon of the university but also employs other trappings of the middle-class academic culture (i.e., manner of dress such as the navy or black business suit, heels, and sculptured nails as well as mastery of academic "dinner party small talk," a language of its own!).

However, the ability to pass successfully presumes the presence of a degree of insider knowledge, and the degree of knowledge required varies across types of passes (i.e., "process" versus "event" passing). For instance, an event passer may need to be to some extent bilingual, or able to speak the language of the "other," whereas the process passer must not only be able to *speak* the language of the "other," but more important, be able to *use* it like a native (i.e., know its formal and informal structure and be able to apply linguistic rules situationally). Over and above linguistic concerns, an effective pass requires a wide knowledge of the culture of the "other," particularly if the pass is longer in duration (i.e., passing for an evening requires less attention to performative detail than does passing for a lifetime). Thus, the repertoire of the successful "process" passer must be quite extensive. In short, the more continuous and the longer in duration the pass, the more complex the identity performance, and the more cultural knowledge required.

Tactical Focus

In a perfect world, one's sexual orientation would be a private matter and irrelevant to one's job. This isn't a perfect world. Arizona Congressman Jim Kolbe lived that truth last week. Faced with the threat of an "outing" by a national gay magazine, Kolbe confirmed publicly for the first time that he is gay. "This is the best day of my life, really," Kolbe told me in a phone interview from Washington last Friday, the day the news broke. "I feel a tremendous burden lifted. It's a relief. I'm being totally honest about myself to my friends and family. It feels wonderful." (Willey, 1996, p. B2)

As the case of Congressman Jim Kolbe illustrates, passing involves an objective of some sort. Sometimes the objective is to *be accepted* as "one of them" (whoever "them" might be in a given con-

text), or to *attain some privilege* that "they" have. So in corporate America, a gay man may pass as a heterosexual (i.e., as one of the boys), a single man may pretend to be married, or a woman may take on a "tough" (i.e., masculine) persona if these tactics are seen to advance one's career, or at minimum, equalize one's chances of upward mobility. Passing may also be used to *gain reentry* into "neighborhoods" of desirability (i.e., when the nouveaux riches pass as "old money" in order to move into blueblood social circles). Passing can also be used as a *form of play*, such as in some "drag" shows wherein the most "authentic" gender performance wins a prize. Last, passing can be used as a *tactic of resistance* to arbitrary rules about identities and attendant rewards. One such example of passing as resistance is that of Pat from the television program *Saturday Night Live*. Pat is an androgynous character whose sex is undeterminable. The anxiety and discomfort of others around her/him and the many ploys they utilize in order to discover what Pat's sex "really" is illustrate the potential of passing as a disruptive force to fixed ideas of identity.

In summary, passing proves to be a multidimensional tactic of the marginalized involving unidirectionality (i.e., up/down), temporality (i.e., process/event), actionality (i.e., active/passive), performative content, and tactical focus (i.e., resistance/play/acceptance). We should note that these elements tend to operate in combination. For instance, one might pass "up" while at work by actively re-presenting oneself in a middle-class coded manner in order to gain the social approval of one's peers or superiors that in turn is related to tenure and monetary rewards; and when away from work, one might pass "down" when in the company of friends from one's class culture of origin.

The Limits of Passing

For all our boyish clothes and mannerisms (known as being "butch") we women did not pass as men or boys. We dikes did not want to be taken for men and were insulted and ashamed (I certainly was, anyhow) when someone said we were "trying to be men" or when a clerk called me "Sir." (Grahn, 1984, p. 32)

I can pass for straight, if by some bizarre turn of events I should want to. Or I can pass for a compliant woman who accepts the patriarchal hegemony. But I cannot pass as white in this society. (Gomez, 1995, p. x)

As the words of Grahn and Gomez indicate, passing as an adaptive tactic is not without limits or limitations. Two caveats about passing bear mentioning. First, although passing often involves a degree of *choice,* sometimes people are made to pass without their permission (as in the case of Grahn), and second, as Gomez suggests, not everyone is able to pass. Common instances of the first caveat are those wherein light-skinned Blacks and Latinos are assumed to be White, or those in universities where everyone is assumed to be, at minimum, middle class.

More important, the presence of choice in passing usually indicates that a *degree of privilege* already exists because, regardless of desire, not everyone *can* pass. For instance, dark-skinned people cannot pass for White, poor people who do not have the material resources or the cultural know-how cannot present themselves as upper class, certain kinds of bodies cannot pass for others. In short, passing as an adaptive tactic is not without bounds. Conversely, those with more resources and higher status positions are more likely to be able to exercise choice in regard to passing. For example, a tenured professor raised poor might choose not to pass for middle class with few repercussions, whereas a secretary who refuses to do so may not be tolerated. So, paradoxically, although passing is a tactic of the marginalized, those who have more resources are the most likely to exercise volition in its deployment.

Passing Through Identity

Passing speaks of a secret behind a closed door, which it opens as a space of difference in the heart of the same, disrupting identity. (Tyler, 1994, p. 213)

In the earlier discussion of the social practice of passing, I suggested that passing illustrates the problematic nature of identity-as-essence. I exam-ined some of the ways in which passers trouble the boundary lines between "us" and "them," finding that such marks are often drawn in sand rather than cement. Passing proves to be a creative response to oppressive conditions, an adaptive tactic by which the "consent" of the dominant group for membership is won by presenting oneself as already a member! Adaptive strategies such as assimilation work by making the subordinate group member appear more "acceptable" to members of the dominant culture (i.e., more like "them"), but because that acceptance is won on the terms of the dominant group, such tactics lose much of their liberatory potential. When viewed from "below" (i.e., the perspectives of subordinate cultures), assimilationist tactics are often seen as "selling out" (Daniel, 1992).

Conversely, the passer deploys a pass in/on his/her terms. When viewed "Other/wise" (Nakayama, 1994), passing offers a more politicized notion of identity and adaptation that takes into account the perspectives of those for whom passing is an issue, and one that renders the social relations underlying the need or desire to pass more transparent. In addition, when viewed through the lens of passing, intercultural communication concepts such as adaptation take on a different face. For instance, Berry (1992) suggests four ways that people adapt: assimilation, separation, integration, and marginalization. The problem with these avenues to adaptation is that the terms for adapting are usually set by the dominant or host culture, and these avenues are not available to all. For instance, one wonders if assimilation or even integration is a real possibility for African Americans, Mexican Americans, or Vietnamese Americans in the United States. This country's history has shown us that assimilation and integration are most often open only to certain groups of people (usually people of European ancestry) and that separation (in the form of segregation) and marginalization are the avenues often afforded to "undesirables" (usually people of color).

While passing is not an unproblematic response to relations of domination, as a tactic of the marginalized, it enables them to find a way to make a way in conditions not of their own choosing. In addition, passing highlights power relations rather than obscures them, and makes us realize the vulnerability of the categories we produce to separate "us" from "them." Passing, then, offers a useful perspective for rethinking intercultural communication grounded in a view from "below," one that reminds us that categories are never truly closed, that difference cannot be controlled and disciplined no matter how diligent our efforts to do so. Passing disrupts notions of group homogeneity and our identifications with one another that formulate and support the concept of group identity (Tyler, 1994). Passing opposes notions of identity-as-essence and points us in the direction of conceptualizing identity in "other" terms.

REFERENCES

Baudrillard, J. (1988). Simulacra and simulations (P. Foss, P. Patton, & P. Beitchmena, Trans.). In M. Poster (Ed.), *Jean Baudrillard: Selected writings* (pp. 166–184). Stanford, CA: Stanford University Press.

Berry, J. W. (1992). Psychology of acculturation: Understanding individuals moving between two cultures. In R. W. Brislin (Ed.), *Applied cross-cultural psychology* (pp. 232–253). Newbury Park, CA: Sage.

Bradshaw, C. K. (1992). Beauty and the beast: On racial ambiguity. In M. P. P. Root (Ed.), *Racially mixed people in America* (pp. 79–88). Newbury Park, CA: Sage.

Caughie, P. L. (1992). "Not entirely strange, . . . not entirely friendly": *Passing* and pedagogy. *College English, 54*(7), 775–793.

Creef, E. T. (1990). Notes from a fragmented daughter. In G. Anzaldúa (Ed.), *Making face, making soul: Haciendo caras* (pp. 82–84). San Francisco: Aunt Lute Books.

Daniel, G. R. (1992). Passers and pluralists: Subverting the racial divide. In M. P. P. Root (Ed.), *Racially mixed people in America* (pp. 91–107). Newbury Park, CA: Sage.

De Certeau, M. (1984). *The practice of everyday life* (S. Rendall, Trans.). Berkeley: University of California Press.

Garon, P. (1995). White blues. *Race Traitor, 4,* 57–66.

Gomez, J. (1995). Repeat after me: We are different. We are the same. *Oral tradition: Selected poems old and new.* Ithaca, NY: Firebrand Books.

Grahn, J. (1984). *Another mother tongue: Gay words, gay worlds.* Boston: Beacon Press.

Hitchcock, P. (1994). Passing: Henry Green and working-class identity. *Modern Fiction Studies, 40*(1), 1–31.

Larsen, N. (1986). *Passing.* New Brunswick, NJ: Rutgers University Press. (Original work published in 1929)

Lefebvre, H. (1971). *Everyday life in the modern world* (S. Rabinovitch, Trans.). London: Penguin.

Maitland, S. (1986). *Vesta Tilley.* London: Virago.

Martin, J. N., Krizek, R. L., Nakayama, T. K., & Bradford, L. (1996). Exploring whiteness: A study of self labels for white Americans. *Communication Quarterly, 44,* 125–144.

Millett, K. (1971). *Sexual politics.* London: Sphere.

Moon, D. G. (1996a). Concepts of "culture": Implications for intercultural communication discourse. *Communication Quarterly, 44*(1), 70–84.

Moon, D. G. (1996b). [White women and the construction of social class identity]. Unpublished raw data.

Nakayama, T. K. (1994). Show/down time: "Race," gender, sexuality, and popular culture. *Critical Studies in Mass Communication, 11*(2), 162–187.

Nakayama, T. K., & Krizek, R. L. (1995). Whiteness: A strategic rhetoric. *Quarterly Journal of Speech, 8*(3), 291–309.

Pepper, J. (1982). *A man's tale.* London: Quartet Books.

Piper, A. (1994). Passing for white, passing for black. In J. Frueh, C. L. Langer, & A. Raven (Eds.), *New feminist criticism* (pp. 216–247). New York: IconEditions.

Robinson, A. (1994). It takes one to know one: Passing and communities of common interest. *Critical Inquiry, 20,* 715–735.

Tanno, D. V. (1997). Names, narratives, and the evolution of identity. In A. González, M. Houston, & V. Chen (Eds.), *Our voices: Essays in culture, ethnicity, and communication* (2nd ed., pp. 28–33). Los Angeles: Roxbury.

Tyler, C. A. (1994). Passing: Narcissism, identity, and difference. *Differences: A Journal of Feminist Cultural Studies, 6*(2/3), 212–248.

Willey, K. (1996, August 4). Gay lawmaker gets priorities straight. *Arizona Republic*, p. B2.

Wood, J. T. (1997). *Gendered lives: Gender, culture, and communication* (2nd ed.). Belmont, CA: Wadsworth.

KEY TERMS

passing	power
identity	culture
adaptation	intercultural commu-
sojourner	nication

DISCUSSION QUESTIONS

1. Moon describes how passing can change the ways in which one thinks about identity. Can you think of how other intercultural concepts such as intercultural competence might be rethought through the lens of passing?

2. In her essay, Moon differentiates between passing and appropriation. Do you agree with the distinction that she draws between these two concepts? Why or why not?

3. Moon argues that passing as an adaptive tactic is one way of taking some control within social systems into which we are born. What are other adaptive or resistance tactics that people use?

4. Moon suggests that the social practice of passing problematizes the notion of group identity. What membership groups do you claim? On what basis do you make claims to membership in these groups? What reference groups do you claim? Why do you choose these groups rather than others?

5. In Moon's essay, she suggests that the phenomenon of passing draws attention to the "politics of identity." What does she mean by this phrase? What does the need or desire to pass tell us about social relations in the United States?

PART EIGHT

COMMUNICATION AND INTERCULTURAL RELATIONSHIPS

Essays in this part highlight the importance of intercultural communication in family, acquaintance, friendship, romantic, and marital relationships across sexual orientation. Not all families look alike, any more than all marriages look like the romantic images we see in mainstream film and television. The intercultural nature of the family is often overlooked, despite its tremendous importance in the development of cultural roles and socialization.

Different kinds of families and different kinds of relationships require sensitivity to intercultural communication, as we see in this section. These essays offer different ways to think about relationships as well as practical suggestions for developing intercultural relationships. Essays range from a discussion of how broad cultural values influence relationships, to identifying cross-cultural differences in relational communication and development, to explorations of how social and legal contexts constrain relationships. Other essays explore the unique challenges and joys of friendship and romantic intercultural relationships.

Consider these questions as you read the articles in this part:

How are intercultural relationships similar to or different from intracultural relationships?

Do relationships develop in similar ways in most cultures?

How do social constraints influence whom we come in contact with, whom we develop relationships with, and how we feel about our relationships?

In "The Role of Family and Macrocultures in Intercultural Relationships," Carley H. Dodd and John R. Baldwin explore how two levels of culture, family and national or ethnic (macrocultures), influence intercultural relationships. Specifically, they show how family and macrocultures shape identity and also communication styles in intercultural relationships, including notions of supportiveness, cohesion, adaptability, receptivity, and availability. They also provide cross-cultural perspectives on these various aspects of intercultural relationships. Note that they are most interested in broad cultural differences that are fairly consistent across contexts.

In "I, We, and They," social psychologist Geert Hofstede discusses how one core cultural value (individualism-collectivism) influences interpersonal relationships. Like E. T. Hall's work, Hofstede's extensive cross-cultural studies in IBM subsidiaries worldwide have formed the bases for many social science studies in intercultural communication that predict how cultural values (e.g., individualism-collectivism) influence communication behavior. In this reading, Hofstede shows how these cultural preferences are reflected in family, education, and work relationships. He also discusses implications of these cultural differences for building relationships across cultures.

Ling Chen, in "Chinese and North Americans: An Epistemological

Exploration of Intercultural Communication," provides a description of how broad cultural differences can affect communication and intercultural relationships—particularly in initial interaction. She contrasts North American and Chinese "structures of consciousness" and shows how the Chinese collectivist consciousness and the North American individualistic orientations can lead to misunderstandings and embarrassment on both sides. Note the causal relationship between cultural membership (North American and Chinese) and communication behavior—assumed to be consistent across many contexts.

To further explore intercultural relationships, Mary Jane Collier discusses "Intercultural Friendships as Interpersonal Alliances." Based on Cultural Identity Theory, her interpretive ethnographic research identifies three issues central to intercultural friendships: (1) power and unearned privilege, (2) acknowledgment of history, and (3) emergent orientations toward cultural differences, the relationship, and the other persons. She explores how these issues work in successful friendships that span national, ethnic, and gender differences. Note that Collier's work is interpretive in that she assumes a dynamic, reciprocal relationship between cultural identity and communication. Also, notions of power *emerge* from her study rather than being part of the assumptive foundation of her research.

The last two essays focus on romantic intercultural relationships. Melanie Payne, in "Waiting for Lightning to Strike," discusses the role of social support in interracial relationships. She indicates that although interracial couples are increasingly more prevalent, they still face stigma from the larger U.S. society. She points out that social support of friends and family plays an important role in all romantic relationships but is especially important for interracial couples. From her own experience and the results of an exploratory study, Payne identifies common verbal and nonverbal messages from friends, family, and society at large that support or negate interracial relationships.

Providing a critical perspective on intimate romantic relationships, Jacqueline Taylor, in "Performing Commitment," describes commitment in her family relationships—with her partner and two daughters. For her, commitment in a lesbian relationship can only be understood by considering current social, political, and legal contexts. She explores how commitment is performed communicatively in bridging the gap between *her family's* lived experience and the laws and customs within which family commitments are traditionally organized and performed. Her family's public and private rituals of commitment include a "marriage of addresses," anniversary celebrations, and rituals of adoption. She describes how ritual, ceremony, language, custom, and laws all interact to construct and constrain conceptions of family.

35
THE ROLE OF FAMILY AND MACROCULTURES IN INTERCULTURAL RELATIONSHIPS

CARLEY H. DODD / JOHN R. BALDWIN

Baldwin and Lindsley's (1994) listing of 206 definitions of culture demonstrates many competing notions of culture today. Much of the literature about intercultural relationships has looked at "culture" in a traditional way, as relatively large groups of people who share the same way of life (Gudykunst & Kim, 1992). However, many scholars, such as Collier (1997), are now suggesting that *any* size group can share a way of life, and for that group, this becomes a culture. Thus, in this essay, we refer to the "large groups of people" who share a way of life, even if those are ethnic co-cultures within a nation, as *macrocultures*.[1] But, as we will suggest shortly, each family comes to develop its own way of life. We suggest in this essay that partners in a relationship bring both the elements of their macrocultures and the elements of their family cultures into the relationship.

In recent years, intercultural specialists have looked at "culture" and "intercultural" communication at a variety of levels, from the culture shared by large groups (Gudykunst & Kim, 1992) to that shared by cultural, regional, age cohort, and even family groups (Collier, 1997; Dodd, 1998). This expanded view, including numerous co-cultures, also involves several relationship dynamics that together with the larger culture help explain intercultural and intergroup communication. Indeed, the impact of relationships on culture and of culture on relationships—and of both on human communication—is an area of growing interest.

Gudykunst and Kim (1992) discuss intercultural encounters using the metaphor of meeting a stranger. They propose that such meetings create a cognitive "head-response" of uncertainty (trying to understand the other's behavior) and an affective "heart-response" of anxiety (fearing some negative outcome). Dodd (1998) combined this approach with a "Third Culture Perspective" to propose that as partners resolve their anxiety and uncertainty, they develop a new, common culture. By initiating positive attitudes, images, and actions invested in building a relationship climate, the partners achieve functional outcomes including accurate information, friendship, mutual goals, and respect.

These writers and others conclude that intercultural communication occurs when people experience or perceive some group-level difference. As we encounter someone different, this intuitive perception of sameness or difference shapes the resulting relationship. This internal classification, resulting from a perceived level of difference, can be accurate or flawed but, regardless, frames attitudes and actions toward others.

This essay explores how intercultural relationships are linked with one of our deepest sources of intercultural perception and emotion, the family. In effect, the family intersects with "culture" in at least three ways. First, the family of each partner in a relationship reflects to some degree the culture of origin of that family. Gushue and Sciarra (1995) note that this influence is one of the major new waves in multicultural counseling:

> Different cultures [have] different ways of understanding "appropriate" family organization, values, communication, and behavior. Although the family perspective had revolutionized the individual view of the client by taking the family context into account, it now needed to understand its own unit of analysis (i.e., the family) in light of an even larger context: culture. (p. 588)

Also, Rohrlich (1988) referred to family communication as an extension of intercultural communication. From her vantage point, the metaphor of culture accurately describes family and is a major influence over intercultural communication.

Second, as noted above, after two partners decide on more than just a casual acquaintanceship, they begin to adjust to one another, to develop rules and behaviors in some ways unique to them. Thus, the communication partners become, in some sense, a *culture*.

Third, the family itself comes to be seen as a "culture" much as organizational researchers have treated organizations as cultures. Family therapists have long looked at families as *systems*—with interrelated parts whose behavior influences one another. But with the emergence of broader definitions of culture that include *any* "historical system of symbols, meanings, and norms" (Collier, 1997, p. 36), families can be said to be *cultures* in that, through family norms, rituals, rewards, and communication, each family develops its own sense of functioning, its own way of life. One family may resolve conflict by arguing or physical aggression; another may use inuendo and moodiness; and another may subterfuge the conflict by moving on to some other activity. In this regard, Falicov (1986) suggests that "strictly speaking, we all intermarry, even if we marry the boy next door" (p. 429).

Thus, family cultures are fundamental perceptual frameworks influencing relationships. Relationships, in turn, are pivotal arenas for intercultural encounters. What happens when a family's culture provides an acceptable set of rules, roles, norms, symbols, social style, stories, myths, and interpretive framework to see the world for Person A, while Person B comes from a family quite opposite? This essay attempts to answer that question along with cultural differences.

Family as Culture: Identity Through Family

First, we must again underscore the nature of family as culture. The case of Maria and Richard's struggling marriage illustrates our core position:

"You never believe a thing I say!" said 28-year-old Chilean-born Maria to her 29-year-old

American husband, Richard. "Every time I talk, all you do is turn on the TV. You're always paying attention to television, or your newspaper, or your friends far more than to me." After another one of their long, drawn out arguments, Maria concluded that the only thing to do was to dissolve their 5-year marriage. Despite the fact that they were so much in love when they first met, barriers seemed all too apparent. As Maria sat in the therapist's office, tears streamed from her eyes as she recounted their dating, courtship, and the 5 years of their marriage. "It seemed so promising," she said, "for Richard and I both knew we were in love. My heart told me and led me to this relationship." Both revealed their missed expectations of how each other's families "always were the perfect pattern" for their marriage, and how disappointed they were of each other.

Maria's story presents many aspects of intercultural marriages. While Richard was paying much more attention to his friends, football games on television, and his computer, cultural factors and family tradition factors also became apparent. He complained of value differences and how Maria never did things like his mom. These perceptions overlooked the comparative richness of Maria's culture and its contrast of time, relationship building, and emotional expectations. The therapist originally overlooked culture and its link within the family system as a cause of their difficulties, but the conditions soon illustrated to the couple and to the therapist that indicators associated with both culture of origin (macroculture) and family culture explained their difficulty.

Maria and Richard's situation reminds us of family culture's powerful ability to frame events and relationships. According to intergroup theory, if there is a significant, positive identity development—that is, if a person has a group that he or she can rely on as a primary group—then there is social identity (Gudykunst & Gumbs, 1989). Families clearly provide this social identity. I am a McClintoch. I am a Johnson. I am a Martinez. I am a Schleyermacher. I am from the family of Lin Chan. My father is Professor Ito. In this sense, family is a cultural unit defining *identity quali-*

ties such as security, intimacy, self-worth, and confidence.

Second, not only does family culture serve to instill these identity qualities, but it is a source of norms regarding interaction and communication style. Each family culture generates ways of thinking, feeling, and acting. For example, Elizabeth Stone (1996) interviews men and women from different ethnic cultures to find out how the stories families tell, be they about maternal sacrifice, male heroes, or sibling rivalries, teach family members how to act in relationships, influencing family members to communicate a certain way. This "way" often develops into a pattern or a linguistic norm that becomes a preferred and expected communicator style. While families are not the only cause of individual communicator style, family, other co-cultures, macroculture, personality, education, and other experiences contribute to linguistic norm development in communities.

Families are made up of people in relationship. Wood (1996) suggests that *relational cultures* are "privately transacted system[s] of understandings" that include the partners' (or family members') identities, attitudes, and actions. As relational cultures, families demonstrate and engage varying interaction patterns, norms, rules, attitudes, values, space, time use, dress, systems of reward, tools, and roles. They have stories, special symbols, myths, and images. They live within an external environment such as a town, a state, and a nation. A family can be characterized as having a unique personality and a resulting communicator style. Some families have an aggressive, assertive style, while others are laid-back and easygoing. Some families are meditative; some are active and fun loving. Some families encourage total dependency, others encourage autonomy.

Therefore, when family culture interfaces with one's macroculture, an enriched source of intercultural communication emerges. To conclude our case example, Maria's family culture (with all its assumptions, procedures, etc.) and her macroculture (Chile) are jointly part of the interaction "package" with Richard. Richard's family habits and outlooks interlocked with his U.S. culture in his talking and listening to Maria. There were at least two cultures influencing their communication and relationship. Her cultures (macro and family) emphasized people first and task accomplishment second, whereas his cultures underscored task orientation above all else. She tried to nurture the relationship, but he seemed to take her for granted while he advanced his career. Relationship expectations were missed, and the marriage was dissolved.

Still other writers on intercultural marriage, such as Romano (1988) or the various writers in Tseng, McDermott, and Maretzki (1977) give countless instances of misunderstandings. The father (from a Polynesian island culture) rewards conformity in the children, while the mother (an Anglo American) rewards independent thought. The man from one culture defines the marriage (in terms of mutual sexual fidelity) differently than the woman from another. The man from a Central Asian culture wants to fulfill financial obligations to extended family, but the woman from a Western culture sees the nuclear family as having sole ownership over time and financial resources.

Elements of Family Culture Impacting Intercultural Communication

What specific aspects of family culture imprint upon intercultural communication and relationships? Earlier we stated that family is identified as a culture. As a system it can be tightly woven or loose, functional or dysfunctional, adaptable or not adaptable, but unmistakably a system composed of contributing elements and people. If Dad loses his job, certainly the attitudes and actions of all family members can be affected. If an unmarried daughter becomes pregnant, the siblings and parents often change. In other words, what happens to one affects the whole family system. To understand these relationships, a number of systemic elements can be analyzed that help us better understand the nature of this culture. Since intercultural studies involving extensive use of categories of family culture are in development, we will select foundational elements from classic literature focusing on such elements.[2]

Supportive Communication

Some families encourage various degrees of what family researchers term *supportive communication,* defined here as the quality of affirming family members during crisis. We can illustrate from the case of a family in central Mexico where the father, upon learning of his 16-year-old daughter's pregnancy, literally abandoned her, ordering her out of the house and refusing to talk with her. Although this case is extreme, family rigidity during crisis can take many more subtle forms where families freeze relationships and increase distance. Some silently nurse grudges, ruling out the possibility of healing or happiness. As a result, a person from a nonsupportive family may "act out" in a way that creates dysfunctional communication (Galvin & Brommel, 1996).

It is not hard to see how people from two diverse family systems can experience group clash: one from a supportive family culture and the other from a nonsupportive family culture, each acting from a vantage point modeled by family. Affirming families are able to engage in a number of important communication behaviors. Among those behaviors is the ability to provide reassurance, forgiveness, nurturing, competency, accomplishment, and understanding. Sadly, not every family capably assures affirmation expected in that culture. For example, one father in therapy, over a period of several weeks, refused to look at his teenage son during the sessions. He literally looked straight across the room, craning his head around his son to be able to look at the therapist, despite repeated efforts to encourage father-son communication. As a result, the son failed to resolve his aberrant behavior and remained in an adolescent facility isolation unit until the family's communication source of the problem was corrected.

In addition to the influences of the family culture, macrocultural influences may impinge upon a couple in two ways. First, different cultures may not only define *supportiveness* differently but place a different value on it. For example, Hecht,

Collier, and Ribeau (1993) cite much research suggesting that for African Americans goal attainment (in a sense of social support) is a primary goal both in interpersonal interaction and in friendships. This seems to correspond with the values of the African American *Kwanzaa* festival of *ujima* (collective work and responsibility) and *ujamma* (cooperative economics) (Bowers, 1997). African American families might, according to these principles, highly value *supportiveness*, but in a different way from Caucasian families. Although the latter might define supportiveness in terms of "open communication," the former might define it in terms of goal accomplishment, especially in terms of accomplishing tasks together in the face of an unequal power structure.[3]

The second way that family-culture supportiveness may impinge on intercultural families is in the way the support of extended family is expressed in cases of intercultural or interethnic marriage (Baldwin, 1992). Graham, Moeai, and Shizuru (1985) find that interculturally married couples in Hawaii perceive more of their problems to be caused by "external" factors such as cultural differences and pressure from family, rather than "internal" factors such as personal differences. We hold that, as in all intercultural interaction, two main influences might be present in intercultural romantic relationships: The first is *real cultural differences* brought from the macro or family cultures; but the second, pertinent here under a discussion of supportiveness, is the support from the surrounding family and community. Writers in Tseng, McDermott, and Maretzki (1977) suggest that the success of an intercultural family goes up as the distance from either family of origin increases! Falicov (1986) suggests that boundary management (keeping the in-laws out of nuclear family business) is one of the major issues for intercultural families.

Cohesion

Another important family system variable is cohesion. Cohesion refers to a feeling of closeness, and includes two dimensions. The first dimension is a sense of separation or independence, in which family members feel the freedom or desire to "do their own thing," to spend time alone or with friends apart from the family. The second dimension is a sense of connection or interdependence, in which members want to spend time together. Wood (1996) suggests that relationships exist in "dialectic"—or tension between various extremes. She and other dialectic writers would suggest that all relationships have both extremes constantly in tension with one another. "Healthy" relationships (including families) have a balance of the two extremes (Olson, 1976, defined these extremes with combinations across axes of cohesion and adaptability). Often, difficulties arrive when the family members are trying to emphasize different ends, such as when the parents want a *family* vacation and the teens want to go off with their friends and increase their autonomy.

Family cultures characterized by either extreme can be considered potentially unhealthy. On one hand, family members can develop extreme patterns of exclusivity in relationships, expectations of autonomy, and lack of teamwork. Partners and other family members become *isolated* from one another. In contrast, other family cultures might become what some family-system experts refer to as "enmeshed." In this case, interdependence is so extreme that an individual cannot be extricated from his or her family network. Thus, when autonomy is needed, an individual is not able to draw upon independent dimensions of thought. In fact, the evidence indicates that enmeshment can create learned dependency and helplessness (Lewis, Dodd, & Tippens, 1992).

However, notions of connection, enmeshment, and isolation must be reconsidered also from the standpoint of other cultural standards. Shon and Ja (1982), for example, suggest that "Asian cultures"[4] are more "collective." As such, the connections that are important to a particular Asian culture might be as much to the father's family, to society at large, or to some other collective rather than to the nuclear family; and, within the Buddhist or Confucionist cultural framework, this would be "natural" rather than "unhealthy." Such an orientation toward connection influences even verbal and nonverbal patterns, leading Asian Americans to frequently prefer more indirect means of conflict (preserv-

ing connection), whereas Caucasians might prefer more direct conflict styles (preserving autonomy). In similar fashion, Gaines (1995) notes the *familism* (a high value on the family) in Latino American relationships and the *collectivism* (preference for the group) in African American families. As familism or collectivism increases, he suggests, Latino American and African American mates would express more respect and affection for their partners. In the cases of any such collective culture, functioning alone, without consultation of the "collective" with which the partner identifies, is rare.

In these and other cases, even the definition of "attachment" or "cohesion" differs. For example, Sprecher et al. (1994) discuss several different types of love that partners may feel for each other, such as *ludus* (game-playing love), *eros* (romantic, passionate love), and *storge* (friendship love). They found that couples in America, Russia, and Japan differed not only in which form of "love" they preferred, but also in the way they approached attachment in general. Thus, we can see how levels and definitions of connectedness impact intercultural relations and communication where two individuals come from very different family or macrocultural traditions.

Family Rules and Cultural Adaptability

Family rules are the teachings of obligations and expectations of behavior, the dos and don'ts within the family. Family rules can include anything from what you should or should not do at a family reunion to what you should or should not do in cleaning up your room. Every family has its methods of doing things, sometimes taught explicitly, sometimes by example. For instance, an older student returning to college tells a story that illustrates family rules:

> My parents were very rigid. Everything we did had to be done just as they had done them. On one occasion, after I had married and had a baby, I had to move home for a short while because my husband was stationed with the air force in Morocco. My parents had no washer or dryer, and all of our clothes were washed at a

laundromat and hung up. To save folding time, I hung the baby's diapers already folded in half. My parents thought this practice was absolutely ridiculous! Their ridicule helped me decide it didn't matter anymore, as long as the job got done. At least I wasn't being called "lazy" anymore.

As this case underscores, rules are not always deliberate, well-thought-out, consciously placed guides to action. Whatever their source, rules guide family norms, influence thinking, feeling, and behavior, and affect relationships in intercultural communication. We have shown that persons A and B experience different family rules that lead to areas of difference in expectation and communication. Sometimes the rules are particular to a family culture, and sometimes they are products of the larger macroculture, such as our earlier example about rewarding children's independence or conformity.

From an intercultural vantage point, Shon and Ja (1982) suggest that shame, or the reflection an action makes on the collective, is more important to collective Asian American cultures than guilt, or the personal responsibility one feels for an action. Thus, an "external" accountability in a collectivist culture may be more motivational in this situation than an individually grounded "internal" application of rules.

Based on our cultural assumptions, we recommend "mindfulness" (Gudykunst & Kim, 1992) about rules—rules should be thought about, considered, and often treated with some flexibility. Children who have rules and are taught "why" understand a sense of permeability. They see why the rules exist, and when conditions change, they can adapt based on the principles involved. In contrast, children raised in families where the reasons for the rules are rarely explained may be at risk in relationships where intercultural communication is needed. As adults, they may experience less ability to cope with adaptation in intercultural environments. One family's rules of cleanliness were so well ingrained that their daughter suffered in her adaptability in New Guinea where village cleanliness standards were very different. Despite her other excellent intercultural skills, this inflexibility about cleanliness

impeded her adjustment in the new environment. In sum, many of our intercultural communication encounters can be explained by family rules: decision-making routines, everyday procedures, methods of interaction, finding the right time to talk, who takes responsibility for which task, gender-role expectations, how much to talk and listen, and so on. We learn from this idea to examine the many unconscious rules that define and structure our relationships.

Cultural Adaptability

Family specialists often view adaptability as a family system's characteristic to change its power, roles, and rules based on situational stress or developmental conditions experienced by one or all of the family members (Galvin & Brommel, 1996; Pearson, 1992). Cultural adaptability is important for the intersection of family and culture in two ways. First, families from nondominant cultures must learn to adapt to their new culture or to a culture that marginalizes or discredits their way of life.[5] Gudykunst & Kim (1992), for example, suggest that a major factor in cultural adaptation (which we extend to families) is the receptivity of the new environment.

The second way in which cultural adaptability is important is in dual-culture relationships or multicultural families. Whether the differences in rules are based on family culture or on macrocultures, the family must make a choice of which cultural pattern to follow. Tseng (1977) suggests five possible patterns for adaptation: (1) *One-way adjustment*, in which the family consistently adopts the cultural standards of one of the spouses—"a total capitulation to the culture" of one member (p. 99). For example, a Filipina wife married to an Anglo husband might speak only English, learn to cook hamburgers, and so on, giving up her own culture. (2) In *alternative adjustment*, the partners or family adopt first one culture, then the other—Filipina food tonight, American food tomorrow night (this example is simplistic and ignores deeper underlying value differences that are not so easily reconciled or alternated!). (3) *Mixing* has partners adopting elements of both cultures at the same time. A family might practice Chinese acupuncture or Native

American herbal medicine while still consulting the local (Western medical system) doctor. An example of (4) *midpoint compromise* would be to give money to extended family members but negotiate the amount. Finally, Tseng discusses (5) *creative adjustment,* in which "both partners decide to give up the cultural behavior of both sides and invent a completely new behavior pattern" (p. 100). This is similar to the Third Culture Perspective we mentioned earlier.

Rohrlich (1988) suggests that in all dual-culture marriages, *power* might be an issue. We suggest that in issues of cultural adjustment, this is especially the case. Partners from dual cultures (including dual family cultures) must ask themselves questions such as: Who determines *which* rule we follow? (For example, Should we automatically adjust to the husband's culture?) How are such decisions made? Do they treat all family members equitably? Mutual agreement to these questions can facilitate adaptation.

Communication Receptivity

Another major category in understanding family culture is *communication receptivity,* defined here as each family's degree of openness to communication and ability to incorporate and apply new information into family member relationships. When this quality is present, family members are "askable." They are open and they listen. Their communication conveys the attitude, "It is OK to ask any question, or express any feeling. No issue is off-limits in this family. I will not condemn. I will listen with understanding."

When receptivity is absent from a family's culture (avoidance), family members respond differently depending on one's macroculture. For instance, low communication receptivity among U.S. American Caucasians is often viewed as "unhealthy." Failure to be receptive in dealing with taboo subjects illustrates how some children will find relevant information and may experiment outside the family culture. It should not be surprising that communication and family experts assert that avoiding communication may be the worst possible strategy, particularly in sensitive family topics. For example, clinical experience points to Roberta, who remembers her innocent questions about sex when she was 8 years old. Out of his own discomfort, her father responded, "We don't talk about that here." When she was 9, she was sexually abused by an uncle. She tried again to talk to her father, this time about the uncle's abuse. Her father's only response, "We don't talk about that here." At 10, she was molested by her grandfather and once more heard from her dad, "We don't talk about that here." At 34, as a patient in a psychiatric hospital, trying to cope with the trauma of a recent rape, she painfully shared with her father four other instances of sexual abuse. She remembers her father saying the same words, "We don't talk about that here." Today she is a psychotic, locked in a fantasy world, in part because of her father's denial.

In addition, macroculture influences communication receptivity. For example, Rohrlich (1988) suggests that cultural self-disclosure differences should be considered in intercultural marriages. Indeed, much research on initial conversations and developing relationships suggests that different cultures see different topics as intimate or taboo. For example, whereas the "only two subjects you shouldn't discuss are politics and religion" in many American circles, Friday (1997) suggests that for U.S. Americans interacting with Germans, politics, philosophy, and even religion are very appropriate topics. In the same manner, our personal experiences suggest that for many South Americans, death is not a taboo topic.

Communication receptivity is not simply a matter of revising daily schedules. Rather, it may be a deep-rooted cognitive, emotional, and behavioral construct expressed in a pattern of interaction habits affecting intercultural communication. In a study in five Latin American countries, Norton (1984) found that the degree of interpersonal openness was a major contributor to U.S. expatriates' intercultural adjustment. While this study did not examine family culture in detail, many respondents said that family interaction, viewed as a by-product of family culture, helped them adjust to a new country.

A related feature associated with communication receptivity is *availability.* It is one thing to be culturally approachable and appropriately open, but still another to be available. Alex, a rather enterprising young man, was frustrated by having so little time to talk with his very busy father. Under an assumed name, he made an appointment with his father's office. When Alex appeared at the arranged time, his dad quizzed, "Why are you here, Alex? I have an appointment with someone else. Sorry." The teen replied, "Dad, I had to make an appointment under a fictitious name or you never would have seen me. We really have to talk." Time allotted to family members thus contributes to the nature of family and its expectations.

We value these communication characteristics and think they would improve families cross-culturally. At the same time, we recognize that other cultures might have different means of expressing communication receptivity. The family-systems perspective, discussed above, has an element called *equifinality*—that is, a system can reach the same end-state or goal through different means. Although our research suggests that approachability and availability *within the family system* are a key way to have positive family relations and outcomes for individual members, other cultures might meet this goal through other means. For example, some West African cultures expand communication receptivity to significant—and culturally prescribed—roles outside the nuclear family. The Ashanti culture (Ghana) expects a communication receptivity role through a person's maternal uncle.

So, on one hand, low communication receptivity (or avoidance) on the part of an intercultural family member can work against the resolution of cultural and individual differences in the family. On the other hand, conflict literature suggests that many cultures around the world deliberately avoid conflict in order to "preserve the face" or protect the public self-image of the people in the interaction (Ting-Toomey, 1988). The intercultural family must be aware not only of the usefulness (from the U.S. American standpoint) of "open discussion" but also of the need to culturally preserve the "face" of the others in the family.

Overall, we learn here that a lack of communication receptivity can be associated with a number of other communication issues: perception of communication accuracy, contributing to a positive communication climate, risk taking, understanding, encouragement, and listening. What we experience in intercultural communication as negative stereotyping, poor empathy, inadequate relationship development skills, ethnocentrism, stress reactions, and the like can grow from deep taproots related to family culture. Further, conflicts can arise through our assigning negative *personal* characteristics to partners who come from conflict-avoiding macrocultures.

Conclusion

This essay focused on two mutually important levels of culture and their roles in intercultural relationships. First, family culture is a rich source of unexplored social interactions that serve to affect intercultural communication. The family system incorporates rules, roles, myths, customs, communication style, expectations, and the like that alter intercultural relationships.

The macroculture of partners and family members in intercultural relationships offers a second and parallel level of culture affecting intercultural relationships. Thus, outcomes within intercultural relationships such as bonding, nurturing, affirming, cohesion, autonomy, adaptation, codes, rules, social identity, self-worth, and adjustment are defined differentially in the intercultural relationship, from the perspective of *two* cultural units. By blending these two forces, family culture and macrocultural differences, this essay offers a more robust explanation of intercultural relationships.

NOTES

1. We do not here intend to present the *only* definition of culture, or a definitive definition. It is merely that this "communicative" definition works more for the purpose of our essay.

2. This list of factors is not intended to be all-inclusive, but rather to provoke thought on the part of the reader. We recognize that our discussion may reflect the biases of our own cultural identities (we are both Caucasian American males) and of the traditional social science framework from which this essay is written, such as the citation of Olson's often

quoted categories and his FACES instrument, which has influenced major streams of thought in the family literature.

3. Our cultural examples here are primarily from African, Latino, and certain East Asian ethnicities. This is not to "privilege" these ethnicities, but because these are some of the ethnicities most represented in the United States. The various authors of McGoldrick, Pearce, and Giordano (1982) give extensive discussion of families from 19 different cultures, sometimes even noting regional value and communication differences between co-cultures of a given background (e.g., "British Americans").

4. We recognize that there are vast differences between and within the various Asian American groups (Filipino Americans, Japanese Americans, Korean Americans, Chinese Americans, etc.). We adopt this label here only following the authors we are citing.

5. This sort of adaptability is a major theme of cross-cultural counseling books such as McGoldrick et al. (1982).

REFERENCES

Baldwin, J. R. (May, 1992). *Dual-culture marriages: An annotated bibliography.* Presented at the annual conference of the Society for International Training, Education, and Research (SIETAR), Montego Bay, Jamaica.

Baldwin, J. R., & Lindsley, S. L. (1994). *Conceptualizations of culture.* Tempe, AZ: Urban Studies Center, College of Public Programs, Arizona State University.

Bowers, D. L. (1997). Capturing the spirit of *Kwanzaa.* In A. González, M. Houston, & V. Chen (Eds.), *Our voices: Essays in culture, ethnicity, and communication* (2nd ed.). (pp. 121–124). Los Angeles: Roxbury.

Collier, M. J. (1997). Cultural identity and intercultural communication. In L. A. Samovar & R. E. Porter (Eds.), *Intercultural communication: A reader* (8th ed.) (pp. 36–44). Belmont, CA: Wadsworth.

Dodd, C. H. (1998). *Dynamics of intercultural communication* (5th ed.). New York: McGraw-Hill.

Falicov, C. J. (1986). Cross-cultural marriages. In N. S. Jacobson & A. S. Gurman (Eds.), *Clinical handbook of marital therapy* (pp. 78–90). Rockville, MD: Aspen Systems Corporation.

Friday, R. A. (1997). Contrasts in discussion behaviors of German and American managers. In L. A. Samovar & R. E. Porter (Eds.), *Intercultural communication: A reader* (8th ed.) (pp. 297–307). Belmont, CA: Wadsworth.

Gaines, S. O., Jr. (1995). Relationships between members of cultural minorities. In J. T. Wood & S. Duck (Eds.), *Understudied relationships: Off the beaten track* (p. 88). Thousand Oaks, CA: Sage.

Galvin, K., & Brommel, B. (1996). *Family communication: Cohesion and change* (4th ed.). Glenview, IL: Scott, Foresman.

Graham, M. A., Moeai, J., & Shizuru, L. S. (1985). Intercultural marriages: An intrareligious perspective. *International Journal of Intercultural Relations, 9,* 427–434.

Gudykunst, W. B., & Gumbs, L. I. (1989). Social cognition and intergroup communication. In M. K. Asante & W. B. Gudykunst (Eds.), *Handbook of international and intercultural communication* (pp. 204–224). Thousand Oaks, CA: Sage.

Gudykunst, W. B., & Kim, Y. Y. (1992). *Communicating with strangers* (2nd ed.). New York: McGraw-Hill.

Gushue, G. V., & Sciarra, D. T. (1995). Culture and families: A multidimensional approach. In J. G. Ponterotto, J. M. Casas, L. A. Suzuki, & C. M. Alexander (Eds.), *Handbook of multicultural counseling* (pp. 586–606).

Hecht, M. L., Collier, M. J., & Ribeau, S. A. (1993). *African-American communication: Ethnic identity and cultural interpretation.* Newbury Park, CA: Sage.

Height, M. (1984). Satisfying communication and relationship labels: Intimacy and length of relationship as perceptual frames of naturalistic conversations. *Western Journal of Speech Communication, 48,* 201–216.

Lewis, D., Dodd, C. H., & Tippens, D. (1992). *Dying to tell.* Abilene, TX: ACU Press.

McGoldrick, M., Pearce, J. K., & Giordano, J. (Eds.). (1982). *Ethnicity and family therapy.* New York: Guilford.

Norton, M. L. (1984). *The effects of communication effectiveness and cognitive complexity on culture shock*. Master's thesis, Abilene Christian University, Abilene, TX.

Olson, D. (1976). *Treating relationships*. Lake Mills, IA: Graphic.

Pearson, J. (1992). *Communication in the family* (2nd ed.). New York: Harper & Row.

Rohrlich, B. (1988). Dual-culture marriage and communication. *International Journal of Intercultural Relations, 12*, 35–44.

Romano, D. (1988). *Intercultural marriage: Promises & pitfalls*. Yarmouth, ME: Intercultural Press.

Shon, S. P., & Ja., D. Y. (1982). Asian families. In M. McGoldrick, J. K. Pearce, & J. Giordano (Eds.), *Ethnicity & family therapy* (pp. 208–228). New York: Guilford.

Sprecher, S., Aron, A., Hatfield, E., Cortese, A., Potapova, E., & Levitskaya, A. (1994). Love: American style, Russian style, and Japanese style. *Personal Relationships, 1*, 349–369.

Stone, E. (1996). Family ground rules. In K. M. Galvin & P. Cooper (Eds.), *Making connections* (pp. 59–67). Los Angeles: Roxbury.

Ting-Toomey, S. (1988). Intercultural conflict styles: A face-negotiation theory. In Y. Y. Kim & W. B. Gudykunst (Eds.), *Theories in intercultural communication* (p. 213). Newbury Park, CA: Sage.

Tseng, W.-S. (1977). Adjustment in intercultural marriage. In W.-S. Tseng, J. F. McDermott, Jr., & T. W. Maretzki (Eds.), *Adjustment in intercultural marriage* (pp. 93–103). Honolulu: University of Hawaii.

Tseng, W.-S., McDermott, J. F., Jr., & Maretzki, T. W. (Eds.). (1977). *Adjustment in intercultural marriage* (pp. 93–103). Honolulu: University of Hawaii.

Wood, J. T. (1996). Communication and relational culture. In K. M. Galvin & P. Cooper (Eds.), *Making connections* (pp. 11–15). Los Angeles: Roxbury.

KEY TERMS

family
family culture
family systems
intercultural relationships
cultural identity
communication style
supportiveness
cohesion
social change
rules
roles
enmeshment
communication avoidance
approachability
availability
affirmation
cultural adjustment
cultural adaptability

DISCUSSION QUESTIONS

1. What is the difference, according to Dodd and Baldwin, between family culture and macroculture? What is the relationship between these two? (How are they alike and different? Do they influence each other in any way?)

2. How can people from diverse family backgrounds and cultures develop balance and harmony in their relationships?

3. It is easy to lapse into comfortable "restricted" codes in our relationships, codes that only you and a few others understand. Unfortunately, restricted code usage lacks overlap in experiences, buffer, explanation, and other relationship-building features badly needed for relationship development. How can language and code be an effective beginning point for cultural differences perceived from family differences?

4. Imagine that you and your partner are from different types of cultures (family or macro)—one culture values direct conflict ("laying the cards on the table") and the other prefers avoiding conflict ("saving face"). How might you resolve a conflict, say, over household chores or how to spend time together?

5. Interview couples from two different macrocultures and family cultures and ask them to comment on each person's perception of how they are alike and how they are different from one another.

6. If you were to interview a couple from two different cultures (family or macrocultures) where there were *cultural* reasons for doing something, how might one partner understand and explain the other's behavior ("attribution")? What are the implications of these internal explanations on resolving family differences?

7. What role(s) do you find yourself playing in your family system? How do those roles affect other family members? Your friends and significant others?

36
I, WE, AND THEY

GEERT HOFSTEDE

A medium-size Swedish high-technology corporation was approached by a compatriot, a businessman with good contacts in Saudi Arabia. The company sent one of their engineers—let me call him Johannesson—to Riyadh, where he was introduced to a small Saudi engineering firm, run by two brothers in their mid-thirties, both with British university degrees. Johannesson was to assist in a development project on behalf of the Saudi government. However, after six visits over a period of two years, nothing seemed to happen. Johannesson's meetings with the Saudi brothers were always held in the presence of the Swedish businessman who had established the first contact. This annoyed Johannesson and his superiors, because they were not at all sure that this businessman did not have contacts with their competitors as well—but the Saudis wanted the intermediary to be there. Discussions often dwelt on issues having little to do with the business—like Shakespeare, of whom both brothers were fans.

Just when Johannesson's superiors started to doubt the wisdom of the corporation's investment in these expensive trips, a telex arrived from Riyadh inviting him back for an urgent visit. A contract worth several millions of dollars was ready to be signed. From one day to the next, the Saudis' attitude changed: the presence of the businessman–intermediary was no longer necessary, and for the first time Johannesson saw the Saudis smile, and even make jokes.

So far, so good; but the story goes on. The remarkable order contributed to Johannesson being promoted to a management position in a different division. Thus, he was no longer in charge of the Saudi account. A successor was nominated, another engineer with considerable international experience, whom Johannesson personally introduced to the Saudi brothers. A few weeks later a telex arrived from Riyadh in which the Saudis threatened to cancel the contract over a detail in the delivery conditions. Johannesson's help was asked. When he came to Riyadh it appeared that the conflict was over a minor issue and could easily be resolved—but only, the Saudis felt, with Johannesson as the corporation's representative. So the corporation twisted its structure to allow Johannesson to handle the Saudi account although his main responsibilities were now in a completely different field.

The Individual and the Collective in Society

The Swedes and the Saudis in this true story have different concepts of the role of personal relationships in business. For the Swedes, business is done with a company; for the Saudis, with a person whom one has learned to know and trust. As long as one does not know another person well enough it is convenient to have present an intermediary or go-between, someone who knows and is trusted by both parties. At the root of the difference between these cultures is a fundamental issue in human societies: the role of the individual versus the role of the group.

The vast majority of people in our world live in societies in which the interest of the group prevails over the interest of the individual. I will call these societies *collectivist*, using a word which to some readers may have political connotations, but it is not meant here in any political sense. It does not refer to the power of the state over the individual but to the *power of the group*. The first group in our lives is always the family into which we are born. Family structures, however, differ between societies. In most collectivist societies the 'family' within which the child grows up consists of a number of people living closely together; not just the parents and other children, but, for example, grandparents, uncles, aunts, servants, or other housemates. This is known in cultural anthropology as the *extended family*. When children grow up they learn to think of themselves as part of a 'we' group, a relationship which is not voluntary but given by nature. The 'we' group is distinct from other people in society who belong to 'they' groups, of which there are many. The 'we' group (or ingroup) is the major source of one's identity, and the only secure protection one has against the hardships of life. Therefore one owes lifelong loyalty to one's ingroup, and breaking this loyalty is one of the worst things a person can do. Between the person and the ingroup a dependence relationship develops which is both practical and psychological.

A minority of people in our world live in societies in which the interests of the individual prevail over the interests of the group, societies which I will call *individualist*. In these, most children are born into families consisting of two parents and, possibly, other children; in some societies there is an increasing share of one-parent families. Other relatives live elsewhere and are rarely seen. This type is the *nuclear family* (from the Latin *nucleus* meaning core). Children from such families, as they grow up, soon learn to think of themselves as 'I'. This 'I', their personal identity, is distinct from other people's 'I's, and these others are not classified according to their group membership but to individual characteristics. Playmates, for example, are chosen on the basis of personal preferences. The purpose of education is to enable the child to stand on its own feet. The child is expected to leave the parental home as soon as this has been achieved. Not infrequently, children, after having left home, reduce relationships with their parents to a minimum or break them off altogether. Neither practically nor psychologically is the healthy person in this type of society supposed to be dependent on a group.

Measuring the Degree of Individualism in Society

• • •

The new dimension is defined as follows. *Individualism* pertains to *societies in which the ties be-*

tween individuals are loose: everyone is expected to look after himself or herself and his or her immediate family. Collectivism as its opposite pertains to *societies in which people from birth onwards are integrated into strong, cohesive ingroups, which throughout people's lifetime continue to protect them in exchange for unquestioning loyalty.*

Degrees of individualism obviously vary within countries as well as between them, so it is again very important to base the country scores on comparable samples from one country to another. The IBM samples offered this comparability.

• • •

The dimension to be identified with individualism versus collectivism was most strongly associated with the relative importance attached to the following 'work goal' items. For the individualist pole:

1. *Personal time*   Have a job which leaves you sufficient time for your personal or family life.

2. *Freedom*   Have considerable freedom to adopt your own approach to the job.

3. *Challenge*   Have challenging work to do—work from which you can achieve a personal sense of accomplishment.

For the opposite, collectivist pole:

4. *Training*   Have training opportunities (to improve your skills or learn new skills).

5. *Physical conditions*   Have good physical working conditions (good ventilation and lighting, adequate work space, etc.).

6. *Use of skills*   Fully use your skills and abilities on the job.

If the IBM employees in a country scored work goal (1) as relatively important, they generally also scored (2) and (3) as important, but (4), (5), and (6) as unimportant. Such a country was considered individualist. If (1) was scored as relatively unimportant, the same generally held for (2) and (3), but (4), (5), and (6) would be scored as

TABLE 1   Individualism Index (IDV) Values for 50 Countries and 3 Regions

Score rank	Country or region	IDV score	Score rank	Country or region	IDV score
1	USA	91	28	Turkey	37
2	Australia	90	29	Uruguay	36
3	Great Britain	89	30	Greece	35
4/5	Canada	80	31	Philippines	32
4/5	Netherlands	80	32	Mexico	30
6	New Zealand	79	33/35	East Africa	27
7	Italy	76	33/35	Yugoslavia	27
8	Belgium	75	33/35	Portugal	27
9	Denmark	74	36	Malaysia	26
10/11	Sweden	71	37	Hong Kong	25
10/11	France	71	38	Chile	23
12	Ireland (Republic of)	70	39/41	West Africa	20
13	Norway	69	39/41	Singapore	20
14	Switzerland	68	39/41	Thailand	20
15	Germany F. R.	67	42	Salvador	19
16	South Africa	65	43	South Korea	18
17	Finland	63	44	Taiwan	17
18	Austria	55	45	Peru	16
19	Israel	54	46	Costa Rica	15
20	Spain	51	47/48	Pakistan	14
21	India	48	47/48	Indonesia	14
22/23	Japan	46	49	Colombia	13
22/23	Argentina	46	50	Venezuela	12
24	Iran	41	51	Panama	11
25	Jamaica	39	52	Equador	8
26/27	Brazil	38	53	Guatemala	6
26/27	Arab countries	38			

relatively more important. Such a country was considered collectivist.

• • •

. . . The factor scores for the individualism dimension were multiplied by 25 and a constant number of 50 points was added. This puts all scores in a range from close to 0 for the most collectivist country to close to 100 for the most individualist one.[1]

The individualism index (IDV) scores can be read from Table 1. . . . The scores represent the *relative* positions of countries. What can immediately be recognized by inspecting Table 1 is that nearly all wealthy countries score high on IDV while nearly all poor countries score low. There is a strong relationship between a country's national wealth and the degree of individualism in its culture; it will be further explored later in this chapter.

Sweden scores 171 on IDV and the group of Arab-speaking countries to which Saudi Arabia belongs scores an average of 38, which demonstrates the cultural roots of Johannesson's dilemma. Of course, the Arab countries differ among themselves, and impressionistically the Saudis within this region are even more collectivist than some other Arabs like Lebanese or Egyptians. In the IBM sample the latter were more strongly represented than the Saudis. Sweden's rank among 53 countries and regions is 10–11 and the Arab countries' rank 26–27, so there are still a lot of countries scoring more than the Arab average. As stated above, collectivism is the rule in our world, and individualism the exception.

• • •

Individualism and Collectivism in the Family

At the beginning of this chapter individualism was associated with a nuclear family structure and collectivism with an extended family structure, the latter leading to the distinction between ingroup and outgroups. The relationship between the individual and the group, like other basic elements of human culture, is first learned in the family setting. The fact that Japan scores halfway in Table 1 (rank 22/23, IDV 46) can at least partly be understood from the fact that in the traditional Japanese family only the oldest son continues to live with his parents, thus creating a 'lineal' structure which is somewhere in between nuclear and extended.

There is a correlation between the degree of collectivism in a society as measured by the IDV and the likelihood that sons will share the occupation of their fathers (Hofstede, 1980, p. 257; 1984, pp. 169–170). In more individualist societies the chances are greater that sons of fathers in manual occupations will move to nonmanual occupations and vice versa. In more collectivist societies this happens more rarely, an obvious outcome of sons staying within the extended family sphere.

The child who grows up among a number of elders, peers, and juniors learns naturally to conceive of itself as part of a 'we'; much more so than the nuclear family child. An extended family child is seldom alone during the day or at night. An African student who came to a Belgian university

to study told us that this was the first time in her life she had ever been alone in a room for any sizeable length of time.

In a situation of intense and continuous social contact the maintenance of *harmony* with one's social environment becomes a key virtue which extends to other spheres beyond the family. In most collectivist cultures direct confrontation of another person is considered rude and undesirable. The word 'no' is seldom used, because saying no *is* a confrontation; 'you may be right' or 'we will think about it' are examples of polite ways of turning down a request. In the same vein, the word 'yes' should not necessarily be seen as an approval, but as maintenance of the communication line: 'yes, I heard you' is the meaning it has in Japan.

In individualist cultures, on the other hand, speaking one's mind is a virtue. Telling the truth about how one feels is the characteristic of a sincere and honest person. Confrontation can be salutary; a clash of opinions is believed to lead to a higher truth. The effect of communications on other people should be taken into account, but it does not, as a rule, justify changing the facts. Adult individuals should have learned to take direct feedback constructively. In the family, children are told one should always tell the truth, even if it hurts. Coping with conflict is a normal part of living together as a family.

A former Dutch missionary in Indonesia (a country with IDV 14, rank 47/48) told about his parishioners' unexpected exegesis of the following parable from the Bible: 'A man had two sons. He went to the first and said "Son, go and work in the vineyard today"; he replied "I will go, sir", but he did not go. The man went to the second and said the same to him. He replied "I will not", but afterwards he changed his mind and did go. Which of the two did the will of the father?' (St. Matthew 21: 28–31; Moffatt translation). The biblical answer is 'the last', but the missionary's Indonesian parishioners chose the first; for this son observed the formal harmony and did not contradict his father. Whether he actually went was of secondary importance.

In the collectivist family children learn to take their bearings from others when it comes to opinions. 'Personal opinions' do not exist: they are predetermined by the group. If a new issue comes up on which there is no established group opinion, some kind of family conference is necessary before an opinion can be given. A child who repeatedly voices opinions deviating from what is collectively felt is considered to have a bad character. In the individualist family, on the contrary, children are expected and encouraged to develop opinions of their own, and a child who only ever reflects the opinions of others is considered to have a weak character. The behavior corresponding with a desirable character depends on the cultural environment.

The loyalty to the group which is an essential element of the collectivist family also means that resources are shared. If one member of an extended family of 20 persons has a paid job and the others have not, the earning member is supposed to share his or her income in order to help feed the entire family. On the basis of this principle a family may collectively cover the expenses for sending one member to get a higher education, expecting that when this member subsequently achieves a well-paid job the income will also be shared.

In individualist cultures parents will be proud if children at an early age take small jobs in order to earn pocket-money of their own, which they alone can decide how to spend. In the Netherlands, as in many other individualist Western European countries, the government contributes substantially to the living expenses of students. Recently the system has been changed from an allowance to the parents to an allowance directly to the students themselves, which stresses their independence. From now on the government will consider both boys and girls as independent economic players from age 18 onwards. In the USA it is quite normal for students to pay for their own study by temporary jobs and personal loans; without government support they too are less dependent on their parents and not at all on more distant relatives.

Obligations to the family in a collectivist society are not only financial but also ritual. Family celebrations like baptisms, marriages, and, especially, funerals are extremely important and should not be missed. Expatriate managers from individualist societies are often surprised by the family reasons given by employees from a collectivist host society who apply for a special leave; the expatriates think they are being fooled but most likely the reasons are authentic.

In an individualist culture when people meet they feel a need to communicate verbally. Silence is considered abnormal. Social conversations can be depressingly banal, but they are compulsory. In a collectivist culture the fact of being together is emotionally sufficient; there is no compulsion to talk unless there is information to be transferred. Raden Mas Hadjiwibowo, an Indonesian businessman from a Javanese noble family, recalls the family visits from his youth as follows:

'Visits among Javanese family members needed no previous appointment. Actually that could easily be done, for although the telephone had not come into common use yet, one could always send a servant with a letter asking for an appointment. But it was not done, it never occurred to one that a visit would not suit the other party. It was always convenient. Unexpected visitors did not exist. The door was (and still is) always open.

The visitors were welcomed with joyful courtesy and would be asked to take a seat. The host and hostess hurriedly withdrew to change into more suitable attire than their workaday clothes. Without asking, a servant brought in coffee or tea. Cookies were offered, while in the meantime the host and hostess had joined the party.

There we sat, but nobody spoke. We were not embarrassed by this silence; nobody felt nervous about it. Every now and then, thoughts and news were exchanged. But this was not really necessary. We enjoyed being together, seeing each other again. After the first exchange of news, any other communication was utterly redundant. If one did not have anything to say, there was no need to recite platitudes. After an hour or so, the guests would ask permission to leave. With mutual feelings of satisfaction, we parted. In smaller towns on the island of Java life is still like this.'[2]

US anthropologist and popular author Edward T. Hall distinguishes cultures on the basis of their way of communicating along a dimension from 'high-context' to 'low context' (Hall, 1976). A high-context communication is one in which little has to be said or written because most of the information is either in the physical environment or within the person, while very little is in the coded, explicit part of the message. This type of communication is frequent in collectivist cultures; Hadjiwibowo's family visit is a case example. A low-context communication is one in which the mass of information is vested in the explicit code, which is typical for individualist cultures. Lots of things which in collectivist cultures are self-evident must be said explicitly in individualist cultures. American business contracts are much longer than Japanese business contracts.

Next to harmony another important concept in connection with the collectivist family is *shame*. Individualist societies have been described as *guilt* cultures: persons who infringe upon the rules of society will often feel guilty, ridden by an individually developed conscience which functions as a private inner pilot. Collectivist societies, on the contrary, are shame cultures: persons belonging to a group from which a member has infringed upon the rules of society will feel ashamed, based upon a sense of collective obligation. Shame is social in nature, guilt individual; whether shame is felt depends on whether the infringement has become known by others. This becoming known is more of a source of shame than the infringement itself. Such is not the case for guilt, which is felt whether or not the misdeed is known by others.

At last concept bred in the collectivist family is *face*. 'Losing face', in the sense of being humiliated, is an expression which penetrated into the English language from the Chinese; the English had no equivalent for it. David Yau-Fai Ho, a Hong Kong social scientist, defines it as follows: 'Face is lost when the individual, either through his action or that of people closely related to him, fails to meet essential requirements placed upon him by virtue of the social position he occupies' (Ho, 1976, p. 867). The Chinese also speak of 'giving someone face', in the sense of honor or prestige. Basically, 'face' describes the proper relationship with one's social environment, which is as essential to a person (and that person's family) as the front part of his/her head. The importance of face is the consequence of living in a society that is very conscious of social contexts. The languages of other collectivist cultures have words

with more-or-less similar meanings. In Greece, for example, there is a word *philotimo*; Harry Triandis, a Greek–American psychologist, writes:

> A person is *philotimos* to the extent in which he conforms to the norms and values of his ingroup. These include a variety of sacrifices that are appropriate for members of one's family, friends, and others who are 'concerned with one's welfare'; for example, for a man to delay marriage until his sisters have married and have been provided with a proper dowry is part of the normative expectations of traditional rural Greeks as well as rural Indians (and many of the people in between). (Triandis, 1972, p. 38)

In the individualist society the counterpart characteristic is 'self-respect', but this again is defined from the point of view of the individual, whereas 'face' and 'philotimo' are defined from the point of view of the social environment.

Collectivist societies usually have ways of creating family-like ties with persons who are not biological relatives but who are socially integrated into one's ingroup. In Latin America, for example, this can be done via the institution of *compadres* and *comadres* who are treated as relatives even if they are not. In Japan younger sons in past times became apprentices to craftsmasters through a form of adoption. Similar customs existed in medieval Central Europe.

Individualism and Collectivism at School

The relationship between the individual and the group which has been established in a child's consciousness during its early years in the family is further developed and reinforced at school. This is very visible in classroom behavior. In the context of development assistance it often happens that teachers from a more individualist culture move to a more collectivist environment. A typical complaint from such teachers is that students do not speak up in class, not even when the teacher puts a question to the class. For the student who conceives of him/herself as part of a group, it is illogical to speak up without being sanctioned by the group to do so. If the teacher wants students to speak up, she or he should address a particular student personally.

Collectivist culture students will also hesitate to speak up in larger groups without a teacher present, especially if these are partly composed of relative strangers: outgroup members. This hesitation decreases in smaller groups. Personally I obtained broad participation when teaching a collectivist class by asking students to turn around in their seats so that groups of three were formed. I asked the students to discuss a question for five minutes, and to decide who would report their joint answer to the class. Through this device students had an opportunity to develop a group answer and felt comfortable when speaking up before the class because they acted as the small group's representative. I also noticed that in subsequent exercises the students arranged for the spokespersons to rotate. Taking turns in group activities is a habit which exists in many collectivist cultures.

The desirability of having students speak up in class is more strongly felt in individualist than in collectivist cultures. Because most collectivist cultures also maintain large power distances, their education tends to be teacher-centered with little two-way communication. . . .

In the collectivist society ingroup–outgroup distinctions springing from the family sphere will continue at school, so that students from different ethnic or clan backgrounds often form subgroups in class. In an individualist society the assignment of joint tasks leads more easily to the formation of new groups than in the collectivist society. In the latter, students from the same ethnic or family background as the teacher or other school officials will expect preferential treatment on this basis. In an individualist society this would be considered nepotism and intensely immoral, but in a collectivist environment it is immoral *not* to treat one's ingroup members better than others.

In the collectivist classroom the virtues of harmony and the maintenance of 'face' reign supreme. Confrontations and conflicts should be avoided, or at least formulated so as not to hurt anyone; even students should not lose face if this can be avoided. Shaming, that is invoking the group's honor, is an effective way of correcting offenders: they will be put in order by their ingroup members. At all times the teacher is dealing with the student as part of an ingroup, never as an isolated individual.

In the individualist classroom, of course, students expect to be treated as individuals and impartially, regardless of their background. Group formation among students is much more *ad hoc*, according to the task, or to particular friendships and skills. Confrontations and open discussion of conflicts is often considered salutary, and face-consciousness is weak or nonexistent.

The *purpose* of education is perceived differently between the individualist and the collectivist society. In the former it aims at preparing the *individual* for a place in a society of other individuals. This means learning to cope with new, unknown, unforeseen situations. There is a basically positive attitude towards what is new. The purpose of learning is less to know how to do, as to know *how to learn*. The assumption is that learning in life never ends; even after school and university it will continue, for example through recycling courses. The individualist society in its schools tries to provide the skills necessary for 'modern man'.

In the collectivist society there is a stress on adaptation to the skills and virtues necessary to be an acceptable group member. This leads to a premium on the products of *tradition*. Learning is more often seen as a one-time process, reserved for the young only, who have to learn *how to do* things in order to participate in society.

The role of diplomas or certificates as a result of successful completion of study is also different between the two poles of the individualism–collectivism dimension. In the individualist society the diploma not only improves the holder's economic worth but also his or her self-respect: it provides a sense of achievement. In the collectivist society a diploma is an honor to the holder and his or her ingroup which entitles the holder to associate with members of higher-status groups; for example, to obtain a more attractive marriage partner. It is to a certain extent 'a ticket to ride'. The social acceptance that comes with the diploma is more important than the individual self-respect that comes with mastering a subject, so that in collectivist societies the temptation is stronger to obtain diplomas in some irregular way, such as on the black market.

Individualism and Collectivism in the Workplace

Employed persons in an individualist culture are expected to act according to their own interest, and work should be organized in such a way that this self-interest and the employer's interest coincide. Workers are supposed to act as 'economic men', or as people with a combination of economic and psychological needs, but in either case as individuals with their own needs. In a collectivist culture an employer never hires just an individual, but a person who belongs to an ingroup. The employee will act according to the interest of this ingroup, which may not always coincide with his or her individual interest: self-effacement in the interest of the ingroup belongs to the normal expectations in such a society. Often earnings have to be shared with relatives.

The hiring process in a collectivist society always takes the ingroup into account. Usually preference is given to hiring relatives, first of all of the employer, but also of other persons already employed by the company. Hiring persons from a family one already knows reduces risks. Also, relatives will be concerned about the reputation of the family and help to correct misbehavior of a family member. In the individualist society family relationships at work are often considered undesirable as they may lead to nepotism and to a conflict of interest. Some companies have a rule that if one employee marries another, one of them has to leave.

The workplace itself in a collectivist society may become an ingroup in the emotional sense of the word. In some countries this is more the case than in others, but the feeling that it should be this way is nearly always present. The relationship between employer and employee is seen in moral terms. It resembles a family relationship with mutual obligations of protection in exchange for loyalty. Poor performance of an employee in this relationship is no reason for dismissal; one does not dismiss one's child. Performance and skills, however, do determine what tasks one assigns to an employee. This pattern of relationships is best known from Japanese organizations. In Japan it applies in a strict sense only to the group of permanent employees which may be less than half of the total work force. Japan scores halfway on the IDV scale. In individualist societies the relationship between employer and employee is primarily conceived as a business transaction, a calculative relationship between buyers and sellers on a 'labor market'. Poor performance on the part of the employee or a better pay offer from another employer are legitimate and socially accepted reasons for terminating a work relationship.

Christopher Earley, a management researcher from the USA, has illustrated the difference in work ethos between an individualist and a collectivist society very neatly with a laboratory experiment. In the experiment, 48 management trainees from southern China and 48 matched management trainees from the USA were given an 'in-basket task'. The task consisted of 40 separate items requiring between two and five minutes each, like writing memos, evaluating plans, and rating job candidates' application forms. Half of the participants in either country were given a group goal of 200 items to be completed in an hour by 10 people; the other half were given each an individual goal of 20 items. Also, half of the participants in either country, both from the group goal and from the individual goal subset, were asked to mark each item completed with their name, the other half turned them in anonymously.

The Chinese, collectivist, participants performed best when operating with a group goal, and anonymously. They performed worst when operating individually and with their name marked on the items produced. The American, individualist, participants performed best when operating individually and with their name marked, and abysmally low when operating as a group and anonymously. All participants were also given a values test to determine their personal individualism or collectivism: a minority of the Chinese scored individualist, and these performed according to the US pattern; a minority of the Americans scored collectivist and these performed like the Chinese (Earley, 1989).

In practice there is a wide range of types of employer–employee relationships *within* collectivist and individualist societies. There are employers in collectivist countries who do not respect the societal norm to treat their employees as ingroup members, but then the employees in turn do not repay them in terms of loyalty. Labor unions in such cases may replace the work organization as an emotional ingroup and there can be violent union–management conflicts, as in parts of India. There are employers in individualist societies who have established a strong group cohesion with their employees, with the same protection-versus-loyalty balance which is the norm in the collectivist society. Organization cultures can to some extent deviate from majority norms and derive a competitive advantage from their originality. . . .

Management in an individualist society is management of individuals. Subordinates can usually be moved around individually; if incentives or bonuses are given, these should be linked to an individual's performance. Management in a collectivist society is management of groups. The extent to which people actually feel emotionally integrated into a work group may differ from one situation to another. Ethnic and other ingroup differences within the work group play a role in the integration process and managers within a collectivist culture will be extremely attentive to such factors. It often makes good sense to put people from the same ethnic background into one crew, although individualistically programmed managers usually consider this dangerous and want to do the opposite. If the work group functions as an emotional ingroup, incentives and bonuses should be given to the group, not to individuals.

Within countries with a dominant individualist middle-class culture, regional rural subcultures have sometimes retained strongly collectivist elements. The same applies to the migrant worker minorities which form majorities among the work force in some industries in some individualist countries. In such cases a culture conflict is likely between managers and regional or minority workers. This conflict expresses itself, among other things in the management's extreme hesitation to use group incentives in cases when they are the only things that really suit the culture of the work force.

Management techniques and training packages have almost exclusively been developed in individualist countries, and they are based on cultural assumptions which may not hold in collectivist cultures. A standard element in the training of first-line managers is how to conduct 'appraisal interviews': periodic discussions in which the subordinate's performance is reviewed. These can form part of MBO [management by objectives] . . . , but even where MBO does not exist, conducting performance appraisals and the ability to communicate 'bad news' are considered key skills for a successful manager. In a collectivist society discussing a person's performance openly with him or her is likely to clash head-on with the society's harmony norm and may be felt by the subordinate as an unacceptable loss of face. Such societies have more subtle, indirect ways of communicating feedback: for example by the withdrawal of a normal favor or verbally via an intermediary. I know of a case in which an older relative of the poorly performing employee, also in the service of the employer, played this intermediary role. He communicated the bad news to his nephew, avoiding the loss of face which a formal appraisal interview would have provoked.

The Sensitivity Training (T-Group) fashion of the 1960s, the encounter group fashion of the 1970s, and the transactional analysis fashion of the 1980s have all been developed in the USA, the country with the highest individualism index score in Table 1. Each of them is based on honest and direct sharing of feelings about other people. Such training methods are unfit for use in collectivist cultures. There, sensitivity training is felt to be training in *in*sensitivity; daily life is filled with encounters so that no special groups have to be formed to this purpose. Relationships between people are never seen as 'transactions' between individuals: they are moral in nature, not calculative.

The distinction between ingroup and outgroups which is so essential in the collectivist culture pattern has far-reaching consequences for business relationships, beyond those between employers and employees. It is the reason behind the cultural embarrassment of Mr Johannesson and his Swedish superiors in Saudi Arabia related at the beginning of this chapter. In individualist societies the norm is that one should treat everybody alike. In sociological jargon this is known as *universalism*. Preferential treatment of one

TABLE 2   Key Differences Between Collectivist and Individualist Societies. . . .

Collectivist	Individualist
People are born into extended families or other ingroups which continue to protect them in exchange for loyalty	Everyone grows up to look after him/herself and his/her immediate (nuclear) family only
Identity is based in the social network to which one belongs	Identity is based in the individual
Children learn to think in terms of 'we'	Children learn to think in terms of 'I'
Harmony should always be maintained and direct confrontations avoided	Speaking one's mind is a characteristic of an honest person
High-context communication	Low-context communication
Trespassing leads to shame and loss of face for self and group	Trespassing leads to guilt and loss of self-respect
Purpose of education is learning how to do	Purpose of education is learning how to learn
Diplomas provide entry to higher status groups	Diplomas increase economic worth and/or self-respect
Relationship employer–employee is perceived in moral terms, like a family link	Relationship employer–employee is a contract supposed to be based on mutual advantage
Hiring and promotion decisions take employees' ingroup into account	Hiring and promotion decisions are supposed to be based on skills and rules only
Management is management of groups	Management is management of individuals
Relationship prevails over task	Task prevails over relationship

customer over others is considered bad business practice and unethical. In collectivist societies the reverse is true. As the distinction between 'our group' and 'other groups' is at the very root of people's consciousness, treating one's friends better than others is natural and ethical, and sound business practice. Sociologists call this way of thinking *particularism*.

A consequence of particularist thinking is that in a collectivist society a relationship of trust should be established with another person before any business can be done. Through this relationship the other is adopted into one's ingroup and from that moment onwards is entitled to preferential treatment. In Johannesson's case this process of adoption took two years. During this period the presence of the Swedish businessman as an intermediary was essential. After the adoption had taken place it became superfluous. However, the relationship was with Johannesson personally and not with his company. To the collectivist mind only natural persons are worthy of

trust, and via these persons their friends and colleagues, but not impersonal legal entities like a company. In summary: in the collectivist society *the personal relationship prevails over the task* and should be established first; in the individualist society *the task is supposed to prevail over any personal relationships*. The naive Western businessman who tries to force quick business in a collectivist culture condemns himself to the role of outgroup member and to negative discrimination.

Table 2 summarizes the key differences between collectivist and individualist societies described so far.

• • •

Individualism, Collectivism, and Ideas

Individualist societies not only practice individualism but also consider it superior to other forms of mental software. Most Americans feel that individualism is good, and at the root of their country's greatness. On the other hand, the late Chairman Mao Tse Tung of China identified individualism as evil. He found individualism and liberalism responsible for selfishness and aversion to discipline; they led people to placing personal interests above those of the group, or simply to devoting too much attention to one's own things. Table 1 contains no data for the People's Republic of China but the countries with a predominantly Chinese population all score very low on the individualism index (25 for Hong Kong, 20 for Singapore, 17 for Taiwan).

Economics as a discipline was founded in Great Britain in the eighteenth century; among the founding fathers Adam Smith (1723–1790) stands out. Smith assumed that the pursuit of self-interest by individuals through an 'invisible hand' would lead to the maximal wealth of nations. This is a highly individualist idea from a country which even today ranks near the top on individualism. Economics has remained an individualist science and most of its leading contributors have come from strongly individualistic countries like the UK and the USA. However, because of the individualist assumptions on which they are based, economic theories as developed in the West are unlikely to apply in societies in which not individual interest, but group interests prevail. Unfortunately there are few alternative economic theories yet to deal with collectivist economies. The Dutch sociologist Cas Vroom, describing the situation of Indonesia, contrasts the Western orientation towards 'return on investment' with an Indonesian 'return on favors' (Vroom, 1981).

The French Revolution, the bicentennial celebration of which took place in 1989, had as its slogan *'liberté, égalité, fraternité'*: freedom, equality, brotherhood. This was the slogan of political idealists who wanted to have their cake and eat it, for it does not recognize that in politics there is an inescapable trade-off between freedom and equality, and very little brotherhood. Not much of the revolutionary ideal was realized in France, as we know: it led to the Reign of Terror and subsequently to the dictatorship and military adventures of Napoleon. . . .

• • •

The degree of individualism or collectivism of a society will affect the conceptions of human nature produced in that society. In the USA the ideas of Abraham Maslow (1908–70) about human motivation have been and are still quite influential, in particular for the training of management students and practitioners. Maslow formulated his famous 'hierarchy of human needs' in 1943. It states that human needs can be ordered in a hierarchy from lower to higher, as follows: physiological, safety, belongingness, esteem, and self-actualization. In order for a higher need to appear it is necessary that the lower needs have been satisfied up to a certain extent. A starving person, that is, one whose physiological needs are not at all satisfied, will not be motivated by anything other than the quest for food, and so forth. At the top of Maslow's hierarchy, which is often pictured as a pyramid, there is the motive of self-actualization: realizing to the fullest possible extent the creative potential present within the individual. This means 'Doing one's own thing', as it was called in the US youth culture of the 1960s. It goes without saying that this can only be the supreme motivation in an individualist society. In a collectivist culture, what will be actualized is the interest and honor of the ingroup which may very well ask for self-effacement from many of the ingroup members. As the interpreter for a group of American visitors to China remarked, the idea of 'doing your own thing' is not translatable into Chinese.

Maslow's main book in which he explained his theories (Maslow, 1970) is based on a concept of personality which is common in Western thinking, but which is not universal. The Chinese–American anthropologist Francis Hsu has shown that the Chinese language has no equivalent for 'personality' in the Western sense. Personality in the West is a separate entity, distinct from society and culture: an attribute of the individual. The closest translation into Chinese is *jen* (*ren* in the modern transcription), which stands for 'person' as a 'human constant', which includes not only the individual but also his or her intimate societal and cultural environment which makes his or her existence meaningful (Hsu, 1971).

• • •

The Future of Individualism and Collectivism

The deep roots of national cultures make it likely that individualism–collectivism differences, like power distance differences, will survive for a long time. Yet if there is to be any convergence between national cultures it should be on this dimension. The strong relationship between national wealth and individualism is undeniable, with the arrow of causality directed, as shown above, from wealth to individualism. Countries having achieved fast economic development have experienced a shift towards individualism. Japan is an example: the Japanese press regularly publishes stories of breaches of traditional family solidarity. Care for the aged in the past was considered a task for the Japanese family, but provisions by the state have become necessary for cases where the family stops fulfilling its traditional duties.

Nevertheless, even at a level of per capita income equal to or larger than Western countries, Japanese society will very likely conserve distinctive collectivist elements in its family-, school-, and workspheres. The same holds for differences among Western countries themselves. Next to a noticeable convergency towards individualism under the influence of a common economic boom, relationships between the individual and the group continue to differ between, say, the UK, Sweden, and Germany. The cultures shift, but they shift together, so that the differences between them remain intact.

As far as the poor countries of the world are concerned there is no reason why they should become more individualist as long as they remain poor. The IBM data bank allowed for measurement of the shifts in individualism during the four-year period from 1968 to 1972. Out of 20 countries which had been surveyed in both periods, 19 had become richer, and all of these had shifted towards greater individualism. The only country in the set that had become poorer, Pakistan, shifted slightly towards the collectivist end of the scale.

Differences in values associated with the individualism–collectivism dimension will continue to exist and to play a big role in international affairs, for example in negotiations between rich and poor countries. Individualism versus collectivism as a dimension of national cultures is responsible for many misunderstandings in intercultural encounters. . . .

NOTES

1. Using factor scores as a basis for country indices was very easy for the initial IBM study but makes it difficult to compute index values in later follow-up studies. The scoring guide for the 1982 values survey module issued by the Institute for Research on Intercultural Cooperation (IRIC) therefore contains an approximation formula, in which the individualism index value can be computed by simple mathematics from four of the 'work goals' mean scores.

2. From a speech by R. M. Hadjiwibowo to Semafor Senior Management College, the Netherlands, September 1983. Translation from the Dutch by GH with suggestions from the author.

SELECTED REFERENCES

Earley, P. C. (1989). Social loafing and collectivism: A comparison of the United States and the People's Republic of China. *Administrative Science Quarterly, 34,* 565–581.

Hall, E. T. (1976). *Beyond culture.* Garden City, NY: Doubleday Anchor Books.

Ho, D. Y.-F. (1976). On the concept of face. *American Journal of Sociology, 81,* 867–884.

Hofstede, G. (1980). *Culture's consequences: International differences in work-related values.* Beverly Hills, CA: Sage.

Hofstede, G. (1984). *Culture's consequences: International differences in work-related values,* abridged edition. Beverly Hills, CA: Sage.

Hsu, F. L. K. (1971). Psychological homeostasis and *jen:* Conceptual tools for advancing psychological anthropology. *American Anthropologist, 73,* 23–44.

Maslow, A. H. (1970). *Motivation and personality* (2nd ed.). New York: Harper & Row.

Triandis, H. C. (1972). *The analysis of subjective culture.* New York: Wiley-Interscience.

Vroom, C. W. (1981). *Indonesia and the West: An*

essay on cultural differences in organization and management. Jakarta: Catholic University.

KEY TERMS

individualism
collectivism
power distance
organizational
  communication

cultural values
family
work

DISCUSSION QUESTIONS

1. In what ways are your relationships with your friends more or less individualistic or collectivistic?

2. What advice would you give international students from collectivist cultures about making friends at a U.S. university?

3. How do you think individualistic-collectivistic behavior might vary from context to context? For example, might your behavior be more collectivistic in family contexts, less so in work contexts?

4. Hofstede's research was conducted from a social science perspective. How might an interpretive or critical research investigate national values?

5. What are the dangers (limitations) of making generalizations about behaviors based on nationality?

37

CHINESE AND NORTH AMERICANS: AN EPISTEMOLOGICAL EXPLORATION OF INTERCULTURAL COMMUNICATION

LING CHEN

The Issue of Knowing

Being and knowing, two fundamental philosophical issues that can be traced to ancient Greece, are still intriguing and controversial today. The two can often be reduced to one, that of knowing, because any ontological position naturally leads to the epistemological question: "How do you know?" The importance of this question to communication is that the definition of communication would be totally different, given different viewpoints (Gregg, 1984; Littlejohn, 1989). In the West, the issue of knowing generates disagreement shown in such opposing propositions as: (a) people know because the world exists for them to perceive; or (b) people know because humans have the ability to reason.[1] The two positions lead logically to differing views of communi-

cation. The knowing-is-perceiving position presupposes an objective world that is the criterion for the truthfulness of knowledge. It follows that if the truth is knowable, it is communicable. Thus, communication is regarded as a tool for transferring or reflecting truth. This is the more traditional view of rhetoric as an ancient discipline of speech communication.[2] The knowing-is-reasoning position, on the contrary, invests great faith in humans as rational beings, capable of creating and using symbols. Such symbolic practice leads to reasoning and the production of knowledge. This is the epistemological root of another view of communication—that it is itself a process of knowing. This view can be found in some contemporary scholarship.[3] The distinct epistemological positions of empiricism versus rationalism reflect the Western tradition of the mind–body dichotomy extant since the 17th century. Each tradition recently has been challenged again in the scientific community and in rhetorical studies (Gregg, 1984). The field of communication also has attempted to establish a middle-of-the-road position between the two extremes, with varying degrees of success. Many such efforts, however, either finally sided with one of the two positions in a more subtle way or are regarded to have done so by others.[4]

In studies of language philosophy, Fodor (1976, 1981) provides an enlightening argument on the acquisition of concepts (as expressed by linguistic symbols) as knowing at the earliest stage of development. He points out that the point of dispute between nativism (rationalism) and empiricism has been misrepresented by those who state that the former believes in the power of mind, whereas the latter favors experience of an objective world. He argues that the opposite can be proved: The nativist continues to rely on experience, whereas the empiricist, in fact, also lives by reasoning. He posits that innate capacities for concept acquisition may operate only when triggered by external stimuli, whereas the processes of learning (or knowing) through experiences operate through inductive reasoning that either confirms or rejects concept formation. It can be shown that both positions are rooted in the common belief that the acquisition of a primitive concept is a function of environmental stimulation, that is, contingent upon the activation of the sensorium. Moreover, both assume that complex concepts are formed from primitive concepts through some kind of combination apparatus. This argument from studies on the most fundamental level of knowing (concept acquisition) forcefully advances the concept that, whereas different views may place different emphasis on which is more important, there is no denying the implicit position; that is, people know as a result of interaction between the innately capable mind and the external world.

This position is supported by studies on concept categorization in cognitive science. Human beings are assumed to be active processors of information (Eiser, 1980) who make sense or acquire knowledge by categorizing sensory information input. Findings in cognitive, linguistic, anthropological, and developmental research (for more references, see Chen, 1987) have indicated that, as a process of generalization, human categorization operates in a hierarchical manner, classifying information into levels of categories by degree of abstractness from the most specific (i.e., a category of one case) to the most general (i.e., a category that includes all cases that share even the slightest common feature). The findings indicate further that there exists a basic (generic) level of categories where abstraction is such that members of these categories are perceptually identifiable and are usually identified with a single word, for example, *dog* or *cat* (Rosch, 1978). This is the last level wherein categorization is based largely on ostensive sensory data. Beyond this level, the categories are too abstract to provide a typical exemplar of a category member. For example, we can readily point to a particular dog to exemplify *dog*, the concept; however, it is hard to do the same to exemplify the concept *animal*. People see a dog or a cat, but not an animal. It follows from this that one can plausibly assume that categorizations on more than basic levels are largely based on symbolic data. Symbolic data, however, are generalizations of sensory data. It has been suggested that the basic level most clearly points to the probability of innate capabilities: Names of basic categories have been found to always be the first words children (including those with a handicapping condition such as blindness or total hearing loss) learn in any culture and are almost all encoded into lexical items in most languages. Differences occur only on levels either above (superordinate level: more abstract and general), or below the basic level (subordinate levels: with greater or more specific details).

The significance of this thesis is that it suggests a way to account for cultural variation as well as universal aspects of cultures. Coding and categorizing of information from the environment are the same in all cultures at the basic level; variation among cultures would be represented by categorization discrepancies on levels that are either more general or more specific. Different cultures may put the same basic information in different categories at more abstract levels, that is, interpret it differently. From this standpoint, communication is symbolic expression and/or symbolic exchange of that which is perceived (Gregg,

1984). It may not coincide perfectly with the external world or between communicators, but there is enough overlap to allow communication.

Structure of Consciousness

Among obvious cultural differences is that which exists between the East and the West. The differences between the two may even seem to defy comparison. However, careful examination will reveal a commonality as well. To suggest that cultures are different from, and at the same time similar to, one another is a paradox.

The complexity of culture demands a macrocosmic analytic system, so that the study of cultures can be systematic, elaborate, inclusive, and manageable. Gebser's (1985) theory on the origin and mutation of culture provides a viable solution to this problem. Gebser proposes the concept of the structure of consciousness as a framework for studying culture in societies. The consciousness structure consists of the universal dimensions of time, space, sensory perception, ego, existence, and so forth; these are the fundamentals of any culture's understanding of the world, that is knowing, in a broad sense. Consciousness structures are modes of human consciousness with different orientations toward the environment and everything in it, including the society and the properties of humans. From a different perspective, this conceptualization process is analogous to human categorization: There is something basic to all cultures that stands in testimony to existential universals (being cultural–general). Gebser analyzes numerous myths, legends, folklores, epics, tales, and prehistoric artwork, as well as social systems from cultures all over the world. His analyses present convincing evidence of the link between nature and human consciousness manifesting in various dimensions. Even the concept of *negation*, noted by Burke (1968) as a unique human invention, is shown to be related to the natural contrast between day and night, life and death, and presence and absence (see later discussion on polarity). This notion is echoed in psycholinguistic studies where it is demonstrated (Clark & Clark, 1977) that these are, indeed, universal dimensions (represented in such linguistic universals as terms for spatial and temporal relations, terms for basic colors, etc.) shared by all cultures, reflecting the natural world in which we live. These are basic aspects of life perceptually accessible to all human beings.

The structure of consciousness is conceptualized as the mode knowing, which is associated closely with human activities, dreams and imaginings, emotions, rationality, and self-awareness. Therefore, it is taken as given that different consciousness structures would generate differences in all human pursuits and reactions. Gebser (1985) suggests five structures as the possible major modes of consciousness, distinguished only by variation in their status relative to one another.[5] These structures coexist in all modern cultures. Features of one consciousness structure (i.e., the way each of the basic dimensions is oriented outward or internalized), which are most distinct in one culture because they constitute its dominant mode of consciousness, may be latent in another culture because that structure may have only minor status there. Dominance of a particular type of consciousness structure, therefore, accounts for a culture's differences from other cultures that use other consciousness structures. At the same time, coexistence of dominant and nondominant consciousness structures provides a base of commonality among all cultures. This model can also be understood in terms of the concept of categorization hierarchy. It was mentioned that cultures, in a sense, differ only in their categorizations at superordinate or subordinate levels. Consciousness structures can be thought of as categorization schemes, whereas basic-level categories developed on the basis of the fundamentals of consciousness are analogous to the universal basic dimensions perceived by the action of external stimuli on the sensorium and its corresponding internal systems. Cultural variation is caused by alternative categorization schemes. Features such as social conventions and traditional values pertaining to interpretations of sensory data (direct observation) thus are on a more abstract level than the basic level in the categorization scheme, which is parallel to the manifestation of basic dimensions that vary in consciousness structures. This way, the seemingly vast differences in the ways that various cultures interpret identical things can be seen as consequences of different categorization or dominance of a structure of consciousness. The presence of non-dominant structures of consciousness renders possible alternative categorization schemes outside the mainstream culture. Generalization of basic categories (i.e., interpretation of sensory data) at more abstract levels may be influenced by other factors, for example, regional natural environments and ways to survive in those particular environments (Meggers, 1954), which are important conditioners of a culture's categorization.

This is the position of this article. It has been argued that the external world, known through species-specific human mental capabilities, provides all cultures with more or less identical basic knowledge. However, a particular cultural tradition directs its members to observe the world from different perspectives or criteria for judgment and to interpret it differently. According to Weaver,[6] cited in Foss, Foss, and Trapp (1985), culture is defined as symbolic manifestations of learned rules/orientations in ecologically (with possible overlap) distanced societies. Given fundamental commonality, a culture has the potential of recategorization above the basic level, which would bring forth the latent features of nondominant structures of consciousness to open the door to a different view, thus allowing for intercultural communication. The present article offers a qualitative comparison of the similarities and differences between two different cultures, the Chinese and the North American, as representative of the vastly different cultures of the East and West, in an attempt to find a common ground among many phenomenological differences. The comparison is based on what is available in the literature, as well as on folk wisdom from both cultures. This is followed by an examination of some common problems in intercultural interaction between Chinese and North Americans that show a potential of dissolution by "returning to the basics." Data in the intercultural section of analysis are selected from personal observations and interviews with people in both societies accumulated over a period of 10 years.

Common Domains of Consciousness

It is widely acknowledged that the Western way is predominantly a perspectival approach to every-

thing/anything, with linear/causal thinking and a strong sense of ego/individual, whereas the Eastern way, is the opposite in virtually every respect (e.g., Cheng, 1987; Gebser, 1985; Oliver, 1971; Servaes, 1988; Yum, 1988). But just how different are the two in terms of their consciousness mode? Without directly following the typology, the three most common domains are specified here to compare differences and similarities (time, space, and ego, with relating orientation toward nature, individual, and society) in order to see how traditions and conventions stem from the basic dimensions to make an impact on social interactions.

According to Gebser (1985), the concept of space provides an index of the human concept of self-identity: Lack of spatial awareness is accompanied by a lack of ego awareness, and it is closely related to the conception of time. The recognition of space provides an individual with his or her own visibility and a measure of control of time. Awareness of a time and space relationship not only defines the external world, including the self, but also defines the corresponding internal world as the territory of emotion, imagination, or abstract (rational) thinking. All this is absolutely essential for understanding the differences between the structures of consciousness. The absence of the perspective of view, or spatial consciousness, is characteristic of the Chinese mode of consciousness, whereas its presence is distinct in the North American mode.

Time and Space

The impression that Chinese culture,[7] in general, is dominated by lack of perspectives in the domain of space/ego consciousness is true to the extent that thinking without perspective is the default mode; in other words, existence of perspectives, or three-dimensional space, is not totally absent, but it is latent, and it is only pushed into attention as specific occasions demand. The customary practice is without perspective. Such familiar sayings as "Listen to all sides and be enlightened; heed only one side and be benighted" (*jian ting ze ming, pian ting ze an*) and "One inch of time is one inch of gold, while one inch of gold cannot buy one inch of time" (*yi cun guangyin yicun jin cun jin nan mai cun guangyin*) are circulated mostly among persons of status and reserved for use only at critical times. The first saying is ruling advice for an emperor, whereas the second is used to motivate a scholar to work hard so that he or she can pass the national examination and qualify to be appointed as a government official, a position of high status and prestige (Creel, 1953). The perception of time reflected in those sayings is close to the modern Western concept, prominent in the United States (Hall, 1977), of time that is spatialized, materialized, quantified, and hence measurable. This mode of thinking, however, is not common among the Chinese. The Chinese are guided mostly by a two-dimensional view of things. The above instances are examples of the latent presence of nondominant mode(s).

Traditionally, for the Chinese, time is simply there (Oliver, 1971). People do things as they see fit; there are few deadlines to beat and no rush. Some things must be done at a particular time, not because of a schedule but because of the natural circumstances. For example, planting starts in spring because it is warm and wet then—just right for planting; having a sick relative is a good reason for putting off overdue obligations—these can always be done some other time. Here we see a connection to the Tao, which advocates following the natural course and avoiding constraints from human efforts (Cheng, 1987; Ma, 1990; Oliver, 1961, 1971). A similar lack of perspective can be seen in traditional Chinese brush painting, where all the objects or figures are depicted on a flat, two-dimensional surface, with no attempt to present the actual, spatial configuration, in contrast to the detailed, realistic Western painting style. Westerners will appreciate this art form more when they realize that brush painters do not strive for a reproduction of a true-to-life image; rather, they present the spirit, the imagination, or an impression (akin to Western impressionist works—an example of a nondominant mode in Western societies). The difference in perspective, nevertheless, springs from the same root—the awareness of space and time, which holds out the promise of a possible understanding between the two peoples.

Lack of perspective renders a flat view of things that is identical to all; that is, everything and anything is the same to everyone and anyone, with totally interchangeable standings. This view is reflected in a saying from Confucius, "not to do onto others what you want not to be done on yourself" (*ji suo bu yu wu shi yu ren ye*), compared to the Golden Rule in the Christian culture of the West,[8] an indication of the presence of a latent mode in the North American culture. Clearly, it is taken for granted that what is good or bad for one person is equally good or bad for another person. This is in sharp contrast to what is implied in the Western saying "One man's meat is another man's poison," where individual differences are stressed through differentiation. In daily social contacts, this uniformity of viewpoints is shown in the Chinese emphasis on interpersonal relations. People are willing to share personal opinions and offer advice on almost all matters, without the least consideration of their acceptability in practice and in emotion, because these are rarely questioned. Friends or acquaintances will not hesitate to render opinions about what you should wear or how you should talk to or deal with various people, including your own family. Moreover, they will tell you how to live your life, as if it were their own. Such liberties in interpersonal interactions are likely to be regarded in the West as poking one's nose into another's affairs, to say the least. However, in China, these are common, daily interactions at work, at school, and elsewhere (Sun, 1989). Here again, the distinctions between self and others are recognized in both cultures, despite the different meanings and the different associated values. Thus, Chinese in Western countries can, and often do, learn to do as "the Romans do," by readjusting the balance between oneself and one's fellows.

Human and Nature

Hand in hand with the space-unconscious mode is the ego-unconscious mode of mind, resulting in a tendency toward polarization. The world, and everything in it, is seen as a whole with complementary halves: Heaven and earth, earth and sea, human and animal, creature and plant, night and day, sun and moon, death and life, and so forth; naturally, there is no place for individual entities (human or other). Such polar opposite categories, covering all natural objects and phenomena in folk taxonomy, reflect polarities rooted in nature. Other examples are the more abstract polar opposites such as evil and virtue, devil and god, truth and falsehood, and motion and motionlessness. This complementary principle, known as the opposites of *yin* and *yang* (representing all listed above), is fundamental to all traditional schools of thinking and is especially emphasized by Taoism (Cheng, 1987; Creel, 1953). The Chinese polarization, distinct from the dichotomy familiar to Westerners, is opposed to upholding (either of) the extremes but advocates a balanced, complementary unity of the two to achieve ultimate harmony in the whole. Here again, we see a common ground between the two cultures in the concept of the whole with two halves. The differences lie in where the emphasis is placed: on the halves for the North Americans, and on the whole for the Chinese.

Hierarchies in society are one manifestation of such thinking, which, for thousands of years, has been regarded as natural as the sky and the earth and which should not be questioned.[9] Just as the sky is above the earth, so is the Emperor, as the Son of Heaven, above all other people on earth, who likewise are dichotomized into nobles and the common people below them, each governed by different sets of *li* (rites/ethical codes), just as day has the sun and night has the moon. This analogy between the natural world and the human world, itself a polar, complementary contrast, is the core of Confucianism (Cai, 1984), an important component of the Chinese cultural tradition. For Confucius, such is the way things should be in order to remain orderly and harmonious.

Another persistent manifestation of polarizing can be found in the position of animals in the Chinese mind. Humans and animals are distinct creatures that are not discussed in the same terms. In the Chinese language, different characters are used to name the sexual differences in humans and animals. Classifiers[10] and pronouns also are distinct for humans and animals. Unlike English, and many other Western languages, where both human and nonhuman organisms are distinguished by the terms *male* and *female* for gender differences, the Chinese language has distinct terms for this in humans versus nonhuman creatures: *nan* (male) and *nü* (female) are for humans, whereas *gong* (male) and *mu* (female), for

example, are for animals. (Use of the latter as attributes for a human is derogative or insulting.) The use of pronouns is similar. Chinese discourse, oral or written, rarely uses a pronoun for nonhuman references; in cases of real necessity, the purpose is served by the pronoun *ta* (it), which writes two entirely different pronouns (*he* or *she*) for humans, in spite of the identical standard pronunciation for all three terms. As a result, use of the personal pronoun for a nonhuman referent, as in some cases in English (e.g., *she* for a ship and *she* or *he*, and even *girl* or *boy*, for a pet), is absurd to a Chinese.

The profound impact of this last polar contrast can be seen in the tradition of good manners. Because animals are part of the external world, the natural environment outside the human, to distinguish humans from animals completely, the natural aspect of human beings, as reflected in emotions, desires, passions, and so forth, must be restrained, while the rational or human aspect is stressed through enforcement of self-control and conformity to standard courtesy, etiquette, and manners in addition to lexical coding. An important component of being human, in contrast to being animal, is the ability to know the way, to have reason. The above mentioned *li* is the criterion, stipulating how one should behave on what occasion to whom and discouraging natural expressions. As a result, the nonverbal bodily or facial expressions in interaction are much more subtle than is the case for North Americans, with the exception that smiles (under particular circumstances) are an important means for expressions of humbleness, friendliness, courtesy, and hospitality that are often required by *li* as good manners. Otherwise, open displays of intense feelings or emotions in social interactions are to be avoided, as such displays are deemed uncivilized. Also frowned upon are touching behaviors or physical closeness in social contacts among adults (for children there are different rules), so that Chinese are classified as belonging to the noncontact culture. This is especially true for physical closeness in interaction, or touching between people of the opposite sex, both of which are seen as signs of sexual behaviors—the most animallike of all behaviors to the Chinese mind. This mentality is clearly expressed in the motto

"Lewdness is the chief of all evils" (*wan e yin wei shou*). North Americans are also listed as a noncontact culture, but for totally different reasons—territoriality and privacy (Watson, 1970).[11]

Ego and Society

The mode of thinking that presupposes that all share the same viewpoint as parts of the collective whole is called *collectivism* and is typical of Eastern cultures, as opposed to the *individualism* of most Western cultures (Sun, 1989; Triandis, 1989). Status of the person as an independent, unique individual with all the divine rights so natural to North Americans is generally ignored, or almost nonexistent, although not entirely denied recognition, in China (less so now than in the past, but still not categorically different). Folk sayings testify to this: "Gun will shoot the bird that flies higher than others" (*qiang da chutouniao*) and "The rafter that stands out rots first" (*chutoude yuanzi xian lan*). Because *li* and its later variations are criteria for behaviors, those who deviate are exemplars of the higher-flying bird or the out-standing rafter, not tolerated and often sneered at as showing off or punished, as a "horse that brings disgrace to its herd" (*hai qun zi ma*), depending on the extent of his or her perceived damage. The virtue and/or evil of a person is determined according to the benefit to the community from his or her deeds, which often may be nothing more than being nice to others and not disgracing one's parents by deviant behaviors rather than active contributions, so that everybody can get along peacefully and harmoniously, as life is meant to be. Everyone is expected to be concerned about everyone else's business, as if it were his or her own, because everyone is tied together to share the joy of honor or the suffering of shame. It is not surprising that Bond (1983) and Bond and Forgas (1984) discovered that the criterion for trustworthiness in personal judgment for the Chinese is conscientiousness, as contrasted to emotional stability and extroversion for North Americans and Australians.

The collective identity is also realized in the manner of socialization, with *li* and other social conventions not only shared but internalized—the Chinese all have similar expectations of various specific settings; explicit reference to expectations is a signal that something is out of order. Children are taught early to follow adults as models and not to ask questions; it is a long-held belief that "examples are better than verbal instructions" (*yanchuan buru shenjiao*). For example, in social contacts, hosts are expected to make guests feel at home, and the visitors are expected to be modest and humble. The best treat for somebody coming home is something good to eat, things that are taken without any question as pleasing to the visitor, because they are such to the host. On the other hand, enjoyment of eating is a behavior closer to that of animals. Thus, a typical scene of visitor-receiving in China is that of the host continuing to offer food while the visitor continues to thank the host for about three or four rounds of persistent offering before partaking. In comparison, the North American host does the asking/offering while the visitors decline, accept, or request an alternative, more or less literally, consistent with the principle of respect for the individual wish.

A tacit understanding among people about specifics in a wide range of typical social situations is such a common phenomenon that it places the Chinese into the category of high context culture (Hall, 1977), which is a manifestation, in the epistemic domain, of the culture's great reliance on first-hand experience (as opposed to information via language codes or logical reasoning) as a base of knowledge and, indirectly, of the polar contrast of human versus nature. The great extent to which social knowledge of a situation is shared, as characteristic of a society with collective consciousness, does not call for verbal explanations of specifics. Thus, typically, students do not ask questions in class about any administrative procedures; they expect to be told whatever they need to know. The teacher knows that an acceptable explanation will follow an absence from class; the students are expected to attend class except for a good reason. Customers are not attended before they ask for help; no one expects or says "thank you" for such small favors as collecting the mail for a neighbor or giving someone information that is needed. Such acts may be seen as the goodwill one should offer to other members of the community, and one can rely on getting the same from them. Typically such acts are viewed as part of life, unlike a personal favor, as understood in the West.

The emphasis on role of experience in knowledge is the best expression of the nonexpressive/inexpressible in the culture, as captured in Lao Zi's (Lao Tsu) famous saying "He who knows does not speak, he who speaks does not know" (*zhizhe bu yan yanzhe buz zhi*). Here again, we can think of the Chinese brush paintings that present things that can be sensed but not expressed, as is the case for much other knowledge about the world (also see Becker, 1991, and Cheng, 1987, on the Chinese view of language and knowledge). People are expected to take whatever is told them and to repeat and repeat, or practice and practice, until they develop a sense of it through their own experience or discover that it is nonsense. It is not Chinese to prove through pure logical argument; Chinese would seek truth in practice, including social practice bound by conventional wisdom, sometimes not entirely logical. Judged by modern scientific standards, some practices that have been followed for generations in China might seem irrational. The best example is traditional Chinese medicine, which treats with methods from experience accumulated over thousands of years. It has its own theories, which, again, cannot be taught logically but must be learned through experience, under the direction of experienced doctors, and has some practices not explained in (scientific) modern medical theories. However, the Chinese trust it more for its contribution to their overall health, although its effect is certainly slower than that of Western medicine, which is, in Chinese eyes, faster and effective but takes care of only the troubled part—as in the saying "Treat the head when the head aches and treat the foot when the foot hurts" (*tou teng yi tou jiao teng zhi jiao*), meaning treat the symptoms but not the disease. Here we have a good illustration of the holistic, polar, and experience-oriented mode of Eastern thinking, in contrast to the causal, linear, and reason-oriented mode of Western thinking.

Another example of lack of ego in the Chinese mode of thinking, again in sharp contrast to the North American, is the case of children. In the United States, children are little individuals, with things and space that they claim to be their own, accepted and respected by adults. They prepare for their total independence when they come of age, and they are ready to be "launched." The government and the society see to it that children are not forced in any way against their wills, and in social settings people of different generations interact more or less as equals. An entirely different picture is found in China. In this still patriarchic society Chinese children are treated differently than adults. They are loved and protected, as all young are; however, they are at the lowest level of the family hierarchy, and they remain so as long as the older generation lives. The young should not have an opinion that differs from that which they are told to have by an elder. Instead, everything is decided for them, on the grounds that what is good for the family is good for each member. The elder's choices are for the benefit of everyone, as part of the family.[12] Naturally, the responsibility of the elder for the younger (physical, emotional, financial, social, and so forth) ceases only on their last day of life, as does the obedience of the younger in every possible way—"Filial piety comes before all virtues" (*baixing xiao wei xian*) is the other half of the motto about lewdness mentioned above. The responsibilities of the elder warrant overt expressions of their love and care toward the young: Nothing is more expected than the adult's picking up, hugging, and kissing a child, even if they do not know each other, because such actions express nothing short of kindness and good will, if not love. They embody an extension of the concept of family. Thus, in social settings, children are the most convenient ice-breaking topics.

A final point can be made about the Chinese judicial system, criminal and civil, as a testament to its two-dimensional view. Until some years ago, there were no laws in China, as we know them in the West, where there are social formations that exist only where human behaviors are presumably spatialized and not only measurable for direction (right vs. wrong) but also quantifiable (how much wrong). A legal system reflects the recognition of individuals as equals before the law. For hundreds of years in China, criminal cases, and rare instances of civil conflicts, have been dealt with in a court, which was totally different from that which exists in the United States.

The Chinese court operated on the basis of custom or common sense. The judge was usually a local government chief, supposedly a person of wisdom and reputation, as well as authority. Civil conflicts were settled mostly in the neighborhood or community, with the help of relatives and friends of the parties involved, who mediated according to custom and common sense, getting the parties to see their own deviations from what was expected and/or socially acceptable in particular circumstances, and persuading the parties to come to terms with each other by mending each one's ways. There were no written codes to follow, except for tacit knowledge shared in the society.

Chinese Meeting North Americans

With such discrepancy between the two peoples in the structures of consciousness dominating their thinking it is only natural that they have difficulty understanding each other, even in the most ordinary daily routines. Many Chinese in America were confused the first few times they received a "thanks" from a shop assistant or someone they visited, because they saw no reason for it whatsoever. They found it more peculiar to see family members thanking one another, which to them was akin to thanking oneself: It made no sense. Their first impression, then, was that North Americans were overly polite. Excessive politeness, especially among peers, for Chinese equates with aloofness; it is not a sign of respect for the individual, even in most trivial matters or in an intimate relationship. Similarly, some North Americans visiting China were appalled by the rudeness of the Chinese, who pushed their way in the crowded streets, not stopping to apologize to the pushed (a common scene there that does not bother the natives because they know the pushers are in a hurry, and mean no harm).

A story common to Chinese first visiting the United States is that North Americans are friendly but superficial and absent-minded or forgetful, if not arrogant. Unused to explicitly expressing their feelings, many Chinese were overwhelmed by meeting with North Americans for the first time, impressed or even moved by the latter's hospitality (from the Chinese standard), with many

pleasant verbal expressions (e.g., "I am so glad to see you," "It is a pleasure to know you," "I am so pleased that you came," etc.),[13] accompanied by rich facial expressions and enthusiastic gestures (e.g., broad smiles, assuring nods, firm handshakes, friendly shoulder-patting). They seemed to be so outgoing, relaxed, and approachable. The Chinese would regard such behavior as an indication of their acceptance into the community. They never would have imagined that their new friends often would have totally forgotten their meeting at some time later. This was a great surprise to the Chinese and a source of deep embarrassment. For people with a collective mode of consciousness, it is, at first, difficult for them to comprehend how one part could no longer know another part of a collective whole in a single existence: One never fails to recognize one's family. With the passage of time, many Chinese came to realize that the basic unit in the North American society is the individual. Then it made sense when things that did not directly concern an individual did not usually get much attention from that person, and that the expressiveness in social interaction was no more than a gesture of respect and goodwill. Such understanding is not possible without the assumption that both cultures recognize the relationship between the part and the whole. On this basis, the Chinese need to make a shift from the whole to the part as the point from which to know North Americans.

Another Chinese impression of North Americans is that they are ready to lend a helping hand, but it is hard to make genuine friendships with them. Many Chinese in North America have experienced timely help from their North American friends. Fellow passengers would take them home for the night and help them find a place to live; people they met would offer all kinds of help or information to solve their settling-down problems. Naturally, these people are considered friends. The term *friend*, however, has different connotations in the two cultures. For the Chinese, it often means someone you know really well, to the extent that you know everything, not only about each other, but about each other's family, past, and present. Note that a typical Chinese way for one to know anything is through experience, which is acquired only in context. In the case of a person, the context is his or her background in every respect: family, education, job, friends, habits, income, and other parts of personal life. Habitually, the Chinese would expect exactly the same from their new North American friends, to know everything (a rather threatening situation to many North Americans) through typical Chinese chatting with the person involved and with related others. However, they found it difficult to strike up such conversations with many North Americans, who are jealous of their privacy and are not used to casual self-disclosure and other exposure with great detail.

Many North Americans in China have comparable impressions of their Chinese hosts. They find the Chinese friendly and hospitable but too noisy and gossipy. Also, the Chinese way of making them feel at home sometimes "drives them nuts," because they are constantly being asked after their well-being and time and again are offered food, regardless of repeatedly declining. Some feel their host is intrusive, because they rarely have time alone; rather, they always have company to keep them from being "lonely." It is a great breach of etiquette in China to leave a guest alone; this would imply that the visitor is not welcome, the last thing a Chinese would do. The visitor is expected to feel welcome, even at a most "inconvenient moment" to the visited, which by the way is not an original Chinese concept. A genuine Chinese expression would be, even with the most "disliked person," as is consistent with the egoless consciousness, that members of the collective whole would not openly express dislike of such a person because to do so would be to risk their interdependent existence.

To think in perspective is characteristic of North Americans. Reflecting on interpersonal relations in daily life is to see people from many different sides. This puts many Chinese in a quandary. It takes some time for them to discover that North Americans do not usually put people into one of the two categories, kind and unkind (good or bad), as Chinese constantly do with their two-dimensional, polar view of the world. It sounds strange and inconsistent to the Chinese ear that someone can be "kind and not easy to talk to." Consequently, an attribution would often fol-low that the person making such a statement is insincere, or reluctant to be honest about his or her personal opinion. What matters about a person for Chinese is his or her conscientiousness; thus, besides being kind or unkind, other things about a person are not important enough to be worth mentioning. Here we also trace the mark of lack of ego consciousness: As part of a whole, there is no need for uniqueness in a person, only for a conscience for the collective good. Being kind to fellow human beings promotes harmony (Yum, 1988).

Conclusion

As different as the Chinese culture is from that of North Americans, it has been argued that traditions and values are associated with the most basic dimensions encompassing all aspects of life. Manifestations of different modes of consciousness in different cultures do not come from a void but stem from basic concepts and evolve into traditional or conventional value differences. Traditions and values are two of the many elements of culture that might account for some, but not all, cultural characteristics. They are the most conspicuous aspects of the source of what sets cultures apart phenomenologically, whereas the more fundamental, deeply rooted dimensions are often taken for granted. The acceptance of this position has led to the proposition that, in intercultural communications, communicators from cultures with a different dominant consciousness structure have the potential to understand one another, provided that cultural variations can be put in perspective in light of the basic dimensions of concept. Once on an equal footing at the basic level, the two minds become congruent: They can think in similar terms and see in a similar light.

As in all studies, the foregoing qualitative analysis inevitably reflects the bias of a researcher. However, it presents a point of view accessible to those who would take a particular position similar to this one. Further studies of knowing and intercultural communication can go in several directions. One is to substantiate the model further with more diverse and extensive empirical data of various cultures in order to demonstrate specific cultural practices as manifestations of modes of consciousness. Efforts to gather evidence of coexisting modes of consciousness in a single culture are especially valuable, because such evidence will have added implications for intercultural education: How different modes are accommodated in a culture may enlighten us about ways of intercultural accommodation and intercultural understanding. Another avenue to examine is specific instances of communication failure in intercultural settings. The aim is to specify the extent to which we can attribute communication breakdown to participants' thinking in different modes. Operating in an invariate mode is at the bottom of such unsuccessful attempts to communicate. The point is to pin down exact points of failure on the epistemic level. Alternatively, successful intercultural interactions can be examined—for example, when interactants can laugh at the same joke—to find the common ground, the underlying epistemic roots that allow us to operate between modes of consciousness.

NOTES

An earlier version of this paper was presented at the International Communication Association Annual Conference, 1990, Dublin, Ireland. The author thanks Young Kim, William Starosta, Hui-Ching Chang, and Gao-Ming Chen for their constructive comments and suggestions on earlier versions.

1. Other views on this matter, for example the Christian mystic tradition, are excluded, because they are beyond the scope of this discussion.

2. This is evident from various definitions of rhetoric provided by generations of rhetoricians, that it is "the practice of enchanting the soul with words" (Socrates and Plato, 1874), "the art of finding available means of persuasion" (Aristotle, see Jebb, 1909), "the art of effective persuasion" (Cicero, see Clarke, 1963), "the art or talent by which the discourse is adapted to its end" (Campbell, in Bitzer, 1963), "to apply Reason to Imagination for the better move of Will" (Bacon, see Dick, 1983); and "linguistic description of reality" (Cherwitz & Hikins, 1983).

3. Such as Toulmin (1958, 1972), Scott (1967), and Foucault (1970, 1972).

4. For example, the theory of constructivism by Delia and colleagues (e.g., Delia, 1977, Burlson, 1987) explicitly proffers knowledge following interactions between cognitive structure and external factors. Nevertheless, the theory is often regarded as dealing with personal traits; thus, it is biased toward empiricism. Because their works are part of a collection on personality and communication (McCroskey & Daly, 1987), proponents of the theory were prepared to defend their behaviorist approach against those who favored a phenomenological approach (SCA convention program 1990, pp. 91, 102). On the other hand, this approach is criticized as one of interpretivists, who believe in the human construction of reality (Bostrom & Donohew, 1992).

5. These are subtypes; see Gebser (1985) for a discussion of this. To put it simply, the major five are archaic, magic, mythical, mental–rational, and integral structures. Consciousness within the archaic structure has no sense of time or space but has an internal latency. Consciousness within the magic structure has a sense of natural time but not space and has emotion as the instinctive drive. Consciousness within the mythical structure is aware of both time and space in a two-dimensional sense and is disposed to imagination. Consciousness within the mental–rational structure not only knows the space as it is but also spatializes everything else with rational abstraction. Consciousness within the integral structure manifests a time-free and space-free emphasis, and renders concretion transparent. Features of all types of structures are present in every culture, but one has dominance over the others.

6. About his view of culture as "imagination, the spirit, and inward tendency" governed by the "Tyrannizing Image," see discussions in Foss et al. (1985).

7. The approach here to the Chinese culture is somewhat different from the usual one. Ancient Chinese thinkers are quoted not to discuss their influence on the culture—which they indeed have—but to present them as representative of Chinese thinking, or the Chinese mode of consciousness. These thinkers grew from the cultural soil, and they have, in return, cultivated the culture; the two are interdependent, nourishing each other.

8. The author thanks Drs. Donald Cegala and

William Starosta for bringing this to her attention. Also see Oliver (1971) for a discussion of this in terms of "reciprocity."

9. This is not quite the same in recent decades, as there are indications of a small, but steadily growing, influence of other structures of consciousness (Chen, 1991; Sun, 1989).

10. When modified by numerals, Chinese object nouns must, at the same time, be modified by classifiers following the numeral to designate the category to which the noun belongs. These classifiers are similar to such English lexical items as *piece* and *loaf,* as in "a piece of paper" and "a loaf of bread."

11. Watson neither distinguishes between the cultures of the same category based on the criterion of "contact" nor provides specific rationales for differences in categories, other than differences in tradition.

12. The contemporary young generation enjoys much more independence than ever before; however, the spirit of seniority–superiority is still deeply rooted, as can be seen in the cases of children under the current one-child policy enforced by the government: The main concern of the public is that there will be a whole generation of "spoiled children" who will want to have their own way.

13. Part of the reason may be the Chinese translation of these expressions. Lacking equivalent phatic communion, the Chinese language adds to the literary translations an extra enthusiastic flavor not found in English. However, this sheds light on the status of the individual there: The individual is recognized neither socially nor linguistically. Even phatic expressions in Chinese are of a different topic/nature, usually in the form of a question about the addressee's whereabouts or activities, which are often too inquisitive to a North American's ears.

REFERENCES

Becker, C. B. (1991). Reasons for the lack of argumentation and debate in the Far East. In L. A. Samovar & R. E. Porter (Eds.), *Intercultural communication: A reader* (6th ed.). Belmont, CA: Wadsworth.

Bitzer, L. F. (Ed.). (1963). *The philosophy of rhetoric.* Carbondale: Southern Illinois University Press.

Bond, M. (1983). Linking dimensions of person perception to dimensions of behavior intention: The Chinese connection. *Journal of Cross-cultural Psychology, 14,* 41–63.

Bond, M., & Forgas, J. (1984). Linking person perception to behavior intention across cultures: The role of cultural collectivism. *Journal of Cross-cultural Psychology, 15,* 1–27.

Bostrom, R., & Donohew, L. (1992). The case of empiricism: Clarifying fundamental issues in communication theory. *Communication Monographs, 59,* 109–129.

Burke, K. (1968). *Language as symbolic action.* Berkeley: University of California Press.

Cai, S. (1984). *The ideological system of Confucius.* Shanghai: Peoples' Literature.

Chen, L. (1987). *Semantic relations, conceptual categorizations, and lexical structures: An investigation into some aspects of the vocabulary of Mandarin Chinese.* Unpublished master's thesis, University of Essex, England.

Chen, L. (1991). Culture, politics, communication, and development: A tentative study on the case of China. *Gazette, 48,* 1–16.

Cheng, C.-Y. (1987). Chinese philosophy and contemporary human communication theory. In D. L. Kincaid (Ed.), *Communication theory: Eastern and Western perspectives* (pp. 23–43). New York: Academic Press.

Cherwitz, R. A., & Hikins, J. W. (1983). Rhetorical perspectivism. *Quarterly Journal of Speech, 69,* 249–266.

Clark, H. H., & Clark, E. V. (1977). *Language and psychology: An introduction to psycholinguistics.* New York: Harcourt Brace Jovanovich.

Creel, H. G. (1953). *Chinese thought from Confucius to Mao Tse-tung.* New York: New American Library.

Dick, H. C. (Ed.). (1983). *Selected writings of Francis Bacon.* New York: Modern Library.

Eiser, J. R. (1980). *Cognitive social psychology.* London: McGraw-Hill.

Fodor, J. A. (1976). *The language of thought.* New York: Crowell.

Fodor, J. A. (1981). *The modularity of the mind.* Cambridge, MA: MIT Press.

Fodor, J. A. (1983). *Representations.* Cambridge, MA: MIT Press.

Foss, S. K., Foss, K. A., & Trapp, R. (1985). *Contemporary perspectives on rhetoric.* Prospect Heights, IL: Waveland.

Foucault, M. (1972). *The archaeology of knowledge.* New York: Pantheon.

Foucault, M. (1970). *The order of things: An archaeology of human sciences.* New York: Pantheon.

Gebser, J. (1985). *The ever-present origin.* Athens: Ohio University Press.

Gregg, R. B. (1984). *Symbolic inducement and knowing: A study in the foundations of rhetoric.* Columbia: University of South Carolina Press.

Hall, E. (1977). *Beyond culture.* Garden City, NY: Anchor.

Jebb, R. C. (1909). *The rhetoric of Aristotle: A translation.* Cambridge: Cambridge University Press.

Littlejohn, S. W. (1989). *Theories of human communication* (3rd ed.). Belmont, CA: Wadsworth.

Ma, H. K. (1990). The Chinese Taoistic perspective on human development. *International Journal of Intercultural Relations, 14,* 235–249.

McCroskey, J. C., & Daly, J. A. (1987). *Personality and interpersonal communication.* Newbury Park, CA: Sage.

Meggers, B. J. (1954). Environmental limitations on the development of culture. *American Anthropologist, 56,* 801–824.

Oliver, R. T. (1961). The rhetorical implications of Taoism. *The Quarterly Journal of Speech, 15,* 27–35.

Oliver, R. T. (1961). *Communication and culture in Ancient India and China.* Syracuse: Syracuse University Press.

Plato. (1874). *The dialogues of Plato.* (B. Jowett, Trans.) New York: Scriber Armstrong.

Rosch, E. (1978). Principles of categorization. In E. Rosch & B. Loyd (Eds.), *Cognition and categorization.* Hillsdale, NJ: Lawrence Erlbaum.

Scott, R. L. (1967). On viewing rhetoric as epistemic. *Central States Speech Journal,* 18 February, 1967.

Servaes, J. (1988). Cultural identity in East and West. *The Howard Journal of Communications, 1,* 58–71.

Speech Communication Association Annual Meeting Program (1990, pp. 91, 102).

Starosta, W. J. (1988–1989). Sources in intercultural communication. *The Howard Journal of Communications, 1,* 232–237.

Sun. (1989). *The deep structure of Chinese culture* (2nd ed.). Taiwan: Tangsan.

Toulmin, S. (1958). *The uses of argument.* Cambridge: Cambridge University Press.

Toulmin, S. (1972). *Human understanding, vol. 1: The collective usage and evolution of concepts.* Princeton: Princeton University Press.

Triandis, H. C. (1989). Cross-cultural studies of individualism and collectivism. *Nebraska Symposium on Motivation.* Lincoln: University of Nebraska Press.

Watson, O. M. (1970). *Proximic behavior: A cross-cultural study.* The Hague: Mouton.

Yum, J. O. (1988). The impact of Confucianism on interpersonal relationships and communication patterns in East Asia. *Communication Monographs, 55,* 374–388.

KEY TERMS

epistemology	interpersonal communication
consciousness	
time	initial interaction
space	individualism
ego	collectivism
China	

DISCUSSION QUESTIONS

1. Chen identifies Chinese sayings that reflect a collectivist approach, such as "Gun will shoot the bird that flies higher than others." Can you think of contrasting English sayings that reflect an *individualistic* orientation?

2. According to Chen, could an ad campaign based on the "time is money" U.S. approach work in China? If not, what kind of approach or persuasive strategies might work?

3. Chen's findings are based on qualitative, interpretive study. How might a social science researcher investigate these same cultural differences?

4. Based on this essay, what advice would you give U.S. exchange students in China about adapting their nonverbal behavior to fit in better in China?

5. Do you think Chinese visitors would have an easier time getting to know people in different parts of the United States? Would regional and urban or rural differences in communication style make a difference?

38
INTERCULTURAL FRIENDSHIPS AS INTERPERSONAL ALLIANCES

MARY JANE COLLIER

In the United States, as in many countries, anti-immigration laws are being debated and Affirmative Action policies are being reconsidered. In several states, laws barring discrimination against gays and lesbians are being challenged, and membership in self-proclaimed racist groups such as the KKK and militia organizations is increasing (Southern Poverty Law Center Report, March 1996). Racism has become a part of our everyday language, as have other forms of "isms" toward many groups.

It is in this sociohistorical, cultural milieu that we find ourselves today. All of us must manage a series of identity dialectics or seemingly contradictory tensions. At the national level, we struggle to manage the tension between the need to be international citizens and the need to maintain a unique national identity. Paradoxically, we have increased our technological abilities and access to international sites and, at the same time, increased our need for defining and protecting our group boundaries.

As ethnic group members we struggle to manage the tension between being U.S. Americans and being, for example, Cuban or Japanese. We recognize that men and women aren't limited to a particular sexual orientation, or a gendered style of speaking, and that families and friendship relationships take many forms. As individuals, we are members of many groups and relationships, yet we maintain some degree of individual uniqueness.

My purpose in this essay is to explore how individuals who have satisfying friendships with people from different cultural backgrounds maintain their friendships as well as demonstrate respect for one another's cultural differences. I am proposing that some intercultural friendships become interpersonal alliances. The word "ally" connotes partner, advocate, collaborator, and supporter, and "alliance" means to be associated, connected, pledged, and joined in a united front. Although most commonly we think of alliances in contexts of war or violence, they arise in different contexts and take various forms within and between many national, ethnic, sex, class, religious, and political groups.

Our everyday talk includes numerous explicit and implicit references to ingroup and outgroup distinctions. We define our own identities in comparison to other groups. Frequently, an "insider" comes to think of and describe others as "outsiders," one of "them" instead of "us." Insider-outsider boundaries are constructed, defended, and challenged through communication; our words and actions create the borders and shared spaces of our world. We become who we are as well as negotiate power through communicating within and across such boundaries.

In an alliance, the insider-outsider distinction becomes open to question and critique. Alliances require at least two people who are both responsible for and dependent upon the quality of their relationship. Often, in regions torn by violent conflict and war, women form alliances to work for peace. When Palestinian and Israeli women march together for peace in the streets of Jerusalem, an observer can't identify who is an insider and who is an outsider; one can see only the alliance.

Intercultural friends must manage not only feelings of being both the insider and outsider at different times but also various tensions. Such relationships are often filled with paradox and dialectical tension between contradictory forces—toward being both separate and together, unique and divided, independent and interdependent.

In the remainder of the essay I describe my orientation to intercultural communication in friendships by explaining an approach based in cultural identity(ies). First, I explain how four group identities—race, sex, ethnicity, and nationality—are formed. Second, I describe how cultural identities become the basis of intercultural friendships. Finally, I identify three critical components important in developing and maintaining intercultural friendship alliances.

Developing Cultural Identities: Race, Sex, Ethnicity, and Nationality

Rather than studying culture as the *place* where people come from, or as an independent variable from which researchers and scholars can predict specific conduct, I focus on the communication processes through which people construct culture and their identities. I define culture to be an enduring and changing, situated and transcendent, co-constructed set of communicative practices and interpretive frames shared by a group. Membership occurs when people self-identify as group members, their membership is bounded and salient, and members of the group confirm the membership (Carbaugh, 1990). In addition, the communicative practices and interpretations must endure to some degree and be invoked for new members while simultaneously being re-constructed and changed.

According to the criteria outlined here, not all groups have a culture. When a culture does emerge, the particular character of the communicative system that individuals, friends, and group members enact is cultural identity. In this essay, I focus on cultural groups whose members self-identify on the basis of biological characteristics (male, female, skin color), shared ancestry and heritage (ethnicity) or nationality (birth or naturalization), and social and historical construction.

Membership in some cultural groups is more involuntary than voluntary. An individual's sex and race are designated at birth for most people and thus membership is more involuntary. In general, scholars conceive of race in one of two ways. The first focuses on physically inherited characteristics based on generations of geographical and climatic adjustment. But being born into a group and sharing race, for instance, does not mean that each group member will communicate in similar

ways or have a similar group identity. The second, more recent approach, is to define race as a social/historical construction. Scholars in this tradition argue today that because of intermarriage and changes in the definitions of racial categories, one can no longer base categories of race on biological or genetic conceptions. They maintain that race as a categorization system has been used throughout history to identify outsiders in order to exert and maintain power. From this perspective, race is a way of creating an identity hierarchy and ascribing to others an identity that allows members of the group in power to keep their power.

Sex is another primarily involuntary group category. Sex, like race, is determined at birth (or is very difficult to change). It should be pointed out, nonetheless, that women (and men) do not all share the exact same identities or even assumptions about how to be women (or how to be men). Men and women in many countries adopt aspects of a masculine or feminine style.

Gender identity is socialized, contextualized, and emergent. Although male children are taught to use a masculine style and female children are taught to be feminine in many countries and contexts, and gender is still a basis for discrimination against women all over the world, gender identity variations are increasing for both sexes.

Race and sex are important because outsiders often use these categories to apply stereotypes of group members, attribute values and beliefs, allocate resources, determine policies, and pursue or avoid relationships. Media examples of such stereotypes and attributions abound. Insiders also use race and sex as markers of group identity and to teach the young norms of expected conduct for males and females within the group. Sex and race categorizations frequently result in different standards for evaluation and often affect the self-concepts of men and women in different groups.

In addition to race and sex, ethnicity and nationality are two other categories of group membership. Ethnicity refers to one's ancestry and heritage from a different nation-state of residence, or to residence in the current nation-state from a time preceding the creation of the nation-state (Banks, 1987). Nationality refers to the nation in which one is born or holds citizenship.

Ethnicity designates not only the group of ancestors with whom one shares a sense of history and place of origin but also the history and association with a group in the current nation-state of residence. This is why many ethnic groups choose labels that include both places from which their group identity is constituted, for example, Mexican American.

Ethnicity tends to be involuntary in that one's ancestors cannot be changed. Unlike race and sex, however, some individuals such as White U.S. Americans have the choice of "putting on" or "taking off" their British German U.S. ethnicity so that others cannot identify their ethnic heritage. In that sense, then, ethnicity, for some, may be a more voluntary group affiliation than sex or race.

Although nationality still commonly refers to the nation in which an individual is born, increasing numbers of people change their citizenship and hold dual citizenship. We can generally think of nationality as an affiliation that is more voluntary than race, sex, or ethnicity (recognizing that there are some circumstances in which a group of people opt to leave a country involuntarily to escape persecution or violence).

Although individuals may share membership in national or ethnic groups, they may not share the intensity with which they enact their national or ethnic identity, or the importance they place on that identity relative to other identities (Collier & Thomas, 1988). For example, Collier and Bornman (in press) found that South Africans of Dutch and British descent talked about their national identity in very different ways. Afrikaners focused on pride in their families, clear standards of acceptable behavior to which any respectable South African should hold, and optimism regarding the "new South Africa." In contrast, the British Whites talked more about Black-White crime and individual responsibility for behavior and had less optimism about the future.

In addition, interpretations of what it means to be a member of an ethnic group may differ dramatically in different regions of the country. For example, individuals of Mexican descent in New Mexico often see their origins as more Spanish; those in Oregon are more closely tied to Mexico. Members of ethnic groups may have different preferences for identity labels (e.g., African American, Black American, or Black) because of what each connotes about political standpoints and history of the group. Dolores Tanno (1997) points out that categorizing her ethnicity with one label misrepresents the complexity of the cultural identity process in that in some situations she is Chicana, in others Mexican American, and in still others, Spanish. Age and generation may also affect perceptions of the language and codes that are viewed as appropriate. For example, third-generation Chicano/a college students may view speaking Spanish with their friends as being more important than do their Mexicano/a grandparents.

In summary, race, sex, ancestry, and citizenship are used by ingroup as well as outgroup members as one set of markers about identity. Such characteristics are often the basis of stereotypes by outgroup members and can be one of the initial criteria used to determine membership for insiders. But these criteria can be very limiting. They may falsely presume a relationship between the inherited or ascribed category and cultural conduct; they may be gross overgeneralizations that include neither the group members' experiences of what it means to be a member of the group nor the historical, social, and contextual variations in how the group membership is constituted and reinforced. Perhaps most important, these criteria ignore the role of power and privilege in determining the categories and outcomes of being assigned to particular categories. Some people, for example, are formally registered as Indians in the United States but may not be considered to be "real" Indians by most of the group (Weider & Pratt, 1990).

Understanding the difference between the involuntary, ascribed group membership and emergent, enacted identity of the group at a particular time and place may help you in several ways in building intercultural relationships. First, it can help you recognize when you are making unwarranted assumptions and applying stereotypical expectations to members of groups. Second, knowing that we are socialized through institutions such as education and religion, and through multiple channels and forms of media as well as messages from parents and friends, can help you understand how others come to know how to be who they are. Third, it can help you understand the origins of *your* own cultural identities. What can also be useful to you is coming to understand the differences in what it takes to be an accepted member of your and others' cultural groups and what it takes to behave appropriately and effectively with people whose cultural identities are different from yours.

Now that I've explained how several group identities are developed and maintained, let's examine Cultural Identity Theory. This theory is one of many useful theories to help us build our knowledge about intercultural friendship communication, and it is the primary theory that I apply in my research on intercultural friendships. It is based on several assumptions about how we come to know who we are and what to believe (epistemological premises) as well as how to be an accepted, competent member of the cultural group (ontological premises).

Cultural Identity Theory

The main premises of the theory are that people have multiple cultural identities and the identities are constituted through discourse with others. We come to know who we are in relationship to others through our talk with others (Hecht, Collier, & Ribeau, 1993). For example, a respondent interviewed for a course project on interethnic friendship said, "If someone says '*Yo soy Chicana*' then we can talk politics. If she says 'I am Mexican American,' I know we may have different views about politics and the importance of history, but we can acknowledge that our people share a history and our ancestors come from the same place."

Next, I outline nine properties of Cultural Identity Theory helpful to build understanding of how cultural identities are defined with one another (Collier & Thomas, 1988; Hecht, Collier, & Ribeau, 1993). The first and second properties relate to avowal and ascription processes.

Avowal, or subjective identity, consists of the perceived identity enacted by the self or group members in a particular context. A Cuban American in a recent study said, "I am always Cuban American, I can't ever not be Cuban American; I

am a successful Cuban businessman who holds American citizenship." In sum, avowal is evident in self-perceptions of the discourse "this is who I am as a member of my cultural group(s) in this context" (Collier, Thompson, & Weber, 1996).

Ascription of identity is the individual's perception of the identity attributed to self by other. Ascription is evident in self-perceptions of others' discourse when individuals note, "this is how you are seeing me as a member of my cultural group(s) here and now." We all hold ascriptions about others, and such ascriptions include prejudices and stereotypes. Such stereotypes and prejudices often serve to reinforce ingroup solidarity (our group is better than they are), but negative ascriptions from others can also affect self-esteem and evaluations of one's cultural group.

Avowal and ascription processes are important to recognize in intercultural friendships because when two people are avowing different cultural identities, inaccuracies can lead to misunderstandings and conflict. Avowal and ascription affect relationship tone, content of what is talked about, and desire to continue the friendship. Ascription is particularly important to many U.S. ethnic groups designated as minorities because who they are is strongly affected by ascriptions by socioeconomically dominant European Americans.

Typically, avowals are individually framed, whereas ascriptions are communally framed. Even when questions are asked of the "other," they are posed to the group because that is how we most easily understand others—as group members. There is also a trend to use labels that make fine and more detailed distinctions among members of our own group and to use a broad, overgeneralized label to designate members of the outgroup. For example, outsiders might label a group's members as Latino/a, but insiders may make distinctions and refer to Chicano/a, Mexican, Mexican American, Spanish, Puerto Rican, or Nicaraguan.

Cultural identities are *enduring* and *changing*—the second and third properties relevant to intercultural friendships. They are enduring because they are group identities that are handed down to new members. What is handed down reflects a history and, for national and ethnic groups, a past orientation. However, cultural identities are also changing and affected by context. How young adult Navahos define their ethnic identity as Indians in Denver, for example, may be different from how older Navahos living on the reservation define theirs.

The fifth and sixth properties of cultural identity relevant to intercultural relationship processes are *content* and *relationship* dimensions. What is talked about in the way of topics discussed and information shared as well as themes and core symbols in the talk are all content dimensions. Members of cultural groups are taught norms about what topics to discuss with whom. Collier & Shimizu (1993) found that Japanese and U.S. friends differed in that U.S. friends talked more openly about their family, were more likely to criticize family members or friends, and were more likely to share positive accomplishments with their friends.

Relationship issues include connection, inclusion, coordination, interdependence, emotional attachment, and quality of contact. Relationships are constructed through the changing quality of nonverbal and verbal messages, and power is one of the most critical relational dimensions for intercultural relationships. Members of ethnic "minority" groups are aware of European Americans' unearned privilege, whereas many European Americans are unaware of such privileges. Perhaps the friends develop explicit ways of dealing with their unequal privilege, or perhaps they negotiate power and control in more implicit ways. This is a question that warrants more attention and research.

Because they are members of multiple groups with shared histories and bounded codes and norms, individuals have a range of cultural identities that can become salient in any given context. Thus, a seventh property of cultural identity relevant to the study of thriving intercultural friendships is *multiple types of identity*—national, ethnic, gender, religious/spiritual, regional, professional, and so on. Some identities have broad scope, that is, numerous people share national identity; others have narrow scope—fewer persons share the cultural identity, such as in a regional or corporate affiliation. Acknowledging each individual's range of identities may help limit our tendencies to overgeneralize about the group members.

Context and power affect which identity(ies) is(are) enacted. European Americans, one of the groups having the greatest socioeconomic and sociocultural power in the United States, are highly individualistic and may have the most flexibility in featuring national identity or gender identity or ethnic identity. Members of ethnic groups with lower socioeconomic and sociocultural power, such as African Americans, U.S. Indians, and Latinos, do not have the same freedom of choice because of the frequency and absoluteness with which European Americans or other outgroup members ascribe negative stereotypes and set up expectations for conduct. A Lakota Indian explained, "I can't be Lakota at work. I cut my hair, I wear the tie" (Collier, Thompson, & Weber, 1996).

Salience and *intensity* of avowal are the eighth and ninth properties relevant to the study of intercultural friendships. Salience refers to relative importance of one or two identities to others. One reason salience is so important is that when allies begin enacting ethnic distinctiveness and perhaps move toward conflict, they may remind each other, in explicit or implicit ways, that the friendship is the most salient identity. From that frame of reference or shared assumption, cultural differences can be accommodated or accepted. In South Africa, Asians recommended that all groups needed to first learn about and then accept cultural differences in order to form lasting intercultural relationships (Collier & Bornman, in press).

Another reason salience is so significant is because it may be possible for individuals to enact multiple identities at once. Perhaps friends are both friends and ethnically different at the same time. Identity enactment probably isn't a matter of making choices between polar opposites; it may be a matter of dialectical tensions between ethnic identity and friendship identity. Further, the intensity with which people avow particular identities may change as topics change or as others enter a conversation. As people become proud or threatened, they may more or less intensely avow a particular identity. Iranian Americans talked about the effect of stereotypes during the Persian

Gulf War and their resulting desire to correct mis-perceptions by speaking up (Collier, Thompson, & Weber, 1996).

An African American male interviewed for a course project related that he doesn't think his ethnic identity is important in his friendship with a Japanese American, whereas when visiting his family in the neighborhood where he grew up, he feels less choice about how to be. "At home I'm surrounded by Blacks, so I'm Black." An African American woman said that she is a "proud Black woman" wherever she goes, whomever she is with, and the only thing that changes is how others respond to her.

Enacting Different Cultural Identities in Friendships

As stated earlier, what we say and do constitutes who we are. When we constitute our relational partner as "other," as a member of a different ethnic group or sex, we are constituting our relationship in a particular way. Intercultural relationships are not experienced or constituted in the same way as intracultural relationships. A South African noted in discussions of politics, "My White friends and I have to work harder at understanding each other . . . maybe compromise . . . another Coloured can understand the situation perfectly well because her upbringing was the same" (Collier & Bornman, in press).

What does it take to be a good relational partner in intercultural friendships? Intercultural competence involves two friends who are avowing different cultural identities behaving appropriately and effectively for their friendship in the particular context. This means that friends can benefit from acknowledging that communication is a problematic and dynamic process and that the most appropriate and effective conduct requires some flexibility and negotiation.

Collier & Thomas (1988) suggest that intercultural competence is the continuing match between avowed and ascribed cultural identities; in other words, both people treating each other appropriately and effectively for the particular cultural identity(ies) being enacted throughout

the conversation. Thus, allies must develop the knowledge and ability to track and sometimes adapt to their partner's cultural identities. Certainly, people do not shift arbitrarily or necessarily frequently from identity to identity in each conversation in chameleonlike fashion, but they may change the intensity with which their ethnic identity is being advanced.

While friends are negotiating their cultural identities in intercultural communication, they are also negotiating their relationship as friends. Let's look more closely at intercultural friendship.

Although individuals have their own ideas and unique experiences about what friendship is, generally, good friends have relationships characterized by warmth, affection, trust, self-disclosure, commitment, and an expectation that the relationship will grow and endure. Cross-cultural investigations of friendship show that friendships include helpful, supportive behaviors more than fighting or avoidance, asking for advice rather than offering criticism, intimate rather than role-governed behaviors, and overt, visible, rather than covert, hidden, behaviors. In addition, Argyle and Henderson (1984) found that privacy was respected and that debts, favors, and compliments were repaid, in the United Kingdom, Japan, North America, Hong Kong, and Italy.

However, relationships are inherently filled with contradictions, or dialectic tensions. That is, friends usually want both independence and interdependence, openness and privacy, and novelty and predictability. Such contradictions are simultaneously present in friendships, and the presence of opposing forces creates change and the potential for dynamic relationships. Communication scholars Leslie Baxter and Barbara Montgomery (1996) explain that taking a dialectical perspective also includes recognition of praxis, wherein individuals are both actors and acted upon by the partner through the totality or full range of dialectic tensions.

A key to interpersonal alliances across cultures is that while all the aforementioned dialectics are present, there is an additional one—in that both partners maintain a mutually satisfying *relational* identity while simultaneously maintaining *divergent cultural* identities. The relational alliance does not mean that distinct cultural identities lose their importance. It may be that friends with different ethnic identities prefer to simultaneously be friends and be culturally different, rather than seek to develop intimacy based on individual or personal selves. This is different from the process described in more traditional models of interpersonal relationship development predicting that the message content and predictions about the other develop from intercultural to intimate (Taylor & Altman, 1987). Given the important dialectic of autonomy and connection, perhaps in intercultural relationships, friends are able to simultaneously be autonomous in their cultural distinctness and be connected in their relationship.

Emergent Issues in Intercultural Alliances

Three broad issues have emerged from past research that I propose may be central to intercultural friendships: power and unearned privilege; acknowledgment of history; and orientations to affirm differences in cultural identities and the importance not only of the relationship but of the "other" as an individual.

Power and Unearned Privilege

Power differences are a salient and ever-present issue for ethnic group members as they negotiate their cultural identities through avowal and ascription processes. Collier & Bowker (1994) concluded that unearned privilege and unstated power were evident in the talk of European American women describing their own and ideal intercultural relationships. This unstated power was identified by women who were classified as ethnic minorities in the United States, who read the responses of the European American women. They observed that European Americans advising all friends to "be open" included a tacit presumption of power. That is, they noted that the "White women risked less with openness than did the women of color or immigrants." These women of

color questioned whether their European American friends *really* wanted them to be open and to voice what they might in the way of anger and rage.

Recognition of power differences is also consistent with acknowledging the dialectic tension between being open and vulnerable and being closed and protected. Understanding how members of intercultural relationships with ethnic, gender, and class differences manage their power issues may help you understand why conflict emerges and why some conflict-management processes may be more competent than others.

Impact of History

In addition to recognizing power differences and unearned privilege, it may also be important for intercultural friends to recognize the impact and relevance of history and past experiences of discrimination. In South Africa, Afrikaners and British both recommended that in order to build relationships with people from diverse race groups, the Blacks in particular were going to have to "forget the past" and "recognize that this is not 1964, Sharpeville, or Soweto, anymore" (Collier & Bornman, in press). In contrast, the Blacks and Coloureds recommended acknowledging the impact of history and apartheid and said, "All people in South Africa live with the results—the legacy of the past." This suggests that the importance of history is seen differently by the relatively powerful and powerless.

Standpoint theory may be very useful in helping us understand how these differing perspectives evolve and affect interpersonal relationships. Standpoint theory points out that by regulating members' experiences, a culture reproduces distinctions (hierarchies) among groups. "Through this process, societies sustain social hierarchies and, with those, distinct standpoints of individuals in different groups" (Wood, 1995, p. 37). For example, the different experiences of Blacks and Whites in South Africa led to clearly different standpoints from which they view the relative importance of history. Another important requirement for intercultural alliances, thus, may be recognizing the standpoints for self and other and the processes through which such standpoints are developed and maintained.

Orientations of Affirmation

A third theme in intercultural alliances is an orientation or type of conduct that demonstrates positive regard. What characterized successful intercultural friendships for the women studied by Collier and Bowker (1994) was the women perceiving an intention to value differences *and* affirm the other person as a member of a culturally different group. Such intentions were often evident in the discourse and were explicitly addressed in requests to be taught about an aspect of the other person's culture, storytelling, historical accounts of experiences, talk about family, or in conflict.

Another example of an orientation to affirm the other's cultural identity can be seen in Latino friends' descriptions of norms of appropriate behavior in their friendships, showing respect for and the desire to learn more about, the other person's ethnic identity (Collier, 1996). One respondent talked about how much he enjoyed spending time with the friend's family: "I go to his house and get to hear his family talk about their country." An African American male respondent said, "He knows that we show respect for our history." A female noted, "She appreciates that we take pride in our roots."

Friends in intercultural alliances also affirm the value of their relationship. Such affirmations occur within the norms of what the two friends consider appropriate for the friendship. Some friends may have more need for privacy or autonomy, and affirming messages may occur less frequently than in other friendships. Such messages may be explicit verbal messages, such as this comment from a Latina: "She tells me I am a good friend." The messages may take the form of nonverbal support, as with as an Asian American friend who said, "We always listen to anything and everything, and show we care" (Collier, 1996).

Sometimes, perceiving an intention to affirm may be strong enough to compensate for conduct that has a negative impact on one of the friends. For example, an African American woman noted that she continued her friendship with a European American woman—even when the European American friend "has no clue about how much privilege she has every day, and why I object when she says something like, 'Doesn't everyone want their kids to get a college education, be president of their own company, and live in a nice house?'" She explained that she maintained the friendship because her European American friend kept "coming back for more" and showing that "she was committed to the friendship and wanted to be able to hear my anger and frustration in being Black in the U.S." (Collier & Bowker, 1994).

Friends are more likely to maintain their friendship when their self-concept as well as the value of the relationship is similarly affirmed. It is also important that this affirmation occurs throughout the history of the relationship. For instance, Planalp (1993) found that friends can be distinguished from acquaintances by their mutual knowledge and their sense of continuity—their ability to refer to their past, to a future together, and to a continuous present.

Wrestling with the issues of power, history, and intention to affirm may help you better understand your friend's points of view and conduct and your own reactions, and may perhaps help you to manage conflict when it arises. Making these issues explicit and talking about them with friends may be ways to show respect for the other person's cultural identities and the contextual factors affecting salience and intensity of avowal, thus increasing the potential that your intercultural friendship will endure.

REFERENCES

Argyle, M., & Henderson, M. (1984). The rules of friendship. *Journal of Personal and Social Relationships, 1,* 211–221.

Banks, J. A. (1987). *Teaching strategies for ethnic studies* (4th ed.). Boston: Allyn & Bacon.

Baxter, L., & Montgomery, B. (1996). *Relating: Dialogues and dialectics.* New York: Guilford Press.

Carbaugh, D. (1990). Intercultural communication. In D. Carbaugh (Ed.), *Cultural communication and intercultural contact* (pp. 151–176). Hillsdale, NJ: Lawrence Erlbaum Associates.

Collier, M. J. (1991). Conflict competence within African, Mexican, and Anglo American friendships. In S. Ting-Toomey & F. Korzenny (Eds.), *Cross-cultural interpersonal communication* (pp. 132–154). Newbury Park, CA: Sage.

Collier, M. J. (1996). Communication competence problematics in ethnic friendships. *Communication Monographs, 63,* 314–336.

Collier, M. J., & Bornman, E. (in press). Intercultural friendships in South Africa: Norms for managing differences. *International Journal of International Relations.*

Collier, M. J., & Bowker, J. (1994, February). *U.S. American women in intercultural friendships.* Paper presented at the Speech Communication Association conference, New Orleans, Louisiana.

Collier, M. J., & Shimizu, M. (1993, May). *Close friendships: A cross-cultural comparison of males and females in Japan and the United States.* Paper presented at the International Communication Association conference, Washington, DC.

Collier, M. J., & Thomas, M. (1988). Identity in intercultural communication: An interpretive perspective. In Y. Kim & W. Gudykunst (Eds.), *Theories of intercultural communication* (pp. 99–120). International and Intercultural Communication Annual, XII. Newbury Park, CA: Sage.

Collier, M. J., Thompson, J., & Weber, D. (1996, November). *Identity problematics among U.S. ethnics.* Paper presented at the Speech Communication Association conference, San Diego, California.

Geertz, C. (1973). *The interpretation of cultures.* New York: Basic Books.

Hecht, M. L., Collier, M. J., & Ribeau, S. (1993). Ethnic identity. In *African American communication* (pp. 59–81, 114–158). Newbury Park, CA: Sage.

Planalp, S. (1993). Friends' and acquaintances' conversations II: Coded differences. *Journal of Social and Personal Relationships, 10,* 339–354.

Schneider, D. (1976). Notes toward a theory of culture. In K. Basso & H. Selby (Eds.), *Meaning in anthropology* (pp. 197–220). Albuquerque: University of New Mexico Press.

Southern Poverty Law Center Report, Vol. 26, Number 1, March 1996. Montgomery, AL.

Tanno, D. (1997). Names, narratives and the evolution of ethnic identity. In A. González, M. Houston, & V. Chen (Eds.), *Our voices* (2nd ed., pp. 28–34). Los Angeles: Roxbury.

Taylor, D., & Altman, I. (1987). Communication in interpersonal relationships: Social penetration processes. In M. Roloff & G. Miller (Eds.), *Interpersonal processes: New directions in communication research* (pp. 257–277). Newbury Park, CA: Sage.

Weider, D. L., & Pratt, S. (1990). On being a recognizable Indian among Indians. In D. Carbaugh (Ed.), *Cultural communication and intercultural contact* (pp. 45–64). Hillsdale, NJ: Lawrence Erlbaum.

Wood, J. (1995). *Relational communication.* Belmont, CA: Wadsworth.

KEY TERMS

intercultural communication	avowal
cultural identity	ascription
friendship	salience of avowal
relationship	intensity of avowal
alliance	standpoint theory

DISCUSSION QUESTIONS

1. What are examples of defining culture as place, as a predictor of communication conduct, and as a system of discourse? What are strengths and weaknesses of each approach?

2. Why is it important to talk about involuntary aspects of membership in groups based on race, sex, nationality, and ethnicity? How might you respond to someone who argues, "Why don't we treat each person we meet as a unique individual, and do away with these kinds of group categories?"

3. How can you apply the properties of cultural identity outlined in the essay to your own intercultural friendships? How can discussing such processes as avowal and ascription, having multiple identities, or differences in salience and intensity help friends understand each other and perhaps manage conflict differently?

4. How do you know when an intercultural friendship is an interpersonal alliance? How do intercultural allies manage the dialectical tensions in

their friendship? For instance, when and how should allies explicitly talk about differences or prejudices or historical oppression?

5. To what extent do you agree that giving attention to the three issues of power, history, and intention to affirm can improve intercultural friendships? Specifically, how might friends demonstrate their intention to affirm each other as an individual, a person with a different cultural identity that is valuable to know, and the salience of the friendship?

39
"WAITING FOR LIGHTNING TO STRIKE": SOCIAL SUPPORT FOR INTERRACIAL COUPLES

MELANIE PAYNE

As I walked to the student union one day, I overheard two women suck their teeth and loudly state, "Umm, they must have jungle fever." Curious, I turned to see whom they were talking about and quickly realized that they were referring to an interracial couple walking hand in hand into the union. "Jungle fever," or a state of mind brought on by intense heat that causes a person to do something driven purely by delirium, is a term often used to describe romantic relationships between Black and White[1] people, with the jungle being the figurative African American "heritage," and the fever being the only rational explanation for why these two people are together. This term has been bantered around the African American community as a descriptor for interracial relationships, as seen in Spike Lee's movie *Jungle Fever*. Inherent in this notion is an underlying feeling that these relationships are not natural or normal and should not even be tolerated. Yet, interracial coupling persists, with increasing numbers of people getting married to those outside of their own racial and ethnic heritage.

Social support, or the support provided by friends and family, seems to be important in most couples' relationships. In fact, research suggests that social support is one of the key factors that will determine whether or not a relationship will last. On the other hand, the lack of social support or the negative interference of friends and family often leads to disastrous consequences for couples. These outside circles of friends, family, and acquaintances have a decided effect on our perception of self, of others, and of our relationships.

Questions are raised when you start to consider how social support may be different for intercultural relationships. Not all friends and families express support in the same fashion, and different cultures look at support in a variety of ways. Since all cultures have norms about who we are to date and marry, is one type of social support even suitable when looking at different types of relationships? This essay examines the role of social support for one kind of intercultural relationship—interracial couples. But first, let's describe characteristics of interracial relationships, and then look at the importance of social support.

Interracial Relationships

"Of the various couplings . . . the world at large likes this kind the least . . ." (Rosenblatt, Karis, & Powell, 1995, p. 121). The quote refers to an interracial relationship, a union between a White person and a Black person. Imagine the strain on people just knowing that the choice they made in their relationship is considered socially unacceptable. It is not enough that couples must answer to their respective friends, families, and partners about their choice in mates, but they must also answer to a hypocritical society—a society that speaks in terms of freedom of speech and freedom of choice yet still clings to stereotypes and belief systems that make it uncomfortable to exercise such freedoms.

Keeping in mind that the United States had laws against racial intermarriage up until 1967,[2] most of the research in the area of interracial relationships has focused on actual occurrence, attitudes about interracial relationships, motivations of individual partners, and overall societal acceptance of these relationships (Aldridge, 1978; Pascoe, 1991). By and large, the majority of the research has been attitudinal based, meaning that researchers were interested in the attitudes of one group of people about the other, especially when it came to dating and marriage. Researchers were interested in how immigrants, for example, were assimilating into the larger American culture, giving up their native language and ways of doing things while replacing them with American ways. If a particular ethnic or racial group was at the stage of intermarriage into a larger "Americanized" group, that was the mark of their assimilation. At the time, the researchers were not interested in what was introduced by the "ethnic" partner to the marriage, or in how the marriage was received by each partner's family and friends.

Why do people enter into interracial relationships? One researcher, Jeanette Davidson, reviewed at least 60 years of existing research focused on interracial relationships and discovered six reasons "why" researchers believe people date interracially: (1) social or economic mobility for the Black partner, (2) rebellion against the family (or society) on the part of the White partner, (3) mental illness of the White partner, (4) sexual curiosity of both parties, (5) "hostile" preoccupation of White women by Black men, and (6) exhibitionism, or showing off by both parties (Aldridge, 1978; Davidson, 1991). What this review suggests is that the researchers Davidson highlights relied more heavily on stereotypes, faulty thinking, and prejudice rather than on an objective look at why these couples have come together. Davidson clearly shows that these researchers never considered supporting interracial relationships: their reasons "why" illustrate that there must be something "wrong" with these individuals, that they cannot possibly be "just in love."

Interracial marriages are on the rise, and currently there appears to be a tide of goodwill in gaining acceptance of such relationships. However, it is extremely important to understand that on the whole these relationships meet with disapproval from society at large. For instance, couples in one study report familial and social disapproval, everything from lack of understanding to lack of recognition that the partner is even in the room, to disownership for letting the family down (Rosenblatt et al., 1995). Because of this general tendency in society and within families, one of the biggest complaints stated by couples in interracial unions is that they feel detached from their friends and families (Brown, 1989). In fact, "interracial marriages are often plagued by patterns of secrecy and relative familial isolation established during the courtship" (Brown, 1989, p. 35). Too afraid to face their families and too in love to end the relationship, interracial couples are forced into a corner with no easy exit. Do they distance themselves from the partners they love, or do they distance themselves from the families? To understand the depth of this question, let's consider the possible role that social support has in our lives.

Social Support in Relational Development

An old cliche says that a chain is only as strong as its weakest link. The same holds true for a relationship. Without the strength of social support from family and friends, the couple's link to the social world, a relationship grows fragile and eventually breaks. The strength of the support network is often evident in the strength of the relationship. "Social support refers to verbal and nonverbal communication between recipients and providers that reduces uncertainty about the situation, the self, the other, or the relationship, and functions to enhance a perception of personal control in one's life experience" (Albrecht & Adelman, 1987, p. 19). This link serves to bring the couple together, keep them together, or help them break apart.

In the Beginning . . .

Social support is usually viewed in the context of close, intimate relationships. Within the confines of a close relationship, the size of the social support network either grows or shrinks, dependent upon the stage of the relationship. In other words, in the beginning of a relationship, the partners have individual support, but as the couple grows closer, the support network expands to encompass both families and both sets of friends. George Levinger (1980) proposes a model of "pair relatedness" that describes how relationships develop with respect to social networks. In the first stage, two people are aware of each other but are relatively unaffected by each other. This stage may be similar to attraction or even mate selection "where one person judges the other without the second person's awareness" (p. 513).

As the relational dance continues, the pair grows closer to each other. In Levinger's model, this second stage is represented by a slight overlap of two circles, indicating initial interactions between two people or even repeated interactions, such as those on an acquaintance level. Social support becomes crucial to the formation of the couple at this dating stage. For example, friends and family react to the couple, inviting them together to functions, asking about a partner who is absent, thinking of them together and ensuring that they *are* together (Lewis, 1973). This may help to "push" an uncertain couple together. How we choose to view our self and our relationships is dependent upon the type of support we receive from others in our network. If your family and friends believe that the person you brought home is ideal, for instance, you may begin to view that person as such, especially when your mind was not made up in the first place (Parks & Adelman, 1983).

Maintaining the Relationship

As the relationship continues and the interactions become increasingly personal and unique, the pair enters into the third and final level of

"pair relatedness." This level includes "mutuality" where the overlapping circles, representative of two people coming together, indicate interdependence. This overlap clearly draws a path to transitivity. Transitivity allows that if Fred likes Susie, and Susie likes Jane, then Fred will either like Jane as well, or will learn to like Jane because he likes Susie (Parks, Stan, & Eggert, 1983). This model is fundamental to social network involvement. If a romantic couple has reached the third level in Levinger's degrees of closeness and are truly interdependent, they become more involved with each other's social support network. The more involved they become with one another, the closer they are to the network and so on.

The circle of social support becomes increasingly clear. The more involved we are in relationships, the more involved we are with the social network, leading to higher involvement in the relationship (Parks et al., 1983). In other words, as a couple becomes closer, they become closer to each other's friends and families, which makes the couple even closer. Moreover, social networks not only keep people close, they act as a barrier against relational dissolution. This barrier implicitly ensures that a couple will stay together, as fear of life outside the network may keep individuals from leaving the union.

Maintaining a relationship is clearly easier with social support. With the help of interdependence, barriers, and transitivity, couples with strong social support networks report stronger relationships (Kim & Stiff, 1991). For same-race couples, such strong support may lead to relational commitment, whereas interracial couples with inadequate support may be on the road to relational dissolution.

Relational Commitment or Dissolution

If positive support leads to positive relationships, then negative support or its extreme form, interference, should lead to an eventual breakup. One study shows specifically how interference from a social network can lead to relational dissolution. Statements such as "perhaps you should spend less time with your partner, X" and so on from support networks increase as it becomes clear that the couple is moving away from the larger network. In fact, the greater the negative interference is from family, the more likely the relationship will not last (Johnson & Milardo, 1984).

We can see how interference can quickly become opposition in interracial relationships because family and friends are more likely to disapprove from the beginning. However, this interference and opposition may backfire—the "Romeo and Juliet effect." This effect states that couples, particularly interracial, stay together *because* of the disapproval and interference of their support network. Motivated by the negative support, the couples stay together, perhaps out of anger, rebellion, or other familial problems. Although research provides little support for this effect, the myth of Romeo and Juliet still drives a great deal of thought when it comes to interracial couples.

Social support from friends and family is crucial to developing and maintaining intimate relationships. However, there seems to be little support for interracial couples in today's society. Furthermore, the current understanding of social support is not geared to interracial couples, or to any type of intercultural relationships for that matter. The theory of social support is based only on same-race couples and makes no mention of social or historical aspects of support. So, we are left to wonder how interracial couples seek and receive support. Do they utilize traditional social support networks, melding their individual support into a larger, combined network, or do they create a new one that supports their differing needs? Finally, what role does social support play in identity formation, couple formation and dissolution, and opposition? These questions, left unanswered by current research, are discussed in the remainder of this essay. Based on personal experience, research, and observation, I discuss how interracial couples deal with support in this racially aware and racially tense time.

Society as a Constant Couple Member[3]

The word "couple" means two: two people, two partners, and in the case of interracial couples, two cultures. Within interracial unions there is often another member, sometimes silent, sometimes outspoken—society at large. Few same-race couples would consider "society" as a member of their network or a force in their relationship. However, for interracial couples, this figurative third wheel communicates, reacts, and interacts with a couple just as the two partners relate with one another. This member, be it from the Black community, the White community, or both, is a part of the couple's existence. The consistent and often negative societal intrusions affect actions, movements, and choices for the interracial couple.

Communication is vital for any relationship. This also holds true for the relationship that interracial couples have with society at large. Society sends a variety of messages, but three seem consistent among the people I spoke with: verbal de-coupling messages, nonverbal de-coupling messages, and messages about how involved members of the interracial couple should be within their communities.

Verbal and Nonverbal De-coupling Messages

Society has a tendency to react to interracial couples in a negative fashion. This reaction can be simple, commonplace, and often overlooked. Christopher describes how these reactions can be bothersome and tiring:

> Some of the things that you get are . . . in a store together or something and they will ask her if she needs help and then they will ask me. We'll say we're together and then there is a pause, the shock "Oh." That's, you know, little things, but it's there. If we were the same race, that wouldn't be an issue, they wouldn't question both of us. . . . At a bank, we walk up to the teller together, obviously we are together, there's no need to say "Can I help you next." It's things like that. And we just get looks and some people look and you can see that disapproving look or whatever. Nothing really, no comments or anything. But sometimes that's worse than . . . "If you are thinking it why don't you go ahead and say it?" But usually it's really subtle.

For this narrative, Christopher mentions two reactions, a verbal and a nonverbal one. The verbal reaction is of course the "de-coupling" that he and his wife experience when they run errands together. The societal member does not see Christopher and Jill as a couple. One might expect that as a member of a social network, society would always assume that couples like Jill and Christopher are together rather than display the shock followed by the embarrassed "Oh." This de-coupling is difficult to interpret for it may be a simple mistake or a blatant disregard for the possibility of an interracial union. Christopher prefers to interpret the reaction as the latter, stating that if they were of the same race, their togetherness "wouldn't be an issue."

Another type of de-coupling message is the nonverbal stares that Christopher mentions. Other interracial couples consider furtive glimpses, curious faces, and nasty glances par for the course. Christopher, however, sees them as a silent, cowardly reaction to his union, that these people do not have the dignity to state what is on their mind. He says that somehow these stares are "worse" than the verbal reactions offered by sales clerks and bank tellers.

De-coupling is not the only societal response. Messages from the "community" often indicate the level of involvement it wishes to have with the couple, communicating what they think about that union. When I asked Michael about the "African-American" things he does with his wife, he described how the community relates to them:

> You know, not much, and the reason is that I have had such negative feedback from the Black community that I don't think that would be wise. There would be times that she may have suggested it, and I sorta downplayed it. . . . I came to the realization that it was really a square peg in a round hole situation. After a few months of trying to fit in, I decided that it wasn't my thing.

The Black community in Michael's case has let him know that he and his White wife do not "fit in." It has also stipulated to some extent that there may be consequences if Michael were to push this issue with the community, as he states that it "would not be wise" to do so. Of course, he neither spells out what would happen if he were to participate more fully in the community nor indicates what type of response he has to this "negative feedback" other than avoidance. Nevertheless, Michael interprets this to mean that he no longer

belongs in the Black community because of his choice in partners, or as he says, "the square peg in the round hole."

Interracial couples view their relationships as interacting with society, be it avoiding stares, clarifying togetherness, or heeding messages about involvement. This invisible yet constant member figures more prominently in this network. More research needs to be done in this area because this "third wheel" may have more to do with making or breaking a relationship than previously thought.

Interference

Under the guise of "helping," couples (interracial and otherwise) are often faced with a support network that is insistent upon interfering in their lives. A theory suggested by Johnson and Milardo (1984) discusses the influence such involvement by family and friends has on relational commitment or dissolution. By interfering in relationships, support networks attempt to coerce couples to change some part of their relationship. The act of interference can be as simple as offering statements of disapproval or as complex as actually physically interfering, such as keeping a couple separated. The notion of interference becomes a serious and explicit threat to the survival of interracial couples. The network uses fears, stereotypes, and faulty constructions of race and gender to explain its feelings, in hopes that it can change the mind of the "deviant" friend or child. These intrusions happen at all levels of relational growth and continue to happen even after marriage, as the following examples will illustrate.

Helpful advice is the most frequently used tool for interference. The interference is subtle, attempting to cast doubt on the validity of the relationship more so than actually breaking up the union. Nevertheless, interracial couples are often plagued by "free" advice that is primarily based on outdated, stereotypical constructions of others, as Michael's narrative illustrates:

> He was trying to convince me that ahh, I think that he was trying not to get too personal, but to make his point which was that white women are nothing but trouble. Umm . . . that was the

basic thrust of his argument and different ways of saying they were trouble, they were trouble financially, they were greedy, they were trouble emotionally because they were somehow overly delicate emotionally. He had a number of ways he thought they were trouble and he was very upset that I had ever dated them.

The depiction of this "white lily," or the belief that White women are "delicate" and "emotional," is a construction of femininity created during the height of slavery. This type of interference can be more damaging because its logic is faulty. Rather than suggesting that they are not well suited for each other on a social, spiritual, or intellectual level, Michael's friend suggests that Michael and Catherine are poorly suited on a race-based level. The underlying implication of interference such as this is that "Black men marrying White women are weak." As his acquaintance suggests, a strong Black man would not tolerate the delicacy, the temperament, or the trouble that White women cause.

Another strategy of interference is the use of persuasion. Casting doubt on personal decisions and playing on fears is an effective way to keep a couple separated and perhaps influence them that they made the wrong decision. Jill describes the time when she was heavily persuaded to stay home by her family:

> Yeah, they were trying to keep me home when I went home for my dad's funeral. My brother said, "Why don't you stay a month and think about what you are going to do?" . . . They said "Why don't you stay home for a month? You know, you're not really making any headway back there." . . . It was almost as if I was a prisoner . . .

By suggesting that she was not making any headway, implying that she was better off at home, the interference was a way to keep the couple physically separated, encouraging eventual dissolution. According to the interference theory, negative influence provided by the family is the most powerful (Johnson & Milardo, 1984). By keeping Jill from seeing Christopher, the family was in fact holding her "prisoner" under the

auspices of helping her. This forced Jill to eventually make a difficult decision, placing her needs over those of her family:

> Then I realized that I was being held prisoner and said to my mother, "No way. . . . this is for the birds." Even if I am totally isolated from the family, I am still moving back because that is where I live.

Interference happens to many couples, usually in the middle of their relationship when the individuals are still deciding whether or not to commit to their partners. Although not unique, the role that interference takes is somewhat different for interracial couples. Instead of hearing negative support suggestions such as "Spend less time with X," couples may be faced with more insidious interference based in outdated stereotypes, fears, and coercion. Their battle becomes one of independence from the network as well as resistance to the messages the network is sending. If social support theory understood the context interference for interracial couples more clearly, the theory itself could prove more useful to these couples.

Creation

Whereas interference may be a negative aspect to being involved within an interracial union, the ability to create may be a more positive aspect. Faced with support networks that include society as a third wheel, family and friends that may or may not understand the uniqueness of the union, interracial couples have had to adapt and create a support network that works best for them. This creation is obviously one of the strengths of the unions.

Once the couple has reached the level of interdependence, social support theory holds that their individual network decreases in size, while the mutual network grows (Milardo, 1982). Interracial couples are much more selective about how the mutual network grows. Choosing friends becomes an act of adaptation for them because the better the network, the better the support. As Michael points out, any possible problems are best dealt with as the relationship grows: "There were those peripheral friends that were kinda iffy [about interracial couples] that we dropped as we went along." Rather than cling to the network as it stood, Michael and Catherine cleaned house and ended relationships with people who were not supportive.

Following in this same vein, another way that interracial couples create supportive networks is to use the "interracial" aspect of their union as a litmus test to determine membership in the network. Making membership closed, they gauge how people will respond to their union and make friends on that basis.

> No, umm, like I said before, I have had people insinuate things about me and tell me about their disapproval of the relationship, but it didn't make me reconsider the relationship, it made me reconsider my affiliation with those people.

By dropping any possible "dissenters" before they became a problem, Catherine and Michael create a more effective and supportive network. This may help to prevent any possible external pressures, such as people who would have suggested ending the relationship. Moreover, it drew a clear line between those who were inside and those who were outside of their social network.

While Catherine and Michael were quietly creating a network that would work for them, Kay was confronting her family and developing her network based on ultimatum:

> If you have a problem with anything that I do, then you remove yourself from life. . . . If you just can't accept it, then accept the fact that I will no longer consider you a part of my family, I will no longer consider you a part of my family network.

Here, Kay is creating a very definitive family network. By confronting members in her family who "love and support her," she is asking for that love and support to be extended to her partner. Should that member be unwilling, Kay will simply remove him or her from her network. While confrontational, Kay is creating her network in much the same way as Michael and Catherine. She goes

on to say that "we have enough problems from the outside world that we don't need internal conflict." It is vital to her that all the members of the network be up front and communicate to her whether they support her.

The couples I spoke with suggest that they surround themselves with like-minded people, end relationships with those they are not sure of, and completely cut off those that do not pass the test of acceptance to their satisfaction. This may limit the size of their network more severely than it would that of a same-race couple. It might also alienate the interracial couple from important support givers such as family.

From there, the couples were not clear on how they related to their networks. By so strongly limiting who was allowed to be in the networks, it would stand to reason that interracial couples at some point turn to their customized social support and rely on it in much the same way as do same-race couples. Nevertheless, the couples interviewed adapted to the strain placed on them and managed to survive. Their ability to create a system that works for them is clearly a small triumph for the successful couple that may distinguish them from interracial couples that did not survive.

Discussion

As I stood outside the union, watching these two women make loud and degrading judgments about that couple, I was appalled. Not because it is the "right" reaction to have after such a comment, but because I pictured my boyfriend and me walking in the same manner and receiving the same, unsolicited feedback. I began to wonder whether or not that comment was really what people thought about me and my partner—was I sick with the fever? What does all of this *mean*?

As I started this research, I tossed aside the notion of a "color-blind" society I had so quickly bought into as a child. There are colors, and there are boundaries. Should you cross them, you risk everything from public embarrassment to disconnection from what you previously believed to be your loving friends and family, to actual physical harm. Notice that I said *risk*—it is, at some level, risky to be in an interracial relationship. As Catherine, Michael's wife, stated, her experience being in an interracial relationship was often like "waiting for lightning to strike." It's statistically possible, but you cannot put your life on hold waiting for the lightning.

Nevertheless, being in an interracial couple has its benefits. I am able to learn about my partner's culture as he learns about mine. I am offered another viewpoint on the world, because the world seen through his eyes is drastically different from the world I look at every day. Finally, I am offered some small amount of satisfaction knowing that we work every day to understand each other in the context of our own culture—and if we can communicate, maybe there is still hope for society at large.

My preliminary research suggests that to some extent, success for the interracial couple is based not on a strong network, but on strong individuals. To weather the storm of disapproval, both publicly and privately, most couples seem to emerge unscathed. This may be part adaptation and part denial on their part, but many interracial couples make it work.

There seems to be some similarity between how same-race couples and interracial couples relate to their social support. They are both dependent to some extent on the vital support offered in relational development and maintenance. However, the steps taken to get to that point are completely different and are sometimes contrary to what social support theory suggests. This contrary finding leads me to question this theory, as it obviously never considered any type of diverse relationship. This theory leads us to believe that it represents all couples rather than a select few. As researchers, it is important that we challenge this inclusiveness and start to understand people within their own context. Only then will we discover a more encompassing and dynamic explanation of interracial couples, beyond the whys and the hows.

Interracial couples deserve to be heard and should be celebrated for finding a way to overcome personal and socially constructed differences. As I said earlier, I consider interracial couples to be the very model of effective intercultural communication, for two cultures have come together into one relationship. Only the relationship that makes room for both cultures and experiences will survive and flourish.

NOTES

1. For the purposes of this paper, "Black" refers to those from an African American ancestry, and "White" refers to those of European American ancestry.

2. "Laws in sixteen states still forbade interracial marriage until 1967, when the Supreme Court ruled that such laws were unconstitutional" (Davidson, 1991, p. 14).

3. Some of these observations were based on personal experience as well as interviews with three interracial couples as a part of a course research project in spring 1996.

REFERENCES

Albrecht, T., & Adelman, M. (1987). *Communicating social support*. Newbury Park, CA: Sage.

Aldridge, D. (1978). Interracial marriages: Empirical and theoretical considerations. *Journal of Black Studies, 8*, 355–368.

Brown, P. (1989). Black-White interracial marriages: A historical analysis. *Journal of Intergroup Relations, 16*, 26–36.

Davidson, J. (1991). Black-White interracial marriage: A critical look at theories about motivations of the partners. *Journal of Intergroup Relations, 18*, 14–20.

Davidson, J., & Schneider, L. (1992). Acceptance of Black-White interracial marriage. *Journal of Intergroup Relations, 19*, 47–52.

Johnson, M., & Milardo, R. (1984). Network interference in pair relationships: A social psychological recasting of Slater's theory of social regression. *Journal of Marriage and the Family, 46*, 893–899.

Kim, H., & Stiff, J. (1991). Social networks and development of close relationships. *Human Communication Research, 18*, 70–91.

Levinger, G. (1980). Toward the analysis of close relationships. *Journal of Experimental Social Psychology, 16*, 510–544.

Lewis, R. (1973). Social reaction and the formulation of dyads: An interactionist's approach to mate selection. *Sociometry, 36*, 409–418.

Milardo, R. (1982). Friendship networks in developing relationships: Converging and diverging social environments. *Social Psychology Quarterly, 45,* 162–172.

Parks, M., & Adelman, M. (1983). Communication networks and the development of romantic relationships: An expansion of Uncertainty Reduction Theory. *Human Communication Research, 10,* 55–78.

Parks, M., Stan, C., & Eggert, L. (1983). Romantic involvement and social network involvement. *Social Psychology Quarterly, 46,* 116–131.

Pascoe, P. (1991). Race, gender, and intercultural relations: The case of interracial marriage. *Frontiers, 12,* 5–18.

Rosenblatt, P., Karis, T., & Powell, R. (1995). *Multiracial couples: Black and White voices.* Thousand Oaks, CA: Sage.

Spigner, C. (1990). Black/white interracial marriages: A brief overview of U.S. Census data, 1980–1987. *Western Journal of Black Studies, 14,* 214–216.

KEY TERMS

interracial couples   jungle fever
social support   de-coupling message
social networks   interference
stereotypes

DISCUSSION QUESTIONS

1. Payne discusses the tension interracial couples feel between pleasing their families and pleasing their partners. In what way, if at all, have you experienced this same type of tension? How did you react to it?

2. How does social support theory fall short in explaining a successful interracial relationship? How is the theory adequate?

3. What types of norms have you been taught about dating and marriage? How would your family and friends react if you broke those norms and dated someone outside your religion, race, ethnicity, age, or class?

4. Payne suggests that social support theory should be more context based. What is she referring to?

5. Examine the history of race relations between Whites and Blacks in this country to understand the six reasons "why" researchers believe couples become involved interracially. What stereotypes are these reasons based upon?

40
PERFORMING COMMITMENT

JACQUELINE TAYLOR

I grew up in a small Southern town, where I lived right smack next door to the large Baptist church my daddy pastored. Although the role of preacher's daughter was often trying, one advantage was that I was almost always invited to any wedding my father performed. As a result, I became something of a professional wedding guest.

Saturday afternoons often found me racing around the church parking lot on my second-hand green Huffy bicycle. Moments before the music was scheduled to begin, I clattered into the parsonage to exchange Keds, shorts, and shirt for my Sunday best. As the first organ notes began to sound, I settled myself in the front row of the church balcony, leaning perilously over the rail to scrutinize the flowers, the guests, the ushers, the music, at last the bridesmaids, and then finally, climactically, the bride. My father stood facing the important couple and intoned the words that transformed them mysteriously and abruptly from two separate people into one flesh. The power to transform was vested in him by church and state. "I now pronounce you husband and wife," he would say, and the ceremony was complete.[1] The bride and groom kissed, and the happy sounds of the recessional burst from the organ pipes.

I drank in all this lovely, lavish ritual from my aerial perch, evaluating each facet of the performance, dreaming myself into the starring role. After the ceremony, I headed to the basement of the church to partake of the typical Baptist wedding reception fare: gooey white cake, salted nuts, pastel mints, and sweet, oh-so-sweet punch laced with nothing stronger than ginger ale.

If the day was sunny, I sometimes grabbed my cake and nuts and ran. But if the weather was bad or the bride was especially beautiful, I stayed until the uncontested star of this extravaganza had changed into her "going-away outfit" and run hand in hand with the groom down the steps of the church toward a car fitted with tin cans, signs, and streamers. We untied the ribbons on our little satin packets of rice and pelted the lucky pair as they shrieked and giggled past us. We Baptists didn't recognize the ritual shower of rice as an invocation of the favors of an ancient fertility goddess who would bless their union with children; we just found it good fun and unquestioned custom to rain rice on the giddy couple.

I'm 35 years away from that preadolescent girl who leaned over the balcony rail to watch wedding after wedding. But I got another glimpse of her a few years ago during a visit with my parents. My daughters, Lucy and Grace, began complaining of the lack of toys. From the top shelf of a bedroom closet, I pulled down a small, round, yellow suitcase. I flipped the catch with a satisfying snap that recalled to me the hundreds of times I had

opened this case as a child. Inside was Charlene, my Miss Revlon doll, a 1950s precursor to Barbie. She rested on the vast wardrobe lovingly sewn for her by Grandmama and Aunt Clarice. As I began to unpack my doll, Lucy's and Gracie's wide dark eyes grew wider and darker. Grace began to brush Charlene's gorgeously flipped red hair, while Lucy combined lounging pajamas and a lace stole in a one-of-a-kind outfit. The doll wardrobe included evening gowns, dresses, purse, heels, coats, jeans, hats, nylons, bra, girdle, petticoats—in short, everything a well-dressed young woman of those days would require. Most particularly, she had not one but two wedding gowns. Grandmama had made her a white voile summer gown, trimmed in lace. From Aunt Clarice she had a full-skirted satin gown for winter. Both gowns included veils.

At the bottom of the case we found Tom, the only male doll near enough Charlene's size to make a suitable groom. I remembered it all. Obsessed with weddings and wedding plans, I determined to make Charlene a bride. Tom came from the dime store dressed in a gray jumpsuit of the sort garage mechanics wore. With his painted-on hair and too-large head, Tom was not the same calibre doll Charlene was, but the groom was only a minor player in these events, anyway. Aunt Clarice was enlisted to sew him a black suit. We couldn't find shoes to fit him, so we covered his feet in black tape. My sister and two friends were invited for the event. We procured or improvised flowers, cake, punch. I probably preached.[2] In any case, the bride and groom dressed up, said "I do," and then changed into their "going-away clothes" and headed off for a honeymoon.

Of course, a girl wouldn't have to grow up as the preacher's daughter in order to develop an acute interest in weddings. Growing up female in this culture is sufficient to produce this common preoccupation. But the frequency with which I at-

---

[1] In the fifties and sixties, when I was watching all these weddings, most wedding ceremonies used the language "man and wife." My father, then and now unlikely to be identified as a feminist, was nevertheless more thoughtful than most of his contemporaries about male and female roles. He used the language "husband and wife" because he wished to stress the equality of the marriage partners. Indeed, his boiler-plate language for wedding ceremonies talked about God's creation of Eve from Adam's rib: "from under his arm, that she might be protected by him, from out of his side, that she might be equal to him, and from near his heart, that she might be loved by him."

[2] I have written elsewhere about my gradual discovery of the extent to which I have come, as an adult, to emulate my preacher father. My text, of course, is somewhat different from his, but even these essays function as a variation on testimony that we Baptists were encouraged to practice. See "On Being an Exemplary Lesbian: My Life as a Role Model," unpublished essay and performance piece.

tended wedding ceremonies and the role my father played in the marrying gave me frequent cause for reflection on the nature and meaning of this ritual.

Weddings as Rituals

Cultural anthropologists direct our attention to the ways in which weddings reinforce the traditional social ties between individuals. A wedding is not simply a celebration. Through this event the actual status and relationship of the couple within the community is altered. The participation of family and friends enacts their investment in the success of the relationship. Community ties and beliefs and cultural values are communicated and solidified. Clifford Geertz (1973, pp. 168–169) reminds us that the ritual does not always merely replicate and reinforce the cultural structure. Particularly at times of social change or at points of intercultural contact and influence, rituals can reveal tensions between the cultural framework of meaning and the patterning of social interaction.

Put simply, the variations from the traditional script in the performance of wedding ceremonies may highlight the disparity between convention and actual social practice. Such rituals employ a range of communicative acts to both strengthen the social structure of the community and perform the evolution of that social structure. Often, through the highly symbolic communication that characterizes weddings, the couple engages in a process of identity negotiation. Bride and groom may come from different cultural backgrounds. Or marriage partners may stake out a cultural terrain that differs from either family's traditional practices. Ting-Toomey (1993) defines effective identity negotiation as "the smooth coordination between interactants concerning salient identity issues, and the process of engaging in responsive identity confirmation and positive identity enhancement" (p. 73). This process of effective identity negotiation within novel communication episodes is essential to Ting-Toomey's definition of intercultural communication competence. Because each couple desires to put their own stamp on this familiar ritual, each wedding is both familiar and novel. Richard Schechner (1985,

p. 120) draws our attention to the way ritual performances engage in a continuous process of rejecting and replacing. The wedding becomes interesting not only because of the mastery with which a familiar cultural script is performed, a mastery that reveals communicative competence, but also because of the ways in which the familiar script is altered. These alterations may, as we shall see below, communicate intercultural conflict and cultural transformation.

Negotiating Identity Within the Context of Ritual

I married for the first time in 1970, at the age of 19, on a Saturday morning in August. (The time was 10:30. It was important to have the wedding on the half hour, so the hands of the clock would be headed up rather than down.) The antimaterialist and antitraditionalist impulses abroad in the land in 1970 influenced the plans for what my young man and I intended as a simple wedding. The voile dress I wore was one my mother-in-law-to-be and I made ourselves. My sister was my only attendant. We sewed her long skirt and peasant blouse. I insisted on decorating with and carrying wildflowers—Queen Anne's lace, daisies, black-eyed Susan's, baby's breath—picked and arranged by my mother and me. We wrote our own vows, which I no longer remember, and no one gave me away. I took my husband's name. The church was packed.

Each choice was freighted with meaning and symbolic value. Family and friends from near and far assembled to participate in this ritual that marked my passage from girl to woman and our passage as a couple from private sweethearts to public kin. Unfortunately, the passage was rocky. Before our third anniversary, we were divorced.

A full decade went by and my second marriage began with hope and promises and ended in divorce before I came to understand that no man would ever fill the empty place in my heart. Raised within a culture of compulsory heterosexuality and primed with images of wedding ceremonies that led inevitably into happily ever after, I have a heart that yearns toward women. All those sleeping princesses in the fairytales of my childhood made sense to me at last when the touch of a woman awakened me to a dimension of life that I had thought existed only in dreams.

Crossing Cultures

For over 13 years I have created family within the context of my commitment to Carol, my partner and longtime companion. The law says we are not a couple, but two single women. No church or state has blessed or ratified our union. Although our property and our finances are by this time as entwined as our hearts and lives, the state does not apply its joint-property laws to us or give us the right to inherit from each other in the absence of a will. I cannot include her on the family insurance benefits my university offers. The only place we can purchase a family membership is at the women's bookstore.

Eight years ago we became mothers together, with the adoption of our first daughter, Lucy. One year later we adopted Grace. The law recognized us not as one family, but as two—two single mothers living in the same house with our two adopted children. No blood ties unite any of the four of us. We are a family not because but in spite of the social and legal structures that refuse to name us so. Because our status as a family has been ignored or denied by the laws and customs of our society, our existence as a family can never be taken for granted but must be constantly created and recreated. That our family differs in some significant ways from conventional notions of what constitutes a family means that our creation of family must simultaneously affirm and critique familial structures.

Although the field of intercultural communication has given scant attention to gay culture (see Majors, 1994, for an exception), Martin (1993) argues that "the notion of culture needs to be extended . . . beyond national culture" (p. 28). When gay men and lesbians break cultural norms in their communicative practices, they do so not because of a lack of communicative competence but because the dominant communicative practices erase or deny the existence of gay people. So what happens to the performance of commitment when the family operates outside the legal and social definitions of family? And what happens to intercultural communication when the culture where one finds oneself most at home is not the culture of origin? (Most gay men and lesbians grow up in heterosexual families, sometimes experiencing a substantial degree of alienation in contexts that are quite literally familiar.) In what follows, I describe some of the strategies our family has developed to communicate our commitment and connection and the contexts within which we perform this commitment.

Identity Negotiation Within the Wedding Ritual

Because the dominant culture defines marriage as necessarily heterosexual, gay and lesbian weddings become an important site for the negotiation of identity. Gay and lesbian couples create commitment ceremonies both within and against the grain of the wedding ceremonies that sanctify and legitimate heterosexual unions. Our ceremonies become engaged in the continuous process Schechner (1985) identified as rejection and replacement of these more familiar, and certainly more public, spectacles of heterosexual privilege.

Gay and lesbian weddings have become increasingly common in the nineties. Common enough, in fact, that a 1996 episode of the situation comedy *Friends* portrayed a lesbian wedding. They were almost unheard of in 1985, when Carol and I moved in together. We were already in a committed relationship by the time we set up housekeeping. Living together signified a deeper commitment to our shared life; we wanted to mark this passage with a celebration. We decided to throw ourselves a party.

The party mimicked a wedding reception. We issued weddinglike invitations announcing the "marriage of our addresses" and inviting the recipients to a party in celebration of this union. We followed the Baptist traditions of my youth by having a three-tiered cake, pastel mints, salted nuts, and a guest register, but we also served a catered buffet (my tastes had gone uptown, or at least upstairs, since the basement wedding receptions of my youth). Yet, in our mimicking of tradition, the cultural critique appeared, for the cake was topped by two brides rather than the traditional heterosexual pair.

The question of what to wear occupied a good deal of our attention. The choices we made signaled our connections both to traditional wedding celebrations and to our lesbian community. We also used clothing to reveal the playful approach we took to the whole event. We wore tuxedo shirts, bow ties, and casual pants (one pair black, the other pink). One of us donned high-top sneakers; the other wore black flats and lace socks.

On the appointed day our friend Diane arrived early, wearing a pair of white tennis shoes and an aqua chiffon mother-of-the-bride number she had found at the nearby Goodwill. She played the piano for the event. A lush rendition of "Feelings" had Carol and me whirling around the living room in our best version of the happy couple's first dance. Lesbian friends, work friends, my sister, and one of Carol's sisters ate and drank and celebrated together for hours.

Our "marriage of addresses" party was both a thoroughly camp send-up of wedding receptions and a public performance of the commitment Carol and I so deeply felt. The structure of the party allowed us to make the reference to heterosexual ceremonies explicit while its tongue-in-cheek tone provided us with a technique for distancing ourselves in some ways from the very ritual we were invoking. The differences between our "ceremony" and heterosexual rituals became as telling as the similarities. The fundamental difference, of course, was that the party celebrated the union of two women rather than a man and a woman, a union the state refuses to acknowledge. Perhaps the staging of a reception that was its own reason for being rather than a postceremony party was the most significant variation of all. The event was an allusion to our permanent commitment, but that commitment was deliberately not spelled out or defined in permanent terms.

If I am honest, I must admit that we felt uncertain about the response our heterosexual friends, families, and co-workers would make to our celebration. It is telling that neither of us invited our parents. We did not think they would come and did not want the pain of a refusal. I warned a woman I worked with that she would be getting an invitation from me and should remember that it had been issued with tongue planted firmly in cheek. I felt I had to give her permission not to take us seriously at the same time that Carol and I were both in absolute earnest about the life we were creating together.

Family Rituals

In the wedding ceremonies of my youth, the showers of rice augured for and foreshadowed the children that would issue from these unions. In the event Carol and I created, nothing foretold the children who would transform us publicly and irrevocably into a family. When we joined our lives together in 1985, the social and legal definitions of family had sufficiently influenced my dreams that I assumed that we would not, rather than that we would, have children. I, who had always dreamed of motherhood, had come to believe that this was a loss in my life with which I must make my peace. So there were no little satin packets of rice when Carol and I performed our commitment to a permanently shared life.

But 4 months after that party, Carol's sister gave birth to a daughter with whom Carol fell hopelessly in love. Carol had never really pictured herself as a mother, but I believe now it was her love of Ardy that caused her to dream of a child of her own. As Carol tells the story, she stood in the airport one day, waiting to board a flight to join me in New Orleans. She saw a mother with a baby, and suddenly she realized that she did not want to go through her life without mothering a child. Within a few weeks we were researching and then initiating the adoptions that made us mothers.

In 1989 in Illinois two unmarried adults could not apply together to adopt. In order to create our family, we each adopted one of our daughters, acting as separate single parents. The pledge we made to each other to parent our two daughters together was belied by the entire adoption process, which with each adoption recognized only one mother. The other mother was at best regarded as good friend, at worst, disregarded altogether.

The process of knitting ourselves into a family has taken years and has been characterized more by daily and, yes, mundane performances of commitment than by rituals and ceremonies. Yet we have also participated in public rituals that have helped us to construct ourselves.

The arrival of our babies was greeted by four different showers thrown by friends. Each of our workplaces and two sets of friends organized parties. The various communities we participate in have worked hard to fill the gap between what the law and convention define as family and what our experience reveals. The four of us create our own rituals, as well.

On the occasion of our 10th anniversary, Carol and I planned a modest celebration in the form of an intimate dinner at a nearby Indian restaurant. The babysitter was scheduled to arrive at 6:00. At 5:15, her mother called to say, "Nina has the flu. She can't sit for you tonight." I quickly called four other sitters, none of whom, of course, were available. Our anniversary celebration appeared doomed. In an exuberant attempt to resuscitate it, Lucy suggested that she and Grace come along. Before we knew it, we were working with a whole new dress code. Our daughters decked themselves out in party shoes and party dresses almost before I had finished dialing the last babysitter. "Wear dresses," they instructed us, and so we did—probably the first time we had both been so dressed up for an anniversary in 10 years.

The girls grew giddy at their inclusion in this anniversary of "the day Mama-Jackie and Mama-Carol fell in love." We toasted 10 years by clinking our ice-water together and passed the Tandoori drumstick to Grace. For the umpteenth time, we told the story of the night I opened the door to the newcomer at my lesbian book group and fell under the spell of Carol's twinkling eyes and devilish smile. Our young daughters capped our celebration by leaping from the table and bursting into a rousing improvised floor-show rendition of "Cruella Deville," the theme song from their then-favorite *101 Dalmations*. This was certainly not the romantic anniversary celebration we had anticipated. Nor was it an anniversary we even in our wildest dreams could have predicted at the beginning of our relationship. Yet after it had happened, we recognized it as exactly the most appropriate of celebrations imaginable for this children-dominated period of our lives. In any case, it was as unforgettable an anniversary as we are ever likely to have.

We have not come effortlessly to the space we now occupy, the space in which we name ourselves family and perform our commitment for one and all. When we brought Lucy home from Peru, she was only 5½ months old. We did not yet realize how soon this bright-eyed little gal would be repeating, commenting on, and questioning everything she heard us say. We knew we were both mothers to this daughter; we knew she would call us Mama-Jackie and Mama-Carol. We just didn't know how quickly it would all become public.

Within a few months we perceived that unless we were going to begin our children's lives with impossible explanations about how wonderful our family was but how embarrassed we were about it in public, we would have to get ourselves entirely out of the closet and stay there. Small children don't understand homophobia, and they don't make refined distinctions between what you tell to your best friend and what you tell to the meter reader, but they do understand when they have a mother who is not claiming them or a mother who seems ashamed of her family.

As the importance of educating people in our community became clear to us, we began to welcome opportunities to let the world know that families like ours not only survive but thrive. So when someone from WBEZ, the Chicago affiliate of National Public Radio, called to invite our participation on a program covering single parent adoption, we accepted without hesitation.

During our interview, we told stories about the discrimination we faced as lesbians wishing to adopt. We also talked about how we worked with and against the grain of the systems put in place to support heterosexual parents' adoption.

For Carol and me, that radio interview was an important coming-out ritual. We left the station with a deeper sense of commitment. In the absence of other defining rituals, it helped us in the ongoing project of defining ourselves as a family. For the next several days, we encountered neighbors and co-workers who had heard us on the radio. We're out now, we said to ourselves and each other. We agreed that out is right where we have to be if we're going to make our family strong and the world safe for our daughters.

Carol reminds me that the most important

performance of commitment is the daily care and love we give to our daughters. Parents communicate commitment every day through the constant and repetitive tasks that children's survival depends on—changing diapers, wiping up spills, kissing "owies"—and later on, supervising homework, chauffeuring to sports and music lessons, listening to their stories. For heterosexual families perhaps this is enough. But we gay and lesbian (and adoptive) families create family outside the context of the social and legal structures that allow traditional families to take themselves for granted, and so we must do more.

Thus, we have learned to use language consciously, carefully, and repetitively to define ourselves to each other and our social world. *"Family"* we say, over and over. "Thank you for carrying that package. You are helping our *family.*" "This party is just for our *family.*" "In our *family,* we don't hit."

Each time we choose a pediatrician, a school, a church, we take care to introduce our whole family and to make sure the relationships are clear. Lucy and Grace are now 7 and 8. For as long as possible, we want them to be surrounded by people who accept and support their family as it is. The forms we fill out have spaces for mother and father. Again and again, we cross out "father" and write in "mother," then complete the form. We always feel nervous when we do this. Will there be someone on the staff who will refuse to treat our family with respect? Each public definition of our family is an act of faith.

So far, we have been blessed with teachers and administrators who have valued Lucy's and Gracie's family as it is. Yet the culture's norms and assumptions bombard us. At 3½, Lucy worked with her preschool class on a special Christmas program. Carol and I sat with all the moms and dads. Along with several dads, I trained my camcorder on my talented child. Lucy hopped by right on cue, fluffy bunny tail attached to her bright green pants. We clapped and clapped.

That night in the kitchen, Lucy announced, "My mom and dad came to see my Christmas program today." I swallowed my surprise. "Oh yeah? It looked like your mom and mom to me." "No," said Lucy. "Carol was my mom but you were my dad." I smiled. "Lucy, honey," I said, "anytime you need a dad, I'll be your dad, you just say the word."

Legal Ties

On a sizzling day in July 1995, I picked up a copy of the *Chicago Tribune* and started to toss it into the back seat. Suddenly, my eye caught on the headline—"State court says gays have right to adopt" (Fegelman, 1995). I quickly called Carol and then Rosemary Mulryan, our attorney. Rosemary assured us that with our long history as a couple and as mothers, and with home studies from our original adoptions long since complete, we made what she considered an ideal test case of the new ruling. Within days, Rosemary entered our petition for co-parent adoptions on each of our daughters—a petition that, if successful, would convert our two single-parent adoptions into two-parent adoptions.

We knew we were family before we arrived at the Daley Center shortly after lunch on that hot August afternoon and made our way to family court. Yet when we entered Daley Center dressed in our best, it was with a powerful sense of excitement and anticipation, and, yes, anxiety. What if the judge saw our petitions for co-parent adoptions and decided to block them?

We gathered, along with several other families awaiting their turn, in a toy-filled waiting room that adjoins the Family Court. After 20 anxious minutes we heard our names called. We stepped into the courtroom, each mom holding a daughter by the hand. The judge was a kind and intelligent looking woman about our age. After a brief conversation with me and Carol, she turned to the girls. To get the conversation started, she asked them what school they attended. "Inter-American Magnet School," they answered solemnly. "Are you girls sisters?" she asked next. Carol and I stopped breathing. She was trying to find out whether they understood themselves to be related to one another. "Yes," Lucy and Gracie answered clearly and firmly. Of this answer both girls were comfortably, happily certain, so certain, in fact, that a year later Lucy recalled the judge's query with the words, "What a ridiculous question! Why would a judge ask such a ridiculous question?" And yet it was not until we walked from the court a few minutes later with our temporary custody orders, that the law began to catch up with these sisters' lived reality.

The power of these legal ties and public rituals of commitment can be measured in part by the feelings of exuberance that Carol and I shared as we left Daley Center with our temporary custody orders. Six weeks later, we experienced a similar rush of emotion, when the final adoption decree arrived in the mail.

Carol and I are married in all the ways that matter most. After 13 years and two children together, we don't need a piece of paper to strengthen or cement our commitment. What we do need are the legal benefits and protections that the state provides to families. We also share with other families the longing to perform our deepest commitments and connections through public and private rituals and to have our family supported and embedded within a rich web of kin and community.

In our early years together, we feared the response of family and friends and so gave ourselves a tongue-in-cheek celebration that simultaneously asserted and denied our real commitment. The children in our family have consistently led us toward more public performances of the ties that bind us.

Ritual, ceremony, language, custom, law—all of these interact to construct and constrain our conceptions of family. To the extent that one's family goes against the grain of traditional definitions of the nuclear family, to that extent one must work to make a space for that family.

A couple of years after Carol and I became mothers, I was ranting to one of my lesbian friends about the ignorant, insensitive, and sometimes downright obnoxious and offensive things that strangers say to us—regarding adoption, skin color, ethnicity, or the curious spectacle of two mothers mothering together. My friend gave me an indulgent smile. "Jackie," she said, "you're exactly right. But you must admit you are asking them to take in an awful lot all at once." Well, yes. Even as I write about performing commitment, I realize that writing about these issues as they pertain to our lesbian-parented family leads me into writing about performing commitment within our adoptive and interethnic family.

Our family doesn't fit anybody's mold. But we are a family, held together by ties of love, loyalty, commitment, and daily life. Because our family does not conform to traditional definitions of family, the performances that connect us to the social fabric and to one another take on even greater importance. Through the anniversaries, ceremonies, rituals, and holidays that mark our years and the repeated mundane actions of commitment that mark our days, we perform the bonds that make us kin. Meanwhile, we dream and struggle toward the day when the laws of the land and the expectations in people's hearts and minds catch up to our reality—that family is a group of people who live together and love each other, bound by their shared commitment to the health, growth, and welfare of all.

REFERENCES

Fegelman, A. (1995, July 19). State court says gays have right to adopt. *Chicago Tribune*, pp. 1, 15.

Geertz, C. (1973). *The interpretation of cultures.* New York: Basic Books.

Majors, R. (1994). Discovering gay culture in America. In L. Samovar & R. Porter (Eds.), *Intercultural communication: A reader* (7th ed.) (pp. 165–171). Belmont, CA: Wadsworth.

Martin, J. (1993). Intercultural communication competence: A review. In R. Wiseman & J. Koester (Eds.), *Intercultural communication competence* (pp. 16–29). Newbury Park, CA: Sage.

Schechner, R. (1985). *Between theater and anthropology.* Philadelphia: University of Pennsylvania Press.

Taylor, J. (1995, January). On being an exemplary lesbian: My life as a role model. Performance presented at the University of Texas at Austin.

Ting-Toomey, S. (1993). Communicative resourcefulness: An identity negotiation perspective. In R. Wiseman & J. Koester (Eds.), *Intercultural communication competence* (pp. 72–111). Newbury Park, CA: Sage.

KEY TERMS

adoption	culture
coming out	family

gay
gay and lesbian
    weddings
homophobia

lesbian
marriage
ritual
wedding

DISCUSSION QUESTIONS

1. This essay is predicated on the notion that there is a dimension of cross-cultural communication in the communication between this lesbian-parented family and their community. What characteristics of cross-cultural communication do you see illustrated here? In what ways do these experiences differ from models of cross-cultural communication?

2. What sorts of rituals or performances has your family used to define itself as a family? How is culture embedded in and negotiated through those rituals?

3. Consider the argument that weddings can serve as sites for the negotiation of identity. Can you think of examples from your experience of such identity negotiations?

4. If you did not grow up in a household with gay or lesbian parents, imagine that you are one of the estimated 6 million to 10 million children in the United States who are living in such a household. What communication problems do you think you might encounter? What sorts of changes (legal, social, cultural) would make communication easier for you and your family?

5. It's easy to see that this family encounters some struggles. Can you see any advantages that flow from their ongoing efforts to communicate and perform family relationships?

PART NINE

CONFLICT, COMMUNICATION, AND CULTURE

The following essays explore various intersections among culture, communication, and conflict in domestic and international contexts. In conflict situations, people often experience physiological reactions that may lead them to overlook the intensely cultural aspect of conflict. Yet, conflict—how it is experienced, maintained, negotiated, and avoided—is highly cultural. These cultural differences can often lead to further conflict rather than to resolution.

Consider these questions as you read the articles in this part:

How do you deal with conflict? How did you develop your own approach to conflict?

How do your conflict-management strategies vary across contexts?

What role does power play in conflict communication?

The authors of these essays offer insights about how cultural groups vary in approaches to conflict and how best to manage intercultural conflict. In these readings conflict is seen as interpersonal conflict or mediated, as causally related to national and ethnic cultures or as dynamically negotiated, and as occurring in international or domestic contexts. The final essay cautions us that study of intercultural conflict should not be limited to interpersonal contexts but should extend to global media contexts as well.

In "Intercultural Conflict Competence," Stella Ting-Toomey provides a useful overview and framework for thinking about broad cultural differences in conflict management and resolution. She addresses two questions: How do various cultural groups deal with conflict? How can individuals deal effectively with intercultural conflict? Based on a review of social science research, she shows how basic cultural values (individualism-collectivism, personal self-construals, high-context/low-context communication) can influence how individuals approach interpersonal conflict. She points out a fundamental problem—we all approach conflict with ethnocentric lenses. Finally, she identifies components of conflict competence (knowledge, motivation, and skill) and gives practical suggestions for dealing with intercultural conflict.

Peter Ogom Nwosu, in "Negotiating with the Swazis," provides an interesting case study of conflict resolution that stands in contrast to most North American models. In an interpretive study based on personal experience and participant observation, Nwosu describes the important characteristics of Swazi negotiation, including credibility, relationship-building, and indirect communication. This study is a good example of Ting-Toomey's description of a collectivist cultural approach to conflict resolution.

In "Views from the Other Side," Benjamin J. Broome provides an interesting case study of interethnic conflict in an international context—Turks and Greeks in Cyprus. From his own extensive experience and ethnographic research he provides some background with which to understand this long-enduring conflict. The contrasting Greek- and Turkish-Cypriot perspectives reveal the dynamic relationship between external forces of media and family influences and the personal fears and ideas about the conflict and what the future holds for Cyprus.

Shifting to interethnic conflict in domestic contexts, Karen Lynnette Dace and Mark Lawrence McPhail, in "Crossing the Color Line," provide a way to think beyond interracial conflict. In narrative form, these two authors each explore how empathy has impacted their understanding and behavior as they relate to "the gulf that exists between African and European Americans." Taking a critical-interpretive perspective, they examine their relationships with European Americans and emphasize the importance of resisting "racial reasoning," the tendency to see Black-White interactions in Black and White terms. They present a new way of thinking about empathy—where empathy is more than rational understanding. It is rather *implicature,* or thinking *and* experiencing, both objectively and subjectively, the worldview of others.

In "Mass-Mediated Communication and Intercultural Conflict," Fernando Delgado challenges us to think about conflicts beyond interpersonal contexts. Taking a critical perspective, he examines broad international and mediated contexts where power inequities lead to cultural conflict. He provides two examples: The first concerns debates about control and domination over media technology in which Third World nations express concern over the rapid growth of technology and control of media by First World nations. The second example is an analysis of cultural dominance debate. In this conflict, non-U.S. cultural critics express concern over the dominance of U.S. popular culture, its ubiquitous nature, and its influence on other cultures.

41
INTERCULTURAL CONFLICT COMPETENCE

STELLA TING-TOOMEY

Intercultural miscommunications and misattributions often underscore intercultural conflict. Individuals coming from two contrastive cultural communities bring with them different value assumptions, expectations, verbal and nonverbal habits, and interaction scripts that influence the conflict process. Intercultural conflict is defined as the *perceived incompatibility of values, norms, processes, or goals between a minimum of two cultural parties over identity, relational, and/or substantive issues.* Intercultural conflict often starts off with different expectations concerning appropriate or inappropriate behavior in an interaction episode. Violations of expectation, in turn, often influence the effectiveness of how members of two cultures negotiate their interests or goals in the interaction. If inappropriate or ineffective negotiation behavior continues, the miscommunication can very easily spiral into a complex, polarized conflict. The following dialogue between two intercultural strangers trying to get acquainted in the Los Angeles International Airport lobby illustrates this type of conflict.

Example 1

Mr. Gass (a young, enthusiastic Euro-American businessman, shaking hands with Mr. Lim vigorously): Welcome to L.A., Mr. Lim. Nice meeting you, finally. My name is William Gass. Just call me Bill. Here is my business card. [*Bill forwards the card with his right hand.*]

Mr. Lim (an elderly Korean businessman): Nice meeting you, Mr. Gass. I'm Peter Pyong Gap Lim. Here is my business card. [*Mr. Lim forwards his card with both hands.*]

Mr. Gass: Please, call me Bill. I hope we'll be doing a lot of business together here in L.A.

Mr. Lim: Yes, I hope so too.

Mr. Gass (glancing quickly at Mr. Lim's card): Pyong Gap, I'll give you a call tomorrow after you get some rest in your hotel. Maybe we can have lunch together.

Mr. Lim (with a polite smile): Yes, maybe, Mr. Gass. Please call me tomorrow. I will await your phone call.

When members of different cultures greet one another in an initial encounter, they often draw on their own cultural scripts to guide their behavior. In Example 1, Mr. Gass is very pleased with the initial encounter with Mr. Lim. He is especially pleased that he called Mr. Lim "Pyong Gap"—his client's Korean name rather than his American name. Mr. Gass feels that he has succeeded in building an informal, symmetrical relationship with Mr. Lim by addressing him on a first-name basis and paying attention to his Korean ethnicity. Mr. Gass believes that they will be able to work well together, since Mr. Lim departed with a smile and a firm handshake.

Mr. Lim, on the other hand, is very uncertain about the initial meeting with Mr. Gass. First, Mr. Lim feels uncomfortable that Mr. Gass forwarded his business card using only one hand. In the Korean culture, a business card represents the face, or public self-image, of an individual. It should always be treated with proper respect and dignity. Mr. Gass should have forwarded his card with both hands and received Mr. Lim's business card with both hands. Second, Mr. Gass should have taken the time to read and admire Mr. Lim's card carefully before putting it away in his wallet. Third, Mr. Lim was uncomfortable and insulted when Mr. Gass addressed him by his Korean name. He would have preferred that Mr. Gass address him more formally as "Mr. Lim"; after all, Mr. Lim is the client and is much older than Mr. Gass.

As an older Korean businessman, Mr. Lim would like to see more asymmetrical deference and respect from Mr. Gass. If Mr. Gass insists on being informal, he should at least address Mr. Lim as "Peter" rather than "Pyong Gap," since Mr. Lim created his western name "Peter" just for the sake of informal interaction in American business transactions. Mr. Lim smiled because he was embarrassed by Mr. Gass's imposed intimacy. His smile was to cover his own embarrassment for the "face loss" incurred in the first few minutes of the initial encounter.

Both Mr. Gass and Mr. Lim have been conditioned by their own cultural norms or standards to behave in a certain way. While Mr. Lim is already anticipating difficulty in working with this "overbearing" American, Mr. Gass has no idea that he has offended his client in so many ways in the first few minutes of interaction. Although no explicit, interpersonal disagreement took place in Example 1, the seeds of potential disagreement or perceived incompatibility were sown. If similar miscommunication between Mr. Gass and Mr. Lim becomes a pattern in subsequent interactions, Mr. Gass may not be able to secure the business contracts he wants from Mr. Lim. Even though both Mr. Gass and Mr. Lim attempted to be sensitive to each other's cultural background, their effort created a cultural chasm.

Not all intercultural conflicts are caused by miscommunication or misunderstanding. Some intercultural conflicts arise because of deep-seated hatred, centuries of antagonism, and clear understanding. However, most everyday intercultural conflicts that we encounter can be traced to cultural miscommunication or ignorance. As cultural beings, we are socialized or "programmed" by the values and norms of our culture to think and behave in certain ways. Our family, peer groups, educational institutions, mass media system, political system, and religious institutions are some of the forces that shape and mold our cultural and personal values. Our learned values and norms are, in turn, expressed through the way we communicate.

The study of intercultural conflict in contemporary U.S. society is especially critical today for several reasons. First, in the United States, immigrants (many of whom are non-English speakers), members of minority groups, and women represent more than 50 percent of the present work-force. Second, by the year 2000, 85 percent of the *entering* workforce in the United States will be new immigrants, minority group members, and females (Loden & Rosener, 1991). Third, four out of every five new jobs in the United States at present are generated as a direct result of foreign trade (Lustig & Koester, 1993). As the global economy becomes an everyday reality in most societies, we will inevitably encounter people who are culturally different in diverse workplace and social environments. Learning to manage such differences, especially in intercultural conflicts, can bring about alternative perspectives and multiple solutions to an existing problem. Competence in intercultural conflict means managing cultural differences appropriately, effectively, and adaptively.

This chapter examines some of the cultural background factors . . . that influence face-to-face intercultural conflict. . . . First, the cultural variability perspective of individualism/collectivism, in conjunction with self-concept and low/high-context communication, is presented; second, some underlying factors that contribute to intercultural conflict are identified; third, a competence-based approach to intercultural conflict management is discussed.

A Cultural Variability Perspective

Culture refers to a group-level construct that embodies a distinctive system of traditions, beliefs, values, norms, rituals, symbols, and meanings that is shared by a majority of interacting individuals in a community. Simply put, culture refers to a patterned way of living by a group of interacting individuals who share similar sets of beliefs, values, and behaviors. A complex frame of reference influences our thought patterns, our feelings, and our everyday functioning. In order to understand differences and similarities in the assumptions and behaviors in conflict across cultures, we need a perspective or framework to explain in depth why and how cultures are different or similar.

Although there are many potential dimensions in which cultures differ, one dimension that receives consistent attention from intercultural researchers around the world is *individualism/collectivism*. Individualism/collectivism explains group-level differences between cultures. . . . A value-based dimension such as individualism/collectivism, can provide us with a more in-depth understanding of why members of two contrasting cultures (for example, American and Korean cultures) approach conflict differently. In addition to this dimension are the dimensions of self-concept and low/high-context communication. The former explains individual-level approaches to conflict; the latter explains cultural differences in conflict style.

As a whole, a cultural variability perspective emphasizes the following three dimensions: individualism/collectivism, self-concept, and low/high-context communication. These three dimensions influence the values we hold in approaching or avoiding conflict, the way we attribute meanings to conflict events, and the way we communicate in specific conflict episodes.

Individualism/Collectivism

Individualism refers to the broad value tendencies of people in a culture to emphasize individual identity over group identity, individual rights over group obligations, and individual achievements over group concerns. In contrast, *collectivism* refers to the broad value tendencies of people in a culture to emphasize group identity over individual identity, group obligations over individual rights, and group-oriented concerns over individual wants and desires (Hofstede, 1980, 1991; Triandis, 1995). Individualism is expressed in interpersonal conflict through the strong assertion of personal opinions, the revealing of personal emotions, and personal accountability for any conflict problem or mistake. Collectivism is manifested in interpersonal conflict through the representation of collective opinions or ideas, the restraint of personal emotional expressions, and group accountability, if possible, for the conflict problem. . . .

. . . we can also find "both individualistic and collectivistic elements in *all* . . . countries, in different combinations" (Triandis, 1995, p. 2). In

addition, considerable differences within cultures have been uncovered in many pluralistic societies. For example, within a pluralistic society such as Canada or the United States, different ethnic communities can display distinctive individualistic and group-oriented value tendencies. Cultural miscommunication and conflicts often arise because of our ignorance of different value priorities and modes of behavior in different cultures. Moving beyond the general discussion of culture-level differences, we can examine individual-level differences within and across cultures.

Self-Concept

An alternative way to understand individualism and collectivism focuses on how individuals within a culture conceptualize the sense of self. . . . Individuals with a strong sense of *independent self* tend to see themselves as autonomous, self-reliant, unencumbered agents of change, and as rational choice makers. Individuals with a strong sense of *interdependent self* tend to see themselves as group-bound, role-based, interconnected, obligatory agents, and as harmony seekers. Both types of self-concept exist within a culture. Overall, however, whereas independent concepts of self are more common in individualistic cultures, interdependent concepts of self are more common in collectivistic cultures.

• • •

Independent-self people tend to make sense of their environment through autonomous-self lenses; interdependent-self people tend to make sense of their surroundings through group-bound–self lenses. Independent-self individuals tend to worry about whether they present their individualistic self credibly and competently in front of others. Interdependent-self individuals tend to be more reflective of what others think of their projected face image in the context of in-group/out-group relations (which are discussed later in the section on *Conflict Norms*). Finally, while independent-self individuals tend to practice direct verbal communication, expressing their own thoughts and feelings, interdependent-self individuals tend to practice responsive communication, anticipating the thoughts and feelings of the other person. Direct verbal communication is a low-context way of communicating; responsive communication is a high-context way of communicating. . . .

Low/High-Context Communication

According to Hall (1976), human interaction can be divided into low-context and high-context communication systems. Low-context communication emphasizes expressing intention or meaning through explicit verbal messages. High-context communication emphasizes conveying intention or meaning through the context (for example, social roles, positions) and the nonverbal channels (for example, pauses, silence, tone of voice) of the verbal message. In general, low-context communication refers to communication patterns of direct verbal mode, straight talk, nonverbal immediacy, and sender-oriented value. In low-context communication, the speaker is expected to construct a clear, persuasive message that the listener can decode easily. In contrast, high-context communication refers to communication patterns of indirect verbal mode, ambiguous talk, nonverbal subtleties, and interpreter-sensitive value. . . . In high-context communication, the listener or interpreter of the message is expected to read "between the lines," to infer accurately the implicit intent of the verbal message, and to observe the nonverbal nuances and subtleties that accompany the verbal message. High-context communication emphasizes the importance of multilayered contexts (for example, historical context, social norms, roles, situational and relational contexts) that frame the interaction. . . .

As Barnlund, in commenting on the communication style differences between Japanese and Americans, observes:

> Conflict is far less common in Japanese society for a number of reasons. First, the emphasis on the group instead of the individual reduces interpersonal friction. Second, an elaborate set of standards emphasizes "obligations" over "rights," what one owes to others rather than deserves for oneself. Third, the value attached to harmony cultivates skill in the use of ambigu-

ity, circumlocution, euphemism, and silence in blunting incipient disputes. The ability to assimilate differences, to engineer consensus, is valued above a talent for argument. (1989, p. 39)

Individualism and independent-self concept in the United States promote the need for verbal self-assertion, and verbal self-assertion often promotes individual differences and competitions. In contrast, collectivism and interdependent-self concept in Japan promotes the need for verbal circumspection, and verbal circumspection often promotes face preservation and relational harmony.

To summarize, while independent-self individualists engage in low-context styles of conflict management, interdependent-self collectivists engage in high-context styles of conflict negotiation. Overall, the cultural variability dimensions of individualism/collectivism, independent/interdependent-self concept, and low/high-context communication patterns help guide us toward a general understanding of conflict between members of individualistic and collectivistic cultures.

Factors in Intercultural Conflict

Drawing from the key ideas of a cultural variability perspective, this section identifies the underlying factors that create intercultural frictions and conflicts between individualists and collectivists. These factors include differences in conflict assumptions, conflict rhythms, conflict norms, conflict styles, and ethnocentric lenses.

Conflict Assumptions

The values of individualism versus collectivism, and how these values are linked to individual self-concepts and low/high-context communication patterns, affect our assumptions about conflict. Cultural assumptions about conflict color our attitudes, expectations, and behaviors in the conflict episode. Different cultural assumptions toward conflict are one factor contributing to intercultural miscommunication and conflict.

For individualists, the resolution of interpersonal conflict follows an outcome-oriented model.

For collectivists, however, the management of interpersonal conflict follows a process-oriented model. An *outcome-oriented model* emphasizes the importance of asserting individual interests in the conflict situation and moving rapidly toward the phase of reaching tangible outcomes or goals. A *process-oriented model* emphasizes the importance of managing mutual or group face interests in the conflict process before discussing tangible outcomes or goals. "Face," in this context, refers to upholding a claimed sense of positive public image in any social interaction (Ting-Toomey, 1994a). From the collectivistic perspective, face is not about what one thinks of oneself, but about what others think of one's worth, especially within the in-group/out-group context.

For individualists, effective conflict negotiation means settling the conflict problem openly and working out a set of functional conflict solutions conjointly. Effective conflict resolution behavior (for example, emphasizing the importance of addressing incompatible goals or outcomes) is *relatively* more important than appropriate facework behavior. For collectivists, on the other hand, appropriate conflict management means the subtle negotiation of in-group/out-group face-related issues—pride, honor, dignity, insult, shame, disgrace, humility, trust, mistrust, respect, and prestige—in a given conflict episode. Appropriate facework moves and countermoves are critical before tangible conflict outcomes or goals can be addressed.

In commenting on face issues in collectivistic cultures, Cohen observes, "For the representatives of interdependent cultures the experience of international negotiation is fraught with considerations of face. The very structure of the situation, in which competing parties pit their wills and skills against each other, is uncongenial to societies that see social harmony, not confrontation, as the desired state of affairs" (1991, p. 132).

To summarize, independent-self individualists tend to operate from the following outcome-oriented conflict assumptions:

1. Conflict is perceived as being closely related to the goals or outcomes that are salient to the respective individual conflict parties in a given conflict situation.

2. Communication during conflict is viewed as dissatisfying when the conflict parties are not willing to deal with the conflict openly and honestly.

3. Communication during conflict is viewed as satisfying when the conflict parties are willing to confront the conflict issues openly and share their feelings honestly (that is, assertively but not aggressively).

4. Conflict is perceived as unproductive when no tangible outcome or plan of action is reached or developed.

5. Conflict is perceived as productive when tangible solutions are reached and objective criteria are met.

6. Effective and appropriate management of conflict means that individual goals are addressed and differences are dealt with openly, honestly, and properly in relation to timing and situational context.

Interdependent-self collectivists follow the conflict assumptions of a process-oriented model:

1. Conflict is weighed against the threat to face that is incurred in the conflict negotiation process and is interpreted in the webs of in-group/out-group relationships.

2. Communication during conflict is perceived as threatening when the conflict parties push for a discussion of substantive issues before properly managing face-related issues.

3. Communication during conflict is viewed as satisfying when the conflict parties engage in *mutual* face-saving and face-giving behavior and attend to both verbal and nonverbal signals.

4. Conflict processes and outcomes are perceived as unproductive when face issues are not addressed and relational or group feelings are not attended to properly.

5. Conflict processes and outcomes are defined as productive when both conflict parties can claim that they have "won" with respect to both face-related and substantive issues.

6. Appropriate and effective management of conflict means that the faces of both conflict

parties are saved or even upgraded in the interaction, and the parties have dealt with the conflict episode strategically in conjunction with substantive gains or losses.

Thus, while individualists are concerned with resolving conflict problems, collectivists are concerned with the dynamic issues of in-group/out-group face. These implicit conflict assumptions are superimposed on the rhythms and pacing of intercultural conflict resolution.

Conflict Rhythms

The consciousness of conflict management rhythms varies along the individualism/collectivism divide. Differences in conflict rhythms are the second factor contributing to intercultural conflict between individualists and collectivists. Individualistic values tend to foster *monochronic-time rhythms*, and collectivistic value tendencies tend to cultivate *polychronic-time rhythms*.

As Hall and Hall explain: "In monochronic cultures, time is experienced and used in a linear way—comparable to a road . . . M-time [monochronic time] is divided quite naturally into segments; it is scheduled and compartmentalized, making it possible for a person to concentrate on one thing at a time. In a monochronic system, the schedule may take on priority above all else and be treated as sacred and unalterable" (1987, p. 16). Hall and Hall identified Germany, Scandinavia, Switzerland, and the United States as prime M-time examples. In contrast, they note: "Polychronic (P-time) systems are the antithesis of M-time systems. P-time is characterized by the simultaneous occurrence of many things and by a great involvement with people. There is also more emphasis on completing human transactions than on holding schedules. . . . P-time is experienced as much less tangible than M-time, and can better be compared to a single point than to a road" (Hall & Hall, 1987, pp. 17–18). Many African, Asian, Latin American, Eastern European, Caribbean, and Mediterranean cultures are prime examples of P-time systems.

M-time people prefer to deal with conflict using a linear approach; P-time people prefer to handle conflict from a spiral viewpoint. For M-time individuals, conflict management time should be filled with problem-solving or decision-making activities. For P-time individuals, time is a "being" idea governed by the smooth implicit rhythms in the interactions between people. When two P-time individuals come into conflict, they are more concerned with restoring the disjunctive rhythms in the interaction than with dealing head-on with substantive issues.

M-time people tend to emphasize agenda setting, objective criteria, and clear time schedules to accomplish certain conflict goals. P-time people, in contrast, tend to work on the relational atmosphere and the contextual setting that frame the conflict episode. For M-time individuals, effective conflict negotiation means reaching and implementing tangible conflict outcomes within a clearly established timetable. For P-time individuals, the arbitrary division of clock time or calendar time holds little meaning if the relational rhythms between people are out of sync. For M-time people, a signed contract or written agreement signals joint explicit agreement to the solution of the conflict problem. For P-time people, however, once the appropriate level of relational rhythm or rapport is established, their words can mean more than a signed contract. Likewise, if they perceive that the relational rhythms are disjunctive, renewed face-related negotiation is needed to restore that delicate, face-honoring point. M-time people tend to define conflict using a short-term time line; P-time people tend to view time from a long-term, historical process. For P-time members, "deadline" is always subject to renegotiation, and human deadlines should be dealt with flexibly and patiently.

People move with different rhythms in conflict negotiation. Intercultural conflict between individualists and collectivists is magnified when the implicit rhythm of time plays a decisive role in the encounter. M-time individuals want to move faster to address substantive problems and resolve the conflict. P-time individuals prefer to deal with relational and contextual issues before concrete, substantive negotiation. M-time persons want to establish a clear timetable to achieve specific conflict goals and objectives. P-time people want to spend more time building trust and commitment between the conflict parties. Different rhythms of monochronic time and polychronic time thus can further polarize the individualists and the collectivists in the intercultural misattribution process.

Conflict Norms

Differences in norms of conflict interaction are the third factor compounding intercultural conflict. Norms are standards or guidelines for behavior. They are reflected in our expectations of what constitutes proper or improper behavior in a given setting.

. . . The *equity norm* emphasizes the importance of individual reward and cost calculations, and of obtaining equitable rewards in resolving the problematic issue. The *communal norm* stresses the importance of taking in-group expectations into account in the calculation, and of satisfying the face needs of the in-group members that are involved in the conflict.

While the equity norm reflects the individualistic, outcome-oriented model in conflict, the communal norm reflects the collectivistic, process-oriented model. In addition, in collectivistic cultures different norms govern conflict interaction with in-group and out-group members. According to Triandis, *in-groups* are groups of individuals "about whose welfare a person is concerned, with whom that person is willing to cooperate without demanding equitable returns, and separation from whom leads to anxiety" (1995, p. 9). In-groups usually consist of people who perceive a "common fate" or shared attributes. *Out-groups* are groups of individuals "with which one has something to divide, perhaps unequally, or are harmful in some way, groups that disagree on valued attributes" (Triandis, 1995, p. 9). For very important conflicts, collectivists (similar to the individualists) prefer to use the equity norm when competing with out-group members (for example, people from another company) for needed resources (Leung & Iwawaki, 1988). However, for less important conflicts, collectivists prefer to use the communal, smoothing norm with either in-group or out-group members. Each culture also has different rules and meanings for proper or improper conflict behavior in dealing with in-group or out-group members in different situations.

By the norms of emotional expression, conflict is an emotionally distressing experience. In two extensive, detailed reviews of culture and emotions (Mesquita & Frijda, 1992; Russell, 1991), clear cross-cultural differences in emotional expression and interpretation are uncovered. On the basis of these reviews, we can conclude that there are cultural norms that regulate displays of aggressive or negative emotional reactions in conflict interaction such as anger, fear, shame, frustration, resentment, and hostility. For example, in many individualistic western cultures, open expressions of emotions in conflict are viewed as honest, engaging signals. In many collectivistic Asian cultures, however, restrained emotions are viewed as self-disciplined, mature signals in handling conflict. Thus, while basic emotions such as anxiety, shame, and fear can be viewed as pancultural conflict emotions, cultural display rules of when to express which nonverbal emotions (to whom and in what context) differ from one cultural community to the next. For example, for collectivists, the masking of negative emotions is critical to maintain a harmonious front during conflict. When collectivists feel embarrassed or perceive face threat in conflict, they may sometimes smile to cover up their embarrassment or shame.

Thus, different norms and rules govern the way individualists and collectivists deal with specific conflict issues. When an individualist prefers to use the equity norm to deal with a conflict issue and a collectivist prefers to use the communal norm, the hidden factor of normative expectations further splinters intercultural communication. In addition, the nonverbal/verbal dimension of emotional expression in conflict can vary along the individualism and collectivism schism, creating further tensions and gaps.

Conflict Styles

. . . Differences in conflict styles are the fourth factor in intercultural conflict negotiation. Cultural differences in conflict style generate intergroup attribution errors and biases. For example, the following dialogue between Ms. Gumb (an African-American supervisor) and Mr. Lee (a recent Chinese immigrant) in a U.S.-China joint-venture firm illustrates differences in conflict styles and attribution processes.

Example 2

Ms. Gumb (in the main office): Lee, where is your project report? You said you'd get it done soon. I need your part of the report so that I can finish my final report by the end of this week. When do you think you can get it done? [*Attribution: Lee is very irresponsible. I should never have trusted him. I thought I was giving him a break by putting him in charge of this report.*]

Mr. Lee (hesitantly): Well, Ms. Gumb . . . I didn't realize the deadline was so soon. . . . I will try my best to get it done as soon as possible. It's just that there are lots of details I need to cross-check. . . . I'm really not sure. [*Attribution: Ms. Gumb is sure a tough lady. Anyway, she is the supervisor, why didn't she tell me the exact deadline early on? Just last week, she told me to take my time on the report. I'm really confused. In China, the supervisor always tells the workers what to do.*]

Ms. Gumb (frustrated): Lee, how soon is soon? I really need to know your plan of action right now. You cannot be so vague in answering my questions all the time. I believe I've given you plenty of time to work on this report already. [*Attribution: Lee is trying to be sneaky. He does not answer my questions directly at all. I wonder if all Chinese are that sneaky? Or maybe he is not comfortable working for a black female? Anyway, I have to press him to be more efficient and responsible. He is in America; he has to learn the American way.*]

Mr. Lee: [*a long pause*] . . . Well, I'm really not sure, Ms. Gumb. I really don't want to do a bad job on the report and disappoint you. I'll try my best to finish it as soon as possible. Maybe I can finish the report next week. [*Attribution: Ms. Gumb is sure a pushy boss. She doesn't seem to like me and she is causing me to lose face in front of all my peers. Her voice sounds so harsh and blunt. I have heard American people are hard to work with, but she is especially rude and overbearing. I better start looking for a new job tomorrow.*]

In Example 2, while Ms. Gumb is assertive and direct in dealing with the problem, Mr. Lee is hesitant and indirect in answering her questions. Ms. Gumb has a "straight-talk," low-context approach to dealing with the work problem; Mr. Lee has a "face-talk," high-context approach. If both understand concepts such as low-context and high-context communication styles, they may arrive at a better understanding of each other's behavior.

Conflict style differences between cultural or ethnic group members profoundly influence the meanings we attach to each other's behavior. We typically use our own habitual scripts and interaction styles as a baseline to judge and evaluate others' behavior. While Mr. Lee is using his high-context scripts to evaluate Ms. Gumb's behavior as rude and overbearing, Ms. Gumb is using her low-context attribution (for example, "Lee is trying to be sneaky") and historical script (for example, "maybe he is not comfortable working for a black female") to make sense of Mr. Lee's high-context approach. If Ms. Gumb and Mr. Lee understand the cultural and historical conditioning of their own and the other's behavior, they may learn to be more culturally sensitive in their attribution process. They may learn to respect each other's stylistic scripts and work more adaptively in achieving a common ground in their interaction.

Ms. Gumb may learn to talk privately to Mr. Lee rather than to engage in such direct face-threatening behavior in public. Mr. Lee may learn to be more direct and open in answering his supervisor's questions and to pause and hedge less in their interaction. On the strategy level, individualists in conflict appear to prefer direct verbal assertions, direct verbal questioning, direct requests, and direct clarifications and answers in conflict. In contrast, collectivists prefer qualifiers (for example, "*perhaps* we should meet this deadline together"), tag questions (for example, "*don't you think* you'll feel better if you finish it and get it out of the way?"), disclaimers (for example, "*maybe I don't understand* what's going on here"), and indirect requests (for example, "*if it's not too much trouble,* let's try to finish this report together") to convey a softened approach to working out differences.

. . . Silence is a critical strategy in dealing with both in-group and out-group conflicts in collectivistic cultures. Silence may signal approval or disapproval in collectivistic conflict interaction.

In silence, the conflict parties incur no obligations. Silence may also be interpreted as an ambiguous "yes" or "no" response. On the other hand, silence may be viewed as an admission of guilt or incompetence in an individualistic culture.

Finally, several researchers indicate that collectivists tend to prefer an *informal* third-party conflict mediation procedure (such as seeking help from relatives or from wise teachers or gurus) more so than individualists (Cohen, 1991; Leung, 1987, 1988; Ting-Toomey, 1985, 1988). In mediated conflicts individualists prefer objective advice and facilitation from an impartial, formal third-party mediator . . . , and collectivists prefer to seek help from someone who already is informed about the conflict and whom they can trust and respect.

Different cross-cultural conflict styles create different attribution biases and tensions. In attributing meanings to collectivistic, indirect conflict styles, individualists tend to view collectivists in the conflict as trying to sidestep genuine issue discussions. Conversely, collectivists tend to perceive individualists as pushy, rude, and overbearing because of their confrontational conflict style.

Ethnocentric Lenses

Although we often rely on the knowledge of our own cultural approach, rhythms, norms, and styles to explain the behavior of other people from our culture, the same criteria may not be applicable to another culture. Being unfamiliar with the other party's cultural norms creates problems that can exacerbate an already tense intercultural conflict episode. An examination of such problems is a natural extension of the discussion on differences in conflict styles.

Ethnocentrism is defined as "the view of things in which one's own group is the center of everything, and all others are scaled and rated with reference to it" (Sumner, 1940, p. 13). When members of different cultures believe that their own approaches are the correct or natural ways to handle conflict, they tend to see the conflict behaviors of other cultures as deviant from the standard. . . .

Individualists with strong ethnocentric tendencies tend to view the outcome-oriented model as superior and more efficient in conflict resolution than the process-oriented model. Conversely, collectivists with strong ethnocentric lenses tend to view the process-oriented model as more desirable and personable than the mechanistic outcome-oriented model. Ethnocentrism reflects our comfort with familiar cultural habits and practices. Individuals are often unaware of their own ethnocentric behaviors and evaluations. They have internalized the standards and norms of their culture as the "proper" and "right" ways of behaving.

Individualists and collectivists also may engage in different attribution processes during interpersonal conflict. Overall, individualists tend to use more dispositional attributions than do collectivists to explain the conflict problem. Individualists might explain conflict by making negative personality statements such as "She's late because she's lazy" or "He's just too dumb to get it." Collectivists, on the other hand, tend to use more situational attributions than do individualists to explain problems. For example, they make statements such as "Maybe she's late because the traffic is really bad" or "Maybe he's confused because the manager did not explain the project clearly." Individualists tend to hold the person accountable for the conflict; collectivists tend to emphasize the context that contributes to the conflict.

Individualists and collectivists sometimes use similar attributions in making sense of conflict. Stewart and Bennett, in commenting on how ethnocentrism leads to more intensified intercultural miscommunication, observe: "When communicators engage in mutual negative evaluation, the recriminatory interaction may be enough to block communication. If the communicators then attempt to overcome the difficulty through ethnocentric procedures, the communication event may deteriorate even further. . . . With each turn of this regressive spiral, negative evaluations are intensified" (1991, p. 165). The lack of specific information about each other's conflict assumptions or styles often creates negative interaction spirals that deepen the cultural schism. The lack of communication skills to handle such problematic intercultural episodes appropriately and effectively also compounds the miscommunication chasm.

Our ethnocentric lenses push us to judge the behavior of another culture evaluatively and negatively. Ethnocentrism creates biased attributions and expectations in intercultural conflict. Thus, cultural differences in conflict assumptions, conflict rhythms, conflict norms, conflict styles, and ethnocentric lenses act as invisible barriers that widen the gap of intercultural conflict. Individualists and collectivists typically collide over their use of an outcome-oriented model or process-oriented model in dealing with conflict. They also collide over the rhythms, the norms, and the styles of how to approach conflict appropriately and effectively. Ethnocentric lenses creep into our attribution process and create further evaluative biases and binary mind-sets (that is, my way is the *right* way and your way is *wrong*).

Competence in Intercultural Conflict

. . . *Knowledge* is the cognitive or experiential understanding that helps one communicate effectively and appropriately in a given situation. *Motivation* is the cognitive or affective readiness, or mind-set, to communicate effectively and appropriately with others. *Skill* is the ability to perform behaviors that are considered effective and appropriate in a given situation. This section examines the effectiveness and appropriateness criteria of competence in intercultural conflict and concludes with some recommendations for enhancing our knowledge, motivation, and skill in managing intercultural conflicts competently. . . .

Knowledge, Motivation, and Skill in Intercultural Conflict

To act effectively and appropriately in interactive conflict, individuals have to enhance their cultural knowledge and motivation in applying adaptive interaction skills. Of all the dimensions of managing intercultural conflict, knowledge is the most important and underscores the other dimensions of competence.

Without culture-sensitive knowledge, parties cannot learn to uncover the implicit ethnocentric "lenses," or assumptions, they use to interpret and evaluate events in different intercultural conflict situations. "Knowledge" here refers to in-depth understanding of certain phenomena via a range of information gained through conscious learning and personal experiences and observations.

In addition to individualistic and collectivistic value tendencies, individual differences within cultures, such as independent-self versus interdependent-self concept, contribute to the interpretation of intercultural conflict. To manage intercultural conflict competently, we must take other people's cultural perspectives and personality factors into consideration. If others are interdependent-self collectivists, we may want to pay extra attention to their process-oriented assumptions about conflict. If others are independent-self individualists, we may want to be sensitive to their outcome-oriented assumptions about conflict. Although this chapter provides general knowledge for understanding individualistic and collectivistic cultures, knowledge concerning cultural and ethnic conflict assumptions and styles should also be pursued. This chapter emphasizes intercultural conflict differences rather than ethnic differences (for example, African-American versus Mexican-American interaction style in the United States) in conflict. However, the general concepts (that is, differences in conflict models, rhythms, norms, styles, and ethnocentric lenses) should serve as a good working basis in managing any kind of group-based difference in conflict. Both general and specific knowledge of other cultures and ethnic groups can increase our motivation and skill in dealing with people who are culturally and ethnically different.

In addition, while individualists and collectivists have different frames of reference in conflict negotiation, it is important to remember that most conflicts involve some common interests. Rather than harping on positional differences in conflict, parties to intercultural conflict should learn to uncover or cultivate common interests that bind them in the conflict (Fisher & Ury, 1981). Learning about cultural differences and moving toward mutual interest–based negotiation (for example, we both want the computer project to be on time, even though we have different ways of approaching this problem) can serve as the first step toward competent intercultural conflict management. If conflict parties do not develop in-depth knowledge of the implicit theories or scripts that drive intercultural conflict, the root causes of the intercultural conflict may remain unresolved.

"Motivation" in intercultural conflict competence refers to our cognitive and affective predispositions with regard to communicating with people who are different from us. Motivation is a conflict *mind-set* issue. To have an open mindset in dealing with people who are different, we need (1) to suspend judgment of unfamiliar behavior, (2) to develop a mindful attitude in conflict, and (3) to engage in ODIE (observe, describe, interpret, evaluate) analysis.

Suspending evaluative judgment in intercultural conflict requires us to accept the fact that we engage in ethnocentric evaluations of culturally unfamiliar behavior. Ethnocentrism colors our attitudes and behavior in any intergroup conflict. To act competently in intercultural conflict, we must first acknowledge the ethnocentric lenses we put on in interpreting and judging unfamiliar behavior. As Stewart and Bennett comment:

> Participants in a cross-cultural situation need to consider first the possibility that a negative evaluation might be based on unrecognized cultural difference rather than the result of astute cross-cultural analysis. Each person needs to be aware that he or she is evaluating the other, often on similarly ethnocentric grounds, and seek to suspend these kinds of evaluations until the potential spiraling effects of the action have been considered. . . . swift evaluation is likely to be ethnocentric and detrimental to effective intercultural communication. (1991, p. 167)

Acknowledging our own ethnocentric biases and suspending our reactive evaluations are critical aspects of managing intercultural misattribution. By withholding our gut-level negative judgments about unfamiliar behavior, we are giving ourselves and others a chance to understand the cultural nuances that exist in a problematic situation.

Mindfulness is a motivational concept in managing intercultural conflict competently. Langer's (1989) concept of mindfulness encourages individuals to tune in consciously to their habituated mental scripts and expectations. According to Langer, if mindlessness is the "rigid reliance on old categories, mindfulness means the continual creation of new ones. Categorization and recategorization, labeling and relabeling as one masters the world are processes natural to children" (1989, p. 63). To engage in a mindfulness state, an individual needs to learn (1) to be open to new information, (2) to create new categories, and (3) to be aware that multiple perspectives typically exist in viewing a basic phenomenon (Langer, 1989, p. 62).

To acquire new information in conflict interaction, conflict parties must listen responsively to each other even when they are disagreeing. In intercultural conflict, disagreeing parties have to learn to listen attentively to the cultural perspectives and assumptions expressed in the interaction. They have to learn to listen responsively, or *ting* ("聽," the Chinese character for "listening" means listening with our "ears, eyes, and a focused heart") to the sounds, tones, gestures, movements, nonverbal nuances, pauses, and silence in the conflict situation. They must mindfully notice the verbal, nonverbal, and meta-nonverbal contexts that are being conveyed in conflict negotiation. Creating new categories means learning to create or apply culturally sensitive concepts such as low/high-context communication styles in making sense of variations in conflict behavior. Finally, being aware that there are multiple perspectives means that individuals can apply different frameworks (for example, both individualistic and collectivistic perspectives) in analyzing and interpreting conflict and can come up with a creative, synergistic solution.

The third aspect of motivation is *ODIE analysis* (observe, describe, interpret, and then evaluate). Rather than making snapshot, evaluative attributions, we should first learn to *observe* attentively the verbal *and* nonverbal signals that are being exchanged in the conflict process. We should then try to *describe* mentally and in behaviorally specific terms what is going on in the conflict situation (for example, "she is not maintaining eye contact when speaking to me"). We should then generate *multiple interpretations* (for example, "maybe from her cultural angle, eye contact avoidance during conflict is a proper behavior; from my cultural angle, this is considered an improper signal") to make sense of the behavior we are observing and describing. Finally, we may decide to accept or respect the differences as genuine cultural differences and to adapt our-selves by integrating the differences or by *evaluating* them (for example, "I understand that eye contact avoidance can be either a cultural or a personal habit, but I still don't like it, because I feel invalidated by the person's lack of eye contact"). The idea of the sequence observe-describe-interpret is to allow ourselves a more open-ended evaluation or judgment of unfamiliar behavior. We may realize that the discomfort we experience in the conflict negotiation process is based, in part, on communication style differences. We may want to sample a wide range of people (in a wide variety of contexts) from this cultural group to de-termine whether eye contact avoidance is a cul-tural or individual habit. Or we may decide to approach the person (with the low/high-context styles in mind) directly or indirectly to talk about such differences.

Interaction skills, abilities that help us com-municate effectively and appropriately in a given situation, are useful in promoting competence in intercultural conflict. The three skills that ap-pear to be most pertinent are face management skills, trust-building skills, and communicative adaptability.

Parties to intercultural conflict should learn to cultivate *face management skills* in order to deal competently with intergroup conflicts. Face man-agement skills address the fundamental issue of social self-esteem. Most human beings like to be respected and affirmed in their daily interaction with colleagues and loved ones. However, the be-haviors that reveal the need for self-respect and that show respect and dignity to others differ from one culture to the next.

Individualists may want to learn to "give face" to the collectivists in the conflict negotiation pro-cess. Giving face means not humiliating or em-barrassing the collectivists in public, and ac-knowledging collectivists' in-group concerns and obligations. Collectivists, on the other hand, may want to reorient face maintenance concerns and learn to pay more attention to the substantive (or task-relevant) issues. Collectivists may also want to recognize that individualists often separate substantive issues from socio-emotional issues in conflict. Conversely, individualists may want to pay more attention to the link between substan-tive issues and facework or relational issues when negotiating disagreements with collectivists. Thus, although the concern for face maintenance is universal, how we manage face issues is culture-specific.

Critical to competent management of inter-cultural conflict are *trust-building skills*. If parties in conflict do not trust each other, they tend to move away (cognitively, affectively, and physi-cally) from each other rather than struggle side by side. According to Fisher and Brown (1988), trust is often viewed as the "single most important element of a good working relationship" (1988, p. 107). When we do not trust someone's words or actions, we tend automatically to turn off our lis-tening devices in conflict. We may hear the words, but we are not listening. Trust building is both a mind-set and a communication skill. Especially in intercultural conflict situations, when we are experiencing high anxieties with unfamiliar be-havior (for example, accents, nonverbal gestures), we may automatically withhold our trust. Well-founded trust is critical in any effective and ap-propriate management of intercultural conflicts. Trusting someone, however, entails risks.

In emphasizing the importance of developing a good working relationship as a base for conflict management, Fisher and Brown (1988) recom-mend that we learn to be "trustworthy" but not necessarily "wholly trusting." We should also learn to carefully analyze the risk of trust in an intercultural conflict situation. To be trustworthy means we should make our behavior more reli-able so that others can depend on our words or actions over time. To avoid wholly trusting some-one, we should be neither more nor less trusting than the risks dictate. Well-founded trust is based on a mindful analysis of risk. For individualists, such analysis probably is based on the conflict sit-uation at hand. For collectivists, such analysis is often based on a long-term, contextual view of the layers that enwrap the conflict situation. Well-founded trust, in short, is a mind-set, an attitude. It is also a behavior that is developed via consis-tent, competent communication skills of manag-ing differences.

Communicative adaptability is one of the key interaction skills in the negotiation of inter-cultural conflict. Communicative adaptability is the ability to change conflict goals and behaviors to meet the specific needs of the situation (Duran, 1985). It signals our mindful awareness of the other person's perspectives, interests, and/or goals, as well as our willingness to modify our own interests or goals to adapt to the conflict situation. Communicative adaptability can also imply behavioral flexibility. By mindfully observing what is going on in the intercultural conflict situation, both parties may modify their nonverbal and/or verbal behavior to achieve more synchronized interaction.

Summary

Competence in intercultural conflict requires that we communicate effectively and appropriately in different intercultural conflict negotiation situations, and effective, appropriate communication requires adaptation. To manage conflict competently, we must understand and respect different world views and ways of dealing with conflict. We must be sensitive to the differences and similarities between individualistic and collectivistic cultures. We must also be aware of our ethnocentric biases and culture-based attributions in making snapshot evaluations of other conflict management approaches.

Competent conflict negotiation promotes flexible, adaptive behaviors in attuning to both the process and the outcome of an intercultural conflict episode. Although intercultural conflict is complex, understanding conflict along the individualism/collectivism continuum is the first step toward understanding cultural variations on conflict.

SELECTED REFERENCES

Barnlund, D. (1989). *Communicative styles of Japanese and Americans: Images and realities.* Belmont, CA: Wadsworth.

Cohen, R. (1991). *Negotiating across cultures: Communication obstacles in international diplomacy.* Washington, DC: U.S. Institute of Peace.

Duran, R. (1985). Communicative adaptability: A measure of social communicative competence. *Communication Quarterly, 31,* 320–326.

Fisher, R., & Brown, S. (1988). *Getting together: Building relationships as we negotiate.* New York: Penguin Books.

Fisher, R., & Ury, W. (1981). *Getting to yes.* Boston: Houghton Mifflin.

Hall, E. T. (1976). *Beyond culture.* New York: Doubleday.

Hall, E., & Hall, M. (1987). *Hidden differences: Doing business with the Japanese.* Garden City: Anchor Press/Doubleday.

Hofstede, G. (1980). *Culture's consequences: International differences in work-related values.* Beverly Hills, CA: Sage.

Hofstede, G. (1991). *Cultures and organizations: Software of the mind.* London: McGraw-Hill.

Langer, E. (1989). *Mindfulness.* Reading, MA: Addison-Wesley.

Leung, K. (1987). Some determinants of reactions to procedural models for conflict resolution: A cross-national study. *Journal of Personality and Social Psychology, 53,* 898–908.

Leung, K. (1988). Some determinants of conflict avoidance. *Journal of Cross-Cultural Psychology, 19,* 125–136.

Leung, K., & Iwawaki, S. (1988). Cultural collectivism and distributive behavior. *Journal of Cross-Cultural Psychology, 19,* 35–49.

Loden, M., & Rosener, J. (1991). *Workforce America! Managing employee diversity as a vital resource.* Homewood, IL: Business One Irwin.

Lustig, M., & Koester, J. (1993). *Intercultural competence: Interpersonal communication across cultures.* New York: HarperCollins College Publishing.

Mesquita, B., & Frijda, N. (1992). Cultural variations in emotions: A review. *Psychological Bulletin, 112,* 179–204.

Russell, J. (1991). Culture and the categorizations of emotions. *Psychological Bulletin, 110,* 426–450.

Stewart, E., & Bennett, M. (1991). *American cultural patterns: A cross-cultural perspective.* Yarmouth, ME: Intercultural Press.

Sumner, W. (1940). *Folkways.* Boston: Ginn.

Ting-Toomey, S. (1985). Toward a theory of conflict and culture. In W. Gudykunst, L. Stewart, & S. Ting-Toomey (Eds.), *Communication, culture, and organizational processes.* Beverly Hills, CA: Sage.

Ting-Toomey, S. (1988). Intercultural conflict styles:

A face-negotiation theory. In Y. Kim &
W. Gudykunst (Eds.), *Theories in intercultural
communication.* Newbury Park, CA: Sage.

Ting-Toomey, S. (1994). Managing intercultural
conflicts effectively. In L. Samovar & R. Porter
(Eds.), *Intercultural communication: A reader*
(7th ed.). Belmont, CA: Wadsworth.

Triandis, H. (1995). *Individualism and collectivism.*
Boulder, CO: Westview Press.

KEY TERMS

conflict

individualism

collectivism

high context

low context

self-construal

ethnocentrism

conflict style

conflict competence

DISCUSSION QUESTIONS

1. Individualism and collectivism promote two
rather different orientations to conflict. How are
these differences reconciled in an intercultural
conflict? One person could completely adapt
(conform) to the other person's orientation.
For example, a collectivist could take on an
individualist orientation during conflict with
an individualist. Would this approach be communicatively competent? Why or why not? What
are some alternative ways for reconciling differences in values so that conflict can be managed
successfully?

2. Think of a difficult conflict you've had with a
relative stranger (possibly someone from another
culture). Can you explain any of the difficulty
in the conflict as being due to the fact that you
and the other person had (1) different conflict
assumptions, (2) different conflict rhythms,
(3) different conflict styles, or (4) different ethnocentric lenses? What happened that leads you to
infer any of these differences?

3. Among the dimensions that facilitate communicative competence, knowledge is the most
important for managing intercultural conflict.
What is meant by knowledge? Do you agree or
disagree? Why or why not? Can knowledge about
another's culture ever lead you to be incompetent? If so, how? (Hint: If you meet a Chinese
man and presume he possesses collectivistic
values and treat him accordingly, do you run the
risk of unduly stereotyping him?)

4. The desire to maintain face seems to be culturally universal, even though face issues are
managed differently in different cultures. Does
this universality suggest any general guidelines
that would help communicators seek common
ground when managing intercultural conflict?

5. How might power differentials come into play
in cross-cultural conflicts?

42
NEGOTIATING WITH THE SWAZIS

PETER OGOM NWOSU

*I feel like a man sitting in my house facing
a poised snake. I am trying to be very calm
and avoid sudden movement. Meanwhile, my
friends outside the door are throwing rocks at
the snake. I am the one endangered, not they.*
—Late King Sobhuza of Swaziland

Negotiation

Negotiation or bargaining[1] has been defined as a
process in which two or more players with different needs, different interests and perspectives "attempt to settle what each shall give and take, or

perform and receive in a transaction between them" (Rubin and Brown, 1975). Since the players involved in the process are interdependent, they use proposals, counterproposals, and compromises to reach agreements based on mutually acceptable terms (Putnam and Jones, 1982).

In their article "Reciprocity in Negotiations: An Analysis of Bargaining Interaction," Putnam and Jones (1982) note that:

> Although we typically associate bargaining with labor-management disputes, the process of negotiating occurs in a number of settings. Specifically, companies bargain with suppliers, customers bicker with sales personnel, politicians and diplomats make international trades [or agreements], and lawyers bargain case appeals with clients and judges. In effect, we rely on bargaining as a dominant mode of conflict management in a variety of interpersonal and organizational contexts (p. 171).

Noting that negotiation [in some cultures or situations] "employs trade-offs as the dominant modus operandi for managing conflict or resolving issues," Putnam and Jones (p. 172), however, warn that negotiation involves more than an assimilation of trade-offs. More important, "it is a communicative process involving persuasion, and is characterized by the exchange of information, arguments, and strategic maneuvers." Shelling (1960) shares a similar view. According to him, communication allows players in a negotiating encounter "to discover patterns of individual behavior that make each player's actions predictable to the other, to test each other for a shared sense of regularity [and] to exploit . . . impromptu codes for signaling intentions and for responding to each other's signals" (p. 4).

However, when the players have become socialized in different cultural milieu—when they "do not share the same ways of thinking, feeling, and behaving"—the process of negotiation at either the domestic or international level becomes much more complex. As Fisher (1980) puts it, the "potential for misunderstanding will be greater [here]; more time will be lost in talking past each other. More complete explanations of positions may be needed, or a special kind of persuasive

skill called for" (p. 1). And Fisher warns that "it is naive indeed to venture into international negotiation with the untempered self-assurance that after all people are pretty much alike everywhere."

In fact, no two nations actually negotiate in the same way. Each country's style of negotiation is shaped by [its] culture, historical circumstance, political ideology and its place in the international community (Binnendijk, 1987). Adler (1986), for instance, notes that "countries vary on such key aspects as the amount and type of preparation for a negotiation, the relative emphasis on task versus interpersonal relationships; the use of general principles versus specific details; and the number of people present and the extent of their influence" (p. 152). The ability of an individual, therefore, to understand a country's negotiating style, including the nuances, enhances that individual's effectiveness as a negotiator, and *ceteris paribus*, the atmosphere for the peaceful resolution of issues.

This paper describes the negotiating style of the Swazi, a Bantu-speaking[2] people inhabiting a small but strategically located kingdom in Southern Africa. The paper is based on interviews conducted with Swazi nationals and government officials, as well as on selected literature on the country, and on the subject of negotiation in general. Among issues addressed are the players and the social situation, the negotiation process including strategies and tactics, style of decision making, as well as the impact of national character and cross-cultural "noise" on negotiations.

Swazi Approaches to Negotiation

The story is told of a prominent British evangelist who had come to Swaziland to negotiate a piece of land where he would build a church for his Christian ministry. He was brought before the *Ngwenyama*[3] (King Sobhuza) by an intermediary. The intermediary, while introducing the evangelist to the king, eulogized the evangelist's healing power. He told Sobhuza that the evangelist had come to seek the king's support so that he could live in Swaziland and perform the same miracle works he had carried out in Britain. King Sobhuza listened attentively. After a long pause, he responded by first welcoming the evangelist. He thanked him for his interest in the kingdom and the people. He then turned to his officials after another pause and remarked, "Go and find out if there are people in Britain who still need healing. If there are no such people, then give this gentleman every support that he needs, including a piece of land!" Strong words. Of course the evangelist went back home and never returned. Several months later, reports had it that this evangelist had been jailed for defrauding the government! (M. Dlamini, Personal communication, April 14, 1988).

This story underscores a key, but often overlooked, aspect of Swazi negotiation style—the assumption that the Swazis bring to the bargaining encounter. To the Swazis, the other party is guilty of deception until proven innocent. The American notion that a person is innocent or trustworthy until proven guilty does not prevail during negotiations.

Hilda Kuper (1986), a noted authority on Swazi history, remarks that most Swazis prefer that the *umlungu* (a term used for a foreigner, particularly a white person) must prove himself before he could be received as *umuntfu* (a person). Another scholar explains:

> Swazis are very skeptical of foreigners—in whatever form. They want to know by whose authority you come. They want to know why that authority is not personally present. And they want to know whom to go to if a problem arises. Someone has to be accountable for your presence. (M. Dlamini, 1988)

The cautious, or perhaps suspicious approach of the Swazis toward negotiations, notes Carlton Dlamini, Acting Ambassador of the Kingdom of Swaziland to the United States, is a reflection of the country's historical past as well as its geopolitical position in Southern Africa. "Our open approach to issues in the past, and our acceptance of people on the face value have created problems for us. In addition, we are sandwiched between two systems of government that are completely different from ours. Such situations dictate that we maintain some form of caution" (C. Dlamini, Personal communication, April 21, 1988).

Traditionally, when visitors come to a Swazi homestead or any part of the countryside, the Swazi family is obliged by custom to let the visitor in, even if they do not know the person. In most cases, they allow the visitor to occupy a bedroom, even if it means having the occupants of the household sleep in the living room or in the kitchen. This African concept of hospitality, or the "spirit of accommodation" as it is called, which has been extended to the negotiating encounter, formed the basis for the acceptance into Swaziland of many foreigners (mostly Europeans) during and after the nineteenth century. But as Booth (1983) notes, the European's appetite for Swaziland's resources (particularly the land and its wealth) turned the kingdom into a pawn in the scramble for Africa and eventually into a British protectorate. By 1968, when the country became independent, over fifty percent of Swazi Nation Land had been expropriated, and some ceded to South Africa, under dubious land deals. Today, modern-day Swaziland, a small landlocked kingdom (slightly larger than the state of New Jersey in the United States), and certainly one of the smallest countries in Africa, finds itself bordered on three sides by the Republic of South Africa, and by Mozambique on its eastern side. Negotiations are still continuing with South Africa to recover some of the lost lands.

The Swazis believe that the first step in the negotiation process, either at the domestic or international level, is to establish the legitimacy or credibility of the negotiators. What this entails, for instance, is that a foreigner coming to conduct negotiations, particularly business negotiations, for the first time in Swaziland must develop "legitimate contact." Legitimate contact, according to Martin Dlamini, a member of the Swazi Royal Family, implies an "intermediary," or "go-between," who will be responsible for "clearing the road" for the foreigner before the actual negotiation begins. Usually the intermediary is a prominent person within the community, and his responsibility involves taking the foreigner to meet the "right" people at the "right" time. In the process, the intermediary helps build the credibility or legitimacy of the foreigner, prior to the negotiations. Ambassador Dlamini remarks that the use of intermediaries, or go-betweens, during negotiations is a highly valued aspect of Swazi culture. "In a sense, it shows the seriousness of the issue" (C. Dlamini, 1988).

Generally, the Swazis do not like to be taken by surprise, and by using an intermediary, the negotiation path is smoothed and the element of surprise removed. In the same manner, when a Swazi official is coming to another country, for instance, the United States, to conduct business either at the World Bank, the International Monetary Fund, or the State Department, "we prefer to send a person who makes the initial contacts, thus making things easier for our negotiators" (C. Dlamini, April 21, 1988).

An intermediary may not necessarily be a Swazi national but could be someone from another culture who has spent some time in Swaziland and understands the culture and the people. It could, for instance, be the U.S. Ambassador to Swaziland or any top member of the diplomatic corps; or the director of Peace Corps activities in Swaziland. The subject matter determines the choice of the intermediary. While intermediaries may clear the way or smooth the negotiation path, they do not necessarily guarantee the success of a negotiation. As the story of the British evangelist suggests, the foreign negotiating team must convince the Swazis of the authenticity of their mission. According to Martin Dlamini, "the Swazis will receive a foreigner given their traditional concept of hospitality, but we know we do not have to agree with you until we have verified your authenticity."

Martin Dlamini recalls the negotiation that took place in 1980 during the hiring of a national soccer coach for the country. Two foreigners—one from Poland and the other from Hungary—had been invited for discussions. While the Polish coach engaged in much self-praise, the Hungarian (Coach Ted Dumitru), on the other hand, was reportedly very low-profile, soft-spoken, less abrasive and less pushy in his comments. He was consequently chosen, even though it would cost the Swazi Government more to hire him!

The Swazis are quick to attribute motives when a person, during negotiations, is very pushy, engages in too much self-praise, or acts like he or she knows everything. "People who talk a lot are not welcome. Be calm, but not too calm that they suspect you are up to some mischief," remarks an official of the Swazi Embassy in Washington, D.C. Indeed, there is such a thin line between talkativeness and calmness, that it is difficult for a foreigner to understand when one is being "too talkative" or "too calm." Hence, Swazi insistence or suggestion that an intermediary be used.

Typically, Swazis employ what Adler (1986, p. 149) calls an "affective approach" to negotiating. An affective approach to negotiations emphasizes the development of a strong sense of relationship. To the Swazis, it is not the piece of paper, the contract, the agreement, or the substance of the negotiation that necessarily counts, but rather the relationship of trust that is developed with the other party.

Thus, prior to the negotiations, they treat the foreign negotiating team to a number of events or ceremonies, including, in some instances, courtesy calls on the *Ngwenyama* (the king) or the *Ndlovukazi* (The Lady Elephant or Queen Mother), or other relevant functionaries of the government. Swazis use such events or occasions to get to know more about the other negotiators. In fact, the development of a fairly strong relationship at the early stage of the negotiations or bargaining process reduces the element of suspicion. It also provides a basis or context for further interaction or deliberations. While many Americans may downplay these ceremonies and protocol, Swazis cherish them. For them, it is simply not appropriate to sit down to discuss business without, at least, some form of social interaction taking place first. Many foreign negotiators, frustrated by the delays, have actually marred the negotiation process by their impatience and the insistence that they "get down to business immediately" (M. Dlamini, April 14, 1988).

Swazis do not like to be rushed or be expected to negotiate within a specific time frame. A Swazi embassy official remarks that "the worst thing you can do in terms of negotiating with the Swazis is to place a time limit upon them." The issue has to be of national significance and immediacy to require a rush or a time limit. The official advises foreign negotiators to "be prepared to spend a lot more days during negotiations. Come there, knowing that the first day is for protocol and socializing" (Personal communication, April 20,

1988). Where the issue is of a certain magnitude, he adds, it may require the final approval of the *Ngwenyama*, or the Ngwenyama-in-council, and this may take more days.

In a sense, Swazi concepts, structure, and perceptions of time, like those of all Africans, are dictated by nature. This is not the situation in case-particularistic societies such as the United States, where time has been reified, and placed at the center of all social, economic, political, and personal activities. Time, as Burgoon and Saine (1978) remark, is the master, Westerners [Americans] its slaves. In Swaziland, as in the rest of Africa, time is the slave, Swazis its masters. As Awa (1987) notes, if a person comes to a meeting "late," he or she does not feel obligated to apologize. And when a paramount chief, for instance,

> summons his cabinet, through a messenger, to convene at daybreak [i.e. at the crow of the cock] and some arrive at 5:30 a.m. and others at 6:00 a.m, none of them will be perceived as late. Decisions by "chiefs-in-council" require full representation and participation of all section heads, and such decisions are generally preceded by a social event—the ritual breaking of Kola nut, a prolonged libation ceremony— deliberately calculated to allow time for a quorum to be attained. (Awa, this volume p. 139).

Strategies

During the actual negotiations, the Swazis employ a "traditional" negotiating style. In essence, it is not a give-and-take approach but, instead, it is based on what Martin Dlamini calls the "concept of listening." "We do not throw out all our cards on the table. We first listen to what the other party has to say. If we do not have an immediate response, we may then ask for adjournment to enable us to put our heads together and prepare one."

This may take a few hours or even days, and this could be frustrating to the foreign negotiator. Throughout the negotiating encounter, waiting and silence, as is the case with the Barai of Papua New Guinea (near Australia) or the Japanese, become frequent. To the Swazis, long pauses and si-

lence during negotiations provide an opportunity for them to analyze the implications of what is being said by the other party. Where the language of the negotiation is English, French, or any foreign language other than *SiSwati* (Swazi language), silence enables the Swazis to "think through" the information given by the other party. To Westerners, however, gaps of silence during negotiations can be a terribly discomforting cultural "noise." As Olsson notes, such noise could indicate a lack of interest in the issue being discussed.

Generally, Swazi culture does not allow for open confrontation or disagreement with the outsider. Such would be seen as a negation of the idea of relationship-building which the Swazi prize so much. So when Swazi negotiators become too uncomfortable or have misgivings about an issue, they may ask for an adjournment, rather than engage in an argument.

During the negotiation process, Swazis express disapproval over an issue by looking at each other without saying a word. This non-verbal eye-to-eye contact message is interpreted or decoded by the Swazi negotiating team as a time to call for adjournment. Meetings could resume the same day or the following day by which time the Swazi team may come up with responses, new strategies, or concessions.

Indeed, the vocalization of this intent (that is the adjournment) is one of five of the verbal tactics used by the Swazis during negotiations. The other four are: to postpone the negotiation *indefinitely*, in order to make a point; to provide alternative suggestions or counterproposals; to employ the concept of sympathy; or to use the notion of a small but powerful country. (Personal communications with M. Dlamini, April 14, 1988, and C. Dlamini, April 21, 1988).

Although postponing negotiations *indefinitely* is a tactic in the bargaining arsenal of the Swazis, it is rarely used, except in circumstances where they feel very strongly about certain principles. One example is the question of publicity during negotiations. The Swazis are a very low profile people; hence press coverage of negotiations when, in fact, the negotiations have not been concluded, are frowned upon.

Hilda Kuper (1986), in her book *The Swazi: A South African Kingdom*, notes the national consternation that resulted in 1982 when the South African press reported a controversial land deal between the Republic of South Africa and the Kingdom of Swaziland. The South African press had reported, albeit wrongly, that the government of Swaziland was negotiating with South Africa for the incorporation (into South Africa) of territories inhabited by ethnic Swazis. The truth of the matter was that the Swazi government was negotiating with the government of South Africa for the return to Swaziland of *Ka Ngwane*—the areas inhabited by ethnic Swazis in South Africa and which the South African government had granted the status of *Bantustans* or dependent homelands.

Negotiations for the return of these areas had started long before South Africa formulated its policy of Bantustans. According to Kuper, following the establishment of the Union of South Africa in 1910, Swaziland had negotiated the territories through the British. In 1966, when *Ka Ngwane* was pronounced a Bantustan, the *Ngwenyama*, King Sobhuza, requested the British to ask the South Africans "to hold the matter in abeyance." Direct negotiations were resumed soon after Swazi independence in 1968. These negotiations, spanning several years, were highly secretive. Sobhuza operated in the background, acting through emissaries, especially his minister of Foreign Affairs, R. V. Dlamini. Most Swazi officials, according to Kuper, were neither consulted nor kept informed. All dealings were with accredited representatives of the South African government "on the grounds that international boundaries could only be negotiated by heads of independent states, not leaders of Bantustans or dependent homelands" (Kuper 1986, p. 156). While it is not exactly clear why the South Africans released their version of the negotiation to the press, that version evoked a feeling of betrayal and outrage in Swaziland.

Sobhuza responded by postponing the negotiations *indefinitely*, and calling a meeting later (March 19, 1982), at his *Lozitha* palace to clarify the position of his government. In attendance were heads of diplomatic missions in Swaziland, as well as all of Swaziland's ambassadors and high commissioners called home from abroad, and by members of parliament, permanent secretaries, and the Swazi National Council. He also

dispatched a team of top-level officers to different African countries to explain the position of his government to African leaders.

Another verbal strategy that the Swazis employ during the bargaining process is to provide alternative suggestions or counterproposals. As Adler (1986, p. 176) notes, counterproposals involve negotiators responding to their opponents' proposals by simply offering their own proposal. Counterproposals are frequently used by the Swazis especially when the concept of sympathy, or appeal to emotions, as a verbal strategy fails. In some instances, notes Martin Dlamini, Swazis have occasionally, even in a subtle manner, prefixed their responses to negotiations with emotion-laden appeals. For example, a Swazi negotiator may refer to Swaziland's small size or that it is a disadvantaged developing country, as a tactic for winning concessions from the other party. However, as Fisher (1980) discovers in his study of Mexican negotiating styles (and this applies to Swaziland as well), "where this approach crosses the line from being a sincere position to calculated tactics is not easily determined" (p. 25). Ambassador Carlton Dlamini further remarks that while the concept of sympathy may not be as pervasive as other strategies during negotiations, the Swazis may play, in a positive way, on the size of their country, the strength of their economy, their geographical location, and their peaceful coexistence with their neighbors as a basis for winning concessions. In reality, Swazis describe their country as the "Switzerland of Africa." Clearly that notion of its peace and stability in a region of great conflict, in addition to its large deposits of natural resources, make it a more important country in Southern Africa than its size would indicate. These factors embody the concept of a small but powerful country, which the Swazis often bring to the negotiating table as a strategy for influencing the bargaining process and outcomes.

Swazi verbal responses to requests sometimes leave the other party wondering what they have said or what they mean. When he is not sure how he wants to respond, a Swazi negotiator, as Martin Dlamini reveals, may use such phrases as, "Oh, I see, I see," while at the same time nodding his head. The nodding of the head does not necessarily indicate that he agrees with what the other party is saying. This behavior often creates problems for the foreign negotiating team. Again, when he is not sure of what responses to provide, a Swazi negotiator may use the phrase, "Well, I think this may need the approval of the king."

Negotiators

We turn now to the negotiators themselves. How are they selected? In general, a Swazi negotiating team is composed mainly of a wide range of officials appointed because of their status and loyalty to the *Ngwenyama*, their experience in the bureaucracy, and their technical expertise. Because Swaziland is traditionally a monarchy, there is a conscious effort to include a symbolic representative of the king in the negotiating teams. The king's representative is selected on account of his age, wisdom in traditional precedence, and loyalty to the royal family. He is perceived as the *Ngwenyama's* "ears" and "eyes" at the meetings, even though he may have no knowledge of the subject matter. Usually the official chief negotiator is a senior person with sufficient status and experience to serve as a symbolic representative of the domestic consensus. He could be a cabinet minister or a permanent secretary, for example. Then there is a person(s) with the technical expertise—usually a younger person. While the chief negotiator may know and say little about the subject matter, he usually refers the matter to the younger person with the specialized knowledge. As a rule, many of these younger specialists have acquired their education and training at colleges and universities in the United States, the United Kingdom, or at the University of Swaziland. In dealing with foreigners, particularly whites, Western education is recognized as an asset, and young people with this qualification are occupying important positions within the bureaucracy (Kuper, 1986, p. 35).

Like the selection process, the process of decision making is highly centralized in Swaziland. Swazi negotiators do not have a wide latitude to commit the country to certain deals, without the approval of higher authorities. Certain issues, for example, the land negotiations with South Africa, require the final approval of the *Ngwenyama* or the full *Ligogo* (the inner council).

In general, trying to influence the process of decision making in Swaziland is a delicate issue, as the Swazis are suspicious of attempts by foreigners to manipulate them or to goad them into making precipitous and costly decisions. The story is told by a prominent observer of Southern Africa that he was conversing with the late King Sobhuza about the problem of South African political refugees—and even freedom fighters—using Swaziland as a base for operations. Although Swaziland did not allow its territory to be used as a base by the freedom fighters, there was considerable pressure from other African leaders for it to do so. Sobhuza, an aging but astute politician, commented, "I feel like a man sitting in my home facing a poised snake. I am trying to be very calm and avoid sudden movement. Meanwhile my friends outside the door are throwing rocks at the snake. I am the one endangered, not they" (Grotpeter, 1975).

While caution predominates the Swazi approach to bargaining, it must be noted that increasing contact with the outside world, both economic and political, means that Swaziland must adjust certain aspects of its "traditional" negotiating style. "The status quo is already losing its touch," says Martin Dlamini. He recalls several negotiations with the World Bank and the IMF for loan agreements, pointing out that "Swazi negotiators are abandoning our traditional approach to negotiations, and instead, are throwing their cards first on the drawing board, without first *listening* to what the other party has to offer. In the final analysis, too little is achieved, too much concessions are made to the detriment of Swazi national interests."

We have already noted certain aspects of protocol and formalities in negotiations with the Swazis, but suffice it to state (and this is important) that the American custom of addressing people (negotiators) by their first names is not accepted by them. During the December 1987 Reagan-Gorbachev meeting in Washington, D.C., President Reagan informed the American audience that he and Soviet General Secretary Gorbachev have agreed to call each other by their first names—Ronnie and Mikhail. But this egalitarian behavior has long been recognized as a threat to international protocol. Swazis frown at such cross-cultural noise. Nobody ever addresses the *Ngwenyama* by his first name; only by his official title. Both the *Ngwenyama* and the *Ndlovukazi* receive elaborate deference during official ceremonies. Royal speeches, according to Kuper (1986, p. 158), are punctuated with flattering titles: "He is 'The Lion,' 'The Sun,' 'The Milky Way,' 'Obstacle to the Enemy.' She is 'The Lady Elephant,' 'The Earth,' 'The Beautiful,' 'Mother of the Country,'" and so on. Other Swazis, as a rule, prefer to be addressed formally during negotiations.

Also, when shaking hands with Swazi officials prior to the actual negotiations, the Swazis prefer that the foreign negotiators do so the "Swazi way," using both hands, with the left hand holding the arm very close to the wrist of the extended right hand. Swazis consider this a sign of respect, and the behavior comes from Swazi philosophy that in receiving something from a person, you must do so fully and sincerely. Putting one hand in one's pocket while shaking hands with the other, notes Martin Dlamini, is considered noise, a mark of disrespect, and could create a barrier to effective communication during negotiations.

Finally, as a people steeped in tradition, the Swazis like their culture to be esteemed. Knowledge of a few Swazi words places the foreign negotiator at an advantage. It opens up the door to relationship building, an important aspect of Swazi negotiating style. In the final analysis, a foreign negotiator must learn to be patient, and gradually build the trust that is needed for negotiating successfully with the Swazis.

NOTES

1. The terms *negotiation* and *bargaining* are used interchangeably in this paper. This position is supported by some theorists such as Shelling (1960) and Putnam and Jones (1982), who argue that the processes and characteristics of bargaining and negotiations are similar to one another. The difference, however, may be in the degree of interactions. While bargaining may involve interactions among small units, negotiations often involve interactions among large social units. But such differences do not obviate the fact that at both levels of interaction, the interactants may use similar approaches or strategies to argue their cases.

2. *Bantu* literally stands for "People," in siSwati, the Swazi language. It is a linguistic label derived from the root *ntu*, meaning "person," and the plural prefix *ba*. For a detailed analysis of the Swazi people and their history, see, for example, Kuper, Hilda, *The Swazi: A South African kingdom. Case studies in cultural anthropology, 1986.*

3. *Ngwenyama* is a Swazi word for "The Lion." It is a title used for all Swazi kings, including the current one—twenty-year-old King Mswati III.

REFERENCES

Adler, N. (1986). *International dimension of organizational behavior.* Boston, MA: Kent Publishing Company.

Awa, N. (1987). *Communication in Africa: Implications for development planning.* Paper presented at the 37th Annual Convention of the International Communication Association, Montreal, Canada.

Binnendijk, H. (Ed.). (1987). *National negotiating styles.* Washington, DC: Foreign Service Institute, Department of State.

Booth, A. (1983). *Swaziland: Tradition and change in a southern African kingdom.* Boulder, CO: Westview Press.

Burgoon, J., and Saine, T. (1978). *The unspoken dialogue. An introduction to non-verbal communication.* Boston: Houghton-Mifflin Press.

Fisher, G. (1980). *The cross-cultural dimension in international negotiation.* Rev. discussion paper prepared for the Foreign Service Institute, Washington, DC.

Grotpeter, J. J. (1975). *Historical dictionary of Swaziland.* Metuchen, NJ: The Scarecrow Press, Inc.

Kuper, H. (1986). *The Swazi: A South African kingdom.* New York: Holt, Rinehart and Winston.

Olsson, M. (n.d.). *Meeting styles for intercultural groups.* Washington, DC: Society for Intercultural Education, Training and Research.

Putnam, L., and Jones, T. (1982). Reciprocity in

negotiations: An analysis of bargaining interaction. *Communication monographs, 49,* 171–191.

Rubin, J., and Brown, B. (1975). *The social psychology of bargaining and negotiation.* New York: Academic Press.

Shelling, T. (1960). *The strategy of conflict.* Cambridge, MA: Harvard University Press.

KEY TERMS

bargaining	emic
negotiation	Africa
conflict resolution	communication style
Swaziland	

DISCUSSION QUESTIONS

1. How does the Swazi style of conflict resolution compare with U.S. conflict resolution styles?
2. What is the role of intermediaries in Swazi negotiation?
3. What advice would you give Swazi students studying at a U.S. college about how to best deal with conflicts they may have with U.S. friends?
4. Nwosu researches from an interpretive perspective. How might a social science researcher investigate negotiation styles?

43
VIEWS FROM THE OTHER SIDE: PERSPECTIVES ON THE CYPRUS CONFLICT

BENJAMIN J. BROOME

Introduction

During the past 2½ years, I have lived and worked on the eastern Mediterranean island of Cyprus, which is the legendary birthplace of Aphrodite, the ancient goddess of love and fertility. Unfortunately, there are few signs today of Aphrodite's legacy, as the country is engaged in a long-standing conflict that has resulted in the physical division of the country between two ethnic communities, the Greek Cypriots and the Turkish Cypriots. I was in Cyprus as a Fulbright Scholar, offering seminars, workshops, and training programs in communication and conflict resolution. I worked in both communities and in a bicommunal setting with individuals of all ages, professions, and political persuasions. My initial goal was to introduce concepts and skills that might help members of the two communities work together more productively. In the process of offering these programs I became a third-party facilitator for bringing members of the two communities together across a dividing line that has proven to be even stronger than the Berlin Wall.

The Cyprus conflict has become one of the most protracted international disputes of modern times. Almost immediately after Cyprus gained its independence in 1960, intercommunal violence started between the Greek Cypriots and the Turkish Cypriots, who at the time were living in mixed or neighboring villages and towns. Disputes over changes in the constitution led to the withdrawal of the Turkish Cypriots from the government in 1963, and violent clashes later that same year resulted in the formation of Turkish Cypriot enclaves scattered throughout the island. United Nations peacekeeping troops were brought in to help prevent further bloodshed. Unrest between the two communities continued, however, and in 1974 a coup against the Cyprus government, staged by the military dictatorship of Greece, led to intervention by Turkish troops. Thousands of Greek Cypriots were forced from their homes and businesses in the northern part of the island, and almost all Turkish Cypriots fled their homes in the southern part of Cyprus and were resettled in the north. This resulted in ethnic partition of the island, enforced to this day by the heavy military presence of the Turkish army. United Nations peacekeeping forces patrol a buffer zone that divides the island across the middle from west to east. In spite of continuous diplomatic activity mediated by the United Nations, the United States, Great Britain, and the European Union, no settlement of the Cyprus conflict has been reached in over 22 years of negotiations.[1]

Although Turkish Cypriots and Greek Cypriots speak different languages and follow different religions, they share many common cultural characteristics, the results of over 400 years of living together on a small island. Their social values, their lifestyles, their traditional crafts, and many of their songs and dances are similar. They have a large shared vocabulary, and they have much in common in their communication style—both speak a dialect of their respective languages, and these dialects share common rhythmic patterns. Both Greek Cypriots and Turkish Cypriots feel connected to the island in similar ways, and they face similar difficulties when they travel to their respective "motherlands," Greece and Turkey. Even in their physical characteristics they are difficult to distinguish. On many occasions I have shown photos of bicommunal groups to outsiders, and it was impossible for them to indicate the ethnic background of the participants. Even Cypriots themselves usually cannot identify members of the other community by physical appearance alone.[2] Yet the mental pictures that each holds of the other and of the past are totally different. There are few places in the world where two communities living in a single geographical area who share so much in common are so far apart on issues that divide them.

One of the primary factors contributing to the stalemate in Cyprus is the almost total lack of contact between the two communities. Although it is never easy to deal with conflict situations, it becomes even more difficult when there is no direct communication between the parties involved. Without an exchange of ideas and perceptions, negotiation and compromise are unlikely, and it is impossible for relationships of

trust and empathy to develop.[3] Although the avoidance of communication is sometimes a conscious choice of the conflicting parties, the Greek-Cypriot and Turkish-Cypriot communities in Cyprus are trapped in a situation where communication is actually prohibited or very tightly controlled. Almost all forms of direct interaction are nearly impossible because of the absence of normal communication links between the two communities—only with the help of third parties such as the United Nations can residents contact each other via telephone, mail, or personal visits, and there is almost no business exchange between the two communities. During the past 30 years, the primary images each has developed of the other have come through the mass media, the education system, and political propaganda. The forced separation has created a gap that will make it very difficult to find a solution to this tragic conflict.

The de facto partition of Cyprus has meant that a generation of Turkish Cypriots and Greek Cypriots have grown up without knowing anyone from the other community. Many of these people are now university students, and they have very different perspectives about the conflict on their island and distorted perceptions of each other. Most important, they hold very different beliefs about what must be done to resolve the conflict. This article gives an account of these seemingly incompatible realities, as they are described by the younger generation. It presents two letters, each addressed to you, a person who lives outside Cyprus and who may not be familiar with the situation. The letters come from Cypriot students—one from a Greek-Cypriot university student living and studying in the Greek-Cypriot-administered part of the island, one from a Turkish-Cypriot university student living and studying in the Turkish-Cypriot administered part of the island.

In these letters, the authors try to explain their understanding of the Cyprus conflict, as they have learned about it from their family, in their school, and from the media. Neither of the letters was written by a single person; rather, each one is based on numerous discussions I have had with students in Cyprus during the past 2 years. Most of the students are undergraduates at universities in their respective communities, in some cases studying only a few kilometers from each other but living in very different worlds. Of course, students hold a variety of views about the Cyprus situation, so as you read these letters keep in mind that any particular Cypriot student may disagree with some of the points. Nevertheless, each letter represents a composite of attitudes and views that are widespread throughout the respective communities.

As you read the letters, note the similarities and differences in the two points of view. The Cyprus issue is very emotional for all those involved, making it difficult for anyone caught up in the conflict to listen to the other. At the end of this article I provide a brief analysis of the two perspectives. Before reading my comments, ask yourself if there is any possibility of bridging the differences between the two communities. What do you think are the primary obstacles to building empathy? Can you find common themes upon which empathy might be built? Do you believe it is possible for the two individuals to understand each other?

A Greek Cypriot's View of the Cyprus Conflict [4]

Hello, my fellow student. I am glad to know that you are interested to learn something about the conflict in my beautiful but tragic country, and I will do my best to explain the situation to you. I don't know if you have heard much about Cyprus, but I am sure that you learned many things in your school about Greece because it gave the world the concept of democracy and provided the basis for all of Western science, art, medicine, and philosophy. Well, Cyprus has been part of the Greek world for more than 3,000 years, and if you visit my island you will see all the ancient Greek temples and other archeological sites. We have been speaking the Greek language here since the earliest Greeks arrived, just after the Trojan war described by Homer, the great poet of antiquity. Of course, we have endured many conquerors since that time, but none of them have been able to take away our language and culture. We were subjugated

by many empires, including the Romans, the Franks, and the Venetians, but we suffered the most under the Turks, who invaded our island over 400 years ago and kept us under their yoke for over 300 years.

When the Turks were ruling Cyprus they sent many soldiers and farmers here, who settled in many of our villages and towns. Today these people make up the Turkish-Cypriot population, who comprise about 18% of the total. These newcomers to our island speak a different language (Turkish) and follow a different religion (Islam). We Greek Cypriots are very hospitable, however, so we used to get along quite well with the Turkish Cypriots. Most of them learned to speak Greek, and we lived together in harmony as good neighbors. After Turkish rule ended in the late 1800s, we became a British colony. The Turkish Cypriots stayed, and we let them keep their lands, houses, and businesses.

Although the British made some positive contributions to the island, particularly in improving our roads and other means of communication, they wouldn't let us join with Greece, our mother country, to whom we felt we belonged (at least at that time). The British wanted to keep us as their colony, but eventually we managed to get rid of them, thanks to our heroic EOKA (or freedom) fighters. Unfortunately, we were not able to achieve our goal of union with Greece, but we became an independent country, the Cyprus Republic, in 1960. However, our constitution was drawn up by outsiders, and it was very unfair, giving too much power to the Turkish Cypriots who were only 18% of the population. We tried to make it work, but the Turkish Cypriots were always blocking legislation, making it impossible for the government to function effectively. When we wanted to introduce some changes that would make the system more workable, the Turkish Cypriots decided to stop participating in the government. This happened near the end of 1963, and although I don't know much about what took place, I remember there were troubles that occurred when Turkish-Cypriot terrorists killed some people. After that, the Turkish Cypriots chose to abandon their homes and villages and live together in areas they controlled. I guess they felt safer there, although they had nothing to fear from us. In any case, life went back to normal for a while.

Unfortunately, Turkey started getting involved in Cyprus around this time, and things took a turn for the worst. I think that Turkey was behind the Turkish Cypriots leaving the government and convinced them to be afraid of us. You see, Cyprus is only about 60 kilometers from the Turkish coast, and the expansionist plans of Turkey have always called for takeover of Cyprus. Turkey was waiting for the right opportunity, and it tried to create trouble several times. In 1974 we Greeks gave it the excuse it needed. There was a military dictatorship in Greece at the time, and it overthrew our government, installing its own leader in Cyprus in place of our democratically elected president. We were too weak to do anything about it, even though no one liked what happened. In any case, Turkey immediately sent in an invasion force to take over Cyprus, claiming it was intervening to protect the Turkish Cypriots.

When the Turkish army came, it was a savage and barbaric onslaught against a defenseless people. The army killed innocent civilians, raped the women, burned our forest, stole valuable icons. We put up a brave resistance, but the Turks had too many soldiers, tanks, and airplanes. We didn't stand a chance. The army landed on the north coast, and as it advanced, the soldiers forced all the Greek Cypriots from their homes and businesses, turning them into refugees within their own country. The Turks took many prisoners, and 1,619 of them are still missing. Finally the army stopped and drew a line across the middle of Cyprus, dividing the island into the north and south. After chasing all the Greek Cypriots from the northern part, the army took all the Turkish Cypriots and moved them to the north to live in our homes. In the end, it was a very effective job of ethnic cleansing.

My own family suffered greatly at the hands of the Turks. My father's brother was killed trying to defend against the invasion, and the son of my mother's sister was taken prisoner. We have never found out what happened to him. Our family came from a beautiful village on the north coast called Lapithos, in the Kyrenia dis-

trict. My mother's family had lived there for generations, and we had a beautiful house and many orchards of cherry and almond trees. The view from our village was the best in Cyprus, since you could see all along the coast of the beautiful Mediterranean, while behind you were the magnificent forested slopes of the Pendedactylos mountains. There were some beautiful churches in Lapithos, with famous icons and centuries-old paintings, all of which were stolen by the Turkish army. When the Turks came, we had to leave quickly. We had no time to pack anything. Everything was left behind, including all the wonderful lace and tablecloths my mother had made and even the photos of my parents' wedding. Now some Turkish military officer or some settler from Anatolia is probably living in our house, and who knows what condition it is in.

It was not easy to overcome the loss inflicted upon us by the Turks. My father and mother had three children, and they had to live in tents for many months before they could find a suitable house. I was born just after they found an apartment. Fortunately, my father worked for a bank in Kyrenia, so he was able to keep his job by transferring to another branch in Paphos. So we slowly recovered, in spite of the pain from the loss of my uncle and the tremendous anxiety about the fate of my cousin. Some of my friends were not so fortunate—they lost all means of supporting their families.

In spite of all that has happened to us, and in spite of the way the media reminds us daily of the losses we suffered, I never learned to hate the Turkish Cypriots. I have always known that it was the Turkish army that created all the trouble, and I am sure that if we could get rid of the army, we could live in peace with the Turkish Cypriots. Although most of my friends are more fanatic, my parents are peace-loving, and they have always said only kind things about Turkish Cypriots. My grandfather used to have many Turkish Cypriots working for him, especially during the time of the year when the fruit was ripening and the land needed working. We paid them well, and they always brought us things, such as the nice sweets made from the green almonds. My grandfather was one of those who learned to speak Turkish, so all the Turkish Cypriots liked him a lot.

I am worried, however, because the Turkish Cypriots are being taught a lot of propaganda about us, and I am not sure if the new generation will think of us so positively. I feel sorry for the Turkish Cypriots, because they have to live daily with the Turkish army, and I don't think they like the soldiers any better than we would. More disturbing is the fact that so many of them are leaving Cyprus and going to England or Canada because their economy is so poor and there are no job opportunities for them. It's ironic that they took the best part of Cyprus and yet they are in such bad condition. Turkey doesn't really care about the Turkish Cypriots, and the illegal regime of Denktash has brought in tens of thousands of uneducated farmers from Anatolia who are Islamic fanatics. Soon we won't have any Turkish Cypriots left in Cyprus, just a bunch of settlers that we could never live with.

Now the Turkish Cypriots have declared an illegal state in which they have their own pseudopresident and pseudoparliament. Everyone knows there is no democracy, and their leader, Mr. Denktash, is intent on keeping his power by maintaining the division of Cyprus. They talk about peace, but it is clear that they don't mean it. The Turkish army occupies nearly 40% of my island and doesn't intend to give up any of it. I'm afraid that Turkey wants the whole island and is just looking for the right excuse to continue the invasion. Lately, the Turks have been engaging in many provocative acts to create trouble. Our side has responded with restraint, but I'm sure that one day war will break out and we will lose everything and have nowhere to go.

In order to bring about a settlement to the Cyprus problem, the United States has to exert a lot of pressure on both Turkey and Mr. Denktash. Our side has compromised so much over the years, and yet there has been no movement from their side. The Turkish army continues its occupation of our country, even though there have been many United Nations Security Council resolutions calling for its withdrawal. I don't understand why countries such as the United

States are willing to send in their armies to throw Saddam Hussein out of Kuwait but won't do anything about the illegal occupation of our country. Somehow, Turkey has become the "pet" of the Western world, and it can get by with anything. The whole international community ignores the blatant violation of human rights by Turkey, and the rest of the world doesn't seem to care that so much injustice exists right here in Europe. There can never be real peace in Cyprus until the Turkish army leaves, the settlers are expelled, and we Greeks are allowed to go back to our homes. Even though I was not born at the time, I have strong images of our home, and I believe that one day I will be able to return.

Well, I hope I haven't depressed you with my description of the situation in Cyprus. Myself, I am not very optimistic about the future. I live every day with the fear of another invasion. I really hope for a solution soon, because I know that both we and the Turkish Cypriots will be better off in a united Cyprus. Sometimes I come home and find my mother crying because she can see the Pendedactylos but cannot go there. She wants to visit her mother's grave and put flowers there. She goes every Sunday to church and prays for the day when she can go home again. It really hurts me to see the pain in her heart, and I hope that before she finishes her life, she is able to live again in her own house.

A Turkish Cypriot's View of the Cyprus Conflict [5]

Greetings from Cyprus. It is a great honor to accept your invitation to explain a few things about the situation in this troubled place we call home. You probably think that Cyprus is a Greek island, and you may be surprised to learn that I speak Turkish, worship in a mosque (occasionally), and travel often to Turkey. I've never been to Greece, although I hope I can visit there someday. Unfortunately, the world understands very little about Cyprus and even less about the Turkish population of our little island. When I go abroad and tell people I am from Cyprus they always say something to me in Greek or ask something like "How is Zorba (or Zeus or some other Greek character)?" I find this very offensive, although I can forgive them because I know it is not their fault. The blame must be put on the Greeks and Greek Cypriots, who have managed to create many problems for this little island by spreading the myth that it belongs to Greeks. I apologize for starting off on such a negative tone, but you must understand that my people have suffered much in the past 40 years because of the Greek Cypriots, and I cannot escape these feelings.

The Turkish presence in Cyprus goes back to 1571, when the island became part of the Ottoman Empire and a population of Turks were brought to settle here and help the island grow and develop. At that time Cyprus was ruled by the Venetians, who subjugated the Orthodox Christian population and tried to convert them to Catholicism. The residents of the island welcomed the Ottomans as liberators, and the Orthodox church was given a great deal of autonomy and independence. In fact, it became an important part of the Ottoman administration, responsible for taking care of the affairs of the Christian population. The freedom and prosperity brought to the residents of Cyprus by the Ottomans was similar to that brought to other lands that became part of the Ottoman empire—the Ottomans were the first rulers to take a multicultural approach in the administration of vast territories. As Turkish Cypriots, we are proud of our Ottoman heritage and the many contributions our ancestors made to art, science, engineering. In Cyprus their influence is everywhere—in the design of houses, in the traditional clothing styles, in the music and dance, in the handicrafts, and in the foods we eat. We remained part of the Ottoman Empire until 1925, when we became a British colony. I should point out that England had actually governed the island from 1878, after the initial breakup of the Ottoman Empire, until Cyprus gained its independence in 1960. In any case, it is important to remember that the Turkish population has been in Cyprus for more than 400 years, before the first English settlers came to North America, and that for most of that time we were the ruling class.

The current troubles started in the 1950s, when Cyprus was still a British colony. The Greek Cypriots tried to achieve what they call *enosis*, or union, with Greece—in essence to become a Greek island, like Crete or Rhodes. If you see what happened to the Turkish population of those islands when they became part of Greece, you will understand why the Turkish Cypriots did not want *enosis*—it would have meant the end of our existence. In fighting for *enosis*, the Greek Cypriots told us to stay out of the way, that it was their business and that we shouldn't worry because they would take care of us. Even while they were fighting against the British, there were several killings and even some massacres of Turkish Cypriots, so it is easy to see how they meant to "take care of us." Of course, the Greek Cypriots were not the only culprits, because the British were following their normal policy of "divide and rule," which helped turn us against each other. Actually, there were quite a lot of good Greek Cypriots who helped us and were very friendly as neighbors. But they let the extremists get away with destroying the relations between us. They should have stopped them while they had the chance, because now too many minds have been poisoned.

When Cyprus achieved independence in 1960, the constitution created a partnership between the Greek Cypriots and the Turkish Cypriots. Although it was not a completely equal sharing of power, there were certain guarantees built in to the system to ensure that the Turkish Cypriots, who were much fewer in number, would not be completely dominated by the Greek Cypriots. As you might expect, the Greek Cypriots did not like this system, and they set about trying to destroy it from the very first moment. Even though the constitution specifically ruled out the possibility of any kind of union with another country, the Greek Cypriots began immediately trying to find a way to continue their campaign for *enosis*. The EOKA movement started again, and the Turkish Cypriots suffered almost immediately. In fact, the Greek Cypriots created the "Akritas Plan," which called for the extermination of Turkish Cypriots. Apart from that, they made it difficult for Turkish Cypriots to travel abroad, to get loans, to build businesses, and in other ways to live as full citizens of the Cyprus Republic. We were constantly harassed when we tried to travel from one place to another for work, to visit relatives, and even to get medical attention. We were treated as second-class citizens from day one.

In 1963 we were thrown out of the government by the Greek Cypriots. They tried to change the constitution from a partnership to a Greek-Cypriot state in preparation for another attempt at *enosis*. In December of the same year, they began to implement the plan to exterminate the Turkish Cypriots, and we had no choice but to flee our homes and villages and gather in enclaves where we could protect ourselves. We left everything behind and became refugees in our own country. The Greek Cypriots looted our houses and sometimes would not allow basic supplies to come through to the enclaves. We had no work and no place to live that we could call our own. In some cases we were sleeping 20 people to a room, for months on end. It was a terrible existence. We began to hope that Turkey would come to our rescue. Before this, we had never felt that close to Turkey, but now we were forced by the Greek Cypriots to look to our motherland for protection.

Finally, in July of 1974, the Greek Cypriots went too far. They used military force to overthrow their own leadership and installed a known terrorist in power who could be a puppet of Greece. The Turkish prime minister went to Great Britain, one of the three guarantor powers of the independence of Cyprus (along with Greece and Turkey), and asked for intervention to prevent this illegal takeover. When Britain refused to take action, Turkey had no choice but to come to our rescue. It had shown great restraint several times during the previous 10 years, but it decided to act this time. Turkey feared additional massacres of Turkish Cypriots if it waited any longer, so on July 20 it began the rescue operation aimed at protecting the Turkish Cypriots and restoring the independence of the Cyprus Republic. War is never a pretty sight, and many people on both sides were killed. Many brave Turkish soldiers died while trying to protect us from the Greek Cypriots, who were intent on carrying out further

massacres. It was decided that the only viable solution was to divide Cyprus into two zones, one administered by the Turkish Cypriots and the other by the Greek Cypriots. So we again had to give up our homes and become refugees. Almost all the Turkish Cypriots fled to the north part of Cyprus, and the Greek Cypriots decided to go to the south. A border was drawn across the middle of Cyprus, and at last the Turkish Cypriots felt safe and ready to start a new life.

My own family suffered so much from the Greek Cypriots between 1963 and 1974, and life has not been easy for us since that time. We had a beautiful house in a small village near Polis, one of the loveliest parts of the island. The sea there is so calm and clean, and there are wonderful wildflowers everywhere. In 1963 we had to abandon our house because of the threats by the Greek Cypriots, and even though we returned from time to time, we spent most of the next 10 years crowded together at my aunt's house in a nearby village, protected by sentries. I was not born until after the events of 1974, but I have heard so many stories from all my family, so the events between 1963 and 1974 seem very real to me. When the coup happened in 1974, my father, who was well respected in both communities, was shot by some Greek Cypriots belonging to EOKA, for no reason other than that he was a Turkish Cypriot. Fortunately, he survived, but we became refugees again, leaving the area where my parents' ancestors had lived for generations. We left everything behind and went by bus, under the protection of the United Nations, to our new home in Lapta (what the Greeks used to call Lapithos). Because our family had been well-off, we were given a nice house, but because it was not ours, we had a hard time getting used to living there.

Because of all the things that have happened, I don't know if we can ever live together with the Greek Cypriots again. Although many people from the older generation hate the Greek Cypriots, I don't personally have anything against them. We have to move beyond the past and never allow it to repeat itself. However, the only solution is to live separately, at least for one or two generations. When I hear my parents talk about the Polis area, I know they miss it, even though they have no desire to return to their former homes and face the difficulties and dangers of living among the Greek Cypriots.

In any solution the most important thing is our security, both physical and social. There is always the danger of attacks by Greek-Cypriot extremists, and given the record of the United Nations in other places around the world, the only force we can count on for protection is the Turkish army. I know the Greek Cypriots don't like this, but they have to face reality and understand that the Turkish Cypriots will never agree to a solution that does not guarantee their security. However, security is more than protection from physical attack. Since 1974 we have been able as a community to build up our own institutions and forms of government. Before 1974, we were just second-class citizens under the Greek Cypriots. It takes time for a community like ours to break out of a past in which we were so suppressed, so we still have many problems, and we are more dependent on Turkey than we would like. But if we have enough time, I know we can overcome these difficulties and feel proud of ourselves and what we have accomplished.

The primary obstacle to our development as a community is the extreme isolation we face in the world. The Greek Cypriots have managed to turn almost everyone against us, and they have placed an economic and diplomatic embargo against us that makes it almost impossible to develop our economy or our ties with other countries. They have managed to trick the world into viewing them as the sole legal representative of Cyprus, even though it should be obvious that we have no voice in their government. No one will trade with us or establish diplomatic ties because they are afraid they might upset the Greeks. I don't understand how the Greeks became such "darlings" of the western Europeans and the Americans. I think most of it has to do with the fact that we are Muslims, and the Christian world is not ready to accept us, in spite of their talk about tolerance and cooperation. I face this isolation every time I travel. I have to use the Turkish passport rather than my own, and because there are no international embassies on our side, I have to get my visas

from Istanbul. My father's business does not qualify for any of the loan programs that the Greek Cypriots have access to from the European Union, and even the local chapter of the Rotary Club cannot belong to the international bodies because it is considered "illegal." We are always referred to as the "pseudostate" or the "illegal regime." This kind of treatment only hardens our attitudes, and I worry about how the young people like myself will ever develop a desire to make peace with the Greek Cypriots. Unfortunately, most of us won't stay in Cyprus after we finish our education, because there are few opportunities for meaningful jobs. The Greek Cypriots have pushed us away with their embargoes and the political isolation they have imposed on us, and soon the only people left in the north will be the hard-line politicians and the poor farmers coming here from Anatolia.

I'm sorry if I confused you with so many details, but the Cyprus situation is very complex. I am not very hopeful about the possibility for working things out in the near future, but I hope that someday I will be able to cooperate with the Greek Cypriots. Every day I wonder if the Greek Cypriots will start another war. They are buying so many arms and making constant talk about fighting. They won't stand a chance against the Turkish army, but if war comes, we will all suffer. My parents are getting older now, and the anxiety they have felt for the past 30 years gets stronger all the time. I hope that before they leave this earth, they can feel the peace in their hearts that comes from not having to worry about the possibility of war, harassment by Greek Cypriots, or becoming refugees again.

An Analysis of Conflicting Views

It is difficult to read these two letters without feeling some degree of hopelessness about the situation in Cyprus. Indeed, if you focus on the differences in *content* of the two letters, they seem so far apart that you must wonder if there is any possibility for a peaceful settlement to the conflict. The Greek Cypriots see the 1974 events as the starting point of the conflict, whereas the Turkish Cypriots see the 1963 events as the most crucial.

The Greek Cypriots refer to 1974 as an invasion of the Turkish army, but the Turkish Cypriots refer to it as a peace operation. The Greek Cypriots believe that the two communities lived together happily before the division, and the Turkish Cypriots remember their unpleasant treatment as a minority. The Greek Cypriots believe that the island is undeniably Hellenic in character, and the Turkish Cypriots emphasize the Ottoman influence. The Greek Cypriots see the use of an economic embargo and political isolation of the Turkish Cypriots as the only way to force concessions, but the Turkish Cypriots see these as part of a continued attempt to push them off the island. The Greek Cypriots seek complete freedom of movement and settlement within the island, whereas the Turkish Cypriots seek a self-administered area with a great deal of autonomy. The Greek Cypriots vehemently insist on the withdrawal of all Turkish troops from the island, and the Turkish Cypriots insist that the troops are required for their protection. The Greek Cypriots demand a return of their homes and property in the north, but the Turkish Cypriots have little or no desire to go back to their homes in the south. The list of differences could continue ad infinitum. One could easily conclude that there is no possibility for empathy to develop.

Unfortunately, the points listed above are exactly where the disputants get bogged down in their attempts to negotiate with one another—they focus exclusively on the content and fail to discuss aspects of the *process* that are holding them back. If we examine the two letters from a more analytical perspective, it becomes clear that both of the writers are trapped by a similar manner of approaching the events, and it is this approach—not the different views on the subject—that prevents empathy. Specifically, the letters illustrate five major barriers to empathy:

1. *One-sided interpretation of history.* It would be misleading to suggest that anyone can be completely objective about the past, but the deliberate distortion of history to serve primarily political purposes creates unnecessary division and presents a serious obstacle to reconciliation. The writers of both letters are very selective in their memory of past events, and their description of these events is far from objective. For example, the Greek Cypriot emphasizes the long history of

Hellenic influence in Cyprus and totally ignores the positive contributions of the Ottoman period. In the current school curriculum of the Greek Cypriots, the Ottomans are portrayed as barbaric tyrants who treated the Greek-speaking population as slaves. Most accounts of this period clearly show that the Ottomans gave a great deal of autonomy to the Christians, putting mechanisms in place that allowed the Orthodox church to become very powerful in running the affairs of the island. The church was much better off under the Ottomans than under the Venetians or other previous conquerors. The Turkish Cypriot emphasizes the massacres by the EOKA militia during the 1950s and 1960s but does not point out that a similar organization created by the Turkish Cypriots (called TMT) was guilty of equally hideous crimes. Many reports document that TMT instigated killings of their own people and then placed the blame on EOKA in order to generate greater fear of the Greek Cypriots among the Turkish Cypriots. These examples are typical of the way in which the past has been distorted beyond recognition by the educational systems and political propaganda of both sides. Such one-sided interpretations of historical events push the two communities further apart and allow little room for healing processes.

2. *Negative portrayals of the other.* It is difficult to share a small geographical area with someone you don't like, respect, or otherwise consider as your equal, and it is especially difficult if the other is considered your enemy. Both the Greek Cypriot and Turkish Cypriot paint a negative image of each other. The Turkish-Cypriot description is especially harsh, portraying the Greek Cypriots as suppressors and murderers. Although there is acknowledgment of the "good Greek Cypriots," the overall image is one of extremists intent on exterminating the Turkish Cypriots. Historically, it is true that the Turkish Cypriots suffered a lot at the hands of Greek Cypriots, and even though the majority of the population was not directly involved in committing acts of violence, it took no steps to prevent the extremists from carrying out their deeds. However, most Greek Cypriots feel a degree of warmth toward the Turkish Cypriots, even if this warmth is sometimes condescending. At first glance it might seem that the Greek Cypriot

was less negative in the portrayal of the Turkish Cypriots, especially given the reference to the kindness of Turkish-Cypriot neighbors and their affection for the grandfather. However, it becomes clear upon closer examination that the Turkish Cypriots are not viewed with respect or equality. In the mind of the Greek Cypriot, Turkish Cypriots occupy a minority status and should not expect to be treated as equals. Their proper role is seen as workers and laborers for the more prosperous Greek Cypriots. Such images of the other do not make it easy to enter into productive negotiations about issues that divide communities.

3. *Placement of blame on the other*. It is rare that full responsibility for a problem can be attributed solely to one party. In Cyprus the case can be easily made that both parties share the blame equally (along with Turkey, Greece, the U.K., and the United States). Yet each of the letter-writers places almost full blame for the situation on the other. The Greek Cypriot claims that the troubles of 1963 started when Turkish-Cypriot terrorists killed people; however, most international reports state that Greek Cypriots started the troubles. Similarly, the Greek Cypriot implies that the Turkish Cypriots created the constitutional crisis by withdrawing from the government; but most people outside of Cyprus recognize that it was the Greek-Cypriot attempt to take away Turkish-Cypriot rights that left the Turkish Cypriots no choice but to withdraw. Although some acceptance of responsibility is acknowledged for the role of the coup, the Greek Cypriot focuses almost exclusively on the expansionist policies of Turkey and the resulting invasion. There is no mention of the guarantor rights under the 1960 constitution that Turkey declared in carrying out its intervention. Similarly, the Turkish Cypriot lays primary blame for the current troubles on the *enosis* movement but does not acknowledge the current strong movement among Turkish-Cypriot officials toward *enosis* with Turkey. The Turkish Cypriot blames the Greek Cypriots for enforcing an economic embargo against their products but never brings up the failure of Turkey to heed numerous United Nations resolutions calling for the prompt withdrawal of Turkish troops from the island. This kind of blaming places each of the parties in a defensive position, causing each to focus on attacking the other rather than acknowledging its own responsibility for creating and maintaining the situation. Such blaming actions quickly spiral into a mutually destructive exchange of accusations, making it impossible for the two sides to consider concessions to the other.

4. *Mistrust of the other*. No relationship can last long without the existence of mutual trust. Lack of confidence in the intentions of the other leads to continuous questioning of each other's motives. It is clear that each of the letter-writers is suspicious of the motives of the other's community. This is particularly true for the Turkish Cypriot, who believes that the Greek Cypriots will take the first opportunity they find to continue their attempt to dominate and suppress the smaller Turkish population. The Greek Cypriot is convinced that Turkey is waiting for the right time to take over the whole island. Both sides are caught in a vicious trap, with one afraid to live without the protection of the Turkish army and the other living each day in fear of further attack by this same army. Even more serious, each side doubts the sincerity of the other about wanting an agreement. Each believes that the other is gaining positive benefits from the current situation and stands only to lose if the conflict ends. Such mistrust leads to continuous posturing by both sides, resulting in a game of exaggerated demands and resistance to backing off first for fear that one will take advantage of the other.

5. *Unwillingness to make offers of friendship toward the other*. No deadlock can be broken until one side or the other makes the first conciliatory gesture. If each side maintains a hard-line stance, it offers no way for the other to take positive steps that might relax the situation and lead to a positive climate for negotiation. In this case, it is not so much what one or the other says or does as it is what they *fail* to say or do. Although each of the letter-writers hints of possible cooperation, neither offers suggestions that might help defuse the tension. Each is afraid of taking the first step toward building confidence. The Greek Cypriot is waiting for the Turks to withdraw their troops and allow the Greeks to return to their homes, and the Turkish Cypriot is waiting for the Greek Cypriots to lift the embargoes and other restrictions. In order for fruitful discussions to take place between

the two sides, each needs to offer an opening toward peace, a window in which a future could be built together.

Is Empathy Possible?

The dismal picture created by the students' letters does not become any more optimistic with the process analysis just completed. At first glance, the existence of the barriers in combination with the incompatible positions seems to create an impossible situation. However, an awareness of these barriers offers hope for improving the situation. In conflicts where so much divides the parties, it is not always advisable to enter into direct discussions about the contentious issues. These discussions will almost certainly fail, as negotiations have failed numerous times in Cyprus. It is more productive to encourage different ways for the two sides to view each other and to communicate with each other. Each needs to develop a less one-sided view of history, to construct more positive perceptions of each other, to learn to accept responsibility for its own community's mistakes, to build a greater sense of trust, and to create ways of breaking the deadlock by taking steps toward the other. Only by overcoming these barriers can they develop a relationship characterized by genuine trust and empathy.

In both of the letters, the writers provided a small but significant opening on which to build a positive relationship. The Greek Cypriot expressed hope for a solution in the near future, and the Turkish Cypriot expressed hope that it will be possible to cooperate in the future with the Greek Cypriots. These hopes can provide an entry point for working together to overcome some of the prejudices and biases in their attitudes toward each other. As part of my work in Cyprus, we started a group of university students composed of over 50 individuals from each community who were willing to come together in a bicommunal setting for the purpose of learning about one another. Prior to our workshops, most of these students had never met anyone from the other community. They came in with a variety of attitudes toward the other community and a range of perspectives about the Cyprus problem. Through our meetings, these students began to overcome most

of the barriers illustrated in the letters. By listening to one another, each learned more about how the history of the conflict is seen by the other side. Through their interactions, they gained more positive perceptions of one another. By discussing the effects of various events on each community, they took significant steps toward recognizing how their own community had contributed to the current situation. In working together on common projects, they slowly started the process of trust building. Finally, by accepting one another as partners in the struggle for peace, they started thinking about ways to express friendship across the buffer zone that divides them. Of course, this group has a long way to go, but it has taken a giant leap toward reconciliation.

Fortunately, the student group is only one of many such bicommunal groups that are now operating in Cyprus.[6] Groups of young business leaders, young political leaders, educators, management trainees, women, journalists, policy leaders, and citizens from all walks of life are participating in workshops and seminars in which they attempt to overcome the obstacles to building peace on their island. Our experience has shown that under the appropriate conditions and using an appropriate methodology, groups can move beyond the barriers described above and develop a stronger basis for working together in the future.[7] Without such work, the two communities are destined to move further apart and remain forever trapped in a cycle of mistrust and misunderstanding.

NOTES

1. For helpful descriptions of the Cyprus conflict, see Attalides (1979), Bahcheli and Rizopoulos (1996), Hitchens (1984), Markides (1977), Koumoulides (1986), and Stearns (1992).

2. On several occasions we have been able to schedule bicommunal meetings outside the buffer zone. When we have coffee together in the afternoon or eat lunch or dinner together, we often ask the owner of the coffeehouse or restaurant to tell us which members of the group are Greek Cypriot and which are Turkish Cypriot. The man's usual response, after a quick look at the group, is to throw up his hands and shake his head, saying that it is impossible to make the distinction. During a recent visit by

a bicommunal student group to each community leader's office, it was clear that both Mr. Clerides and Mr. Denktash have the same problem.

3. I use the term "empathy" in the relational sense rather than in the psychological sense of the term. That is, I believe that empathy is a characteristic of the relationship between individuals rather than something that one person has for another. Viewed in this manner, empathy does not develop simply through the efforts of one person to understand another. Instead, it requires communication between individuals in a climate characterized by a willingness to learn. See Broome (1993) for a more complete description of relational empathy and its role in resolving difficult conflict situations.

4. For a more complete exposition of the Greek-Cypriot point of view see Clerides (1988). Also write to the Press and Information Office of the Republic of Cyprus, Nicosia, Cyprus.

5. For a more complete exposition of the Turkish-Cypriot point of view, see Denktash (1988). Also write to the Press and Information Office of the "Turkish Republic of Northern Cyprus" in Lefkosa, Mersin 10, Turkey. Volkan (1979) provides a psychological analysis of the Cyprus conflict that helps explain many of the Turkish-Cypriot fears toward the Greek Cypriots.

6. A written description of my initial work in Cyprus with peace-building groups is contained in a report that is available for the cost of copying and postage. Write to Anna Argyrou at the Cyprus Fulbright Commission (P.O. Box 4536, Nicosia CY1385, Cyprus) and ask for a copy of *Designing the Future of Peace-Building Efforts in Cyprus: Report of Design Workshops with the Conflict Resolution Trainers during 1994 & 1995*, initially written in January 1996 and updated throughout the year.

7. Many of these groups are using a problem-solving and design methodology called "interactive management," described in Broome and Keever (1989) and Broome and Chen (1992).

REFERENCES

Attalides, M. A. (1979). *Cyprus: Nationalism and international politics*. Edinburgh, UK: Q Press.

Bahcheli, T., & Rizopoulos, N. X. (1996, Winter). The Cyprus impasse: What next? *World Policy Journal*, 27–39.

Broome, B. J. (1993). Managing differences in conflict resolution. In D. J. Sandole & H. van der Merwe (Eds.), *Conflict resolution theory and practice: Integration and application* (pp. 95–111). Manchester, UK: Manchester University Press.

Broome, B. J., & Chen, M. (1992). Guidelines for computer-assisted group problem-solving: Meeting the challenges of complex issues. *Small Group Research, 23*, 216–236.

Broome, B. J., & Keever, D. B. (1989). Next generation group facilitation: Proposed principles. *Management Communication Quarterly, 3*, 107–127.

Clerides, G. (1988). *My deposition* (Vol. 1). Nicosia: Alithia Publishing.

Denktash, R. R. (1988). *The Cyprus triangle*. New York: Office of the "Turkish Republic of Northern Cyprus."

Hitchens, C. (1984). *Cyprus*. New York: Quartet Books.

Koumoulides, J. T. A. (Ed.). (1986). *Cyprus in transition: 1960–1985*. London: Trigraph.

Markides, K. C. (1977). *The rise and fall of the Cyprus Republic*. New Haven, CT: Yale University Press.

Stearns, M. (1992). *Entangled allies: U.S. policy toward Greece, Turkey, and Cyprus*. New York: Council on Foreign Relations Press.

Volkan, V. (1979). *Cyprus—War and adaptation*. Charlottesville: University Press of Virginia.

KEY TERMS

empathy	Cypress conflict
conflict	bicommunal
Greek Cypriot	communication barriers
Turkish Cypriot	content-process

DISCUSSION QUESTIONS

1. This essay emphasizes how the lack of direct communication between parties over long periods of time creates obstacles toward efforts to resolve protracted conflicts. Do you believe this is always the case, or can you think of situations where the absence of contact can make problem-solving easier?

2. The two letters contained in this article show that a great divide exists between Greek Cypriots

and Turkish Cypriots. Do you think that differences of this magnitude exist between any cultural groups in the United States?

3. Broome suggests that it is more productive to focus on changing the form of communication between parties in conflict than to allow disagreements about issues to lead to a stalemate. How difficult do you think it is for parties to de-emphasize content and focus on process?

4. The five major obstacles to empathy illustrated in the letters could make any conflict situation more resistant to resolution. How might they be applied to conflicts with which you are familiar (either intergroup or interpersonal)?

5. At the end of his article, Broome mentions several bicommunal groups in Cyprus that are meeting regularly. He implies that through their interactions, they are overcoming the five major obstacles to empathy. What are some of the activities such groups might use to accomplish this aim?

44

CROSSING THE COLOR LINE: FROM EMPATHY TO IMPLICATURE IN INTERCULTURAL COMMUNICATION

KAREN LYNNETTE DACE / MARK LAWRENCE MCPHAIL

In 1903 the African American historian W. E. B. DuBois (1982) argued that "the problem of the Twentieth century is the problem of the color line" (p. xi). When DuBois died three score years later, the line that divided African and European Americans seemed finally to be at a point where it would be erased, where individuals would be judged not by skin color but by character. As we approach the beginning of the 21st century, however, Blacks and Whites in this country continue to live in different emotional, intellectual, and material worlds, divided as much by psychological separation as by physical segregation. "It's sad," writes Nathan McCall (1994) in his bestselling book *Makes Me Wanna Holler*, "this gulf between blacks and whites. We're so afraid of each other" (p. 349). McCall's autobiography tells an emotionally powerful story of an African American man's personal growth and transformation, of a journey from the streets of a working-class neighborhood to prison, and finally to a position working on one of America's most prestigious newspapers, *The Washington Post*.

It is in the culmination of McCall's (1994) journey and in his own ambivalent feelings about racism that he articulates an important recognition of the problems and possibilities created by the color line in American society: "I have come to believe two things that might be contradictory," he writes. "Some of our worst childhood fears *were* true—the establishment *is* teeming with racism. Yet I also believe whites are as befuddled about race as we are, and they're as scared of us as we are of them. Many of them are seeking solutions, just like us" (p. 414). Although he frames his understanding in a language of difference, in the terms of "us" and "them," McCall's belief that both Whites and African Americans experience the fear and sadness of racial divisions, and that both may be seeking the same solutions, illustrates an attempt to cross the color line by finding common ground, an attempt to establish what psychologists and communication scholars call "empathy," the ability to "feel with" another human being. It is in the psychological concept and communicative practice of empathy that, we believe, students and scholars of intercultural communication will find a strategy for addressing the difficulties of human difference and division, and for facilitating interracial identification.

This essay will present the perspectives of two African American communication researchers, one male and one female, both of whom have focused on issues of interracial communication and interaction, and both of whom believe that the concept of empathy holds significance for communication theory and practice in general and addresses issues of interracial interaction in particular. First, we discuss how the concept of empathy has been examined in various areas of communication scholarship, and how it might be usefully extended to the discussion of interracial communication. Then we each present personal narratives that illustrate, in our own voices, how empathy functions in our lives not only as a theoretical concept but as a practical strategy for understanding and dealing with racial differences. Finally, we extend the concept of empathy beyond its cognitive and affective emphases to suggest its potential as an ontological and epistemological principle that holds transformative possibilities for human consciousness, communication, and culture.

Empathy as Understanding and Sharing: Addressing the Problem of Being Human

Webster's New World Dictionary (1987) defines empathy as "intellectual or emotional identification with another" (p. 201), and the concept is generally seen as the psychological capacity to "feel with" another human being. Psychologist Carl Rogers (1967) defines empathy as the ability to understand another's "inner world of private personal meanings as if it were your own, but without ever losing the 'as if' quality" of the experience (p. 89). At its best, then, empathy encourages individuals to respect and appreciate cultural differences instead of simply erasing or ignoring them, and encourages communication that is nonjudgmental and accepting of others. Numerous scholars have considered how empathy might be useful in addressing rhetorical, interpersonal, intercultural, and performative aspects of communication. Charles Kelly (1973) offers a rhetorical consideration of "empathic listening," which involves

"participation in the spirit of an environment as receiver" (p. 264) and "full attention to total communication environment" (p. 270). Brant Burleson (1983) discusses the concept of "emotional empathy," noting that "in emotionally empathizing with another, one does not merely recognize another's emotions, but also *shares* these emotions" (p. 297). He suggests that it is not sufficient to simply possess empathic skills, but that one must also be motivated to understand and share the experiences and feelings of others. The emphasis on both understanding and sharing exemplified in the rhetorical and interpersonal approaches to empathy also emerges in its intercultural and performative considerations.

Benjamin Broome (1991) explains that empathy is "a central characteristic of competent and effective intercultural communication" (p. 235), and Larry Samovar and Richard Porter (1995) echo Broome's findings when they note that "empathy can be increased if you resist the tendency to interpret the other's verbal and nonverbal actions from your culture's orientation. Learn to suspend, or at least keep in check, the cultural perspective that is unique to your experiences" (pp. 286–287). Samovar and Porter suggest that, in addition to its conceptual aspects, empathy also involves specific communicative behaviors. Myron Lustig and Jolene Koester (1996) offer an explanation of empathy similar to that presented by Rogers in that it emphasizes the "as if" dimension of empathy, noting that although it is impossible to put oneself in another's place, it is possible to "behave as if one understands the world as others do" (p. 331). Empathy, they believe, contributes to intercultural awareness and understanding and is an important indicator of communicative competence.

Empathy also plays an important role in the study and practice of performance, as Jill Taft-Kaufman (1985) points out: "Through an understanding of theories of empathy, interpreters seek to explain the subtle process by which a performer becomes involved in a text and an audience becomes involved in an experience" (p. 171). Taft-Kaufman notes that the concept of empathy has evolved over time to reflect both its complexity and its importance for human interaction. Ronald Pelias (1982) considers this evolution in terms of the directions it offers for the field of performance and presents an integrative approach to understanding the concept. For Pelias, empathy is "a qualitative, developmental process in which individuals not only come to share and understand another's feelings but also consider the reasons and context that inform the other's feelings" (p. 527). Pelias calls for further amplification of the concept of empathy, both beyond its affective and cognitive dimensions and toward its implications for human being and knowing.

Such an amplification involves extending the concept of empathy beyond abstract psychological experience to the concrete emotional and intellectual practices of communicative behavior. We attempt to facilitate this amplification through personal narratives that illustrate how empathy has impacted our own understanding and behavior as they relate to interracial communication. Both narratives address the "gulf" that exists between African and European Americans and offer strategies and insights to suggest ways in which the conceptual and cultural divisions that separate us might be bridged. Karen Dace's narrative addresses the interpersonal and intercultural implications of the color line, and Mark McPhail considers how the study and practice of performance might enable us to cross that line. Together, they illustrate how the communicative practice of empathy can be extended to inform our theoretical understanding of difference through the idea of "implicature"—the notion that human beings are linguistically, materially, psychologically, and spiritually interrelated and interdependent, or "implicated" in each other. The move from empathy to implicature, we believe, represents a transformative evolution of the symbolic and social possibilities of dealing with dissonance and difference in communication between European Americans and African Americans.

Karen Lynnette Dace: Empathy as an Escape from Racial Reasoning

Before reading McCall's *Makes Me Wanna Holler*, I had never spent a great deal of time analyzing my friendships with European Americans, but I had always been aware that these friendships fell into at least three distinctions or categories. One rela-

tionship type is best characterized by our ability to discuss anything pertinent to our existence, including race and culture. A second relationship type consists of "guilty liberals" who pity my oppression more than they value my culture. Although these friendships provide an opportunity for an open and frank discussion of race, class, and gender, the tone is often apologetic—that is, these "guilty liberal" European Americans recognize what McIntosh (1986) identified as their "white privilege" and accept blame for every oppressive act perpetrated against people of color since the beginning of time. The third intercultural relationship type includes those European American friends with whom I can discuss anything, except race and culture. The fact that an essential part of who I am (and who they are) is taboo is a constant source of frustration. Similar feelings result when I am not allowed to discuss my concerns as an African American woman in my relationships with some African American men. Other than being aware of these distinctions, I gave very little thought to what makes these relationships work. On some level, they did work. That was all I needed to know.

That changed when I read the short but powerful chapter "Danny" in McCall's autobiography. I began to see similarities between McCall's relationship with the European American man after which the chapter is named and my relationship with a European American man named Bill. McCall's Danny lives in an African American neighborhood and is well-read in African American literature. Bill lived on Chicago's North Side in a predominantly European American neighborhood and was well-versed in blues. Although McCall does not talk about developing respect for Danny explicitly, as I read his narrative, that is what comes through. I developed respect for Bill when I learned that on two nights a week he coached a basketball team of kids from the Cabrini Green Housing Project. They played other "Green" kids every Saturday. The neighborhood is infamous, and certainly there are European Americans and African Americans who refuse to go anywhere near the area. The fact that Bill worked with these kids was not what impressed me. The fact that he kept his coaching a secret for some time, coupled with the knowledge that he was not required to do any type of community service by our employer or any other entity, moved me. I loved the fact that he never bragged about his participation in that league as if what he was doing deserved special recognition. When asked why he participated, Bill explained that he loved the kids and the sport.

I believe my respect for Bill and trust in the sincerity of his motives for friendship grew out of what I perceived as his empathy for the children at Cabrini Green. Unlike so many do-gooders from all cultures, Bill never asserted himself as a savior the kids should worship and be grateful to have in their lives. He was not condescending and neither looked for nor expected recognition. Bill was most concerned with understanding the kids' needs and being available to them at times and in ways that were important to them. He worked hard not to impose himself and his beliefs on the kids and their families. Bill's relationship with the children of the Cabrini Green Housing Project created the space for our relationship to grow.

McCall (1994) writes of Danny, "whenever he said something to me, there was a straightforwardness, a childlike honesty, that I didn't get from most other white people" (p. 343). The first time I read that passage, Bill came to mind. A few years ago, after I left the firm for graduate school and Bill left to work at a local radio station, he called me, deeply concerned. His new employer, a nationally recognized industry giant, instituted a service program in which a group of European American men worked as softball coaches for another group of inner-city, mostly African American, kids. This new program included weekly talks and workshops to help these men interact with the children. The night Bill called, their guest speaker had been an "angry African American woman." Bill explained, "Everything she said was full of anger and fury. It was like she hated us." What separated Bill from the other men in the group, many of whom vowed not to return, was that he genuinely wanted to "understand her anger." We spent several hours that night discussing the source of that fury.

"Are *you* angry?" he wanted to know.

"Yes," I explained, quoting Toni Morrison's (1970) observation in *The Bluest Eye*, that "anger is better. There is a sense of being in anger. A real-

ity and presence. An awareness of worth. It is a lovely surging" (p. 43). We talked about all major social movements resulting from anger. He tried to understand. What was most important to me was his wanting to understand. He tried to understand the source of African American anger, and he was willing to suspend his own preconceived notions and judgments in an effort to permit space for another point of view and experience.

My relationship with Bill has taught me three important things. First, all of my friendships with people outside of African American culture are initiated by those people. There are no instances where I did any of the preliminary work. Although I understand why this might be the case for most people of color, I am also struck by the problematic nature of this truth. Second, these relationships are characterized by sincerity on both our parts. Neither of us is out to prove we are exceptional because we have friendships across cultural lines. Instead, an empathic understanding drew us together and was sufficient to keep us interested in one another long enough for the development of deeper bonds. Finally, there has always been a certain sense of freedom on the part of those European Americans with whom I have developed friendships—that is, they feel comfortable enough to ask uncomfortable questions. Like Danny, these friends often ask "the damnedest things out of the blue." McCall (1994) recalls that Danny asked the questions most European Americans wanted to ask but refused to out of fear of being labeled racist:

> But Danny didn't seem to care. I concluded it must have been because he was secure in his mind that he wasn't racist, and he had nothing to hide. He was simply curious. He didn't know, so he did what any intelligent person should have done: He asked rather than assume. I respected that about him and found that, in spite of myself, there was something about this dude I really liked. (p. 343)

When Danny left the newspaper where he and Nathan McCall once worked, he informed his African American friend that "you may not believe this, but there are several white people in the newsroom who are *really* good people. You should give them a chance before writing them off as racists. Get to know some of them. You might be pleasantly surprised" (pp. 348–349). There are times when I wonder if I might open myself up more and be more pleasantly surprised. My friendships with European Americans like Bill, though valuable, are also outnumbered by equally enduring relationships with African Americans. I am often curious about whether I have refused— out of fear—to admit others who are different (not just European Americans) to my circle of friends.

Understanding and addressing this fear may be the most important lesson that I have learned from my relationship with Bill. He has helped me deal with what Cornel West (1993) describes as "racial reasoning," the tendency to see interactions between European and African Americans in rigidly Black and White terms (pp. 37–38). McCall (1994) explains racial reasoning to Danny when he informs him that race "affects every facet of my life" (p. 346). Although Danny has the luxury of not having to think or feel about race, McCall does not: "I can't get away from it, man. I stay so mad all the time because I'm forced to spend so much time and energy reacting to race. I hate it. It wearies me. But there's no escape, man. No escape" (p. 246). As an African American woman, I can certainly empathize with McCall; yet, I can also appreciate Danny's recognition that the feelings of hate often reflected in reacting to race "ain't healthy" (p. 346). Danny, like my friend Bill, confirms that relationships between European and African Americans, like relationships in general, are seldom Black and White. Indeed, both these European American men give me some hope that there may be some escape from the prison of racial reasoning, and that empathy might just be the key.

Mark Lawrence McPhail: Unlocking the Self Through Empathic Performance

I teach a course called "African American Experiences" in the ethnic studies program at our university, and in it I require a final performance from a selection of African American literature. I relate performance to the African American experience through exploration of the oral influences on the culture, and also through a discussion of how the act of performance offers the opportunity to "get us out of our own heads," and experience—if only for a moment—what it might be like to be in someone else's. One student, a young European American man, performed a selection from the conclusion of the chapter entitled "Danny" in McCall's (1994) *Makes Me Wanna Holler* and stated in his introduction that it gave him "some sense of what it must be like to be a Black person." The section that he performed clearly illustrated the empathic potential of performance for both the writer and the reader: "The notion that one of them cared, really cared, about what I thought moved me. Danny was the first white person I met whom I actually saw trying to understand," recalls McCall. He also explains that his relationship with Danny helped him "better understand the fear and ignorance behind prejudice" and realize "that the education system in this country has failed white people more than it's failed anybody else. It has crippled them and limited their humanity" (p. 347). This failure reflects what is perhaps the greatest pitfall of racial reasoning.

In considering my own encounter with the difficulties of racial reasoning, I wish to reflect on the influence that two White men, the poet Robert Penn Warren and the rhetorical scholar Richard Lanham, have had on my personal and professional development. Their work has had particular impact on my own writing and performance. Warren's poetry has stayed with me throughout my educational and professional career and influenced my own writing perhaps most powerfully in a piece I authored in college entitled "Between Two Cities." The poem attempted to imitate the aesthetic qualities I admired in Warren's (1978) "American Portrait Old Style," which ends with the statement that "love is a hard thing to outgrow" (p. 7). Lanham's (1976) discussion of "the rhetorical ideal of life" (pp. 1–35) helped me come to grips with what it meant to be "between two cities," not only in relation to the "double-consciousness" that W. E. B. DuBois (1982) saw as an essential aspect of the African American experience (p. 45), but also in terms of the human struggle between emotion and reason, between what Lanham (1976) calls the "social" and "central" selves (p. 6).

I wrote "Between Two Cities" as a tribute to Warren when I was a junior in college, and it continues, to paraphrase the late James Baldwin (1974), to "spell out the language of my life" (p. 65). It embodies the experience of the intersections between communication and culture that have shaped my life since high school, where I was first introduced to the writings of an elderly southern White man whose words spoke to me in powerful ways, influencing my writing of poetry in college and my study of performance in graduate school. Perhaps more important, the poem reflects the tensions that occur when one chooses to live emotionally and intellectually between the opposing poles of Whiteness and Blackness that circumscribe racial reasoning, to accept and embrace one's Africanness as well as one's Americanness. Critics on both sides of the color line might view the acceptance and embracing of both Blackness and Whiteness as indecision at best, or "collaborating with the enemy" at worst, but I choose to view this as a manifestation of the "twoness" spoken of by DuBois (1982, p. 6), a two-ness that is paralleled in the personality of what Richard Lanham (1976) calls "Homo Rhetoricus": rhetorical man (p. 6).

The distinguishing characteristic of that personality is, in Lanham's (1976) account, the love of language and performance. "Rhetorical man is an actor; his reality public, dramatic. His sense of identity, his self, depends on the reassurance of daily histrionic reenactment. He is thus centered in time and concrete local event" (p. 4). This performative quality of existence emphasizes emotion and empathy. As Lanham explains, rhetorical man "usually has the sense of humor to know that he—and others—not only may *think* differently, but may *be* differently. He pays a price for this, of course—religious sublimity, and its reassuring, if breathtaking, unities" (p. 5). The "rhetorical ideal of life" offers a way of knowing and being that recognizes interdependence and interrelatedness. It is, like love, a hard thing to outgrow. Yet it is a way

of knowing and being from which racial reasoning attempts to free us. But, as Lanham states, we cannot be free from it:

> If truly free of rhetoric, we would be pure essence. We would retain no social dimension. We would divest ourselves of the very mechanism of forgiveness. For what is forgiveness but the acknowledgment that the sinner sinning is not truly himself, but plays a misguided role. If always truly ourselves, which of us shall scape hanging? (p. 8)

We would, in short, rid ourselves of the capacity for emotional connection, of empathy. We would be trapped in, as Lanham describes it, "the nightmarish prison of unchanging essence" (p. 8), and we would lose what Vincent Crapanzano (1985) calls "that small space of freedom that is at the heart of humanity and enables us to engage in a vital manner with those about us" (p. 20). Our ability to connect to one another would indeed be crippled, and our humanity limited, and our differences would continue to divide us from one another, in the segregated cells of a prison of our own making.

What I have learned from Warren and Lanham, however, is that performative empathy—the rhetorical ideal of life—may be the key to unlocking these cells. Embracing Warren's aesthetic influence and performing his poetry have taught me that the spaces that connect us, a young African American and an old southern American, are potentially just as powerful as those that separate us. Lanham's criticism has shown me a transformative vision of language, life, and method, one that transcends material realities and touches the spiritual ideals of our humanity, despite our differences of race, age, or ideology. These two White men have taught me important and lasting lessons about the problems and possibilities of racial identity, and had I not been willing to listen to and experience their words, I would not be who I am today. Perhaps the young European American student who encountered McCall's words will be similarly moved and will become another in the chorus of voices speaking into being a more coherent understanding of human interaction, one that resists racial reasoning. Such an understanding is certainly needed, for as Cornel West (1993) observes: "Either we learn a new language of empathy and compassion, or the fire this time will consume us all" (p. 8).

From Empathy to Implicature: Creating a New Language of Compassion

The concept of empathy provides an important touchstone for transforming how we think about and enact language practices, and its significance for communication cuts across the various divisions within the discipline. Although empathy has been explored in terms of its emotional and intellectual dimensions in rhetorical, interpersonal, intercultural, and performance studies, we might look beyond the surface of the concept to consider its larger implications for human knowledge and existence. Empathy, as traditionally conceived, assumes a view of the world in which self and other are essentially separate and distinct. This view of the world, however, has been challenged dramatically in a number of disciplines, from philosophy to physics, by the notion that our separateness is an illusion, and that *in reality*, we are all essentially implicated in each other. From this perspective, empathy is a state of mind that reflects an underlying state of being, an experience of reality that is defined not by separateness but by wholeness, or what we have chosen to call "implicature."

One of the most powerful expressions of implicature is seen in the writings of the late David Bohm (1987), a physicist who explains how our prevailing beliefs about existence and knowing separate us from one another psychologically, physically, and spiritually. Bohm contends that this view of reality deals only with its "explicate" manifestations, and that another view, one that recognizes the "implicate order" of existence, will enable us to better deal with the divisions and fragmentation that affect human individual and collective experience. The implicate order reflects "the unbroken wholeness of the totality of existence as an undivided flowing movement without

borders" (p. 7). It represents an empathic connection not only with human beings, but with reality itself, because it assumes that just as we all are implicated, at a fundamental level, in one another's lives, so too are all aspects of existence implicated in one another.

Implicature extends the notion of empathy from the psychological to the physical by acknowledging that self and other are never separate and distinct, but are always interdependent and interrelated. Whereas empathy reflects psychological aspects of human experience and understanding, implicature reflects the lived, "dialogic" experience of otherness in which, according to Mikhail Bahktin (1986), "I realize myself through others." Bahktin's conceptualization of dialogue points to the intersection of experience and consciousness that undergirds implicature: "Just as a body is formed initially in the mother's womb (body), a person's consciousness awakens wrapped up in another's consciousness" (p. 138). Implicature intimates that the separation of self and other that begins at birth can be attenuated in those intimate spaces of interaction in which separation and division is transformed through a conscious and embodied embracing of difference.

Recognizing and cultivating implicature is a critical task for students and scholars of communication, and the exploration of the significance of empathy for human symbolic and social interactions is certainly a step in the right direction. Still, we believe that more theoretical and practical work is needed, especially if we are serious about healing the divisions created by differences of communication, culture, and consciousness. In the realm of interracial relations, the need for continued inquiry and action is clearly evident. If, as Karen Dace (1994) suggests, the present state of African and European American symbolic interaction "leads one to wonder if there can ever be a different kind of communication between these two groups" (p. 18), then it is imperative that we begin to examine existing concepts, as well as to articulate new ones, that will enable us to reframe our interactions and relationships. In this essay, we have attempted to suggest through theoretical insight and practical experience that the move from empathy to implicature might facilitate such a reframing. If we are correct, then perhaps the problem of the 21st century will no longer be the problem of the color line.

REFERENCES

Bahktin, M. M. (1986). *Speech genres and other late essays*. Austin: University of Texas Press.

Baldwin, J. (1974). *If Beale Street could talk*. New York: Dial Press.

Bohm, D. (1987). *Wholeness and the implicate order*. London: Routledge and Kegan Paul.

Broome, B. (1991). Building shared meaning: Implications of a relational approach to empathy for teaching intercultural communication. *Communication Education, 40,* 235–249.

Burleson, B. (1983). Social cognition, empathic motivation, and adult's comforting strategies. *Human Communication Research, 10,* 295–304.

Crapanzano, V. (1985). *Waiting: The whites of South Africa*. New York: Random House.

Dace, K. (1994). Dissonance in European-American and African-American communication. *Western Journal of Black Studies, 18,* 18–26.

DuBois, W. E. B. (1982). *The souls of black folks*. New York: New American Library. (Original work published in 1903)

"Empathy." (1987). *Webster's new world dictionary*. New York: Warner Books.

Kelly, C. (1973). Empathic listening. In J. Trent, J. Trent, & D. O'Neill (Eds.), *Concepts in communication* (pp. 263–272). Boston: Allyn and Bacon.

Lanham, R. (1976). *The motives of eloquence*. New Haven, CT: Yale University Press.

Lustig, M., & Koester, J. (1996). *Intercultural competence: Interpersonal communication across cultures*. New York: HarperCollins.

McCall, N. (1994). *Makes me wanna holler: A young black man in America*. New York: Random House.

McIntosh, P. (1986, April). *White privilege and male privilege: A personal accounting of coming to see correspondence through work in women's studies*. Paper presented at the Virginia Women's Studies Association Conference, Richmond, VA.

Morrison, T. (1970). *The bluest eye*. New York: Pocket Books.

Pelias, R. (1982). Empathy: Some implications of social cognition research for interpretation study. *Central States Speech Journal, 33,* 519–532.

Rogers, C., & Stevens, B. (1967). *Person to person: The problem of being human*. New York: Simon & Schuster.

Samovar, L., & Porter, R. (1995). *Communication between cultures* (2nd ed.). Belmont, CA: Wadsworth.

Taft-Kaufman, J. (1985). Oral interpretation: Twentieth century theory and practice. In T. Benson (Ed.), *Speech communication in the 20th century* (pp. 157–183). Carbondale: Southern Illinois University Press.

Warren, R. P. (1978). *Now and then: Poems 1976–1978*. New York: Random House.

West, C. (1993). *Race matters*. Boston: Beacon Press.

KEY TERMS

color line	implicature
dialogue	racial reasoning
double-consciousness	rhetorical ideal of life
empathy	wholeness
implicate order	

DISCUSSION QUESTIONS

1. Discuss how the move from empathy to implicature might be achieved in any of the following arenas of interaction: religion, gender, class, ability.

2. What are some of the barriers that exist between African Americans and European Americans that make empathy difficult? How might implicature help us understand these barriers?

3. How might we think of implicature in terms of the intimate relationships we have with others in our lives? Is it possible, or desirable, to extend the type of intimacy we experience with those who are close to us to others who are significantly different?

4. Karen Dace suggests that the present state of race relations between African Americans and European Americans "leads one to wonder if there can ever be a different kind of communication between these two groups." Respond to

Dace's suggestion by discussing your perceptions of existing communication between African and European Americans as well as what a "different kind of communication" would look like.

5. Mark McPhail suggests that performance can provide opportunities for people from different backgrounds to experience "otherness" in positive and productive ways. Do you agree or disagree? Give concrete examples from your own experience to support your answer.

45
MASS-MEDIATED COMMUNICATION AND INTERCULTURAL CONFLICT

FERNANDO DELGADO

Conflict has typically been conceptualized and examined by communication scholars as an interpersonal issue. For example, communication scholar Mary Jane Collier (1991) suggests that "conflict occurs when *relational partners* perceive incompatibility in such diverse areas as ideas, values, emotions, needs, access to resources, and constraints on action" (p. 132). Intercultural communication textbooks also tend to reinforce this interpersonal perspective (Gudykunst & Kim, 1992, pp. 84–87; Lustig & Koester, 1993, pp. 268–271).

This essay takes a different approach to intercultural conflict. I share with intercultural scholars the perception that conflict is an integral part of intercultural contact, and that it often results from clashes between dissimilar cultural experiences and meaning-making systems. However, I also believe that culture transcends the dyad and exists at all levels of communication, from the interpersonal to the mass-mediated. Therefore, I argue that intercultural conflict should be examined in contexts other than interpersonal communication, specifically in mass-mediated and popular culture forms.

In what follows I review and assess the interpersonal emphasis in intercultural communication study. I then describe and discuss two forms of conflict related to the transmission and reception of mass-mediated and popular culture. Such moves are important if we are to enrich what we do in intercultural communication research.

Interpersonal Emphasis in Intercultural Communication

As I have already noted, intercultural scholars mainly study interpersonal contact. The intimate relationship between interpersonal and intercultural communication has developed principally because of the theoretical, methodological, and disciplinary biases of many intercultural researchers. For example, William Gudykunst (1984) has noted several shortfalls of intercultural research; nevertheless, he bases his perspective of intercultural communication on the presumption that *dyads* are the ground for intercultural inquiry.

Nwankwo (1979) has written that "some communication scholars have tried to limit intercultural communication to the interpersonal level of interaction and to distinguish it from such other forms of communication as interracial, interethnic, international, and cross cultural communication" (p. 325). Nwankwo suggests that these tendencies among intercultural scholars reflect personal and collective research biases rather than actual human (and cultural) contact or behavior. Intellectual choices are often made to delimit an area of inquiry and justify teaching activities, but in this case they reduce our understanding of culture in the context of intercultural contact.

Therefore, when intercultural communication scholars examine conflict, it is not surprising that they envision an interaction between two people of dissimilar cultural backgrounds with different motivations, goals, behaviors, and symbol systems. For example, Ting-Toomey (1988) explains that "conflict is a pervasive phenomenon that penetrates all forms of social and personal relationships in all cultures. Partners in a conflict situation typically bargain over many facets of the conflict process" (p. 213). This perspective, however valid, provides only a partial view of culture, communication, and conflict. If conflict is a clash between cultures' values, norms, symbols, ideologies, and political autonomy or national sovereignty (as in the cases of the former Yugoslavia or Soviet Union), then the interpersonal perspective is too restrictive.

On the other hand, if we take culturalist approaches (Hall, 1959) literally—that communication is culture and vice versa—any symbolic activity that crosses or links cultures can be defined as intercultural contact without distinguishing or privileging levels or even contexts of interaction. Let us look at how intercultural conflict can be seen as something more than a clash between dissimilar interactants of a dyad.

Culture, Conflict, and the Media

Most intercultural scholars share the perspective that communication and culture are dynamically interrelated. Robert Shuter, in Part One, argues that practical concerns—economic, political, technological, social—should inform a return to the study of culture by communication scholars: "Compelling global conditions require intercultural researchers to alter their research agenda and return culture to preeminence in their studies" (p. 42). Such research could involve interpersonal, small group, and organizational as well as rhetorical, media, and political research. Intercultural communication can include

more than two people, and conflict often involves a level of cultural contact beyond the dyadic interaction. For example, when nations negotiate in diplomacy, they do so with political and national concerns in mind but through members who reflect cultural perspectives and imperatives. Such contact is clearly more than interpersonal communication. Moreover, when we broadly consider the exchange of symbols and meanings from one group to another, the possible interactive contexts and levels expand to include peace (and diplomacy) communication (see Korzenny & Ting-Toomey, 1990) as well as the interrelated areas of mass-mediated communication inquiry, which include developmental communication, global and world communication, and international communication (Mowlana, 1986; Nordenstreng & Schiller, 1993).

The reality of international politics, the development of communication and transportation technologies, and the expansion of globalized economics mean that cultural contact through various forms of mediated and unmediated forms of communication is a given. Nations must negotiate to reach agreements, develop alliances, and engage in and resolve international conflicts. The prevalence and power of mediated forms of communication (computer technology, telephone, television, film, even radio) make intercultural contact—communication that crosses cultural and national borders—all the more pervasive. But such contact can lead to intercultural conflict because of economic and political conflicts as well as clashes over values.

In the following sections, I examine two interrelated aspects of intercultural conflict at the macrolevels: First, I survey debates over media domination related to information and media flows. Second, I examine ideological and cultural critiques of American culture based on structural rather than interpersonal contact.

International Communication: New World Information and Communication Order Debates

In this first example I examine how mass communication can be understood as a form of cultural, and hence intercultural, contact that leads to conflict. More specifically, by surveying intellectual and ideological debates regarding media domination (or imperialism) and a world information order, we can see that intercultural conflict is a reality beyond interpersonal contact. Sean Macbride and Colleen Roach (1993) explain that "[r]esolutions, meetings, and manifestos [often involving UNESCO and the United Nations] calling for a 'new order' in international information structures and policies became a feature of the world scene in the early 1970s and generated intense dispute" (p. 3). The debate regarding the control and domination over media technology and cultural forms, and the broader arguments over media imperialism, are examples of macrolevel intercultural conflict.

Briefly, the New World Information and Communication Order (NWICO) debates arose from nonaligned and developing (Third World) nations' concerns over the pattern and speed of national and international communication systems; the role of the mass media in the international sphere (with special emphasis on the political and economic impacts); and potential for egalitarian and democratic restructuring of international information systems (Kleinwachter, 1993, pp. 15–17). These abstract concerns are more concrete when seen from a communication perspective. Much of the debate centers on (1) the unequal distribution of and control over means of communication; (2) the related imbalance or inequity of the flow of media products; and (3) the distortion of media coverage regarding developing regions by more powerful First World nations (Galtung & Vincent, 1992, pp. 1–24; Kleinwachter, 1993).

The United States, with its vast technological resources and economic development, is at the forefront of these debates and conflicts. As *the* communication power, the United States dominates global cultural and entertainment markets. As former president Ronald Reagan approvingly noted:

> [O]ur culture is as powerful and transcendent as our military. In 1989, America made the top five movies in Greece, Ireland, Italy, the Netherlands, Norway, Switzerland, Hungary, Bolivia, Brazil, Australia, and Japan. In October 1991, almost half of the top fifty T.V. entertainment programs in Italy and Spain were American—including programs like *Cheers* and *Golden Girls*. (Cited in Lincoln, 1994, p. 152)

Such cultural dominance, though celebrated at home, can spark intercultural conflicts because it inhibits the development of other nations' indigenous popular culture products, stunts their economic development, and foists U.S. values and perspectives on other cultures. These effects, in turn, often lead to resentment and conflict. For example, Henry Comor, in defending Canadian cultural products, has observed that "American television has made the development of a Canadian cultural identity almost impossible" (in Schiller, 1992, p. 123). Comor's sentiments are reflective of nations' desires to defend their industries and culture from undue outside influence.

Although a critique of technological control or of the dominance over the economic benefits related to media and entertainment industries is valuable, several scholars have also focused on the impact of the ideas and values that international media flows can transmit (Tunstall, 1994). Taken as a whole, the elements of mass media can pose a threat to national sovereignty as well as cultural development and identity (Garnham, 1993). For example, the economic needs of a commercialized television network alter the relationship among entertainment product, corporate entity, audience, and consumption values in ways that may not be typical or "natural" to a culture; though, retrospectively, these relationships appear natural to Americans.

Herbert Schiller (1992) argues that U.S. massmedia corporations are part of a militaryindustrial complex that seeks world domination by pursuing pocketbooks as well as minds, as reflected in Reagan's remarks. This is achieved, for example, when American media companies pursue a strategy similar to that of Japanese electronic companies allegedly "dumping" their products in the United States. Media scholar Jeremy Tunstall (1994) describes how this happens:

> [T]he standard American practice in all media fields is to initially undercut the opposition through price competition; this follows from

the enormous numbers of publications and broadcast outlets in the U.S.A. The policy is wide sales at low prices. (p. 42)

The effect of such practices is that products from Hollywood and New York dominate the markets in Europe, Asia, Latin America, and Africa. It is this kind of market domination that has sparked the conflict and debate over the control of information and communication technology.

Critical and Marxist scholars such as Schiller note the interconnectedness between our global economic and political domination and the diffusion and penetration of our cultural products. In short, what we might consider a TV sitcom in the United States might be considered, or function as, propaganda elsewhere. Joseph Straubhaar (1991) argues that there is an asymmetrical interdependence among most nations when it comes to popular and media culture forms. In practicality what that means is that movie houses, television stations, and record stores in faraway lands display many of the cultural products we experience here. The reverse, although possible, is not nearly as prevalent or obvious. For example, India produces many more films than Hollywood, but few Indian films are available in the United States. Although American films (or television programs) are arguably aesthetically pleasing, they indisputably transmit cultural perspectives and values that often clash with and overrun local cultures.

The New World Information and Communication Order debates are fundamentally about access, equality, and flow of communication, and hence culture. It is clear that multinational entities, which do not respect national borders, are increasingly paying for the expansion and diffusion of media technologies and content. The domination of technological markets and entertainment industries has political as well as economic and cultural effects. Cultural groups who feel that they are being economically and culturally dominated predictably react with feelings of resentment. The rise of multinational corporations and alliances shifts the debate somewhat, but experience tells us that the United States, along with its culture and ideology, will remain a leader in the hierarchy of popular and media culture dissemination. At the same time, it is also clear that developed and

developing nations will resent that presence and dominance.

Cultural Criticism: Ugly America, Ugly Americans

Indirectly related to the New World Information and Communication Order debate, another form of intercultural conflict is reflected in the work of cultural critics. These cultural critics include academicians, journalists, and politicians who speak and write about issues affecting their respective cultures. They often write about the preservation of the best of their home cultures and at the same time are highly critical of other cultures. As a highly visible cultural superpower, the United States has been on the receiving end of several such satirical and scathing critiques. These critiques often reflect intercultural conflict in mediated rather than interpersonal levels of conflict.

As a teenager, I spent time in Europe and was able to see how American media and culture existed in a foreign context. In one instance I was struck by the incongruity of seeing street graffiti admonishing "Yankees go home!" and the same day seeing *How the West Was Won* dubbed in Spanish for Spain's national network. The incongruity grew as my Spanish friends and I sat around in our Rolling Stones t-shirts, Levi's, and Adidas tennis shoes and drank Coca-Cola. It was during this time that French cultural minister Jack Lang began to criticize media imperialism; these critiques turned into protectionist policies with respect to the culture industries of France (issues revisited during the 1993 General Agreement on Trade and Tariffs [GATT] negotiations). Lang's rhetoric was both protectionist in defending France's cultural autonomy and chauvinist in attacking the cultural value of U.S. cultural products. In both of these examples we can see mediated, rather than interpersonal, intercultural contact and conflict.

During a recent trip to Europe, I again noticed the presence of anti-American sentiments. For example, graffiti, newspapers, and television programs in Spain and France disparaged the U.S. policy toward the former Yugoslavia and continued to label the United States as an imperial power. At the same time, youth fashions, popular music, television, film, and now automobiles bore the unmistakable imprint of U.S. products. Only fast-food outlets, perhaps the ultimate sign of American cultural exportation, seem to be out of fashion or in decline. Yet, a palpable sense of resentment, frustration, and disdain among the locals coexisted with an amazement at the penetration of U.S. popular culture.

Politics, economics, and technology clearly accelerate networks for intercultural contact while blurring national borders and cultural boundaries—consequently provoking intercultural conflict in many instances. European scholars, grappling with the cultural dilemmas caused by the European Union, continue to note the presence and impact of U.S. culture and products on foreign soil. Whether we call it internationalization or globalization, political and economic forces are bringing cultures together. During my stay in Spain, I was also struck by the availability of American television there, now in network form via cable systems rather than dated reruns. Indeed, in Madrid one could catch Conan O'Brien, in English, through the National Broadcasting Company's (NBC) feed. But television watchers could just as easily choose from programming offered by ESPN and CNN. Satellite and cable communications have indeed shrunk the physical space of the world. But a shrunken global village does not necessarily make for a global community or foster a sense of unity.

Three noted European critics—Umberto Eco, Jean Baudrillard, and Vicente Verdú—have assessed American culture with varying degrees of vitriol, amazement, and shock as they analyze various forms of cultural conflict brought on by the forces of globalization. Eco (1986), often in cautious terms, finds ways to compare (rather unfavorably) European popular and "high" cultures with the cultural activities and life found in the United States. Exemplars of European popular culture are often described by Eco as "subdued, [and] diffident [whereas] their American counterparts are loud and aggressive" (p. 12). Indeed, Eco's assessment of American popular culture is peppered with adjectives such as "crude," "loud," "fake," and "violent." It is as if Eco were shocked by the sheer scale and intensity of U.S. popular culture. Noting a culture rife with imitations, il-

lusions, and the absence of authenticity, Eco writes that "the ideology of this America wants to reestablish reassurance through Imitation. But profit defeats ideology, because the consumers want to be thrilled not only by the guarantee of the Good but also by the shudder of the Bad" (p. 57).

In his book *Travels in Hyperreality*, Eco (1986) visits the United States and finds a world of playgrounds, wax museums, zoos, and amusement parks and observes reconstructions of environments that never were. We too can see the incongruity in American culture: a resort in Las Vegas that purports to recreate the physical structures and inner soul of New York; a Disneyland that gives tourists "a small world" to cavort in while elsewhere reconstructing a politically correct "Pirates of the Caribbean" ride. Or perhaps we could look at department stores touting "genuine virgin acrylic" or "authentic reproduction" in order to sell blankets and collectibles. Between the lines of his writing we can almost hear Eco, the Italian intellectual, noting that Europe retains its experience while the United States copies just enough so that what was real can be marketed to those who seek safe, sanitary, and entertaining approximations.

In a direct indictment of the restructuring and recontextualizing of experience that is at the heart of American popular culture, Eco (1986), promoting and hoping for an alternative path for Italian culture, asks "what could happen when we attain the levels of institutionalized cultural showmanship that have been reached in the United States?" (p. 155). Eco answers his own question and simultaneously delivers a devastating critique of American culture:

> If cultural performance is going to follow this road, then we have little to be content about. Not because the show is "cultural," but because it is a "show" in the worst sense of the word: a false life depicted on the stage so that the witnesses, in silence, may have the illusion of living, through an intermediary. (p. 156)

It is clear that Eco is concerned about cultures, specifically European, becoming infected by the corrosive inauthenticity and crass commercialization he sees in American popular culture. The cultural conflict is insinuated, the European communities, more sensitive to history, are contrasted with the constructed and commodified audiences of the United States.

If Eco worries about the simulations that mark American popular culture, Jean Baudrillard revels in them. In his travelogue, *America,* Baudrillard (1988) picks up on Eco's themes: "America ducks the question of origins; it cultivates no origin or mythical authenticity; it has no past and founding truth. Having known no primitive accumulation of time, it lives in a perpetual present" (p. 76).

Baudrillard (1988) is amazed at what Americans have created in the United States, yet there is also a sense of mocking, a subtle and stinging critique of U.S. culture, in his work. Baudrillard is clear to distinguish, as Eco did, Europe from America: "[T]he confrontation between America and Europe reveals not so much a rapprochement as a distortion, an unbridgeable rift. There isn't just a gap between us, but a whole chasm of modernity" (p. 73). It is as if Baudrillard is suggesting that Europe grew with all the ugliness, dirtiness, and naturalness that is human existence whereas America is like a test-tube baby subsequently raised in a sterile environment with no past, only brilliant present and future, and Utopia within its grasp. But reading Baudrillard, one is also led to believe that if Americans could not find Utopia, they would manufacture a close approximation of it and sell tickets to the attraction.

As with Eco, Baudrillard (1988) seems to be descriptive, assessing what he sees but not being overly judgmental. That is deceptive. In Baudrillard's work we can observe the seeds of cultural conflict between the old and new worlds. The old world evolved, learned, and matured; its weaknesses documented, its strengths to be protected. The United States has different origins and elements, "America is neither dream nor reality . . . America is a giant hologram" (pp. 28–29). Baudrillard respects the technical acumen and commitment that has created America, appreciates the success that Americans have achieved in short order, and notes the sheer egoism of our culture. But he does not see these achievements and values as possible or desirable in other cultural contexts. In fact, Baudrillard can be read as particularly disdainful of Americans: "For me there is no truth of America. I ask only of the Americans that they be American. I do not ask them to be intelligent, sensible, [or] original" (p. 27).

If Eco and Baudrillard are seductive, even playful in their critiques, Vicente Verdú (1996), in his *El Planeta Americano* (The American Planet), is blunt. Verdú finds the United States and the American people easy to critique as boorish, vulgar, overly prideful. His text is a polemic against the United States' global economic, ideological, and cultural hegemony. In short, his work is a warning to Europeans to avoid all that is culturally American. Briefly, several examples illustrate Verdú's position. On the U.S. secondary education system Verdú writes,

> [A]t that level we are talking about a vocational education that, more than anything, attempts to form determined citizens, with a strong dosage of self-esteem and self-confidence. Strong and apt to develop within the United States, where they not only are but where they believe the world will come to be. (p. 15; Verdú's work is in Spanish, all translations are mine)

Verdú perceives a destructive cultivation of individual ego and collective ethnocentrism among Americans that is also present in our culture and social institutions.

Verdú (1996) finds much to criticize. Whether it be our incongruent celebration of religion and obscenity or our anti-intellectualism, Verdú perceives American culture to be of questionable value. The incongruity of the church next to the porn palace, cultural elites complaining about nudity in film while celebrating rapacious violence, and the denigration of educated people as "impractical" confuses and dismays Verdú. For example, if Americans were to say they have the best cinematic resources, Verdú would ask then why are Arnold Schwarzenneger and Sylvester Stallone films so popular? Any culture that makes Beavis and Butthead cultural icons is difficult to defend against Verdú's thesis. Indeed, Verdú even finds a way to critique our core value of individualism by noting our related tendency toward exhibitionism (exemplified in reality, tabloid, and talk television) (pp. 96–97). The combination of exhibitionism and individualism suggests to Verdú that American culture is immature, egotistical, and not something to be invited in or emulated by other cultures.

From Verdú's perspective as a Spanish intellectual, the United States is a nation to be interrogated for its excesses, sanctimony, and greed. When Verdú (1996) is critiquing Americans' approach to capitalism, he might also be talking about our politics and culture as well, noting that "the history of the United States is constructed of winners of a certain style, opportunistic, audacious, and aggressive" (p. 65). In sum, these characteristics are what Verdú finds to be at the core of American culture and, consequently, why he feels compelled to warn the world away from us. Verdú shares with Eco and Baudrillard an appreciation for America's accomplishments, but a disdain over what effect U.S. values and habits might have in other cultural contexts. For these critics it is enough to experience our culture, but one gets the sense they would not live here.

Returning to the issues of conflict, these three European scholars are engaging in mediated forms of communication rife with conflict. Each is demonstrating his own biases toward the United States, reflecting on meanings, values, and identities (of another culture) that trouble them, and ultimately arguing against U.S. culture and for their own. In short, the content of these three writers' respective efforts are examples of intercultural conflict—a clash over ideas, values, and norms.

Conclusion

In this essay I have briefly surveyed a series of debates and perspectives that demonstrates how cultural conflict is not simply found in, or processed through, interpersonal communication. Intercultural conflict is based on a clash over competing and opposing systems of symbols, meanings, and values carried by multiple channels and forms of communication. If intercultural communication scholars are going to meet the challenges of the next century, we must expand our conceptual repertoire and become more creative in examin-

ing conflict. Intercultural scholars must attend to conflict in its many contexts and many levels of interaction.

I have no doubt that intercultural communication is complex and confounding to researcher and student alike. But as the examples in this essay demonstrate, we might likely face greater complications before we find the answers. As Robert Shuter's essay indicates, culture is the key concept in intercultural communication. As illustrated here, culture and communication coincide in various forms that affect our daily lives. We are each emblematic of our own cultures; we are created by and subsequently re-create the structures of cultures and societies. But if Baudrillard (1988) is correct in noting that "New York and Los Angeles [and therefore the United States] are at the centre of the world" (p. 23), Americans owe it to themselves to understand how cultures relate and how conflict is generated culturally.

REFERENCES

Baudrillard, J. (1988). *America.* (C. Turner, Trans.). New York: Verso.

Collier, M. J. (1991). Conflict competence within African, Mexican, and Anglo American friendships. In S. Ting-Toomey & F. Korzenny (Eds.), *Cross-cultural interpersonal communication* (pp. 132–154). Newbury Park, CA: Sage.

Eco, U. (1986). *Travels in hyperreality.* San Diego, CA: Harcourt Brace Jovanovich.

Galtung, J., & Vincent, R. G. (1992). *Global glasnost: Toward a new world information and communication order?* Cresskill, NJ: Hampton Press.

Garnham, N. (1993). The mass media, cultural identity, and the public sphere in the modern world. *Public Culture, 5,* 251–265.

Gudykunst, W. B. (1984). Intercultural communication: Current status and proposed directions. In B. Dervin & M. J. Voigt (Eds.), *Progress in communication sciences 5* (pp. 1–46). Norwood, NJ: Ablex.

Gudykunst, W. B., & Kim, Y. Y. (1992). *Communicating with strangers: An approach to intercultural communication* (2nd ed.). New York: McGraw-Hill.

Hall, E. T. (1959). *The silent language.* New York: Doubleday.

Kleinwachter, W. (1993). Three waves of the debate. In G. Gerbner, H. Mowlana, & K. Nordenstreng (Eds.), *The global media debate: Its rise, fall, and renewal* (pp. 13–20). Norwood, NJ: Ablex.

Korzenny, F., & Ting-Toomey, S. (Eds.). (1990). *Communicating for peace: Diplomacy and negotiation.* Newbury Park, CA: Sage.

Lustig, M. W., & Koester, J. (1993). *Intercultural competence: Interpersonal communication across cultures.* New York: HarperCollins.

Macbride, S., & Roach, C. (1993). The new international information order. In G. Gerbner, H. Mowlana, & K. Nordenstreng (Eds.), *The global media debate: Its rise, fall, and renewal* (pp. 3–12). Norwood, NJ: Ablex.

Mowlana, H. (1986). *Global information and world communication: New frontiers in international relations.* New York: Longman.

Nordenstreng, K., & Schiller, H. I. (Eds.). (1993). *Beyond national sovereignty: International communication in the 1990s.* Norwood, NJ: Ablex.

Nwankwo, R. L. (1979). Intercultural communication: A critical review. *Quarterly Journal of Speech, 65,* 324–346.

Reagan, R. (1994). Remarks by President Ronald Reagan at the National Association of Broadcaster's 70th Annual Convention, 13 April 1992. In B. Lincoln, *Authority: Construction and corrosion* (pp. 147–153). Chicago: University of Chicago Press.

Schiller, H. I. (1989). *Culture Inc.: The corporate takeover of public expression.* New York: Oxford University Press.

Schiller, H. I. (1992). *Mass communications and American empire* (2nd ed.). Boulder, CO: Westview Press.

Shuter, R. (1998). Revisiting the centrality of culture. In J. Martin, T. Nakayama, & L. Flores (Eds.), *Readings in cultural contexts* (pp. 38–47). Mountain View, CA: Mayfield Publishing.

Straubhaar, J. D. (1991). Beyond media imperialism: Asymmetrical interdependence and cultural proximity. *Critical Studies in Mass Communication, 8,* 39–59.

Ting-Toomey, S. (1988). Intercultural conflict styles: A face-negotiation theory. In Y. Y. Kim & W. B. Gudykunst (Eds.), *Theories in intercultural communication* (pp. 213–238). Newbury Park, CA: Sage.

Tunstall, J. (1994). *The media are American: Anglo-American media in the world* (2nd ed.). London: Constable.

Verdú, V. (1996). *El planeta americano.* Barcelona: Editorial Anagrama.

KEY TERMS

developing nations	imperialism
First World nations	intercultural conflict
globalization	international communication
ideology	

DISCUSSION QUESTIONS

1. Delgado argues that intercultural communication and conflict can be seen in different ways. How can conceptions of intercultural conflict vary?

2. Delgado discusses debates relating to the flow of communication products and technology. What are these debates called and what are the key issues involved in them?

3. Delgado's essay makes a case for a way to examine intercultural conflict. What are the benefits of looking at conflict in this way? What are the limitations of his perspective?

4. Given Delgado's perspective, how are culture and communication linked in mass-mediated communication?

5. Delgado introduces three critical thinkers—Eco, Baudrillard, and Verdú. Of the three, who is the most vigorous critic of American culture? Why? Who is the kindest critic? Why?

PART TEN

ETHICS
AND
INTERCULTURAL
COMMUNICATION

Ethics is an important series of considerations in any intercultural interaction. Because we live in a world that is increasingly hostile, violent, and conflicted, the study of ethics has become much more significant in intercultural communication. The following readings address questions of how to behave ethically in an increasingly complex and hostile world. Although there is no one correct way to be ethical, it is vital that you think about ethical considerations. The essays in this section explore various ethical issues involved not only in being competent intercultural communicators but also in studying "others." In discussing ethical issues in researching "others," we revisit some of the issues raised in Part One.

Consider these questions as you read the articles in this part:

Are there ethical considerations in what we choose or choose not to study?

Are there ethical and unethical ways of using intercultural communication knowledge?

Are there ethical and unethical ways to study other people?

How responsible is the researcher for the ways in which research is shared with communities?

In "Ethical Issues in Intercultural Communication," Judith N. Martin, Lisa A. Flores, and Thomas K. Nakayama outline a theoretical framework for developing a metaethic of intercultural communication. They first define ethics and issues of concern for ethical communicators. Then they propose three principles to guide ethical intercultural interaction: humanness, dialogic, and speaking "with" and "to." Finally, they identify and discuss everyday dilemmas in intercultural communication practice and study.

In "Joint Performance Across Cultures," Mary Catherine Bateson describes how the canon of humanness may be applied in actual intercultural encounters. She recounts the story of taking her daughter to a religious celebration in Iran, which involved the ritual killing of a sheep. Bateson describes this intercultural encounter as a "joint improvisation" in which, as is often the case, the scripts are not written for intercultural interaction. Instead, individuals participating in the ritual together create a common script. She also describes the culture-learning that occurred in that encounter for her daughter and herself, and she emphasizes the importance of *experience* in understanding intercultural communication.

We then turn to ethical issues in studying about intercultural communication and learning about others. Mike Allen, in "Comparing Views of Science," describes the ethical issues that arise in two different research perspectives: the social science and the critical. He stresses that the answers are not easy and that each faces unique but important ethical dilemmas.

Dolores V. Tanno and Fred E. Jandt join this discussion and address the challenge of how to study "others" ethically. In "Redefining the 'Other' in Multicultural Research," they suggest that cultural communities should not be seen as research objects, but as research participants. They propose action research as a means of including participants and offer ways in which participants can play a more active role in research.

Finally, in "Painting the White Face Red," María Cristina González provides a good example of a researcher who meets the ethical challenges of studying "others." Her interpretive ethnographic study investigates how some White Americans appropriate Native American spirituality. Her study, from methods to analyses, reveals an ethical commitment to the community involved. Her "Four Seasons" methodology—based on Native American thought—assumes that the researcher is not in charge, that research is instead the natural unfolding of experience. Her concern for ethical issues leads her to present her findings through poetry rather than through traditional academic writing. Her poems reveal the complexity and intensity of this intercultural contact between Indians and non-Indians.

46
ETHICAL ISSUES IN INTERCULTURAL COMMUNICATION

JUDITH N. MARTIN / LISA A. FLORES / THOMAS K. NAKAYAMA

How do we decide what is right and what is wrong for ourselves and others? We usually rely on our personal sense of ethics or morals to guide us in making important decisions and in evaluating our own actions and the actions of others. We learn a sense of right and wrong by explicit teaching and by implicit example from our families, religion, and other cultural experiences. However, what is considered right in one cultural context may be considered wrong in another.

These different ethical systems sometimes collide in intercultural interactions. A common example in international business is that of taking bribes. What is considered just compensation in many Asian countries is considered unethical bribery for U.S. managers (Howell, 1982). Another example is absolute honesty versus relative honesty. In some countries it is more ethical to save face than to tell an unpleasant truth (Kras, 1989). Or it may be unethical to date, even casually, without a promise of commitment to marriage.

There is currently no accepted metaethic, no universal guides for ethical communication in intercultural encounters. Perhaps this is not surprising, given the complexity of the challenge. As communication scholar Dean Barnlund (1982) predicted more than 15 years ago:

> The ethical systems we know are each tied to and reflect the premises of a particular body of people. . . . Until a metaethic . . . can be articulated in ways that gain wide allegiance, or until a common one emerges from the thousands of daily confrontations, confusions, and antagonisms that characterize such encounters, we shall continue to conduct intercultural affairs in a moral vacuum. (p. 381)

Based on an assumption that there are no easy answers, this essay seeks to join the search for ethical guidelines in intercultural encounters. In the first section, we define ethics and describe the relationship between culture and ethics. We then review four common ethical models in communication. Finally, we propose several principles to guide ethical intercultural communication and explore how these principles might work in everyday life.

Culture and Ethics

Ethics or morals have to do with what is considered right and wrong, "the practical, specific, generally agreed-upon, culturally transmitted standards of right and wrong" (Johannesen, 1990, p. 1). Some scholars distinguish between morals and ethics, reserving ethics to mean the study of morals, but in this essay we use the two terms interchangeably.

Ethics tells us what is right and wrong, and our cultures tell us what is right and wrong. They both provide frameworks for assessing others' behavior and for guiding us in important choices. However, not all cultural patterns are ethics statements. Cultural values are those fundamental beliefs that tell us what is "good" and what "ought to be"—for example, individualism, desirability of material wealth, equality, hard work, efficiency. Although these may motivate us and function as criteria for making choices and judging others, communication scholar Richard L. Johannesen (1990) suggests that ethical judgments focus more precisely on *degrees of rightness and wrongness* in human behavior than do cultural values (p. 1). For example, we may criticize someone for being inefficient, conformist, extravagant, lazy, or late, but we probably would not also claim that he or she is unethical.

However, some value standards such as honesty or directness, promise-keeping, fairness, and humanness *are* used in making ethical judgments of rightness and wrongness. So there is some overlap between cultural values and ethics standards. Put simply, all values standards are not ethics, but most ethical decisions are probably related to cultural values.

Different cultural ethics are not much of a problem when cultural groups are isolated. For example, it isn't of great consequence if cultural groups have two different ethics of telling the truth. Each system can be understood within its cultural contexts. However, if members of those cultures are trying to communicate "truthfully" to one another, then a more universal metaethic would be helpful. What we are searching for are some principles that can guide everyone—regardless of cultural background—in intercultural interactions. Continuing the explorations of culture and ethics, let's review contemporary communication models of ethics.

Review of Ethical Models in Communication

Communication scholars Janet Metzger and Jeffrey Springston (1992) argue that the lack of insight on intercultural ethics arises from the limitations of accepted communication models. They review four common communication models and describe how each addresses ethical issues.

The traditional mechanistic model represents communication as comprised of several distinct components (e.g., sender, receiver, channel, message, and noise). In this model, good (successful) communication occurs when the message received is the same as the message sent. That is, there is good communication when there is no noise, for example, cultural differences in the channel. A related psychological model views cultural differences as conceptual filters that influence the encoding or decoding of messages. In both the mechanistic and the psychological models, the skillful (ethical) communicator is one who understands, deals with, and minimizes the impacts of cultural differences. Both these models take an individual-centered approach and do not

specifically address ethical issues. We could surmise, however, that ethical guidelines in these models would involve trying to understand other cultural patterns as well as developing empathy and other skills that lead to maximum understanding. For example, understanding different definitions of truth and dishonesty would go a long way in resolving conflicts about truth-telling. However, as we know, people can understand each other very clearly and still behave unethically in doing violence and harm to one another and to society.

Moving from the individual-centered models to social ethics, Metzger and Springston (1992) review models based on a systems approach to communication. A systems model of communication emphasizes the interconnectedness of human communicators to each other and to their environment (the cultural context in which communication occurs). Any change in one element of the system affects other elements and ultimately the entire system. In this model, ethical communication occurs when there is a fit between communicators and the cultural environment. Change agents may adapt a systems approach in helping resolve ethical dilemmas across cultures—by helping individuals or organizations adapt their communication to meet the challenges of the cultural environment.

In symbolic interactionism, the locus of communication is in role-taking, and culture is viewed as an outworking of ideas. Good communication needs to be looked at on a case-by-case basis, either as what participants define as good or as what the researcher, using her or his own frame, determines to be good. Intercultural communication consultants often use this approach in helping individuals learn to take various roles and perspectives and work for the good of the group. However, ethical, moral, and class concerns are not specifically addressed and are generally brought in by other means of analysis.

Metzger and Springston (1992) argue that what is needed for intercultural communication is an integration of the individual level, which is relatively amoral and acultural, with the concerns of social ethics for justice. In a case study of fishing rights concerns in Wisconsin, they show

how each of the previously mentioned ethical systems is limited in capturing and resolving the individual, social, historical, political, and religious complexities of this case (pp. 79–81).

Three Principles for Ethical Intercultural Communicators

In our search for a metaethic, it may be useful to apply a dialectical approach, where ethical communication must be both individually and socially oriented. There are three principles that might provide the foundation for such a framework.

1. The Humanness Principle

Although proposed by several scholars, the following description of the humanness principle is from philosopher Christopher L. Johnstone:

> to be human suggests that one's conduct is guided by a respect for and a tenderness toward others' beings. . . . a humanist ethic requires that the individual be responsive in his or her actions to the impact they might have on the humanity of those affected by the act. It demands, finally, that one conduct oneself so as to maximize opportunity for cultivating in oneself and in others an awareness and appreciation of humanness. (Johnstone, quoted in Johannesen, 1990, p. 56)

This principle seems sound and has led to other general ethical principles such as the peace principle (Kale, 1994). This metaethic, the peace principle, prescribes addressing others with respect, describing the world as accurately as possible, recognizing the uniqueness of all groups, and trying to identify (empathize) with others. We can ask ourselves what violating these principles of humanness might mean for us in our everyday lives. Might violating the ethic of peace mean denying access to discourse in public settings? Another violation might be to make fun of others' communication styles or cultural beliefs, or to portray cultural groups as stereotypical caricatures in conversations or in media representations. However, we need to search for more specific communication guidelines. A more specific principle is the dialogic principle.

2. The Dialogic Principle

This principle concerns specific attitudes of communicators toward each other and is particularly apt for intercultural communication. It is based on many different strands of philosophical thought. It stresses the centrality of *relationships* in the human experience, that we become most human in the "betweenness" of relationships. This principle is both in contrast and complementary to the more self-centered principle of humanness (see Buber, 1958; Friedman, 1960). Applying the dialogic principle to communication means turning outward, reaching for and developing relationships with others. Particularly appropriate for intercultural communication is the emphasis on trying to understand and share the lived experience of another—which implies developing empathy with others. Benjamin Broome (1991) refers to *relational empathy*, which is dynamic and provisional and allows two individuals to move toward *varying degrees* of understanding (p. 241). He also stresses that relational empathy takes time. It develops when people are willing to open themselves to new meanings, to engage in genuine dialogue, and to respond to new meanings emanating from the situation (p. 243).

A related notion is the ethics of caring. The ethics of care extends the ethic of justice because it promotes seeing the world as "a web of relationships, or circles and chains of people" (Metzger & Springston, 1992, p. 81). This means that using other principles of ethics may result in good but not necessarily moral communication. This is quite striking when we consider that from this ethic, communication without a sense of relationship may be immoral, that reaching out is not just a nice thing to do, but an ethical obligation. This challenges much of our individualistic way of thinking.

There are specific guidelines for following this relationship-centered dialogic principle, for example, authenticity, inclusion, confirmation, presentness, a spirit of mutual equality, and a supportive climate. However, these seem to be limited in that they reflect cultural biases of Western individualism and as such, do not provide a metaethic (Johannesen, 1990, pp. 62–63). We can see again a strong emphasis on empathy. The practical implications of following the dialogic principle in intercultural encounters lead to three challenges: cultural constraints of empathy, power differentials, and considerations of contexts.

Cultural Constraints   Scholars have pointed out that empathy, central to the dialogic principle and the individual-centered communication ethics model, is culture bound. That is, empathy works best among people who share similar cultural backgrounds and experiences. In order to meet this challenge, communication scholar Milton Bennett (1979) suggests replacing the Golden Rule of "Do unto others as you would have them do unto you" with the platinum rule "Do unto others as they themselves would have done unto them" (p. 422). How do we truly understand what others would want done unto them? How do we learn about "others"? In many ways, this is the crux of success in intercultural encounters— knowing about others' experiences. It is easy to imagine learning about other cultures in an intellectual way, but as Karen Lynnette Dace and Mark Lawrence McPhail suggest in their essay in Part Nine, we must go beyond empathy to implicature. Implicature is a fusing of both knowledge about *and* feelings for in reaching out empathically across cultural boundaries. Like Broome's (1991) notion of relational empathy, implicature can happen only when individuals take time and make the effort to nurture and develop intercultural relationships.

We are bombarded daily by messages about others' behavior, and we often make ethical judgments about these behaviors. Although contrasting worldviews sometimes stand in the way of empathy, there is another challenge that must be considered: the role of power.

The Role of Power   Power is an omnipresent but often hidden part of all intercultural interactions. What does power have to do with empathy and understanding others? One of the characteristics of power relations is that those with less power usually understand those with more power rather than the other way around. For example, women often direct more energy toward understanding men (e.g., those articles in "women's magazines" telling women how to understand and be successful in relationships with men) than men direct toward understanding women. Individuals from ethnic minority groups often know more about White experiences in the United States than vice versa (Miller, 1992).

For example, studies contrasting various ethnic groups' notions of effective communication show that U.S. Whites approach communication assuming equality, whereas African American models include elements of power and powerlessness (Martin, 1993). The point is, in order to approach an empathic understanding or to understand the limits of empathy, we have to (1) understand how power works and (2) examine our position(s) with respect to power (Collier, this volume). Ethical dilemmas require an analysis of power relations. For example, Metzger and Springston's (1992) analysis of the fishing controversy in Wisconsin showed how different groups had different access to power (pp. 82–85).

Understanding Contexts   A third challenge in following the dialogic principle is that we cannot understand the human experience (or human communication) without understanding the contexts in which this experience is lived. For example, to study communication between Whites and Blacks in the United States without a firm grounding in the historical contexts of slavery and African diaspora is limiting. In studying interaction between Arabs and Jews, we must incorporate historical events of the Middle East.

In order to develop empathy and really learn about others, we interculturalists need to understand how our own contexts have shaped our lives and discourses as communicators. If we are White Americans, we may approach intercultural interactions with little distrust or apprehension, assuming that if we are nice and polite that others will like us. If we are African American or members of another U.S. ethnic minority, we may approach some intercultural interactions with mistrust. The challenges of cultural constraints, power differentials, and considerations of contexts lead to questions of how to ethically learn about others and of who can speak for others. Our third principle provides some answers by extending the relational dialogic principle to *communication*.

3. The Principle of Speaking "With" and "To"

Given the challenges identified in the previous section, perhaps it seems discouraging to learn about others and to pursue ethical intercultural relationships. Yes, intercultural understanding is challenging, but the answer is not to stop learning about others or to say that only members of a particular group can speak for this group (e.g., only White women can speak for White women). This can be a cop-out because if you speak only for yourself, no one can criticize your position and you don't have to reach out to others. Linda Alcoff (1991/1992), a cultural studies scholar, proposes a *"speaking to"* position, which promotes the practice of speaking *with* and *to* rather than speaking *for* others (p. 23). This promotes "listening to" others as opposed to speaking for others. She equates speaking "for" others with speaking "about" others and suggests that the impetus to speak for must be carefully analyzed and approached carefully. What does this mean for students of intercultural communication?

It may mean that one should *approach scholarly descriptions of others with a critical eye*. Intercultural communication students are often asked to read descriptions of various cultural groups. However, scholars are relatively privileged people and, like anyone else, cannot transcend their own location easily. Alcoff suggests that when scholars speak for (or describe) cultural patterns of less privileged people, they sometimes reinforce the oppression of the group spoken for (p. 7). These descriptions are coming more and more under criticism from members of those oppressed groups (Rosaldo, 1989).

Be Self-Reflexive In order to recognize and understand contextual influences and the role of power, ethical intercultural communicators should examine the "location" from which they are speaking (Rosaldo, 1989). So we, the authors of this essay, as middle-class academicians must think carefully about how our social position influences the way we see the world. What do we know about working-class life? Or student life, for that matter? How do our experiences influence our descriptions and our understanding of intercultural communication?

These are not easy questions to answer, but they *form the foundation* of an ethical approach to intercultural interactions. We must think about the bearing and location and context on what we are saying—to first articulate the possible connections between our location and what we are saying (but not as a disclaimer). Also, our speaking about others should carry an accountability with it.

Listen One of the most difficult things to do is to truly listen. We are often struck by the resistance of people to really listen, particularly on the part of people who speak from relatively privileged positions. Power and listening are related. People who are privileged are often less motivated to listen. Oppressed groups always know more about the lives, motivations, and desires of the powerful than vice versa. This is unfortunate for both (Miller, 1992).

Perhaps a crucial part of listening is not only asking but educating ourselves and not waiting for others to educate us. Gloria Yamato (1995), in "Something About the Subject Makes It Hard to Name," emphasizes that we shouldn't expect others to educate us. She suggests that especially for U.S. Whites who want to be allies of people of color,

> Do not expect that people of color should teach you how to behave non-oppressively. Do not give in to the pull to be lazy. Think, hard. Do not blame people of color for your frustration about racism, but do appreciate the fact that people of color will often help you get in touch with that frustration. Assume that your effort to be a good friend is appreciated, but don't expect or accept gratitude from people of color. Work on racism for your sake, not "their" sake. Assume that you are needed and capable of being a good ally. Know that you'll make mistakes and commit yourself to correcting them and continuing on as an ally, no matter what. Don't give up. (p. 73)

For people of color:

Remember . . . various groups have been oppressed in a variety of ways. Educate yourself
about the ways different peoples have been oppressed and how they've resisted that oppression. Expect and insist that whites are capable
of being good allies against racism. Don't give
up. (p. 73)

Engage in Dialogue   Just listening is limiting. If
individuals are committed to stronger intercultural relations, they need to commit to those relationships, and that means both listening to
and dialoguing with others across cultural boundaries. But, how to engage in dialogue that is
guided by a speaking with and to ethic? It's tricky
to know when to speak and when to listen. Sometimes it's important to speak up—to engage others. If one can remember that *speaking with and to*
builds on the principles of self-reflexivity and
listening, it is possible to avoid a *speaking for.*
Tanno and Jandt (1994 & this volume) provide
very specific guidelines for reaching across cultural boundaries to engage "others" in collaborative culture-learning.

Ethical Dilemmas in Everyday Intercultural Interaction

Our insistence on the relative nature of ethics is
not meant to argue that any behavior can be ethical. Instead, we insist that the character of ethics
is deeply embedded in cultural ways of living. Cultural differences take on heightened significance
in the realm of ethics. The old saying, "When in
Rome, do as the Romans do," is only a partial
guide to navigating the tricky waters of intercultural communication ethics.

Given the enormous number of cultural differences around the globe, we cannot hope to be able
to offer any reasonable lists or guides to ethics in
culture-specific contexts. Instead, we offer the following examples to help you think about ethics
and intercultural communication. As you unpack
the ethical issues in each of these examples, think
about the ways that people deal with these inter-

cultural situations in everyday life. Intercultural
communication takes place on a number of levels, and our examples highlight different aspects
of that interaction. Ethical issues arise in interpersonal intercultural interactions with tourists,
business people, refugees, and migrants. They
also arise in newspaper and television reports and
popular culture representations. They occur in
ingroup jokes and other interactions that are not
directly addressed to members of another cultural
group. Ethical concerns also arise both in the way
intercultural communication is studied and in the
way different cultural groups are characterized in
those studies. Finally, intercultural communication students should be concerned with how they
(and others) use the results of those studies. Let's
look at some examples.

Example 1: In his class in intercultural communication, John learned that, when shopping,
Japanese often consider it insulting to count the
change given by the cashier. Counting change in
front of the cashier is often taken as an accusation of either mathematical incompetence or deliberate shortchanging. John works in a tourist-
related industry with many Japanese clients. He
surmises that they are often well-to-do, as low-
income Japanese do not have the luxury of leisure
travel. How unethical is it for him to shortchange
these clients? Does it depend upon his financial
needs? What if he feels the tourist-related company is underpaying him?

Example 2: Maria is interested in studying a
particular cultural group, but she is not interested
in being very involved in that cultural community.
She does not read their ethnic newspaper; she
does not participate in any of their community activities. She only interacts with members of that
cultural group as students in her courses. She
uses her courses to recruit these students as respondents in her studies. Her use of intercultural
concepts is derived from journal articles, not
from the community she is studying. Is this kind
of intercultural communication research ethical?
In what ways is it ethical? In what ways is it
unethical?

Example 3: The concept of X is important in
Mark's cultural group. He utilizes this concept to
study another cultural group. In interviewing

members of this other group, he finds that they have difficulty expressing how the concept of X functions in their group. He concludes in his study that this other cultural group is less developed and less sophisticated and needs to learn how to enact X more effectively, if it is going to compete effectively on the world market. Is he being unethical in his assessment of this other cultural group? How might his methods of gathering information (interviewing) influence his conclusions about cultural behavior?

Example 4: Diane has read studies about the aggressive nature of men in the country she is visiting. She is wary when she is there, particularly as she is traveling alone. She consciously avoids intercultural communication with men in that country. Is she being sexist? Racist? Is she using her intercultural communication knowledge ethically?

Although these examples are hypothetical, they illustrate the kinds of issues in intercultural communication that call for ethical judgments. By returning to the framework we provided earlier and the ethical challenges we presented, we can examine these issues from an ethical perspective.

First, let's consider John, who was deciding how much change to give to the Japanese tourists he helped. The cultural constraint of empathy requires us to position ourselves within the other culture as we decide how to act. Bennett's revised Golden Rule asks that we "do unto others as *they would have you do unto them.*" With this as an ethical guide, what should John do? It is likely that the tourists he is helping, regardless of their financial position, would like all of their change. For John to shortchange them violates an ethical norm of empathy.

However, the answer may not be quite so simple. Empathy and ethics in intercultural communication also hinge on power. Who has greater power in this situation? From one perspective, John can be seen as having power. He is a member of the host culture, and he has the knowledge of cultural customs that allows him to consider the possibility of shortchanging the tourists. And yet, there may be other factors that are important here. If John is dependent on his job for his living

and the tourists seem to have greater resources, enough to allow for this trip, might his "miscalculation" of a dollar here or there help to level the power difference?

John's musings here, on the Golden Rule and on power differences, might require him to remember another ethical guide—self-reflexivity. Before John makes any decisions, he should think about his thought processes. What cultural values are influencing John's decision? Does John's own class position affect his attitudes about international travel? Is he operating from a dualistic perspective, thinking that *either* you have enough money to travel *or* you have to work hard for your living? John's notions of right and wrong develop out of his cultural location. However, if he wants to make an ethical decision in this intercultural interaction, his recognition of the cultural influence on his decision can help him assess the situation in a more complex manner. As you first read Example 1, you may have had an immediate response, such as, "Well, that's a simple question; of course John should. . . ." The ethical guides that we are proposing here suggest that before we go for the "easy answer," we stop and think about the intercultural implications of the situation.

What happens if we turn to Maria, whose interest in a particular cultural group is based on her research interests? To what extent is she, as an intercultural communication scholar, obligated to the cultural community she studies? One consideration she might want to make is to use a critical eye when reading scholarly research on this cultural group. She might want to consider whether the research that is available on the cultural group has been done by members of that group or by nonmembers. If the scholars she is reading are not members, she might want to think about power differences—are they members of a more dominant group? Why is this an important ethical consideration? As we mentioned, the growing body of research being done within African American, Asian American, and Latino/a studies, gay and lesbian studies, and women's studies, by members of those groups, calls into question much of the existing research. Because even intercultural scholars have to reflect on the biases we bring to our research, Maria should use the avail-

462   Part Ten: Ethics and Intercultural Communication

able research carefully, so that she does not impose meaning on the group she is studying. Does this mean Maria should not read scholarly literature on the cultural group? Or should she read only research that has been done by members of the group? No. But it does mean that Maria cannot accept the conclusions of the existing research without thinking about the subject positions of the authors and of herself. This critical lens should also be used when she reads work that has been written by members of the group. Biases exist in all of us and affect all the work that we do.

In addition to thinking critically about the work, Maria can also extend her knowledge by turning to individual members of the group. By listening to the members talk about their community, their interests, their goals and needs, Maria can balance her background in the scholarly literature with the knowledge that comes from people who can tell her about daily life. This moving toward listening can then lead to dialogue between Maria and members of the group. If Maria begins by speaking with and to the members of the group she is studying, she can gain a whole new perspective on the ethical issues that surround her research. She can identify the kinds of knowledge that would benefit the members of the group, and she can merge her scholarly interests with those of the group so that both she and the community she is studying can benefit from her research.

Think now about Mark and Diane. What questions should they consider as they decide how to act? We leave you to unpack these last two examples. How might Mark follow suggestions of listening, being self-reflexive, and engaging in dialogue in order to more ethically communicate in these unfamiliar intercultural contexts? Similarly, how might Diane use these suggestions to more ethically learn about and understand the cultural group she is visiting?

As you can see from our discussion, the ethical principles and challenges offered here provide a beginning. They are offered to help you think in more complex ways about ethical dilemmas in intercultural encounters. The intercultural situations faced in everyday life are often difficult and cannot be answered easily or quickly. Cultural differences in what is considered right and wrong, good and bad, mean that as we think about ethics,

we must approach situations from many perspectives. The place to start is by reflecting on the humanness of others, establishing and nurturing dialogic relationships, and speaking with and to others across cultural boundaries.

REFERENCES

Alcoff, L. (1991/1992). The problem of speaking for others. Cultural Critique, 5–32.
Barnlund, D. C. (1982). The cross-cultural arena: An ethical void. In L. Samovar & R. E. Porter (Eds.), Intercultural communication: A reader (3rd ed., pp. 378–383). Belmont, CA: Wadsworth.
Bennett, M. J. (1979). Overcoming the Golden Rule: Sympathy and empathy. In D. Nimmo (Ed.), Communication yearbook 3 (pp. 407–422). New Brunswick, NJ: Transaction Books.
Broome, B. J. (1991). Building shared meaning: Implications of a relational approach to empathy for teaching intercultural communication. Communication Education, 40, 235–249.
Buber, M. (1958). I and thou (2nd ed., R. G. Smith, Trans.). New York: Scribners.
Cooper, T. W., Christians, C. G., Plude, F. F., & White, R. W. (Eds.). (1989). Communication ethics and global change. New York: Longman.
Friedman, M. S. (1960). Martin Buber: The life of dialogue. New York: Harper Torchbook.
Grice, H. P. (1978). Logic and conversation. In R. J. Fogelin (Ed.), Understanding arguments (pp. 329–343). New York: Harcourt Brace Jovanovich.
Gudykunst, W. B. (1980, November). Communication, ethics, and relativism: The implications of ethical relativity theory for intercultural communication. Paper presented at the annual meeting of the Speech Communication Association, New York City.
Hatch, E. (1983). Culture and morality: The relativity of values in anthropology. New York: Columbia University Press.
Howell, W. S. (1982). The empathic communicator. Belmont, CA: Wadsworth.
Johannesen, R. L. (1990). Ethics in human communication (3rd ed.). Prospect Heights, IL: Waveland Press.
Johnstone, C. L. (1981). Ethics, wisdom, and the

mission of contemporary rhetoric: The realization of human being. *Central States Speech Journal, 32,* 177–188.

Kale, D. W. (1994). Peace as an ethic for intercultural communication. In L. Samovar & R. E. Porter (Eds.), *Intercultural communication: A reader* (7th ed., pp. 435–441). Belmont, CA: Wadsworth.

Kant, I. (1949). *Fundamental principles of the metaphysics of morals* (T. Abbott, Trans.). Indianapolis, IN: Library of Liberal Arts/Bobbs-Merrill.

Kras, E. S. (1989). *Management in two cultures: Bridging the gap between U. S. and Mexican managers.* Yarmouth, ME: Intercultural Press.

Martin, J. N. (1993). Intercultural communication competence: A review. In R. L. Wiseman & J. Koester (Eds.), *Intercultural communication competence* (pp. 16–29). Newbury Park, CA: Sage.

Metzger, J. G., & Springston, J. K. (1992). The skillful, the loving, and the right: An analysis of ethical theories and an application to the treaty rights debate in Wisconsin. *The Howard Journal of Communications, 4,* 75–91.

Miller, J. B. (1992). Domination and subordination. In P. S. Rothenburg (Ed.), *Race, class and gender in the United States* (pp. 20–26). New York: St. Martin's Press.

Rosaldo, R. (1989). *Culture and truth: The remaking of social analysis.* Boston: Beacon Press.

Tanno, D. V., & Jandt, F. E. (1994). Redefining the "other" in multicultural research. *The Howard Journal of Communications, 5,* 36–45. (Reprinted in this volume)

Wellman, C. (1988). *Ethics and morals* (2nd ed.). Englewood Cliffs, NJ: Prentice-Hall.

Yamato, G. (1995). Something about the subject makes it hard to name. In M. L. Andersen & P. H. Collins (Eds.), *Race, class, and gender: An anthology* (2nd ed., pp. 71–75). Belmont, CA: Wadsworth.

KEY TERMS

ethics	dialogic
cultural values	humanness
ethical issues	

DISCUSSION QUESTIONS

1. What ethical dilemmas have you encountered in intercultural relationships?
2. How might one go about researching a universal metaethic for intercultural communicators?
3. In what ways does cultural background constrain development of empathy?
4. How might power differentials constrain the development of empathy in intercultural relationships?
5. In applying Bennett's platinum rule, how can you discover how others want to be treated in intercultural relationships?

47
JOINT PERFORMANCE ACROSS CULTURES: IMPROVISATION IN A PERSIAN GARDEN

MARY CATHERINE BATESON

Often when I speak I start with a story or example that I can turn at different angles, a story that fits with my subject in multiple ways. Today I want to begin by describing an episode that happened in a Persian garden. Before you let your imagination go too far in thinking of what that garden might be like, let me warn you that it is winter. But still we are dealing with a classic walled garden, full of fruit trees and rosebushes, with a watercourse down the center. I have just arrived in Tehran with my husband and our two-and-a-half-year-old daughter Vanni for the beginning of a period of research, teaching, and institution building. It is twenty years ago, pre-revolutionary Iran.

The day before, we had gone to drink tea at the home of the landlord and landlady of the apartment we had just moved into. When they heard that I was an anthropologist and that I would be learning about Iranian culture, they invited us to come with them the following day to the garden where we are now gathered, on family land in a village near Tehran, to celebrate Eyd-e Qorban, the Feast of Sacrifice.

At the same time of year that pilgrims are going to Mecca and going through the ritual steps of the Meccan pilgrimage, Muslims around the world are also celebrating some of the steps of that multi-day ritual, one of which is the sacrifice of a sheep or a camel. They tell me that in Saudi Arabia there are so many sheep and camels slaughtered by pilgrims, as part of their observance, that they are simply plowed under the ground by bulldozers. Originally they were given to the poor, but this has become unmanageable given the numbers involved. In any case, many families in Iran do sacrifice a sheep on the Feast of Sacrifice, and when our landlady invited us, although my husband couldn't come, well of course I said yes. That's my business. Then I stopped and thought briefly and I said, "I'm afraid I'll have to bring my daughter Vanni with me." And they said fine.

Then, in the car, on the way to the village, it suddenly occurred to me to wonder what I had gotten myself into. I am taking my two-and-a-half-year-old daughter to see a sheep killed. What am I going to say? How bloody will this be? How am I going to handle this so that it is not disturbing to her? What I thought about in the car was motherhood, not anthropology. It seemed to me that the key was going to be to keep her close to me and to give her a running commentary. This is the advice that is given about some of the horrors that children see on television: they are not so horrifying if they are watched in the company of an adult who provides a model for how to respond. So given that set of ideas it seemed to me I knew how to deal with the slaughtering of the sheep.

So there we were: myself and Vanni, our host

and hostess, their gardener, who would do the slaughtering, and his wife who was wearing a coarse village *chador* (veil), and their three children—all gathered outdoors in the cold for this ritual. My landlady had the most elegant high-heeled French boots on, and a fur coat. You have a sense of the contrasts of all this.

Such a garden, you know, is a cosmological statement. Most of you have not seen a Persian garden, but you have seen models of them if you have seen a Persian carpet, for there is a metaphorical relationship between them. A garden is bounded, walled. Inside, it is fertile and hospitable, and there is always an awareness of an outside world that is not so fertile and hospitable. Water is part of every garden. The Shah used to have a palace in the northern part of Tehran, at the high edge of the city, where there was a garden with a fountain, and the water from that fountain symbolically went down through the city to his subjects. A garden is also a model of the paradise to which the faithful will go after death.

To be in that garden was to stand in the middle of a complex statement about the world. There was also a statement there about the social structure of Iran at that time. The sophisticated, affluent Westernized urbanites, the villagers, the performing of a ritual that rooted them in the past—all of these things going on implicitly and explicitly in that setting.

The gardener gave the sheep a drink of water, turned it to face toward Mecca, prayed in the name of God the merciful and the compassionate, and slit its throat in the ritually correct manner. He then proceeded to clean and dismember the sheep. The way he removed the fleece from the sheep was by making a little cut next to one of the hind hooves, and blowing through it to separate the skin from the body. Then he put the fleece down and started laying the different organs out side by side. I was holding Vanni, figuring that body contact was going to be important here, and giving her a running commentary: "You see, that's the sheep's *heart*. You have a heart, and the heart is pumping blood around the body. Put your head here and you can hear my heart beating. See, that's a liver. And those are intestines."

And then I had one of those moments when you notice what you are doing: I was taking advantage of the visual aids to give a little mini-lecture about each organ in a vocabulary appropriate to a very verbal two-and-a-half-year-old. But just at the point when I was saying, "That's a lung . . ." I realized: it's HUGE. Then it occurred to me that although I could identify it as a lung, I had never actually seen the lung of a substantial-sized mammal. The knowledge that was allowing me to recognize a lung was entirely theoretical—as for many of the other organs I was giving a commentary on. What I was passing on to her was not knowledge based on previous experience of the dissection of large mammals, but an entirely abstract set of labels, the theoretical character of which was not accessible to me, until I was shocked by a feature that I had failed to anticipate.

And you know, just as I could say, "That's a heart, that's a lung," we go through life, and we say: "I must be in love," "Oh, this is an orgasm," "This is a midlife crisis," "This is sea sickness." We are provided with the labels, the culturally-constructed labels, long before we encounter the realities—up to the point even of saying: "This is a heart attack," "I must be dying."

Now, I became aware of this because of the dissonance of my different roles in that situation. To be an anthropologist is a complicated role anyhow, because one is a participant—a performer—and an observer at the same time; and quite often the dissonance there will break through. It may pull you closer to the experience when you've distanced it and thought of yourself as an observer. Or it may push you away again when you have identified with what was happening. So I was there as a learner, as an observer, as an outsider. And yet because I was there as a mother, I was simultaneously a teacher, an authority on what was happening, trying to establish an interpretation that would be intelligible and *educational* for my daughter. And out of that dissonance, I believe, came the possibility for an extra layer of awareness.

This is one of the things that I have been writing about in relation to women—that the effect of being under multiple simultaneous role demands is to stretch awareness and to force you out of particular stereotyped interpretations of what is going on in a particular situation. This is not something that is unique to women, of course, but it has been experienced by most women through

history for two reasons: because they are subject to multiple demands of spouse and children at different developmental stages who require different kinds of attention and response in the same setting, and because women's work includes all those things that can be done simultaneously with something else, namely caring for a child. Women must be one thing to one person and another to another person simultaneously, and must see themselves through multiple eyes and in terms of different roles. This is something that women have experienced that leads to a kind of multiple vision which, if you limit roles to separate contexts, you may not have.

One of the things that has struck me as I look back on that day in the Persian garden is that it has come to represent for me what is wrong with much of our thinking about education. We tend to think of classrooms as places in which there are teachers who know and students who don't know, instead of seeing education and learning as a two-way process all the way through, in which all the participants often have to play multiple roles as both teachers and learners.

Furthermore, what I was forced to do in that setting was to improvise, and, incidentally, to improvise responsibly. I did not know the rules. I had just arrived in Iran. I had no way of knowing what was going to happen. I had indeed no real sense of the depth of my own ignorance of the situation. But even so I was trying to put together a way of performing in accordance with what I believed to be the nature of my relationship with my child and my relationship with my profession. And this was improvised: there was no previously-given set of rules for that improvisation. What I was doing was stringing together elements of previous knowledge in accordance with patterns that I did have in advance.

This, you know, is how improvisational art works. I do think one of the most important things that Noam Chomsky ever pointed out is that most of the sentences that most of us speak day in and day out have never been spoken before. We have the components and we have the rules for combining them, but we generate novel performances.

Vanni of course was generating a novel performance too. Let me not get so preoccupied with my own navel that I forget that she was also facing something she had never seen before, having an experience she'd never had before, and trying to figure out who to be and how to react. And those of you that have had much to do with children will know that she got some of her cues from me, but she also kept a watchful eye on the children of the Iranian gardener. She picked up from them their sense of occasion combined with their sense that this was an ordinary, unfrightening, matter that was taking place in front of them.

So there we were, eight or nine people, differing in at least three dimensions: adults and children, Iranians and Americans, affluent urbanites and villagers, with differences of language and religion falling along the same cleavages. We were sustaining a joint performance in spite of the fact that, as performers, we did not share a common code. What was happening had different meanings to us according to where we fell in these different categories. The contrasts were as great between the sophisticated urban people and the villagers, who were all nominally Muslims and Iranians, as between the American outsiders and our hosts. We were going through the performance of a ritual, with a beginning and an end, and a certain festive but serious quality to it. We were sharing in sustaining that joint performance without working from the same codes or the same systems of meaning.

I had, at that point, come from a period of research on mother-infant communication. When my daughter was born, I had decided that since I was going to be distracted for some time to come, I would arrange my professional work in such a way that the distraction would be beneficial. I had been working at the Research Lab of Electronics at MIT where another researcher, Margaret Bullowa, had collected a corpus of films of mother-infant interaction, and I was studying those films and tapes and then dashing home to nurse Vanni when the babies on the film reminded me that it was time. I had set my work up that way, working on infants between one and two months old, because I was convinced that I would see and be able to document interactions in the film that I was seeing and responding to in my own relationship with my daughter. And indeed I found myself describing a pattern of playful vocalizations between mother and infant that I spoke of in terms of the epigenesis of conversation.

What interested me about these proto-conversations was that whereas the mother was speaking sentences to the infant, using the words and grammatical patterns of adult language, the infant was responding with little coos and gurgles, so that the internal structure of the infant's behavior was quite different from the internal structure of the mother's behavior, but together they were collaborating in sustaining a joint performance that looked like a conversation. And that joint performance preceded the differentiation of linguistic structure—learning words or grammar or rules of sentences. Just as, in this later scene in the Persian garden, Vanni was able to be a participant in a scene with a very complex history and set of cultural references which she knew nothing about and did not need to know in order to be a participant.

This relates to another line of thought about the classroom. Classes, like the giving of speeches and the presentation of papers at conferences, involve joint productions shared in by people with only partially overlapping systems of meaning, constructing in the process the categories with which they subsequently work. Vanni was also, I suppose, learning something about my stance in a situation of that sort. She doesn't remember this occasion now, but she would have remembered it over the next few months, and other experiences would have been matched with it and sorted out in her learning process. She was going through experiences of immersion in a new culture and having to learn not only the things that adults can tell you about being a guest, but also the things they don't know about how children are expected to behave in that setting. And even as a two-year-old she was playing multiple roles.

I was struck, several years later, when my daughter was about twelve, with a comment of hers: "Gee, Mom, it must be awfully hard on you and Daddy that I'm not interested in any of the things you're interested in." Now what do I say? Because she was coming up on adolescence, maybe she needed that sense of distance and contrast: on the other hand, maybe she didn't. So I asked, "How do you mean?" She said, "You're social scientists, and I'm an actress." Which she is, in fact; this is an interest that has continued. She said, "I'm not interested in writing books or giving lectures or being in a university or any of that stuff; I'm interested in acting." And I said, "Well, it does seem to me that to be a good actress you have to be good at observing people and trying to understand their motivations and the meanings they're working with—trying to empathize with them. It seems to me that you use a lot of the same skills that your daddy and I use, in a different setting." I was praying that this was the right response, and I think it was, because she's been repeating a version of it to people ever since. It gave her a reframing, a way of connecting the meaning of what she cared about doing with a relationship that she cared about. That reframing was based on a true connection between observation and performance. Vanni subsequently joined an improvisational theater group and got me thinking about improvisation as central to the way we really behave. What I didn't know enough to mention that day was that we, the social scientists, are also performers—actors—not only in classrooms and lecture halls, but in our conduct as we find our way into the settings and relationships from which we learn most.

As I look at the anthropological literature, I find discussions of enculturation that seem to imply that the knowledge of a culture is packed into children in childhood, and then they know it. You find a little more in sociology, in terms of discussions of adult socialization as you enter a new institution or a new role, and in recent years there's been discussion of how one learns to be a widow, how one learns to be a retired person, of learning new roles as these come up in different stages of the life cycle. But even so, the assumption is that you first learn a role and then you perform it. Now I'm arguing that this often happens the other way around. You have to begin performing a role before you learn it, and the learning never ends.

There are moments when one experiences this very sharply, like the moment of arriving home from the hospital with a new baby. You're in the role, and you're learning it as you go along, and improvising. As time goes on you get a little more skilled. As for the father, depending on the era he belongs to, he knows he's supposed to pace in the waiting room or to count breaths in the delivery room, but he too has to make it up as he goes along. You have to improvise, you have to invent, all the way. The available scripts are fragmentary at best. The invention of how to be the person you are at a moment in time takes place in a social and communicative context where you are also instructing the other person, like most teachers, in something you don't know too much about yet yourself.

Recently, I've been experimenting with a phrase that may help address some of the issues that we live with at the moment: the notion of a canon of human experience, as contrasted with a canon of great books. On the one hand, there are the experiences represented in this story by the sheep's liver and pancreas and heart—the realities of biological life: learning one's own body, one's maturation, sexuality, illness, the biological possibilities of being human. But you can't even begin to think about these commonalities without encountering cultural differences, because the world—and even the body—is experienced differently through the interpretive systems of different cultures. When you encounter (let us say) the body in the context of cultural difference, in the context of the contrasting patterns that we've seen in that garden, you attend in a new kind of way. This is true even of death. If you go to the funeral of an immigrant, there will be present at the funeral relatives from the old country who mourn in a different way. When you mourn in your Anglo-Saxon-influenced American way while someone else is there wailing, the juxtaposition of the two reactions to the same biological phenomenon offers a deepening of your sense of that experience. This is the "canon" we need exposure to.

We have gotten ourselves into a terrible pickle today, where the term "multiculturalism" has apparently come to mean we ought to have (in the classroom) a dose of role models and historical figures for every ethnic group, and then each cluster of people can refuse to learn about other people's traditions. That's not what multiculturalism is about at all. I would hope "multiculturalism" would mean everyone in that classroom being exposed to the traditions of the others. Multiculturalism refers to a situation in which the world is not fixed because of this or that customary arrangement, like the 1950s vision of domesticity. A husband and wife in the suburbs with two children, a station wagon, and a puppy is not a model of "family" given by the laws of nature, but one of several ways of doing things and by no means the healthiest or most adaptive; so we can all benefit from exposure to alternative models, not one but several. If you look at "family" cross-culturally, you are liable to conclude that children are better off with more than one caretaker, but a household with only two adults is also pretty skimpy, and children may be best off with five or six caring adults, in all sorts of possible arrangements. This is what multiculturalism should mean: access to a very wide range of experiences.

Anthropologists get away with murder, you know. One day we claim, rightly, the status of a science, and the next day we apply to the National Endowment for the Humanities for a grant. There's a great deal to be said for this, because the divisions are artificial. One reason I like to talk about the canon of human experience is that when you expose yourself to the culture of another human community, you are exposing yourself to a masterpiece, to a work of art, to the invention of a form of humanness that has been made over a long period of time. This then allows the thinking of ways to connect, to share, in spite of disparate codes. We hear all this concern at the moment about what we are going to do if we don't have all the same central ideas, if we haven't read all the same books, if we don't have a core on which we agree. Well, you know, we may do what mothers and infants do. We may do what often enough strangers do. We may work together to sustain joint performances, joint institutions, joint conversations in the larger sense, including the entire process of political discourse, in spite of not sharing a single, uniform code. And do everything we can to make those shared performances contexts for learning.

Somebody once described to me what used to be called "the U.N. gesture": you are walking down the hall and you sort of move your right hand part way forward because you are trying to figure out whether the person walking toward you comes from a culture where people shake hands; you're ready to shake hands if shaking hands is the appropriate thing to do. That search for cues, that

willingness to improvise, is not a bad starting point in human relations.

After I got married, my husband and I went on our honeymoon to Beirut to visit his family. There are a lot of good stories about that but I'm only going to tell you one, which happened at the airport on our last day. It is quite interesting learning to be a Middle Eastern daughter-in-law. My husband's family is Armenian, and there they were at the airport saying goodbye to us. And I thought, oh dear, I forgot to ask Barkev whom I'm supposed to kiss. Well, there was his mother: easy, I was sure I should kiss her. And there was his brother. I wasn't absolutely sure, but I figured, let's do it. There was the other brother, I kissed him. There was his sister: easy. There was his sister's husband, and next to him was the sister's husband's brother. Well . . . the question was, *how many people to kiss?* There was not much to go on in this process because they were also having to work out how to deal with a foreign daughter-in-law. You have to meet a situation like that with the sense that the traditional frameworks within which individuals repeat traditional patterns are themselves works of high art, but that the improvisations are also works of art. So I kissed the sister's husband, and I could feel in the set of his shoulder muscles that I had done the wrong thing, and at least I knew better than to kiss his brother. I was only a little off in this particular improvisation, and there was good will to spare.

This is really the kind of issue we all face, not always with sufficient good will. We are only going to be able to feel comfortable in this world of multiculturalism, in this world where we struggle to sustain joint performances with disparate codes, if we combine with the improvisation that has to go on a sense of the aesthetic values involved in this process: the sense that the traditional frameworks within which individuals carry on their improvisations are themselves works of high art and of improvisation as an art form.

Improvisation is central to living in periods of change, when it is very hard to prepare for a specific future and you have to find ways of combining skills that are not given in existing models. The roles of women are changing, at the moment, faster than the roles of men, which means that there are some contexts in which, willy nilly, women are the pioneers. It is women who are figuring out how to adapt to a very different shape of life cycle, in ways that I believe will be true of men as well. But of course it is women and men together who have to learn to sustain joint performances, both learning and teaching at the same time. I see an analog between my situation as a bride, newly arriving in another country, and that of a child newly arrived in a particular society, or the situation of refugees, as there are today many refugees from Iran, trying to reconstruct their lives. These issues arise for people dealing with other discontinuities too: lost jobs, changing technologies, political upheaval; the need to re-invent constantly, and therefore to improvise. But you see, we have a library we can draw on, the canon of human experience that teaches as much by its diversity as by its specific details.

Sometimes it is helpful to have a fresh metaphor that changes the way you are focusing your attention in a given situation. A lot of women have talked about "juggling" their multiple roles. Just thinking of that metaphor makes me uncomfortable, because it does have a truth but it primarily conveys the sense of anxiety about whether one will in fact be able to sustain the performance: whether one of these many balls in the air is going to fall down. Real jugglers are highly skilled, and they perform with great grace, yet the metaphor evokes anxiety. By contrast, the metaphor of an improvisational art form, putting together different elements, dealing with the unknown in a way which sustains performance and connects it with other systems of meaning, can make us celebrate the uncertainties with which we are beginning to live.

For some reason, which is not fully clear to me, I have been recycling this episode in the Persian garden which has recently come to seem pregnant with the meaning that can be drawn out of it. I should tell you how the story ends, to the extent that such a story ever does end. The theoretically correct behavior is to give the meat of the sacrificed sheep to the poor. In fact, the fleece and the internal organs were given to the gardener as a reward for his work, and the landlord and landlady packed up the meat to take back to Tehran to share with family members. We got in the car and drove to the city, with Vanni falling off to sleep on my lap. I went on with trying to learn Persian and Iranian customs. By now, as you know, it is quite

likely that the landlord and landlady are outside of the country. Perhaps one or two of that gardener's sons died in the war with Iraq. A lot of time has passed, a lot of changes. But the revolution that eventually occurred was present in that garden. It was present in the class differences, and in the ambivalent relationship to tradition of the wealthy urban landowners, the cultural disparities between them and the villagers they were employing. Even the presence of a foreigner, I think you would have to say that Iran was a society in which the codes did become unmanageably disparate, so I cannot use that episode only to say that it is possible to sustain a joint performance across vast differences. But I can use it to make people aware that when we talk about multiculturalism we are talking about the opportunity to learn, and that multiculturalism is only viable if we combine it with the expectation of life-long learning. When we talk about going beyond the traditional canon, we are talking about opening up a library not of great books, but of versions of humanness—some of them never written down in any form at all. A lifetime is long enough for multiple versions without, in the end, scanting one's own tradition.

My emphasis on improvisation and on learning going on all the time is a way of escaping from the notion that you are supposed to get something under your belt, some fixed body of knowledge: control it, have it, be educated and then live a life. If we can get away from that we may be able to reshape the current, very badly shaped, debate about education in such a way that we have some sense of the resources available for learning and of how life can keep on unfolding as an artistic performance, as a graceful and creative improvisation, for people of every age.

KEY TERMS

performance	Persia
ritual	Iran
culture learning	experience

DISCUSSION QUESTIONS

1. According to Bateson, how is intercultural communication a "joint performance"?
2. Bateson writes from an interpretive perspective.

How might a social science scholar investigate this topic of intercultural learning?

3. How do you think the different power positions of the people present in this Persian garden (e.g., male-female, U.S.-Iranian) might influence their communication with each other?

4. Do you think the international relations between the United States and Iran would have influenced the intercultural relationships of the people in this essay? Do you think this kind of interaction would be different today?

5. To what extent does Bateson think experience is important in intercultural learning and scholarship?

48

COMPARING VIEWS OF SCIENCE: IMPLICATIONS FOR INTERCULTURAL RESEARCH[1]

MIKE ALLEN

Research scientists are supposed to produce knowledge. But to what degree is a researcher responsible for how that knowledge is ultimately used? The process of generating and using scientific knowledge often becomes linked to ideological considerations. The question that this essay considers is how ethics, values, politics, and ideology are linked to the research process, particularly in intercultural communication research. Rather than proposing a final answer, the essay explores competing views of this process and the issues raised.

Ethical Issues in Research

Consider the social scientist asked to study the values of a foreign culture by a tobacco marketing company. Shouldn't the scientist expect that the knowledge produced will be used to increase tobacco (probably cigarette) sales in that country? If cigarette smoking constitutes a health risk, isn't the researcher participating in a process of commercial exploitation leading to death?

What about a researcher asked to help the World Health Organization (WHO) conduct an investigation of barriers to the use of condoms in a country experiencing the spread of HIV? The goal of the research is to assist the WHO in increasing the use of condoms. Although many would consider this research beneficial to the country, if the society has values that condemn the use of condoms, then isn't the researcher assisting in the undermining of those values?

The problems faced by intercultural communication researchers require examination and consideration. There exists no "magic" answer or solution to the ethical, moral, and ideological dilemmas raised. Rather, the researcher must decide to establish some principles as a basis for action that provide guidance in resolving such ethical issues.

This essay compares two views of research offered by critical theorists and traditionalists. The critical view argues for an ideology justifying and requiring action on the part of the scientist to address social issues—that is, critical researchers take an active interest in defining and solving social problems. In contrast, the traditional view of science does not require the need for social action in order to generate or evaluate the production

[1] An earlier version of this essay dealing with general issues in communication scholarship appears in Allen (1993).

of knowledge; rather, the traditional view places the scientist in the role of an observer reporting on the truth. For the traditionalist, action or advocacy is unrelated to the process of knowledge creation.

This paper argues that these differences in ideologies remain unresolvable and that both traditional and critical approaches present potential dangers. However, it is important to understand how each view provides a set of expectations about the process of research. Awareness of the implications of the decisions made by the scientist permits an evaluation and conscious choice between the alternative views.

These differences assume practical importance where the abstract world of the scientist and the everyday world of action overlap. For example, communication scholars are asked to apply their expertise to real-life problems. Several scholars (including myself) work on the issues surrounding making AIDS prevention education more effective. The problem is that the people capitalizing on that information may be divergent in perspectives (e.g., some groups oppose information about "safe" sex on moral grounds). The nature of the responsibility a scientist has toward the connection between knowledge and action becomes a serious source of concern.

In many respects, the divergence between the critical and traditional ideologies about science stem from the differences over the definitions about what eventually constitutes valid scientific practice. The distinction hinges on the view of the relationship of the scientist with the rest of society. The next section of this essay considers how ethics plays a part in science.

Let's examine ways in which ethical issues are played out in scientific research. The failure to employ potentially fruitful methods entails an ethical choice, in that advances may not occur as rapidly if methods remain restricted. For example, cures for diseases or new or more efficient means of producing goods may not occur. Similarly, some questions and issues become more deserving of research because of the centrality of the phenomena to a theory or to the issues of a society. The society must find a way of allocating the resources of science by determining what directions scientific investigation should pursue. Every

one of these decisions involves a question about the ethics of scientific practice.

The traditional approach to social science justifies the search for knowledge for the sake of knowledge. Finding knowledge because of the desire to know justifies the effort. The approach mandates no particular purpose that the knowledge must fulfill. The scientist pursues research projects for various reasons, perhaps because he or she finds a research question personally interesting or is paid by a corporation or government for pursuing particular research questions.

In contrast, critical theory justifies knowledge on the basis of how such research improves or emancipates human beings—that is, the practice of science cannot be separated from the practices of society. In fact, science, in serving society, must deal with the same issues confronting the progress of society. Science and scientists must practice a method and produce an end that satisfies the needs of the members of society.

The traditional ethical standards used to judge social science experimentation assess the methodological procedures, not the substance or goal of science. Ethics represent a set of procedures and guidelines to which the process adheres. One generally does not evaluate the ethics of the goal of the researcher. For example, a scientist producing knowledge for monetary rewards is judged as ethical on the basis of the procedure, not on the basis of the goal or the motivation. In this view, a researcher helping a tobacco company market cigarettes overseas would therefore not be considered inherently unethical.

A critical view begins with the premise that science serves the social system. Lynd (1939) notes, "There would be no social sciences if there were not perplexities living in culture that call for solution" (p. 181). This quotation focuses on two aspects: (1) problems deserving a search for solutions, and (2) knowledge providing insight for successful solutions. Scientists engaged in seeking information to increase the sales of cigarettes would probably not be viewed as ethical. They are using the process of science to harm individuals.

This comparison of ethical assumptions should not be considered as the sole basis for accepting or rejecting either system. This distinction *recognizes* rather than evaluates the practices of the scientist. Each system of scientific ideology indicates some features of desirable and undesirable practices. Justifying the choice a scientist makes provides a basis for comparing these competing systems. The next section considers how different views of what constitutes ethical scientific practice contribute to the evaluation of the two views.

What Should Science Accomplish?

The first issue that divides the two views is the definition of what a person should expect science to produce. The choice of how one perceives the scientific process becomes the basis for the view that one selects for science. Each view describes a relationship between the knower (scientist) and the known (knowledge).

Knowledge can be "discovered" or "created" by the investigator. The traditional definition of science defines science as a search for truths. Such truths will be "ahistorical," "pancultural," and "objective" (Cappella, 1991). This view of science does not require that knowledge serve an identifiable function. For example, some types of communication research examine how persons cognitively process information. Although such investigations may eventually have uses and applications, it is often not immediately clear what social improvement or change such information is intended to create.

In support of a more critical view toward the creation of knowledge, McGee (1985) comments on how he wearies of description and wishes to see some creation. This argument implies that the production of knowledge is within the control of the scientist. The researcher *chooses* to seek and generate knowledge claims. The creator bears the moral and ethical responsibility for the effect of this knowledge.

A *discoverer* simply finds, observes, and reports. The discoverer possesses no moral responsibility in the passive role. The traditional approach views researchers as passive observers who simply seek to find the truth. Science becomes a game played by process rules that the scientist must follow with regard to the method of discovery. Anyone can make a discovery; the fact that a particular scientist is credited with the discovery is important, but any other scientist would make the same finding. The discoverer does not create knowledge—Columbus did not cause North America to come into existence; he merely bumped into it, as would anyone else making that sail. Although one might credit Columbus with the journey, one should not credit him with the existence of the continent.

The argument between the two views contrasts the role of the scientist within the process by demonstrating the alternative responsibilities of the passive observer versus the active creator. Consider the scientist asked to conduct research for the tobacco company relating to cigarette attitudes. The creator of knowledge provides the existence of information to a corporation and must bear some level of responsibility for the impact of that information. If the scientist believes that the information on the culture will hurt members of that society, the scientist must accept responsibility for that outcome. The discoverer simply reports accurately the information and is not inherently responsible for the actions resulting from that information.

The critical view places the scientist within a set of historical, social, political, and moral forces and sees such outcomes as fitting within this framework. The traditional approach to science does not necessarily make this claim or place any such burden on the scientist to consider such issues. The issue raised is simply, to what degree must the scientist take responsibility for the research process?

The ideological difference between critical and traditional views shapes the divergence of positions among scientists. The next section considers the process of making claims, something both views advocate. Both views of science may even agree on the existence of particular facts. The difference between the two views, however, lies in the implications of these findings and the critique of the outcomes.

Making Empirical Claims

Establishing and verifying empirical claims about the world comprise the scientific enterprise. Both critical and traditional views share this definition.

But beyond that very basic assumption, vast differences exist between the approaches.

Describing Versus Prescribing

Consider how each view would respond to the generation of a finding from research. Consider a study comparing two cultural groups on the basis of empathy in interaction. One culture is found to exhibit higher levels of empathy in interaction than those of another culture. Consider the implication and impact that such a statement might have on the attitudes of people toward each other.

The finding excites and disturbs the members of the academic community. The research spawns a whole host of repetitions, each considering how various cultures exhibit degrees of empathy. The researchers use a variety of measures and cultures to examine this question. A decade passes and dozens of studies exist on this topic, examining a large variety of cultures.

The entire body of studies is demonstrated as mathematically consistent with the first study. The conclusion from the available data is that cultures differ in levels of empathy exhibited in interaction. Both the critical and traditional scientists would agree on those "facts" that exist.

The problem is that scientific findings affect not only scientists but the rest of society and potential decision makers (legislative, commercial, and personal)—all want to benefit from the information. What would finding that cultures vary in the levels of empathy imply for potential decisions? Would various political, social, or economic groups use such a finding to promote an agenda? Facts exist within a society as a social force for possible change. Knowing something provides a basis for action.

Consider if the information had no utility or application. Research costs a great deal of resources as measured in the time of the scientist and support facilities (computers, libraries, laboratories, etc.). Conducting dozens of studies to find divergent levels of empathy requires some justification. Why should scientists spend effort on this issue as compared to other potential issues?

Traditional scientists would accept the finding and work to establish controlled experiments and causal models for explanations and predictions.

If the findings imply some undesirable outcome, the goal of the explanation and prediction would probably involve a quest to find ways to improve the situation.

A critical view usually takes one of two directions (sometimes both) with regard to unpleasant research findings: (1) criticism of the community or (2) criticism of the social system producing these relationships. Consider the former: Many feminists and Marxist theorists criticize empirical findings as sexist or capitalist. The critique focuses on the scientist as a source of the information. Some critical approaches view such information as an interpretation of the universe created by the investigator; then one can critique the subjective bias of the scientist.

Critical theory requires examination of the scientist. Communication scholar Sonja Foss (1996) talks about the need for feminist theory to oppose the patriarchal system by creating alternative views. She rejects the traditional approach to the study of persuasion because it legitimizes the oppressive structure of a male-based system. For example, persuasion studies focus on the use of "evidence," but the term refers typically to statistics and expert testimony rather than to the lived experiences of the communicator (a more feminine view of support for assertions). Although she notes disagreements among feminists, she points out that feminists all share the search for alternatives to the existing system. Notice that the element introduced requires a different type of "union card" that empowers one group (women) but tends to displace or compete with another group (men). Foss talks about the need to create a cultural space for women apart from men, to distance them from the patriarchy.

A central feature here is the consideration of the motivation of the scientist. For example, was the research financed by some outside agency or condoned by some institutional force? Intercultural research is often influenced by economic and social factors. For example, whether the United States permits Spanish (or ebonics) to be spoken within the schools, jobs, and governmental agencies impacts on the acceptability of language research. The prevailing view of the Nation of Islam determines whether the study of Black Muslims in the United States will receive sanction and approval. The ever changing fortunes of

Israelis and Arabs impact on the labels applied to groups (terrorists, imperialists, freedom fighters, religious zealots) as part of the ongoing process of investigation. The critical view interprets the impact of societal norms as the basis for research agendas.

The second version of critical theory would accept the findings but argue that the findings reflect some social situation that needs changing. For example, at one convention, I heard a paper's findings critiqued because it supported "the White male middle-class patriarchal system that oppresses and subordinates the goals and aspirations of women and minorities." The argument contained in this criticism does not indict the accuracy of the description or invalidate the finding. Instead, the statement argues that the results of the research, however valid, work to promote antisocial goals. The critique argued against the *value* of the findings and implies that the research should not continue.

From a critical theorist's perspective, research not providing the means to empower the participants or the persons under study constitutes a failure of the method. The researcher must consider the issues from the point of view of the person responding. Dealing with empathy, did the researcher consider how labeling a culture as nonempathic might be viewed? Did the investigator view the culture from within the culture to determine whether persons in that culture consider themselves lacking in empathy? Even if the findings are accurate, what does knowing this about the culture provide as a basis for the empowerment for change? Critical research views typically require some consideration of the implication of the knowing for the social system under study.

The Goals of Research

Critical views of science view the goal of science to be to improve the society, whereas the traditional view of science sees the process as one generating knowledge claims. These competing views establish sources of inspiration that translate into research agendas for the scholar.

Consider the example provided by Leeds-Hurwitz (1990 & this volume) of the Foreign Service Institute (FSI) associated with training United States Department of State diplomats. The goal of the training was to make diplomats more effective intercultural communicators. The FSI employed culture and communication specialists. The scholars conducted research and training involving the cultures considered important to the Department of State.

Obviously, the FSI administration wanted to make the diplomats more effective at promoting United States interests overseas. What role should the scientists play in contexts such as these? Each scientific ideology, traditional and critical, would view the endeavor differently.

Traditional scientists would be concerned with the accuracy of the knowledge and the representations provided. The goal would be to conduct research that accurately reflects the culture and transmits that understanding to the participants of the institute. On the other hand, critical theorists would examine United States foreign policy, particularly for that region or diplomatic destination. If the aims of foreign policy are imperialistic, then participation in the FSI would constitute an immoral act because the scientist would be helping to oppress part of humanity. The information to the FSI must not only be culturally accurate, but framed in a manner that promotes the empowerment of the people in the culture.

Evaluating Scientific Claims

Truth Versus Social Value

Scientists function not as mere spectators to social events, but should they serve as moral forces? The question deserves consideration when determining the function of the scientist within the framework of society. Do organizational communication scholars simply serve the task of making organizations more effective (as measured by productivity) or some higher value that requires increasing the power of the employee within the workplace?

The divergence comes not from the findings but from the function of those findings. The traditional view generates information but provides no inherent function for such knowledge. Critical approaches on the other hand seek solutions involving empowerment. Any social problem ultimately faces the need for contextualization of findings. How are both problems and solutions to be contextualized for the generation of understanding? The traditional view offers little guidance, whereas the critical view offers an abundance of potential positions. The next section explores that difference.

The Need for Contextualizing Research Findings

The traditional view of science provides no moral or ethical guidance for scientific knowledge. Knowing how to do something, such as changing genetic codes for humans or creating dinosaurs (like those in the movie *Jurassic Park*), does not inherently speak to whether or not one should. The understandable concern of the critical tradition is to consider the social context of a finding. The critical school not only considers the application of knowledge but considers what knowledge to create.

However, the process of contextualizing introduces values. Put another way, into *which* context should empirical findings be designated? Ideological decisions provide the goal and in essence designate the context of the findings. The purpose of the research and the claims generated are contextualized by the ideological choices of the scholar. In addition, the society provides a framework for the interpretation of any scientific finding. If a scientist knows that the finding will be used by a tobacco company or the United States government, what implications should exist for the researcher? Not all United States foreign policy, for example, is desirable or reprehensible. And disagreement exists: Was the attack during Desert Storm a justified use of military force for peace or another example of the United States intervening in the local political system of a region? Were the United States troops in Somalia an invasion or a humanitarian use of force to save millions? The answer to the question determines whether one views the participation of a scholar as unethical or honorable.

Criticism by Hanna (1991) of the scientific ideal provides a set of problems for critical theory. How are ideological goals compared and con-

trasted when evaluating such goals? It is insufficient to say that knowledge should empower, because often knowledge empowers different people differently. The differential impact of findings on individuals remains an issue unaddressed by either critical or traditional ideologies of science.

Critical theory provides no answer to the ability of the scientist to generate knowledge that empowers or affects different individuals in different manners. This means that the agenda-setting function of the scholarly community increases in importance. Under critical theory, the empowerment stems from research, and the choice of agenda translates into a choice of who to empower.

Critical theory empowers according to the whim or preference of the scholar to work with particular topics. This means that the goal of equality is limited by the preference of the scholar in the same way that the agenda-setting of traditional scholars determines what topics continue to receive attention. The ascendancy of particular critical paradigms ultimately falls prey to the same kinds of criticism as traditional views of research. The critical research makes a choice among groups to empower; some groups will not be empowered as quickly. The inhumaneness of the traditional approach to science and the cold-hearted view of the process certainly creates a problem. However, this is matched by the possibility of caprice and error by uniting both the knowledge producers and the action takers within the critical view.

Conclusions

The struggle over a social scientist's responsibility as a member of the community represents a contest between two competing ideologies. Both systems seek a particular definition of what constitutes "truth" within an ideological framework. Both viewpoints seek knowledge but disagree on the role of scientist with regard to those findings. The struggle should not be viewed as a struggle between good and bad or right and wrong. The struggle is between two ideologies with divergent sets of values and currently no method of attaining consensus or resolution. Ultimately, every scientist must either consciously, willingly, and voluntarily or unconsciously, unwittingly, and involuntarily subscribe to ideological values. The degree to which those become explicit or implicit should generate some concern. However, the recognition and respect for the right to freely choose an ideology must be maintained.

A set of issues remains for traditional views of science. What to do with findings that are socially divisive and explosive? How to handle or promote a sense of social consciousness among the members to solve problems? How to promote sensitivity to social problems (racism, sexism) and maintain a sense of remoteness? Traditional views of science permit racism and sexism and make no allowances for the state of the human condition. Traditional scientists deplore such problems and view their findings as working to limit or eradicate these troubles, but they have no necessary and direct commitment to finding a solution.

For the critical theorist, the issues are problematic. How does one deal with unappreciated findings? How does the discussion of scientific issues proceed without degenerating into name calling and questioning motives? On what basis does the scientist make decisions between competing values when considering research?

A useful way to approach this dilemma is to establish that such matters are ideological and based on some tenet of faith. Ideological struggles are not resolvable with evidence, but require resolution on the basis of conscience. In the movie *Indiana Jones and the Last Crusade*, the hero, to save his father's life, must ultimately sacrifice scientific principles and rely on faith. The "leap from the lion's head" becomes a requirement to complete the journey. The taking of such leaps of faith is not irrational or unproductive to the process of scientific investigation. Leaps of faith serve a prerequisite for the conduct of ethical scientific investigation. Such leaps carry the potential for error and human caprice, an inherent part of all science. However, such leaps should ultimately come from the courage of human conviction that such a leap carries the process toward a desirable goal. The function of ideology in communication research becomes how such leaps serve to establish and reach goals.

REFERENCES

Allen, M. (1993). Critical and traditional science: Implications for communication research. *Western Journal of Communication, 57,* 200–209.

Cappella, J. (1991). The biological origins of automated patterns of human interaction. *Communication Theory, 1,* 4–35.

Foss, S. (1996). Re-sourcement as emancipation: A case study of ritualized sewing. *Women's Studies in Communication, 19,* 55–76.

Hanna, J. (1991). Critical theory and the politicization of science. *Communication Monographs, 58,* 202–212.

Leeds-Hurwitz, W. (1990). Notes in the history of intercultural communication: The Foreign Service Institute and the mandate for intercultural training. *Quarterly Journal of Speech, 76,* 262–281.

Lynd, R. (1939). *Knowledge for what? The place of social science in American culture.* Princeton, NJ: Princeton University Press.

McGee, M. (1985). The moral problem of *Argumentum per Argumentum.* In J. Cox, M. Sillars, & G. Walker (Eds.), *Argument and social practices: Proceedings of the Fourth SCA/AFA Conference on Argumentation* (pp. 1–15). Annandale, VA: SCA.

KEY TERMS

critical theory	ethics
epistemology	methodology
ideology	research practices
social responsibility	

DISCUSSION QUESTIONS

1. What responsibility does a scholar have when conducting research? Does knowledge carry a sense of moral imperative?

2. To know something, does that knowledge imply an action? Knowing that something is true, does that carry the implication of an action one ought to advocate or pursue?

3. Is knowledge created or discovered by the scientist? What relationship exists between knowledge and the knower?

4. Commercial or governmental research involving

culture and intercultural issues involves the acquisition of information for action. How does one distinguish between endeavors that are ethical and desirable and those that are not?

5. Consider the essay's examples of research conducted for a tobacco company or the World Health Organization. How does a scientist evaluate the appropriateness of the endeavor?

49

REDEFINING THE "OTHER" IN MULTICULTURAL RESEARCH

DOLORES V. TANNO / FRED E. JANDT

Science may date from human prehistory, but at least since the time of Aristotle we have believed that to explain an event we must give its causes. However, societies differ in the extent to which science is an accepted way of knowing, as Malinowski (1948) has pointed out. Science, as a methodology as well as a body of knowledge, has influenced Western thought since the 17th and 18th centuries. Its impact has been so strong that it is still often perceived as the only legitimate way to determine what constitutes knowledge.

The position that very little in social science exists without a parallel in physical sciences has given rise to fierce debate. One side argues that by the nature of social data, physical sciences cannot serve as a model, observing that social scientists have not succeeded in confirming any laws. The other side argues that it is not the physical science model per se but rather the underlying reasoning that is significant: that is, establishing facts as empirically verifiable observations about social relations.

This paper does not continue the debate over the adequacy of the physical science model for studying human society, a debate described by Maulana Karenga (1993) as one of "power and place" in which power is given exclusively to the researcher as definer and evaluator. Rather, this paper examines the *consequences* of research based on the physical science model in the *multi-cultural context*, in which concerns about the production and ownership of knowledge lead to questioning who is the "other" in the multicultural research process. Any research model based on the physical sciences will, by definition, lead the researcher to consider and talk about "others" as objects who are subject to observation and manipulation. In addition, this model assumes a monologic, monocultural perspective through which the "other" is studied, a perspective that underscores the researcher's position of power and authority.

Before we proceed further, we want to provide the rationale for our specific focus and to define our terms. We have chosen to focus on multicultural communication studies because they offer a unique research opportunity insofar as other cultures have generally been understood by superimposing on them the accepted epistemological, ontological, and methodological assumptions of another, more dominant culture.

We have used the word *multicultural* for two reasons. First, it serves an inclusive function, since it subsumes all the communicative acts previously defined as occurring in intercultural, cross-cultural, and international contexts. Second, because the common emphasis in these contexts is the study of communication as it is affected by cultural traditions, rituals, and so forth, we adhere to Prosser's (1978) definition of culture as "the traditions, customs, norms, beliefs, values, and thought-patterning which are passed down from generation to generation" (p. 5). We define the multicultural "other" broadly as including all participants in any multicultural study, as well as the cultural collectives to whom study conclusions are often generalized. We agree with McPhail's (1991) argument that the language of research should be "a *rhetoric of coherence,* one that defines and constructs reality in such a way as to resolve the problem of privileging one position at the expense of another" (p. 10). The idea of dialogue here implied is articulated by Broome (1991) in his study of empathy in the intercultural context; Broome argues that "instead of trying to understand the other as a separate objective entity, the focus is on co-creating with the other a shared reality" (p. 247).

Redefining the multicultural "other" is an attempt to humanize research through a multidisciplinary effort that seeks empowerment through dialogue with those previously labeled and perceived as subjects for observations. For example, in the field of communication studies, Altman and Nakayama (1991) address empowerment by arguing that it is essential to have "difficult dialogue" about the ways "differences . . . are constructed in social interactions and in public discourse" (p. 116). Nakayama and Altman (1992) also advocate dialogue as one critical strategy whereby we can "emphasize multivocality and inclusiveness" in multicultural studies (p. 10).

The researcher can be empowered in new ways. Anthropologist Dan Rose (1990) suggests the need for researcher empowerment by calling attention to graduate schools' strong conformist ideology that constructs our research persona, as well as the persona of the "other" whom we study. This socialization not only creates a gap between the "expert" and the "other" but also inculcates the fixed belief that our true audiences, the ones for whom our knowledge is produced, are fellow experts.

Buchler (1955) recounts that philosopher Charles Peirce argued there are four general ways of "fixing belief": tenacity, authority, a priori, and science. *Tenacity* refers to firmly held truths; *authority* refers to established beliefs; *a priori* refers to self-evident assumptions; and *science* refers to

the method by which beliefs are determined by "nothing human, by some external permanency, by something upon which our thinking has no effect," by which all can reach the same ultimate conclusion (p. 18). Clearly, the research persona has resulted from socialization according to the scientific way of inculcating ideas.

Over 30 years ago, Thomas Kuhn's book *The Structure of Scientific Revolutions* (1962) challenged the scientific community to examine its perceptions of an objective reality as resulting from socially accepted beliefs that he called "paradigms" (p. 10). Kuhn argued that science progressed by way of paradigm shifts or changes in scientists' beliefs. A new paradigm is created when the old paradigm fails to provide solutions for critical problems. In early times, for example, the Ptolemaic paradigm in astronomy was replaced by the Copernican paradigm when the increasingly complex understanding of the heavens did not lead to a concomitant increase in predictive accuracy. Kuhn's thoughtful analysis clearly showed that paradigms act as filters that screen our experiences and our perceptions. Kuhn asserted that advocates of differing paradigms cannot communicate with one another because the meanings of their respective concepts can be contradictory.

More recently, Bohm and Peat (1987) have contended that the break in communication between persons holding different paradigms calls for the establishment of a true dialogue, a dialogue that acknowledges any point of view "as it actually is whether one likes it or not" (p. 241) and that requires exploring the other's point of view. Bohm and Peat describe the major barrier to this dialogue as the rigidity in the tacit infrastructure of rules governing how interactions should occur. This rigidity is also in place in the research process, and it often prevents us from engaging in a dialogue. Bohm and Peat thus help explain why various marginalized groups are increasingly challenging the adequacy of the science-based research paradigm to provide truly accurate and complete understanding of their respective cultures.

Clearly, our attempts at understanding our diverse society have not been as successful as we hoped. Our studies have provided great amounts of information, but they do not seem to have resulted in the self-reflection, self-definition, and self-understanding that can lead to the empowerment of those we study. While the discovery of the boiling point of water at various elevations does not change the *nature* of water, multicultural studies have the potential of changing the *nature* of how groups perceive themselves: discovering contributing factors to school dropout rates among different marginalized groups, for example, has the potential of forever changing group identity whenever members internalize and act on that information. Klaus Krippendorf (1989) has argued that "we have to take *responsibility for the kind of image . . .* we portray in our theories of human communication and human participation in social affairs" (p. 79).

Even as our studies have failed to empower multicultural research participants, our approaches to research have largely reflected our unwillingness as researchers to work outside the constraints of a science-based model. One notable exception is Kenneth Bancroft Clark's body of work, which challenged the paradigm that led to the "tendency to replace notions of biological inferiority with notions of cultural inferiority" (Steinberg, 1989, p. 118). That Clark's challenge contributed to civil rights reform and thus to some degree of empowerment is evidenced by the extensive citation of his work in the 1954 *Brown v. Board of Education* decision. Other examples of questioning the science-based model include some feminist, ethnographic, performance-based, and critical studies.

It seems we are operating under a dominant paradigm that can no longer deal with the complexities of a multicultural society. Once we accept that proposition, the characteristics of a new paradigm should be sought. We want to argue that the "others" in multicultural research should be perceived as being co-owners and co-producers of knowledge, as having the ability to ask questions and assist in gathering and validating data, and as becoming the primary audience to whom our findings should be addressed. In attempting to redefine the "other," this essay represents a beginning point. We have organized it around three paradigmatic issues, the first epistemic and the latter two ontological, as well as method-

ological: "The 'Other' as Co-Producer/Owner of Knowledge," "The 'Other' as Participant," and "The 'Other' as Audience."

The "Other" as Co-Producer/ Owner of Knowledge

The first characteristic of the new paradigm concerns the epistemic issue of production and ownership of scholarly knowledge. We have long been accustomed to the idea that once publication occurs, we move on to more and we hope, better studies. We presume that the academic community owns the knowledge that results from such studies. But what if the "other" participated in all aspects of the research process and thus could claim co-ownership? We offer here three examples that suggest such participation can and should occur: the first describes shared production of knowledge, the second addresses the purpose of research, and the third raises the question of owning knowledge.

Shared production of knowledge that approaches research as dialogue or co-production of knowledge is found in Alberto González's (1989) study of WMEX-FM radio in Ohio. González wanted to understand the role played by this Mexican-American radio station in simultaneously helping to maintain cultural identity and reducing intercultural distance. Of particular significance in this study is the way González made the DJs active participants:

> Throughout the study, I attempted to make my observations accessible to and understood within the social world encompassed by the site. Periodically during the two-and-one-half years of research, I explained my observations and interpretations to the DJs and gave them opportunities to clarify their perceptions. . . . In the summer of 1985, the original DJs met a final time . . . to re-tell their experiences with WMEX and to respond to my interpretations. (p. 399)

González and Peterson (1993) reiterate the importance of real participation when they address feminism and intercultural communication: "Rather than *determining* whether the lot of women has improved or worsened, feminists studying intercultural communication should demonstrate their respect for those women they study by *asking them*" (p. 268).

Both González's radio study and González and Peterson's admonition demonstrate that understanding how discourse is used to promote ethnic pride, as well as participation in the larger society, occurs at two levels. Thus in the former case we see *intracultural* understanding occurring because the DJs were intimately involved in the study from beginning to end, as well as the *intercultural* understanding that adds to the collective knowledge of how a particular marginalized group perceives itself in the greater society. Together these two levels of understanding suggest a degree of empowerment.

The second example, taken from an anthropological study, points to the attitudinal stances of researchers that we will have to recognize, define, and reassess before we can move toward a research-as-dialogue process of understanding. In *Living the Ethnographic Life*, Rose (1990) makes a compelling argument "urging a more radical democratization of knowledge" that "deprivileges our academic inquiry while serving to help recover ideas and practices from other points of view—whether of marginal or oppressed people, whether close to home or geographically and culturally remote" (p. 11). Rose urges researchers toward self-study, toward questioning why we do research and what is the impact of the knowledge we find. If knowledge about cultures is to be richer and truer, the logic of inquiry demands that our methodologies must mirror cultural realities and needs. This understanding will occur when we acknowledge that "people have the right to define their own reality, establish their own identities, name their history" (hooks, 1989, p. 42).

Concerning the ownership of knowledge, we offer our third example: the Maori. Biculturalism was asserted in the 1840 Treaty of Waitangi between the British Crown and the Maori of New Zealand. But since the signing of the treaty, the relationship between the two cultures has been one of domination and marginalization of the Maori people (Walker, 1990). To cite one significant example, schools were established on the English

model, which valued the written over the oral in marked contrast to the Maori-preferred modes of knowledge transmission.

Social-science research *on* the Maori has concentrated on identifying the characteristics that contribute to "subcultural" and "dysfunctional" behaviors of group members in the dominant majority culture (Smith, 1991). Much research has belittled or otherwise adversely affected the Maori and their history even as it benefitted the researchers and the non-Maori academic community. Academic theory even has the Maori crossing the Pacific by the winds of chance, thus effectively denying their skills as navigators.

Today a growing number of Maori insist that Maori research should be done by Maori people only. From a more moderate position, Ohia (1989) argues that the place of Maori in the research is as initiators of the process; it is the Maori who best understand what is necessary to promote their own improvement and empowerment.

Maori opposition to traditional social science research raises questions about the initiator, the controller, the interpreter, and the owner of research. It is not difficult to project this scenario onto cultures represented in the Americas. Unless we change our attitudes and practices, we may have no "participants" at all.

The "Other" as Participant

The second characteristic of the new paradigm is a redefined role of the participant. Over the years, many small steps have been taken away from thinking of individuals as passive sources of data. One example is the informed consent requirement, which resulted from concern voiced about the possibility of harm to those being studied. Another example is rhetorical in nature and signals an understanding of the power of language. We have largely replaced *subjects* with *participants*, hoping to establish the idea of a more dialogic approach to research. Yet the language of the American Psychological Association's 1982 Code of Research Ethics still assumes an authoritative position of power on behalf of the researcher: "The investigator always retains the responsibility for ensuring ethical practice in research," or "The investigator protects the participant," or "After the data are collected, the investigator provides the participant with information." A clear separation of the "expert" and the "nonexpert" serves to dehumanize the "other." Moreover, the use of *subjects* still finds favor in recent publications. In *Planning Ethically Responsible Research,* Sieber (1992) argues for the use of the term as follows:

> Many have argued that the term *research participant* is more respectful than the term *subject.* For some purposes, I would agree. For the purposes of this book, however, I would prefer to use the term that continually reminds the reader that the person being studied typically has *less power* than the researcher and must be accorded the protections that render this *inequality morally acceptable* [italics added]. (p. 13)

We italicized language in this quotation to demonstrate the deeply rooted assumptions underlying the traditional research paradigm. Understanding the power of language, Karenga (1993) argues that to replace "slave trade" with "the holocaust of enslavement," for example, permits greater insight into African American culture, and to replace "colonization" with the "holocaust of colonization" allows for a perceptual stance that would allow researchers to see Latino and Native American cultures in a different light.

The examples taken from the Code of Ethics and those provided by Karenga illustrate Kuhn's contention that different paradigmatic stances lead to different perceptions. More important, these examples illustrate that ultimately the words that shape the paradigms possess transformative power. In a multicultural context, such transformation can lead either to generally empowering those involved or to maintaining a power schism between the expert and the so-called nonexpert.

To diminish the gap between researcher and participant, we must begin thinking of the "other" as someone who possesses the ability, means, and willingness to participate in creating and understanding knowledge. We must acknowledge that the "other" can contribute not only the data upon which we impose our methodologies but also the questions that guide our research, the interpretation of data, and the validation of conclusions. As

Karenga (1993) suggests, we need to generate research questions from within cultures. According to anthropologist Renato Rosaldo (1989), the postmodern view of participants is that they can and do "critically interrogate" (p. 2). Furthermore, as Anthony Giddens (1989) observes, participants are human agents, and "all human agents know a great deal about the conditions of their activity" (p. 57). Thus the idea of passive subjects or participants is an illusion that offers us a comfortable intellectual distance because of "our sense of possessing intellectual control . . . [and] a reliance on ourselves to interpret [studies] successfully by appropriately modifying our framework of anticipations," as Michael Polanyi (1962, p. 103) has stated. Instead, Polanyi gives us a new definition of the "other" as knower when he writes of "personal knowledge," or the "*personal participation* of the knower in all acts of understanding" when "comprehension is neither an arbitrary act nor a passive experience" (p. vii). Perceived in this way, the redefined "other" in multicultural research can be invited to become the co-originator of research questions and the co-validator of research results.

Clearly, if we begin talking about the research process using terms such as *true participation* and *dialogue* and the "other" as *expert* about his or her life conditions, these rhetorical changes may help us synchronize the multicultural research process with the multicultural social reality.

The "Other" as Audience

A third characteristic of the new paradigm is the incorporation of research participants and cultural communities into our concept of *audience.* This particular change can occur if we ask ourselves questions proposed by Bishop (1992): Who needs to have access to research findings? To whom is the researcher accountable?

Currently, we are accountable only to one another, and thus our research is directed at a specialized few—in the language used to formulate the questions we ask, in the methodologies we use to answer those questions, in the language of the conclusions themselves, and in the dissemination of those conclusions.

There is the sense that participants become constructed *before* the research begins. This perception can happen when the results of earlier studies on particular ethnic groups are unquestioningly accepted as accurate and truthful representations of their cultures (the Maori are a case in point). We ask research questions and accommodate the methodology on the basis of *a priori* construction. But we know that answers are often embedded in the questions we propose; therefore, we end up finding that which we seek. Such commitment to the received view at the expense of true understanding is "unconscionable," as Krippendorf (1989) argues:

> By making an objective and observer-independent reality the principal ruler over the constitution of scientific knowledge, *this dominant paradigm in effect absolves scientists from taking responsibility for their constructions.* (p. 78)

The question then becomes: what can we do to take responsibility? One answer is that we can begin making conscious efforts to turn the "other" into the audience of our research results.

If research questions and data collection are co-designed by the "other" and if results are owned by the "other" as well, researchers become consultants or participants in a dialogue. Viewing the "other" from within this new paradigm has the potential to change study results in important ways. For example, if we use a traditional approach to the problem of birth control in a society, we may assume that a public medium is the most appropriate channel for disseminating information and thus may conclude that radio or television programming would be the most effective means. However, by redefining the "other" and inviting true participation, we may discover that birth control is viewed as so personal an issue that more private channels of information dissemination not only are perceived as more appropriate but also are more effective. The multicultural "other" might, for example, recommend messages on calendars because not only are they inexpensive but also they are more private and are consulted daily in every home.

Another aspect of making the "other" an audience is to stop writing only for each other, beginning instead to communicate our knowledge back to participants. We know very few people outside any given discipline who regularly read academic journals. A first step would be to identify the primary information outlets of each culture we study and attempt consistently to use them in conveying information about studies. To publish in other than "legitimate" journals is professionally risky, but to take the risk is to take responsibility for our part in the social construction of cultural images.

We recognize the paradox of publishing these ideas in an academicians' journal. In fact, a reviewer astutely asked, "Aren't you, the authors, by publishing an essay in an academic journal, merely perpetuating the very practice that you are criticizing?" At this time, the only honest answer to this question is "Yes." But we perceive that two trends are developing in multicultural research. The first is that the "other" is increasingly becoming more actively critical about the process of sharing knowledge about his or her culture. The second is that a growing number of researchers and critics[1] are actively examining the role of traditional research in the multicultural context to find, as Broome (1991) argues, that it has "offered more confusion than inspiration and more discouragement than motivation" (p. 245). We can add only that the traditional research paradigm has largely failed to acknowledge the power of the other. We raise the possibility that what we describe here is a need to reduce uncertainty between the researcher or critic and the multicultural "other." We hope that as the need for a paradigm shift becomes more obvious and as more researchers conduct studies that adhere to these new definitions, we will increasingly find access to a wider variety of information outlets, while at the same time becoming more comfortable with our roles as participators in a research dialogue.

Conclusions

In effect, we argue for closing the gap between the expert and the presumed nonexpert. William Foote Whyte (1991) has proposed the label *participatory action research* (PAR) to describe studies that involve participants in the entire research process, from initial design, to data-gathering and analysis, and finally to conclusions and actions arising out of the research. Whyte's *Street Corner Society,* published in 1943, was a precursor in using this methodology. In 1991, Whyte continued to promote PAR as "the alternative view . . . that it is important, both for the advancement of science and for the improvement of human welfare, to devise strategies in which research and action are closely linked" (p. 8). Although PAR has been used primarily in industrial and agricultural studies, PAR-like methodologies are appropriate to multicultural research because of the approach's concern for improvement and empowerment through participation. PAR is clearly different from "applied research" as it is commonly understood: the researcher is the professional expert who controls the design, the collection of data, and the interpretation of findings, and who ultimately makes the recommendations. With methodologies like PAR, the gap between participant and researcher is considerably lessened as they work together throughout the research process.

The dialogue between researcher and participant is clearly one of the most important benefits gained when we redefine the "other." Through research dialogue, the empowerment of both participant and researcher is potentially increased. But other benefits may be gained, most notably the shared production and ownership of knowledge and the promise of a deeper understanding.

We will encounter obstacles, however, as we redefine the "other" in multicultural communication research. The most obvious is that the research enterprise we have described will be much more time consuming. The less-obvious—but perhaps the most difficult—obstacle is the uncertainty we will experience about the different roles we must play in the research process. Ultimately, the clearest evidence of our willingness and ability to change how we view the multicultural "other" will be the willingness and ability to change how we view our role as researchers and critics.

NOTE

1. In addition to those cited, other examples include B. Broome (1991), "Bridging the Gulf Between Two Realities: Personal Reflection and Essay,"

International Journal of Intercultural Relations, 15, 323–326; B. Broome (1993, November), "Collective Design of the Tribal Future," paper presented at the annual meeting of the Speech Communication Association, Miami Beach; A. Mirande & D. V. Tanno (1993), "Labels, Research Perspective, and Contextual Validation: A Commentary," *International Journal of Intercultural Relations, 17,* 149–155; A. Mirande and D. V. Tanno (1993), "Understanding Interethnic Communication and Research: 'A Rose by any Other Name Would Smell as Sweet,'" *International Journal of Intercultural Relations, 17,* 381–388. In addition, the 1992 SCA convention included a seminar, "New Agenda in Intercultural Communication," that addressed new ways of thinking about intercultural communication.

REFERENCES

Altman, K. E., & Nakayama, T. K. (1991). Making a critical difference: A difficult dialogue. *Journal of Communication, 41,* 116–128.

American Psychological Association. (1982). *Code of research ethics.* Copyright 1973, 1982.

Bishop, R. (1992, July). *Toward a paradigm for participant driven empowering research in a bicultural context.* Paper presented at the Summer Workshop for the Development of Intercultural Coursework at Colleges and Universities, East-West Center, Honolulu.

Bohm, D., & Peat, F. D. (1987). *Science, order, and creativity.* London: Routledge.

Broome, B. (1991). Building shared meaning: Implications of a relational approach to empathy for teaching intercultural communication. *Communication Education, 40,* 235–249.

Buchler, J. (Ed.). (1955). *Philosophical writings of Peirce.* New York: Dover.

Giddens, A. (1989). The orthodox consensus and the emerging synthesis. In B. Dervin, L. Grossberg, B. O'Keefe, & E. Wartella (Eds.), *Rethinking communication: Volume 1, paradigm issues* (pp. 53–65). Newbury Park, CA: Sage.

González, A. (1989). "Participation" at WMEX-FM: Interventional rhetoric of Ohio Mexican Americans. *Western Journal of Speech Communication, 53,* 398–410.

González, A., & Peterson, T. R. (1993). Enlarging conceptual boundaries: A critique of research in intercultural communication. In S. Bowen &

N. Wyatt (Eds.), *Transforming visions: Feminist critiques in communication studies* (pp. 249–278). Cresskill, NJ: Hampton Press.

hooks, b. (1989). *Talking back: Thinking feminist, thinking black.* Boston: South End Press.

Karenga, M. (1993, April). *Multiculturalism in the university: The multidimensional challenge.* Paper presented at the Second International East Meets West Conference in Cross-cultural Communication, Comparative Philosophy, and Comparative Religion, Long Beach, CA.

Krippendorf, K. (1989). On the ethics of constructing communication. In B. Dervin, L. Grossberg, B. O'Keefe, & E. Wartella (Eds.), *Rethinking communication: Volume 1, paradigm issues* (pp. 66–96). Newbury Park, CA: Sage.

Kuhn, T. S. (1962). *The structure of scientific revolutions.* Chicago: The University of Chicago Press.

Malinowski, B. (1948). *Magic, science and religion, and other essays.* Glencoe, IL: Free Press.

McPhail, M. L. (1991). Complicity: The theory of negative difference. *The Howard Journal of Communications, 3,* 1–13.

Nakayama, T. K., & Altman, K. E. (1992, October). *Rhetorics of culture.* Paper presented in New Approaches to Intercultural Communication (W. S. Lee & P. Wander, Chairs), seminar conducted at the meeting of the Speech Communication Association, Chicago.

Ohia, M. (1989, Summer). *Research for Maori education.* Paper presented at New Zealand Association for Research on Education Conference, Trentham.

Polanyi, M. (1962). *Personal knowledge: Towards a post-critical philosophy.* Chicago: The University of Chicago Press.

Prosser, M. H. (1978). *The cultural dialogue: An introduction to intercultural communication.* Boston: Houghton Mifflin.

Rhetorics of culture. Paper presented in New Approaches to Intercultural Communication (W. S. Lee & P. Wander, Chairs), seminar conducted at the meeting of the Speech Communication Association, Chicago.

Rosaldo, R. (1989). *Culture and truth: The remaking of social analysis.* Boston: Beacon Press.

Rose, D. (1990). *Living the ethnographic life.* Newbury Park, CA: Sage.

Sieber, J. E. (1992). *Planning ethically responsible research.* Newbury Park, CA: Sage.

Smith, T. L. (1991). Te Rapuna I Te Ao Marama: Maori perspectives on research in education. In R. Morss, Jr., & T. J. Linzey (Eds.), *The politics of human learning: Human development and educational research* (pp. 46–55). Dunnedin, New Zealand: University of Otago Press.

Steinberg, S. (1989). *The ethnic myth: Race, ethnicity, and class in America* (rev. ed.). Boston: Beacon Press.

Walker, R. (1990). *Ka Whawhai Tonu Matou: Struggle without end.* Auckland, New Zealand: Penguin.

Whyte, W. F. (1943). *Street corner society.* Chicago: The University of Chicago Press.

Whyte, W. F. (1991). Introduction. In W. F. Whyte (Ed.), *Participatory action research* (pp. 7–15). Newbury Park, CA: Sage.

KEY TERMS

"other"

multicultural research

ownership of knowledge

researcher role

researcher responsibility

DISCUSSION QUESTIONS

1. Tanno and Jandt suggest that dialogue should be a central feature of intercultural communication research. Can we use their notion of dialogue in our daily intercultural interactions?

2. If we follow Tanno and Jandt's suggestion that the "other" be redefined in multicultural research, how will this new direction in research change the way we think about and do intercultural communication?

3. What responsibilities do we have as researchers in intercultural communication to the field we are studying? To the people we are studying? If these responsibilities come into conflict, what guidelines should we use to negotiate that conflict?

4. What should be the primary goal of intercultural communication research? Does our conception of the participants in the research affect that goal?

5. If we follow Tanno and Jandt's redefinition of the "other," and see the "other" as co-producer and owner of knowledge, as participant, and as audience, how might our research change? What strengths and limitations would there be in doing the participatory action research that Tanno and Jandt advocate?

50

PAINTING THE WHITE FACE RED: INTERCULTURAL CONTACT PRESENTED THROUGH POETIC ETHNOGRAPHY

MARÍA CRISTINA GONZÁLEZ

It is claimed that the Native American spiritual leader Sitting Bull once stated that "if the Great Spirit had wanted me to be a white man, he would have made me one." Each of us is born into a particular set of circumstances, familial and cultural, racial and historical, that despite the changes in our lives, we can never really escape. Phenomenologists call this phenomenon "thrownness"—that great inexplicable sense of not having had any "say" over certain aspects of our experience. In the "great United States," we live with the myth that we can do, say, or be whatever or whomever we wish. In many ways, this myth allows us as individuals to challenge the thrownness of our social experience. It provides a belief system by which we can reject the undesirable or personally unacceptable in favor of a preferable reality.

Intercultural contact provides us all with opportunities to get to know how others view the world, how they experience day-to-day realities and differences in personal cultural identities. When this happens, we are able to examine our own worldview, experiences, and identities. Sometimes the boundaries we have established for our own identities are rigid and impermeable, not allowing for the changes that intercultural contact invites. Many of our efforts to improve intercultural relations focus on the negative attributions of "others" that occur and interfere with the potential for good relations when persons of different cultures meet. What is different is seen as bad, threatening, or offensive. As long as these views of the "other" remain, it is unlikely that good relations can develop between cultures.

Having a belief system that allows people to create their own identities creates the potential for a different sort of intercultural challenge. If for some reason an individual is unhappy with his or her social experience or personal identity, meeting people who live a different cultural reality can become a door of opportunity. New routines, values, forms of language, and norms for personal relationships can offer someone a "way out" of a lifestyle or cultural experience that is "not working" for one reason or another. When the social and cultural myths we live by support the idea of freedom to shape one's own identity, the potential for this possibility is increased.

The emphases on postmodern identities in contemporary social research, which allow for the simultaneous existence of many different identities, can also work to enable individuals to believe identity is something that can simply be chosen, as from a menu. The idea that all of our realities are socially constructed is often used as a philosophy for methodology and research. If we are not careful, such philosophies can lead to intercultural research that doesn't take into account the importance of the meaning of identities and realities that are constructed by particular cultural groups.

Often, contact with a different culture opens us to see possibilities for our own existence. By deconstructing our current identities and identifying the multiple forces that have influenced the "way we turned out," it is possible to imagine the ways we would have turned out if we'd had more freedom to be ourselves "naturally." The idea of returning to a more organic source of identity can be empowering.

These ideas create an interesting backdrop for the study that captured my attention for a 3-year period. In a nation where the freedom of personal choice is valued (if not practiced), and where cultural studies are leading us to see that no aspects of our social experience are by nature fixed, some people decide to choose to consciously reject aspects of their selves, to change who they are, to become "new persons," even if it means assuming a totally different ethnic identity. Some make new families, recreate histories, and even go so far as to alter their biological features of gender, race, and ethnicity.

For this study, I became interested in people who were deciding to "become Indian" (native American), even when they had no legitimate claims to the identity. Specifically, I was interested in those non-Indians who began practicing native American spirituality,[1] sharing with and learning from native Americans engaged in indigenous spiritual traditions.[2] In the United States it is common for people to acquire artifacts and features of many of the cultural groups who make up the U.S. society, to share in rituals and traditions as part of a multicultural experience. This is not the phenomenon that caught my attention. Rather, I was interested in people who gradually rejected their everyday ways of life in favor of an "Indian" lifestyle, transforming their living environments, adjusting their schedules, and altering their personal relationships in order to live in accordance with how they perceived the native American spiritual traditions they were learning and practicing.

In my personal experience of learning about my own family history of Lipan Apache and Tarahumara origin, I remembered that I was of-ten asked if I was tribally enrolled to prove my claims of Indianness. I learned that there was a trend of "ethnic fraud" and cultural appropriation sweeping "Indian country" in the United States, and that it often showed itself most vividly in the arena of spirituality. This theme recurred throughout my ethnographic study of non-Indians sharing and learning native American spirituality.

Somehow, although identities are socially constructed and in many ways arbitrary, the phenomenon of people deciding to acquire new identities rooted in cultures not indigenous to their own experience or history can create an experience of violation. In this study, the respect of boundaries for ownership of and access to their own cultural experiences was integral to the cultural identity of the native Americans who shared (either voluntarily or involuntarily) their spiritual traditions.

This concept of respect for indigenous cultural experience and identity seemed to be vital to the understanding of what it was to "be Indian." It was a concept held to be central to the personal identity and spiritual and emotional harmony of all peoples. As such, the non-Indian desire to become Indian was a mystery and perplexing. As each individual's life was by nature complex, it was baffling for anyone to want to add to that complexity. Why would someone want to add to the confusion of personal identity by attempting to take on an identity judged to be inauthentic, or as many asked, "why would someone want to be who they're not?"

As a scholar of human communication, the questions were equally as intriguing as they were perplexing. If I were to study this phenomenon of identity-shaping through the sharing of spirituality, what would I find? It was truly an intercultural process, one in which some seemed to be participating voluntarily, of which others claimed to be victims. As I read books and talked to people involved with native American spirituality, I found some to take a disciplined, studious approach, others to be undoggedly faithful to their teachers and traditions, and still others who seemed guided by an invisible and spurious intuition and sometimes by powerful personal preferences. Given this array of participants, how could an understanding of the boundaries of identity ever be reached?

As an ethnographer, my purposes were to eventually write about the intercultural experiences I witnessed, attempting to build understanding. I used the methods of participant observation and conversational interviewing over a period of 2½ years, devoting another half year to writing the ethnography. For this work, I encountered many who were seeking to learn and practice Native American spiritual traditions. I found them in sweat lodge ceremonies, craft supply stores, New Age bookstores and workshops, public lectures, college campuses, museums, on and off Indian reservations. They were an international lot, prevalently from the United States, but with a growing interest and presence of European inquirers. A smaller contingent of Latin Americans were present. Also included in the groups were Native American and Chicana and Chicano individuals attempting to regain their own cultural identity through a commitment to practicing ancient traditions.

Although there was a largely intertribal "Indian" population involved, the traditions that I saw shared were primarily Lakota (which many non-Indians referred to as "Sioux"[3]). Because of the Lakota influence, much of my field immersion took place at sites and ceremonies to which I was invited on the Pine Ridge and Rosebud Reservations in South Dakota. I also attended ceremonies and gatherings in both private and public locations throughout the southwestern United States. I did not attend any private events to which I was not invited by a participant, family, or tribal member.

Because much of my work was done during actual ceremonies and in the events that surrounded these ceremonies, I did not choose to record in any traditionally academic way the experiences I witnessed. Instead, I chose to make impressionistic notes that triggered my recall of what I witnessed. For example, instead of recording verbatim the prayers or taking photographs of a ceremony, I would jot down phrases that captured the images for me. More ritualistic forms of expression, or the words used "every time" by "everyone," I would use in their verbatim form. In the few instances in which I conducted more formal interviews or attended lectures, I did make tape recordings and write notes.

As I proceeded with the study, I used the Four Seasons (González, 1996) as the guide for methodology, employing a combination of traditional ethnographic methods with introspective, reflective techniques. These methods, familiar to all ethnographers, I organized around a cycle of naturally occurring seasons of activity and based them in an ontology (assumptions of what is real) that privileges natural experience as determinant of action.

From the Four Seasons approach, natural experience is seen as having a powerful "say" in how one's research is done. It is therefore possible that the study you start out doing will look significantly different when you finish, based on what develops as you engage in the study. The validity of a study is based on its groundedness in real experience that determines its form and outcome, even if not preferred professionally or personally by the researcher or his or her discipline.

So, although the "four seasons" may seem on the surface to simply be a scheme for organizing methods in which others already engage, it is actually a worldview for doing research, one that says that the researcher is not in charge; rather, it is the natural unfolding of experience that determines the process and outcomes of the study.[4] This powerful role of naturally occurring experience, both personal and social, was infused into the study by regularly asking the following questions throughout observation, interviews, analysis, and writing:

♦ Do I know why am I doing this study, both personally and professionally? (purpose, motives)

♦ Is this the right time for engaging in the method I choose to use, or is there a better time—or none—for doing what I want to do? (appropriateness)

♦ Am I open to all available sources of information in my data, even if it is not in agreement with my "hypotheses" and preconceived notions and wishes for this research? (rigor)

♦ Will my study accomplish what I intend without distorting the nature of what others have shared with me, or the relationships I developed? (ethics)

♦ Should I change my study or its focus given what I have learned? (adaptability)

It is the openness to radical change in direction or purpose of one's study that characterizes methods that reflect the ontology of natural experience. It is much the same as the unexpected late frost that thwarts a farmer's plans for a particular harvest, or a fire starting from a lightning bolt forcing whole natural populations to migrate. In this study, the passage of the seasons resulted in a nontraditional report of my "findings" through poetry.

Most ethnographies are written in prose. I chose to report through poetry for various reasons. Among those reasons was the growing awareness of the culture and personal experience involved in the phenomena I was studying. As I maintained my discipline of the Four Seasons and repeatedly asked myself the questions related to my study, I was concerned with the anonymity of the actual persons about whom I wrote, as well as respecting the sacredness of the ceremonies and spiritual practices shared. I would often remember how as a child raised Roman Catholic, I had been taught to revere the chalice at Mass; no one except those specially designated could touch it—the wine and crumbs from communion had to be disposed of in a special manner and in a special place. I chose to remember this type of reverence when dealing with traditions equally sacred to the people who were sharing them, and it allowed me to learn very much.

It also led me to realize that traditional academic writing would distort what had been shared with me in ways that would very likely offend or hurt. As I sifted through my notes and recollections, photographs and recordings, and discussed what I had experienced with participants, it also became increasingly obvious to me that to write the ethnography in prose that purported to express intercultural "facts" about the groups I observed, both Indian and non-Indian, would not capture the integral nuance of the phenomena. The dialectic tension would be removed by reporting units of knowledge, rather than by presenting both the positive and negative, the strong and the weak, the admirable and shameful, as it existed in the real experience. It was during this "fall harvesting" of my ethnographic process that I realized I would write the ethnography in poetry because poetry enabled the dialectic tension to be maintained and allowed for the experience of the spiritual through poesis.

I wrote almost 60 poems as the record of my study and shared these poems with members of the groups with whom I had shared experiences. I gave them the opportunity to respond to the versions of their experience I had represented poetically. In traditional ethnographic language, this is the process of "member-checking," of validating one's report through a checking of its content with members of the cultural groups. Had they disagreed with the versions I presented, or protested in some fashion, the required ethical response would have been to either change the poems or omit them entirely from the final ethnographic collection. Two poems were thus eliminated, being poems that reflected more my own editorial opinions and reflections than actual experiences. Others were deleted because of ambiguity resulting from the way in which they were written.

The 52 poems that resulted all describe phenomena that are based on actual situations that occurred during the 2½-year period of my participant observation; in other words, they are about "things that really happened." The names were all changed except when they referred to actual places and public gatherings, or when a dedication was made to a specific individual. Dedicated poems were shared with the persons to whom they were dedicated or with family members, if the person was deceased.

Many of the poems contain a composite of similar situations; as such, they are functioning as textual categories of field experience. The poems are able to give us the sense of an entire category of experience without the use of hierarchical outlines or axiomatic structures. Rather, they are contextually situated in a poetic form that allows for a simultaneous manifestation of emotion, spirit, intellect, and description.

Each poem contributes a piece toward a "whole" experience. They mirror the actual feelings and experiences of the events I observed. Some of the poems seem to reflect an attitude of support for the sharing of spirituality; others seem to oppose it; still others seem to have no opinion. Although my personal agenda as an individual may lean more in one direction or another, as an ethnographer in this study it was to be descriptive. By choosing to write the text in poetry, decisions could be left to the readers, in much the same way that they would be left to decide if a part of the situations was described. Any opinions expressed in the poems were actual opinions expressed in conversations in the field.

The following poems are selected from the 52 poems in the ethnography to demonstrate how they represent aspects of the intercultural experience of sharing culture through the sharing of spirituality. I hope you will come to understand aspects of what occurs within the intercultural arena of the sharing of native American spirituality by reading these poems. I further hope that you will recognize that each poem presents small holograms of the entire experience, which although expressing the nature of the phenomenon are not as accurate alone as when read with others. Finally, I hope that you will find in these glimpses of this particular intercultural context evidence of what characterizes intercultural communication across other contexts in which traditions are being shared, learned, protected, or challenged.

She Sees No One

When I look in the mirror
    I see no one
she said.
no legacy
no traditions known or treasured
nondescript mousy brown hair
pale skin the color of silly putty
I see no one.

And so she puts on feathers
and turquoise

and feigns a downward glance
when she talks to friends
They think something's bothering her
because she doesn't look at them anymore
she pretends it is a noble tradition
she has always practiced
though she still has to concentrate
when she catches herself looking
into somebody's
Eyes.

So when a well-meaning friend asks
"what's up?"
she can voice defiance
anger
disgust with *the System*
with white supremacy
with European culture
why do we have to look at each other?
it's so invasive.
it's a Native American tradition . . .
to look . . .
inward.

And somehow she feels noble
for defending an Indian way
when her friend only wondered if she was okay.
yesterday she was white.

When she looks in the mirror
she sees feathers
and turquoise
fringe and frill around the
nothing
she saw before
and she is frightened to take them off
because even in her noble
lack-of-eye-contact
newfound Indian ways
she still sees
No One.

Getting Smudged[5]

What's that smell?
is someone burning something in here?
it smells just like . . .
just like what?!
getting purified smells
like it's against the law

to your citified nostrils
and intellectualized senses
illicit Indian smells
trigger fear.
getting clean
feels like getting dirty.

Seminar Lady

Calls herself Starfeather Woman
and runs these seminars
on walking the sacred road
they cost a couple of hundred dollars
and people actually pay for it.
Starfeather Woman
man, she was nobody but little
Jane Doe
when she first came around here
who gave her that name anyway?

The "Open" Sweat [6]

They hovered around the firepit
with towels and
t-shirts and gym shorts
fluorescent white legs with
curly golden brown leg hair
the women in big baggy dresses
towels draped over their breasts
some less modestly over their arms
standing, watching
watching each other—

He has his towel *on*
he *doesn't*
I wonder which is *right?*
her dress has sleeves
hers is short
Hers is a solid color
I thought
you weren't *supposed* to wear jewelry
why are they holding sage
why are they wearing sage on their ears?
do I need some?

Have you ever noticed
how the air feels like
it's tangled

when everyone is busy
watching everyone
trying to learn
from others trying to learn
    . . . from others trying to learn
        . . . from others trying to learn

They say it is "traditional"
to learn by watching.
but was there ever a tribe
where only a couple of people
knew *how*
and the rest didn't?

Loop Hole

You guys could probably
make lots of money
if you sold
sweat lodge kits
tobacco prayer tie [7] kits
just put in everything for them
some little squares of cloth
some string
a package of tobacco
a little bit of sage
some matches
sell it for ten dollars
if you put it in a basket
you could sell it for fifteen
then the sweat could be free
and you wouldn't have to
worry about charging
for ceremonies.

Feminist Friends

Stop cooking so much!
don't feed the men first!
be liberated!
They come to help the women
to see their oppression
they want to show them a better way
a way to come out
from under
Male
oppression

so they instigate
motivate
tempt
and disrupt
leave a mess
in the same place
they found them
and go home
to their liberated condos
and nine-to-five jobs.

Indians Only

With a sense of entitlement
he walks into the meeting.
"I want to help;
I understand you."
No words uttered in response
a mass of pursed lips
as he takes a seat
amongst their circle
about to *help* them.

I understand you
he says.
I am glad to be here
I am not Indian
but I understand you.

Perhaps in saying it a *fourth* time
he will understand
that if he understood us
he would understand
that part of helping us
is to stay away
and let us help ourselves
decide
when *we* want to
invite others
into our circle.

Questions Like Speeding Bullets

Your desire to know
has a speed all its own
a speed that is so fast
it often surpasses my ability
to tell you

in the right way
what it is I have
what it is I know
what it is I have inherited
from my grandfathers.

Asking in a Good Way

If you want to know something
you don't have to ask any questions.
the Grandfathers know
and if we are the ones to tell you
then you will learn from us
but more likely
you will learn from you
and only *think*
that you are learning from us.

When you ask your questions
peering over our shoulders to
watch what we are doing
you act as if knowledge is something
that is scheduled
and your deadline for knowing is now.

In our ways,
there is no problem
when there are no answers
when we ask questions
you cannot force water
from a cloud
that is not a rain cloud.

The rain will come when it comes
or when it is asked
in the right way
in a good way

And no, we cannot tell you what that means.

Unwelcome Visitor

I really don't know what the problem is
or if there *is* a problem
or if there should *be* a problem
am I really not welcome here?

I know you've told me about *others*
but I thought that meant—

I thought that meant
I was different
I thought that meant
you trusted me
I thought that meant
you saw more than
the color of my skin

You gave me an Indian name
you stayed at my house
I bought your groceries
and I fixed your car
you taught me about spirit
and that we are all related
but right now
right now I feel like
you want me to go home.

I feel something
something that feels like
hatred
disdain
I'm confused
can't you see
that I changed my whole life
to be with you?

Moment of Truth

Generations
and Imposed Borders
separate *me*
from the people around me
always
forcing me to be stronger
to stand more firmly
in my place
Wherever I am,
in my place.
Always a visitor—
in my place.
Learning to be present
with self-respect
even when there's no
invitation.

The Talking Stick

Feeling respect
in a new way
they hold the Talking Stick
reverently
fingering the beadwork
the smooth sanded knots
gripping it solidly
like "Warriors."

Head warrior explains
it is an old tradition . . .
nodding solemnly
no one dares smile
and they pass the stick.

Each man speaks once
it moves in a circle
from man to man
warrior to warrior
each sharing words
feelings
thoughts
from the depths of his
feminine masculinity
each focusing on words
speaking poetry
and feeling good when all have
Spoken.
feeling good *that*
all have Spoken.

Not realizing that the true wonder
was that they all had
listened.

Painful Screams

Make tobacco ties
and pray.
face the Spirits of the
      West
      North
      East
      South
send smoke to the sky
touch your fingers to the earth

know that the pain in your heart
is good.

Learn to feel comfort
from
the pain
do not avoid it.

It is the voice of your spirit
sending health
and help.

Listen.

Your pain is the screaming voice
of spirit
telling you how to heal.

Inipi[8] Pain

I do not think
that until we see clearly
as in the sweat lodge
Inipi
as when we smoke the pipe
Chanunpa[9]
or offer up our ties
black
    red
        yellow
            white
blue and green

I do not think
that until that begins
that we know
what we are doing.

My pain now
is like the pain of the sweat lodge
I have chosen it.
crawled to my place
seated in revealing darkness
burning
because it will purify me
because it will heal me
because it is good.

Mundane Medicine Men

Who are the medicine men
who are the healers
that are placed on sacrificial altars
and granted special status

Some would have it that they are
somehow
more than human
somehow
somehow
men who have transcended
what it is to be human
what it is to be mundane on the earth.

Placed on pedestals
so that all can hear
so that all can see
that his feet no longer
touch the ground
and when we no longer
walk on the ground
we do indeed escape
what it is to be human
what it is to be mundane.

So we help medicine men healer gurus
to leave the ground
out of respect
we do this to them
out of respect
and awe
we take away their source of power.

A Spirit People

Everything we have
and have had
have had for ages
and will have—
everything
is Good.
Good.
we are Good.
no power on earth could make me claim
    otherwise.
no power in heaven would make me try.
the united spirit of us

a people
is stronger than you
or
me.
the united spirit of *us*
a people
will live on forever
they cannot kill our spirit.

Sitting Bull Freedom

Thousands of you came
hundreds of years ago
and keep coming today
like scurrying ants
that have forgotten
where the farm is
fleeing religion
fleeing oppression
fleeing family distress
and because you never dealt with it
came and created the same things here
invited us along for the ride.

They say Sitting Bull
sat in the middle of a battle
bullets and arrows flying past
and around him
never touching him
just sat there.

If you came here to escape
you're in the wrong place
turtle island[10] freedom
Is not about moving
Turtle Island freedom
being Indian
is about staying put
even when you are moving.

NOTES

1. Readers are encouraged to read the work of Ed McGaa (1990, 1992) for treatment of the tradition of spirituality that was shared, as well as commentary from the perspective of those who support it.

2. A note on my terminology: I am calling "Indian" those with legitimate claims to Indianness, whether through tribal enrollment, family history

and tradition, or acknowledgment by an Indian community. Those I call "non-Indian" are those who cannot make these claims. I also include within the category of "non-Indian" those who claim to have "rumors" of a past Indian ancestry but whose families have no proof of this fact, more significantly, no incorporation of Indian culture into the accepted ways of the family. The term "native American" is used at times to refer to the traditions.

3. Many attribute the incorporation of Lakota spiritual practice into other tribal "traditions" to the Lakota spiritual leadership of the intertribal American Indian Movement, especially in the early 1970s, inspiring a resurgence and return to traditional spiritual practices nationwide by many "urban" and culturally displaced (through adoption into non-Indian families) native Americans. For more history and cultural context, readers are directed to Peter Matthiessen's (1991) treatment.

4. "Spring" focuses on the preparatory phases of the study, heavily emphasizing personal introspection, relevant reading, increasing one's awareness of assumptions and motives, and striving for appropriate access to the phenomena of interest. "Summer" then serves as the season of one's actual immersion in cultural phenomena, with much emphasis on the lessons derived through interpersonal contact, conflict, and personal dilemmas and stress. "Fall" is the season of harvesting one's efforts, celebrating the findings with the persons who supported the study, preparing for the isolated task of writing, and recognizing the resources available (including data) for the actual report. "Winter" is then the season of figurative hibernation, of writing one's report and determining its best form and purpose, based on the experience and knowledge gained in the previous seasons. Each season emphasizes its own activities, but several questions are asked constantly. They are based on the awareness that the research does not control the seasons; rather, the seasons will determine the research.

5. "Smudging" is the practice of burning herbs such as sage, sweetgrass, cedar, or pine in order to use the smoke as a form of purification or vehicle for prayer. This is done at many times, but routinely at the beginning of ceremonies or prior to important meetings or discussions.

6. "Sweat" is the name used for a purification ceremony in which steam is used to purify individu-

als. An "open" sweat was one to which non-Indians were allowed.

7. "Prayer tie" is the name used by some to describe the small pouches filled with tobacco and tied together with string as offerings of prayer.

8. *Inipi* is the Lakota word for what is, in English, referred to as a sweat lodge.

9. *Chanunpa* is the Lakota word for the pipe used in ceremony and prayer.

10. Turtle Island is the reference made by many indigenous (native American) peoples to the lands that make up what is known as North America.

REFERENCES

González, M. C. (1996, February). The four seasons of ethnography. In Martin, J. (Chair), *Ethnicity and Methodology*. Symposium conducted at the 1st Conference on Ethnicity and Methodology at Arizona State University, Tempe.

Matthiessen, P. (1991). *In the spirit of Crazy Horse*. New York: Viking Penguin.

McGaa, E. (1990). *Mother Earth spirituality*. New York: Harper.

McGaa, E. (1992). *The Rainbow Tribe*. New York: Harper.

KEY TERMS

throwness   indigenous
contact   ethnic identity

spirituality   tradition
ethnography   postmodern identities
ethnic fraud   Native American
cultural myth

DISCUSSION QUESTIONS

1. According to the author, why is the form of a research report important? What does poetry contribute to a report on intercultural communication?

2. Select one poem that you believe demonstrates how intercultural contact heightens the awareness of a person's cultural identity. Based on the insights of the poem, what could be done to increase the quality of intercultural communication?

3. How likely is it that individuals would have a totally positive response to a culture very different from their own? How do the poems reflect the struggles between two such cultures?

4. Based on these poems, what should people be aware of when they begin to learn about another culture?

5. Do you think it is possible to become a member of another culture by choice?

CREDITS AND ACKNOWLEDGMENTS

Reading 2 Leeds-Hurwitz, Wendy. (1990). Notes in the history of intercultural communication: The Foreign Service Institute and the Mandate for Intercultural Training. *Quarterly Journal of Speech, 76,* 262–281. Used by permission of the Speech Communication Association and Wendy Leeds-Hurwitz at the University of Wisconsin, Parkside. All but five footnotes deleted.

Reading 7 Spellers, Regina E. Happy to be nappy! Embracing an Afrocentric aesthetic for beauty. Opening quotation from *Untitled* by Me'Shell N'Degeocello. © 1993 WB Music Corp. (ASCAP), Askia Music (ASCAP), & Maverick Music Company (ASCAP). All rights administered by WB Music Corp. All rights reserved. Used by permission of Warner Bros. Publications U.S. Inc., Miami, FL 33014.

Reading 12 Baldwin, James. (1955). Stranger in the village. From *Notes of a Native Son* by James Baldwin. © 1955, renewed 1983, by James Baldwin. Reprinted by permission of Beacon Press, Boston.

Reading 15 Giles, Howard, & Noels, Kimberly A. (1977). Communication accommodation in intercultural encounters. Figure 1: Some increasing variants of convergence and divergence. Adapted by permission from H. Giles, R. Y. Bourhis, & D. M. Taylor (1977). Towards a theory of language in ethnic group relations. In H. Giles (Ed.), *Language and intergroup relations* (p. 324). London: Academic Press. Figure 2: Degree, direction, and mutuality of accommodation. Adapted by permission from C. Gallois & H. Giles (in press). Accommodating mutual influence in intergroup encounters. In M. Palmer (Ed.), *Mutual influence in interpersonal communication: Theory and research in cognition, affect, and behavior,* vol. 20 of Progress in Communication Science Series. Greenwich, CT: Ablex Publishing.

Reading 17 Carbaugh, Donal. (1995). "I can't do that!" but I "can actually see around corners": American Indian students and the study of public "communication." In Jaakko

Lehtonen & Leena Lahtinen (Eds.), *Critical perspectives on communication research and pedagogy* (pp. 215–234). St. Ingbert, Germany: Röhrig Universitätsverlag. Reprinted by permission of the publisher and the author.

Reading 19 Fitch, Kristine L. (1990–1991). A ritual for attempting leave-taking in Colombia. *Research on Language and Social Interaction, 24,* 209–221, 223–224. Reprinted by permission of Lawrence Erlbaum Associates, Inc., and Kristine Fitch, University of Iowa.

Reading 20 Bowers, Detine L. (1996). When outsiders encounter insiders in speaking: Oppressed collectives on the defensive. *Journal of Black Studies, 26,* 490–503. Copyright © 1996 by Sage Publications, Inc. Reprinted by permission of Sage Publications, Inc.

Reading 21 Hall, Edward T., & Hall, Mildred Reed. (1990). Key concepts: Underlying structures of culture. In E. T. Hall & M. R. Hall, *Understanding cultural differences: Germans, French, and Americans* (pp. 3–31). Reprinted with the permission of Dr. Edward T. Hall and Intercultural Press, Inc., Yarmouth, ME. Copyright 1990.

Reading 22 Kim, Min-Sun. (1992). A comparative analysis of nonverbal expressions as portrayed by Korean and American print-media advertising. *Howard Journal of Communications, 3,* 317–339. Excerpted by permission of the *Howard Journal of Communications.*

Reading 23 Philipsen, Gerry. (1976). Places for speaking in Teamsterville. *Quarterly Journal of Speech, 62,* 15–25. Used by permission of the Speech Communication Association and the author.

Reading 26 King, Janis L. Cultural differences in the perceptions of sports mascots. Excerpts from Tim Giago, Notes from Indian country, *Indian Country Today,* reprinted by permission of Tim Giago.

Reading 27 Seiter, Ellen. (1990). Different children, different dreams: Racial representation in advertising. *Journal of Communication Inquiry, 14* (no. 1): 31–47. Reprinted by permission.

Reading 30 Dion, Michel. (1994). Madonna in the French press (Trans. T. K. Nakayama). In Michel Dion (Ed.), *Madonna: Érotisme et pouvoir.* Paris: Éditions Kimé. Used by permission of Michel Dion and Éditions Kimé.

Reading 31 Kim, Young Yun (1995). Cross-cultural adaptation: An integrative theory. In R. L. Wiseman (Ed.), *Intercultural communication theory* (pp. 170–193). Thousand Oaks, CA: Sage Publications. Excerpted by permission of the Speech Communication Association and the author.

Reading 36 Hofstede, Geert (1991). I, we, and they. In *Cultures and organizations: Software of the mind* (pp. 49–79). New York: McGraw-Hill. Reprinted with the permission of The McGraw-Hill Companies.

Reading 37 Chen, Ling (1993). Chinese and North Americans: An epistemological exploration of intercultural communication. *Howard Journal of Communications, 4,* 342–357. Used by permission of the *Howard Journal of Communications.*

Reading 41 Ting-Toomey, Stella (1997). Intercultural conflict competence. In William R. Cupach & Daniel J. Canary (Eds.), *Competence in interpersonal conflict* (pp. 121–147). New York: McGraw-Hill. Reprinted with the permission of The McGraw-Hill Companies.

Reading 42 Nwosu, Peter Ogom (1988). Negotiating with the Swazis. *Howard Journal of Communications, 1,* 145–154. Used by permission of the *Howard Journal of Communications.*

Reading 47 Bateson, Mary Catherine. (1993). Joint performance across cultures: Improvisation in a Persian garden. *Text and Performance Quarterly, 13,* 113–121. Used by permission of the Speech Communication Association and the author. Portions of this material were included in Chapter 1 of Mary Catherine Bateson, *Peripheral Visions.*

Reading 48 Allen, Mike. Comparing views of science. An earlier version of this reading appeared in Allen, Mike (1993). Critical and traditional science: Implications for communication research. *Western Journal of Communication, 57,* 200–209. Reprinted by permission of the Western States Communication Association.

Reading 49 Tanno, Dolores V., & Jandt, Fred E. (1994). Redefining the "other" in multicultural research. *Howard Journal of Communications, 5,* 36–45. Used by permission of the *Howard Journal of Communications.*

◆ INDEX

Aboud, F., 140
Abril, K., 230–231
Accent, speech, 135, 136, 143, 155
Acceptance/fellowship face, 310, 311
Accommodation, 141–146, 157
    asymmetrical, 143
    and gender, 146
    mutuality of, 143, 144
    objective, 143
    optimal level of, 144–146
    psychological, 143
    subjective, 143
Acculturation, 296, 297
    challenges to traditional models of, 320
Active communication strategies, 313
Active modes, of coping with reentry, 309
Adaptation
    versus compulsion, 325
    to social environment, 295
    See also Cross-cultural adaptation
Adler, N., 307, 309, 415, 417, 419
Adler, P. S., 297
Adoption, by gay and lesbian couples, 393–394
Advertising
    Burrell commercials, 262
    directed at children, 259–261
    multiracial representation of children in, 258–263
    nonverbal expressions across cultures, 206–207, 210–215
    in non-Western cultures, 206, 214
    nostalgia myth in, 259
    perpetuation of racial divisions in, 240

reinforcement of cultural images by, 240–241
    relationship to culture, 207, 214–215
    use of children in, 257
Africaans, 139
African Americans
    as consumers, 279–280
    context of interaction with Euro Americans, 8
    forced defensive postures, 186
    importance of family collectivism to, 338, 339
    intercultural conflict with European Americans, 399
    internalized racism, 74–77
    marginalizing of in social science research, 72
    oppositional cultural criticism, 276
    portrayal in *Space Traders*, 277–281
    portrayal in television advertising, 257–263
    power and powerlessness in communication models, 458
    and racist rhetorical condition, 186–192
    rage of, 116
    socially constructed cultural experience of, 280, 283n5
    uniqueness of history, 118–119
    women's role of in Civil Rights movement, 279
African diaspora, 8
Afrikaners, 104, 106–107, 108, 372, 376
Afrocentric theory, 71, 76–77
"Akritas Plan," 427

Alcoff, L., 459
Alienated mode, of coping with reentry, 309, 313
Al-Khatib, M., 146
Alliance, 370
Allport, G. W., 121
Altman, K. E., 478
America (Baudrillard), 446, 447, 448
American Council of Learned Societies, 18
American culture
    clothing and body exposure in, 210
    communication patterns in, 208
    dominant racial ideology, 278
    eye behavior in, 209
    hand and arm gestures in, 208
    low-context low-information communication in, 201
    narrative of Americanness, 269, 272–273
    nonverbal expression in advertising, 206–207, 210–215
    racial relations in, 118–120, 434
    territoriality in, 202
    white supremacy in, 119
    See also American popular culture; Western culture
American Dream, 270, 273
American Foreign Service Journal, 17–18
American Indians, 494n2. *See also* Native Americans
American popular culture
    European criticism of, 446–448
    exhibitionism in, 448
    and intercultural communication, 237–241